W9-BZY-550

LATIN AMERICA AND ITS PEOPLE

COMBINED VOLUME

LATIN AMERICA AND ITS PEOPLE

COMBINED VOLUME

Third Edition

Cheryl E. Martin
University of Texas at El Paso

Mark Wasserman
Rutgers University

Prentice Hall

Boston   Columbus   Indianapolis   New York   San Francisco   Upper Saddle River
Amsterdam   Cape Town   Dubai   London   Madrid   Milan   Munich   Paris   Montreal   Toronto
Delhi   Mexico City   Sao Paulo   Sydney   Hong Kong   Seoul   Singapore   Taipei   Tokyo

Executive Editor: Jeff Lasser
Editorial Project Manager: Rob DeGeorge
Editorial Assistant: Julia Feltus
Senior Marketing Manager: Maureen E. Prado Roberts
Marketing Assistant: Samantha Bennett
Production Manager: Kathleen Sleys
Cover Designer: Suzanne Behnke
Cover Photo: Jordi Camí/Alamy
Full-Service Project Management/Composition: Hemalatha/Integra
Printer/Binder/Cover Printer: R.R. Donnelley & Sons, Inc.
Text Font: 10/13 New Baskerville

Credits and acknowledgments borrowed from other sources and reproduced, with permission, in this textbook appear on page C-1.

Copyright © 2012, 2008, 2005 Pearson Education, Inc., publishing as Prentice Hall. All rights reserved. Manufactured in the United States of America. This publication is protected by Copyright, and permission should be obtained from the publisher prior to any prohibited reproduction, storage in a retrieval system, or transmission in any form or by any means, electronic, mechanical, photocopying, recording, or likewise. To obtain permission(s) to use material from this work, please submit a written request to Pearson Education, Inc., Permissions Department, One Lake Street, Upper Saddle River, NJ 07458.

Library of Congress Cataloging-in-Publication Data
Martin, Cheryl English
  Latin America and its people / Cheryl E. Martin, Mark Wasserman.—3rd ed.
    p. cm.
  "Combined volume."
  ISBN-13: 978-0-205-05470-1 (alk. paper)
  ISBN-10: 0-205-05470-6 (alk. paper)
  1. Latin America—History.   I. Wasserman, Mark   II. Title.
F1410.M294 2012
980—dc22
                                                    2010046656

10 9 8 7 6 5 4

Prentice Hall
is an imprint of

PEARSON

www.pearsonhighered.com

ISBN 10:   0-205-05470-6
ISBN 13: 978-0-205-05470-1

Plate 1 A mural at the Maya site of Bonampak showing a battle scene.

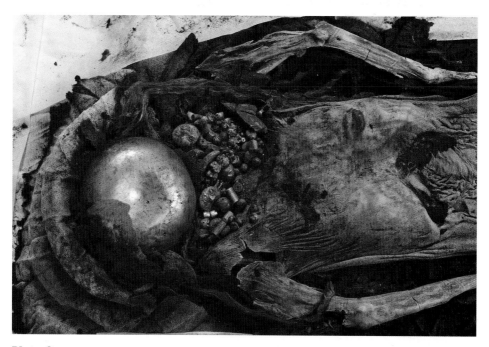

Plate 2 Mummified remains of a Moche woman who died about 450 c.e., discovered by archaeologists in 2005. She was a woman of high status, but what is most remarkable about her tomb is that it contains not only needles and other artifacts usually associated with female gender roles but also war clubs and spear throwers, suggesting that perhaps she was a warrior or a ruler. Note the tattoos on her arms.

Plate 3 The temple complex at Monte Albán, Oaxaca, Mexico. Archaeologists believe that the building in the foreground served as an observatory.

Plate 4 A textile from the fifteenth century C.E. depicting jaguars, a recurrent motif in Andean artwork. This piece is from Chancay, north of present-day Lima. Chancay was conquered by the Incas at about the time the textile was made.

Plate 22 Mexicans celebrate the Day of the Dead with colorful decorations of grave sites.

Plate 23 Juan O'Gorman, *La marcha de la lealtad* (*The March of Loyalty*). Francisco I. Madero, Mexico's first revolutionary president.

Plate 24 Latin American cities with more than one million inhabitants.

To the students of Rutgers University
and the University of Texas at El Paso,
who have inspired us.

CONTENTS

1

THE FIRST PEOPLES
OF THE AMERICAS   1

2

AMERICANS AND IBERIANS ON THE EVE OF CONTACT 31

3

THE EUROPEAN CONQUEST OF AMERICA 64

4

THE IBERIANS' NEW WORLD   96

5

THE AMERINDIANS' CHANGING WORLD 126

6

A NEW PEOPLE AND
THEIR WORLD   155

7

THE SHIFTING FORTUNES OF COLONIAL EMPIRES   186

8

THE NEW NATIONS
OF LATIN AMERICA 216

9

REGIONALISM, WAR,
AND RECONSTRUCTION: POLITICS
AND ECONOMICS, 1821–1880 242

10

EVERYDAY LIFE IN AN UNCERTAIN AGE, 1821–1880 271

11

ECONOMIC MODERNIZATION, SOCIETY, AND POLITICS, 1880–1920   300

12

BETWEEN REVOLUTIONS: THE NEW POLITICS OF CLASS AND THE ECONOMIES OF IMPORT SUBSTITUTION INDUSTRIALIZATION, 1920–1959   327

13

PEOPLE AND PROGRESS, 1910–1959   352

14

REVOLUTION, REACTION, DEMOCRACY, AND THE NEW GLOBAL ECONOMY: 1959 TO THE PRESENT   375

15

EVERYDAY LIFE:
1959 TO THE PRESENT 401

LIST OF FEATURES

Slice of Life

LIST OF MAPS
AND COLOR PLATES

Maps

Color Plates

Front of book

Gulf of Mexico

ATLANTIC

OCEAN

Nassau ● BAHAMAS

Havana ● CUBA

DOMINICAN REPUBLIC

PUERTO RICO

Mexico City ●

HAITI

VIRGIN IS.

JAMAICA

Kingston ● Port-au-prince

Santo Domingo

San Juan ●

ST. KITTS & NEVIS

ANTIGUA & BARBUDA

GUADELOUPE

DOMINICA

MARTINIQUE

BARBADOS

GRENADA

TRINIDAD & TOBAGO

BELIZE

Belmopan

GUATEMALA

Guatemala City

HONDURAS

EL SALVADOR

Tegucigalpa

San Salvador

NICARAGUA

Managua

Caribbean Sea

ST. LUCIA

ST. VINCENT

THE GRENADINES

COSTA RICA

San Jose

Panama City

PANAMA

Caracas ●

L. Maracaibo

Orinoco

Georgetown

Paramaribo

Cayenne

VENEZUELA

GUYANA

FRENCH GUIANA

SURINAM

Bogotá ●

GALAPAGOS

ISLANDS

COLOMBIA

Quito ●

Amazon R.

ECUADOR

BRAZIL

Lima ●

São Francisco R.

PERU

L. Titicaca

La Paz

Brasília ●

BOLIVIA

Paraguay R.

Paraná R.

PACIFIC

OCEAN

PARAGUAY

São Paulo ●

Rio de Janeiro ●

Asuncion ●

CHILE

Cordoba ●

URUGUAY

Santiago ●

Buenos Aires ●

Montevideo ●

ARGENTINA

FALKLAND/MALVINAS

ISLANDS

Tierra del Fuego

● National Capitals

PREFACE

Our aim in writing *Latin America and Its People* has been to provide a fresh interpretative survey of Latin American history from pre-Columbian times to the beginning of the twenty-first century. The millions of "ordinary" Latin Americans are the central characters in our story. We look at the many social and political institutions that Latin Americans have built and rebuilt—families, governments from the village level to the nation-state, churches, political parties, labor unions, schools, and armies—but we do so through the lives of the people who forged these institutions and tried to alter them to meet changing circumstances. The texture of everyday life, therefore, is our principal focus.

NEW TO THIS EDITION

Chapter 2
- REVISED: Map of "The Valley of Mexico" has been revised to indicate more accurate placement of *chinampas*

Chapter 3
- NEW: Latin American Lives: Domingos Fernandes Nobre

Chapter 6
- NEW: Illustration: Blacks in Trujillo, Peru

Chapter 7
- NEW: How Historians Understand: Latin America and the Atlantic World

Chapter 8
- NEW: Latin American Lives: Manuela Sáenz

Chapter 9

- NEW: Latin American Lives: Francisco Solano López

Chapter 11

- NEW: Latin American Lives: Evaristo Madero

Chapter 14

- UPDATED: Narrative updated throughout to reflect recent events and new scholarship
- UPDATED: Pink Tide
- NEW: Indigenous Political Movements

Chapter 15

- UPDATED: Narrative updated throughout to reflect recent events and new scholarship
- NEW: Environment: Natural Disasters
- EXPANDED: The Great Migrations
- NEW: Informal Economy: Narcotics Trade

The list of suggested readings at the end of each chapter, Learning More about Latin America, has been updated throughout, with some older titles having been replaced by recent publications.

THE TEXTURE OF EVERYDAY LIFE

Life has not been easy for most Latin Americans. Poverty, hard work, disease, natural calamities, the loss of loved ones, and violence have marked many people's lives. Many have lacked educational opportunities and the chance to speak their political opinions openly. In the chapters that follow, we will devote a lot of attention to the daily struggles of men, women, and children as they faced these difficult challenges and adapted to changing times. We are also interested in how people managed to find meaning and enjoyment in their lives. Even in the midst of hardship and tragedy, they came together as families and communities to celebrate, dance, eat and drink, flirt, marry, and pray. Our readers will meet the people of Latin American history "up close and personal," in their houses and on the streets, on the shop floors and in the fields, and at work and at play, for it is the texture of everyday life that makes the history of Latin America so fascinating and compelling.

THE DIVERSITY OF LATIN AMERICA

Latin Americans are a very diverse people. They have spoken Spanish, Portuguese, Nahuatl, Quechua, Maya, Aymara, Guaraní, and scores of other languages. Their ethnic and cultural roots can be traced to the indigenous civilizations of the Americas and to many generations of European, African, and Asian immigrants. A few have been very rich, but many more have been very poor. They have adapted to many climatic zones, some at altitudes as high as 11,000 feet above sea level. Many Latin Americans have lived in rural areas, but they have also built some of the world's most sophisticated cities, from the Aztec and Inca capitals of Tenochtitlan and Cuzco to such modern industrial giants as São Paulo, Brazil, and Monterrey, Mexico, to cosmopolitan urban centers like Mexico City and Buenos Aires. Following their independence from Spain and Portugal, they have experimented with a variety of political regimes—monarchy, liberal democracy, oligarchy, socialist revolution, and brutal military dictatorships, to name a few.

Despite this diversity, Latin Americans have faced certain common challenges. European conquest and subsequent shifts in world economic and political configurations have shaped the region's history over the past five centuries. Latin America's rich natural resources have attracted foreign investors who have profited handsomely, while the people who worked in the mines and oilfields have seldom garnered an equitable share of the bounty. The region's ability to produce a stunning variety of agricultural staples has shaped patterns of landholding and labor throughout the region, again to the detriment of the many and the benefit of the few. How to achieve political stability in nations divided by class, ethnic, and regional differences has been an enduring conundrum for Latin Americans, even if they have tried many different means of resolving that dilemma.

Our goal, then, is to explore Latin Americans' common history without losing sight of their diversity, and to compare how the many different peoples of the region have responded to similar situations. We have therefore organized our text thematically rather than proceeding country by country. There are too many countries and too much time to cover for us to thoroughly document the history of every Latin American nation. No doubt, some country specialists will feel their area slighted, but textbooks are as much about the choices of what to exclude as they are about what to include. Unlike many other texts on Latin American history, *Latin America and Its People* interweaves the history of Brazil with that of its Spanish-speaking neighbors, rather than segregating it in separate chapters, while also pointing out the special features that distinguish it from other Latin American countries. Volume I includes coverage of those portions of the present-day United States that were once part of the Spanish colonial empire.

Our underlying assumption is that, in order for our students to gain an introductory (and, we hope, lasting) understanding of Latin America, it is best not to clutter the narrative with too many dates and names. We believe that students will remember the major themes, such as the struggle to control local affairs, the impact of war, the transformation of women's roles, and the social changes wrought by economic development. And they will remember, perhaps even more clearly, that many Latin Americans lived and continue to live in overwhelming poverty.

VOLUME I

Volume I of *Latin America and Its People* looks at the ways in which people have continually reinvented the hemisphere that Europeans called the "new world." This world was first "new" for the nameless ancestors of today's Native Americans, who migrated across the Bering Strait and fanned out across North and South America over the course of many millennia. Generation after generation, they adapted to the many different climatic zones of the hemisphere and gradually accumulated the surpluses necessary to found the great civilizations of the Aztecs, the Inca, the Maya, and so many others. Chapter 1 is devoted entirely to the long trajectory of cultural development in the Americas down to the year 1400 C.E., while Chapter 2 includes an extensive comparative discussion of the Aztec and Inca empires and the simultaneously emerging national monarchies of Spain and Portugal.

Spanish and Portuguese colonists not only found this world very different from what they had known but also remade it as they discovered its potential for yielding silver, gold, sugar, and other commodities of value to them. The changes introduced by European conquest and colonization profoundly altered the world of the indigenous peoples of the Americas. Over the course of three centuries, the hemisphere witnessed the rise of a new people, the biological and cultural offspring of native peoples, Europeans, and Africans, who yet again made this world something new. Chapters 3, 4, 5, and 6 explore the constantly changing worlds of Latin American peoples under Spanish and Portuguese rule. Chapters 7 and 8 look at the transformation of Latin American society in the eighteenth and early nineteenth centuries, the period known to historians as the "Age of Revolution."

The most important theme of Volume I is how ordinary people built these successive new worlds and continually renegotiated the complex and overlapping hierarchies of class, ethnicity, political status, and gender that supposedly governed their lives. Native peoples endured military and political conquest, catastrophic epidemics, highly oppressive labor regimens, and the imposition of a new religion. Yet, despite these enormous challenges, they survived and rebuilt their communities, selectively incorporating cultural elements introduced by the Europeans along with traditional practices and beliefs as they formed their new society.

Against what might seem like insurmountable odds, Africans brought to the Americas as slaves managed to retain something of the life they had known before, especially in places where their numbers were sufficiently great that they could form some kind of identifiable community. Some found ways to escape the bonds of slavery and passed that freedom to successive generations of descendants. Like the indigenous peoples, they too borrowed selectively from European cultures.

Throughout three centuries of Spanish and Portuguese colonial rule, Latin Americans of all races and social classes contested, sometimes successfully, sometimes not, the many "rules" that dictated how men and women should behave and how people in subordinate social positions should render deference to those who supposedly ranked above them. Volume I argues that it was not just kings and priests and other authority figures who built the world of colonial Latin America. Men, women, and children of all classes and all racial groups had at least some say in the outcome, even if the colonial state sometimes wielded enough power to silence the most vocal among them.

VOLUME II

The overarching theme of Volume II is how ordinary people struggled over the course of two centuries to maintain control over their daily lives. This meant that they sought to determine their own community leaders, set their local laws and regulations (especially taxes), establish and keep their own traditions, practice their religion, supervise the education of their children, live by their own values and standards, and earn a living. This endless struggle came to involve more than just the narrow view and experience of their village or urban neighborhood or their friends and neighbors. Rather, it brought ordinary people and their local lives into constant, not always pleasant and beneficial, contact with the wider worlds of regional (states, provinces, and territories), national, and international politics, economy, and culture. Although the local struggle forms the backbone of the narrative, we must include summaries and analyses of the contexts in which these struggles occurred, as well. Because all Latin Americans, regardless of country, participated in this struggle, the economic and political narratives proceed thematically and chronologically.

Volume II offers three chapters (Chapters 10, 13, and 15) that describe the everyday lives of Latin Americans at different points in time. We want students to know what people ate and drank, how they had good times, how they worshipped, where they lived, and what their work was like. The descriptions are individual and anecdotal and collective and quantitative. Thus, it is our hope that students will remember how a Brazilian small farmer raised cassava, or the tortuous efforts of Chilean copper miners. Perhaps, readers will remember the smells of the streets of nineteenth-century cities or the noises of late twentieth-century megalopolises. The struggle for control over everyday life and the descriptions of daily life are related, of course, for the struggle and its context and the reality were joined inseparably. Students should know what the lives were like for which so many bravely and often unsuccessfully fought.

There are other themes interwoven with that of the struggle for control over everyday life. Unlike many other texts in the field, our book gives full and nuanced coverage to the nineteenth century, incorporating the most exciting new scholarship on that period. In the nineteenth century, we assert, chronic war (external and internal) and the accompanying militarization of government and politics profoundly shaped the region's economy and society. We maintain, as well, that race, class, and gender were the crucial underlying elements in Latin American politics. Moreover, warfare, combined with the massive flow of people to the cities, most particularly transformed the place of women.

In the twentieth century, conflict between the upper, middle, and lower classes was the primary moving force behind politics. No ideology from either Left or Right, nor any type of government from democracy to authoritarianism, has brought other than temporary resolutions. We also follow the continued changes in the role of women in society and politics in the face of vast transformations caused by technology and globalization.

It is also our belief that the history of Latin Americans is primarily the story of Latin America and not of the great powers outside the region. To be sure, Europeans and North Americans invested considerable sums of money and sometimes intervened militarily in Latin America. Their wars and rivalries greatly affected Latin America's possibilities. We do note the importance of such key developments as Mexico's loss of half its national territory to the United States in 1848, the impact of the Cold War on Latin America, and the training that right-wing Latin American military establishments received at the hands of U.S. military forces in the late twentieth century. But we prefer to keep the spotlight on the people of Latin America themselves.

SPECIAL FEATURES

In addition to the main narrative of our book, we have included three separate features in each chapter. Each chapter offers a feature called "Latin American Lives," a biography of an individual whose life illustrates some of the key points of that chapter. Many of these figures are not well known.. Chapter 2, for example, highlights Tanta Carhua, a young woman sacrificed to the Inca sun god in Peru, while Chapter 4 discusses a seventeenth-century Spaniard who made a fortune mining silver in Bolivia. We also give a "Slice of Life" for each chapter—a vignette that takes students to the scene of the action and that illustrates in detail some of the social processes under discussion. We include, for example, deliberations of the Spanish cabildo at Cuzco, Peru, in 1551, living conditions in Chilean copper mining camps in the late nineteenth century, and the circumstances that provoked Mexico City's so-called "Parián Riot" of 1828.

We hope, too, to convey a sense of the methods that historians have used in bringing that texture of everyday life to light and the many debates the intriguing history of Latin

America has generated. Each chapter therefore includes a piece entitled "How Historians Understand," designed to give readers better insights into the way that historians go about their work or the ways in which historical knowledge is used and transformed according to the concerns of a particular time and place. Chapter 5, for example, describes how historians have measured Indian acculturation under colonial rule by analyzing the incorporation of Spanish words into indigenous language sources. In Chapter 9, we show how changing political conditions in Mexico are reflected in the many myths and interpretations that have arisen concerning the life of President Benito Juárez.

AIDS TO LEARNING

Because students are at the heart of this enterprise, we have included a number of aids to learning. A glossary explains technical terms and Spanish and Portuguese words used in the text. Discussion questions at the end of the special features Latin American Lives, Slice of Life, and How Historians Understand are intended to stimulate classroom discussion and individual research projects. We have also included suggestions for further reading at the end of each chapter. In keeping with our emphasis on everyday life in Latin American history, we have chosen books that give readers especially clear views of "ordinary" men, women, and children as they went about their daily lives and made Latin America what it is today, at the beginning of the twenty-first century.

ACKNOWLEDGMENTS

Textbooks are inherently collective enterprises. In synthesizing the work of other scholars we have come to an extraordinary appreciation for the remarkable researches and analyses of our colleagues all over the world. We have tried to use the best old and new discoveries to illuminate Latin America's past. The list of those to whom we are beholden is endless. Because space constraints forced us to eschew scholarly apparatus, we have not presented formal recognition of these contributions. Many will recognize their work on our pages. They should regard this as our highest compliment. Some, but by no means all, we mention in our "Learning More about Latin Americans" at the end of each chapter. But the latter include only books in English that primarily pertain to everyday life, so it is incomplete.

We would like to thank the editors at Longman, especially Erika Gutierrez, whose patience and encouragement fostered the project. Thanks, too, to Danielle E. Wasserman, who read and commented on the chapters in Volume II, and to our colleagues Sandra McGee-Deutsch and Samuel Baily for their helpful suggestions. To Marlie Wasserman and Charles Martin, our gratitude for putting up with us during the years that this book was in the making. Special thanks to the many students who have taken our courses at Rutgers

University and the University of Texas at El Paso over the last three decades. Their questions and enthusiasm for learning about the people of Latin America helped inspire this book.

Finally, we would like to thank the following reviewers for their helpful comments and suggestions:

Ida Altman, *University of Florida*

Thomas Benjamin, *Central Michigan University*

Christina Bueno, *Northeastern Illinois University*

Nicola Foote, *Florida Gulf Coast University*

Orlando A. Hernandez, *New York University*

Michael K. Ward, *Ventura College*

Cheryl E. Martin

Mark Wasserman

ABOUT THE AUTHORS

Cheryl E. Martin has taught Latin American History at the University of Texas at El Paso since 1978. A native of Buffalo, New York, she received her bachelor's degree from the Georgetown University School of Foreign Service and her M.A. and Ph.D. from Tulane University. She studied at the Universidad de Cuenca, Ecuador, on a Fulbright Fellowship and was a visiting instructor at the Universidad Autónoma de Chihuahua, Mexico. Her publications include *Rural Society in Colonial Morelos* (1985) and *Governance and Society in Colonial Mexico: Chihuahua in the Eighteenth Century* (1996). She also coedited, with William Beezley and William E. French, *Rituals of Rule, Rituals of Resistance: Public Celebrations and Popular Culture in Mexico* (1994).

Professor Martin has served on the council of the American Historical Association and on the editorial boards of the *Hispanic American Historical Review, The Americas,* the *Latin American Research Review,* and H-Borderlands. She has received two fellowships from the National Endowment for the Humanities and Awards for Distinguished Achievement in both teaching and research at the University of Texas at El Paso. She is the proud grandmother of Mackenzie and Zachary.

Mark Wasserman is a professor of history at Rutgers, the State University of New Jersey, where he has taught since 1978. Brought up in Marblehead, Massachusetts, he earned his B.A. at Duke University and his M.A. and Ph.D. at the University of Chicago. He is the author of three books on Mexico: *Capitalists, Caciques, and Revolution: The Native Elite and Foreign Enterprise in Chihuahua, Mexico, 1854–1911* (1984); *Persistent Oligarchs: Elites and Politics in Chihuahua, Mexico, 1910–1940* (1993); and *Everyday Life and Politics in Nineteenth Century Mexico: Men, Women, and War* (2000). He also coauthored the early editions of the best-selling *History of Latin America (1980–1988)* with Benjamin Keen. Professor Wasserman has twice won the Arthur P. Whitaker Prize for his books. Professor Wasserman has received research fellowships from the Tinker Foundation, the American Council of Learned Societies/Social Science Research Council, the American Philosophical Society, and the National Endowment of the Humanities. He has been Vice-Chair for Undergraduate Education of the Rutgers Department of History and Chair of the Department's Teaching Effectiveness Committee. Professor Wasserman was an elected member of the Highland Park, New Jersey, Board of Education for nearly a decade and served as its president for 2 years. He is an avid fan of Duke basketball and enjoys reading mystery novels, hiking, and travel.

1

THE FIRST PEOPLES
OF THE AMERICAS

WHEN WE THINK of the pre-Columbian past of North and South America, the images that come most readily to mind are perhaps the spectacular empires of the Aztecs of Mexico and the Incas of Peru, whose splendid architecture, art, and social organization dazzled the Spanish conquistadors of the sixteenth century. But the Incas and the Aztecs had risen to prominence little more than a century before the first Europeans arrived. They succeeded in building their great cities and empires only because they could draw upon the technical and cultural achievements of previous societies in the Americas.

For thousands of years, human beings had occupied the lands that would one day be home to the Incas and the Aztecs and many other peoples. Through a long process of trial and error, they had learned how to make those lands productive enough to feed growing numbers of people who devoted their time to endeavors beyond mere subsistence. They observed the movements of stars and pondered what cosmic forces were responsible for the origins and sustenance of human life. They also discovered how to organize growing populations into complex but cohesive units capable of building monuments to their gods and palaces for their leaders. In this chapter, we will explore how these early Americans learned to harness the resources of their natural environment and how they built their communities and refined the cultural legacies of their ancestors.

THE FIRST AMERICANS

The first human inhabitants of the Americas had no sense that they were entering a "new world" when they walked across the frozen Bering Strait from Siberia to Alaska, or paddled small canoes along the coast, probably in pursuit of mammoths, mastodons, bison, antelope,

1

caribou, and wild horses. Nor, of course, did they think of themselves as "Americans." Each person probably identified only with the small group with whom he or she traveled. Only much later would they begin to identify with larger communities. Not until Europeans arrived in this hemisphere, just over 500 years ago, was the word "America" even coined. Many more years elapsed before the people for whom this was a very "old" world came to call themselves "Native Americans." But for want of better terminology, we shall speak of them as the earliest Americans.

Coming to America

The timing of the first migrations to the Americas is subject to debate, but most authorities believe that they probably began more than 35,000 years ago and continued until about 14,000 years ago. Then the climate began to warm, and the ice bridge gradually melted. Although some theorists claim to have found evidence of occasional contact between the two hemispheres after that time, the "new world" remained separated from the "old" for more than 10 millennia. The migrants spread throughout North and South America, adapting to the changing ecological conditions they found. Again, scholars dispute the chronology of this movement. Some cite evidence of human habitation in northeastern Brazil as many as 30,000 years ago, and many others assert that the Andean highlands of South America have been occupied for over 15,000 years. Virtually all experts agree that human beings had reached southern Chile by at least 10,000 and perhaps as many as 14,000 years ago.

Subsistence Strategies and the Development of Agriculture

These early Americans were foragers, subsisting on fish, leaves, eggs, insects, lizards, nuts, and fruits, as well as whatever game they could trap and kill. People in central and southern Mexico, for example, obtained animal protein from deer, foxes, gophers, rabbits, and tortoises. These hunter-gatherers of aboriginal America moved from place to place as food supplies fluctuated with the changing seasons, sometimes stopping to camp a while, or even permanently, where foods were abundant in one place. Foraging also provided fibers that could be fashioned into baskets, fishnets, and textiles; animal hides that were used for clothing and shelter; as well as dyestuffs, stimulants, and hallucinogens.

WESTERN HEMISPHERE	EASTERN HEMISPHERE
35,000 BP–14,000 BP Migrations from Siberia to North America	
10,000 BP Human settlements in southern Chile	
	7000–4000 BCE Spread of agriculture in the Middle East
6500–3500 BCE Transition to agriculture in Mesoamerica	
5000–2000 BCE Transition to agriculture in Peru	**2600 BCE** Building of the first great pyramid in Egypt

2000 BCE
Fully sedentary communities and first ceremonial centers found in Mesoamerica and Peru

1500 BCE
Metalworking in Peru

1200–400 BCE
Olmec civilization in Mexico

900–200 BCE
Chavín de Huantar in Peru

500 BCE–700 CE
Monte Albán in Oaxaca, Mexico

300 BCE–800 CE
The Classic Maya

250 BCE–1000 CE
Tiwanaku in Bolivia

100 BCE–750 CE
Teotihuacan, Mexico

100–750 CE
The Moche and Nazca in coastal Peru

500–850 CE
The Wari Empire, Peru

700–1200 CE
Mixtec ascendancy, Oaxaca, Mexico

800–1517 CE
The Post-Classic Maya

900–1200 CE
The Toltecs, central Mexico

1150–1532 CE
The Chimu Kingdom, Peru

1798–1750 BCE
Rule of Hammurabi in Babylon

1000–870 BCE
King David in Israel

470–430 BCE
The height of Greek civilization at Athens

27 BCE
Augustus founds the Roman Empire

476 CE
The fall of Rome

700–800 CE
Spread of Islam

1066 CE
Norman Conquest of England

Gradually, aboriginal Americans discovered that they could plant seeds at propitious locations and return later to harvest a crop, and that they could carry seeds with them to new places. They began supplementing their diets with a few cultivated plants without making a conscious "transition to agriculture." Farming involves hard work and a delay between the planting of crops and the consumption of food, while foraging offers more instant gratification. Thousands of years passed before these early Americans derived the bulk of their nutritional needs from crops they had planted and nurtured. The gradual extinction of mammoths, horses, and other large game after about 8000 BCE gave them an extra incentive to find new sources of food.

People in Mexico and Central America—what archaeologists call Mesoamerica—developed some of the earliest complex agricultural systems. Gourds were evidently the first plants to be cultivated, perhaps as early as 6500 BCE Next came squashes, beans, peppers, and avocados. With the domestication of maize by about 3500 BCE, the Classic Mesoamerican diet was born. These crops supplied essential carbohydrates, vegetable proteins, fats, and vitamins, which ancient Mesoamericans continued to supplement with animal protein from small game and fish. Meanwhile, they also began cultivating cotton. Agriculture began developing in parts of South America by 5000 BCE. In the Peruvian Andes, people cultivated potatoes and lesser-known tubers such as oca and ullucu. High in caloric content, these crops could be grown even at altitudes above 10,000 feet. At lower elevations, they grew maize, a grain known as quinoa, and various legumes. By 3000 BCE, early Andean peoples as far south as Chile had domesticated guinea pigs for food, llamas as beasts of burden, and alpacas as a source of wool. Images of llamas and alpacas appear in the rock art of these ancient Americans.

The development of agriculture in coastal Peru shows how ancient Americans gradually added cultivated plants to their diet. The ocean, full of fish carried by the Humboldt Current, was the prime "hunting ground" of these early Peruvians. They ate anchovies, sardines, and larger fish, as well as mussels, clams, crabs, sea lions, and marine birds. Beginning perhaps about 4000 BCE, they began growing crops a few miles inland on the flood plains of rivers that flowed from the Andes to the coast. In addition to squash, beans, peppers, sweet potatoes, and manioc, they grew cotton that could be woven into fishnets and gourds that were used as flotation devices for the nets. But only after 2000 BCE, as they added maize to their list of crops, did more of their diets come from agriculture than from hunting, gathering, and fishing.

Maize cultivation had spread over a wide area by 2000 BCE, from the interior of Brazil to parts of what is now the southwestern United States. It reached eastern North America during the following millennium and the Caribbean coast of what is now Colombia by the year 1 CE. Elsewhere, hunting and gathering persisted even longer as the primary mode of subsistence, in some cases until well after the arrival of Europeans in the hemisphere.

Sedentary Communities and Ceremonial Centers

Once they could obtain sufficient food in one place, early Americans became more sedentary. The establishment of permanent villages usually accompanied the domestication of plants, and fully sedentary communities appeared throughout Mesoamerica and the Andes by 2000 BCE. In coastal Peru and Chile, however, fishing provided so much nourishment that a sedentary lifestyle developed long before agriculture provided more than an incidental source of food. In some communities, people obtained more than 90 percent of their diet from the sea.

The establishment of sedentary communities and the growing productivity of agriculture and fishing created pools of labor that could devote energy to nonsubsistence pursuits. As some individuals assumed positions of command and orchestrated collective construction projects, the ancient Americas witnessed the development of public architecture—structures that served purposes other than minimal shelter for humans and storage of food. Most often, these buildings were dedicated to religious rituals aimed at tapping the power of the supernatural. Some of the earliest monumental structures, found in coastal Peru, date from between 3000 and 2000 BCE, roughly contemporaneous with the Old Kingdom pyramids of Egypt and the ziggurats of Mesopotamia. The Huaca de los Sacrificios and the Huaca de los Idolos at Aspero, some 100 miles north of present-day Lima, are sloped stone platforms measuring about 100 by 150 feet at their bases. Atop the platforms sit multiroomed structures, their interior walls adorned with friezes and niches.

Other projects that required collective labor also began to appear in Peru and elsewhere by the second millennium BCE. Most important were irrigation canals in the arid coastal lowlands and agricultural terraces on the slopes of the Andes. Such technical improvements increased agricultural yields, allowing larger populations to thrive. The people of coastal Ecuador, Colombia, and perhaps the Amazon lowlands had learned to make pottery as early as 3000 BCE, and by 2000 BCE potters could be found in many parts of the Americas, manufacturing utilitarian items for storing and cooking foods, as well as figurines and drinking vessels used for ritual purposes.

CEREMONIAL CENTERS IN MEXICO AND PERU

Toward the latter half of the second millennium BCE, more complex societies developed in some parts of Mesoamerica and the Andes. Farmers now produced surpluses sufficient to enable many people to become full-time construction workers, artisans, rulers, and ritual specialists. The result was an increase in the building and use of ceremonial centers, which in turn brought remarkable advances in art and architecture. Religious practices became more elaborate, and social divisions among people of different occupations widened.

The Olmec: "Mother Culture" of Mexico?

One of the first groups in Mesoamerica to develop large ceremonial complexes were the Olmec, who lived in what are now the states of Veracruz and Tabasco, along the tropical coast of the Gulf of Mexico. Fertile soil and abundant rainfall allowed farmers to harvest maize and other crops twice a year, freeing others to build and embellish temples. Of the several dozen known Olmec ceremonial centers, San Lorenzo and La Venta have received the most attention from archaeologists. San Lorenzo reached its greatest splendor between 1200 and 900 BCE, while La Venta flourished somewhat later, between 900 and 400 BCE. Neither center had a resident population of more than about 1000, so they must have drawn on the many surrounding villages for the labor necessary to construct these works.

The first Mesoamerican people to carve bas-reliefs and statues in the round, the Olmec crafted giant basalt heads, more than 8 feet high and weighing 20 tons or more.

How Historians Understand	ARCHAEOLOGY, LITERACY, AND THE STUDY OF HISTORY

Our discussion of early American societies has relied heavily on archaeological evidence—temples, tombs, and homes; the murals and carvings that adorned these structures; and the artifacts left behind by the men, women, and children who lived, died, worked, played, and worshipped at these sites. Through painstaking study of everything from tiny fragments of pottery to enormous pyramids, archaeologists have deduced much about the lives and worldviews of these people. They have even analyzed coprolites (fossilized human feces) to learn what early Americans ate.

New archaeological discoveries are constantly adding to our knowledge, yet enormous gaps remain. For most early American civilizations, we can only give approximate dates, even for specific events such as the founding of Monte Albán or the dedication of Quetzalcoatl's temple at Teotihuacan. Indeed, we do not even know what language was spoken at Teotihuacan, or what its residents called their splendid city. We know much more about their European contemporaries, the ancient Romans. For Rome, we have the names of specific individuals and very precise dates, the kind of data that are the historian's traditional stock in trade. We know, for example, that Julius Caesar was assassinated on the Ides of March in 44 BCE, and his writings allow us to share, word for word, his perspective on military and political matters.

Thus, we can speak of Julius Caesar and the Romans as "historic" peoples in the sense that we know their names, deeds, and dates, while Americans of Caesar's time remain "prehistoric." It is not that they had no stories to tell, nor even that they did not record them for posterity. But instead of using alphabetic script, most of them used pictures and stylized designs that appeared on temple walls, textiles, and pottery.

balam

ba - balam - ma

Maya writing combined symbols that stood for whole words as well as symbols that represented syllables. In this example, the first of the two signs—a picture of a cat's head—represents the word "jaguar" (*balam* in Maya). But scribes added syllabic symbols to distinguish the jaguar from other spotted cats. The element to the left of the cat's head stands for the sound "ba," while the symbols beneath the head signify the sound "ma."

The facial features of each head are so distinctive that archaeologists theorize that they were portraits of specific individuals. The stone used for these figures came from more than 50 miles away and was probably rolled on logs and then transported on wooden rafts along the region's many rivers. The Olmec also created huge mosaics, measuring 15 by 20 feet, in the form of jaguar masks. They excelled in carving smaller pieces, such as ceremonial axes, jewelry, and figurines from jade and other semiprecious stones. Already evident at San Lorenzo by 1150 BCE, their distinctive artistic style often depicted beings

Their priests and rulers knew the meaning of these symbols and used them as memory aids or illustrations in explaining concepts or events, rather like a speaker might refer to notes and display images on a screen for the audience. What is missing is the kind of verbatim transcripts that we have for the famous orators of ancient Greece and Rome.

The Classic Maya and the Mixtecs and Zapotecs of southern Mexico are something of an exception. They left detailed pictures and symbols that expressed abstract ideas, and the Maya developed a form of writing that reproduced human speech. For these people, we can identify specific rulers, their lineages, and the precise dates of their reigns. The glyphs identifying King Pacal of Palenque are phonetic, so we even know what people called this great Mayan lord of the seventh century CE. Even so, they remain much more obscure to us than their contemporaries in Europe.

Our understanding of the ancient societies of the Americas is further limited by events that followed the arrival of Europeans in the sixteenth century. Native priests who might have explained symbols recorded by their ancestors died in the conquest or were driven underground, so much of their knowledge was lost to future generations. Sometimes Spanish priests ordered the destruction of indigenous writings and artifacts, believing that they were the work of the devil. At other times, some of these same missionaries wrote down their observations of native society and religion, providing a valuable view of indigenous culture, at least from the perspective of sixteenth-century Spaniards and their native informants.

The archaeological record itself became obscured over the course of many centuries, as important pre-Columbian sites suffered the ravages of weather, earthquakes, and looters. Even today many sites remain unexplored. But it is important to remember that the people who built Chavín de Huantar and Teotihuacan were as culturally sophisticated as their contemporaries in Greece and Rome.

Questions for Discussion

Does the absence of written texts about most ancient American societies affect the way we think about their descendants in our own times? How would our attitudes toward classical Greece and Rome be different if we only had archaeological remains to tell us about them?

that combined human and jaguar-like features. Spindle whorls found at San Lorenzo also indicate that they were experts in textile production.

Because the Olmec showed many cultural traits that reappeared in later civilizations in Mexico and Central America, scholars have portrayed them as the "mother culture" of Mexico. They were evidently among the first to play the Mesoamerican ball game, a ritual that had profound religious overtones. Rubber is abundant in the Gulf Coast area, and indeed the name "Olmec" (literally, "people of the place with rubber") is what centuries

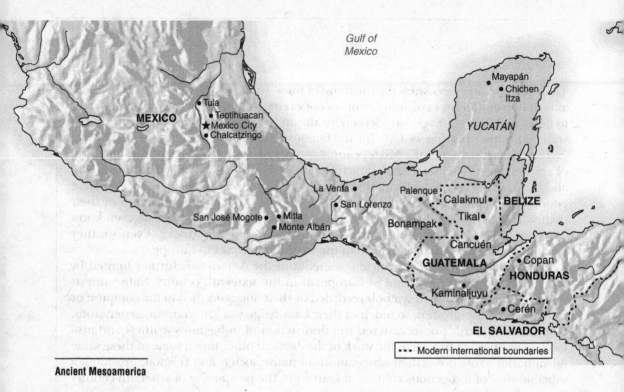

Ancient Mesoamerica

later the Aztecs would call those who lived there. The Olmec began manufacturing rubber balls as early as 1200 BCE, eventually exporting them throughout Mesoamerica. Their 260-day ritual cycle was still central to Mesoamerican religion when Europeans arrived some 2500 years later. They also had a rudimentary writing, in the form of glyphs using dots and dashes. Although archaeologists have not succeeded in deciphering these symbols, they were probably calendar notations.

Another important cultural innovation that apparently developed in various parts of Mesoamerica during the later stages of the Olmec era was the tortilla. Although Mesoamericans had eaten maize for several millennia, it was in the form of roasted ears or a gruel known as *atole*, both of which were perishable and not easily portable. Production of tortillas—grinding the maize and shaping it into flat pancakes and toasting them on a ceramic griddle called a *comal*—was highly intensive labor, usually performed by women. Unlike atole and roasted ears of corn, tortillas lasted for several days and were easily transported. Archaeologists surmise that they served as a convenient "fast food" for merchants or armies in transit and may have had a significant impact on the economic and political transformation of Mesoamerica.

Whether or not the Olmec in fact were the originators of Mesoamerican culture, they maintained extensive contact with their contemporaries as far south as El Salvador. Some of their jade came from the state of Guerrero in western Mexico, and they acquired obsidian from Oaxaca in the south. Evidence has been found of an Olmec colony at Chalcatzingo in Morelos, just south of modern-day Mexico City, dating from about 900 BCE.

Chavín de Huantar in Peru

At about the same time that Olmec civilization was developing in Mesoamerica, the Andes entered a new cultural phase with the rise of the ceremonial site known as Chavín de Huantar, located in northern Peru at an altitude of more than 9000 feet. Chavín reached its peak between 400 and 200 BCE. Like San Lorenzo and La Venta in Mexico, it served primarily as a center of religious observances, with a resident population that never surpassed 3000. It stood at the juncture of natural travel routes in the Andes, and pilgrims from a wide area came to consult its oracle and attend religious rituals held at its Old Temple. This structure contained more than 1600 feet of internal drainage and ventilation ducts. Water draining through the canals must have produced impressive acoustic effects. An interior staircase enabled priests to emerge at the top of the mound. A sunken courtyard in front of the temple was large enough to hold 500 people. Religious observances at Chavín evidently employed hallucinogens, intoxicants, ritual cannibalism, and sacrificial offerings of llamas and guinea pigs.

Chavín art features images of snakes, jaguars, caymans, and other jungle fauna, as well as tropical crops such as manioc and peanuts, suggesting contact with the Amazon basin east of the Andes. Luxury items found at Chavín include lapis lazuli from as far away as the Atacama Desert of northern Chile and cinnabar (mercuric sulfide, which produces a brilliant red dye), probably from the mountains of southern Peru. Large strombus shells from coastal Ecuador were fashioned into trumpets used in religious ceremonies. The people of Chavín used tools made of obsidian, obtained from more than 250 miles away. These items and goods such as coca, chile peppers, salt, and dried fish were carried to Chavín on the backs of llamas.

Artisans at Chavín were well known for their expertise and innovation in textile design. They combined llama and alpaca hairs with cotton fibers and wove them into fabric. Their textiles featured multicolored

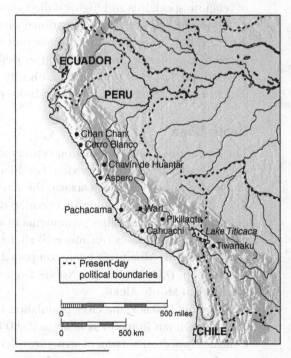

Ancient Peru

designs, some of them painted on and others achieved through techniques similar to tie-dyeing and batik. Metalworkers at Chavín learned soldering techniques and produced silver, gold, and copper alloys. They were evidently the first to craft three-dimensional objects from metal. Chavín exerted cultural influence over a wide area along the coast of Peru and in the highlands as well. Pilgrims visiting the shrine probably brought ritual and utilitarian objects home with them, providing models that could be replicated by artisans who had never been to Chavín.

After 200 BCE, the Chavín cult began to decline, perhaps because of widespread droughts. Building of monumental structures stopped throughout its sphere of cultural influence. Localized artistic designs replaced Chavín motifs on ceramics and other media. But the memory of Chavín de Huantar lived on. Sixteenth-century Spaniards marveled at the old temple, and a stone bridge that crossed the nearby Wachesqa River remained in use for nearly 3000 years, until a landslide destroyed it in 1945.

THE CITIES OF CLASSIC MESOAMERICA

The monumental public architecture of San Lorenzo, La Venta, and Chavín de Huantar served important ceremonial purposes, but these sites cannot be considered true cities, because their permanent populations remained small and probably consisted primarily of religious specialists and highly skilled artisans. In the latter half of the first millennium BCE, however, the size and occupational diversity of a few places in Mexico and Central America took on proportions that warrant their designation as genuine urban centers. Social hierarchies became more sharply defined, and systems of government developed the multiple layers of power and authority characteristic of modern states. The ascendancy of these centers inaugurated a 1000-year epoch known as the Classic period.

Monte Albán

The first of these great population centers was Monte Albán, just outside the present-day city of Oaxaca in southern Mexico. Founded by the Zapotec people in about 500 BCE at the center of the Valley of Oaxaca, the city dominated the surrounding area for more than 1000 years. Archaeologists theorize that Monte Albán owed its existence to the deliberate decision of valley settlements to establish a capital on a neutral site, perhaps for defensive purposes but more likely to settle disputes among themselves. In this respect, Monte Albán has been compared to newly created modern capitals such as Washington, D.C., or Brasilia. Nobles from communities throughout the valley took up residence at Monte Albán.

By about 250 BCE, the city's population reached 15,000, and at its height in the sixth century CE. it was home to as many as 25,000 people. These figures are, of course, rough estimates based on surveys of structures that, in their design or the distribution of artifacts found within them, suggest they served as dwellings for "ordinary" households.

Archaeologists have discovered what they believe are 15 separate residential subdivisions at Monte Albán, many of them situated on carefully created terraces on the sides of mountains. The city's main ceremonial structures sat atop an artificially flattened mountain that towered 1300 feet above the valley. They include a pyramid with an internal staircase leading to the top, numerous sacrificial altars, a ball court, and palaces that probably housed its priestly elite. A defensive wall protected the city on its north and west sides (see Plate 3).

Monte Albán evidently collected tribute in the form of food and other supplies from many smaller communities. Hieroglyphics adorning the palaces may refer to specific locations under its dominion. One of its most famous structures, dating from between 500 and 250 BCE, is the Palacio de los Danzantes (Palace of the Dancers), named for the 150 bas-reliefs of naked, contorted male figures that adorn its exterior walls. Archaeologists now believe that these images represent not dancers but rather prisoners captured in battle, perhaps being tortured, or the corpses of sacrificial victims. The hundreds of stelae (pillars carved with hieroglyphics) found at the site show Zapotec rulers standing on symbols said to stand for conquered territories, also suggesting that their influence spread through military force. Archaeologists have explored nearly 200 tombs at Monte Albán. These enclosures have highly decorated entranceways covered with hieroglyphics and frescoes on some of the interior walls. One particularly impressive tomb features the Zapotec god of maize wearing an elaborate headdress of serpents and feathers. Pottery funeral urns and lavish grave offerings can be found in many of the tombs.

There are many signs of Olmec influence or cultural kinship. The facial features of the "dancers" on the Palacio de los Danzantes resemble Olmec styles. The people of Monte Albán used a form of glyphs, probably associated with calendrical signs and the 260-day ritual calendar, that again are reminiscent of the Olmec. But they built on cultural traditions closer to home as well. A site known as San José Mogote flourished in the northern branch of the Valley of Oaxaca between 1350 and 500 BCE. Its archaeological remains feature figures similar to the danzantes.

Monte Albán's decline set in after 600 CE, as it lost access to merchandise coming from the great central Mexican city of Teotihuacan (see below) and the Zapotec rulers could no longer use these commodities to buy the loyalty of chiefs from other valley communities. By the year 700 CE, the population of Monte Albán had shrunk to about 4000, and the political unity of the valley fragmented.

Teotihuacan

Urban centers on an even grander scale arose in the Valley of Mexico, not far from today's Mexico City. Cuicuilco, at the southwestern edge of the valley, grew in population to more than 10,000 by 300 BCE, but its continued development ceased around 50 BCE, when volcanic eruptions destroyed the agricultural lands on which it depended and created the lava beds that residents of Mexico City today call the *pedregal*. Cuicuilco's decline opened the way for the city that centuries later the Aztecs would call Teotihuacan, "the place of the gods," to dominate the entire valley. Teotihuacan's population had already topped 40,000 by 100 BCE. At its peak 600 years later, it had well over 100,000, and by some accounts as many as 200,000 residents, making it one of the largest cities anywhere in the world at the time. Its ethnically diverse population included a colony of Oaxacans and another of people from Veracruz. At least a third of the city's residents worked at pursuits other than farming.

Teotihuacan is today one of Mexico's leading tourist attractions, and justifiably so. The city's territorial expanse covered about 12 square miles, and everything about it was of monumental proportions. It had about 600 pyramids, including the massive Pyramid of the Sun, more than 215 feet high and measuring half a million square feet at its base, as well as the smaller but equally impressive Pyramid of the Moon. The central prome-nade, now called the Street of the Dead, is 150 feet wide and more than 2 miles long. More than 100 palaces housed priests and other dignitaries. The facades of the Pyramids of the Sun and Moon were once covered with brightly colored stucco designs. Another exquisitely decorated structure, the Temple of Quetzalcoatl, bears carved images of the feathered serpent deity found at many Mesoamerican sites and another identified as the rain god. Pilgrims evidently came from great distances to participate in rituals at Teotihuacan. The city was a haven of artisan and mercantile activity, with a huge market complex and hundreds of workshops for manufacturing ceramics and obsidian tools.

Archaeologists speculate that about 2000 apartment complexes, laid out on a grid pattern and dating from the fourth century CE, housed the city's working population. Excavations of these compounds give a glimpse of everyday life in Teotihuacan. Household artifacts include numerous comales, so the preparation and consumption of tortillas was evidently common. Cooking of other foods was done on small braziers, prob-ably in open-air patios scattered throughout the apartment structures. Their residences contained numerous incense burners and ceramic figurines, suggesting that religious rit-uals were part of the domestic routine.

Although scholars once depicted Mesoamerica's Classic period as a "golden age" of peace and artistic advance, it is now clear that Teotihuacan used military force to extend its influence throughout central Mexico. Large numbers of men were conscripted into its armies. Military motifs appear in murals and ceramics with increasing frequency, espe-cially after 650 CE. Soldiers from Teotihuacan were evidently the first Mesoamericans to use the type of quilted cotton body armor—as much as 2 or 3 inches thick—that Aztec armies wore when they confronted the Spanish. Enemies captured in battle became sac-rificial victims. Mass human sacrifices marked the dedication of the Temple of Quetzalcoatl around 150 CE. Their corpses were buried beneath the pyramid, along with their military accoutrements. It is likely too that some of the city's spectacular population growth can be attributed to the forced relocation of conquered peoples.

Teotihuacan's cultural and economic influence spread even further than its military reach, thanks to its monopoly on obsidian, the sharpest material known to Americans before the introduction of European steel. Its trade networks extended to what is now the southwestern United States and southward to Central America. At the Maya highland center of Kaminaljuyu in Guatemala, many public buildings dating from the early sixth century resembled structures found at Teotihuacan. The art and architecture of Monte Albán also show Teotihuacan influences, and the Zapotec elites became fond of luxury goods imported from the north.

By the sixth century CE, Teotihuacan evidently began losing population. The center of the city was destroyed and burned about 750, probably by its own people, though perhaps by seminomadic groups invading the valley from the north and west. The decline of Teotihuacan probably contributed to the demise of other Mesoamerican sites, whose elites lost access to the goods they had obtained from the great city in the valley of Mexico. Following the collapse of Teotihuacan, a substantial portion of its population dispersed throughout central Mexico. As many as 30,000 residents remained in place for years to come, but the days of Teotihuacan's glory had clearly passed. Several hundred years later, however, the Aztecs believed that a race of giants had lived there, and that it had been the birthplace of the "fifth sun," the universe as they knew it.

Maya Civilization in the Classic Era

The lowland rainforests of southern Mexico, Guatemala, Honduras, and Belize witnessed the rise of another great civilization of the Classic Era, the Maya, beginning in the third century BCE and peaking about 1000 years later. One of the greatest achievements of the Maya was the development of a true system of writing. While other early American peoples used pictorial symbols that sometimes came to stand for abstract ideas and occasionally even sounds, Classic Mayan writing is phonetic—that is, many of the glyphs we see on their carved stone monuments, and in their few surviving books, stood for sounds. The Maya could record the spoken word far more accurately than any other pre-Columbian civilization. Their writing system was, in the words of Maya scholars Linda Schele and David Freidel, "a rich and expressive script, capable of faithfully recording every nuance of sound, meaning, and grammatical structure in the writers' language." Scholars have deciphered close to 90 percent of the Mayan glyphs. Many Mayan writings record the genealogies of local ruling classes, and the Maya are the earliest Americans for whom we can identify specific individuals and exact dates. For individuals such as Pacal, lord of Palenque in southern Mexico, we can reconstruct full biographies and genealogies. But Mayan script also reveals much about religious rituals and the lives of warriors and artisans as well as kings and queens.

Mayan civilization had no single dominant center comparable to Teotihuacan or Monte Albán. Instead, there were more than 50 politically autonomous but interdependent city-states, each drawing tribute from a hinterland that probably extended no more than a day's travel from the center. With a population that neared 50,000, Tikal in Guatemala was one of the largest and most powerful Mayan cities, and one of the most spectacular as well. It boasted several artificial lakes and the tallest known Classic Mayan structure, at 230 feet. Its ruling dynasty was established in 219 CE. Copán in Honduras may have had a sphere of influence comparable in size to Tikal. Glyphs referring to Tikal have been found at Copán, and vice versa, indicting that the two cities had considerable contact with one another.

LATIN AMERICAN LIVES

PACAL THE GREAT, KING OF PALENQUE, 603–683 CE

PALENQUE (the word comes from the Spanish word for stockade) in the southern Mexican state of Chiapas is one of the most frequently visited Mayan sites. It rose to prominence during the final two centuries of the Classic Era by extending its influence over the surrounding region through military conquest and marriage alliances with local rulers. Palenque's most distinctive building, a palace that evidently served as an administrative center and a residence for members of its ruling elite, features a four-story square tower that commanded a stunning view of the city's environs. Archaeologists have found a glyph representing the planet Venus on one of the tower's interior walls, suggesting that it also functioned as an observatory.

Palenque reached its peak in the seventh century, during the reign of King Pacal the Great. Pacal received the throne in 615 from his mother, Queen Zac-kuk, and ruled for nearly 70 years until his death in 683. Painted relief sculptures on many of Palenque's structures chronicle his genealogy and the elaborate rituals that accompanied his funeral. When Pacal was about 70 years old, work began on the Temple of the Inscriptions, the pyramid that would eventually serve as his tomb. Among its carved images is one depicting Pacal's passage from this world to the next.

An interior staircase led from the summit of the Temple of the Inscriptions to Pacal's subterranean crypt. There he was entombed in great splendor, along with half a dozen people sacrificed as part of his funeral rites. His corpse was adorned with a collar, headpiece, earspools, rings, and bracelets, all made of jade. A mask fashioned from jade, shells, and obsidian covered his face. His sarcophagus and the walls of his tomb featured likenesses of Pacal, his mother, and his oldest son and successor Chan Bahlum ("Serpent Jaguar"). These images suggest that in death and perhaps in life Pacal had come to be identified with the Sun god and that his mother was the mother of all the gods.

Great construction projects and important architectural innovations continued during the reign of Chan Bahlum, which officially began 132 days after Pacal's death and continued until the year 702. Especially worthy of note is the Temple of the Cross, built to commemorate Chan Bahlum's accession to the throne. It too contained images of Pacal, again showing him as the Sun god, and the passing of royal authority from father to son. The temple was positioned so that light struck these images only at sunset on the day of the winter solstice.

The builders of the Temple of the Cross intended that Pacal's rule would be remembered for many years to come. Pacal himself probably encouraged them to think in this way, for he left an inscription proclaiming that his successors would celebrate the anniversary of his coronation 8 days following the end of the Mayan calendar's 8000-year cycle. In our calendar, that day will come on October 15, 4772.

Questions for Discussion
How did King Pacal use monumental architecture to enhance his own power? How do you think Mayan commoners would have responded to these building projects? Is there evidence that the rulers of other communities discussed in this chapter used similar methods of promoting themselves?

Each separate Mayan polity had its *ahau,* or king, and nobility, and these upper classes lived in style. In 2000, archaeologists discovered a splendid palace at Cancuén in Guatemala. Before the excavations began, it resembled a hill covered with dense jungle foliage. The absence of visible pyramids at the site caused previous researchers to overlook it. Covering an area larger than two present-day U.S. football fields, the structure contained 170 rooms and 11 courtyards. Inscriptions date the palace from the reign of King Tah ak Chaan, who ruled at Cancuén from 740 to 790 CE. Even Cancuén's commoners were relatively well off, as evidenced by the many objects of jade found in their graves.

Scholars once thought that the Mayan city-states lived in relative harmony with one another, but images on their monuments suggest otherwise. Recent research has shown that Tikal and the city of Calakmul, some 60 miles to the north, engaged in a protracted conflict, with smaller communities often serving as pawns in this contest of Mayan super-powers. Brilliantly colored murals at Bonampak in Chiapas show captives taken in battle undergoing torture (see Plate 1). The ruling classes of the city-states cemented alliances with one another through marriage, but resorted to warfare when such tactics failed. Fighting evidently consisted of small-scale raids of one community against another, for the jungle terrain of lowland Mesoamerica prohibited the movement of the large armies fielded by highland centers such as Teotihuacan. The extent of warfare among the Classic Maya nonetheless remains subject to debate. The palace of Cancuén, for example, shows no evidence that its rulers engaged in war.

Most lowland Mayan communities had similar resource bases, so trade was not particularly important in their relations with one another. Glyphs at Tikal and other locations suggest that they did carry on long-distance exchanges with Teotihuacan, however. Obsidian from central Mexico and Teotihuacan-type pottery have also been found at numerous Mayan sites, and the people of Cancuén evidently served as intermediaries in the obsidian trade. In exchange, the Maya exported slaves, feathers, chocolate, and animal skins.

The Maya excelled in mathematics, using a system based on units of 20. They were apparently the first people to develop the concept of zero—the Hindus began employing the zero in their calculations in the fifth century CE, while Europeans learned it from the Arabs some 800 years later. The Maya had both a 365-day solar calendar and a 260-day ceremonial calendar. They reckoned time in millions of years. Centuries later, by contrast, most Europeans saw the world as no more than 6000 years old. Their knowledge of astronomy was also considerably ahead of that of Europe at the time. Craft specialists,

Bloodletting was an important part of religious observance for many Mesoamericans. The woman kneeling on the right side of this Mayan stone relief is pulling a thorny cord through her tongue.

including jewelers, featherworkers, painters, carvers, and sculptors, could be found in the larger centers. Most Mayan sites featured ball courts. The murals at Bonampak show that the Maya were also musicians, using drums, rattles made from tortoise shells and gourds, and trumpets, flutes, and whistles made from shell, bone, or wood.

A volcanic eruption that occurred about 600 CE near Cerén in present-day El Salvador left a Mayan village buried in ash. Recent excavations have uncovered homes, a steam bath, and a civic center, giving a rare glimpse of how ordinary men, women, and children lived and worked in Classic times. The people of Cerén evidently lived in nuclear family households. In gardens next to their dwellings, they grew manioc, medicinal plants, and the agave cactus that yielded fiber that could be fashioned into textiles. Storage facilities contained large quantities of beans and other seeds, and strings of chile peppers hung from the rafters of their houses. Their diet also included maize and a fermented beverage made from it, as well as squash, avocados, and chocolate, and the meat of deer, dogs, and other animals. Artifacts found in village homes included *metates* used for grinding maize and sharp obsidian blades. Households had many ceramic pots for cooking, storing, and serving food.

Mayan city-states suffered a devastating collapse beginning around 800 CE. Building of temples and carving of stelae halted, abruptly in many centers, more gradually in others. Construction ceased at Tikal after 830, and the last carved date at Palenque is 799. The ceremonial cores of many cities were abandoned to squatters, and the populations of major sites such as Tikal shrank by as much as 90 percent. Numerous factors have been cited to explain the decline of the Classic Mayan sites. A likely hypothesis points to accelerated population growth and resulting food shortages. Competition for scarce resources in turn exacerbated conflicts among city-states and between working classes and privileged elites. In particular, the conflict between Tikal and Calakmul seems to have contributed substantially to the collapse of many Mayan centers. Intrusions from central Mexico may have further upset an already-delicate ecological balance. The deterioration of trade links with Teotihuacan probably also played a role.

PERU AFTER CHAVÍN

The cultural unity fostered by the cult of Chavín de Huantar fragmented in the second century BCE. Within two centuries, however, new regional centers emerged, more urban in their population size, economic diversity, and social stratification. Some of these cities extended their cultural influence and political control over wide areas. The methods they used to dominate growing populations included warfare, intermarriage with local elites, and political tactics that clearly foreshadowed those later adopted by the Incas. Archaeological sites from this period show growing numbers of fortified villages and defensive bastions stocked with stones that could be hurled at approaching enemies.

The Moche

Contemporaries of the builders of Teotihuacan in Mexico, the warlike people known to archaeologists as the Moche inhabited the river valleys along the arid north coast of Peru. Their influence extended for more than 300 miles, and eventually over a hundreds of thousands of people. Scholars once thought that some kind of centralized empire controlled the entire area, but recent work suggests that at least two separate political entities existed. The Moche people were excellent engineers, building flat-topped pyramid mounds, fortresses, roads, and complex irrigation works. They fertilized fields with bird guano, a substance that became an important export from Peru in the nineteenth century.

Two of the most impressive Moche ceremonial structures, the Huaca del Sol and the Huaca de la Luna, can be found at a site known as Cerro Blanco. Building of these works began around 100 CE. and continued for several centuries. The largest structure in the Western Hemisphere for its time, the Huaca del Sol measured 500 by 1000 feet at its base and was 130 feet high. It probably served as a palace and a mausoleum for deceased rulers. Some 143 million molded adobe bricks were used in its construction, many of them bearing an identifying symbol, perhaps signifying which group of people made the brick as part of their tribute obligation. The settlement surrounding these two structures may have housed as

Moche pottery vessel showing a healer and patient.

many as 10,000 people. Near the Huaca de la Luna, archaeologists have unearthed a pottery workshop dating from between 450 and 550 CE.

The Moche lacked a system of writing comparable to that of the Maya, but they were exceptionally skilled artists, producing splendid ceramics, carvings, and textiles, as well as highly detailed murals and friezes that tell us much about their society and ritual practices. A recurrent motif in Moche art is a deity that archaeologists call "the Decapitator," a fearsome fanged creature who holds a knife in one hand and a human head in the other. Further evidence of human sacrifice can be found at the Huaca de la Luna, where more than 40 skeletons of young men have been unearthed. Excavations of Moche tombs show that sacrifices of llamas and humans accompanied the burials of notable men and women.

Moche art also shows humans going about daily activities, from domestic routines, hunting and fishing, to sexual practices and childbirth, giving us some of the most detailed information that we have about gender roles in early American societies. Their portraits of sick people are so realistic that we can even specify their ailments, and we can see detailed drawings of medicinal plants used to treat them. The Moche left images of the elaborate costumes and fine jewelry worn by nobles on ritual occasions, a feature confirmed by rich caches of gold, silver, and copper ornaments and jewelry made from Chilean lapis lazuli found in Moche tombs (see Plate 2). Indeed, the Moche were expert metalworkers, mastering the art of casting objects such as tools and weapons from molds. Moche society began its decline between 600 and 750 CE, due at least in part to drastic climatic fluctuations, as severe drought alternated with devastating floods that destroyed homes, monuments, and irrigation works.

The Nazca

Contemporaries of the Moche, the Nazca flourished for several hundred years in five separate river valleys along the southern coast of Peru. Their environment was even drier than that of the Moche, and they too excelled in hydraulic engineering. In the sixth century CE., they constructed elaborate aqueducts that enabled them to tap underground streams. Remnants of this system continued to be used down to the twentieth century. Their most famous shrine, known as Cahuachi, was located where the Nazca River surfaced after flowing underground for a considerable distance. Pilgrims came from afar to worship and bury their dead during the period of Cahuachi's ascendancy, from about 100 to 500 CE.

The importance of water to the Nazca can be seen in their geoglyphs, the archaeological feature for which they are best known today. These were large designs, often measuring 5 or more miles in length, traced on the desert plains north of the Nazca River. Still visible from the air today, and perhaps originally intended to be visible to the sky gods, the geoglyphs depict animals, people, and abstract shapes. The Nazca made these markings by scraping away the layer of manganese and iron oxides that covered the ground, so that the lighter-colored soil below could be seen. Scholars once thought that

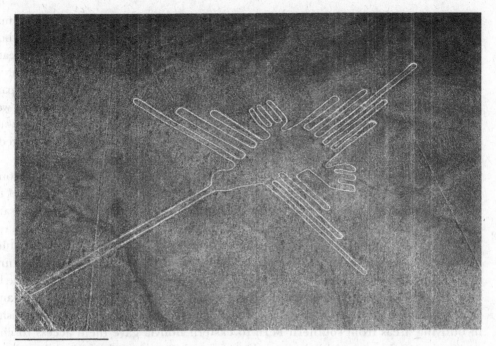

One example of the Nazca lines.

the geoglyphs were aligned with astronomical phenomena, and some people have even seen them as evidence of extraterrestrial contact. Recent research has suggested that the markings pointed to sources of water. One clearly visible line leads from Cahuachi to what appears to have been their most important settlement.

The Nazca excelled in textile production, using alpaca fiber obtained via trade with the highlands as well as cotton grown along the coast. Their textile designs often featured fibers dyed in many shades of the same color. Nazca pottery also employed many different colors. Given the harsh climate of their homeland, the Nazca failed to achieve the population densities of their contemporaries in Mesoamerica or elsewhere in Peru, and their temple mounds and other architectural achievements were more modest in size.

Tiwanaku

Meanwhile, other important centers of South American civilization were developing at much higher inland elevations. One of the foremost of these was Tiwanaku, near Lake Titicaca in present-day Bolivia. Founded in about 250 BCE at an altitude of almost 13,000 feet above sea level, it flourished between 100 and 1200 CE, extending its influence to southern Peru, coastal Chile, and eastern Bolivia through trade and military conquest. At its peak, the city of Tiwanaku covered more than 1000 acres and had a population estimated at between 20,000 and 40,000.

Tiwanaku's most imposing buildings were fitted together without mortar in a manner later copied by the Incas, using large stones transported across Lake Titicaca by boat. The principal ceremonial center sat on an island surrounded by an artificially created moat separating it from the rest of the city. Soil that was dug up to form the moat was then used to create a cross-shaped multilevel platform known as the shrine of Akapana. From its summit, one could see Lake Titicaca and the surrounding mountains that were sacred sites in local religion. Subterranean and surface drainage channels drew water away from the platform and may have produced sound effects similar to those created at Chavín de Huantar many centuries before.

The people of Tiwanaku excelled in weaving, pottery, bone carving, and masonry. Brightly colored stucco designs adorned the walls of ceremonial buildings and the palaces of the elite. One of its most impressive monuments was a 24-foot-high sandstone carving of an elaborately dressed human figure representing either a god or a ruler that today stands in a plaza in La Paz, capital of Bolivia. Tiwanaku's rulers evidently exacted labor from conquered provinces in order to build these structures, much as the Incas would later do. Extensive irrigation works and raised fields made the area surrounding Tiwanaku far more fertile than it is today. People also herded llamas and alpacas and harvested fish and aquatic plants from the lake. Colonies established in outlying areas from southern Peru to eastern Bolivia gave them access to chile peppers, coca leaves, and other produce from different ecological niches. Long-distance trade extended southward to the Atacama Desert in coastal Chile, 500 miles away. Deteriorating environmental conditions, most notably reduced rainfall after about 950 CE, contributed to the eventual decline of Tiwanaku. The city was abandoned by the year 1200.

The Wari Empire

The sixth century CE. witnessed the rise of the Wari Empire, centered near today's city of Ayacucho in Peru and eventually extending over 400 miles to the north, southeast to the plateau around Cuzco, and to the Moche and Nazca areas on the coast. Its capital city, also called Wari, was located 430 miles northwest of Tiwanaku. It served as a ceremonial center and an administrative hub, and housed at least 35,000 residents, who lived in large rectangular compounds separated by narrow streets. Some archaeologists have suggested that Wari began as a colony of Tiwanaku and later asserted its independence. In any event, there is evidence of significant cultural contact between the two cities. The people of Wari also maintained ties with Pachacama, an important pilgrimage site on the coast dedicated to the god Pachacamac, which flourished between 800 and 1000 CE.

The rulers of Wari employed administrative tactics later used so effectively by the Incas. They used *quipus* (knotted cords) to record and transmit information, relocated subject peoples to consolidate their dominions, established centralized control over agricultural production, ordered the terracing of mountainsides to increase the amount of land under cultivation, and maintained large storehouses for maize and other commodities. A network of roads, with rest stops at strategic points along the way, linked its various provincial capitals. Archaeological research at the Wari outpost of Pikillaqta suggests that Wari administrators put the local population to work in return for providing them with food. A separate barracks at Pikillaqta was evidently reserved for female workers who prepared *chicha* (maize beer) and other foods consumed on ritual occasions. Like Tiwanaku, the Wari empire began its decline about the year 850, when its capital was abruptly abandoned.

MESOAMERICA AND PERU, 900–1400 CE

Following the collapse of the Classic centers in Mesoamerica and the Tiwanaku and Wari empires in the Andes, both regions entered a period of political instability that ended only with the spectacular rise of the Aztecs and the Incas 500 years later. Political turmoil was accompanied by increased warfare and mounting human sacrifice. New cities appeared, but they were generally smaller, controlled less territory, and lasted for shorter periods of time than those that preceded them. For several centuries, the pace of cultural and technical advance slowed as well, with the notable exception of metal-workers in Mexico and Central America, who finally caught up with their South American counterparts. Mesoamericans also continued their practice of recording their histories and genealogies in symbols carved in stone or painted on animal skins, so we are able to identify even more specific individuals from these centuries than from the Classic Era.

The Toltecs

Following the fall of Teotihuacan, many groups migrated into central Mexico from the north and west. Native histories characterized them as warlike hunter-gatherers who gradually adopted the more civilized lifestyles they encountered as they settled in their new homes. The Toltecs, builders of the city of Tula some 50 miles from Teotihuacan, were among the most prominent of these migrants. Their rise began sometime after the year 800 CE, especially under the leadership of the legendary ruler Mixcoatl. Tula was evidently settled by refugees from Teotihuacan as well, reaching a population estimated at between 35,000 and 60,000 at its peak. Tula's urban planning was far less sophisticated than that of Teotihuacan, however. Like Teotihuacan, Tula owed its dominance in part to its command of the obsidian trade, but warfare also contributed heavily to its success. Toltec militarism is evident in a series of carved stone warriors over 15 feet tall that can still be seen at Tula today. Murals painted on the walls of Toltec temples also depicted legions of soldiers ready for battle. Skull racks and stone figures holding basins thought to be receptacles for human hearts suggest that human sacrifice figured prominently in their ceremonial life.

Stone warrior statues at Tula.
Source: Imagebroker/Alamy

The cult of the more peaceful plumed serpent god Quetzalcoatl assumed great importance at Tula as well. According to some accounts, Quetzalcoatl demanded only sacrifices of flowers and butterflies instead of the bloody offerings made to other Mesoamerican deities. Mixcoatl's son and successor Ce Acatl was an ardent devotee and eventually assumed the god's name for himself. Mesoamerican legend holds that his political enemies overthrew and expelled him from Tula sometime in the late tenth century. He reportedly headed east, and some accounts say that he went across the sea. Others hold that he and his supporters ended up in Yucatán, and many signs of Toltec influence there tend to support this hypothesis.

Tula collapsed in the twelfth century, again for reasons disputed by specialists, and its population dispersed to other towns throughout the valley. But its cultural reach extended not only to Yucatán but also south to Guatemala. The Toltecs' fame and legacy endured throughout central Mexico down to the eve of the Spanish conquest. Later societies, especially the Aztecs, credited them with great achievements, from the development of maize cultivation to the ability to grow cotton that came in many colors, although in fact they merely borrowed what previous societies had developed. The highest compliment that an Aztec artist could receive was that he or she worked "like a Toltec." For centuries, ruling dynasties in city-states throughout central Mexico legitimized their position by marrying into families that claimed descent from the kings of Tula.

The Mixtecs of Oaxaca

The Mixtecs became the dominant people in Post-Classic Oaxaca, eventually occupying such important Zapotec sites as Monte Albán and Mitla. They were among the first people of Mesoamerica to master the art of metallurgy, crafting exquisite gold jewelry. The Mixtecs also produced fine carvings in wood and bone and beautiful mosaics that adorned their buildings at Mitla, but they are best remembered for the brilliantly colored pictorial "books" they composed on deerskins, some of which record events as far back as 692 CE. Eight of these codices have survived.

These sources chronicle the political history of various communities in Oaxaca and the genealogy of their rulers. We learn, for example, that between the years 963 and 979 a period of conflict known as the War of Heaven followed the decline of Monte Albán. The codices document the reign of a king whom archaeologists call 8 Deer, lord of Tilantongo, located directly northwest of today's city of Oaxaca. His rise to prominence began in 1097. Eventually, he conquered at least 75 cities, including Monte Albán, and imposed his control over a wide area that included highland and coastal settlements. His reign ended with his assassination in 1115, but Tilantongo remained one of Oaxaca's most important kingdoms for more than two centuries thereafter. Toltec influences, including the adoption of the calendar used at Tula, have been attributed to links with the central Mexico established during 8 Deer's reign.

The Post-Classic Maya

During the Classic period, Mayan civilization flourished in Central America, especially in Guatemala and the southern Mexican state of Chiapas. The Yucatán peninsula, though long inhabited by Mayan peoples, had comparatively few great population centers in Classic times. In the Post-Classic period, however, Yucatán flourished, with Chichen Itza as its most important city-state.

The Yucatec Mayan cities had considerable contact with central Mexico in Post-Classic times. Many authorities believe that Chichen Itza and other sites were taken over by invading Toltecs following the fall of Tula, and that these conquerors joined the Itza (Mayan groups from outside Yucatán) in exercising control over much of the peninsula. Other scholars suggest that central Mexican influences spread to Yucatán primarily through trade. In any event, there are many signs of Toltec influence at Chichen Itza. The layout of the city resembles that of Tula, and its great pyramid, known as the Castillo, was dedicated to Kulkulkan, the Mayan name for the feathered serpent of central Mexico. Warlike motifs reminiscent of Tula can also be found in its art and architecture.

Human sacrifice, though certainly not new in Mayan society, played an important role in Post-Classic ceremonial life. Skull racks similar to those of central Mexico can be found at Chichen Itza. The remains of sacrificial victims were thrown into *cenotes*, the deep sinkholes that mark the limestone surface of Yucatán, along with numerous objects made of gold and copper. There is substantial evidence that the huge cenote at Chichen Itza continued to be the site of sacrificial ceremonies down to the sixteenth century.

Like their forebears, the Post-Classic Maya were great astronomers. One of the few surviving pre-Hispanic Mayan documents, the so-called Dresden Codex dating from the thirteenth century, contains an elaborate chart of the cycles of Venus. The traditional Mayan calendar and hieroglyphic writing also survived into the Post-Classic period. Trade contacts with lowland Mayan regions as far south as Honduras also continued. Most of the gold ornaments found in the cenote at Chichen Itza probably came from Central America.

After about 1200, Chichen Itza's dominance of its neighboring city-states ended. For the next 200 years, the city of Mayapán held sway over much of Yucatán. Although some of its architectural features resemble those found at Chichen Itza, everything was on a much smaller scale, and there is little evidence of any great artistic or technical break-throughs during the late Post-Classic period. By the time the Spaniards arrived in the early sixteenth century, Mayapán's control of the surrounding area had deteriorated, and no other town had succeeded in imposing political unity in the peninsula.

Peru After Tiwanaku and Wari

Peru also experienced growing instability and warfare from about 1000 to 1400. Throughout this period a series of regional states vied with one another for power, and the coast again surpassed the highlands in political sophistication and artistic creativity. Many archaeological sites dating from this period once contained enormous caches of gold jewelry and precious stones, but they have been the targets of looters for several centuries.

One of the most important states to emerge along the coast was the Chimu kingdom, which began expanding from its base in northern Peru between 1150 and 1200. Eventually, its territory spanned some 625 miles from north to south. Like other Peruvian rulers both before and after them, the Chimu kings forced their subjects to perform labor for them and maintained satellite administrative centers throughout their sphere of dominance. They distributed luxury goods to local chieftains in an effort to secure and keep their loyalty.

The people of Chimu were still around at the time of the Spanish conquest of Peru, and so our knowledge of them is based on observations of early conquistadors and missionaries as well as on archaeological evidence. They displayed substantial cultural continuity with the Moche, who had occupied much of the same region centuries before. Elaborate irrigation works enabled them to flourish in the dry climate of the Peruvian coast. Their society was highly stratified, dominated by a hereditary nobility and kings who claimed to be divine.

Chan Chan served as the capital of the Chimu kingdom. The city grew steadily as Chimu's power expanded. Each king evidently built himself a new palace complex at Chan Chan when he assumed the throne. By the year 1400, the city covered a territorial expanse of more than 24 square kilometers and boasted a population estimated at between 25,000 and 50,000. Chan Chan's glory days ended with its conquest by the Incas in 1465.

Slice of Life   THE CRAFT WORKERS
OF CHAN CHAN, 1400 CE

THE CHIMU KINGDOM OF COASTAL PERU was especially noted for its fine weaving, wood-working, and metalworking. At the capital city of Chan Chan and at numerous provincial centers, Chimu artisans wove carpets, wall hangings, and other textiles from cotton and alpaca wool. They also manufactured intricate wood carvings with copper inlays, as well as needles, tweezers, and other utilitarian goods made of copper. By the last century prior to the Inca conquest, Chimu leaders and bureaucrats supervised the mass production of these goods, which were then distributed throughout their dominions. The artisans of Chan Chan may have numbered 20,000 or more by the year 1400 of the European calendar. Archaeologists speculate Chimu rulers forcibly recruited craftspeople from conquered provinces and sent them to Chan Chan. Wealth derived from the production of handicrafts supported most of Chan Chan's elite.

Excavations at Chan Chan have revealed something of the lifestyles of these highly skilled men and women who wore distinctive ear ornaments to denote their special standing in Chimu society. They were evidently full-time craft workers dependent on sources outside the city for their food. The artisans lived in their own sections of the city and their remains were buried at sites apart from those of the general populace. Each nuclear family had its own living quarters, complete with a kitchen, storage areas, and workspace. At home they did some of their work. Men probably hammered sheet metal, and women may have spun fiber into yarn. Other tasks were performed in workshops also located within the workers' compounds. Near the center of the city, archaeologists have unearthed structures that housed transport workers who operated the llama caravans that carried goods to and from Chan Chan. These buildings could accommodate several hundred people and featured large communal kitchens. Huge storage facilities for raw materials and finished goods have also been excavated.

Craft production at Chan Chan ceased abruptly in 1465 when the Incas subjugated the Chimu. Many of the city's skilled workers were then taken to the Inca capital at Cuzco in the highlands. Evidently, they had no time to prepare for their journey. They left unfinished textiles, pots of food cooking on their hearths, and copper ingots on the floors of their workshops.

Questions for Discussion

What does the social status of these craft workers tell us about Chimu society? What can we learn about the everyday lives of the Chimu people from the kinds of goods these workers produced?

THE WORLD OF EARLY AMERICANS

For thousands of years after their ancestors unwittingly crossed the Bering Strait, the peoples of the Americas continually tested the potential of the many different physical environments they found as they migrated southward and eastward through North and South America. They hunted, fished, and gathered the fruits of the land, and in many places they domesticated plants and animals. They learned to make tools that lightened their labors and baskets and pottery to carry and store what they produced.

As these early Americans' ability to harness available natural resources grew, so too did the size and complexity of their communities. Some people could now devote a portion of their energies to pursuits other than providing for their own immediate subsistence. Leaders emerged who found ways to force or persuade others to work on construction projects requiring the coordinated labor of hundreds or thousands of people. Men and women also began to explore their creative potential, embellishing utilitarian objects like ceramics and textiles with designs and crafting jewelry to adorn their bodies. A select few spent their time probing the visible heavens and unseen worlds that were the dwelling places of their gods.

Early Americans were open to new possibilities, willing to learn from people they encountered as they migrated from place to place. They readily exchanged material goods, subsistence techniques, strategies of warfare and governance, and philosophical ideas with one another. But they were also careful to conserve what their forebears had taught them about the best ways to meet the specific challenges of their local environment. This selective process of innovation and preservation produced a tremendous variety of cultures throughout the hemisphere.

People and Their Environment

Americans in the year 1400 of the European calendar had gone far beyond the simple quest for food that had lured their hunter-gatherer ancestors from Siberia to North America. They came to know the uses of thousands of plants that grew wild in the hemisphere's many different ecological zones. By lucky trial and tragic error they learned that some plants could satisfy their hunger and alleviate their ailments while others could make them sick or even kill them. They discovered other plants with stimulant or hallucinogenic properties—coca in South America and peyote in Mexico and what is now the southwestern United States, for example.

Over the course of thousands of years, early Americans also domesticated many plants and learned which plants yielded the highest caloric values for the amount of land and labor invested in production—hence the popularity of maize throughout much of the hemisphere and potatoes in the Andes. They also devised ways of preparing and preserving food to maximize its nutritional value. Mesoamericans soaked their maize in water rich in lime, which provided a source of calcium and facilitated the absorption of protein from the beans that were another vital component of their diet. Peruvians learned to freeze-dry potatoes and other foods. Early Americans experimented with ways of seasoning food and made intoxicating beverages, from the *balche* (made from honey and bark) of the Maya to the *pulque* (cactus beer) of the Mesoamericans and the maize beer, or chicha, favored by Andeans.

The natural environment, so full of possibilities to support human life, also posed challenges to the survival of the earliest Americans. Earthquakes and volcanic eruptions were ever-present threats in Mesoamerica and the Andes, while island and coastal peoples continually felt the devastating effects of tropical storms. Droughts lasting a single season or an entire generation could turn fertile fields to wasteland, while too much rain produced ruinous floods and landslides. The atmospheric phenomenon that today we call El Niño wreaked havoc on the lives of ancient Peruvians, bringing torrential downpours to areas that were normally very dry. Archeologists have attributed the decline of the Moche civilization to the effects of El Niño.

Everywhere the ancient Americans went, they left their mark on the physical landscape. Even the simple choice to domesticate certain plants at the expense of others altered the biosphere forever. In the forests of Brazil, they felled stands of virgin trees and cleared fields using slash-and-burn techniques in order to plant crops. People living in more complex societies diverted streams for irrigation, terraced mountainsides to bring more land under cultivation, created artificial islands and lakes, and moved huge stones to build their palaces and pyramids.

Early Americans and Their Beliefs

The belief systems of ancient Americans focused heavily on survival—not so much that of the individual but definitely that of the community and the species. Success in hunting and gathering, agricultural abundance, pregnancy, and birth were all recurrent motifs in their ritual life. Human reproduction depended on the union of male and female, while soil and seed had to come together before plants would grow. Many societies attributed the origins of the world and the human species to some kind of union of opposing forces. Female deities figured heavily in the early American interpretations of the cosmos, as important as male gods and often even more so.

As agricultural peoples, early Americans took careful note of the changing seasons and the movements of the celestial bodies that marked the passage of time. They devised increasingly sophisticated calendars and tracked constellations with growing precision. Many of their temples were carefully positioned to catch sunlight at a particular angle at a specific point in the solar year. Precisely at the moment of the spring and fall equinoxes, the sun strikes the edge of the principal pyramid at Chichen Itza in such a way that the light resembles a serpent running from the top of the pyramid to the bottom.

The Sun and the Moon became deities for many societies. The Moon was often female, probably because its monthly phases suggested a parallel with women's menstrual cycles, while the Sun was usually male. Gods associated with thunder, rain, and lightning were also typically male, while the Earth and particular crops, especially the all-important maize, were more often viewed as female. Many people associated mountains with clouds and rain, and some have speculated that ancient pyramids were meant to resemble mountains. For the fishing people along the Peruvian coast, the sea was a divine force, and fish and other forms of marine life figured prominently in their ritual art. Many societies believed that animals also possessed special powers, and motifs such as serpents and jaguars can be found at many archaeological sites.

Ancient Americans evidently saw themselves at the mercy of powerful supernatural forces that had to be appeased, often with sacrifices of human blood, in order to ward off droughts, plagues, earthquakes, and other calamities. Men and women who could communicate with and satisfy those powers occupied special places in their societies, and locations considered sacred to the gods and goddesses became ceremonial centers that attracted pilgrims from great distances. Monuments constructed at these centers were designed to accommodate huge crowds. For example, a site on the Peruvian coast, built between 1100 and 850 BCE, featured a courtyard big enough for a standing-room audience of 65,000.

Early Americans were also concerned with what lay beyond the present, visible world. Rulers and other elites were buried in elaborate tombs, full of provisions for the journey to the afterlife and often the remains of servants sacrificed to accompany them. Concern for those who had gone before them can also be seen in the special care that many societies showed for the remains of their ancestors. In the Andes, people developed the practice of artificially mummifying their dead as early as 5000 BCE.

Communities, States, and War

The communities that early Americans formed varied in size and complexity, from small hunting bands with no fixed residence to huge, planned urban centers like Teotihuacan. Some people considered themselves part of communities that did not even comprise contiguous spaces. In Peru, kinship groups secured access to land at a variety of different elevations in order to obtain food and other resources from many different microclimates. As communities grew in size, so too did the degree of social stratification—the differences in status, wealth, and power among people. The cooperative, kin-based sharing of labor and resources characteristic of hunting bands and small villages gave way to coercive systems that allowed some people to command others.

Some ancient American communities were large and powerful enough that anthropologists have classified them as states, meaning that rulers emerged who were able to appropriate labor and goods from many people over wide geographical areas, sometimes so large that we can justifiably call them empires. This process began in selected places between about 1000 BCE and 1 CE and accelerated in the millennium that followed. State formation almost invariably led to an increase in warfare, as rulers tried to gain access to vital resources—obsidian, for example—and to build their own power at the expense of rival states. Many states also enhanced their power and extended their cultural influence through long-distance trade.

None of ancient America's great states lasted forever. Teotihuacan, Monte Albán, Tiwanaku, and countless others all "fell," often after hundreds of years of political ascendancy and stunning cultural advance, just as the ancient Mediterranean cities of Athens, Carthage, and Rome all had their own days of glory and retreat. We have virtually no written sources that might help us document the reasons why so many cities of America declined so precipitously, but the archaeological evidence suggests that the causes were complex, ranging from climatic changes to rebellion on the part of subject populations.

CONCLUSION

All available evidence suggests that once the ice bridge linking North America and Siberia melted some 14,000 years ago, the societies we have examined in this chapter developed on their own, without significant contact with people from across the Atlantic or the Pacific. Ever since the voyages of Christopher Columbus revealed the existence of this "new world" to Europeans, many theories to the contrary have been advanced. Sixteenth-century European theologians thought that the natives of the Americas were descended from the lost tribes of Israel and that one of Christ's 12 apostles must have brought the Gospel to the Americas. More recently, observers have noted that Olmec sculptures often have Negroid features, suggesting links with Africa. The propensity of early Americans to build mounds and pyramids has led many people to believe that there must have been some connection to Egypt.

A few early Americans may have had incidental contacts with the "old world" during the thousands of years following the migration of their ancestors to the hemisphere. Polynesians may have occasionally crossed the Pacific, and the twentieth-century Norwegian archaeologist Thor Heyerdahl theorized that ancient Peruvians could have traveled in the opposite direction. There is evidence too that northern Europeans might have made their way across Greenland to North America from time to time. We know for sure that Viking navigators set up an abortive colony in northeastern Canada around the year 1000 CE.

For all practical purposes, however, the Americas developed independently, without "help" or interference from Europe, Africa, or Asia. While archaeologists can cite abundant evidence to show how the ancestors of the first Americans migrated from Siberia to North America, the traditions of Native American peoples offer another kind of truth. They place the origins of human life within their own ancestral homelands and stress the sacred ties of peoples to places. Indeed, it is in the thousands of years of people learning to survive and thrive in tropical lowlands, deserts, grasslands, and mountains that we find the cultural origins of the first peoples of the Americas.

LEARNING MORE ABOUT LATIN AMERICANS

Bawden, Garth. *The Moche* (Oxford, U.K.: Blackwell, 1999). A well-illustrated overview of Moche life and art, incorporating recent archaeological discoveries; one of the series *The Peoples of America*.

Joyce, Rosemary A. *Gender and Power in Prehispanic Mesoamerica* (Austin, TX: University of Texas Press, 2000). An anthropologist's exploration of gender roles among the Olmecs, the Maya, and the Aztecs.

Kolata, Alan L. *The Tiwanaku: Portrait of an Andean Civilization* (Oxford, U.K.: Blackwell, 1993). Another volume in the series *The Peoples of America;* shows how the Tiwanaku developed over the course of many centuries.

Lavellée, Danièle. *The First South Americans: The Peopling of a Continent from the Earliest Evidence to High Culture* (Salt Lake City, UT: University of Utah Press, 2000). Shows how the earliest peoples of South America interacted with the natural environment.

Silverman, Helaine, and Donald Proulx, *The Nasca* (Oxford, U.K.: Blackwell, 2002). Another volume in *The Peoples of America* series by two archaeologists who have done extensive fieldwork in the region; provides an up-to-date explanation of the famous Nazca lines.

2

AMERICANS AND IBERIANS ON THE EVE OF CONTACT

IN CHAPTER 1, we saw how the first peoples of North and South America adapted to the varied environments they found as they dispersed across the continents following their migration from Asia. In some places, they adopted agriculture and built sophisticated irrigation works, while elsewhere they obtained their subsistence through hunting, fishing, and gathering plants. Everywhere they developed systems of belief to explain their world and rituals to propitiate the supernatural forces controlling that world. Ceremonial centers, cities, and states appeared in particularly favored spots.

The fifteenth century in the European calendar witnessed the rise of two great empires in the Americas. The people we call the Aztecs came to dominate much of Mesoamerica, and the Incas controlled the Andean highlands of South America. Both of them drew upon cultural and religious traditions that had developed over many centuries, but they achieved a degree of political organization previously unknown in the Americas. At the same time, a similar process was occurring on Europe's Iberian Peninsula as the monarchies of Spain and Portugal took shape. In 1492, these parallel worlds would meet, with momentous consequences for human history.

MESOAMERICA IN THE FIFTEENTH CENTURY

Mesoamerica was home to many different political and linguistic groups in the year 1400. Most numerous were the Nahuas, so named because they spoke Nahuatl, which was presumably the tongue spoken by the Toltecs. They inhabited many city-states in and around the Valley of Mexico (today's greater Mexico City) and included groups who had long resided in the area and later arrivals who had adopted the languages and cultures of those already there. The Tarascans lived to the northwest, in what is now the Mexican state of Michoacán, while Mixtecs and Zapotecs could be found in Oaxaca to the South. In Central America and Yucatán were the many city-states of the Post-Classic Maya.

Despite their linguistic differences, the peoples of Mesoamerica shared many cultural traits. They lived in sedentary communities that were usually headed by hereditary rulers. Most of their subsistence came from agriculture, and they shared a common diet based on maize, beans, squashes, and peppers. Their religion revolved largely around the agricultural cycle and typically involved human sacrifice and rituals to guarantee successful harvests. These cultural similarities did not lead Mesoamericans of the fifteenth century to view themselves as one people, any more than their contemporaries in Europe saw themselves as such. Warfare consumed increasing measures of human energies and resources in Mesoamerica as rival city-states vied with one another for territorial supremacy.

Mesoamericans also looked down upon neighbors whom they regarded as less culturally sophisticated than themselves. Particularly despised were groups who had only recently migrated to the region and still had far too much in common with the Chichimecas, the nomadic and "uncivilized" people who "lived like dogs" in the arid central plateau of northern Mexico. One such group was the Mexica, who had entered the Valley of Mexico a scant two centuries earlier. Today they are popularly known as the Aztecs, after their mythical homeland of Aztlán, somewhere to the north and west. From their inauspicious beginnings, they became the most powerful state in Mesoamerica by the early sixteenth century.

The Rise of the Mexica

As newcomers, the Mexica had no fixed residence in the valley. Only by attaching themselves to powerful city-states in the region could they secure a place for themselves. First, they served as mercenaries for Culhuacan, at the southern edge of Lake Texcoco, whose kings claimed descent from the mighty Toltecs. By the early 1300s, they had settled on a small island in the middle of the lake, at the heart of what is today Mexico City. Little by little, they expanded the size of their island by dredging soil from the bottom of the lake, and what would become the great city of Tenochtitlan ("Place Next to the Prickly Pear Cactus") took shape. In the 1370s, they established a dynasty that would endure until the arrival of the Spanish conquistadors. Their first king, Acamapichtli, was the son of a woman from the ruling lineage of Culhuacan, and his successors formed marriage alliances with other important powers in the valley. The lowly Mexica had earned a measure of respectability at last.

By the beginning of the fifteenth century, Azcapotzalco to the west of Lake Texcoco had surpassed Culhuacan as the foremost city-state in central Mexico. In 1428, however, the Mexica king Ixcoatl formed an alliance (known as the Triple Alliance) with two other states, Texcoco and Tlacopan, and together they defeated Azcapotzalco. That victory was a major turning point in Mesoamerican history. Tenochtitlan soon became the dominant power within the alliance, with Texcoco a close second and Tlacopan a distant third.

The alliance's domain expanded dramatically over the next several decades. Particularly notable were the conquests achieved by the King Moctezuma I, who ruled at

TIMELINE

700–800
Muslims take over much of Spain and Portugal

1249–1250
Christian reconquest of Portugal and most of Spain

c. 1300
Mexica arrive in the Valley of Mexico

Late 1340s
Black Death in Spain and Portugual

1370s
Mexica ruling dynasty established

1385–1433
King João I establishes Aviz dynasty and political independence of Portugal

1415
Portuguese take Ceuta in North Africa

1418–1472
Rule of Nezahualcoyotl in Texcoco

1428
Triple Alliance gains control of the Valley of Mexico

1438–1471
Rule of Pachacuti Inca Yupanqui

1440–1468
Rule of Moctezuma I in Tenochtitlan

1450s
Droughts and food shortages in central Mexico

1469
Marriage of Isabella of Castile and Ferdinand of Aragón

1478
Spanish Inquisition established

1487
Dedication of the new temple of Huitzilopochtli in Tenochtitlan

1492
Voyage of Columbus; defeat of Granada

1492–1497
Expulsion and forced conversions of Spanish and Portuguese Jews

1493–1525
Rule of Huayna Capac

1498
Portuguese navigator Vasco da Gama reaches India

1502
Expulsion of Muslims from Spain

1516
Charles I becomes first monarch of a united Spain

Tenochtitlan from 1440 to 1468, and his contemporary Nezahualcoyotl, lord of Texcoco from 1418 to 1472. Together they extended their reach well beyond the Valley of Mexico, to Oaxaca in the south and the Gulf Coast to the east. By 1500, the Triple Alliance controlled an area roughly the size of Italy. Subjugated territories paid their new rulers substantial quantities of goods in tribute, including cacao, gold dust, gemstones, cotton textiles, honey, featherwork, and maize. Provinces in the Gulf Coast region provided thousands of rubber balls used in the games played at Tenochtitlan and Texcoco. Local leaders in these conquered regions remained in place, enjoying considerable autonomy as long as they remained loyal to the alliance and handed over the tribute on a regular basis.

There were limits to what the Mexica and their allies could achieve, however. On numerous occasions, conquered provinces rose in revolt and had to be suppressed. Then too, there were enemies too fierce for the Aztecs ever to defeat. In 1479, the emperor Axayacatl suffered a humiliating rout at the hands of the highly militarized Tarascans of Michoacán. Tenochtitlan's armies lost some 20,000 men who either died in battle or were taken prisoner by the enemy. The Mexica also failed to subdue Tlaxcala to the east.

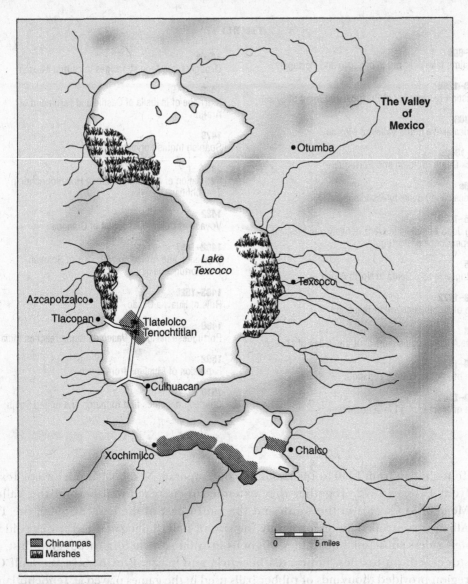

The Valley of Mexico

Mexica Statecraft

In theory, Tenochtitlan and Texcoco were equal partners ruling central Mexico. Each took a 40 percent share of the tribute provided by subject states, while Tlacopan received 20 percent. Texcoco continued to undertake conquests in its own name, even after joining the Triple Alliance. In practice, however, Tenochtitlan gradually eclipsed Texcoco and undermined the position of its ruling class, especially after King Nezahuacoyotl died in 1472.

The Mexica recognized the value of ideology and propaganda. They fabricated a glorious history for themselves, deliberately exaggerating their own role in the victories of the Triple Alliance and downplaying the parts played by Texcoco and Tlacopan. Their official account emphasized the importance of their special god, Huitzilopochtli ("Hummingbird on the Left"), who had guided them safely from Aztlán to the Valley of Mexico. The Mexica were his chosen people, and any evidence that might betray their ignoble origins was carefully suppressed. Thousands of prisoners were sacrificed when a new temple honoring Huitzilopochtli was dedicated in 1487 (see Plate 6).

An Aztec noble named Tlacaelel Cihuacoatl evidently masterminded the rewriting of Mexica history and commanded some of the empire's most important military victories, including the great triumph over Azcapotzalco. He also served as a key power behind the throne for most of the fifteenth century, from the time of Ixcoatl until his death in 1496. Some authorities also suggest that in 1486 he arranged the assassination of the emperor Tizoc, whose 5-year reign was one of the least distinguished in the Mexica line.

Mexica Religion

Aztec religion drew heavily on the centuries-old traditions of central Mexico. Some of their gods, including the feathered serpent Quetzalcoatl and Tlaloc, god of rain, dated back to the time of Teotihuacan. Huitzilopochtli, however, was the Mexicas' most important deity, and a shrine dedicated to him stood alongside Tlaloc's atop the huge pyramid that stood in the center of Tenochtitlan. The Aztec symbol for conquest featured a burning temple, but

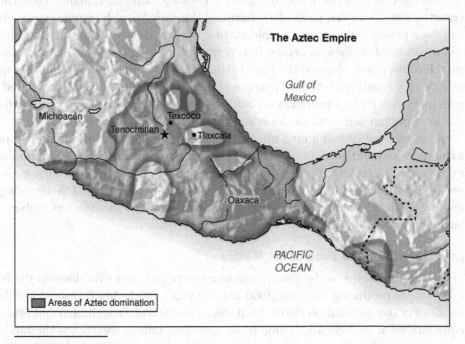

The Aztec Empire

Michoacán

Tenochtitlan ★ • Texcoco
        • Tlaxcala

Oaxaca

Gulf of Mexico

PACIFIC OCEAN

Areas of Aztec domination

The Aztec Empire in 1519

in fact the Mexica allowed subject populations to keep their customary gods as long as they adopted Huitzilopochtli as well. Meanwhile, the Mexica readily adopted gods and rituals of people they conquered.

Dozens of deities therefore populated the Mesoamerican pantheon in the fifteenth century. The creator Ometeotl ("Two-god") was both mother and father to all the other gods, and Tezcatlipoca ("Smoking Mirror") held power over all. Several deities helped assure agricultural and human fertility. The goddess Xochiquetzal represented sexuality, pregnancy, and childbirth, as well as the traditional female occupations of spinning and weaving. Still other gods watched over the masculine pursuits of warfare and hunting.

Religious ritual was an important part of everyday life. The Mesoamerican calendar divided the year into 18 months of 20 days each, with a special 5-day interlude at the end. Each month had ceremonies that were closely related to the agricultural cycle. During the hot, dry period from May 4 to May 23, for example, the Mexica made sacrifices to Tezcatlipoca to guarantee a prompt start of the rainy season and bountiful harvests thereafter.

Almost all Aztec rites included some sort of sacrifice to the gods. Mesoamerican theology held that the gods had given of themselves in creating the Sun, the Universe, and people, and the debt had to be repaid. The world might end if the gods failed to receive their due. Offerings included food, animals, seashells, and incense, but the most precious gift of all was human blood. Men and women of all social classes pierced their earlobes and other body parts at least occasionally in an effort to please the gods, while priests bled themselves daily.

But these sacrifices were not enough—the gods also demanded human lives. The most common ritual, one that particularly horrified the early Spanish conquistadors, involved carrying a person to the top of a temple, excising the heart, and displaying the skull in a rack along with those of previous victims. In ceremonies honoring Xipe Totec, a god of agricultural fertility, priests donned the flayed skins of their victims. Sacrifices also frequently included the ritual eating of small portions of the victim's flesh. Most of those offered to the gods were adult males captured in warfare, but some gods, such as Tlaloc, preferred young children. Women were sometimes sacrificed as well, especially to female deities.

Human sacrifice had a long history in Mesoamerica, and in many other world civilizations as well, but most authorities believe that these rituals increased in number and importance under Aztec domination. Human sacrifice not only pleased the gods but it served the Mexicas' political agenda as well. Priests were closely linked to the ruling class, and highly visible blood rituals impressed everyone—slaves, commoners, nobles, allies, and enemies alike—with the awesome power of the state.

Everyday Life in the Time of the Mexica

Most Mesoamericans in the fifteenth century were peasants who devoted the bulk of their time to producing their own food and the many goods they furnished in tribute to local rulers and imperial overlords. Even some residents of Tenochtitlan and other great cities farmed at least on a part-time basis. The basic unit of society was the household, typically consisting of a married couple and their children, with many duties allocated along gender lines. From May to November, men spent most of their time working in the fields, while during the rest of the year they might serve as warriors or perform compulsory labor for their rulers. Women performed most domestic chores—such as food preparation, housekeeping, and childcare—marketed any surplus produce, and presided over religious rituals within the home. They also wove cloth required for the family's use and for tribute quotas.

Artisans formed another important segment of Aztec society, especially in urban areas. People who farmed for a living often made sandals, pottery, baskets, and other mundane commodities in their spare time, while luxury goods and obsidian weapons and tools usually came from the workshops of full-time craft workers. The Spanish conquistadors marveled at the skill of Aztec goldsmiths, sculptors, and featherwork artists. Recent archaeological investigations have shown that the town of Otumba in the Teotihuacan Valley was an important manufacturing center, specializing in the production of basalt metates and *manos* used for grinding maize, obsidian tools, and the stone ear ornaments and lip plugs worn by nobles throughout Mesoamerica.

Together the peasants and artisans made up the commoner class, the *macehualtin*. A dozen or more households formed a *calpulli*. In theory, the calpulli owned the land that member households farmed and a governing council controlled land allocation, but in practice, families passed their plots from one generation to another as if they owned them privately.

At the opposite end of Mexica society were the nobles, who comprised somewhere between 5 and 10 percent of the population. Tribute and labor supplied to them by the commoners supported their lavish lifestyles. Nobles had special perquisites, including the right to build homes of more than one story and to wear cotton clothing rather than the rough garments of maguey fiber used by commoners. Men of the noble class could also have more than one wife. For a time in the early fifteenth century, it had been possible for male commoners to rise to the ranks of the nobility by distinguishing themselves on the battlefield, but by late Aztec times this avenue to upward social mobility had narrowed considerably. Nobility became almost exclusively hereditary, and nobles generally married within their own class.

The *pochteca*, or long-distance merchants, were another important hereditary group in Mexica society. These men lived in a separate quarter of Tenochtitlan, had their own special gods, and settled disputes among themselves in their own courts. They carried on a rapidly growing trade within the Triple Alliance domains and beyond, as far south as Central America. When traveling in enemy territory, they often served as spies for the Mexica emperors. They made fortunes marketing jewelry, featherwork, stone sculptures, and other luxuries craved by nobles, but as commoners, they were not allowed to display their wealth in public. When returning to Tenochtitlan laden with the profits of a trading expedition, the pochteca snuck into town at night so that no one would see them.

Occupying the lowest ranks of society were slaves, though slavery in Mesoamerica differed markedly from the type of bondage that Europeans would introduce into the Americas when they imported thousands of Africans to perform heavy labor in their

How Historians Understand | COUNTING PEOPLE IN PAST SOCIETIES

Even with state-of-the-art computers and huge cadres of census takers, governments today have difficulty determining the exact size of their populations. Historians face far greater challenges when they try to estimate how many people lived in a given place hundreds of years in the past. This is especially true when it comes to figuring the population of the Americas in 1492.

Many pre-Columbian societies left no written records. Even the Aztecs, long accustomed to putting ideas on paper, were not so much concerned with exact numbers of people as they were with preserving and embellishing their own historical memory and making sure that subject communities paid their tribute. The Incas kept their records on quipus, but few of these artifacts have survived, and scholars have not been able to interpret them all. Nor can population estimates made by early European observers be taken at face value. When they said they saw 10,000 natives at a particular place, they may well have meant just that they saw a lot of people, more

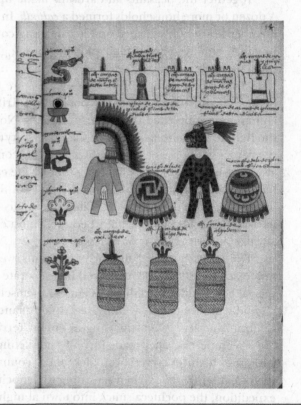

A page from the Mendoza Codex. The symbols in the column on the left stand for five different towns; each town's tribute consisted of 2000 woven cotton mantles, with each symbol representing 400 garments (top row), suits and headdresses worn by Aztec warriors (middle row), 400 loads of chili peppers, and 800 bales of cotton (bottom row).

than they could easily count. Early explorers and conquistadors hoping to gain favor with their monarchs or to encourage other Europeans to invest in colonization ventures had compelling reasons to exaggerate the magnitude of their findings.

Historical demographers working on pre-Columbian societies have had to circumvent the absence of reliable written evidence. Estimates of the population of central Mexico have used documents generated after the arrival of the Spanish that show how much tribute various communities rendered to the Aztecs. One such source is the Codex Mendoza, commissioned by the first Spanish viceroy so that he could better inform the king of Spain about this new dominion. Native artists painted the customary symbols for more than 300 towns that had paid tribute to the lords of Tenochtitlan, and next to them the items and quantities supplied every 80 days. Annotations in Spanish accompanied the pictographic text. Historians have then calculated how many people it would have taken to produce those amounts of goods while also providing for their own subsistence needs.

Historical geographers have also figured how many people a given environment could support, taking into account soil, climate, and available technology. Aerial photography has revealed important evidence of ancient irrigation systems and terraces—signs of intensive agriculture and therefore of high population density. Archaeological remains have yielded further clues, such as the number of houses in a settlement or the amount of labor that might have been required to build a particular structure or manufacture a given quantity of pottery or other artifacts found at a particular site. Still other researchers have used statistical models, working from more accurate data from the 1600s or 1700s to project back to earlier times.

No matter how sophisticated their techniques, however, historical demographers must accept that the results of their studies can only be educated guesses. For this reason, estimates of the total population of the Americas in 1492 vary widely, from as few as 10 million to as many as 100 million or more. For the island of Hispaniola, creditable demographic studies published in the late twentieth century have calculated a precontact population at somewhere between 60,000 and 7 million. What we do know for sure is that the indigenous population of the hemisphere declined drastically following the arrival of Europeans.

Questions for Discussion

Can you think of other types of evidence that might be used in estimating the population of particular localities? What are the connections between population size and cultural achievement in a society?

colonies. In Mexica society, people were not born into slavery. They became slaves as punishment for crimes or because they could not pay their debts or their tributes. In times of economic hardship, such as the great famine that struck central Mexico in the 1450s, many people sold themselves or their children into slavery. Many pochteca traded slaves along with other merchandise. Most slaves worked as servants in the households of nobles.

Mesoamerica on the Eve of the Spanish Invasion

The size of the Mesoamerican population in the year 1500 has been the subject of heated debate among historians and archaeologists. Some estimates for the whole of Mesoamerica run as high as 25 million, but most experts now favor much more conservative numbers. The most reliable recent studies suggest a population of between 1 and 2 million for the Valley of Mexico (today's greater Mexico City) and several million more in the area subject to direct Aztec control. The city of Tenochtitlan alone had over 200,000 inhabitants. As we shall see in Chapter 3, the indigenous population fell precipitously following the Spanish conquest and did not regain pre-conquest levels until the twentieth century.

Whatever the specific numbers, scholars agree that the population of central Mexico grew substantially during the period of Aztec supremacy. Only through an intensification of agriculture could all these people be fed. New lands were opened to cultivation, and irrigation systems were improved. Around the lakes, especially at Xochimilco in the south, people employed a centuries-old technique to turn swampland into productive farmland, building up artificial islands, or *chinampas*. The lakes themselves were another source of food, including fish, insect larvae, turtles, and an algae that Mexica warriors carried in dried form when they set out on their campaigns.

There were signs, however, that by late Aztec times population growth had begun to exceed the limits of available agricultural technology. Severe droughts struck in the 1450s, and food shortages loomed again after 1500. Political unrest mounted as well, even in Tenochtitlan's partner city of Texcoco, where Moctezuma II forcibly imposed his own nephew as ruler following a succession dispute in 1515. But the Mexica state had weathered many crises in the preceding century and may well have proven equal to these new challenges as well. When the Spanish conquistadors first gazed upon Tenochtitlan in November of 1519, they saw a thriving city that was the capital of one of their world's great empires and little to suggest that the power of the Mexica would crumble easily.

THE ANDES IN THE FIFTEENTH CENTURY

While the Mexica were establishing their hegemony in central Mexico, an even larger empire was taking shape in the Andes in South America. The Incas ruled this kingdom, which they called Tawantinsuyu ("The Land of the Four Quarters") from their magnificent capital at Cuzco, 11,000 feet above sea level in southern Peru. Like their Mesoamerican counterparts, they borrowed and built upon the achievements of civilizations that had gone before them. They derived their subsistence from exploiting many different ecological niches of the Andes and practiced centuries-old religious rituals. From art and architecture to strategies of governance, the Incas carried on the cultural traditions of earlier societies.

The Incas, however, attained a level of political consolidation previously unknown in the Andes and even greater than that of the Aztecs or the emerging monarchs of Western Europe in the fifteenth century. On the eve of the Spanish conquest, their dominions extended 2500 miles from the present-day boundary of Ecuador and Colombia in the north, southeast to Bolivia, as far as northern Argentina and central Chile in the south, and eastward beyond the slopes of the Andes, a territorial expanse larger than the Ottoman Empire or Ming China. Some authorities believe that by the early sixteenth century as many as 12 million people lived under Inca domination, but others place the figure closer to 3 million. In the early 1530s, at least 60,000, and perhaps as many as 150,000 men, women, and children resided in Cuzco.

The Rise of the Incas

Following the collapse of Tiwanaku in about 1200, the Andean region had many small chiefdoms, a situation roughly comparable to central Mexico in the same period. The Quechua-speaking Incas of Cuzco were one such group. In the thirteenth century, they began extending their control to neighboring areas. By the time of Pachacuti Inca Yupanqui, their ruler from 1438 to 1471, the Incas had emerged as the premier power in the Andes. Their conquests extended to include Aymara speakers in the region around Lake Titicaca in Bolivia. Pachacuti's successors, Topa Inca Yupanqui (1471–1493) and Huayna Capac (1493–1525), expanded Inca hegemony even further, achieving the definitive subjugation of Ecuador and conducting campaigns southward to Chile as well.

The Incas usually attempted first to persuade regional chieftains to submit voluntarily, offering them incentives including women, gifts, and the promise of retaining their positions. If these tactics failed, they waged war and took the recalcitrant leaders to Cuzco to be executed. The Incas achieved their conquests not through any superiority in weapons or tactics but rather by drafting warriors from previously subjugated provinces into their service. They also exploited the long-standing and bitter divisions among the Andean peoples.

In addition to military service, the people of the empire were forced to perform many other tasks for the lords of Cuzco. They built roads, palaces, temples, and other buildings as dictated by their new rulers. They also cultivated lands, herded llamas and alpacas, and worked gold and silver mines that belonged to the Inca state or to Inca deities. Conquered peoples gave lands to the Incas and provided various commodities in tribute, although apparently not on as great a scale as subjects of the Mexica in Mesoamerica.

Just as the Aztecs found that they could not expand indefinitely, so too did the Incas. They had little luck in subduing people who were not sedentary peasants, such as the inhabitants of southern Chile and the plains of eastern Bolivia. Repeated forays into the tropical forests of eastern Ecuador also ended in failure. The people of the Ecuadorian

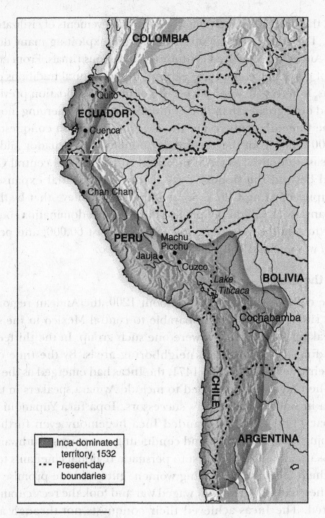

The Inca Empire in 1532

highlands, especially the fierce Cañaris who lived in the region near what is today the city of Cuenca, repeatedly rose in revolt as well. When Huayna Capac died in 1525, a power struggle between his two sons Huascar and Atahualpa divided the empire just as Spaniards were already approaching the coast of Peru.

Inca Statecraft

In many respects, the Incas were more intrusive in the lives of their subjects than the Mexica. Although colonies of conquered peoples could be found at Tenochtitlan, and representatives of the Aztec state fanned out across Mesoamerica, the Incas systematically relocated large populations in an effort to consolidate their hold throughout the Andes. They forcibly moved large numbers of Cañaris from southern Ecuador to Cuzco, along

Silver drinking vessels used in Peru.

with many other recently conquered or notoriously restive peoples. Other groups, including many from Chan Chan on the coast of Peru, were resettled in Cuzco because they possessed specialized craft skills. Some groups originally from Quito were transferred all the way to the environs of Lake Titicaca, while Aymara from the highlands of southern Peru and Bolivia were sent at least temporarily to the lower-lying valley of Cochabamba to the east. At the same time, the Inca rulers dispatched Quechua-speaking *mitmaq*, or colonists, from the heart of the empire to outlying areas. Despite all of these movements, the Incas never succeeded in imposing any kind of cultural homogeneity on the peoples they conquered. Although the use of Quechua certainly spread as a lingua franca, many other languages could be heard throughout the Andes.

To communicate with their far-flung dominions, the Incas constructed 20,000 miles of paved roads, tunnels, causeways, and bridges, a land transportation network far superior to anything in Europe at the time. A series of east–west roads crossed the rugged terrain of the Andes to connect two north–south routes, one on the coast and the other in the highlands. Portions of the roads are still visible today. *Tambos,* or inns, provided shelter along the way.

Using these roads, specially trained relay runners carried messages to provincial governors throughout the empire, covering the distance from Cuzco to the coast in about 3 days' time. They carried knotted, multicolored cords known as quipus, which took the place of written documents in the Andes. The quipus contained census information, details about the labor obligations owed by each community, and other information vital to a highly centralized state. Writing in the early 1600s, the native Andean historian Felipe Guaman Poma de Ayala noted, "With these cords the entire kingdom is governed."

A sense of reciprocal obligation between rulers and the ruled was deeply ingrained in Andean society and essential to Inca administration. The Inca state commandeered men for labor and military service and women to perform special ceremonial roles and to become weavers and brewers of chicha, an intoxicating beverage made from maize. Most subjects had to provide various items in tribute as well. In return, the emperor was expected to take care of his people when they were in need. To this end, the state maintained an elaborate system of warehouses situated at strategic points along its road network. There they stored large quantities of food produced on imperial lands and cloth gathered in tribute. Archaeologists have calculated that the storage capacity of the warehouses at Jauja, for example, exceeded 50,000 cubic meters. These supplies enabled the Incas to play the role of benevolent rulers in times of crisis and provision their armies throughout the empire. State-ordered systems of distribution, rather than market forces, governed the movement and exchange of commodities.

Like the Aztecs, the Incas augmented their hegemony with the use of history. They portrayed themselves as a special people, apart from the rest of humanity, who had brought civilization and order to the land after a long period of darkness and chaos. Cuzco witnessed elaborate ceremonies, including special homage at the tombs of former Inca rulers, all designed to impress everyone with the power and splendor of the state.

Andean Religion in the Time of the Incas

The Incas also sponsored an official state religion that served their political purposes. Their principal deity was Inti, the Sun god, who took on increasing importance as their conquests spread, eventually surpassing the traditional Andean creator god Viracocha. Inca rulers claimed direct descent from Inti, and the walls of his magnificent temple at Cuzco were lined with sheets of gold. They required conquered peoples to incorporate the Sun god and other features of Inca state religion into their worship.

However much the Incas depicted themselves as special, they in fact shared with other Andeans religious beliefs and observances that dated back many centuries and did little to alter the traditional worship practices of their subjects. Few temples to the Sun god or other Inca deities appeared in conquered provinces. Local religious objects from throughout the empire were taken to Cuzco, where they received special attention. Under Inca domination, Andeans continued, as they had for centuries, to venerate the mummified remains of their ancestors as well as hundreds of *huacas*, or spirits attached to particular places, to whom they offered sacrifices of guinea pigs and coca leaves.

Meanwhile, the ancient cult to the god Pachacamac, centered on the coast, continued to thrive. Much as their ancestors had flocked to Chavín de Huántar hundreds of years earlier, pilgrims speaking many different languages from throughout Peru, Bolivia, and Ecuador came to consult the oracle at Pachacamac's shrine and brought coca leaves, food, and textiles in tribute to the god and his ministers. Branch shrines supervised by priests from the central site were set up around the highlands and along the coast.

Chosen women who made textiles and chicha for the Incas, as depicted by the native historian Guaman Poma de Ayala.

Fifteenth-century Andeans included human sacrifice in their religious rituals, as their ancestors had done for hundreds of years. The Incas had no system of pictorial writing, and there are no eyewitness Spanish accounts of human sacrifice in Peru, so we have fewer details about the specific rituals they practiced. We do know that human sacrifice was evidently reserved for special occasions. Children were sacrificed whenever a king died and his successor took over. The sacrifice of enemy warriors taken in battle marked the celebration of important military victories. Young women, considered brides and priestesses of the Sun god, were also strangled and offered to him. At the shrine of Pachacamac, archaeologists have also found the mummified remains of sacrificial victims dating from Inca times.

Human sacrifice was part of the reciprocal relationship that Andeans maintained with their deities. Just as they provided labor and tribute to their rulers in return for help in time of need, they offered gifts to the gods, who in turn gave them protection and special favors. Sacrifices of human beings, animals, textiles, and coca leaves restored harmony between people and the gods. Without such tradeoffs, earthquakes, crop failures, and other calamities inevitably resulted.

Everyday Life in the Time of the Incas

The people of the Inca Empire supported themselves by farming the steep slopes of the Andes, which they fashioned into terraces to prevent water runoff and soil erosion. The basic unit of Andean society, also dating back long before the Incas, was the *ayllu,* a group of people who claimed descent from a single ancestor, worked lands in common, and venerated their own special deities. Here too the notion of reciprocity was important. Everyone shared access to the ayllu's resources and claims on one another's labor. Those who were away from home on military duty or other service could expect other members of the ayllu to fill in for them back home.

The ayllus were not compact, nucleated settlements. Instead, they resembled archipelagos that controlled parcels of land at different elevations, assuring the community's access to a variety of ecological niches, including high areas for pasture and warmer, moister lowlands needed for coca production. This strategy of exploiting the sharply varied terrain of the Andes had been developed over the course of many centuries, and Inca domination did relatively little to disrupt such arrangements. The Inca policy of relocating various groups of people might have helped some ayllus gain access to an even wider range of environmental niches.

Like the people of Mesoamerica, Andeans divided chores along gender lines. Men worked the fields and waged war. Along with childcare and domestic tasks, women's work included spinning yarn and weaving textiles (see Plate 4). To a greater degree than in Mexico and Central America, however, traditional Andean society stressed complementarity between the sexes, with the contributions of men and women valued more equally. Everyone, regardless of sex, had a comparable claim on the resources of the ayllu. Men passed personal property on to their sons, women to their daughters; men traced their ancestry through the male line, women through the female. A woman's performance of

LATIN AMERICAN LIVES

TANTA CARHUA, BRIDE OF THE SUN

AMONG THE MANY MARVELS that caught the attention of the Spanish conquistadors when they arrived in the Inca capital of Cuzco in the 1530s were the large dwellings set aside for specially chosen women. Some Spaniards likened these magnificently arrayed structures to convents, while others compared the women who resided in them to the vestal virgins of ancient Rome or the harems of Muslim potentates. Actually, these women were *acllas,* young virgins appropriated by the state who spent their lives serving the Incas in various capacities.

The selection of local women to be acllas and the construction of a building to house them usually accompanied the Inca conquest of a region. They severed their ties with their ayllus, and all of them were taken at least temporarily to Cuzco. Many returned to their native provinces to be concubines of men who had rendered distinguished services to the state or to perform assigned duties in local religious observances. Others stayed in Cuzco to be wives of the emperor or to weave textiles and manufacture chicha used in ritual celebrations.

A select few acllas were declared brides of the Sun god himself. Tanta Carhua was 10 years old when she was selected for this highest of "honors" during the final years of Inca rule. Her father, a provincial chieftain named Caque Poma, saw the political advantages to be gained from having his only daughter in the service of the Sun god. His role as a crucial intermediary between the empire and his home community was solidified, and he was able to pass that position on to his male heirs. As for Tanta Carhua, her days were numbered, for she was to be sacrificed to the Sun god. First, she participated in a festival known as *capacocha* ("festival of the sacrificed"), held in Cuzco in the presence of the emperor. She then returned to her home province, where she was buried alive on a mountaintop. At the emperor's orders, she was later revered as a special protector spirit, with lands and llama herds designated to support a cult in her honor and her relatives serving as its priests. A hundred years after her death, much to the consternation of Spanish Catholic missionaries, the people of her community continued to offer sacrifices of llamas and guinea pigs at her tomb and to invoke her help in times of trouble.

Questions for Discussion

How did the Incas use Andean gender ideologies to build their own imperial power? How might other young women from Tanta Carhua's province have viewed her experiences?

household duties was considered a service to the community, not to her husband. Andeans incorporated a similar parallelism into their religious practices. Women presided over local rituals in honor of female deities and passed knowledge of these rites on to their daughters, while men performed rites dedicated to male gods and taught

Inca fortress of Machu Picchu. Note the agricultural terraces in the background.

their sons to do likewise. During the final century before the Europeans' arrival in Peru, this complementarity of gender roles deteriorated. The Incas' emphasis on warfare valued men's roles more highly than women's, and women became objects of exchange used to cement bonds between conquered territories and the Inca state.

Reciprocity and theoretically equal access to resources were fundamental principles of Andean life, but this did not mean that there were no social distinctions. Some people, known as *yanaconas*, lived outside the ayllu structure and therefore did not enjoy the privileges that ayllu membership conveyed. They served as personal retainers of nobles or servants of the state or the gods, and their numbers grew during the years of Inca ascendancy. Also on the rise were the ranks of the nobles who had earned special perquisites for their service to the empire. Social stratification was becoming more noticeable in the Andes as the fifteenth century progressed, just as it was in Mesoamerica under the Mexica.

The Aztecs and Incas Compared

Both the Mexica and the Incas gained supremacy a scant 100 years before the arrival of the first Spanish conquistadors. They extended their dominions through military conquest but could only rule these vast territories by co-opting local rulers and leaving them in place. As the empires grew, so too did class distinctions. Both empires demanded that their subjects provide soldiers for their armies and workers who built the great temples and palaces at Tenochtitlan and Cuzco. Aztecs and Incas alike promulgated versions of history that cast themselves in the most favorable of lights, chosen by their special gods to rule over others. Andean and Mesoamerican deities were similarly appeased through human sacrifice.

Model of the marketplace of Tlaltelolco.

Slice of Life   THE MARKETPLACE AT TLATELOLCO

IF TENOCHTITLAN WAS THE RITUAL CENTER of the Aztec empire, its commercial heart could be found at Tlatelolco, an adjacent city annexed by the Mexica in 1473. Its huge market operated daily and attracted as many as 60,000 people, according to sixteenth-century Spanish observers. Its stalls held a dazzling variety of goods, everything from basic staples brought in from the surrounding valley by canoes and human carriers to exotic luxuries that were the stock in trade of the pochteca, the professional long-distance merchants. There were fruits, vegetables, and herbs, as well as maize, tortillas, salt, fish, pottery, baskets, brooms, and tools made of copper and bronze. Precious stones, ornaments made from gold and silver, cotton thread in a multitude of hues, and brilliantly colored parrot feathers were available to those able to afford them.

Other commodities for sale included live animals—rabbits, deer, and small dogs that were all used as sources of protein in the Mesoamerican diet. Male and female slaves were also bought and sold. Indeed, the Tlatelolco market offered many of the services of a twenty-first–century shopping mall. One could stop and eat at the many booths that sold prepared food and drink. Barbers washed and cut people's hair, and porters could be hired to carry customers' purchases home. A trip to the market was also a chance to socialize.

Trade was carefully regulated at Tlatelolco, with cacao beans used as a kind of currency. Vendors were arranged according to the products or services they sold. At the center of the marketplace stood an imposing building where a dozen judges, all of them members of the guild of pochteca, stood ready to adjudicate disputes, while other officials patrolled the stalls, checking for inaccurate measures and other signs of fraud.

The Tlatelolco market was the primary one for the Mexica capital, but there were numerous smaller markets around the city and in smaller towns throughout central Mexico, especially in late Aztec times. Most of them were open only once every 5 days and sold basic commodities, but a few specialized in particular wares—dogs at the town of Acolman near the site of the ancient city of Teotihuacan, for example. When the Spaniards introduced a cash economy in the sixteenth century, the people of central Mexico adapted quickly, for they already had long-established habits of buying and selling.

Questions for Discussion

When Spaniards arrived in Mexico in 1519, the Tlatelolco market was one of the first sights they saw. What would they have thought as they observed it? What, if anything, would have appeared strange to them, and what would have seemed very familiar?

Neither the Aztecs nor the Incas were great cultural innovators, for both drew heavily on preexisting traditions and did relatively little to alter basic patterns of subsistence and belief among their subjects. People in the Andes had domesticated llamas, alpacas, and vicuñas, and they made greater use of metal for utilitarian purposes, but both societies showed great ingenuity in exploiting the natural environment to feed their growing populations, and humans provided virtually all of the muscle power in agriculture. Nowhere in North, Central, or South America did indigenous peoples use wheeled vehicles for transport.

Differences between the Aztecs and the Incas were mostly ones of degree. The Incas achieved significantly greater political centralization through their policies of relocating subject populations and dispatching emissaries throughout the empire over their impressive system of roads. Andeans had traditionally accorded women a greater role in religious observances and community affairs, but in both empires men were considered the heads of households, and the increasing militarization of society placed a premium on males as warriors.

One of the most pronounced differences between these two great civilizations was the way in which commodities were circulated and exchanged. Among the Incas, the state largely controlled the flow of food, cloth, and other necessities, storing these goods in their strategically placed warehouses, ready for distribution in time of calamity. The Aztecs likewise maintained reserves of the many items they received in tribute, but Mesoamericans had a much more fully developed market economy, and merchants comprised an important social group with special privileges.

Whatever their differences, in many ways the Aztecs and the Incas each had more in common with the Europeans of their time than they did with the simpler societies of the Caribbean and coastal South America who would be the first to encounter the European invaders in 1492. When Spanish conquistadors arrived in Tenochtitlan and Cuzco, they were awestruck by the size and splendor of these two great cities, as dazzling as anything they had known in Europe. Once they got over their initial shock at human sacrifice and other rituals they considered grotesque and diabolical, they found much that made sense to them. They could easily relate to temples comparable in grandeur to the cathedrals and mosques they had seen back home, kings who claimed their position by virtue of divine approval, and governments capable of taxing many millions of people and mustering their young men for military service and forced labor.

THE DIVERSITY OF AMERICAN PEOPLES

The systems of social organization of the interior highlands of Mesoamerica and South America ranked among the world's most complex for their time. But to focus exclusively on the great empires of the Aztecs and the Incas would be to minimize the cultural achievements of people who made their homes in areas where the natural environment was less favorable to population growth. We would also miss the tremendous diversity of indigenous societies on the eve of European contact.

Native peoples of the Americas found ingenious ways to eke out a living in many climate zones of the hemisphere. Some provided for virtually all of their own material needs themselves, while others carried on a certain amount of trade. Their types of social and political organization varied from small bands that roamed from place to place in search of wild game and plants for gathering to kingdoms that nearly rivaled the Andeans and Mesoamericans in their level of political sophistication. Some were extremely warlike, while others were more peaceful. Every indigenous society had its shamans or other specialists who communicated with the unseen forces that controlled or influenced the lives of humans. Some practiced human sacrifice and ritual cannibalism, and most maintained elaborate oral traditions that explained the origins of the world and the nature of the gods.

The diversity of native society was readily apparent to Europeans who arrived after 1492. The first peoples they encountered, the Tainos and Caribs of the Caribbean and the Tupi speakers of coastal Brazil, lived far more simply than those they would later encounter in Mesoamerica and the Andes. The people they called the Pueblos of northern New Mexico developed a highly sophisticated society in a challenging physical environment, but the Spaniards who first saw them in the early 1540s found them primitive in comparison with what they had seen at Tenochtitlan and Cuzco.

The Tainos and Caribs

According to some experts, the islands of the Caribbean together contained an estimated 750,000 inhabitants in 1492, but other scholars believe that the population was much larger, perhaps as many as 2 or 3 million. The island of Hispaniola—today's Haiti and the Dominican Republic—was the most densely populated, with perhaps as many as half a million people according to the most reliable population estimates. Cuba and Puerto Rico, by contrast, each had about 50,000 people at most. By far, the most numerous of the Caribbean peoples were the Tainos, whose settlements were located in the Bahamas, Hispaniola, Cuba, Puerto Rico, and Jamaica.

The Tainos were agricultural people who minimized soil erosion and improved drainage by planting their crops in earthen mounds 3 feet high and 9 feet in diameter. Their most important staple was cassava, also known as manioc, a root that could be ground into calorie-rich flour or mashed and fermented to yield intoxicating beverages, but they also cultivated sweet potatoes, maize, peanuts, peppers, beans, tobacco, and cotton. Abundantly available fish, sea turtles, shellfish, lizards, manatees, and small game provided protein. Their settlements were located in the places best suited for agriculture and ranged in size from a few hundred to as many as 5000 people.

Men (and a few women) known as *caciques* ruled over one or more villages. Succession to the chieftainships was reckoned along matrilineal lines. When a cacique died, his oldest sister's oldest son usually took his place. Taino caciques presided over local religious rituals, lived in larger houses than their neighbors, and wore ornaments made from gold mined in the interior mountains of Cuba, Puerto Rico, and Hispaniola, but they received no tribute or labor service from their people.

The ever-increasing social distinctions that characterized life in Mesoamerica and the Andes were unknown among the Tainos. Everyone lived so simply that Christopher Columbus called them "a people short of everything." In the warm climate of the Caribbean there was little need for protective clothing or shelter, and in a region prone to tropical storms it made little sense to build anything more elaborate than mud huts and ceremonial ball courts. But the Tainos had mastered such crafts as woodcarving, weaving of cotton, and pottery, and they carried on trade with neighboring islands.

One of the most peaceful people of the Americas, the Tainos had a hard time defending themselves against their more warlike neighbors or the Spanish intruders after 1492. Smallpox and other European diseases left them all but extinct by the mid-sixteenth century, although liaisons between Spanish men and Taino women assured their contribution to the gene pool of postconquest Caribbean society. Their enduring cultural legacy can be seen in the many Taino words that passed into Spanish and then into English and other languages. "Cacique" became the generic term used by Spaniards throughout their American colonies to describe indigenous rulers and still is used to describe local political bosses. Other words of Taino origin are *canoa* (canoe), *hamaca* (hammock), *barbacoa* (grill, hence the English word barbecue), and *maíz* (maize). Scholars have surmised that had there been no European invasion, the Tainos might have continued their cultural development and established close contact with mainland Mesoamerica.

People called Caribs could be found in the islands known as the Lesser Antilles, from Guadeloupe south to Martinique and Grenada, and in northern South America. Their religious customs and political organization were evidently less well developed than those of the Tainos, but they were much more warlike. Canoes carrying up to 100 men raided Taino settlements and took away women and children as slaves. Male enemies taken in battle were sacrificed and eaten in a form of ritual cannibalism, although sensationalized accounts penned by early Spanish explorers tended to exaggerate the importance of this practice.

In many other ways, the Caribs' lifestyle resembled that of their less violent neighbors. They drew their subsistence from agriculture just as other Caribbean peoples did. When Taino women taken as slaves bore the children of Carib men, they spread Taino cultural traits throughout the region. Meanwhile, the Tainos were becoming more like the Caribs at the beginning of the sixteenth century, fighting back against their aggressors using similar weapons and battle tactics.

The Tupi of Coastal Brazil

The natives of coastal Brazil had much in common with the people of the Caribbean. They too based their subsistence on slash-and-burn agriculture as well as hunting, fishing, and gathering fruits and nuts. Manioc was their principal crop, but they also produced maize, beans, peanuts, and cotton. The importance of shellfish in their diet can be seen in the huge mounds of shells they left behind. The Tupi also possessed a detailed knowledge of the many resources that could be found in the forests that surrounded their settlements. From the tree that the Portuguese would later called brazilwood, the Tupi produced a red dye used to color their cotton garments.

The Tupi lived very simply, and each village was largely self-sufficient. Their lack of interest in accumulating personal possessions mystified sixteenth-century Europeans. One observer noted that among the Tupi "what belongs to one belongs to all." But they did take great pride in adorning themselves with red and black body paint, necklaces, and bracelets made from stones and shells, and lip plugs fashioned from polished jadeite. Brilliantly colored feathers were also used to make headdresses and other garments worn by shamans and other important people.

Tupi settlements usually had from 400 to 800 inhabitants. Groups of up to 60 interrelated nuclear families lived together in large houses. Leadership at the family level and higher was patrilineal. Councils of male elders made decisions for their tribes and preserved the collective memory. Labor was divided by gender. Men felled trees, hunted, and fished, while women planted and harvested crops. Certain crafts, such as the making of baskets and hammocks, were performed by both men and women. Females as well as males also served as shamans or healers in Tupi society.

The Tupi were aggressive people who often fought among themselves. Young men had to distinguish themselves in battle before they were allowed to marry, and men of all ages earned prestige by taking enemy captives. Prisoners were then sacrificed and eaten, but not before they had been carried back to their captor's home and subjected to public humiliation by the women of the village.

The "Pueblo" Peoples of New Mexico

The people who lived in what is now the northern part of the state of New Mexico received their first foreign "visitors" when Francisco Vázquez de Coronado and his entourage arrived in the early 1540s. The Spanish admired their large apartment-like adobe dwellings, calling them *pueblos,* the Spanish word for town. In time, the name came to be applied to the people as well, even though they were in fact made up of several different groups who spoke mutually unintelligible languages.

The dry climate and cold winters of New Mexico forced the Pueblo peoples to work hard to provide for their basic needs. They developed elaborate irrigation systems to water their fields of maize, squash, cotton, and tobacco. They also obtained buffalo hides and other goods by trading with native peoples who inhabited the plains east of Pueblo territory.

Pueblo society stressed social conformity and subordination of the individual to the group. Younger adults were expected always to defer to their elders in matters of leadership and service. Gender roles were also carefully prescribed. Men were hunters and warriors and performed heavy labor in the fields, while women cooked, cared for children, and made pottery and baskets. Women also constructed and maintained the adobe dwellings. Although people traced their lineage through the female line and observed a gender complementarity somewhat comparable to that of Andeans, males dominated Pueblo religion. At least until after menopause, women were not permitted to enter the *kivas,* the circular buildings where sacred objects were kept and important rituals performed.

The Pueblos developed a highly sophisticated culture in a challenging environment, but nothing on the order of what the Aztecs and Incas achieved. In the 1530s, Spaniards in Mexico heard rumors about them and concluded that *otro México*—another Mexico—lay deep in the interior of the continent. Immediately, they organized an expedition to the far north. What they found was a bitter disappointment—adobe buildings that scarcely compared with the temples and palaces of the lords of Tenochtitlan and rulers whose political control reached only to the limits of a single "town." The Pueblos provided sixteenth-century Europeans with yet another example to show that the people they lumped together as "Indians" in fact were even more diverse than the societies they had known back in the "old world."

THE SPANISH AND THE PORTUGUESE

Just as the Inca and Aztec rulers were building their power, a similar process was taking place on the Iberian Peninsula as the emerging national monarchies of Spain and Portugal asserted their control over their political rivals. Like their counterparts in Mesoamerica and the Andes, the new monarchs of Iberia achieved greater political centralization than their predecessors and used history, religion, and ideology to buttress their positions. To a much greater degree than the Aztecs or the Incas, however, they insisted that their subjects conform fully to the officially sanctioned religion and eventually expelled religious deviants from their dominions.

Also in sharp contrast to the lords of Cuzco and Tenochtitlan, the Iberian monarchs showed an interest in what might lie beyond the ocean. Members of Portugal's royal family took the lead, experimenting with new navigation techniques and sponsoring expeditions along the coast of Africa from the early fifteenth century onward. By the time that King Ferdinand and Queen Isabella assumed their thrones in the 1470s, Spain was ready for overseas exploration as well. The Iberians' curiosity would have fateful consequences for the peoples of the Americas.

Centuries of Conquest

Iberia's position at the western end of the Mediterranean meant that for hundreds of years it was exposed to outsiders who indelibly shaped its culture. Between 800 and 1100 BCE, Phoenicians from the eastern Mediterranean established colonies along the southern coast. Phoenician merchants sold oil, wine, jewelry, and ivory to Iberians in exchange for gold, silver, copper, and tin. They also brought new techniques of metalworking and a form of writing that archaeologists have found on tombstones in what is now southern Portugal. Greek traders appeared in Iberia by about 600 BCE, followed in turn by the Carthaginians, who conquered the central and southern parts of the peninsula in the third century BCE and set up a naval base at the present-day Spanish port of Cartagena.

The Romans began their conquest of Iberia in 218 BCE. Dozens of Roman colonies appeared throughout Hispania, the Roman name for the Iberian Peninsula. The Romans' cultural impact was enormous, ranging from law and architecture to language and religion. Latin evolved on the peninsula into modern Spanish, Portuguese, and

Spain and Portugal in 1492

Catalan. Christianity entered Iberia in the Roman period, by the middle of the third century CE. Under Roman rule, the peninsula carried on a thriving trade with the rest of the Mediterranean, exporting olive oil, horses, wine, wool, and metals. Roman domination ended in the fifth century, as the empire itself crumbled. Vandals, Visigoths, and other Germanic peoples crossed the Pyrenees Mountains and set up kingdoms in what are now Spain and Portugal.

In the early eighth century, Iberia witnessed yet another conquest, as Muslims crossed the Strait of Gibraltar from North Africa, took over most of the peninsula, and eventually set up the Umayyad Caliphate that ruled from their magnificent capital at Córdoba. Only the Basque country and the tiny kingdom of Asturias in the north remained under the control of Christian kings who claimed descent from the Visigoths. The Muslims extended religious toleration to Jews and Christians living in conquered territory, but many of the latter chose to convert to Islam.

Intellectual, artistic, and practical pursuits flourished in Muslim Iberia. The newcomers brought with them Arabic translations of texts on astronomy, mathematics, geography, and medicine from Persia, India, and Greece, including the work of the philosopher Aristotle. Christian scholars later rendered these texts into Latin, and subsequently circulated them to the rest of Europe. The Muslims introduced better irrigation techniques and new crops such as sugarcane and rice. They taught Iberians new craft specialties such as silk weaving and leatherworking. Spain's famous steel industry at Toledo also dates from the Muslim occupation. Arabic became the mostly widely spoken language in Iberia, not only among Muslims but among Christians and Jews as well. Christians even celebrated the mass and other rites in Arabic, and hundreds of Arabic words made their way into the Spanish and Portuguese languages.

Medieval Iberia and the Reconquista

By the mid-eighth century, Christians of the northern kingdoms began the *Reconquista,* a centuries-long process by which they wrested control of the Iberian Peninsula from the Muslims. Religion supplied a powerful driving force, but hunger for land to support a growing population also motivated the Christians' advance. As they gradually expanded their domains, the kingdoms of Castile (so named for the many castles, or *castillos,* built along the enemy frontier)—as well as León, Aragón, and Portugal took shape. But medieval Iberia also witnessed long periods of relatively peaceful coexistence between Christian and Muslim states. Often divided among themselves, Christian kingdoms sometimes struck alliances with Muslims against other Christian kingdoms.

The balance of power began shifting in the Christians' favor with the fragmentation of Muslim political unity after 1031. By the mid-thirteenth century, the Reconquista was nearly complete. The capture of the southern region known as the Algarve in 1249 eliminated the last Muslim power in Portugal. Meanwhile King Fernando III of Castile, later canonized as a saint by the Catholic church, conquered Andalusia in the south, including the great cities of Córdoba and Seville. At Córdoba, the victorious Christians reconsecrated the city's splendid mosque as a Catholic church (see Plate 5). In the east, Aragón took Valencia in 1238. Only the kingdom of Granada in southern Spain remained under Muslim control, and its rulers were forced to pay regular sums of money in tribute to the monarchs of Castile.

Centuries of intermittent war with the Muslims left important marks on Iberian society and culture. Knights who led the southward thrust were rewarded with vast tracts of land, and other Christians willing to settle in newly conquered territories received grants as well, thereby setting a precedent that would later be followed in the Americas. The Reconquista also reinforced traditional gender roles and a double standard of sexual conduct. Men were valued for their fighting abilities, and local authorities tolerated their sexual transgressions. Women, on the other hand, contributed to the Reconquista by recreating Christian family life in the new settlements within the seclusion of their homes and under the patriarchal sway of husbands and fathers.

Iberian Christians believed that the apostle St. James, known in Spanish as Santiago Matamoros, "killer of Moors" (Muslims), had aided in their victories. His reputed burial place at Compostela in Galicia became a popular pilgrimage site by the tenth century. Mock battles between Christians and Moors became a part of Spanish folklore that would later be transported to America. Spain's national epic, *El Cid*, also dates from the Reconquista. It tells the story of Rodrigo Díaz, known as "the master," or *al-sayyid* in Arabic, who died in Valencia in 1099. He fought at various times as a mercenary for both Muslim and Christian kings, but legend subsequently made him a great champion of the Christian cause.

Iberian Monarchies in the Fifteenth Century

The defeat of the major Muslim principalities in the thirteenth century failed to bring immediate peace and prosperity to the Iberian Peninsula. Civil wars among the victorious Christian kingdoms continued over the next 200 years. Famines and epidemics added to the misery, especially when the infamous Black Death plague reached Iberia in the late 1340s. Portugal achieved a measure of political stability first. In 1385, King João I of the Aviz dynasty defeated a Castilian rival and assured the political independence of his kingdom, even though intermittent wars with Castile continued. João reigned until 1433, permitting him to trim the power of nobles who had sided with Castile and to consolidate his position with help from a cadre of university-trained bureaucrats.

For Spain, the decisive turning point came in 1469 with the marriage of Isabella, a claimant to the thrones of Castile and León, and Ferdinand, heir to the crowns of Aragón, Catalonia, and Valencia. In 1474, Isabella's partisans defeated those of a rival contender, and she became queen. Five years later, Ferdinand came into his legacy as well. In 1516, their grandson Charles I became the first monarch of a united Spain.

Like the kings of the house of Aviz in Portugal, Ferdinand and Isabella curbed the political power of the feudal nobility and created a professional bureaucracy. They also reorganized the royal armies and dispatched a cadre of *corregidores*, who asserted crown authority over local municipal councils. Meanwhile, Ferdinand and Isabella became the champions of a militant Catholicism, with dire consequences for the many Jews and Muslims of Iberia.

The Breakdown of Iberian "Convivencia"

Despite the intermittent battles of the Reconquista, medieval Iberia enjoyed a measure of coexistence, or *convivencia*, among Christians, Jews, and Muslims. Jews often occupied positions of trust, serving as tax collectors and physicians to Christian kings and as administrators to Muslim potentates. Jews also figured among the peninsula's most prominent merchants and bankers. Although religious leaders of all three faiths exhorted their followers to refrain from participating in the rituals of "infidels," Christians sometimes visited mosques and synagogues with their Muslim and Jewish friends, and Muslims occasionally shared in Christian religious festivities. Muslim rulers officially forbade Christians living in their kingdoms to build new houses of worship, but as early as the ninth century there were various churches under construction not far from Córdoba.

Mutual toleration had its limits, however. In Christian and Muslim states alike, bloody purges periodically took the lives of many Jews, and Christians were sometimes sold as slaves to Muslims in Morocco. Discrimination against Jews grew noticeably in the fourteenth and fifteenth centuries. In Iberia and just about everywhere in medieval Europe, Jews living in Christian kingdoms had to wear special identifying badges and paid higher taxes. Many towns confined them to specific residential enclaves and restricted their economic activities. All Jews were banished from Aragón in the fourteenth century. In the face of rising persecution, many Spanish and Portuguese Jews nominally converted to Catholicism but often continued to practice their ancestral faith in secret. These "New Christians" became targets of popular prejudice and of restrictive laws barring them from certain occupations.

Ferdinand and Isabella thus assumed their respective thrones in a time of mounting religious intolerance. Known as the "Catholic Kings," they used the power of the crown to enforce conformity. In 1478, they received the pope's permission to establish the Holy Office of the Inquisition to discipline New Christians who persisted in the practice of Judaism, as well as other Catholics who entertained ideas that ran counter to the teachings of the Church. Some 2000 New Christians were reportedly executed under Inquisition auspices in the 1480s, while many others were banished from their hometowns. In 1492, the monarchs ordered all remaining Jews to convert to Catholicism or leave Spanish territory. As a result, the number of superficial converts grew. Many Jews fled to Portugal, only to be faced with the same choice of forced conversion or permanent exile just a few years later. Portuguese authorities proved much more lax than their Spanish counterparts in enforcing these provisions, and those who did convert to Christianity fared somewhat better in Portugal because until 1536 there was no Inquisition to scrutinize their behavior.

The growing concern for religious purity brought fateful consequences for Muslims as well. Castile embarked upon a campaign to capture Granada in the 1480s and succeeded in 1492. Zealous clergy, with support from Queen Isabella, then set about converting Granada's Muslims to Catholicism and ordered the burning of thousands of Islamic books. In 1502, all Muslims living in Spain were told to become Catholics or leave. The Portuguese crown had issued a similar decree a few years before. Many Muslims followed the example of the Jews, converting superficially while continuing to practice Islam in secret.

A key figure in Spain's growing religious militancy was Francisco Jiménez de Cisneros, Archbishop of Toledo and head of the Inquisition. While working to eradicate all traces of Islam and Judaism, he also turned his attention to reforming the Spanish Catholic Church from within, exhorting his fellow clergy and the faithful to return to the doctrinal purity and behavioral austerity of the early Christians. The Spanish Church thus purged itself without breaking from Rome and stood ready to defend Catholicism against the Protestant Reformation and to undertake ambitious missionary efforts in the American colonies.

Iberian Society in the Fifteenth Century

Population estimates for Spain and Portugal in the fifteenth century are nearly as uncertain as those for the Americas. The best available figures are about 4 million for the dominions of Castile and another 1 million apiece for Aragón and Portugal. Lisbon, Seville, Barcelona, and Valencia, each with fewer than 50,000 inhabitants, were the only real cities. Most Iberians were farmers, with wheat, wine, and olive oil being the most important products. In the southern part of the peninsula, the warm climate favored the production of citrus fruits and sugarcane. The high and dry central plateau of Castile was best suited for cattle and sheep ranching.

Even though they had seen some of their political power undermined by the emerging monarchies of Spain and Portugal, the titled nobility—dukes, counts, marquises, and the like—still stood at the apex of Iberian society. Many of them purported to be descended from the early Visigoth kings, and most asserted that they or their ancestors had distinguished themselves fighting infidels during the Reconquista. They usually had large landholdings and many vassals who owed them tribute and allegiance. Much more numerous, especially in the north, were the untitled nobles, called *hidalgos* (or *hijos de algo,* "sons of something") in Spain and *fidalgos* in Portugal. These people were often of humble economic status but nonetheless boasted a distinguished lineage. They enjoyed exemption from certain taxes and freedom from arrest by anyone but the monarch's direct representative. Titled or not, all nobles cited their *limpieza de sangre*—literally, purity of blood, which meant that neither they nor their ancestors had ever been Jews, Muslims, or heretics prosecuted and convicted by the Inquisition.

The percentage of titled nobles and hidalgos in the total population varied considerably, from as many as 75 percent, most of them fairly humble hidalgos, in some parts of the north, to as few as 2 percent in the south. At most, they comprised about 10 percent of Castile's total population. The rest were commoners, the most prosperous of whom generally resided in cities and towns. Some were physicians, teachers, lawyers, merchants, and master craftsmen. Others were farmers or day laborers. Africans, both enslaved and free, constituted a small but growing segment of Iberia's population after Portuguese merchants began trading along the coast of Africa in the fifteenth century. Many were domestic servants in the wealthiest households of Seville, Lisbon, Valencia, and other towns, but some worked as stevedores and artisans. In sixteenth-century Seville, crown officials appointed free blacks to help govern the city's rapidly growing African community, and black Catholics created their own religious organizations. Resident colonies of foreign merchants, many of them from the Italian city of Genoa, could be found in the most important ports.

Queen Isabella, as we have seen, was a dynamic leader who brought considerable change to Castile during her long reign. But Isabella became queen only because there were no suitable male heirs in line for the throne. She was an exception to the long-entrenched rule of patriarchy, a system of social relations that vested virtually all authority from the household to the highest levels of church and state in male father figures. Priests and judges exhorted wives to obey their husbands and live modestly within the seclusion of their homes. Denied access to the priesthood, women had no formal roles in official religious ritual comparable to those of their counterparts in Andean society. Even nuns were subject to the discipline of their bishops.

Not all women lived within the rules dictated by patriarchy, however. Lower-class women simply could not remain secluded within their homes; they had to seek whatever work they could find in order to support themselves and their families. More and more women headed their own households, especially as growing numbers of men headed off on the overseas expeditions that began when Portuguese navigators first began probing southward along the African coast. Women also resisted the forced orthodoxy that Catholic authorities tried to impose. It was often mothers who kept Jewish beliefs and rites alive within the privacy of New Christian households, and the Inquisition prosecuted numerous women, old Christians and new alike, for heretical beliefs.

Iberia and the Beginnings of Overseas Expansion

The Mediterranean Sea bustled with commerce in the fifteenth century. At its eastern end, merchants exchanged woolen textiles and other European goods for Asian merchandise transported by caravans along the famous Silk Road of Central Asia or on ships up the Red Sea from the Indian Ocean. Cinnamon, pepper, ginger, cloves, and other spices from India and points eastward had become highly coveted additives to the Western European diet. Asian silks, cotton textiles, sugar, slaves, and precious stones found ready markets in Europe as well. Italians from Genoa and Venice dominated this trade, and they had pioneered sophisticated systems of credit, accounting, contract law, and maritime insurance.

Meanwhile, Europeans were making significant advances in navigation science, including the use of the magnetic compass and new ships that could take better advantage of winds on the open sea. By the fifteenth century, Portugal had taken the lead in these developments, thanks in large part to the initiative of King João I's son Prince Henry (dubbed "the Navigator" by nineteenth-century historians). He gathered experts in navigation and geography and sponsored voyages along the coast of Africa and out into the Atlantic, voyages that would launch his nation as a world power.

Portugal's overseas empire officially began with the seizure of the Muslim stronghold of Ceuta on the Moroccan coast opposite Gibraltar in 1415. Over the next several decades, Portuguese merchants and sailors pushed farther south along the coast of Africa, establishing trading posts where they obtained gold, ivory, and slaves from local rulers in exchange for European horses, saddles, clothing, and tools. In 1498, a Portuguese expedition led by Vasco da Gama sailed around Africa and on to India, and over the next few decades his countrymen established trading posts at Goa on the west coast of India, in present-day Malaysia and Indonesia, and at Macao on the coast of China.

Portuguese merchants no longer needed Italian or Muslim intermediaries to access the wealth of what fifteenth-century Europeans called the "Indies," a term that included not only India but all of Asia and, by extension, any far-off land that might yield exotic merchandise and handsome profits. By no means did they believe that sailing around the tip of Africa was the only way to the lucrative markets of Asia, however. Most knowledge-able people understood that the world was round and that one could sail westward and eventually reach the Orient.

In fact, Iberian navigators had already begun to venture out into the uncharted waters of the Atlantic. During the course of the fifteenth century, Portugal settled the previously uninhabited Azores and Madeira. Both Spain and Portugal fought over the rights to the Canary Islands until the dispute was settled in favor of Castile in 1479. The Guanches, native to the Canaries, were all but destroyed in the process, sharing the fate that would later befall Native Americans. Spanish and Portuguese sugar plantations in the Atlantic islands also foreshadowed the ones they would later set up in Brazil and the Caribbean.

CONCLUSION

The fifteenth and early sixteenth centuries of the Christian calendar witnessed the rise of four great monarchies—the Aztecs and the Incas in the Americas and Spain and Portugal on the southwestern fringe of Europe. As neighbors, Spain and Portugal of course were well aware of one another. Portugal had fought many battles to avoid being absorbed by Castile. The lords of Tenochtitlan and Cuzco may have heard sketchy rumors of one another's existence but devoted their attention entirely to people closer to home that might become new subjects for their expanding dominions.

No one in Iberia or America knew what lay across the Atlantic. The Portuguese and the Spanish, however, were open to the possibility that venturing out to sea might yield great wealth and untold adventure. For many generations, they had heard the tales of China brought back by the thirteenth-century Italian traveler, Marco Polo, and they were familiar with exotic merchandise to be had from Asia. Their religious traditions taught them something of far-off lands as well. Many believed that the apostle Thomas had carried the teachings of Jesus to India, and legends of Christian kingdoms in the east circulated throughout medieval Europe. Their knowledge of distant lands, both real and fictional, spread even more quickly following the invention of the printing press in the mid-fifteenth century.

In matters of geography, the people of Mesoamerica and the Andes had narrower horizons than their European contemporaries. Many of Europe's greatest cities in the fifteenth century—Genoa, Venice, Barcelona, Seville, Lisbon—lay close to the sea, while the most imposing settlements of North and South America were located inland. The Aztecs and the Incas accumulated vast riches from distant places, but these goods came to them chiefly by land, on the backs of llamas and other camelids in the Andes, and of human carriers in Mesoamerica. Waterborne transport was limited to canoes that plied the coast of Central America and the great inland lakes, such as Texcoco in Mexico and Titicaca in Peru.

It was not that the priests and rulers of Cuzco and Tenochtitlan lacked curiosity about distant worlds or kingdoms unseen. Like their forebears, they possessed detailed knowledge of the movements of the stars and the planets, in many ways superior to what Europeans of their time could boast. They maintained, elaborated, and passed on stories that explained the origins of the world they knew and the demise of worlds that had gone before. The underworld, the afterlife, and the realms of their many gods all occupied the attention of the best minds of the ancient Americas.

Nezahualcoyotl, ruler of Texcoco in the mid-fifteenth century, was a philosopher and poet as well as a king. Inside his 300-room palace compound were a library and archive, as well as special quarters for poets, philosophers, and historians. Many of his verses speculated on what awaited humans' discovery in the afterlife. It was not for want of intellectual prowess or curiosity, then, that the existence of flesh-and-blood human beings across the ocean caught the peoples of the Americas by surprise.

LEARNING MORE ABOUT LATIN AMERICANS

Carrasco, David, and Scott Sessions. *Daily Life of the Aztecs: People of the Sun and Earth* (Westport, CT: Greenwood Press, 1998). Places special emphasis on the importance of religion to the Aztec people.

D'Altroy, Terence N. *The Incas* (Oxford, U.K.: Blackwell, 2002). Another volume in *The Peoples of America* series; a comprehensive survey of Inca society, with information on the outlying fringes of the Inca Empire in Ecuador and Chile.

Perry, Mary Elizabeth. *Gender and Disorder in Early Modern Seville* (Princeton, NJ: Princeton University Press, 1990). An excellent social history of the Spanish city that became the chief port for trade with the Americas.

Silverblatt, Irene. *Moon, Sun, and Witches: Gender Ideologies and Class in Inca and Colonial Peru* (Princeton, NJ: Princeton University Press, 1987). A feminist anthropologist shows how the Incas and the Spanish conquerors used ideologies of gender in consolidating their rule, and includes the story of Tanta Carhua.

Smith, Michael E. *The Aztecs* (Oxford, U.K.: Blackwell, 1996). One of the leading authorities on pre-Hispanic Mexico writes this volume for *The Peoples of America* series, with special emphasis on the technical achievements of the Aztecs.

3

THE EUROPEAN CONQUEST
OF AMERICA

WHEN CHRISTOPHER COLUMBUS stepped ashore on the island of Guanahaní in the Bahamas on October 12, 1492, he believed that the continent of Asia could not be far off. Sailing along the north coast of Cuba a few weeks later, he was convinced he had reached Cipango (Japan). His dream of shipping valuable silks and spices to Europe now lay at hand, and he would be Queen Isabella's viceroy, her personal representative, there in what he called "the Indies."

Over the next several decades, it became clear that Columbus had not reached Asia but instead had found a "new world." Isabella and Ferdinand and their grandson King Charles I accordingly expanded their ambitions far beyond the handful of trading posts envisioned in 1492. They now saw the Indies as new kingdoms to enhance the power, wealth, and prestige of Spain, and the natives of these lands—the "Indians"—as dutiful, tax-paying subjects. To administer this vast empire they dispatched a cadre of loyal bureaucrats to supplant the unruly explorers and conquistadors. Meanwhile, the monarchs sponsored a vigorous campaign to convert the natives of this new world to Christianity. By the mid-sixteenth century, the Portuguese crown had set up a colonial government in Brazil and Catholic missionaries had begun working there as well.

Isolated from Europe, Africa, and Asia for thousands of years, the natives of the Americas now became part of emerging empires that spanned the globe. They not only had to swear allegiance to new sovereigns and accept a new religion but also had to contend with the grandiose plans of thousands of Spaniards and Portuguese who followed Columbus across the Atlantic. These settlers saw the "Indians" as a source of labor to help them build their colony and exploit the natural resources of the new continent. When Indians resisted their political, religious, or economic demands, the Europeans resorted to war, killing thousands and enslaving many more. Countless others died of smallpox, measles, and other "old world" diseases to which they had no previous exposure.

The natives who encountered Columbus and his crew on Guanahaní could not have known it, but these travel-weary sailors constituted the advance guard of a massive and brutal occupation of the Americas. The people of this hemisphere did not simply become passive victims of conquest, however. Some persistently fought back or retreated to remote deserts, mountains, and jungles beyond the intruders' reach. Others forged tactical alliances with the invaders in hope of gaining an advantage over long-standing enemies or to assure their personal survival and advancement under the new regime. The result was a colonial society built on indigenous accommodation and resistance as well as on European greed, military prowess, political drive, and religious fervor.

THE EUROPEANS ARRIVE

The people of the Caribbean and coastal Brazil were the first to experience the European invasion. Their settlements, their material culture, and their political organization bore little resemblance to Columbus's hometown of Genoa or the highly sophisticated societies of Asia that the European sailors knew at least by reputation. But ambitious Spanish and Portuguese colonists quickly found other ways to profit from their accidental landfall—gold in the interior of Hispaniola, Cuba, and Puerto Rico and dyewoods in Brazil. Their pursuit of these commodities inaugurated a chain of events that would have profound consequences for the native Caribbeans and Brazilians.

Columbus and the First Encounters

Queen Isabella of Castile was a busy monarch in the early months of 1492. In January, she accepted the surrender of the last Muslim ruler of Granada, and 3 months later she signed a contract with Christopher Columbus, who had finally persuaded her to sponsor a voyage to the west, across the "Ocean Sea." Both the queen and Columbus had high expectations for what the voyage might yield. Isabella accordingly named him admiral, viceroy, and governor of whatever lands he might encounter, and guaranteed him "one-tenth of all merchandise, whether pearls, gems, gold, silver, spices, or goods of any kind, that may be acquired by purchase, barter or any other means, within the boundaries of said Admiralty jurisdiction."

Columbus then proceeded to outfit three ships and 90 men for his voyage. They set sail in early August of 1492. Arriving at Guanahaní, he claimed the island for Castile before heading on to the north coast of Cuba and then eastward to the island of Hispaniola. A triumphant Columbus arrived back in Spain in early March 1493. With him sailed several Taínos he had taken into custody. Eager to persuade the monarchs to finance a return voyage, Columbus gave a glowing report on his discoveries. "I found very many islands, inhabited by numberless people," he proclaimed. Cuba and Hispaniola

TIMELINE

1492
Columbus's first voyage

1500
Cabral's expedition lands in Brazil

1502
Nicolás de Ovando arrives as governor of
Hispaniola, with 2500 colonists

1508–1511
Spanish settlement of Puerto Rico, Jamaica,
and Cuba

1516
Charles I becomes first monarch of a united
Spain

1518
First recorded outbreak of smallpox in the
Americas; first direct slave imports from
Africa to Spanish America

1519–1521
Conquest of Mexico

1532
Pizarro and Atahualpa meet

1536
Revolt of Manco Inca

1537–1548
Civil wars in Peru

1539–1542
Expeditions of Francisco Vásquez de
Coronado and Hernando De Soto

1542–1543
New Laws issued

1549
Tomé de Sousa arrives as governor of Brazil

1556
Philip II becomes king of Spain

1559–1562
Smallpox epidemic in coastal Brazil

1560s
Taqui Onkoy rebellion in Peru

1572
Defeat of the neo-Inca state at Vilcabamba in
Peru

1580
Philip II of Spain becomes king of Portugal

1607–1608
Permanent English and French colonization of
North America begins

1610s
Portuguese authorities defeat santidade
movement in Brazil

1630–1654
Dutch control northeastern Brazil

1640
Portugal declares independence from Spain

constituted nothing short of a tropical paradise, with fertile soil, fine harbors, lush vegetation, fresh water, succulent fruits, and exotic birds. The people of the islands were "exceedingly straightforward and trustworthy and most liberal with all that they have." The natives of Hispaniola, he noted in particular, willingly traded gold for whatever trinkets his crewmen offered. Columbus also found the islanders timid, "readily submissive," and not given to idolatry. He therefore concluded that they would make ideal candidates for conversion to Catholicism.

Columbus's account convinced the queen to outfit 17 ships that set out for the islands in late 1493. Some 1500 people, mostly men, were aboard, along with domestic animals, sugarcane and other plants, seeds, and tools needed to establish a permanent colony on Hispaniola. Meanwhile, word of the new lands spread quickly in Europe, and others hastened to join in the adventure. Columbus and others traveling under Spanish auspices soon reconnoitered the coasts of Puerto Rico, Jamaica, Central America, and

Venezuela, while Portuguese navigators landed on the northeast tip of Brazil in 1500. Within a quarter century of Columbus's first voyage, European explorers and cartographers had sketched a remarkably complete outline of the Caribbean, as well as the eastern coasts of North, Central, and South America, and had crossed the Isthmus of Panamá to the Pacific Ocean. The Italian Amerigo Vespucci's accounts of his journeys circulated so widely in Europe that a form of his first name, "America," began appearing on maps of the new continent.

The Caribbean Colonies

Only Spain and Portugal were at this point ready to form permanent colonies in the Americas. Spanish settlement remained confined to Hispaniola for nearly two decades following Columbus's voyage. The city of Santo Domingo, founded in 1496, became the capital of the new colony. Queen Isabella soon reneged on the broad concessions she had made to Columbus, as the potential riches of Hispaniola became more evident and he proved incapable of establishing order there. In 1500, a new governor took command and promptly had Columbus arrested. Two years later, another 2500 colonists arrived. Between 1508 and 1511, other Spaniards began the permanent occupation of Puerto Rico, Jamaica, and Cuba.

Early settlers in the Caribbean supported themselves by panning for gold in the islands' interior highlands. Adapting practices employed during the reconquest of Iberia from the Muslims, they commandeered local natives to work and raided outlying islands and the southeastern mainland of North America for slaves. Popular legend holds that Juan Ponce de León, a veteran of Columbus's second voyage and conqueror of Puerto Rico, was looking for a "fountain of youth" when he landed in Florida in 1513. In truth, he sought gold and slaves. He never found the former, but native peoples from Florida were forcibly taken off to work in the Caribbean islands. Spaniards who engaged in slave raids assuaged their consciences by arguing that these Indians had resisted Christianity and thus had been legitimately captured.

The indigenous population of the Caribbean region declined dramatically during the first two decades after 1492. Some natives died in battles with the Spaniards, while others succumbed to the exploitive new labor regime. The demands of the European colonists disrupted native agriculture. Sickness, aggravated by malnutrition, also played a significant part. Although the first recorded outbreak of smallpox did not come until 1518, influenza and bacterial infections afflicted Spaniards and natives alike from the 1490s onward.

A few Spaniards rallied to the natives' defense. Foremost among them were a handful of Dominican friars. In 1511, Antonio de Montesinos delivered a fiery sermon to the leading Spanish settlers in Santo Domingo, warning that they faced eternal damnation if they continued in their ways. Later, another Dominican, Bartolomé de Las Casas, took up the cause. In response to pressure from the Dominicans and other clerics, King Ferdinand issued laws codifying the *encomienda* (the practice of distributing Indian workers to individual Spaniards) and stipulated that the holders of these grants, called *encomenderos*, were to protect and Christianize the natives allotted to them.

The Portuguese in Brazil

Like Columbus in the Caribbean, Portuguese navigators were on their way to Asia when they first made landfall in Brazil. Pedro Alvares Cabral's fleet of 13 vessels set sail in 1500 intending to follow up on Vasco da Gama's successful voyage around the southern tip of Africa to India 2 years earlier. By design or by accident, Cabral pursued a more westward course and landed on the coast of Brazil. He and his crew spent 8 days ashore before heading on to their original destination, while one ship hastened back to Portugal with news of the discovery.

In 1501, the Portuguese returned, this time with the express purpose of reconnoitering the land. Early Portuguese impressions of the Brazilian natives were as glowing as Columbus's reports from the Caribbean: "In every house they all live together in harmony, with no dissension between them. They are so friendly that what belongs to one belongs to all." The only commodity of any value the Portuguese found was brazilwood, a dyewood long used by the Tupi to color their cotton fabrics. For the next two decades, the European presence in Brazil consisted of simple trading posts, permanently staffed by just a few individuals, similar to those they had set up in Africa. Natives cut the dyewoods and traded them for European tools, while a few Portuguese men settled in native communities, married local women, and served as cultural intermediaries between Europeans and native Brazilians.

The crown's attention focused on its developing commercial empire in Asia, and there was little reason to set up an elaborate government for a colony that yielded only dyewoods. Kings Manuel I (1495–1521) and João III (1521–1557) relied instead on private enterprise to explore and defend their American claims, awarding monopoly contracts to dyewood merchants willing to take on these added responsibilities. Such initiatives proved ineffective at keeping French interlopers from setting up fortified trading posts along the coast. After a series of naval expeditions failed to dislodge the French, King João sent a large expedition to establish a more permanent Portuguese presence at São Vicente, about 300 miles southwest of present-day Rio de Janeiro.

Meanwhile, King João attempted to promote colonization along the entire length of Brazil's coastline. He divided the coast into 15 captaincies, and granted them to proprietors known as *donatários,* who had proven their loyalty to the crown through government service or participation in the establishment of Portugal's settlements in India. The donatário could recruit colonists, make land grants, found cities, administer justice, collect taxes, and receive a percentage of the profits from the trade in native slaves and dyewoods within his jurisdiction. Most of the captaincies failed for reasons that included hostility from local Indians, poor administration, and internal dissension among the colonists.

A few of the proprietary colonies prospered, however. As donatário at São Vicente, Martim Afonso de Sousa fostered the development of sugar mills, partially financed by northern European investors. A short distance inland from São Vicente, the new town of São Paulo became a base to provide food and supplies for the sugar industry. The captaincy of Pernambuco in the north also succeeded in solidifying the Portuguese presence in Brazil. Proprietor Duarte Coelho Pereira, a former soldier and diplomat in India, recruited numerous settlers and expanded the region's economic base, previously centered on dyewoods, to include sugar production. He also cultivated good relations with Indians in Pernambuco. His brother-in-law married the daughter of a local chief, and the proprietor encouraged other colonists to do likewise.

In other respects, however, the development of these captaincies proved disastrous for the indigenous peoples of Brazil. During the first 30 years after Cabral's arrival, when Portuguese settlers were few in number, the natives retained substantial control over the terms of their interaction with the foreigners. They cut dyewood when and where they pleased and exchanged the logs for knives and other useful tools brought from Europe. The successful donatários and their accompanying entourages disrupted this simple barter economy, as aspiring sugar planters enslaved the natives and appropriated their lands.

THE SPANISH IN MESOAMERICA AND THE ANDES

Meanwhile, the Spanish established sizable permanent colonies, well stocked with familiar plants and domestic animals, and forced indigenous peoples to extract gold from the islands' interior highlands. Almost overnight, the natives of the Caribbean went from trading partners to slaves. At the same time, explorations along the coast of Mesoamerica yielded tantalizing rumors of fabulous kingdoms on the mainland. In 1517 and 1518, two separate expeditions landed in Yucatán. Even in decline, the Mayan city-states were far more impressive than anything Europeans had seen thus far in the Americas. Then in 1519, Hernán Cortés led several hundred of his countrymen over the mountains to the great city of Tenochtitlan. The discovery of the Inca empire followed 13 years later.

Given the formidable military prowess and imperial grandeur of the Aztecs and the Incas, conflict with the invaders was all but inevitable. Victory in battle, almost always with the help of native allies, transformed the Spanish colonial project once again. The mainland held riches far greater than the islands of the Caribbean. The large and highly disciplined populations of Mexico and Peru appeared to be potential subjects of the Spanish crown, converts to Christianity, workers in the colonists' new enterprises, and active collaborators in building a new society.

Cortés and the Aztecs

By 1518, Cuba had become the center of Spanish operations in the Caribbean, and it was from there that the expeditions to Mesoamerica were launched. With word of promising discoveries in Yucatán, Cuba's governor, Diego Velázquez, commissioned a local encomendero, Hernán Cortés, to lead an expedition to the mainland. Cortés prepared energetically for his new assignment, so much so that the governor began to see him as a rival and rescinded his commission. Ambitious and headstrong, Cortés set sail anyway, with 11 ships and about 500 men under his command.

The expedition headed first for Yucatán. There they met Jerónimo de Aguilar, a Spaniard who had shipwrecked there 8 years before and was now fluent in the local Mayan dialect. Aguilar joined Cortés, and they proceeded along the coast to Tabasco, where native chiefs made a conciliatory offering of 20 young women to the Spaniards. As the expedition headed north along the Gulf Coast, Spaniards noticed that one of these women, known to history as Malintzin, could converse with Nahuatl speakers they encountered. She could also speak Mayan with Aguilar, who then translated her words into Spanish. Through these two interpreters, Cortés communicated with couriers dispatched by the Aztec emperor Moctezuma to investigate rumors of intruders on the coast.

The messengers begged Cortés not to venture on toward Tenochtitlan, but he and his men were not to be deterred. Early in the march inland, they learned of unrest within the Mexica empire, as one disgruntled chief offered them several hundred porters to help them carry weapons and supplies. Hearing next of Tlaxcala's long-standing enmity toward the Aztecs, Cortés proposed an alliance. The Tlaxcalans initially rejected his

A map of Tenochtitlan–Mexico City designed by Cortés. In the sixteenth century, the custom of placing north at the top of maps had not yet become standard. In this map, the southern part of the valley of Mexico, with its fresh water lake, is at the top.

overtures, but they sued for peace after a few days' battle. Cortés next set his sights on Cholula, a nearby town only recently under Aztec control. There the Spaniards and their native consorts massacred several thousand warriors as a warning to others who might stand in their way. Meanwhile, Moctezuma could not halt the Spaniards' advance to Tenochtitlan.

On November 19, 1519, Moctezuma and Cortés met on the causeway at the southern entrance to the Mexica capital. Perhaps hoping to placate the strangers, Moctezuma allowed them to enter the city and offered them lodging in a palace at the center of town. An uneasy calm settled over the Valley of Mexico for the next several months, as leaders of surrounding city-states grew increasingly suspicious of the strangers' motives. In the spring of 1520, Cortés learned that Governor Velázquez had sent an expedition from Cuba to oust him. Leaving 80 Spanish soldiers in charge at Tenochtitlan, he headed to the coast, where he defeated his rivals and added several hundred men to his own forces. Meanwhile, the Spaniards' position at Tenochtitlan deteriorated badly, when Cortés's lieutenant, Pedro de Alvarado, ordered an attack on a large gathering of Aztec nobles and the Mexica revolted.

Arriving back in Tenochtitlan, Cortés attempted to restore peace. He brought Moctezuma out on a rooftop to see if he could calm the populace. Instead Moctezuma was killed—by his own people, according to Spanish accounts; by the Spaniards, according to indigenous sources. Cortés and his forces then beat a hasty and undignified retreat, sustaining heavy losses as they fled. They did not abandon hope of taking Tenochtitlan, however. At Tlaxcala, they began preparing for a new assault. In December of 1520, some 550 Spaniards and 10,000 Tlaxcalans set out for the Valley of Mexico once again.

The attack on Tenochtitlan began in May 1521. Swords, pikes, and armor made of steel, as well as crossbows, arquebuses, and cannons gave the invaders a clear advantage over adversaries armed only with wooden and obsidian weapons. Entering the city, however, they encountered fierce resistance. Block by block they advanced, destroying buildings and engaging defenders in hand-to-hand combat. On August 13, 1521, the battle for Tenochtitlan ended as the Spaniards captured the young king Cuauhtemoc. Cortés and his native allies then subdued the surrounding valley, and the mighty empire of the Mexica collapsed. Tenochtitlan became the city of Mexico, capital of the colony that Cortés called "New Spain."

The Search for "Otro México"

After seeing the splendors of Tenochtitlan, the Spaniards reasoned that the new continent must hold other magnificent kingdoms. During the 20 years following Cortés's victory, a flood of new immigrants joined veteran conquistadors in a frantic search for "another Mexico." In so doing, they reconnoitered a vast expanse of territory reaching across what is now the United States from the Carolinas to California, southward to Central America, Peru, and Chile, and the entire length of the Amazon River.

How Historians Understand | MALINTZIN AND THE USES OF HISTORICAL MEMORY

Some historical figures capture the popular imagination, becoming the subjects of myth, fiction, and film. Sometimes too, they come to symbolize the preoccupations of later generations, even becoming scapegoats for collective anger and frustration. In the process, the real person and the historical context in which he or she lived are lost in emotionally charged debate. Such is the case of the Mexican woman baptized as Marina and more commonly known as Malinche or Malintzin.

As Cortés's interpreter, Malintzin played a pivotal role in the Spanish conquest of Mexico, but we know very few details about her life. She was born about 1500, near Coatzacoalcos on Mexico's southern Gulf coast, and spent her early years in a Nahuatl-speaking household. Later, she was sold as a slave to a Maya group and learned their language as well. She was initially "given" to one of Cortés's lieutenants, but when her linguistic ability became apparent Cortés appropriated her for himself. In 1521 or thereabouts, she gave birth to Cortés's son Martín, and a short time later she wed the Spaniard Juan Jaramillo in a Catholic ceremony. When Cortés departed Mexico City for Honduras, she and her husband went along, as did the deposed, captive emperor Cuauhtemoc. Along the way, Cortés charged that Cuauhtemoc was plotting rebellion and ordered him tried and executed. Malintzin reportedly translated as Franciscan friars heard the young king's confession.

The massacre at Cholula, by an Indian artist of the sixteenth century. Malintzin is shown on the right.

Meanwhile, she and Juan Jaramillo had a daughter, and shortly thereafter Malintzin died.

These are all the verifiable biographical details we have about Malintzin. From her own time forward many conflicting images of her have appeared. The conquistador Bernal Díaz del Castillo made her the heroine of his narrative on the conquest of New Spain, describing occasions on which she reportedly saved the Spaniards from ambush and certain death. Sixteenth-century native pictorial representations of Malintzin show her as a powerful figure much honored by her people. Later accounts present a highly romanticized story, full of patently false embellishments. Some, for example, have her traveling to Spain and being presented at the court of King Charles. Indians in Mexico down to today have appropriated her in folk dramas that depict the coming of Christianity.

Other portrayals of Malintzin have not been so kind. Nationalistic Mexicans of the nineteenth and twentieth centuries vilified her for having "sold out" her own people, and the term "malinchista" came to mean "traitor." Because she bore the children of Spaniards, Malintzin has been cast as the archetypal mother of the Mexican nation, raped or seduced by the invaders. The Mexican philosopher Octavio Paz called her *la chingada,* a vulgar and highly pejorative term suggesting both rape and personal dishonor. Still other depictions trivialize her, presenting her as the love slave of Cortés. All of these accounts lack an understanding of Malintzin in the context of her situation. She and countless other native women were sexual objects in the eyes of native and Spanish men alike. What distinguished Malintzin was her linguistic capability. Her childhood experiences gave her knowledge of two languages, but the historical record suggests that she possessed an exceptional ability to understand various dialects in both Maya and Nahuatl. She also apparently learned Spanish readily.

Malintzin did what human beings in most other times and places have done, using her talents to make the best of a difficult situation. Those who blame her for betraying "her people" forget that the natives of the Americas saw themselves as many separate peoples, with no more in common than sixteenth-century Spaniards thought they had with Germans or Swedes. Their common fate as colonial subjects transformed them into "Indians," first in the eyes of Europeans, and only much later in the eyes of native peoples themselves. To cast her as a love-struck girl mesmerized by Cortés or as a duplicitous traitor is to make her something less than human.

Questions for Discussion

If a man had served as Cortés's principal interpreter, would the events of the conquest have been any different? Why or why not? Would the historical memory of a male interpreter have been different? If so, how? If not, why not?

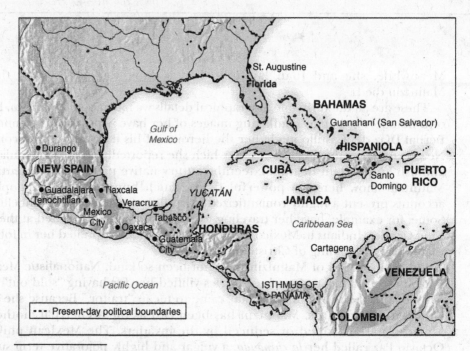

Mexico and the Caribbean in the sixteenth century

Cortés himself spearheaded the quest for new worlds to conquer. He ventured first to Central America, reaching Honduras by 1524, and later sponsored expeditions in the Gulf of California. His key lieutenant, Pedro de Alvarado, founded Guatemala City in 1524. Fifteen years later, Francisco Vázquez de Coronado set off on a journey that took him to the people who became known as the Pueblo in present-day New Mexico, while Hernando De Soto reconnoitered over a wide area from the Appalachians to the Mississippi River, but neither of these expeditions found anything comparable to Tenochtitlan.

The Pizarros and the Incas

In the South American Andes, however, the Spaniards did find "another Mexico." As early as 1523, word circulated in Panama that a large empire lay somewhere to the south. Among those eager to follow up these leads was Francisco Pizarro, a Spaniard who had resided on the isthmus for several years. In 1531, Pizarro sailed with 180 men to the coast of Ecuador and Peru, gathering information as he went. Learning that Atahualpa had defeated his rival and half-brother Huascar, Pizarro hastened to the mountains near Cajamarca, where the new emperor and his army were headquartered.

Pizarro and Atahualpa met on November 16, 1532. The Spaniards had a familiar routine for such encounters. Native rulers were summarily informed that the invaders represented the true God and a great sovereign from across the sea and were "invited" to become Christians and subjects of the king of Spain. Atahualpa was not particularly impressed. His scornful response provided the Spaniards an excuse to attack his troops and take the emperor into custody. Atahualpa then offered a hefty ransom in exchange for his freedom, and arranged to have more than 13,000 pounds of gold and 26,000 pounds of silver brought to Cajamarca. Pizarro and his associates, however, decided that the emperor was a threat to their safety. In a mock trial, they convicted him of plotting against them and executed him in July of 1533. In the meantime, native warriors loyal to Atahualpa had killed Huascar.

Meanwhile, Pizarro seized Cuzco with the help of Indians hostile to the Incas and installed Atahualpa's half-brother Manco Inca as emperor, naively expecting him to cooperate fully with the Spaniards. Pizarro declined to make Cuzco the capital of the new colony of Peru, choosing instead the city of Lima on the coast, the "city of the kings," which he founded in 1535. Lima was well situated for Peru's integration in the emerging Spanish maritime empire, but it left Cuzco as a power base for his enemies, both Spanish and Indian. Other Spaniards marched northward into present-day Ecuador and Colombia.

Early in 1536, Manco Inca led a revolt, attacking Lima and besieging the Spanish settlers at Cuzco for nearly 8 months. Unable to dislodge the Spaniards from either locale, Manco Inca and his forces retreated to the remote mountain fortress of Vilcabamba north of Cuzco, where they maintained a rebel neo-Inca state for more than 30 years. Meanwhile, civil war brewed among the conquistadors. A key player was Diego de Almagro, a former supporter of Pizarro who felt he had not been suitably rewarded for his role in the conquest of Peru. In 1535, Almagro led an expedition to Chile, hoping to find there an alternative kingdom for himself. The venture yielded little, and 2 years later these frustrated would-be conquistadors straggled back to Cuzco to find the city in ruins and governed by Pizarro's brothers Hernando and Gonzalo. Almagro wanted to control Cuzco himself, and launched a revolt against the Pizarros.

The civil war lasted over a decade. Both Almagro and Francisco Pizarro died, and Hernando Pizarro spent 20 years in a Spanish prison for his role in the disturbances. In 1546, Gonzalo Pizarro and his supporters assassinated Peru's first viceroy, Blasco Núñez Vela, sent by King Charles to impose order and to enforce laws requiring that the colonists cease exploiting the Indians. Unrest continued until 1548, when a new governor arrived, defeated Gonzalo's forces, and had him beheaded. Although rivalry among the conquistadors continued, Spanish control of Peru now rested on a more stable base, and by the early 1570s they defeated the native rebels at Vilcabamba.

Military Conquest or Strategic Alliance?

Historians have long debated how just a few hundred Spaniards, far from home and often divided among themselves, succeeded in toppling the Aztec and Inca empires. Without question, European technology—steel swords, gunpowder, Spanish crossbows,

South America in the sixteenth century

- - - Present-day political boundaries

the ships that Cortés constructed for his marine assault on Tenochtitlan via Lake Texcoco—gave them certain tactical advantages. Their weapons enabled them to kill at greater distances than their enemies could. Steel armor provided better protection than the quilted cotton gear of native warriors. Spanish horses gave them superior mobility, at least in open areas. Mastiffs, the huge dogs who accompanied the Spanish forces in Mexico, also inflicted casualties. European technological superiority did not guarantee victory, however. By August of 1521, Cortés's forces had only 80 horses and 16 artillery pieces. Pizarro set off for Peru in 1531 with only 30 horses. Guns proved useless when powder supplies ran out, horses could not maneuver well in the narrow mountain passes of the Andes or on the causeways leading to Tenochtitlan, and native warriors readily seized swords from fallen conquistadors.

Infectious diseases also played a role in the conquests of Mexico and Peru. Smallpox struck Hispaniola in 1518 and apparently reached Mexico in 1520. It then spread to Peru well in advance of the conquistadors themselves. The disease disrupted native leadership, claiming the lives of the Mexica emperor Cuitlahuac, who succeeded Moctezuma, and the Inca Huayna Capac, father of the rivals Huascar and Atahualpa. The smallpox virus undermined the natives' will to resist the invaders, but it killed many native allies of the Spaniards as well.

Some historians and many popular writers have stressed psychological factors in explaining the victories of Cortés and Pizarro. They have portrayed Moctezuma as a fatalistic mystic incapable of decisive action as the bearded strangers drew near his capital. These writers have made much of later Spanish and indigenous reports, compiled well after the fact, that the Nahuas viewed Cortés and his men as gods, but there is no evidence that these claims are anything more than justifications crafted by descendants of those defeated. Cortés's own account shows no sign that the people of Mexico took him for a god.

Perhaps the most decisive factor in the "Spanish conquest" was the assistance of thousands of indigenous people. As many as 200,000 natives assisted Cortés as warriors and porters. Shrewd native chiefs looked to enhance their own political positions by ordering their soldiers to battle, not so much as allies of the Spanish, but as enemies of the Aztec and Inca states. These leaders understood the invaders had a significant technological edge, one that might well bring the downfall of Tenochtitlan and Cuzco. They could not have foreseen the consequences of this tactical maneuver—the creation of a colonial society in which Spaniards claimed the upper hand.

BUILDING A COLONIAL SOCIETY

For the native peoples of the Americas, the brutal slave raids and the defeat of the Aztec and Inca empires constituted just the first phase of the European occupation. Far more deadly were the diseases the intruders unwittingly brought with them. Their burdens mounted as conquistadors looked to translate what they had won on the battlefield into positions of power and wealth for themselves and commandeered native workers to help them build their colonies. Meanwhile, a new society was taking shape, as thousands of European immigrants and African slaves crossed the Atlantic during the sixteenth century.

Engraving by the sixteenth-century Flemish artist Theodor de Bry, based on a woodcut published in 1557 by Hans Staden, a German soldier held captive by Tupis for several years. Images such as this circulated widely in Europe, helping fuel the Black Legend, the idea that the Spanish and the Portuguese were exceptionally brutal conquerors.

The Ecological Conquest

Plants, animals, and unseen microbes that crossed the Atlantic with the human settlers brought about a transformation of the natural environment unprecedented in human history. Smallpox struck some people even before they saw their first European, and it took many victims even as people of Tenochtitlan waged war on Cortés's forces. But these outbreaks were just the beginning of a cycle that repeatedly ravaged native peoples for many generations to come. Periodic episodes of smallpox, measles, influenza, plague, and typhus took thousands of lives and severely disrupted native society. Even those who survived an epidemic could become its victims. When illness struck at a crucial point in the agricultural cycle, few hands were available to plant or harvest crops, and famine loomed. Malnourished and weakened by the invaders' excessive labor demands, native people were in turn left more vulnerable to the next outbreak of disease. Because the epidemics took so many adults in the prime of their reproductive years, birth rates plummeted in native societies, and children who lived might have had no one to care for them.

In the Caribbean, the native population all but disappeared within a couple of generations. Fifty years after Columbus's landfall, fewer than 2000 Indians remained on the island of Hispaniola. Coastal Brazil lost an estimated 95 percent of its aboriginal population during the sixteenth century, so that by 1600 only about 5000 Tupi survived. Estimates of the precontact population of the highland empires of Mexico and Peru vary widely, but there is no doubt that the population declined precipitously, perhaps by as much as 90 percent, over the first century following the Spanish invasion. Central Mexico had at least 10 million inhabitants when Cortés arrived, and perhaps as many as 25 million, while a century later the native population stood at just over 1 million. Only after the mid-seventeenth century, as native peoples began to acquire some resistance to the new diseases, did their numbers begin slowly to climb.

Diseases were just one element in the ecological conquest of the Americas. The Europeans brought many animals previously unknown to the native peoples. Although in time the Indians adopted horses, cattle, oxen, sheep, donkeys, goats, pigs, and chickens for their own uses, the immediate impact of these animals was severe damage to the ecosystem. Animals spread disease, trampled newly planted crops, and polluted water supplies, while their grazing denuded the landscape and led to soil erosion, a problem further exacerbated by the Europeans' insatiable demands for timber and firewood. In coastal Brazil, on the other hand, the forest gained a reprieve with fewer natives to exploit its resources, but with the disappearance of the indigenous population, vital knowledge of the many uses of those resources was lost.

Not all effects of the ecological conquest were negative. Imported animals provided new sources of protein. The natives also supplemented their diets with fruits and vegetables introduced by the Europeans. By the end of the sixteenth century, one could find apples, pears, and plums in many places, and citrus fruits wherever the climate was warm enough. But even when the effects were beneficial, without question the European invasion radically transformed the landscape of the Americas and the daily lives of native peoples.

Transporting horses to America.

Conquistadors, Encomenderos, and Native Peoples

Even before they set foot on the mainland of North and South America, the Spaniards had come to expect that they would tap the native labor supply to help them build their colony. When they learned of the customary arrangements used by the Aztecs and the Incas to compel their subjects to work, they immediately began devising ways to redirect this vast labor supply to their own purposes. Cortés, Pizarro, and other conquistadors gave encomiendas to their favored associates immediately following their military victories. Each of the 168 men who accompanied Pizarro at Cajamarca got encomiendas, and by 1542, Peru had 467 grantees, while in Mexico and Central America their numbers topped 600. Again following pre-Hispanic custom, encomenderos in Mesoamerica and the Andes also received tribute in the form of various commodities from "their" Indians, and they claimed the right to bequeath their encomiendas to their sons and daughters.

Authorities in Spain were not happy with this development. Reformers such as the outspoken Dominican priest Bartolomé de Las Casas had convinced King Charles to abolish the encomienda just as the conquest of Mexico was taking place. When he heard of Cortés's victory, the king reluctantly changed his mind, accepting the argument that the incentive of encomiendas would persuade restless conquistadors to settle down and build colonies. King Charles nonetheless feared that a powerful, hereditary encomendero class might threaten his own control over his new dominions, and over the next three decades he found excuses to confiscate encomiendas from those who flagrantly exploited their Indians and to prevent encomenderos from bequeathing their grants to succeeding generations. According to the "New Laws" of 1542–1543, encomenderos could only demand tribute, and not labor, from natives allotted to them, while other royal orders supposedly forbade the further enslavement of native peoples. Meanwhile, the steady decline in the native population greatly reduced the amount of tribute that encomenderos could expect.

Measures designed to trim the power of the encomenderos met stiff resistance, so prudent royal officials frequently suspended laws emanating from Spain. Those who headed new colonization expeditions to outlying areas got royal permission to grant encomiendas, and settlers in frontier regions from New Mexico to Chile continued outright enslavement of native peoples as well. Even when an encomendero's rights were in fact revoked, the natives got no reprieve. They now just delivered their tribute to the king's treasury and were subjected to forced labor drafts mandated by colonial officials.

A Multiracial Society in Formation

Encomenderos and other veterans of the early expeditions of exploration and conquest were the founders of many of Latin America's most distinguished cities, from Guadalajara and Durango in northern Mexico to Santiago in Chile. Soon, however, growing numbers of people who had not participated in the conquest appeared. A cadre of bureaucrats loyal to the crown arrived to take power from the conquistadors just as they had supplanted Columbus in the Caribbean. And as word spread in Spain that riches could be had in the new lands, thousands of people ventured out to the Indies, especially after rich silver deposits were discovered in Mexico and Peru in the 1540s. A substantial merchant class developed in Lima even during the tumultuous years of civil war. Indeed, some merchants profited handsomely from selling provisions to the rival armies. Meanwhile, hundreds of Spanish artisans plied their trades—tailors, shoemakers, hatters, barbers, carpenters, silk weavers, and blacksmiths, to name a few.

The vast majority—90 percent or more—of the early immigrants to Spanish America and Brazil were male, and most were relatively young, in their 20s and 30s. This preponderance of males, together with a conquest mentality that encouraged both forcible and consensual sex with Indian women, resulted in the birth of racially mixed children called *mestizos* in the Spanish colonies and *mamelucos* in Brazil. A male was called a mestizo or a mameluco; a female was a mestiza or a mameluca. The words "mestizos" and "mamelucos" could denote a group of males or a group composed of both males and females.

Some Spanish conquistadors married newly baptized Indian women in Catholic ceremonies. In fact, the crown encouraged unions between encomenderos and daughters of the Indian nobility as a way of consolidating control over the native ruling class. Children of these marriages grew up as virtual Spaniards in their fathers' households and often inherited considerable wealth and social status. Some mestizos born out of wedlock were recognized and cared for by their fathers as well. Martín Cortés, son of Hernán Cortés and Malintzin, went to Spain with his father and became a page to King Philip II, while Pedro de Alvarado's mestiza daughter married into the Spanish nobility. Many other mestizos born out of wedlock remained with their mothers in Indian communities or were left abandoned in the streets of the new cities of Spanish America. In the eyes of the Catholic Church, they bore the stigma of illegitimacy. Civil authorities saw mestizo boys as a threat to the stability of the colony, although they harbored some hope that girls, if properly educated, could become good wives to future Spanish immigrants.

People of African descent formed another important component of early colonial society. Free blacks from Seville and other Iberian towns joined some of the earliest expeditions to the Americas. Enslaved Africans first appeared during the Caribbean phase of settlement and increased in importance as Spaniards colonized the mainland. Africans shared the Europeans' acquired immunity to the diseases that so devastated the native communities, and Spaniards and Portuguese settlers generally believed that Africans were physically stronger than Indians. At first, King Charles allowed only Christianized slaves who had lived in Spain to enter the colonies, but in 1518 he authorized direct imports from Africa. By the end of the sixteenth century, between 75,000 and 90,000 enslaved Africans had entered the Spanish colonies. Blacks outnumbered Europeans throughout the colonies, sometimes overwhelmingly. Hispaniola's population in 1567, for example, included 30,000 Africans and only 2000 Spaniards.

Spanish and Portuguese law provided various ways for slaves to gain their freedom. Some masters freed at least a few slaves in their wills, and a slave could accumulate money to buy his or her freedom. Still others simply ran away, fleeing to outlying frontiers where they could reinvent themselves as free men and women. Some runaways formed

---

Slice of Life   THE CUZCO CABILDO FOUNDS A CONVENT, 1551

THE DUST had barely settled from Peru's civil wars and the neo-Incas were still holding forth at Vilcabamba when Cuzco's city council convened on April 17, 1551. At the top of their agenda that day were their concerns about the city's growing population of mestizos. The oldest of these were now in their teens, and the boys among them especially were nothing but troublemakers in the councilmen's view. For young women of mixed ancestry (mestizas), however, the city's founders saw a potentially positive role in building Spanish society in the Andes. If these young women were removed from the influence of their Indian mothers and instructed in the ways of Christian womanhood, they might become the wives of Spaniards and the mothers of the next generation of the city's growing Hispanicized community.

Not incidentally, these women could also help the encomenderos to consolidate their position. King Charles had recently reaffirmed his determination to confiscate encomiendas of unmarried men in an effort to get unruly conquistadors to settle down into proper domesticity. As Spanish women were still in short supply, these acculturated mestizas could become an attractive alternative. Although at this point apparently all of Cuzco's encomenderos had Spanish wives, perhaps they were looking ahead to arranging acceptable marriages for the sons who would, they hoped, inherit their encomiendas. Moreover, some of the town's leading Spanish citizens had no surviving children other than ones they had fathered by Indian women. Especially if their mestiza daughters stood to inherit substantial estates, even encomiendas, it was important that they receive a suitable upbringing.

The council therefore voted to establish a convent where these young women might be properly educated while preserving their virginity, a prerequisite for a proper Catholic marriage. Over the next few weeks, the cabildo purchased property from the executor of Hernando Pizarro's estate, using funds donated by one of their number, the wealthy conquistador and encomendero Diego Maldonado. Like most of his fellow councilmen, he had fathered mestizo children, a son and a daughter, out of wedlock. They were his sole heirs, for he and his Spanish wife had no offspring. Their mother was a sister of the Inca emperor Atalhualpa "given" to him by Francisco Pizarro at Cajamarca.

A Spanish widow named Francisca Ortiz de Ayala agreed to serve as the convent's first abbess. Over the next 10 years, dozens of girls, most of them mestizas, entered the Convent of Santa Clara. Some were "orphans," meaning that at least their Spanish fathers were dead or unknown, even if their Indian mothers were still living. A greater number, however, were the daughters of living Spaniards. A few were Indians, like Beatriz Clara Coya, daughter of one of Vilcabamba's neo-Inca emperors, Inca Sayri Tupac, who in the early 1560s abandoned the rebel cause, made peace with the Spaniards, and placed the 6-year-old Beatriz in the convent of Santa Clara. Eighteen of the convent's first cohort became nuns, but nearly twice as many left, and at least 10 married Spaniards. Meanwhile, the convent began accumulating real estate. As early as 1565, its assets included several houses in the city itself and a store on its central plaza, as well as various rural properties and even an encomienda.

In time, the role of the Convent of Santa Clara changed, reflecting the transformations underway in colonial society at large. Growing numbers of Spanish women entered the convent and dominated its internal governance, while mestiza nuns found themselves relegated to second-class status. The crucial role of mestizas as builders of a new empire had passed, as colonial elites found more and more women of Spanish extraction available as wives.

Questions for Discussion

Compare the role of women in the building of the Spanish Empire with that of women in the Inca Empire. What does the history of the Convent of Santa Clara tell us about the position of mestizas in Spanish colonial society?

communities where they defied colonial authorities and resisted all efforts to re-enslave them. Children born to free women were automatically free, regardless of their racial identity or the status of their fathers. Africans both enslaved and free coupled with whites and natives. Offspring of these unions were often called *mulattos* in both the Spanish and Portuguese colonies. Males were mulattos; females were mulattas. By the end of the sixteenth century, a multiracial colonial society was rapidly taking shape throughout Latin America.

THE "SPIRITUAL CONQUEST" OF LATIN AMERICA

To the European mind, the moral justification for Spanish and Portuguese occupation of this new world rested on their commitment to convert the natives to Roman Catholicism. This conversion had to be a total one. Natives were not to be allowed to choose which elements of Christianity they adopted and which elements of their old religions they retained. Missionary efforts made little headway in the early phases of settlement in the Caribbean, but the chance to baptize thousands at a time in Mexico and Peru prompted what some historians have called a "spiritual conquest." In fact, as the missionaries would soon discover, they failed to secure the natives' absolute acceptance of Christianity to the exclusion of all other faiths.

Early Evangelization

The Spanish Church experienced a major revitalization just as the age of overseas colonization was beginning. Monastic orders such as the Franciscans and Dominicans eagerly participated in this attempt to rid the church of corruption and return to a purity and simplicity closer to the teachings of Jesus. The colonies across the Atlantic offered a prime site to build a new church that would more faithfully embody these ideals. Although two priests accompanied Cortés, baptizing the nobles of Tlaxcala even before the defeat of Tenochtitlan, the conversion of the mainland empires began in earnest when 12 Franciscans arrived in Mexico in 1524. These men believed that the end of the world and the second coming of Christ were imminent, and they saw themselves engaged in a struggle with the devil himself for the hearts and minds of the natives. They felt that, once freed from the clutches of Satan, the Indians could become good Christians.

As natives submitted to baptism, the Franciscans' optimism grew. They envisioned the creation of a native priesthood, and they identified promising candidates for ordination, often the sons of local rulers. In 1536, they established the College of Santa Cruz de Tlatelolco in Mexico City, where these young men studied Catholic theology and Latin while also learning to write Nahuatl in the European alphabet. Franciscans emphasized the importance of preparing Indian girls to be good Christian wives and mothers. Missionaries established 10 schools for daughters of the native Mexican elite in the 1520s. Along with their catechism lessons and training in practical skills such as embroidery, pupils learned about Catholic ideals of feminine behavior.

Augustinians, Dominicans, and other orders soon joined the Franciscans. By 1559, some 800 missionaries were at work in Mexico. With the help of thousands of native laborers, they built 160 churches and monasteries, frequently on the sites of pre-Hispanic temples. Evangelization in Peru proceeded more slowly due to the civil wars among the Spaniards, but Franciscans, Dominicans, Mercedarians, and Jesuits were all active in former Inca domains by the 1570s. Meanwhile, Jesuits and other missionaries began work among the Tupi in Brazil.

Missionaries faced the daunting challenge of communicating with their potential converts. They used pictures, pantomimes, and native interpreters, but many priests learned indigenous languages. Dozens of grammar books, dictionaries, confession manuals, and sermons soon appeared in many different native tongues. The first book printed in the Americas was a Nahuatl catechism produced in Mexico City in 1539. In fact, however, missionaries were often hard pressed to learn more than one new language, and they usually concentrated on Nahuatl in Mexico and Quechua in Peru. As the Aztec and Inca empires had extended their dominions in the fifteenth century, each of these languages had become a lingua franca, a means of communication among speakers of other indigenous tongues. In the sixteenth century, universities established in Mexico City and Lima began offering courses in Nahuatl and Quechua for men training to become priests. The spiritual conquest thereby contributed to the continued spread of Nahuatl and Quechua in Mesoamerica and the Andes, respectively.

The Impact of Evangelization

For the native peoples of the Americas, conversion to Christianity meant much more than the substitution of Christian ritual and dogma for traditional ways of ceremony and belief. Family and community life changed dramatically under missionary rule. In many parts of Mesoamerica and the Andes, priests and civil authorities tried to consolidate widely dispersed communities into more compact units, closer to the monasteries, where they could receive more regular indoctrination and where their behavior might be more closely monitored.

Church of Santo Domingo, Cuzco, Peru, built on the foundations of an Inca temple.

Franciscans and Jesuits in Brazil rounded up Tupis in raids that differed little from slave-gathering expeditions. They resettled the natives in compact mission villages called *aldeias* in hopes of transforming them into Portuguese-style peasants. Concentration of the native population helped spread disease among the Tupi. Smallpox swept coastal Brazil between 1559 and 1562, claiming the lives of one-third of the Indians living in the Jesuit aldeias and forcing missionaries and surviving natives to abandon many villages. The missions that remained served as tempting targets for slave raiders, and the Jesuits became outspoken critics of the enslavement of the Brazilian natives. At the same time, however, the missionaries frequently rented Indians out to Portuguese settlers in need of laborers.

Conversion to Catholicism brought many other changes. Native peoples received saints' names at baptism. The Christian calendar with its 7-day week and cycle of holy days replaced old ways of reckoning the passage of time and regulated activities such as market days. Evangelization also altered customary gender roles, especially in Peru, where women had played an important part in traditional religious life by maintaining cults of female deities. Catholic ritual recognized no comparable roles for women. Missionaries tried without much success to suppress what they viewed as indigenous societies' excessive tolerance for premarital sex and divorce. They exhorted couples to marry in Christian ceremonies and expected those living in polygamous relationships to settle down with one spouse. Europeans also believed that the nuclear family consisting of husband, wife, and children was the building block of a civilized society. Franciscan missionaries in Yucatán thus broke up extended family households at a time when smallpox and other diseases were already disrupting native kinship networks.

Resistance to Christianity

Native peoples' responses to the missionaries were ambivalent at best. In many places, they had long been accustomed to accepting the gods and rituals of a conquering people without abandoning traditional deities and practices. The friars' insistence that they reject their "pagan" beliefs entirely and embrace Christian dogma wholeheartedly proved more troubling, especially for those who had reached adulthood before the arrival of the Europeans. For this reason, missionaries targeted young people for indoctrination, often consciously undermining parental authority.

Natives' resistance to conversion dampened the friars' initial optimism about the possibility of turning them into model Catholics and training a native priesthood. Particularly disillusioning were cases of "star pupils" who slipped back into their old ways after having apparently accepted Catholicism. Bishop Juan de Zumárraga of Mexico ordered the public execution of the young Indian chief Carlos Ometochtzin of Texcoco, who had allegedly relapsed after having been considered a prime example of the missionaries' success. Another famous episode occurred in Yucatán in 1562. The Franciscan Diego de Landa became alarmed at reports that Mayas whom he had considered willing converts were in fact continuing customary rites, including human sacrifice. Thousands were taken into custody and interrogated under torture, and Landa ordered the destruction of all pre-Hispanic Mayan books. Only four manuscripts are known to have survived.

In some places, native resistance to Christianity took the form of militant mass rebellions that aimed to overturn European domination and restore the supremacy of ancient gods. One such movement, known as Taqui Onkoy, spread throughout the Andes in the 1560s. Its adherents came from a broad spectrum of native society, including a number of traditional rulers (*kurakas*) as well as Hispanicized Indians who had lived in Spanish settlements. Over half its participants were female. The Taqui Onkoy rebels exhorted Andean natives to set aside their ethnic divisions to form a united front against the Spaniards. They rejected all Christian religious symbols while promoting pre-Inca regional gods. Rebel leaders urged their followers to resist tribute and labor demands imposed by the Spanish. In place of an exploitive colonial society, they promised a new millennium of abundance. The pan-Andean unity projected by the rebels proved difficult to achieve, however, and the rebellion collapsed in the face of brutal repression mounted by Spanish authorities.

Other rebellions utilized Christian symbols while resisting European domination. A series of messianic revolts known collectively as *santidade* swept northeastern Brazil in the late sixteenth century. Indians who had come into close contact with Portuguese settlers, either as aldeia residents or slaves, along with Africans who had escaped from their Portuguese captors, set up their own communities. They envisioned a golden age that would follow the expulsion of the invaders. The rebels fashioned idols that they believed would make them less vulnerable to whites, but they also made free use of such Catholic religious artifacts as the rosary, appointed their own "pope" and "bishops," and sent "missionaries" to spread the word. By 1610, an estimated 20,000 blacks and Indians had fled to santidade communities. Portuguese authorities then ordered an all-out military offensive to wipe them out.

LATIN AMERICAN LIVES

DOMINGOS FERNANDES NOBRE, MAMELUCO OF BRAZIL

The success of the Spanish and Portuguese colonies depended on the cooperation—forced or voluntary—of native peoples and on individuals who understood enough about native cultures and European demands to broker the terms of that cooperation. Sometimes these intermediaries were Indians, like Malintzin of Mexico, and sometimes they were Europeans who had lived among native people. Others were the offspring of European men and indigenous women, like Domingos Fernandes Nobre, born at Pernambuco on Brazil's northeastern coast in 1546, the son of a Portuguese stonemason and an Indian woman. Although baptized a Catholic, fluent in Portuguese, and married to a Portuguese woman, Nobre lived, in the words of historian Alida Metcalf, "on the margins of respectability" in the Brazilian capital of Salvador. He also spent a crucial portion of his life among native people in the *sertão,* the interior of Brazil. There he tattooed his body in the style of the Tupi and adopted the indigenous name "Tomacaúna" ("black antbird") and lived as an Indian, "walking naked as they do" and "neither praying nor commending himself to God."

Nobre's ability to speak the Tupi language and to live in two worlds facilitated his work as a leader of "*entradas,*" expeditions into the interior that captured Indians and delivered them as slaves to sugar plantations along the coast. These activities brought him into direct conflict with Jesuit missionaries, who not only were highly critical of such abuses but also preferred that Indians from the sertão be brought instead to Jesuit villages for indoctrination. A 1585 entrada got him into even greater trouble, however. An ambitious sugar planter named Fernão Cabral commissioned Nobre to lead 100 mamelucos and Indians into the sertão, to round up workers for his estate and, ostensibly, to help suppress an outbreak of native resistance, a santidade.

In fact, however, Nobre and many of the men under his command participated in the rituals of the santidade once they reached the sertão. Nobre personally met Antônio, a baptized Indian who had declared himself "pope," assumed leadership of the rebellion, and even claimed to be God. He joined Antônio in dancing, singing, and smoking tobacco. Acting on instructions from Cabral, Nobre promised the rebels that if they were to accompany him to Cabral's plantation they would be permitted to practice their beliefs without interference. Some 60 adherents of the santidade accepted Nobre's offer and received a warm welcome when they arrived at

Cabral's estate. They erected a "church" there, and Cabral permitted his African slaves to be "baptized" into the rebel sect.

In 1591 a delegation of the Portuguese Inquisition arrived in Brazil to investigate the rampant abuses in the colony. Mamelucos like Nobre, who had enslaved Indians and practiced native religious rituals, were obvious targets. At his trial, Nobre confessed to having had sexual relations with numerous Indian women, including two girls who were his goddaughters. He further admitted that he had bowed down in worship to Antônio and utterly neglected his Christian obligations while in the sertão. He explained to the inquisitor that he had adopted Indian ways so that he would be accepted into native society. Perhaps surprisingly, Nobre received a relatively light sentence for his wrongdoing. He simply had to pay a fine and participate in penitential rites; later he even received a land grant.

But as the sixteenth century ended, Portuguese colonists had secured a powerful enough position that they no longer needed cultural intermediaries like Nobre to subdue natives in those parts of the sertão they were relatively close to the coast. They also turned increasingly to slaves imported from Africa to perform the heavy labor of sugar production.

Questions for Discussion

Why would Indians have been willing to accompany Nobre on his entrada? Why do you think he was not punished more severely?

In the face of the many calamities they endured, natives of the Americas were often unsure which gods they had offended. Were their familiar deities angry because they had submitted to baptism and allowed the Catholic priests to destroy old idols and temples? Or, as the missionaries repeatedly told them, was the Christian god upset because they had not given themselves completely to the new faith? Most people undoubtedly hedged their bets, outwardly conforming to the missionaries' message while continuing to practice traditional rituals as well. In the eyes of the Church, they became *niños con barbas* or "children with beards," incapable of comprehending the full intricacies of Catholicism and in need of constant supervision.

THE CONSOLIDATION OF COLONIAL EMPIRES

The century following Columbus's voyage witnessed the creation of the first empires to span the entire globe. The Portuguese led the way, starting trading ventures along the coast of Brazil at the same time their countrymen were establishing similar posts at Goa in India and Macao in China. Spain was not far behind. Just as Cortés was conquering Mexico, King Charles sponsored the first expedition to circumnavigate the globe, captained by the Portuguese navigator Ferdinand Magellan. Their route took them through what would become known as the Strait of Magellan at the southern tip of South America and then across the Pacific to the Philippine Islands, which became a Spanish colony in the 1560s. Administration of these empires required new institutions of government to insure that European settlers and colonial subjects behaved themselves and maintained respect for royal authority. Especially in Spanish America, an elaborate bureaucracy appeared, charged with the task of overseeing the flow of revenue into the king's coffers. Equally important was the creation of a Church infrastructure to minister to colonists and carry on the work of converting "heathens" to Christianity.

The Viceroyalties of New Spain and Peru

The most powerful colonial officials in the sixteenth century were the viceroys, literally "vice-kings," who represented the king of Spain in Mexico City and Lima. They supervised virtually every aspect of government, from administration of justice to finance and defense, as well as the operations of the Church. The jurisdiction of the viceroy of New Spain included all of what is now Mexico and adjacent portions of the southwestern United States, as well as the Caribbean, Central America, and the Philippines. The viceroy of Peru governed all of Spanish South America.

Those chosen for these positions had to be men the king could trust, not ambitious conquistadors likely to put their own interests first. Antonio de Mendoza, who in 1535 arrived in Mexico City as the first viceroy of New Spain, quickly relegated Hernán Cortés to the sidelines. He enforced a royal order that forbade Cortés to meddle in political affairs or even to enter Mexico City, but the king compensated the conqueror with an encomienda of over 100,000 Indians and the title of Marqués del Valle de Oaxaca. When rumors surfaced that a fabulous kingdom might lie somewhere in the far north of New Spain, Mendoza sent a trusted associate, Francisco Vázquez de Coronado, to investigate them, rather than let Cortés or anyone else be the one to discover "another Mexico."

Viceroy Mendoza supervised the activities of the Church in Mexico and personally established numerous schools and hospitals. He also contributed to the political stability of the colony by negotiating a workable compromise between the king and the encomenderos over the implementation of the New Laws of 1542–1543, a set of regulations aimed at ending the abuse of native peoples and trimming the power of the encomenderos. The consolidation of royal government in Peru proceeded less smoothly. Angry colonists assassinated the first viceroy, Blasco Núñez Vela, when he tried to quell civil unrest and enforce the New Laws. It was not until 1569, with the arrival of Peru's decisive, heavy-handed fourth viceroy, Francisco de Toledo, that Spanish government became firmly established in the former Inca domains. Defeat of the rebel neo-Inca state at Vilcabamba was a top priority, accomplished by 1572, when the viceroy personally ordered the execution of the native leader Tupac Amaru. Meanwhile, he curbed the power of the encomenderos and imposed massive changes on the native population of the Andean highlands. To supply workers for the developing silver mines, he instituted the labor draft known as the *mita,* modeled on pre-Hispanic practices but far more onerous. He also ordered the resettlement of the surviving native population into more compact units, a process that seriously disrupted traditional ayllu networks and forced native peoples to abandon sites sacred in their traditional religious practice. By the 1570s, then, new rulers representing a distant monarch had decisively replaced the lords of Tenochtitlan and Cuzco.

The Spanish Colonial Bureaucracy

Many other individuals played key roles in Spain's rapidly developing machinery of empire. Major Spanish cities, beginning with Santo Domingo in 1511, became seats of *audiencias*, bodies comprising three or more lawyers who acted as courts of appeal and carried out administrative functions over fairly large districts. The audiencia of Mexico City, established in 1527, held jurisdiction over much of central Mexico, while a similar body headquartered at Lima assisted the viceroy in governing Peru. By 1560, additional audiencias had been set up at Guadalajara in Mexico, Quito in Ecuador, and Chuquisaca in Upper Peru (present-day Bolivia). Other audiencias followed, including one established at Santiago, Chile, in 1609.

As direct representatives of the viceroys, provincial governors wielded executive, judicial, and military authority in outlying areas. With the development of silver mining in Mexico and Peru came an elaborate bureaucracy to collect taxes that miners owed to the royal treasury. Town councils, known as *cabildos*, also appeared in the most important Spanish towns. At first, the conquistadors played leading roles in the cabildos, but later merchants and other prominent townsmen replaced them. Among the cabildos' many responsibilities were the administration of justice, supervision of markets, and sponsorship of civic and religious festivals. Local officials, known as corregidores or *alcaldes mayores*, represented crown authority and exercised administrative and judicial functions throughout the colonies. In areas with large indigenous populations, the corregidores and alcaldes mayores shared power with Indian elites. Some of these Indian officials were traditional rulers in their societies; others were opportunistic individuals willing to make deals with the new colonial authorities in order to advance their own positions. These native officers were responsible for maintaining order within their villages and delivering tribute from their communities to encomenderos and royal officials.

In theory, all colonial appointees were supposed to do the king's bidding to the letter of the law, but in practice they had considerable leeway to adjust edicts issued in Spain to suit the situation on the spot. Antonio de Mendoza knew that he depended on the encomenderos to defend New Spain against potential native uprisings, and he realized that he could push these powerful men only just so far, so he suspended what they viewed as the most objectionable features of the New Laws. Whenever colonial officials hesitated to carry out a royal directive, they invoked the phrase "*obedezco pero no cumplo*," literally, "I obey but do not comply." These words signified that they acknowledged the king's authority, but local conditions made enforcement of a particular law impossible or unwise. Many crown appointees no doubt used this formula simply to avoid performing their duties, but a certain amount of flexibility was necessary in order to govern a huge empire, where an order issued in Spain took many months to reach local officials in the colonies.

Royal Government in Brazil

For the first several decades following Cabral's landfall, the kings of Portugal left Brazil in the hands of private entrepreneurs, who managed to settle and defend only a tiny portion of the coastline. By the late 1540s, the continued French challenge to Portuguese control and hopes that silver deposits similar to those recently found in Peru might lay somewhere inland in Brazil prompted João III to tighten his hold on the colony. He therefore appointed Tomé de Sousa to be royal governor-general of Brazil, charged with creating a centralized command that would gradually replace the proprietary captaincies in governing. The king further instructed the new governor to stop the enslavement of Brazilian natives—an impossible task, given the settlers' continued demands for labor.

Sousa arrived in 1549, accompanied by a royal treasurer, a chief justice, other bureaucrats, the first six Jesuit missionaries to serve in the Americas, and 1000 new colonists. He founded the city of Salvador da Bahia de Todos os Santos, located on the coast in a potentially rich sugar-producing area, to serve as capital of the colony. Later governors continued consolidating Portugal's hold on Brazil. With the help of Indian allies, Governor Mem de Sá (1557–1574) finally ousted the French, destroying a settlement they had established on Guanabara Bay and founding the city of São Sebastião do Rio de Janeiro in its place. Mem de Sá also subdued rebellious natives near Salvador and assisted the Jesuits in gathering pacified groups into mission villages. In the three decades following the establishment of royal government in Brazil, the colony's European-born population grew sizably. By the 1580s, Rio de Janeiro had 150 Portuguese households, while in the city of Salvador and its immediate environs more than 2000 Portuguese households could be found.

Never, however, did royal governors in Brazil achieve the power that the viceroys of Mexico and Peru enjoyed in Spanish America. Rather, municipal councils known as *senados da càmara* governed at the local level in Salvador, Rio de Janeiro, and other towns and wielded relatively more power than their counterparts in the Spanish colonies. Drawn from local elites, the councils were especially outspoken in their opposition to any restrictions imposed on their exploitation of native labor. The senados da câmara, along with royally appointed magistrates and a high court (*relação*) located in Salvador, shared responsibility for the administration of justice in colonial Brazil.

The Church in Spanish America and Brazil

The Spanish and Portuguese monarchs justified their occupation of the Americas by arguing that they were bringing Christianity to the natives, and Pope Alexander VI granted them broad powers over the operations of the Church in the colonies. These concessions included the rights to nominate bishops, create new dioceses, issue licenses required for clergymen to travel to the colonies, and approve papal pronouncements before they could be published in the Indies. Although clergymen might dispute civil authorities on the treatment of natives and other issues, in many respects the ecclesiastical establishment served the interests of the colonial powers. In return, the Church received substantial state subsidies for its activities.

Not all clergy were subject to the same degree of crown supervision. Members of religious orders such as Franciscans and Dominicans were known collectively as regular clergy because they lived according to the rule (*regula* in Latin) set by their order's founder. These men operated more freely from royal authority than the secular clergy, who belonged to no order and answered directly to the bishop of their diocese, who in turn owed his appointment to the king. Royal policy envisioned that secular clergy would gradually replace the regular clergy once conversion of the Indians in a particular area was achieved, and the orders would advance to more remote frontier areas to continue the process of evangelization.

Secular clergy were also needed to minister to the growing numbers of non-Indians. Naming of bishops usually followed closely after the initial settlement of new territory. Within 20 years of Columbus's landfall, bishops had been appointed for Santo Domingo and Puerto Rico, and in 1513 the first bishop on the mainland took up residence on the Isthmus of Panamá. Between 1527 and 1561, seven dioceses were created in Mexico, and other bishoprics spanned South America from Cartagena on the Caribbean coast of Colombia to Santiago, Chile. Shortages of suitable secular clergymen led King Charles to appoint members of religious orders as some of the earliest bishops in Mexico and Peru. The Franciscan Juan de Zumárraga, for example, served as the first bishop of Mexico City. Bishops had a wide range of duties. They presided over worship at the cathedral church and oversaw the work of the secular clergy in their dioceses. Acting in concert with viceroys and other high-ranking government officials, bishops supervised the founding and operation of educational and social welfare institutions and convents for women.

Nowhere was the church a monolithic organization. Competition between the regular and secular clergy and among the different religious orders often distracted clerics from their spiritual duties. In Spanish America, many religious orders were also divided within themselves as American-born members vied with those born in Europe for control of the organization's assets and activities. Although divided within itself, the Catholic Church was nevertheless a powerful institution that helped buttress Spanish and Portuguese rule in the colonies.

The Spanish and Portuguese Empires

With the consolidation of the Spanish kingdoms inherited from his grandparents Ferdinand and Isabella, the conquests of Mexico and Peru, and the establishment of Spanish settlements from northern Mexico to Chile, King Charles I was a powerful monarch. His dominions extended well beyond the Iberian Peninsula and the Americas, however. His Spanish possessions came to him through his mother, Juana, daughter of Ferdinand and Isabella, and they included portions of Italy belonging to the crown of Aragón. His paternal inheritance brought him not only territories in northern Europe (Belgium, Luxembourg, and the Netherlands) but also the substantial holdings of the

Hapsburg dynasty of Austria. In 1519, just 3 years after assuming the throne of Spain, he succeeded his grandfather Maximilian I as Holy Roman Emperor (and became known as Charles V), exercising authority over much of modern Germany and Austria. In 1556, Charles abdicated the Spanish crown in favor of his son Philip II, leaving his Austrian possessions to his brother Ferdinand. Philip nonetheless remained the world's first global monarch. In 1565, Spanish navigators established a permanent colony in the Philippine Islands. Vast quantities of silver and other riches of the Indies, both east and west, poured into Spain during his reign. When the last representative of Portugal's Aviz dynasty died without leaving a direct heir, Philip claimed that throne as well, and became king of Portugal in 1580. For the next 60 years, he and his successors, Philip III (1598–1621) and Philip IV (1621–1665), ruled over Portugal and all of its overseas dominions, from Brazil in the west to Goa and Macao in the east.

Students of literature often refer to the late sixteenth and early seventeenth centuries as Spain's *Siglo de Oro,* its golden age. This was the time of Miguel de Cervantes's satiric novel *Don Quixote* and the great playwrights Lope de Vega, Tirso de Molina, and Pedro Calderón de la Barca. In other respects, however, these were troubled years for Spain. In 1566, the Netherlands revolted against Spanish rule, and for the next several decades a good portion of American silver went to outfit Spanish armies that tried unsuccessfully to subdue the Dutch. On more than one occasion, the royal treasury lay empty. Meanwhile, Philip continued King Charles's crusade to advance the cause of Catholicism against its enemies, undertaking naval campaigns against the Ottoman Turks and trying to stop the spread of the Protestant Reformation in Europe. His marriage to Mary Tudor, the Catholic daughter of King Henry VIII and the queen of England from 1553 to 1558, brought Spain into direct conflict with her Protestant successor, Elizabeth I. The English inflicted heavy losses on both sides of the Atlantic, most spectacularly in the defeat of Spain's famous Armada off the coast of Ireland in 1588.

Sixty years of Spanish rule drew Portugal into the international conflicts of the three Philips. The best ships of the "Spanish" Armada were in fact Portuguese vessels that Philip II had appropriated along with his throne. Spain's Dutch enemies attacked Portuguese trading posts in Asia, elbowed their way into the African slave trade, and seized the rich sugar-producing region of northeast Brazil in 1630. Ten years later, Portugal's nobles rallied around the Duke of Braganza, proclaiming him King João IV and successfully asserting their independence from Spain. Meanwhile, Brazilians expelled the Dutch from their territory in 1654. The damage to Portugal's empire had been done, however. During their time in Brazil, Dutch entrepreneurs had learned the business of sugar production, and they used that knowledge to set up rival sugar colonies in the Caribbean, thereby seriously undercutting Brazil's competitive position in European markets.

Iberia's exclusive territorial claims to the Americas were utterly shattered during the first half of the seventeenth century. The first permanent English colonists settled at Jamestown, Virginia, in 1607, followed by the Pilgrims and Puritans of Massachusetts in

1620 and 1630, respectively. A half-century later English colonies extended down the east coast of North America as far as South Carolina. The Frenchman Samuel de Champlain sailed up the St. Lawrence River in 1603 and founded the city of Quebec 5 years later. By the 1680s, French fur traders, missionaries, and explorers had penetrated westward across Canada to the headwaters of the Mississippi River and down the river to the Gulf of Mexico. British, French, and Dutch colonists all permanently occupied various Caribbean islands in the seventeenth century.

CONCLUSION

Columbus's voyage launched a military, biological, political, and ideological invasion of the Americas that led to the creation of the first two seaborne empires of the modern era. By the early seventeenth century, Spanish settlements extended from Santa Fe, New Mexico, and St. Augustine, Florida, in what is now the United States, to Santiago, Buenos Aires, and Montevideo in South America. Meanwhile, Portuguese towns, missions, and sugar plantations dotted the coast of Brazil southward from Salvador to Rio de Janeiro and beyond. The English, French, and Dutch empires, based in part on the riches of the Americas, were taking shape as well. Columbus's first voyage, then, ended several millennia of American isolation from contact with the Eastern Hemisphere. The human and natural resources of the Americas now came to serve the purposes of an emerging world economy and the dictates of European monarchs. To advance the political and military agendas of unseen monarchs thousands of miles away, the indigenous peoples of the Americas found themselves subject to increasingly heavy burdens of taxation and forced labor. Spanish and Portuguese immigrants and their American-born descendants also exploited Indians and the colonies' abundant natural resources for their personal benefit.

LEARNING MORE ABOUT LATIN AMERICANS

Burkhart, Louise. *The Slippery Earth: Nahua-Christian Moral Dialogue in Sixteenth-Century Mexico* (Tucson, AZ: University of Arizona Press, 1989). Explores the exchange of religious and philosophical concepts by Franciscan missionaries and indigenous people during the "spiritual conquest" of Mexico.

Clendinnen, Inga. *Ambivalent Conquests: Maya and Spaniard in Yucatán, 1517–1570* (Cambridge, U.K.: Cambridge University Press, 1987). Traces the early years of the Spanish presence in Yucatán, with special emphasis on the Franciscans' attempts to impose Catholicism.

Cook, Noble David. *Born to Die: Disease and the New World Conquest, 1492–1650* (Cambridge, U.K.: Cambridge University Press, 1998). One of the leading historical demographers of Latin America explores the drastic population decline that followed the European conquest of the Americas.

Crosby, Alfred W. *The Columbian Exchange: Biological and Cultural Consequences of 1492* (Westport, CT: Praeger Publishers, 30th anniversary edition, 2003). Still the classic treatment of the ecological conquest.

León-Portilla, Miguel. *The Broken Spears: The Aztec Account of the Conquest of Mexico* (Boston, MA: Beacon Press, Revised edition, 1992). Aztec sources translated from Nahuatl show how the native peoples of Mexico remembered the Spanish conquest.

Melville, Elinor G. K. *A Plague of Sheep: Environmental Consequences of the Conquest of Mexico* (Cambridge, U.K.: Cambridge University Press, 1994). This award-winning book is perhaps the best concise treatment of the ecological conquest of the Americas.

Metcalf, Alida C. *Go-Betweens and the Colonization of Brazil, 1500–1600* (Austin, TX: University of Texas Press, 2005). A very thorough analysis of Brazilian society in the sixteenth century; details on the life of Domingos Fernandes Nobre are taken from this source.

Restall, Matthew. *Seven Myths of the Spanish Conquest* (New York: Oxford University Press, 2003). Explodes various popular misconceptions about the Spanish conquest of America.

Townsend, Camilla. *Malintzin's Choices: An Indian Woman in the Conquest of Mexico* (Albuquerque, NM: University of New Mexico Press, 2006). Drawing on a wide variety of sixteenth-century sources, this book summarizes all of the known details about the life of Malintzin and her role in the Spanish conquest of Mexico.

4

THE IBERIANS' NEW WORLD

"WE CAME TO serve God, and to get rich." With these words the conquistador Bernal Díaz del Castillo described the motives that supposedly drove him and his fellow Iberians to the Americas. For those first on the scene, this new world offered quick and obvious avenues to wealth—outright plunder and the appropriation of tribute systems in the highly developed societies of Mesoamerica and the Andes, panning for gold in Hispaniola and Cuba, and the gathering of dyewoods in Brazil.

As they became more familiar with this new environment, they saw many other possibilities for self-enrichment. Massive silver deposits lay beneath the Earth's surface in Bolivia and northern Mexico. The varied climate zones of the New World invited the commercial cultivation of wheat, grapes, and other staples of the Mediterranean diet, highly profitable Old World crops such as sugarcane, and even exotic new commodities like chocolate and *cochineal* (a red substance used to dye textiles) that could be exported back to Europe. Wealth derived from mining and commercial agriculture in turn generated lucrative opportunities for trade in everything from the finest lace and silks that dressed colonial elites to maize, potatoes, and dried beef consumed by the laboring populations. The transport of all these commodities provided fortunes for transatlantic shippers and more modest livelihoods for carters and muleteers.

Spanish and Portuguese colonists and their descendants included many talented and ambitious entrepreneurs eager to exploit the American environment for profit. Their plantations, mines, warehouses, and shipyards soon transformed the landscape of Latin America, creating a world that was in many ways "new" for indigenous peoples and immigrants alike. They marshaled native peoples to work in their varied enterprises through outright enslavement or somewhat more subtle forms of political and economic coercion and imported Africans in chains to augment the labor force in the colonies.

Iberian Americas also craved the amenities of life as they had known it—or imagined it—back home. With profits from their business ventures, they erected cities laid out according to European notions of grandeur and propriety. These cities became the seats of civil and ecclesiastical administration, centers of art and learning, and showcases for conspicuous consumption by successful mine owners, merchants, and commercial farmers.

THE LURE OF PRECIOUS METALS

The presence of gold and silver in their New World caught the attention of Spanish explorers and conquistadors within just a few years of Columbus's first landfall. As we saw in Chapter 3, they began mining gold on Hispaniola in the 1490s. Once on the mainland, they saw the magnificent treasure gathered for Atahualpa's ransom and heard persistent rumors of El Dorado—the man of gold—and other tantalizing hints that their New World held fabulous wealth indeed. For centuries, natives of the Americas had worked gold and silver to craft funerary objects, jewelry worn by ruling classes, and the elaborate images and vessels used in religious rituals. Renaissance Europeans likewise valued gold and silver, but for them these precious metals served purposes beyond the decorative and ceremonial. International trade within Europe and with the great markets of Asia revolved around gold and silver coin.

Over time, some Spanish colonists found fortunes of gold in Colombia, southern Ecuador, and Chile, shipping more than 180 tons of it to Europe between 1500 and 1650. Even more substantial gold deposits fell to their Portuguese counterparts who ventured to the interior of Brazil in the late seventeenth and early eighteenth centuries. The real wealth of the Indies lay in silver, however—more than 16,000 tons were mined in the first century and a half following Columbus's voyage. For centuries to come, the silver bullion of Mexico, Peru, and Bolivia became the prime medium of exchange for global commerce, circulating freely from China and India to Europe and the Americas.

The Silver Boom

Already by the 1530s, ambitious Spaniards, including Hernán Cortés himself, had begun mining silver at scattered sites in central Mexico. Then in the mid-1540s, nearly simultaneous silver strikes at Zacatecas in northern Mexico and Potosí in Upper Peru (present-day Bolivia) launched a mining boom that exceeded all expectations. Prospectors at Potosí found literally a mountain of silver and launched a rush to the new town they established at its base. The town had 14,000 residents within 2 years of the silver discoveries, and by 1610 its population reportedly topped 160,000. In the 1590s, Potosí's mines yielded upward of 150,000 kilograms of silver ore per year.

Other bonanzas followed during the sixteenth century, at such sites as Guanajuato, Sombrerete, Durango, and San Luis Potosí in Mexico and Castrovirreina in Peru. Even a faint rumor of silver lured thousands of men and women to distant and unlikely places, and boomtowns appeared wherever deposits were especially plentiful. The successive bonanzas in northern New Spain drew colonists deeper and deeper into the Gran

Chichimeca, the arid and uninviting plateau whose indigenous inhabitants killed the intruders and raided their supply trains. Only after 50 years of warfare did Spanish authorities succeed in subduing them.

Production at many mines began to decline in the seventeenth century, as readily accessible ores were exhausted and mine owners faced shortages of labor, capital, and the mercury used in processing ore. Potosí's output fell more or less steadily after 1610, never to regain the preeminent position it had once enjoyed. Zacatecas and other Mexican mines experienced more gradual falloffs that were partially offset by periodic new discoveries, at Parral and Chihuahua, for example. After 1700, and especially after 1750, governmental subsidies and tax cuts, technical improvements, and more abundant supplies of mercury combined to boost overall silver production far beyond the levels reached earlier, most notably in Mexico.

Labor and Technology in Silver Mining

Mining silver required considerable inputs of capital and grueling labor. Miners cut tunnels and shafts that often extended hundreds of feet underground, and in the seventeenth century, some of the more ambitious entrepreneurs began using gunpowder to deepen and widen the shafts. Workers used picks to loosen silver-bearing rocks, while others shouldered 100-pound sacks of ore and hauled them to the surface.

Then commenced the difficult labor of extracting silver from the ore. Early miners in Peru borrowed smelting techniques that native Andeans had developed centuries before. Only the best quality ores could be smelted in this way, however, and the process required large amounts of firewood, a scarce commodity on the barren plateaus of northern Mexico and Upper Peru. In the 1550s, refiners in Mexico adopted a more efficient method, known as amalgamation, which involved crushing the ore to a consistency resembling sand, then mixing it with salt, copper pyrites, and mercury. In the resulting chemical reaction, the silver bonded with the mercury. When the silver-mercury amalgam was heated, the mercury vaporized, leaving more or less pure silver. In 1563, the discovery of mercury mines at Huancavelica in Peru encouraged more refiners to use this technique.

Workers in mines and refineries worked long hours under extremely hazardous conditions. Those underground worked in dark, damp, and poorly ventilated quarters, and they often fell from the makeshift ladders that led to and from the surface. Shafts and tunnels frequently collapsed or flooded, killing many workers. Those who worked in the refineries were exposed to mercury and the consequent likelihood of a slow, excruciating death by poisoning. Workers in mines and refineries in the Andes routinely dulled their senses by chewing coca leaves or drinking chicha, a fermented beverage made from maize.

Procuring a Labor Supply

Securing a reliable and efficient labor supply posed a major challenge for operators of silver mines and refineries. African slaves were far too expensive for more than occasional use in such hazardous tasks. Mining entrepreneurs therefore preferred to rely on the "cheaper" and more readily available native population. During the 1520s and 1530s, Indians held as slaves and in encomienda worked the mines of central Mexico. By the 1540s, mine owners in areas with substantial concentrations of native population turned to the *repartimiento,* the forced labor draft adopted in New Spain following the formal abolition of Indian slavery and labor obligations for encomienda Indians. Under this system, each Indian community was required to supply a stipulated number of able-bodied men at regular intervals, and government officials allocated these workers to would-be employers.

Miners in Peru made extensive use of forced labor through the notorious mita organized by Viceroy Toledo in the 1570s. Each year, highland communities from as far away as Cuzco in the north and Tarija in the south sent one-seventh of their adult male populations to Potosí, where they worked a full year before being replaced by a new contingent. In the early seventeenth century, approximately 14,000 mita workers, or *mitayos,* were present at Potosí at any given time. Usually, they worked in the mines and refineries for 1 week and then had 2 weeks to rest, but they were often assigned other tasks during their "time off." Mita workers were paid for their labor, but their wages seldom covered the high cost of living in Potosí. Another 2200 mitayos went to the mercury mine at Huancavelica each year.

LATIN AMERICAN LIVES

ANTONIO LÓPEZ DE QUIROGA, BOLIVIAN ENTREPRENEUR

IN THE EARLY 1640s, a Spaniard named Antonio López de Quiroga (1620?–1699) arrived in Lima, one of many thousands of ambitious young men who emigrated to the Americas over three centuries of Spanish rule. Little about him suggested that he would end his days more than a half century later as one of the richest men in all the Indies. Born in the economically backward province of Galicia in the north of Spain, he was an untitled nobleman of modest means, though a distant relative of Pedro Fernández de Andrade, who would serve as viceroy of Peru from 1666 to 1672.

After a brief stint as a merchant in Lima, Antonio headed off for the fabled Potosí. There he established a shop on the *Calle de los Mercaderes* (Merchants' Street), most likely trading in silks and other fine textiles imported from Spain as well as coarser fabrics made in Quito. Within a short time, he had also become a *mercader de plata* (silver trader) who bought silver in bulk from refiners, arranged for payment of the king's one-fifth, and then had the remainder minted into coins, all at a tidy profit to himself. He also supplied credit to miners and refiners who repaid him in still more quantities of silver.

López de Quiroga's next step was to become a silver miner and refiner himself. He pioneered in the use of blasting to dig adits that provided access to silver deposits deep beneath the surface. His willingness to reinvest his profits and to experiment with new mining techniques enabled him to make a fortune even though the best of Potosí's bonanza had already passed. His mines accounted for more than 10 percent of the silver produced in the district of Potosí during the last three decades of the seventeenth century.

By far the richest man in Potosí, Antonio López de Quiroga lived well. He owned two lavish houses just off the central plaza. When his daughter Lorenza married in 1676, her dowry included 20 large sacks of silver coin that together weighed about 3000 pounds, as well as six black slaves, a gilded bed frame, a damask bedspread embroidered in gold, a sedan chair, a writing desk made of ebony and ivory, linens worth 6000 pesos, and numerous pieces of jewelry. He also made generous gifts to churches and charities in Potosí. Like many other successful merchants and miners, Antonio also entered the ranks of the large landowners. In 1658, he paid 52,000 pesos for his first property, a hacienda in the province of Pilaya y Pazpaya, located southeast of Potosí. By the 1670s, he had expanded his holdings there to several hundred square miles. Scores of black slaves worked his properties, producing wine, brandy, beef jerky, tallow, maize, and *chuño* (freeze-dried potatoes) for sale in Potosí.

Antonio López de Quiroga was an astute and hard-headed businessman whose acumen and ingenuity clearly rivaled those of other entrepreneurs who would appear throughout the world in later centuries. But he had another side as well, one that bore greater resemblance to the conquistadors who had settled in Spanish America long before his time. Indeed, he dreamed of being something of a conquistador himself. He spent more than 200,000 pesos outfitting an expedition of discovery and conquest, led by his nephew, to the legendary kingdom of the Gran Patití—another putative lost Inca state rumored to lie far to the northeast of Potosí where today Brazil, Paraguay, and Bolivia meet.

The excursion to Patití yielded nothing, but López de Quiroga still aspired to the power and social status that conquistadors of an earlier time had enjoyed. He longed for a title of nobility—he suggested "the Count of Pilaya and Pazpaya"—with seignorial jurisdiction reminiscent of what Hernán Cortés once had in Mexico. He certainly could have afforded the sizable purchase price of a title, but he never quite convinced authorities in Spain that he merited so lofty a rank. Nor did he ever hold office on the Potosí town council, except for the honorific military titles of captain and field marshal, which allowed him to play ceremonial roles in municipal rituals but carried no real power. His distant kinsman the viceroy paid little heed when López de Quiroga met him personally to ask for in increase in the allocation of mita workers for Potosí. Though he failed to achieve all he wanted, Antonio López de Quiroga attained a level of wealth that other Spanish immigrants could only dream about. His portrait hangs today in the Casa de la Moneda in Potosí, a lasting reminder of the town's grandeur in colonial times.

Questions for Discussion

Would someone like Antonio López de Quiroga feel at home in the business climate of our own time? Why or why not?

The precipitous decline in the native population made it increasingly difficult to muster the numbers of men required for the smooth operation of the repartimiento and mita systems. In the Andes, young men often fled their native ayllus to avoid mita service, further compounding the problem, and those who did submit to the draft sometimes were required to serve more often than every 7 years. Kurakas and caciques often appealed to Spanish courts to seek reductions in the quotas for their communities.

In the Andes, it was possible for Indians who could afford it to buy their way out of mita service by paying for a substitute, so that by 1620 many provinces were providing more than half their allotments in cash rather than labor. In effect, mine owners received direct cash subsidies, known as *indios de faltriquera* ("Indians in the pocket"), instead of actual workers. The miners then used these funds to hire *mingas*, or wage laborers. Sometimes these workers were simply mitayos moonlighting during their off-duty periods, but others were permanent wageworkers. Mingas became concentrated in the more skilled and less dangerous tasks and earned three to four times what a mitayo did—sufficient inducement to convince many Indians to stay on in Potosí following completion of their mita service. As a result, the supply of men available for the mita declined further. Despite the steadily growing importance of wage labor at Potosí, the mita endured until the end of the colonial period. As late as 1789, a total of 3000 mitayos were in residence there.

Paid labor was even more prevalent in northern Mexico, where sparse and often intractable resident Indian populations made forced labor drafts impractical. Mine workers commonly contracted to deliver to their employers a set quantity of ore each workday. Once they met their quotas, they were free to collect additional ore, which they sold directly to refiners. For most workers, these bonuses were far more important than the modest wages, rations, and housing their employers provided.

Goods supplied on credit by their employers constituted an added inducement for many workers in northern New Spain. In theory, indebted workers remained bound to their jobs until they worked off these loans, but many simply fled without paying or contracted with other employers who paid off their existing debts and then extended new credits to get them to sign on. In eighteenth-century Chihuahua, a worker's accumulated debt might easily exceed his nominal annual salary. Silk and linen cloth, fine stockings, and even lace from Flanders figured among the commodities offered to workers on credit during Chihuahua's silver boom in the 1730s. Not everyone fared this well, but throughout colonial Latin America the prospect of material gain continually drew workers to wherever fresh bonanzas might wait.

Gold Mining in Brazil

The case of colonial Brazil offers yet another example of how word of mineral wealth could put people in motion. For nearly two centuries following Cabral's landfall, persistent rumors circulated of gold in the interior, but for the most part, Portugal's American subjects found their treasure in dyewood and sugar, and their settlements

Silver mining and refining in Peru. Here the earlier refining techniques are being used.

remained clustered close to the coast. The vast hinterland remained largely unexplored, except for expeditions led by slave-hunting *bandeirantes* from São Paulo. In the 1690s, however, the bandeirantes struck gold in the sparsely populated region that soon became known as Minas Gerais ("general mines").

A frantic gold rush ensued. Paulistas (people from the area around São Paulo) and northeastern Brazilians, as well as considerable numbers of recent immigrants from Portugal, all flocked to the mining region. A brief civil war pitted the tough Paulista frontier people against the *emboabas* (sometimes defined as tenderfeet), as they derisively labeled the Brazilians and Europeans who encroached on territory they considered their own. The crown intervened to secure the outsiders' access to the gold fields and imposed stricter government control on the region. Meanwhile, the Paulistas continued their prospecting expeditions farther inland, yielding additional finds to the west in Goiás and Mato Grosso. From 1700 to 1799, Brazil produced more than 170,000 kilograms of gold. The discovery of diamonds in the 1720s further en-hanced the attraction of the hitherto uninviting interior.

Most of the gold in Brazil was to be found in streambeds, where panning and other simple techniques were used. Although workers often suffered from pneumonia, malaria, and dysentery, they faced fewer risks to life and limb than their counterparts in the silver mines of Spanish America, and it made greater economic "sense" to use Afro-Brazilian slaves in the gold fields. Indeed, a mining code drafted in 1702 based the size of claims awarded to miners on the number of slaves they owned.

Other factors also abetted the growth of a slave labor force in the mining region of Brazil. Proximity to Africa and a well-established Portuguese slave trade made slaves relatively cheaper than in the Spanish colonies. Furthermore, the sugar industry of northeastern Brazil had entered a period of decline after 1650, and planters sold slaves to would-be miners heading to the interior. Within 20 years of the first gold finds, there were already 30,000 slaves in Minas Gerais alone, and by 1775 the province had more than 150,000 slaves.

AGRICULTURE

Precious metals constituted only one of many avenues to wealth in colonial Latin America. Many Spanish and Portuguese colonists found their livelihoods in the commer-cial production of crops both native to the Americas and introduced from overseas. In addition, those who had made fortunes through mining and trade often diversified their holdings and enhanced their prestige by investing in landed estates. These properties ranged from modest farms in well-watered areas to extensive cattle ranches in the dry Brazilian interior and the northern plateau of Mexico to sugar plantations that required substantial investments in slaves and equipment.

Sugar Plantations

Spaniards and Portuguese were already familiar with the production of sugarcane, a crop native to India, both at home and in the Atlantic islands they had settled in the fifteenth century. The tropical climate of the Caribbean immediately suggested that sugar could be cultivated there, and Columbus brought sugar plants with him when he returned to Hispaniola in 1493. Cortés and other enterprising Spaniards introduced sugarcane in Mexico, while others began planting it in coastal Peru. Sugar achieved its greatest prominence along the coast of Brazil, especially in the northeast around Pernambuco and Salvador da Bahia, where rich soil, abundant rainfall, and easy access to overseas shipping created ideal conditions for the development of plantations. By 1580, Brazil had become the world's leading producer of sugar, a distinction it continued to hold for the next century.

Inside a Brazilian sugar mill, from a drawing made in 1640.

Like silver mining, sugar production required substantial inputs of hard labor, not only for the cultivation and harvesting of cane but also for its processing into sugar. Brazilian planters at first tried enslaving the indigenous population along the coast, supplemented with others rounded up from the interior. By 1545, the six sugar mills in the captaincy of São Vicente had a total of more than 3000 native slaves. Indian captives proved undependable, however. The intense labor involved in producing an unfamiliar crop made little sense to them, and native men resisted agricultural tasks because they considered it "women's work." Those who did not succumb to disease fled at the first opportunity. After a particularly severe series of epidemics devastated the native population in the 1560s, Brazilian sugar planters gradually turned to African slaves. The plantation Sergipe do Conde in Bahia was typical. Africans constituted 7 percent of its labor force in 1574 and 37 percent in 1591. By 1638, there were almost no Indians to be found among its workers.

In 1680, the total slave population of Brazil was about 150,000. Judging from the numbers imported, however, we might expect a much higher number. Some 4000 slaves entered Brazil each year between 1570 and 1630, and the annual figures for the period from 1630 to 1680 average nearly double that. Several factors accounted for the relatively slow rate of natural increase in the slave population. Birth rates among slaves were low, in part because males arriving on the slave ships outnumbered females by two to one.

El Paso

Chihuahua

Parral

Durango
Sombrerete
Gran Chichimeca
Zacatecas
San Luis Potosí

Guanajuato
Querétaro

★Mexico City
Puebla
Jalapa
Veracruz

Cuernavaca

Acapulco

Gulf of Mexico

New Spain

Indeed, sugar planters would have preferred an even higher ratio of men to women, but had to accept the mix of males and females offered by their African suppliers. Lack of prenatal care, malnutrition, and other factors contributed to exceptionally high rates of mortality among children born to slave mothers.

The planters' callous reckoning suggested that it was "cheaper" in economic terms to import adults rather than to bear the costs and risks of raising slave children from birth to the age at which they might become productive workers. They calculated further that it took less than 18 months for an adult slave to produce enough sugar to cover his or her purchase price. As long as sugar prices remained high and Portuguese traders enjoyed access to slave markets on the African coast, recent arrivals figured prominently among the labor forces on the sugar plantations of Brazil. Indeed, everywhere that sugar went—Mexico, Peru, and the Caribbean—African slavery usually followed.

Slice of Life   THE SAFRA IN COLONIAL BRAZIL

ON JULY 30, 1651, the sugar plantation called Sergipe do Conde in northeastern Brazil buzzed with activity as slaves, salaried employees and their families, and farmers from the surrounding countryside gathered to witness the formal inauguration of the harvest season, the *safra*. The priest presiding over the ceremonies prayed for the safety of the workers and a profitable harvest, blessed the mill, and fed the first stalks of sugarcane through it. The same ritual could be seen at engenhos throughout the region year after year in late July or early August. It was a festive occasion for all concerned. Slaves decorated oxcarts with brightly colored ribbons and drove them to the mill for blessing, looking forward to a goodly ration of *garapa* (cane brandy) at the end of the day, while the plantation's owners and their invited guests enjoyed a lavish banquet at the big house.

Festivity soon gave way to nine continuous months of back-breaking, round-the-clock labor. Field hands rose at dawn to begin cutting their daily quota of 2500 to 4000 canes. They worked in teams, typically a male slave who cut the stalks with a heavy scythe and a female slave who then tied them into bundles to be loaded onto boats or carts and transported to the mill. Once cut, the cane had to be processed within 24 hours lest the stalks dry out or the juice become sour. The mill apparatus was a complicated one, driven either by water power or by animals. Seven or eight slaves, usually women, worked inside the mill, some feeding the cane back and forth through a series of heavy rollers until all the juice had been extracted, others hauling away the crushed stalks or cleaning the equipment. The work was dangerous. At one mill, an observer reported that a young woman became completely trapped in the machinery and was "milled with the very cane." Many workers lost limbs to the heavy rollers, but even serious injuries did not spare one from the labors of the safra. A one-armed slave named Marcelina worked at the engenho Santana in the 1730s. Her job was to check the oil lamps that permitted her able-bodied companions to continue milling day and night.

From the mill, the juice was transferred to the *casa das caldeiras* (kettle house) to be heated and reheated until all impurities had been removed. Furnaces beneath the floor burned day and night, consuming enormous amounts of firewood in the process. An Italian Jesuit who visited Engenho Sergipe do Conde in the late seventeenth century described work inside the casa das caldeiras:

> And truly who sees in the blackness of night those tremendous furnaces perpetually burning . . . the cauldrons, or boiling lakes, continually stirred and restirred, now vomiting froth, exhaling clouds of steam . . . the noise of the wheels and chains, the peoples the color of the very night working intensively and moaning together without a moment of peace or rest; who sees all the confused and tumultuous machinery and apparatus of that Babylon can not doubt . . . that this is the same as Hell.

Finally, the purified liquid was poured into cone-shaped forms made of red clay, and slaves carried them to the *casa de purgar* (purging house) where a gradual process of percolation produced crystallized sugar, some of it highly refined and white, some of it lower grade, darker *moscovado,* as well as molasses that was then made into *aguardiente,* or rum. The sugar was then packed in large wooden crates for shipment overseas.

Colonial Brazilians called their engenhos *fábricas,* or factories, and with good reason, for the routines of sugar-making resembled those of modern industry. Men, women, and children all had their assigned tasks. Managers aimed to keep the process moving smoothly and continuously, with workers rotating in shifts. House servants and field hands were often pressed into nighttime duty in the mill. Many mills suspended operations on Sundays and other religious holidays, but some masters, skeptical that the slaves would use their time off for church-sponsored devotions, were reluctant to permit any distractions from the routine. But even the most efficient planning could not prevent a certain amount of down time due to unseasonable rains, shortages of firewood, or equipment breakdowns.

On most days of the safra season, however, slaves had little time to rest. Negative and positive incentives kept them working. Malingerers risked corporal punishment, but overseers hesitated to interrupt milling operations to administer a whipping on the spot. Many slaves had a quota to fulfill, and then they could spend the rest of the day tending to their gardens, where they grew fruits and vegetables for their own consumption or for sale in local markets. They also received periodic rewards in the form of rum or other intoxicants. Slaves who worked in highly skilled or managerial phases of the harvest operations might be given money or some sugar to sell on their own account. Such positions also carried the possibility of upward social mobility within the slave community, and even freedom for a favored few.

The safra ended when the rainy season commenced in early May, but much work remained to be done in the 3 months until the new harvest began. New cane fields were planted and existing ones weeded. Slaves worked at repairing the kettles, forms, and other implements used in the mill. But masters and slaves alike took time in June to celebrate feasts honoring Saints Peter, John, and Anthony. By the end of July, however, it was time for a new safra to begin.

Questions for Discussion
What tactics could the slaves of a sugar mill like Sergipe use to resist the demands of their masters? Would these means have been effective? Why or why not?

Haciendas and Ranches

Meanwhile, other Iberians capitalized on the growing demand for the familiar foodstuffs they had brought to the new continent with them. Spanish colonists in Mexico and Peru began almost immediately to produce the wheat they needed to make bread for the Catholic mass and for their own tables. Early efforts to compel Indians to supply wheat in tribute failed. Encomenderos and others then began producing wheat and crops such as barley, alfalfa, and vegetables on small plots of land, often receiving forced allocations of Indian labor for the harvest season.

As time passed, larger farms, usually known as *haciendas* in the Spanish colonies, appeared wherever people found appropriate ecological niches reasonably close to growing cities and mining centers. The area around Puebla in central Mexico, for example, was well suited to wheat production, and it lay astride the trade route linking Mexico City and the Gulf Coast. Other wheat farms could be found in the region known as the Bajío to the northwest. In South America, Cochabamba in present-day Bolivia soon became a major supplier of wheat and other grains to Potosí, while grain from haciendas in Chile was shipped northward to Peru. Increasing demand for wine, another dietary and religious staple, also prompted colonists to seek out places suitable for growing grapes. Vineyards were planted in coastal Peru and Chile.

Many landowners reaped additional profits from the sale of cattle, horses, oxen, mules, pigs, goats, and sheep. Livestock production stimulated Spanish and Portuguese colonists to settle in areas lacking in mineral resources and unsuitable for large-scale commercial agriculture. Cattle ranches could be found throughout the arid north-central plateau of New Spain and the plains of Venezuela, as well as the Brazilian interior. The gold rush of the eighteenth century brought cattle ranching to Minas Gerais, Mato Grosso, and Goiás in Brazil, while the region around Tucumán in northwestern Argentina supplied mules and cattle for the mines of Potosí.

Sheep ranching and the production of coarse woolen textiles in factories known as *obrajes* spread to many parts of Spanish America by the late sixteenth century. The highland valleys of Ecuador supplied textiles to markets throughout the Andes. The area between Puebla and Mexico City became another important center of textile manufacture. Hispanic colonists also introduced sheep to New Mexico, and they along with their Pueblo Indian neighbors exported large quantities of wool to the south.

Commercial farmers also reaped substantial profits from products indigenous to the Americas. By 1630, most of the maize consumed in Mexico City came from nearby haciendas, and by the late colonial period these estates also supplied much of the city's pulque, the fermented beverage made from the agave cactus that was especially popular among the lower classes. Cacao grown by non-Indian hacienda owners in Guatemala, Venezuela, and coastal Ecuador was shipped to Mexico, where a taste for chocolate spread from the Indian population to Spaniards, mestizos, and blacks. American cacao eventually found rich markets in Europe as well. Haciendas in the Andes produced large amounts of coca for consumption by mine workers at Potosí, as well as chuño, the freeze-dried potatoes consumed since pre-Hispanic times. Meanwhile, tobacco from Cuba and Brazil reached growing numbers of consumers throughout the Americas and in Europe, Africa, and Asia. Indigo, native to both hemispheres, provided profits for hacienda owners in Central America, especially in El Salvador.

Most haciendas had resident workforces that varied in size according to the specific products of the estates. Cattle ranches, for example, required a much smaller resident workforce than haciendas that produced wheat or grapes. Permanent employees were often mestizos and mulattos, although in central Mexico and the Andes there were many Indians as well. Although they were supposed to continue paying tribute and meeting

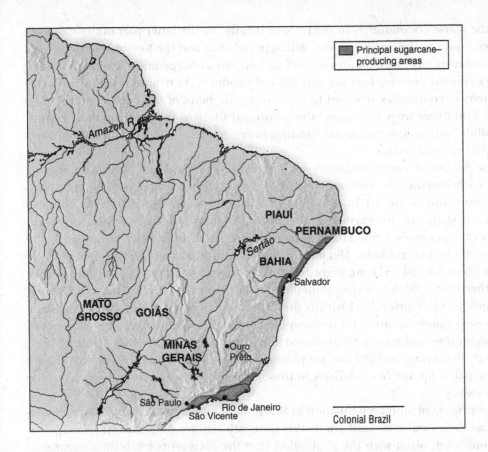

mita and repartimiento obligations, Indian hacienda residents had an easier time evading these burdens than those who remained in their villages.

Landowners offered various incentives to attract resident workers. Customarily, these permanent employees received food rations and perhaps a small plot of land for their own use, along with wages that were normally paid in commodities rather than cash due to the scarcity of coin throughout the countryside. Employers often extended credits to their workers as well, but, like mine workers, many indebted agricultural laborers fled without ever paying. At harvest time and whenever there was extra work to be done, *hacendados* (hacienda owners) recruited temporary laborers from Indian villages in the surrounding countryside, sometimes through forced labor systems such as the repartimiento, in other cases for wages.

Landownership

Large estates did not appear in Mesoamerica and the Andes immediately following the conquest. Densely concentrated indigenous populations occupied the best agricultural land, and the most powerful conquistadors simply skimmed off surplus wealth from the native communities in the form of tribute. By the latter part of the sixteenth century, however, the decline in the Indian population and the forced resettlement of many survivors left vast expanses of land vacant, just as burgeoning cities and mining centers created new markets for agricultural produce. As tribute receipts dwindled and many encomiendas reverted to the crown, the heirs of the early conquistadors had to find other ways to support the privileged lifestyle they had come to expect. Meanwhile, others who had made fortunes in mining or trade diversified their assets by acquiring rural estates.

The process of estate formation was a gradual, piecemeal one. A typical hacienda in the early seventeenth century consisted of a patchwork of properties, not always contiguous and acquired in a variety of different ways. Spanish town councils conferred some of the earliest land grants, often to encomenderos and other prominent Spaniards, while later grants came in the form of titles bestowed by the viceroys of Mexico and Peru. Meanwhile, individual Indians and Indian communities were willing to sell or rent surplus lands to meet past due tribute obligations and other needs. Such transfers sometimes violated protective legislation forbidding non-Indians to acquire land within the indigenous communities. Other aspiring landowners simply squatted on unoccupied land without any formalities whatsoever. Most ambitious landowners accumulated a hefty bundle of papers documenting their holdings. Beginning in 1589 and on various occasions thereafter, the crown allowed them to patch up any irregularities in these titles in exchange for a fee paid to the royal treasury.

The process of land accumulation in Brazil was more straightforward. Many plantations had their origins in land grants that sixteenth-century donatários or royal governors conferred, often with the stipulation that the recipients establish a sugar mill within a specified time. But like their counterparts in the Spanish colonies, aspiring *senhores de engenho* (owners of sugar mills) augmented their holdings through purchase or unauthorized occupation of unclaimed lands.

Religious orders also accumulated substantial landholdings. In Peru, monasteries joined conquistadors in laying claim to lands that had once supported the Inca or the native cults. Franciscans, Dominicans, Jesuits, and others also bought up small parcels of Indian land as readily as laymen. In the early seventeenth century, a Dominican priest in central Mexico purchased for his monastery 31 separate plots, each probably no more than 2 or 3 acres. Individual Indians, villages, and non-Indian hacendados also bequeathed rural property to monasteries and convents throughout Spanish America. The nuns of Cuzco's Convent of Santa Clara received regular shipments of meat, cheese, and tallow from their rural estates.

The Jesuits developed an exceptionally extensive network of rural properties to support their frontier missions and their churches and schools in major cities. Jesuit estates worked by African slaves dominated wine and sugar production in coastal Peru, and it is estimated that the order's haciendas occupied about 10 percent of Ecuador's agricultural land. In Brazil, Jesuits owned several of the largest sugar plantations.

Landed Elites

By the seventeenth century, only those encomenderos who had invested in commercial agriculture, mining, or trade continued to be counted among the elite of Spanish America. Alongside them stood many others who had derived their fortunes directly from entrepreneurial activity. The most successful landowners dominated the cabildos of nearby cities where they maintained their primary residences and where they could be spotted in their linen and velvet finery when they went to mass or other public functions. They frequently consolidated their holdings by arranging marriages of their children to the offspring of other landholding families.

Marriage alliances within the elite helped landowners build estates, but inheritance laws worked in the opposite direction. A select few won royal permission to create an entailed estate whereby the bulk of their property could pass intact to a single heir, often the eldest son, one generation after another. In most cases, however, a landowner's surviving spouse received half the estate and all children, both male and female, divided the remainder equally. When the other parent died, the children split the remaining half, again in equal shares. Thus, rural properties might be subdivided each time an owner died, unless one heir were in a position to buy out his or her siblings' holdings.

Shifting market conditions and the hazards of weather could also undermine the profitability of a hacienda or plantation. Mounting debts posed yet another problem. Proprietors frequently borrowed from convents and other religious institutions to meet operating costs or to finance capital improvements, using their property as collateral. Pious landowners often imposed additional liens on their estates in order to support spiritual and charitable endowments. In Spanish America, haciendas were commonly mortgaged for well over half their market value. Successive owners rarely repaid the principal and often failed to meet the required 5 percent annual interest charges. Time and again, bankrupt estates went up for sale, offering opportunities for more newcomers to enter the landowning class.

Why would anyone purchase a heavily indebted property with uncertain prospects for profit? Schooled in European traditions that associated landownership with nobility, buyers certainly wanted land for the prestige it conferred, especially when a bankrupt estate could be had for little more than a commitment to assume interest payments to lienholders. Landownership also enhanced a family's marriage prospects and signified that an individual was deserving of many other coveted status symbols, such as cabildo membership or an officer's commission in the local militia. Many aspiring landowners probably also looked forward to the kind of deference that resident peons were presumed to owe their employers.

Pragmatic considerations also entered the picture. Buyers could restore a property to profitability by investing in capital improvements or by shifting production to meet changing market conditions. Landowners around Caracas, for example, focused first on producing wheat before moving into tobacco and finally into cacao. Indeed, rural elites displayed considerable willingness to diversify their enterprises. A typical landowner in highland Peru might easily produce wine, wheat, and coca on several different plots, while also investing in mercury mining at Huancavelica and an obraje or two as well.

How Historians Understand   Documenting Colonial Enterprise

Studying the ways in which Iberians transformed their New World in the pursuit of profit is one of the easier tasks confronting historians of Latin America, for the documentation is enormous. The Spanish and Portuguese colonial bureaucracies monitored economic activity in their overseas empires, with an eye to enforcing mercantile restrictions and maximizing revenues for the crown. Such administrative records have obvious limitations, however. They show taxes collected but not those evaded; they itemize goods shipped legally but not those that were smuggled. Historians can use them as rough indicators for tracking fluctuations in production and exchange, but we can never calculate exact totals.

Other kinds of documents help us to reconstruct the histories of many types of colonial enterprises. Copies of land titles ended up in government archives whenever ownership of a property became the object of litigation. Owners and overseers kept careful accounts in their daily operation of mines, haciendas, and businesses.

A document certifying that on February 12, 1693, Blas Albarrán Carrillo took possession of a piece of land that formed a small part of the Hacienda Milpillas near Guadalajara, Mexico. It bears the official stamp required on all legal documents.

Wills typically included information on a person's place of birth, marriages, children, and other heirs, as well as a declaration of the property brought to a marriage by virtue of inheritance, dowry, or personal earnings. Outstanding debts and accounts payable were also listed. Following the testator's death, a meticulous inventory of the estate was taken, complete with the appraised value of all possessions, often down to individual items of clothing and household effects. When heirs fell to squabbling among themselves, the surviving paper trail lengthened.

These records are, of course, skewed toward those who had property of sufficient scale to record, assets worth a court battle among heirs and creditors. Documents are also weighted toward enterprises that remained in the same hands generation after generation. Studies of haciendas have often focused on properties belonging to the Jesuits, not only because members of the order were excellent administrators but also because the governments of Spain and Portugal expelled them from the colonies in the late eighteenth century, confiscating their property and usually depositing their well-kept files in archives that have been accessible to historians. Many of the records detailing the harvesting and processing of sugarcane on Brazilian plantations come from Jesuit estates, and historians have had to take special care in verifying that assumptions made about these properties are valid for others in the region.

The further down the social scale we go, the harder it is to document the activities of specific individuals, but we can track the everyday business of artisans, petty entrepreneurs, and other "ordinary" men and women through the records kept by notaries who certified apprenticeship contracts, bills of sale for all kinds of property, letters granting freedom to slaves, and wills. Those of humble social status appear in court registers too. Alongside hefty bundles of papers dealing with disputes among the great landowners, miners, and merchants, a researcher will often find a slimmer but highly revealing file detailing a complaint brought by a small farmer whose cow had been stolen, or a worker whose boss had mistreated him. Thanks to the fine penmanship and the meticulous record keeping of the thousands of accountants, notaries, clerks, and scribes who plied their trades in colonial Spanish America and Brazil, we are able to trace the varied enterprises of the Iberians' New World.

Questions for Discussion

Most of the documents described in this feature deal with people's property, and not what they were like as people. But suppose we stumbled upon a chest containing documents that belonged to a hypothetical married couple named Juan and María, who between them owned various haciendas in seventeenth-century Mexico. The chest contains Juan's will and documents pertaining to the probate of his estate following his death; an inventory of goods that María brought to the marriage; land titles and records of a lawsuit with a neighboring landowner; an account book listing the names of workers on their haciendas and debts incurred by those workers; and letters granting freedom to several Afro-Mexican slaves, giving information on the liberated individuals' ages and the types of work they performed. What clues can we get from these documents that might tell us something about the personalities and moral values of Juan and María?

Spanish South America

Owners of haciendas and plantations were shrewd entrepreneurs. While they definitely coveted land for reasons of prestige, the lifestyle they aspired to did not come cheaply. Sumptuous townhouses, retinues of slaves and servants, the overseers they hired to manage their properties, and the lavish contributions to religious and charitable causes that were expected of them all required a steady cash flow and unwavering attention to the bottom line. Although they may have been reluctant to toil with their own hands, landed elites could not afford to be idle aristocrats if they hoped to maintain their exalted position in local society.

Rural Society

Large estates were not the only type of landholding in colonial Latin America. Españoles, mestizos, mulattos, and acculturated Indians who worked smaller farms known as *labores* or *ranchos* in Mexico and *chácaras* in the Andes constituted something of a rural middle class. Some held secure title to their lands, while others were squatters, sharecroppers, or tenant farmers. In Brazil, small landholders known as *lavradores de cana* cultivated sugar alongside the great plantations and took their cane to the large mills to be processed. On the outskirts of Salvador and other Brazilian cities, small farms known as *roças* supplied fruits, vegetables, and other staple foods to the urban population and to the sugar plantations.

Lands held by indigenous communities also occupied significant portions of the countryside in many parts of Spanish America. Caciques and kurakas allocated plots of community-owned land to individual Indians, but enterprising non-Indians, including many mestizos and mulattos in Mexico, might receive these allotments by virtue of their residence in the village or their marriage to Indian women. Small farmers known as *labradores* also rented community land. In the Cuernavaca region of central Mexico and in many other places, non-Indian farmers, shopkeepers, and artisans came to outnumber Indians in many villages.

The relative percentages of land held by large estates, small farms, and Indian communities varied from one region to another. In the plains surrounding Bogotá, large estates held about two-thirds of the land by the seventeenth century. In peripheral areas such as Costa Rica and the São Paulo district of Brazil, smallholdings dominated the landscape, while in Oaxaca in southern Mexico substantial lands remained in the hands of Indian villages and their caciques.

Brazilian lavradores de cana sometimes held positions on the governing councils of Salvador and other cities, but most smallholders were not so lucky. They could afford few of the privileges and luxuries enjoyed by the owners of large haciendas and plantations. They remained rural people, without second homes or personal ties to powerful figures in the city. Though they might employ others or even own a slave or two, they could not escape the hard physical labor that agriculture demanded. Nevertheless, they too showed their entrepreneurial side, selling their surplus produce in local and regional markets.

TRADE AND TRANSPORTATION

The Spaniards and Portuguese who crossed the Atlantic and their American-born descendants were no strangers to the profit motive, and we have seen how they eagerly searched for ways to exploit their New World to their economic advantage. They found markets for their produce overseas and in the colonies and spent their profits on merchandise imported from Europe and from other parts of the Indies. The movement and exchange of all these commodities provided many avenues to fortunes great and small for merchants, accountants, shippers, and haulers of freight—as well as embezzlers and thieves. British, French, and Dutch pirates preyed upon international shipping, forcing Spain and Portugal to spend considerable sums defending cargoes and crews.

International Commerce

Gold and silver were by far the most valuable of all commodities transported in colonial Latin America. A substantial portion of these precious metals wound up in Europe. Iberian law considered all subsoil resources the property of the monarch, who granted mining permits on the condition that recipients surrender a portion of their take, usually one-tenth to one-fifth, to royal agents. Some of this treasure stayed in the colonies to finance the administration of the empire, but every year hundreds of silver ingots reached the king's coffers in Madrid. Merchants engaged in the Indies trade also sent large amounts of silver to Europe to be exchanged for merchandise.

Vessels loaded with treasure were attractive targets for plunder by English, French, and Dutch pirates. Part of Cortés's first loot from Tenochtitlan wound up in the hands of French pirates, and in 1628, the Dutch captain Piet Heyn made off with the entire Mexican silver fleet off the coast of Cuba. Spain therefore imposed strict controls on shipping to and from the colonies. All ships bound for the Americas had to embark from the port of Seville and travel in convoys with naval escorts, and they were permitted to call on only a handful of ports in the colonies. Each year, two fleets set out from Seville, one bound for Veracruz on the Gulf Coast of Mexico, the other for Cartagena in northern South America and the Isthmus of Panamá. Their cargoes included Spanish wine, olive oil, salted cod, and other foodstuffs; clothing and tools; and luxury textiles, such as satins, brocades, lace, and linen, often of northern European manufacture.

Once they reached their destination, merchants traveling with the Veracruz fleet headed inland for the famous trade fair at the town of Jalapa, where the climate was healthier and more comfortable than on the coast. Merchants on the South American fleet stopped first at Cartagena and then proceeded to the hot, humid, fever-ridden town of Portobelo in Panama to exchange European wine, textiles, books, and tools for silver, hides, and sugar brought up from Peru. Visitors to the Portobelo fair described how silver lay in heaps in the marketplace as representatives of the most powerful merchants of Lima and Seville haggled over prices. For the return voyage, all ships from both fleets gathered at Havana before setting off together across the Atlantic. Mexican and Peruvian silver crossed the Pacific in the famous galleons that sailed from Acapulco to the Spanish colony at Manila in the Philippines, where resident Chinese merchants eagerly exchanged Asian merchandise for American bullion. The Manila trade brought fine silks, Chinese porcelains, and spices to the growing marketplaces of Mexico and Peru.

Portuguese merchants carried on extensive trade at Goa in India, Macao on the South China coast, and other markets in Asia, bringing exotic commodities back to Europe and thence to Brazil. Meanwhile, the Portuguese developed a trade with Africa that was to endure for more than 300 years. The rise of sugar production in the sixteenth and seventeenth centuries, followed by the gold rush thereafter, created an insatiable demand for African slaves, exchanged for Brazilian gold and tobacco and European tools along the African coast.

Overland Transport

The economy of colonial Latin America also depended heavily on the movement of goods and people over land. Where topography permitted, Iberians introduced ox-drawn wagons and carts. Wagonloads of supplies headed north along the central plateau of New Spain from Mexico City to Zacatecas and on to Santa Fe, New Mexico. But most freight traveled on the backs of mules, especially where rugged terrain or thick vegetation made wheeled transport impossible—up and down the steep slopes of the Andes, and across the Isthmus of Panama, for example. The trail from the port of Guayaquil to Quito was especially treacherous. One observer called it "the worst road in the world, because it always rains on these mountain slopes so that the mules fall into the mire." In dry areas, on the other hand, freight haulers worried about finding enough water and fodder for their animals.

Despite these difficulties, overland transport was a lucrative business. Several thousand mules entered Mexico City each day by the eighteenth century, and in the Andes llamas carried heavy loads to remote mining centers. Many enterprising mestizos, mulattos, and Indians earned their livings as carters and mule drivers, and a lucky few achieved a modicum of upward economic and social mobility. Take, for example, the case of Miguel Hernández, a free mulatto and muleteer who lived in the provincial town of Querétaro, a few days' journey north of Mexico City. The town offered attractive opportunities for profit. Not only was it situated in a fertile agricultural zone and on the route that headed north to Zacatecas, but it also boasted numerous textile factories. By the time of his death in 1604, Hernández had acquired an excellent credit rating, several pieces of real estate in and around Querétaro, and even a black slave. He left numerous documents graced with his elegant signature, and his membership in the prestigious religious confraternity of the Holy Sacrament brought him into close contact with leading local landowners, merchants, and government officials.

Merchants

Merchants formed an important component of colonial Latin American society. Most powerful were the great wholesalers of Mexico City, Lima, and other major cities, many of whom had fortunes worth well over 100,000 pesos—the equivalent of millionaires for their time. Rumor even had it that Lima's most successful merchants slept on mattresses atop hundreds of bars of silver. Often of European birth, the great commercial entrepreneurs built lavish homes at the center of town, bought cabildo positions for themselves or their sons, and diversified their holdings by investing in land, textile production, and urban real estate. In Mexico City and Lima, they organized themselves into merchant guilds, or *consulados,* that settled disputes among them and lobbied for their interests. They also supplied credit to landowners, miners, and other entrepreneurs.

Llamas carrying silver from mines.

Merchants in Salvador provided much of the credit to the sugar planters of Bahia, and many eventually joined the ranks of the planters themselves. Typical was Francisco Fernandes de Sim, a native of the island of Madeira who established himself in the Brazilian capital as a broker in wine and sugar in the 1620s. By the following decade, he owned two ships that plied the Atlantic. His marriage to the daughter of a *senhor de engenho* brought him into the local elite. When he died in 1664, he left three sugar plantations as well as numerous properties in the city of Salvador. Many New Christians, converts from Judaism or their descendants, could be found among the merchant classes of Brazil and the Spanish colonies.

Major wholesalers sent goods on consignment to agents, often their own relatives, who retailed them in smaller towns or turned them over to itinerant peddlers who carried merchandise on pack trains to remote villages, mining camps, and haciendas. During the height of its silver boom in the early seventeenth century, Zacatecas boasted between 50 and 100 shops, most of them specializing either in groceries or cloth, and served as the hub of a trading network that extended several hundred miles farther north.

Through a practice known as the *reparto de mercancías,* the alcaldes mayores, corregidores, and their lieutenants were particularly active in local trade in heavily Indian districts of Spanish America. These men purchased their offices and expected a return on their "investment" beyond their meager salaries. They did so by receiving goods on credit from city merchants and selling them at inflated prices to Indians, and by obliging Indians in their jurisdiction to sell them items of value at deflated prices—all in violation of laws supposedly prohibiting them from engaging in business activities within their jurisdictions.

Mercantile Restrictions

The prohibition on business ventures by political officials was one of many regulations that the Spanish crown imposed on all levels of trade in the Indies. Only Spanish subjects were legally permitted to engage in the Indies trade, and, as we have seen, merchant vessels had to sail from Seville in convoy with the annual fleets. Merchants also paid a variety of taxes.

None of these restrictions daunted ambitious merchants or eager consumers. Tax evasion was commonplace, and contraband flourished, especially after rival European nations began setting up colonies in the Caribbean in the seventeenth century. Spain's growing concerns in Europe undermined its ability to enforce trade regulations or defend its colonies against foreign interlopers, while weaknesses in its domestic economy limited the supply of goods available through legal channels. Foreign merchants residing in Seville simply used Spaniards as fronts for their involvement in the Indies trade, and foreign vessels loaded with contraband merchandise regularly called at Spanish American ports, especially in areas poorly served by the fleet system. Along the coast of Venezuela, for example, smuggling flourished. The Dutch, based in nearby Curaçao, exchanged coveted manufactured goods for high-grade Venezuelan cacao.

Portuguese colonists in Brazil had to contend with fewer trade restrictions than their counterparts in Spanish America. Portugal lacked sufficient shipping capacity to restrict the Brazil trade to its own subjects. Foreign ships were free to travel to and from Brazil as long as they secured a license from the Portuguese crown and paid appropriate taxes. In particular, English vessels often made their way to Brazil. By the seventeenth century, however, mounting defense concerns prompted the introduction of convoys in the Brazil trade as well. The discovery of gold and diamonds in the eighteenth century prompted additional restrictions on economic activity in Brazil.

By exploiting the mineral wealth, varied environment, and cheap labor of the colonies, Spanish and Portuguese Americans generated investment capital and stimulated demand for fine clothing and other luxuries as well as everyday staples—food, shoes, tools, and household utensils. Personal ingenuity turned up new opportunities for profit and creative means of evading constraints on merchants' activities. For example, by the early seventeenth century, the *peruleros* (transatlantic merchants based in Lima) had begun bypassing the Portobelo fairs and the middlemen and tax collectors who did business there. Instead, they went to Spain themselves, purchasing items directly from suppliers in Seville and shipping them back to Peru for resale. Buying and selling were central activities in the Iberians' New World, and the colonial environment furnished ample scope for private initiative.

CITIES AND TOWNS IN THE IBERIANS' NEW WORLD

Colonial Latin Americans, then, derived their fortunes from a variety of sources—from silver mines deep below the surface of the Earth; from fields planted in sugar cane, maize, and wheat; from cattle ranches, goldfields, and textile works; and from the business of moving people and goods over great distances. Regardless of where the wealth came from, however, much of it ended up in the cities and towns that Iberians established throughout their New World. To their way of thinking, the only civilized and proper existence was an urban one. The most successful miners, merchants, and agriculturists of Spanish America and Brazil established their residences and displayed their wealth in the great cities. Cities were also the seats of civil and ecclesiastical power, headquarters of viceroyalties, audiencias, tribunals of the Inquisition, and diocesan sees, as well as the centers of intellectual and artistic life in the colonies. They also became home to the thousands of working men and women, the artisans and domestic servants who supported the lifestyles of the elites.

Capital Cities

Most important among the cities of colonial Latin America were the three great political capitals established in the sixteenth century: Mexico City, Lima, and Salvador da Bahia. Built on the foundations of Aztec Tenochtitlan, Mexico City was in many respects the premier city of the Western Hemisphere. Its population topped 100,000 in the early seventeenth century. The city depended on the vast hinterland of New Spain to supply its necessities, brought in by oxcarts and mules and by canoes that traversed what remained of the valley's lakes.

At the center of Mexico City stood the massive plaza, the *zócalo* that is still the hub of the modern metropolis, surrounded by visual symbols of the colony's power structure: the viceroy's palace, the cabildo headquarters, the cathedral, and the city's principal market. Like many other cities established in Spanish America, it was laid out on a grid pattern. Within a few blocks of the plaza, one could find the lavish homes of the city's elite and dozens of sumptuous convents, monasteries, and churches, as well as the shops of the most prominent retailers and artisans. Elegant coaches trimmed in silk and gold, driven by black and mulatto slaves in full livery, carried the city's rich and powerful citizens as they went about their business. Two large aqueducts, built by Indian repartimiento workers, brought water to the city's many fountains.

Spaniards who settled in Peru intended at first to follow the example of New Spain and use the indigenous capital city as headquarters for their new colony. They soon decided that Cuzco was too inaccessible to serve that purpose, however, and the coastal town of Lima, the "city of Kings," became the capital instead. Lima's population grew to about 25,000 by 1614, and close to 80,000 by the 1680s. Its *plaza de armas,* or central square, was an impressive sight to residents and visitors alike. There, too, hundreds of coaches, some worth more than 3000 pesos, could be seen on city streets. By the eighteenth century, Lima boasted 6 parish churches in addition to its cathedral, along with 11 hospitals, 15 nunneries, and 19 monasteries.

Proudly situated atop a bluff overlooking the entrance to the magnificent harbor known as the Bahia de Todos os Santos, Salvador da Bahia served as capital of Brazil until 1763. There resided the colony's chief political authority, known as the governor-general or viceroy, as well as the high court and the Archbishop of Brazil. Wharves and warehouses lined the waterfront, while government buildings, churches, and the homes of the rich occupied higher ground. Salvador had a population of about 25,000 in the early eighteenth century, and double that number by the end of the colonial period. Leading sugar planters from the surrounding area maintained their principal residences at Salvador, and its local government was dominated by senhores de engenho and lavradores de cana.

Provincial Capitals and Other Towns

Other important cities grew along key transportation routes. Puebla de los Angeles, situated along the road from Mexico City to Veracruz, ranked second only to the viceregal capital among the cities of New Spain and matched Lima in population by the eighteenth century. Puebla's cathedral boasted bell towers higher than those of Mexico City, and its tightly woven local elite tried to outdo their counterparts in the capital in staging elaborate ceremonies to welcome a new viceroy to the kingdom of New Spain.

In South America, Huamanga (known today as Ayacucho) traced its growth to its strategic position along the route linking Lima with Upper Peru. Oruro in Bolivia owed its existence to the success of its silver mines and its location along major trade routes, for the cheapest mode of transporting mercury from Huancavelica to Potosí involved shipping it by sea from Lima to Arica and then overland through Oruro.

Though many a ghost town could be found in the mining regions, major cities developed wherever precious metals proved sufficient in quantity to sustain mining for more than a few decades. In the seventeenth century, Potosí was easily the largest city in South America, and Zacatecas ranked as New Spain's third largest city, with a population that reached 80,000. In the gold fields of Brazil, Ouro Prêto's population numbered upward of 50,000 in the heyday of the mining bonanza (see Plate 7). Communities throughout Minas Gerais boasted elegant, richly ornamented churches.

Still other towns served as regional markets and administrative centers. Quito, today the capital of Ecuador, was the seat of an audiencia and a center of distribution and supply for the many obrajes that could be found in the surrounding valleys. Its Franciscan monastery and Jesuit church remain to this day among the most impressive examples of colonial church architecture in all of Latin America. Cuzco, no longer the center of political power that it had been in Inca times, nonetheless remained an important Spanish city. Spanish churches and convents with precolonial foundations can still be seen in the center of town.

While most of Brazil's important cities were seaports on the Atlantic coast, the heavily fortified port cities of Spanish America—Veracruz, Acapulco, Havana, Portobelo, Cartagena, Guayaquil—ranked among the least impressive of the colonies' urban centers. Most people of any means preferred to live inland, away from the heat, tropical storms, recurrent diseases, and threat of pirate attacks that plagued coastal settlements. The French explorer Samuel Champlain proclaimed Portobelo "the most evil and pitiful residence in the world." An Italian visitor was equally unimpressed with Acapulco, describing it as "a humble village of fishermen."

Urban Amenities

Urban life afforded comforts and amenities not readily available in rural areas. Major cities had paved streets, at least at the center of town, as well as public parks like Mexico City's Alameda. By the end of the sixteenth century, most cities had a number of social welfare institutions, including hospitals, orphanages, and shelters for women, all supported by the church, the state, or pious benefactors. Mexico City even had an asylum that catered to the special needs of the mentally ill.

The viceregal capitals and major provincial towns of colonial Latin America were also active centers of intellectual and artistic life. Printing presses turned out theological and devotional materials in Mexico City, Lima, La Paz, Puebla, and other cities. Santo Domingo, Mexico City, and Lima all had universities dating from the sixteenth century, and by the end of the seventeenth century, universities had also appeared in Quito, Córdoba in Argentina, Guatemala City, and Cuzco. Major cities such as Lima, Salvador da Bahia, and Mexico City, as well as smaller towns such as Cuenca and Latacunga in present-day Ecuador, had Jesuit colleges that trained sons of the elite for the priesthood and other careers. No universities were established in Brazil, but the colony's wealthiest planters and merchants sent their sons to Portugal to study at the distinguished University of Coimbra. Convents located in major urban centers served the intellectual needs of a select group of women.

Architects and artists found ample outlets for their talents in building and adorning the churches and convents in cities and towns throughout the colonies. In Spanish America, the silver bonanza of the late sixteenth and seventeenth centuries spurred an ecclesiastical building boom. Foremost were the great cathedrals that took a century or more to complete. In Mexico City, for example, work on the cathedral began in 1563 and was not concluded until 1700. Richly detailed exterior facades and elaborate gilded

Interior of a church in Salvador, Brazil.

altarpieces characterized the baroque style that predominated in the church buildings of the seventeenth century.

Urban Working Classes

The cities of colonial Latin America were home not only to highly visible political, ecclesiastical, and economic elites but also to thousands of skilled and unskilled workers of all racial groups. In the larger cities, one could observe large numbers of silversmiths, painters, tailors, shoemakers, barbers, candle makers, silk weavers, jewelers, carpenters, masons, bakers, and blacksmiths who organized themselves into guilds in order to maintain the standards of their trades. By the end of the sixteenth century, there were more than 200 guilds in New Spain, most of them located in Mexico City. Hundreds of young men of all racial backgrounds apprenticed themselves to master craftsmen certified by the guilds. Skilled tradespeople played a somewhat less prominent role in Brazilian cities, but in Salvador a popular tribune (*juiz do povo*) represented their interests to the town council.

Blacks and mulattos, both slave and free, could be found in cities everywhere, most notably in Brazil but also in Spanish America. Urban slaveowners often found it profitable for a slave to learn a trade and work for wages, which the master then pocketed. In many cases, however, skilled artisans could accumulate sufficient funds of their own to purchase their freedom or that of their loved ones. Slaves also performed domestic service in the households of urban elites. Blacks were particularly prominent in port cities such as Salvador, Acapulco, Veracruz, Callao, and Cartagena, where they performed a great deal of the labor as porters and stevedores. In the government shipyards of Callao and Guayaquil, black slaves worked as carpenters, joiners, shipwrights, and caulkers, often side by side with their owners.

The urban poor vastly outnumbered the rich and enjoyed few of the comforts that elites took for granted. In Mexico City and elsewhere, many lived in crowded quarters. They enjoyed little privacy, and they spent much of their leisure time in the streets, plazas, and marketplaces, and in the many taverns that catered to a lower-class clientele. Many city dwellers were reduced to begging or petty crime to survive.

At the same time, however, city life offered everyone, even the poor, elaborate spectacles and other diversions. Religious holidays and ceremonies held to honor incoming viceroys and other dignitaries gave elites a chance to show off their wealth and curry favor with powerful leaders of the church and state, but these occasions also featured popular entertainment such as parades, bullfights, and fireworks. As some of the most privileged members of the working classes, members of artisan guilds marched in processions and sponsored comedies for the amusement of the crowds. Festivals also gave the urban poor an opportunity to let off steam and ridicule the pretensions of their prominent and prosperous neighbors. Urban life, then, offered something for everyone, and for this reason, cities were among the most important features of the new world that Iberian Americans created for themselves.

CONCLUSION

From California to Tierra del Fuego, Spanish and Portuguese immigrants found a stunning variety of resources they could exploit: fertile lands suitable for producing crops they had known back home, mineral wealth beyond their wildest expectations, and dozens of exotic new commodities that could be marketed in the "Old" World and the "New." Shrewd and innovative entrepreneurs, they turned rainforests into sugarcane fields, blasted tunnels deep beneath the surface of the Earth, and turned their livestock loose everywhere they went.

Over the three centuries that followed Columbus's landfall in 1492, Iberian colonists, their African slaves and American-born descendants, and the British, French, and Dutch settlers who followed, transformed the physical environment of the hemisphere, making it a "New World" for indigenous peoples and newcomers alike. However much or little they knew of the world beyond the sea, the natives of the Americas became part of a global economy. In Mexico and Peru, they risked suffocation underground and mercury poisoning above, all to provide silver coins that paid Spanish armies in Europe and filled the pockets of merchants as far away as China and India. Europeans became avid consumers of the Aztecs' chocolate, flavored with sugar grown by Africans transported across the Atlantic in chains, while addiction to American tobacco spread throughout Europe and to Africa and the Far East.

To be sure, Mesoamericans and Andeans had engaged in long-distance trade well before 1492, but Spanish colonists refashioned preexisting routes to suit their own purposes. The Nahuas of central Mexico had once obtained their cacao from Colima on the northwest coast and Soconusco in present-day Guatemala, but by the seventeenth and eighteenth centuries their colonial descendants were consuming chocolate produced on haciendas as far away as Caracas and Guayaquil. Spanish and Portuguese Americans carved new trade routes that carried American produce to distant markets in both hemispheres. Transformed into a new world of the Iberians' making, the people and resources of the Americas now answered to the imperatives of an emerging global economy.

LEARNING MORE ABOUT LATIN AMERICANS

Higgins, Kathleen J. *"Licentious Liberty" in a Brazilian Gold-Mining Region: Slavery, Gender, and Social Control in Eighteenth-Century Sabará, Minas Gerais* (University Park, PA: Pennsylvania State University Press, 1999). Shows how the lives of slaves, especially, were shaped by the specific context of Brazil's gold-mining region.

Hoberman, Louisa Schell, and Susan Migden Socolow, eds. *Cities and Society in Colonial Latin America* (Albuquerque, NM: University of New Mexico Press, 1986). Collected essays by leading historians on various groups of people who lived in colonial Latin American cities, including merchants, nuns, artisans, servants, slaves, and criminals.

Hoberman, Louisa Schell, and Susan Migden Socolow, eds. *The Countryside in Colonial Latin America* (Albuquerque, NM: University of New Mexico Press, 1996). A companion volume to *Cities and Society in Colonial Latin America;* essays explore such topics as material culture, conflict, and changing agricultural technology.

Lane, Kris. *Quito 1599: City and Colony in Transition* (Albuquerque, NM: University of New Mexico Press, 2002). A glimpse into the lives of merchants, workers, slaves, and shipwreck victims in colonial Ecuador at the end of the sixteenth century.

Martin, Cheryl E. *Rural Society in Colonial Morelos* (Albuquerque, NM: University of New Mexico Press, 1985). Traces the interaction of native villages and sugar haciendas in the region around Cuernavaca, Mexico.

Schwartz, Stuart B. *Sugar Plantations in the Formation of Brazilian Society: Bahia, 1550–1835* (Cambridge, U.K.: Cambridge University Press, 1985). A prize-winning book that examines life and work on Brazilian plantations.

5

THE AMERINDIANS' CHANGING WORLD

IN 1577, KING PHILIP II of Spain decided that he wanted more detailed information on his American possessions, and he sent a lengthy questionnaire to Spanish officials throughout Mesoamerica and the Andes. The recipients consulted with Catholic priests and indigenous leaders in hundreds of communities. A total of 208 reports reached the king within a few years. These documents graphically demonstrate the profound changes that the native peoples witnessed in the first several decades that followed the arrival of the Europeans in Mexico and Peru.

Typical was the testimony of the Indian caciques of Oaxtepec in what is now the state of Morelos in Mexico. By 1580, the people of Oaxtepec enjoyed many Spanish fruits such as melons, figs, oranges, limes, and quinces. They had become enthusiastic participants in the emerging market economy, with much of their produce destined for sale in Mexico City. Like many other communities, Oaxtepec provided a brilliantly colored map, with both a Catholic church and the indigenous symbol for the community at its center (see Plate 8). But the caciques could not hide their nostalgia for the "good old days" before the coming of the Spaniards, when people worked hard, bathed three times a day, and "did not know what sickness was."

Few of Oaxtepec's caciques were old enough in 1580 to have direct personal memories of preconquest days, and they may well have idealized the years of Mexica domination. But they were certainly correct in their notion of the profound changes the indigenous peoples of the Americas had experienced since 1492. Their material environment had altered forever as Europeans introduced exotic plants and animals and reshaped the landscape to accommodate haciendas, plantations, and mines. The structure of their community life had changed too, as they now answered to new rulers and prayed to new gods. At the same time, Native Americans retained many features of life as they had known it before the arrival of the Spaniards and Portuguese. Long-familiar crops still provided the bulk of their subsistence, and most people continued to speak only the languages their forebears had known for centuries. Behind a facade of adaptation to European forms of community life, indigenous peoples continued many traditional practices and beliefs when they governed themselves and communicated with the supernatural.

This chapter examines both continuity and change among native peoples under Spanish and Portuguese colonization. We will look first at the people who lived in the cores of the great pre-Hispanic empires of the Aztecs and Incas. The presence of mineral and agricultural resources and a native population accustomed to paying taxes and performing forced labor made Mesoamerica and the Andes especially attractive to Spanish colonists. We will turn next to natives of the frontiers of northern Mexico and southern South America, areas less densely settled in precolonial times and less inviting to European colonists. Indians in these regions were often gathered into mission complexes, an experience that triggered even more drastic alterations in their way of life than those experienced by natives in Mesoamerica and the Andes. Finally, we will examine how the indigenous peoples of the Americas resisted and adapted change, and how they reformulated their individual and group identities over time.

NATIVE COMMUNITIES IN MESOAMERICA AND THE ANDES

Spanish colonizers of the sixteenth century gravitated to the highland interiors of Mexico and South America. They marveled not only at the material splendor of Tenochtitlan and Cuzco but also at the sophisticated social and political organization of the great indigenous empires. The simultaneous discovery of great silver deposits in northern Mexico and Upper Peru in the 1540s gave the Spaniards ample incentive to stay, and they looked upon the native peoples of these regions as a convenient source of labor for mining and other enterprises. The colonizers quickly set about reorganizing indigenous community life and adapting traditional systems of forced labor and taxation to their own imperatives.

As a result, the highland peoples of Mexico and Peru experienced more immediate Spanish intrusions into their daily lives than did natives of areas that were more marginal to the European agenda. But Andeans and Mesoamericans also possessed a rich and complex indigenous culture that they could draw upon in fashioning their responses to their changing world.

Shifting Populations in the República de Indios

Official Spanish policy divided colonial society into two separate "repúblicas," one of Indians, the other of Spaniards. In Mesoamerica and the Andes, the "república de indios" was made up of hundreds of peasant communities with no real connection to one another. In theory, these villages were shielded from harmful outside influence,

TIMELINE

1549
First Jesuits arrive in Brazil

1568–1572
Jesuits arrive in Peru and Mexico

1570s
Viceroy Toledo orders massive relocation of
Peru's Indian population

1573
Franciscan missionaries begin work in Florida

1598
Franciscans begin work among the Pueblos of
New Mexico

1610
Jesuit missionaries begin work among the
Guaraní in Paraguay

1615
Felipe Guaman Poma de Ayala completes his
history of Peru

1680
Pueblo rebellion in New Mexico

1690s
Jesuit missionaries active in Sonora and
southern Arizona

1692
Rebellion of Indians and other lower classes in
Mexico City; Spaniards begin reconquest of
New Mexico

1712
Indian rebellion in Chiapas

1769
Franciscans begin building missions in
California

with non-Indians other than priests, corregidores, and alcaldes mayores forbidden to reside within them, while protective legislation supposedly safeguarded community lands. In practice, however, non-Indians infiltrated everywhere, eventually outnumbering the native population in some villages. Meanwhile, labor drafts forced natives from their communities of origin, and the need to supply tribute and other perquisites to the Spaniards drew them into the emerging cash economy of the "república de españoles."

The demographic makeup of the so-called Indian communities was anything but static. European diseases continued to reduce the indigenous population for a century or more until the native peoples began developing greater resistance to Old World illnesses. In order to facilitate missionary efforts and collect tribute, Spanish officials consolidated the survivors numerous times, forcing those living in outlying areas to move to more centrally located villages and sometimes lumping together people who spoke different indigenous languages. This combination of epidemics and forced resettlements left vast tracts of land vacant, facilitating the consolidation of Spanish-owned haciendas.

The most sweeping relocations occurred in the Andes, mandated by Viceroy Francisco de Toledo in the 1570s. In the province of Huarochirí, 100 or so settlements were concentrated into just 17, and in present-day Bolivia Toledo "reduced" some 900 hamlets and 129,000 people into just 44 villages. Toledo's program undermined traditional Andean survival strategies. Prior to the arrival of the Europeans, each community held lands at different elevations up and down the mountainsides, giving them access to several different microclimates and allowing them to grow a variety of crops. Communities created by Toledo's decrees often lost control of outlying ecological niches. The viceroy's program also disrupted cooperative labor arrangements that native peoples had developed over many centuries.

Native peoples did not always comply with forced resettlements. In Peru, some communities lodged official protests with the viceroy and audiencia even before they received their formal orders to relocate, while other groups complied but quickly returned to their former homes. Indians in New Spain appealed to colonial courts and sometimes secured reversals of relocation orders. In 1603, the village of Anenecuilco in the present-day Mexican state of Morelos successfully resisted removal to the village of Cuautla. Three hundred years later, as Mexico's Revolution of 1910 began, Emiliano Zapata rallied his fellow townsmen in Anenecuilco to fight persistent encroachments of nearby sugar haciendas on village lands. Other groups moved voluntarily in the years following the conquest. Andean peoples forcibly relocated by the Incas took advantage of the new colonial regime to return to their places of origin. Particularly notable were the Cañaris, whom the Incas had uprooted from southern Ecuador and resettled near Cuzco and elsewhere.

Many people also moved individually or in small groups. In the Andes, a man who left his community of origin and settled in another native village could escape being drafted for the Potosí mita. Known as *forasteros,* these men were denied membership in the ayllu (the traditional native community organization) and allocations of community land. However, they were also exempt from the payment of tribute. As a result, forasteros often accumulated greater wealth than those native to the community. Many forasteros also gained access to land by marrying local women or making informal arrangements with kurakas (traditional chiefs) in their adopted communities. Kurakas often exacted labor and other personal favors in exchange for these concessions.

Many native people left the república de indios altogether, settling in Spanish cities, haciendas, and mining camps. Meanwhile, favorably situated Indian communities attracted large numbers of mestizos, blacks, mulattos, and people of Spanish descent. By the late eighteenth century, for example, nearly two-thirds of Oaxtepec's people were non-Indians. Though officially barred from political positions in the república de indios, many of these newcomers acquired community lands through purchase, rental, squatting, or marriage to Indian women, and they wielded considerable influence in the Indian villages.

Local Government in the República de Indios

Local government in the villages of Mesoamerica and Peru rested in the hands of an indigenous ruling class deputized by the Spanish to supervise tribute collection, marshal workers for labor drafts, and maintain order. At first, the encomenderos, clergy, and crown officials dealt with whatever hereditary rulers they found in place, as long as these individuals were willing to cooperate. Soon, however, they began attempting to restructure local government to more closely resemble models of municipal organization they had known in Europe.

In each community, the Spanish designated a single individual, always a male, to be the *gobernador* or head of local government. Sometimes the person chosen had a legitimate tie to pre-Hispanic rulers, but in many other cases someone else assumed the position. Other leading figures in the village became *regidores* and *alcaldes* that together formed a governing body that the Spanish called a cabildo, similar to the town councils in Spanish municipalities. Native cabildos also included a bailiff and a scribe trained to record community business in indigenous languages but using the European alphabet. Cabildo members not only received a salary from the village treasury but also claimed food, personal service, and other perquisites from community members and were usually exempt from tribute payment and labor drafts. With such incentives, the number of officers tended to multiply.

The Indian gobernador and his cabildo exercised a wide variety of duties, often following pre-Hispanic custom. They handled the allocation of village lands, supervised the sale and rental of lands by private individuals, and oversaw local markets. They also punished community members for misdemeanors such as public drunkenness, theft, and domestic violence. Thus local government in the indigenous communities rested primarily in native hands, although Spanish district magistrates (corregidores or alcaldes mayores) could and did meddle in village business.

Spanish assumptions that political offices should be reserved for males did not mean that women were completely marginalized from politics in the república de indios. Women raised money to finance lawsuits in defense of community lands and were often at the forefront in village rebellions against colonial authorities. Numerous hereditary *cacicas* (the feminine form of caciques) could be found in the Mixteca region of southern Mexico, and there are scattered references to female kurakas in the Andes. Though excluded from holding office or participating in elections, these women wielded considerable influence within their communities.

Spanish authorities maintained the fiction that indigenous cabildo officers were elected, usually for 1-year terms. Pre-Hispanic custom usually dictated that new rulers were chosen only on the death of an incumbent, so in many places the same individuals were elected year after year. Voting was restricted to a select circle of elite men. Factional disputes abounded in colonial Indian communities, and local elections were sometimes punctuated by violence.

In some places, especially in Mexico, mestizos and others served as village gobernadores and other officers. The Hinojosa family, caciques of Cuernavaca, dominated local politics in the república de indios for several generations in the seventeenth and eighteenth centuries. Biologically mestizos, they perhaps descended from a Spaniard named Francisco de Hinojosa who settled in Cuernavaca in the sixteenth century. They spoke Spanish and maintained close ties with the priests at the Franciscan monastery and with owners of sugar haciendas in the area. The first Hinojosa to be elected gobernador of Cuernavaca was Don Juan de Hinojosa, who attained the office in 1629. Twenty years later, his younger brother Agustín also held the post. Juan boasted descent from the conquistadors of Cuernavaca. Both men openly acknowledged their status as mestizos, although Agustín also claimed Spanish descent on numerous occasions. Agustín married Doña Juana Jiménez, granddaughter of a sixteenth-century gobernador and the sole heir of one of the region's most powerful native families. Their son Antonio served as gobernador for many years. People said he looked Spanish, and his wife was the daughter of a prominent Spaniard and a cacica. Their children's baptisms were recorded not in the book reserved for Indians, but in the volume used for the república de españoles.

The complicity of native officials with the Spanish power structure and their dogged pursuit of personal interests frequently eroded their legitimacy in the eyes of their constituents. Kurakas in Peru who collected tribute and rounded up men to work in the silver mines at Potosí were either unwilling or unable to provide the reciprocal benefits that their forebears had supplied to the commoners, for example.

Subsistence and Survival in the República de Indios

The plants and animals brought by Europeans to their New World and the varied enterprises of Spanish and Portuguese colonists brought profound changes to the physical landscape of the Americas, but Indian peasants continued their traditional modes of subsistence while borrowing selectively from the foreigners. Native crops such as maize and beans in Mesoamerica and potatoes in the Andes remained dietary staples, and Indians were slow to adopt plows and other tools as long as familiar techniques continued to meet their needs. Customary patterns of land tenure officially prevailed, with ownership of most lands vested in the community and native officials in charge of allocating plots to heads of households. In practice, though, passing years saw the increasing privatization of lands, as caciques and kurakas, along with enterprising commoners and non-Indian residents, accumulated more and more lands for themselves.

The greatest challenge the repúblicas de indios in Mesoamerica and the Andes faced was the encroachment on their lands by Spanish estates. In the late sixteenth and early seventeenth centuries, when the Indian population was at its lowest, coexistence was possible, but once native numbers began to increase in the eighteenth century, competition for land and water intensified, especially in areas where Spanish penetration was heaviest. Villages also contended with one another for access to these vital resources, often perpetuating disputes that dated back hundreds of years. They employed a variety of tactics, including forcibly occupying lands, damaging irrigation works, and physically attacking hacienda employees, in an effort to reclaim lands they believed were rightfully theirs. Community leaders also mastered the intricacies of the Spanish legal system and often traveled to Lima or Mexico City to present their complaints in person to the viceroy or the audiencia. They carefully safeguarded sixteenth-century maps and other credentials that supported their case. These papers are replete with references to lands possessed "from time immemorial," long before the arrival of the Spaniards.

Natives also used the courts to get relief from excessive tribute, forced labor obligations, and other abuses. On many occasions they won, in part because the authorities may have still harbored sympathy for the Indians based on the ideals of Bartolomé de las Casas and other sixteenth-century advocates. More importantly, Spanish officials understood the strategic importance of sustaining the native population, for Indians could pay their tributes and serve their labor obligations only if they retained enough land to provide for themselves. Although wealthy landowners might easily bribe a judge to rule in their favor, Indians often proved adept in playing various power figures against one another. They could frequently count on help from their parish priest, whose livelihood depended on the continued viability of the village economy. These victories came at a price, for in resorting to Spanish courts and Spanish laws to defend themselves, native communities tacitly and probably unwittingly acknowledged the legitimacy of colonial rule. On the other hand, one could also say that the authorities' willingness to hear and sometimes act on their complaints earned them a certain measure of legitimacy in the eyes of native plaintiffs.

Slice of Life   THE INDIANS OF OAXTEPEC DEFEND
THEIR LAND AND WATER

AT THE BEGINNING of this chapter, we met the native leaders of the Mexican village of Oaxtepec, who in 1580 looked back on the manifold changes they had witnessed since the Spanish conquest. Little did these caciques know that their community would face continued challenges to its survival for generations to come. These challenges would force their descendants to capitalize on the resources available to them, to enter the cash economy by selling produce native to their land as well as crops brought by the Europeans, and to seek help from sympathetic outsiders. As the caciques gave their testimony in 1580, the area around Oaxtepec—today, the Mexican state of Morelos—stood on the brink of a major shift in patterns of landholding. In the final two decades of the sixteenth century, non-Indians acquired substantial lands near Oaxtepec, lands left vacant by the precipitous decline in the indigenous population, and expanded the cultivation of sugarcane.

From the beginning of the seventeenth century until Mexico's Revolution of 1910, the villagers of Oaxtepec had to compete with sugar haciendas for access to the land and water they needed for their own subsistence and for the fruit, vegetables, and sugarcane they produced for sale. Meanwhile, the village's fertile soil and agreeable climate attracted growing numbers of non-Indians who bought or rented lands from Indian leaders and became permanent residents in violation of royal prohibitions. Officially, however, Oaxtepec remained part of the "república de indios."

A particularly troublesome adversary was a hacienda named Pantitlán, and the object of contention was not land, but water coming from a spring located near the church in Oaxtepec. For many years, Pantitlán lay in ruins, and the villagers enjoyed exclusive use of the water. In 1750, a new owner decided to refurbish the property's sugar mill and expand production. At first, the two parties struck a compromise that allowed each to have access to the water, but by 1776 the hacienda's owner took the villagers to court, charging that they had taken most of the water, halting his sugar mill at the height of the harvest. Protracted litigation and several out-of-court settlements over the next two decades failed to produce a lasting accord. Hacendados in the region circulated rumors that the villagers were planning a general uprising with support from other indigenous communities. Perhaps fear of an insurrection prompted the owner of Pantitlán to agree to build an aqueduct that would enable him to draw water from a nearby river instead of relying exclusively on the contested spring. In this case, then, the villagers won something of a victory; their only concession was to allow a part of the aqueduct to cross their land. The villagers and the hacienda owner continued to bicker over the use of water from the spring, however.

Meanwhile, the villagers carried on a long-standing water dispute with the owner of another hacienda, who accused them of damaging his aqueducts in order to divert water to their crops and to the thousands of banana plants cultivated by the town surgeon, the parish priest, and many other non-Indians who rented village lands. This feud reached particularly acrimonious levels in 1786, central Mexico's famous "year of hunger," when the warm, fertile valleys of present-day Morelos were able to produce extra crops of maize after a devastating crop failure in less-favored locales. For centuries, the Indians and other residents of Oaxtepec had produced irrigated crops of maize in the winter and sold it in the months when supplies were lowest and prices highest, and they stood to make an especially good profit as famine spread and maize prices escalated. A court decision awarded the Indians access to extra water in 1786, but 2 years later the hacendado won a reversal of that verdict. Oaxtepec's response was to renew its battle with Pantitlán over the spring water, continuing their litigation into the first decade of the nineteenth century.

Questions for Discussion

Suppose that the indigenous people of Oaxtepec had decided to close their community to non-Indians and to withdraw completely from the cash economy. Would this strategy have even been possible? Why or why not? Would it have enabled them to better survive the effects of Spanish domination? Why or why not?

When litigation and other means of rectifying abuses failed, a community might resort to violence. Men and women picked up rocks or machetes and attacked a specific target, usually a person or object directly associated with a particular grievance—a priest, government official, or hacienda overseer; a village jail; or a hacienda's irrigation works. Colonial officials met these challenges with a judicious blend of repression and appeasement. Usually, they singled out a few alleged ringleaders for exemplary punishment that might include forced obraje service, fines, public whippings, or exile from the area. They sometimes ordered the construction of a stone gallows in the center of a village to remind residents of the power of the state. Most often, however, the incidents ended with some sort of conciliatory gesture on the part of the authorities. The natives might win at least one round of an ongoing land dispute or gain reprieve from a new increase in taxes, labor obligations, or church fees.

Rarely did these revolts extend beyond a single village, much less challenge the colonial order as such. Most native peoples simply did not see themselves as "Indians" in a way that would have prompted them to unite with neighboring villages with which they had outstanding land disputes and other quarrels. Historian William B. Taylor, who has studied this kind of violence in central Mexico and Oaxaca, concluded that the native villagers in these areas were "good rebels but poor revolutionaries."

Native Communities and the Cash Economy

Indians also made profitable compromises with the evolving cash economy. Income from the sale of agricultural produce and craft items and wages earned laboring in mines and on haciendas provided natives with cash to meet tribute obligations, pay legal fees, buy personal items, make improvements on their churches, and finance community fiestas. In the seventeenth and eighteenth centuries, vendors from Huarochirí in Peru supplied the Lima market with apples, peaches, guavas, chirimoyas (a fruit native to the Andes), maize, and chile peppers, as well as cattle, sheep, goats, and llamas. When they went to Potosí to serve their labor obligations, mita workers carried coca, freeze-dried potatoes, and other commodities to sell at the inflated prices that prevailed in the mining center. Caciques and kurakas used their connections to foster their personal commercial ventures.

A kind of mutual accommodation between haciendas and nearby Indian villages characterized rural society in central Mexico. Large landowners needed extra workers during planting and harvesting seasons, but they wished to avoid the expense of maintaining a large resident labor force. The villages provided a handy reservoir of temporary labor, and it behooved the landowner to see to it that the Indians retained enough land to support themselves during much of the year, but not to the point where they could supply all of their needs without recourse to the cash economy.

Forces other than the need for cash also drew Indians into the larger economy. The *reparto de mercancías,* whereby corregidores and alcaldes mayores pressured natives into buying commodities from them, was common throughout Mesoamerica and the Andes. Sometimes they furnished mules and other items vital to the Indians, but this trade might also involve items for which the natives had no use. Local officials also forced Indians to sell produce to them at prices well below market rates.

In some places, however, Indians willingly participated in the reparto de mercancías because it served their economic interests. In Oaxaca in southern Mexico, for example, Mixtecs and Zapotecs produced cochineal, a red dye extracted from insects that lived on cacti native to the region. Cochineal was highly coveted in Europe, and by the eighteenth century it ranked second only to silver among exports from Mexico. The actual production of this valuable commodity remained almost entirely in native hands, but most Indians needed credit to participate in the trade. At the beginning of each year, local officials advanced them funds to buy the "nests" of pregnant insects that they placed on the cacti. In return, when they harvested their product, they gave their creditors one pound of cochineal for each 1.5 pesos they had received. The Mixtecs and Zapotecs could have gotten higher returns by selling their cochineal in the open market. Without credit, however, they would not have been able to produce it in the first place, and few people other than the corregidores were willing to lend to poor peasants. The 1.5 pesos they received at the start of the season usually exceeded the cost of producing a pound of cochineal, so the arrangement helped them meet other expenses as well. From the natives' point of view, doing business with the corregidores made economic sense.

Families and Households in the República de Indios

The basic unit of production and subsistence in the república de indios was the household. European colonization had brought important changes to indigenous family life. In place of the extended families and other kinship networks common in indigenous society, missionaries attempted to impose the patriarchal nuclear family. They exhorted their converts to accept premarital chastity, monogamy, and the lifelong bonds of Christian matrimony. In the privacy of the confessional, priests evidently probed the most intimate details of the Indians' lives. A confessional manual written in 1631 suggested more than 200 questions that confessors might ask penitents about sexual thoughts and behavior.

The demands of colonialism also upset traditional kinship networks. Widespread mortality left many old and young people without close relatives. Men were gone for weeks or months at a time while they performed forced labor service, and many never returned. Women therefore shouldered heavier burdens at home. When tribute obligations included quantities of woven cloth, women's work further increased. The imposition of highly patriarchal Spanish legal and religious concepts throughout the colonies and the breakdown of the ayllu in Peru disrupted the cooperative and complementary arrangements between men's work and women's work that had characterized gender roles in pre-Hispanic society. Women also found it more difficult to hang on to inherited property in the Spanish legal system. There is evidence of high levels of domestic violence. Spanish social and legal norms recognized a man's right, in fact his obligation, to administer physical "correction" to his wife, children, and other members of the household. Only when such punishments exceeded the bounds considered appropriate did the authorities intervene, and many cases went unreported. Native women were frequent victims of homicide, usually at the hands of their husbands.

Native society thus experienced multiple pressures at the level of the family and the household. Indigenous people nonetheless found new ways to build and maintain kinship networks. Particularly important was the Spanish practice of *compadrazgo,* literally co-parenthood, that created a special bond between a child's parents and godparents. Godparents might also assume guardianship of a child if the parents died. Compadrazgo thus provided an alternative family when migration, disease, and other calamities tore apart natural kinship networks. There is evidence too that the persistence of native notions of community life mitigated against some of the more harmful effects of Spanish patriarchalism. The Mixtecs and Zapotecs, for example, continued as before the conquest to identify women as members of the community as a whole rather than simply as the wives of specific men. When a husband inflicted physical injury on his wife, he had to answer to the entire community.

Native peoples also ignored the church's teachings on sexuality. In Peru, they persisted in the practice of *sirvinacuy,* or trial marriage, in which young couples lived together to test their mutual compatibility before formally marrying in the church. Those who decided not to marry went their separate ways without any loss of personal honor. Children born of these unions, illegitimate in the eyes of the church, bore no such social stigma in Andean society.

RELIGION AND COMMUNITY LIFE IN THE REPÚBLICA DE INDIOS

The evangelization of native peoples in Mesoamerica and the Andes began almost as soon as the Spanish arrived. For many Indians, the first European they met was a priest, whether Franciscan, Dominican, Jesuit, or a member of the secular clergy. Missionaries initially claimed great success in converting the natives, but their early optimism soon waned. They often accused natives of backsliding into pagan rituals and gave up on the idea of creating a native priesthood. Even though colonial Indians were relegated to a decidedly inferior standing within the church, Catholicism as they understood it occupied an important place in their lives. The local church was often a focus of community pride, and Christian festivals gave them regular opportunities to come together and reinforce the ties that bound families and villages together. In an effort to make sense of their continually changing material and cultural world, native peoples freely combined Catholic symbols and dogma with elements of pre-Hispanic religious custom.

Natives as Catholics

Most Indians received rudimentary instruction in the intricacies of the faith. Parents usually brought their infants to church to be baptized within a few days of birth. Children attended catechism classes, where they memorized prayers such as the Our Father and the Ave María and precepts such as the Ten Commandments. Bilingual catechisms used to instruct native children in the Andes suggest that these youngsters were presented with a simplified version of Christian doctrine, reflecting the priests' skepticism about natives' intellectual and spiritual capacities. Priests in Indian parishes enforced regular attendance at Sunday mass.

Catholics were supposed to receive the sacraments of confession and the Eucharist once they reached the age of reason, about seven or eight, although many Indians, especially in the Andes, never did participate in these rites. Perhaps because their indigenous religions had nothing comparable to Christian notions of individual sin and guilt, many Nahuas in central Mexico reportedly avoided the sacrament of confession whenever they could. The incompetence of priests in native languages could also limit the quality of confessions. If a touring bishop reached their community, they might also be confirmed, and whenever possible, priests administered the last rites to the dying. Many adults participated in the sacrament of matrimony as well, although priests continually complained of the number of couples living together without the official blessing of the church.

Relations between Indian peasants and their priests often became strained. Priests demanded perquisites from their parishioners over and above the customary fees they charged for their services. Native women were required to perform domestic chores in the priest's household, for example. Priests sometimes used physical punishment in disciplining their flocks. When secular priests replaced the regular clergy in Indian parishes, they frequently spent so much time on personal business ventures that they neglected their spiritual duties. Parishioners also complained that their priests meddled in village politics and failed to live up to the ideals they preached, especially in the area of sexual behavior. Many priests fathered children by native women.

Belief and Practice in the República de Indios

Native persistence in what priests viewed as vestiges of their old religion, including clandestine rituals that involved the use of hallucinogens and the sacrifice of small animals, proved to be a major source of tension between priests and their Indian parishioners, especially in Peru. Andeans venerated their *huacas*—traditional sacred places and the divinities that inhabited them. Although Indian men often fell under Spanish scrutiny as they performed obligatory labor service, women found chances to retreat to remote locales where they conducted elaborate rituals in honor of these local deities, as they had done in pre-Hispanic times. Native peoples in the Andes also revered the mummified remains of ancestors. They exhumed the corpses of relatives from church cemeteries, dressed them in traditional garb, offered sacrifices of llamas, guinea pigs, maize, and coca, and reinterred them in their old burial grounds.

Numerous campaigns aimed at what churchmen called the "uprooting of idolatry" occurred throughout Peru in the seventeenth century, and a special jail in Lima confined the most recalcitrant offenders. The clergy justified such measures by pointing out that the natives had been converted to the true faith but had relapsed—the same rationale used when non-Indians faced prosecution by the Inquisition. But priests differed among themselves as to what actions constituted dangerous heresy worthy of prosecution and what customs were harmless elements of indigenous culture, inferior to European folkways but not socially disruptive in and of themselves.

Native peoples accepted certain elements of Christianity, retained many old practices and beliefs, and in the end created something new that served personal and community needs through contact with the supernatural. They were more receptive to Christian teachings that fit well with traditional beliefs. For example, native peoples showed particular enthusiasm for the Catholic devotion to the souls in purgatory, perhaps because it meshed with their customary reverence for their dead ancestors.

Priest interrogating an alleged Indian idolater, from the manuscript of the native Andean historian Felipe Guaman Poma de Ayala, who served as an interpreter and assistant to a Spanish priest charged with investigating native idolatry in Peru.

As time passed, the distinction blurred between that which was pre-Hispanic and that which was Catholic. Native Americans showed great devotion to Catholic saints without discarding traditional notions that assumed the presence of the sacred in many animals, plants, and inanimate objects. People in central Mexico, for example, revered bees that produced wax used in the candles that burned on the church altar. Like so many aspects of their life as colonial subjects, the religious experience of Native Americans was a vibrant mix of indigenous elements, European Catholicism, and daily adaptation.

Religion and Community Identity

Whatever the natives' level of doctrinal sophistication or religious orthodoxy, villages took pride in the size and beauty of their principal church, often spending lavish sums on church bells, altarpieces, and other adornments. At the urging of a Franciscan missionary, the Indians of Huejotzingo in central Mexico commissioned a Flemish painter from Mexico City to fashion an altarpiece for their church. Completed in 1586 at a cost of more than 6000 pesos, the altarpiece featured statues of 15 different saints and numerous paintings showing scenes from the life of Christ. Rituals that were at least superficially Catholic, from regular Sunday mass to special feast days, brought the community together on many occasions throughout the year.

A cadre of Indian laymen, known as *fiscales,* helped maintain the church and led devotional services in the absence of a priest. Others served as *cantores* (singers) or sacristans. In central Mexico, these officers were known collectively in Nahuatl as *teopantlaca,* literally, "church people." These positions often carried social prestige, opportunities for personal profit and exemption from tribute. Fiscales in one community near Mexico City required children to bring them gifts of maize when they came to church for catechism class. Following Catholic custom, these positions were restricted to males. Women's roles in official worship services were not as well defined, but in many places they took responsibility for sweeping the church and cleaning the altar linens.

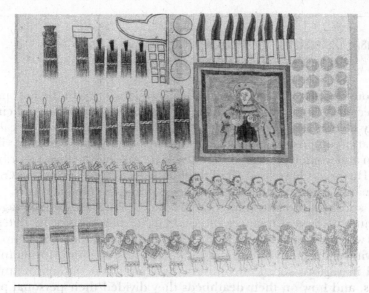

Painting made in 1531 by Indians of Huejotzingo, Mexico, showing goods and services that colonial administrators had demanded of them; one of the items was a banner of gold, silver, and feathers depicting the Virgin Mary and the child Jesus.

Central to religious life in the república de indios were the *cofradías,* organizations that fostered devotion to particular saints and provided spiritual and material benefits to members. Cofradías and the celebrations they sponsored became vehicles for community solidarity. They also provided a kind of life insurance, paying for the funerals of deceased members. Women were very active in the Indian cofradías, sometimes outnumbering male members. Leadership positions, however, were usually restricted to men, and they conferred considerable personal prestige. Indeed, a community's political officials often served in key cofradía offices as well. Specially designated village lands supported cofradía activities. Villagers either rented out these lands or cultivated them collectively, selling the produce and turning the proceeds over to cofradía officers. The Mayan cofradías of Yucatán were noted for their extensive cattle ranches, for example.

Religious holidays that were nominally Catholic became an outlet for indigenous cultural expression. After the obligatory mass and other solemnities that required the presence of a priest, natives often continued the celebration by themselves. Priests decried what they viewed as excesses—bingeing on food and alcohol, elaborate processions and fireworks displays, bullfights, dancing, and lewd behavior—as well as the blatant or subtle traces of traditional custom that accompanied the festivities. The exuberance of their religious fiestas shows how Indians in Mesoamerica and the Andes truly made Catholicism their own, picking and choosing those aspects of the faith that served the spiritual and temporal needs of individuals and communities.

How Historians Understand

MEASURING ACCULTURATION USING INDIGENOUS LANGUAGE SOURCES

As indigenous peoples learned to write their own languages in the European alphabet, they became adept at using their literacy to defend and advance their interests. Community leaders kept written records of the proceedings of their cabildos and cofradías, and composed documents that purportedly substantiated village land claims. Men and women of many different social ranks enlisted native scribes to write their wills. Historians have used all of these sources to gain perspectives on changes within the native communities during three centuries of colonial rule.

Nahuatl speakers of central Mexico produced many native language sources. These documents reveal nuances of colonial life that cannot be detected from documents written in Spanish. We learn, for example, what rituals accompanied land transfers within the native community, what kinds of polite formalities people exchanged in various social encounters, how men and women organized their households, and how on their deathbeds they divided their personal possessions among their kin. Historians using Nahuatl sources have also shown greater continuity in the practice of local government from preconquest to colonial times than what researchers working exclusively from Spanish documents had supposed.

Scholars have also tracked the process of native acculturation by examining the gradual incorporation of Spanish loanwords into Nahuatl. The Spanish brought

Introduction to Nahuatl will and testament of the Indian Juan Fabián, from the town of San Bartolomé Atenco, August 1, 1617.

many objects and concepts for which no Nahuatl equivalent existed. At first, the natives simply used their own words. For horse they said *macatl,* the word for deer, and a firearm was a "fire trumpet." Baptism was *quaatequia,* literally, "to pour water on the head." They did, however, begin adopting a Nahuatlized form of the Spanish word *Castilla* (Castile), which they added to indigenous words to describe other Spanish imports. Wheat thus became "Castile maize."

Within a couple of decades, Spanish nouns began to make their way into Nahuatl. Natives learned to call a horse a *caballo,* and used the words *vaca* (cow) and *mula* (mule) as well. The Spanish *trigo* (wheat) replaced "Castile maize." By the end of the sixteenth century, nouns such as *cuchillo,* the Spanish word for knife, and *camisa* (shirt) had been so thoroughly absorbed into Nahuatl that most Indians probably did not even recognize these items as innovations introduced by the Spaniards.

Natives also adopted words associated with Catholicism such as *misa* (mass), *cruz* (cross), and *Santa Trinidad* (Holy Trinity), along with the days of the week and the months of the year. When Juan Fabián of the town of San Bartolomé Atenco wrote his Nahuatl will in 1617, he began by noting that the day was Monday (*lunes*), the first of August. He then proceeded to invoke the three persons of the Holy Trinity and referred to *Dios* (God) throughout his text.

Terms such as *gobernador, virrey* (viceroy), and *obispo* (bishop) also began appearing regularly in Nahuatl documents by the late sixteenth century. Frequent appearances of the word *pleito* (lawsuit) reflected their growing recourse to the Spanish legal system. In the seventeenth century, Spanish verbs, conjugated as if they were Nahuatl words, began appearing. Especially common were such verbs as *pasear* (to stroll), *confirmar* (to confirm, a reference to the sacrament of confirmation), and *prendar* (to pawn). Even Nahuatl grammar showed some Spanish influences.

This incipient bilingualism reflected native peoples' growing contacts with the cash economy. Scholars have also noted, however, that certain Spanish words failed to appear in Nahuatl. Particularly notable for its absence is the word "indio." The Nahuas persisted in identifying themselves in terms of their local community, despite the strong Spanish tendency to lump all natives together in this category.

Comparisons between Nahuatl sources and colonial documents written in other indigenous languages have suggested that the natives of central Mexico probably experienced far greater exposure to European influence than their counterparts elsewhere in Latin America. Sources from Yucatán, for instance, show far fewer Spanish loanwords incorporated into the Mayan language, and none of the grammatical adaptations common in Nahuatl by the late colonial period.

Questions for Discussion

What similarities and differences are there between the ways Nahuatl speakers began incorporating Spanish words into their speech and the ways people today adopt words from other languages with which they come in contact?

MISSION INDIANS

Colonization took somewhat different forms outside the core areas of Mesoamerica and the Andes. The northern frontier of Mexico, southern South America, and the interior forests of Brazil attracted fewer Spanish and Portuguese settlers. People native to these regions did not escape the negative effects of conquest, however. They too fell victim to imported diseases, and many survivors were rounded up and taken away as slaves to work in distant mines and sugar plantations. Those who remained in their original homelands became the focus of an intense missionary effort. No longer free to roam as they chose, they now derived their subsistence from intensive agriculture rather than hunting and gathering.

Jesuit and Franciscan Missions

The regular clergy spearheaded missionary efforts in Mexico and Peru during the sixteenth century. The presence of orders such as the Franciscans, Dominicans, and Jesuits in Indian parishes was supposed to be temporary. Once they had completed the initial conversion of an area, royal policy dictated that secular clerics replace them and that the orders move on to new frontiers awaiting Christianization. In practice, the regular clergy remained in control of many Indian parishes in Mesoamerica and the Andes until well into the eighteenth century. Meanwhile, though, the orders maintained an ac-

Drawings published in 1614 of Tupi Indians before and after conversion at a mission in Brazil.

tive missionary program on the fringes of Spanish and Portuguese settlement. By far the most prominent among these frontier missionaries were the Jesuits and the Franciscans.

Founded in 1534 by the Spaniard Ignatius of Loyola, the Society of Jesus—the Jesuits—attracted highly educated men from throughout Europe. Ignatius and his followers embraced a militant Catholicism and stressed the need to gain new converts for the faith to compensate for souls lost to Protestantism in Europe. The new colonies of Spain and Portugal offered them an ideal field for their missionary enterprise. The first Jesuits in the Americas were the six who accompanied Governor Tomé de Sousa to Brazil in 1549. They quickly set to work gathering Tupi and other native peoples into the mission villages they called *aldeias*. The numbers of Jesuits working in Brazil grew steadily, reaching 110 by 1574 and 165 in 1610.

Although their detractors accused them of exploiting the native peoples of Brazil, Jesuits could also be found among the most outspoken defenders of the Indians. The most famous of these was Antônio Vieira, who had once served as King João IV's personal confessor and diplomatic emissary. In the mid-seventeenth century, Vieira worked deep within the Amazon territory. Echoing the words of Bartolomé de las Casas and other Spanish Dominicans of the previous century, he declared that those who captured or owned native slaves faced eternal damnation unless they mended their ways. Meanwhile he and his fellow Jesuits rounded up 200,000 natives from the Amazon basin and settled them into 54 mission aldeias close to the coast.

Jesuits arrived in Peru in 1568 and Mexico in 1572. They became especially active in ministering to Indians in the Andes. They also worked briefly in what is now the southeastern United States, setting up missions from Virginia to Florida, until native hostility forced them to abandon their efforts. Beginning in 1610, the Jesuits established a large mission complex among the Guaraní of Paraguay, who saw the missions as refuges from other hostile tribes and Spanish colonists, as well as a place to acquire useful European goods such as iron tools and livestock. By the early eighteenth century, more than 100,000 Guaraní lived in 30 separate mission units, called *reducciones*. These missions extended well beyond the present-day borders of Paraguay, into Brazil and Argentina.

Northwestern Mexico was another important focus of the Jesuits' program. They moved up the coasts of Sinaloa and Sonora and into Baja California in the seventeenth century. By the 1690s, Jesuits had reached the present-day Sonora–Arizona border, where the Austrian-born Eusebio Francisco Kino founded a number of missions. To the east of the Sierra Madre, Jesuit missions included such native groups as Tarahumaras, Tepehuanes, and Conchos.

Franciscan missionaries were also active in areas that would one day become part of the United States. They arrived in Florida in 1573, and by the mid-seventeenth century, their missions extended along the Atlantic coast from St. Augustine north to just below the present site of Savannah, Georgia, and westward across what is now the Florida panhandle. The growth of British colonies in South Carolina and Georgia forced them to scale back their efforts in the eighteenth century, however.

The Franciscans also began work in New Mexico at the end of the sixteenth century. There the natives already lived in sedentary villages, and Spaniards accordingly called them the Pueblo Indians—the word "pueblo" in Spanish means village or town. Therefore, the people of New Mexico continued to live in the same settlements, even the same clustered apartment-like complexes of their ancestors. Indeed, the people of Acoma, New Mexico, today proudly assert that theirs is the longest continuously occupied community in the United States. Still, the transition to Franciscan tutelage spelled enormous change for the Pueblo peoples. As the only ecclesiastical personnel in New Mexico, the friars wielded substantial power, so much so that some historians have called their regimen a virtual theocracy. The Franciscans quarreled frequently with Spanish authorities in New Mexico, even excommunicating the governor on more than one occasion. In the early eighteenth century, they extended their work to Texas, founding a cluster of missions near present-day San Antonio. After 1769, Franciscans established a chain of missions extending up the California coast from San Diego to San Francisco.

Native Peoples in the Jesuit and Franciscan Missions

Resettlement in a mission exposed native peoples to the ravages of European diseases while often requiring the survivors to make drastic changes in their lifestyles. For many Indians, mission life meant a difficult transition from hunting and gathering or semisedentary, slash-and-burn agriculture to residence in a fixed location where their livelihood came from more intensive agriculture and from craft specialties learned from the missionaries.

Ruins of a mission church established by Franciscans in 1626 at Quarai, southeast of present-day Albuquerque, New Mexico. The Quarai church and two others together comprise the Salinas Pueblo Missions National Monument. The church was abandoned in the 1670s and never reoccupied.

This change might in turn alter the natives' customary divisions of labor between males and females. Among the Tarahumara in northern Mexico, men abandoned hunting and warfare and assumed a greater share of agricultural labor under Jesuit tutelage, while women spent more time tending livestock introduced by the Spanish. Resistance was common, and natives were often "reduced" to mission life by force.

Life within the missions was much more structured than what the native peoples had known, even for the Guaraní of Paraguay, who already lived in well-ordered sedentary villages before the coming of the Jesuits. Here as elsewhere, the missionaries set up native governing bodies that at least superficially resembled the cabildos of the república de indios in Mesoamerica and the Andes. Social distinctions became more marked than they had been in precolonial times, as men appointed to these positions claimed exemption from routine labor and other privileges. Denied formal roles in this new hierarchy, native women found their access to community resources reduced as well.

Mission Indians and Colonial Society

In theory, the missions were cut off from contact with the outside world, but in fact the native peoples congregated within them were hardly isolated from the larger colonial society. The Jesuit reducciones of Paraguay offered particularly tempting targets for Brazilian slavers, known as bandeirantes, who operated out of São Paulo. To defend against such attacks, the Jesuits organized mission Indians into militia units. Elsewhere, however, missionaries tolerated or even facilitated the drafting of Indians for various labor obligations and relied on military forces to assist them in rounding up and disciplining their charges.

From Paraguay to Arizona, the missions formed one component of a complex network of Jesuit enterprises. Throughout Latin America, Jesuits accumulated substantial property in the form of haciendas, plantations, and obrajes, using the proceeds to support the missions and the *colegios* where young men trained for the priesthood and other professions. In Brazil and elsewhere, Jesuit estates owned numerous African slaves. As landed proprietors, the Jesuits became shrewd businessmen, and they applied their managerial acumen to their missions as well. Crops and craft items produced by mission Indians sold in regional markets from Sonora to southern South America. The Paraguayan missions became famous for the production of *yerba mate,* a native plant used to make tea. Franciscans showed a similar entrepreneurial bent, shipping mission-grown foodstuffs from Florida to Cuba, for example.

The possibility that the French and the English might somehow penetrate their northern frontier and make off with the treasure of Zacatecas was a constant preoccupation of the Spanish. To secure that frontier, the crown made repeated efforts to lure colonists from the mother country and from central Mexico. Few potential settlers responded, for the bustling cities, fertile agricultural fields, and mining centers to the south offered more attractive possibilities. Many undoubtedly agreed with the Franciscan missionary who called Texas "the land so bad that nobody would want it," and it was just as hard to lure settlers to California later on. Spanish officials therefore saw no alternative but to attempt to make loyal Christian "colonists" out of peoples already native to the northern frontier. The missionary enterprise thus served the king's political purposes, and for this reason the crown provided financial support for the Franciscans in New Mexico, Texas, and California. Local officials in these provinces enlisted pacified natives such as Pueblos and Opatas to join them in fighting Apaches and other recalcitrant tribes.

NATIVE PEOPLES AND THE COLONIAL ORDER

The native peoples of the Americas responded to Spanish and Portuguese colonization in many different ways. Some became so fluent in Spanish that they became known as *ladinos,* a word used in medieval Spain to describe nonnative speakers of Castilian. Quite a few Indians became so thoroughly acculturated that they "passed" as mestizos and no longer functioned as members of the república de indios. Others, like the caciques and kurakas of Mexico and Peru, found powerful incentives to retain their "Indian" identity while collaborating with colonial authorities and wealthy Spaniards. Still others actively participated in the expansion of European hegemony. The Tlaxcalans of central Mexico allied with Cortés to defeat the Aztecs, and their descendants helped colonize the northern frontier of New Spain. At the opposite end of the spectrum were those who remained outside the effective control of the Spanish and Portuguese states.

In the sixteenth century, there were still men and women alive who could remember the days before the coming of the Europeans, and they certainly passed on these recollections to children and grandchildren too young to know anything but the new order of things. Some communities preserved these memories in oral and written traditions that have survived to the present. But in many places, the passing centuries blurred the divide between "pre-Columbian" and "post-conquest" in the historical memory of individuals and communities.

Indians in the República de Españoles

Spanish towns and cities quickly became magnets for Indians. Men wishing to abandon life in their home communities could easily find work in construction, transport, or craft specialties, while native women were in great demand as domestic servants and wet nurses. Native elites sometimes established second residences in Spanish cities and sent their sons to be educated at the Jesuit schools in Mexico City, Cuzco, and Lima.

Mexico City and Cuzco were built on the sites of important pre-Hispanic population centers, and they continued to be home to thousands of natives in the postconquest period, but newly created cities such as Lima in Peru and Puebla in Mexico also had sizable native populations. In its early years, Lima's Indian population included many natives of New Spain and Central America, especially Nicaragua, brought as slaves by the conquistadors, but soon migrants from the Peruvian highlands joined them in the City of the Kings. The population of Bogotá included 10,000 Indians and only 3000 Hispanics at the end of the seventeenth century.

Colonial authorities tried to maintain a separation between the república de españoles and the república de indios even in the cities. They officially reserved some quarters, most often at the center of town, for Spaniards, and required Indians to live in designated neighborhoods on the outskirts. Separate parish churches were set up to minister to Indians and non-Indians. In Mexico City, the cabildo marked off a 13-square-block area at the center of town and declared this the *traza,* the area for españoles. Four native quarters surrounded the traza and together comprised the community known as San Juan Tenochtitlan, and to the north lay another Indian settlement, Santiago Tlatelolco. Both of these communities had a native gobernador and other officers, just like villages in rural areas. Residents of these urban Indian *barrios* (neighborhoods) were subject to tribute and forced labor obligations.

In practice, segregated living patterns were impossible to enforce. As early as 1555, the Mexico City cabildo permitted Spaniards to acquire land within the Indian sector, and Indians had already begun residing in the traza. Most were employed as domestic servants and lived in the homes of their employers. By the end of the sixteenth century, Indians and non-Indians often lived side by side, both inside and outside the traza, and worshipped together at "Spanish" and "Indian" churches alike. In many other cities, local authorities failed to establish even the fiction of separate quarters for the two groups.

Mining towns also drew thousands of Indians, some as forced workers under the mita and repartimiento and others who became permanent wage laborers. Mitayos often brought their families with them when they went to work at Potosí, and many of them stayed on after completing their obligatory service. Native settlements known as *rancherías* surrounded the town. Fourteen churches served the native rancherías at Potosí in the seventeenth century. Similar clusters of Indian residences could also be found on the outskirts of Zacatecas at the height of its mining boom. In the eighteenth century, residents of the northern Mexican mining town of Chihuahua used the generic term "indios mexicanos" to refer to Indians who had migrated there from central New Spain.

Urban Indians mingled not only with Spaniards but also with mestizos, mulattos, and blacks. Many learned Spanish, not only to speak with non-Indians, but also to converse with Indians who spoke different languages. In the process, ethnic distinctions among various groups dissolved. These indios ladinos often found work as court interpreters and town criers. City dwellers adopted many other trappings of a Europeanized lifestyle and became adept at a wide variety of crafts. As early as 1569, one observer noted that the Indians of Mexico City had mastered virtually every trade imaginable. They made swords, saddles, and European-style clothing and hats for the city's growing Spanish population. Spanish artisans came to view them as competitors and did whatever they could to exclude Indians from membership in their guilds.

Despite their considerable acculturation, most natives living in cities maintained a certain identity as Indians, especially through the cofradías that were as important to them as to their counterparts in rural areas. Here as in the peasant villages of the república de indios, native cofradías excluded Spaniards and other non-Indians. In 1585, Lima had seven Indian cofradías, along with six for Spaniards and ten for blacks and mulattos. Local custom often assigned native individuals and their cofradías prominent roles in the public ceremonial life of Spanish towns. Representatives of 82 Indian cofradías from Mexico City and nearby pueblos marched in a procession marking the funeral of King Philip IV in 1665. In 1723, the city of Lima staged an elaborate celebration of the marriage of a member of Spain's royal family. Twelve Indian men, most of whom could claim cacique lineage, marched in the city-wide parade dressed as Inca kings.

Authorities maintained an ambivalent attitude toward urban Indians. The presence of large numbers of native workers was essential to the quality of urban life, but Indians were seen as a threat to social stability in the cities. In 1692, Indians and other lower classes of Mexico City openly rebelled, protesting food shortages and setting fire to the viceregal palace. In the wake of the uprising, city authorities banned the sale of pulque and took other strongly repressive measures against Indian residents, whom they characterized as "lazy, vagabond, useless, insolent, and villainous people."

"Indios Bárbaros"

Despite the sustained efforts of church and crown to bring all the colonies' natives under Spanish and Portuguese tutelage, many groups remained more or less permanently outside their control, living *sin rey, sin fe, sin ley*—without king, without faith, without law. Because they rejected Christianization and subjugation to Spanish rule, Apaches, Araucanians, and others remained *indios bárbaros* (literally, barbarian Indians) in the eyes of settlers and authorities alike.

The Apaches of the northern frontier of Mexico were one group who successfully resisted Spanish encroachments. From the seventeenth century forward, they preyed upon Hispanic settlements in New Mexico and Pueblo villages, carrying off foodstuffs, horses, guns, and tools. In the eighteenth century, as British and French colonies in North America pushed other groups westward into Apache territory, raids extended farther south and west, to Chihuahua and beyond. The many *presidios* (military posts) that appeared along the frontier did little to stop Apache depredations. In southern Chile, the Araucanians posed a similar threat to European settlement throughout the colonial period. Alonso de Ercilla y Zúñiga, a sixteenth-century Spanish military officer who fought against the Araucanians, immortalized their bravery and tenacity in a poetic epic of more than 2000 verses, *La araucana*.

The ability of these peoples to resist was abetted by the fact that they lived in regions that were relatively marginal in the eyes of colonists, lacking precious metals and not well suited to the production of valuable export crops. At the same time, however, they also showed considerable ingenuity in using the tools of the Europeans to preserve their autonomy. Frontier groups acquired Spanish horses early on, and they soon became expert horsemen. By 1600, the Araucanians reportedly had more horses than the Spanish settlers in Chile did. The Araucanians also changed their military tactics, not only learning to fight on horseback but also attaching the tips of Spanish swords to their lances. They even made their own gunpowder to use in weapons they captured from the enemy. These so-called barbarians skillfully adapted their culture to meet the needs of their changing situation. Only with the development of new technology—barbed wire, repeating rifles, railroads, and telegraphs—in the late nineteenth century did the national governments of Chile, Argentina, Mexico, and the United States succeed in finally subduing the natives of their respective frontiers.

Their ability to fend off Spanish rule did not mean that the Apaches and Araucanians were exempted from the hardships and abuses of colonialism. Like other indigenous peoples, they fell victim to the diseases brought to the Americas by Europeans and Africans. Laws forbidding the establishment of new encomiendas or the outright enslavement of native peoples carried no weight on the frontier. Leading citizens of New Mexico, often including the governor himself, reaped substantial profits from the sale of captured Apaches, especially women and children. A similar trade characterized frontier life in Chile. Persistent resistance thus brought no reprieve from the devastating impact of the European invasion of America.

Regional Revolts

In addition to the challenges posed by unsubdued "barbarians," Spanish and Portuguese authorities also had to reckon with acts of open defiance by natives who had supposedly accepted colonial rule. We noted previously that Indians in Mesoamerica and the Andes sometimes employed violence to gain relief from specific taxes, land alienation, or abusive priests and government officials, but seldom did these rebellions spread to surrounding villages. From time to time, however, native revolts assumed a regional character and questioned the fundamental basis of civil and ecclesiastical authority, and these actions provoked more drastic responses from colonial officials. Some were millenarian movements with the stated goal of overturning the existing social order, reminiscent of such early colonial revolts as Taqui Onkoy in Peru. These late colonial rebels made much more extensive use of Christian religious symbols than their sixteenth-century counterparts.

One such upheaval briefly swept Chiapas in southern Mexico in 1712. People from Mayan villages rallied around María López, a 13-year-old native girl who claimed to have seen a vision of the Virgin Mary. Her father Agustín, who served as sacristan in the local parish church in his home village of Cancuc, joined other men in building a chapel on the spot where the Virgin had reportedly appeared. There María took up residence and preached to growing numbers of Mayan pilgrims from other villages. Worsening economic conditions, recent attempts by the Spanish authorities to curb what they viewed as excessive drinking and feasting associated with cofradía celebrations, and the continued abuses of colonialism, many of which fell disproportionately on Mayan women, all enhanced the appeal of a cult led by natives without the intervention of Catholic priests.

Alarmed, officials of church and state pronounced the movement to be the work of the devil, jailed some of Cancuc's native officials, and mustered militia forces to put an end to this challenge to Spanish authority. Agustín López and other Mayan men vowed to defend their shrine with armed resistance of their own, while María reportedly ordered her followers to seize all silver and other ornaments from their churches and bring them to her, "because now there is neither God nor King." In the end, however, Spanish military force prevailed, crushing the rebellion some 4 months after it began.

Sometimes these regional rebellions succeeded in casting off colonial rule altogether, at least temporarily. In 1680, the Pueblo peoples set aside the language barriers and long-standing feuds that had traditionally divided them and mounted a concerted revolt against the Hispanic presence in New Mexico. A long period of drought and the colonial authorities' growing intolerance of the natives' continuing use of pre-Hispanic religious symbols were among the immediate causes. The Pueblo uprising began on August 10, 1680. The rebels burned churches, destroyed Catholic religious images, and slaughtered some 400 Hispanic residents of Santa Fe and other communities, including several Franciscan priests. Hundreds of refugees fled southward to El Paso del Norte—today's Cuidad Juárez, Mexico. The nominal leader of the rebellion, a man called Popé, called for the destruction of all things Spanish, even uprooting European fruit trees that had flourished in New Mexico. He enjoined his followers to wash off their Christian baptism, destroy their rosaries and religious images, and remarry in traditional Pueblo rites. As word of the Pueblos' rebellion spread throughout the northern frontier, other native groups followed their example.

In 1692, colonial authorities began a counteroffensive that restored their control of New Mexico. Numerous factors contributed to the rebels' defeat. Once they had driven out the Franciscans and secular Hispanic officials, the unity they had achieved in 1680 began to crumble. Not everyone was willing to give up all material objects and rituals associated with Spanish domination. Meanwhile, Apaches stepped up their attacks on the sedentary Pueblos, prompting them to renew their alliance with the Spanish for their own protection. Their rebellion won the Pueblos some important concessions, however. They secured an end to the encomienda, and eighteenth-century authorities often looked the other way as descendants of the 1680 rebels kept a number of indigenous religious rituals alive. Although Pueblo warriors now accompanied Hispanic soldiers in campaigns against Apaches and other hostile tribes, they wore their traditional battle gear and war paint as they went.

Native Historical Memory and the Colonial Order

The natives of Latin America have sometimes been called "people without history," in the sense that traumas of the conquest and the deliberate actions of European missionaries and political authorities destroyed indigenous manuscripts and blurred the historical memories contained in oral traditions passed from one generation to another. Although these difficulties should not be underestimated, indigenous peoples in fact preserved at least some memory of their own history.

A few Indian and mestizo intellectuals in Mesoamerica and the Andes produced lengthy treatises documenting their people's history in pre-Hispanic and colonial times. One such individual, Domingo de San Antón Muñón Chimalpahin, was born in 1579 in Chalco on the outskirts of Mexico City. Educated in the capital, in 1620, he completed a lengthy Nahuatl history of his ancestral community. The mestizo Fernando de Alva Ixtlilxochitl, a descendant of Texcoco's ruling family and its gobernador in the early seventeenth century, also wrote a chronicle of his hometown. In Peru, the native historian Felipe Guaman Poma de Ayala composed a monumental history that chronicled the transition from Inca to Spanish rule. His mestizo contemporary Garcilaso de la Vega, son of a Spanish conquistador and an Inca noblewoman, penned another commentary on the history of Peru.

Not many native commoners read these histories, of course, and in some cases the manuscripts were deposited in libraries and archives only to be discovered centuries later by historians. But this did not mean that "ordinary" Indians possessed no notion of their own past. Although only a handful of their pre-Hispanic books survived, the Maya of colonial Yucatán recorded their history in what became known as the Books of Chilam Balam. In each community, elders familiar with ancient oral traditions recited what they could remember, and young men trained in European script wrote down what they heard. From generation to generation, village elders guarded them from Spanish authorities. When native peoples went to court to defend their land and water, they presented elaborate files documenting their historical claim to these resources. Rituals in honor of their ancestors also kept ancient memories alive, and Andean peoples reenacted vestiges of Inca hegemony on many ceremonial occasions.

The histories preserved, retold, and reenacted by native peoples did not always coincide with what we might regard as objective historical fact. The land titles they presented in court were often blatant forgeries or fanciful parodies of Spanish legal documents. Native elites sometime recast community histories to suggest that they had always been Christians. In the seventeenth century, the Otomí caciques of Querétaro in Mexico composed an account that emphasized the contributions of their forebears in the city's founding a century before. Their account never mentioned the coming of the Spanish, and the Otomí are identified as the Catholic conquerors who wrested control of the Querétaro region from the savage, pagan Chichimecas. The caciques did what most other societies have done, blending fact and wishful thinking to create a "usable past" that enabled them to explain their world and cope with the challenges they faced.

LATIN AMERICAN LIVES

FELIPE GUAMAN POMA DE AYALA

BORN IN THE PROVINCE OF Ayacucho just a few years after Pizarro's arrival in Peru, Felipe Guaman Poma de Ayala often stated that his father was an Andean nobleman and his mother the daughter of the Inca emperor Tupac Yupanqui. No historical documentation supports his claims, but whatever his antecedents, Guaman Poma became a prime example of the indio ladino, or acculturated Indian. At the same time, he fashioned a worldview that accommodated both Christian and indigenous Andean teachings.

A native speaker of Quechua, Guaman Poma received a good education, probably under the tutelage of missionaries. He became reasonably fluent in Spanish, learned to write the European alphabet, and read widely in Spanish theology, history, and law. This training made him an ideal candidate to serve as an interpreter for Spanish officials. On one of his most important assignments, he accompanied the priest Cristóbal de Albornoz, commissioned to investigate idolatry in the Andes in the wake of the Taki Onkoy rebellion.

Guaman Poma was not simply a servant of the Spaniards, however. He used his language skills to present lawsuits on behalf of native peoples attempting to defend their lands. On various occasions, he presented native complaints directly to the viceroy in Lima. Some of his grievances against colonial authorities were driven by his own self-interest, however, and pitted him against other indigenous people. He waged a long and ultimately unsuccessful battle against the Chachapoyas, natives from northern Peru whom the viceroy had resettled on lands claimed by Guaman Poma's extended family. His stubborn refusal to accept the viceroy's orders not only discredited his case but earned him a penalty of a public whipping and a 2-year banishment from his home town of Huamanga.

Guaman Poma penned a lengthy history of Peru under Inca and Spanish domination entitled *Primera nueva crónica y buen gobierno*, addressed to King Philip III and completed about 1615. Here he voiced a clear nostalgia for an idealized pre-Hispanic past and denounced the many abuses of the new regime. He deplored the forced resettlements that had removed entire communities from "sites selected by the most important native wise men, doctors, and philosophers and approved by the first Incas for their climate, lands, and water." He had little good to say about Spanish officials and their black slaves. With the coming of colonialism, he wrote, the Andean world had turned upside down. The book also reveals much about Guaman Poma's religious attitudes. Though he embraced Catholicism, he criticized the clergy for their pursuit of worldly gain and their notorious sexual misconduct, especially their forced liaisons with native women. He likewise condemned other officials of church and state who used excessive force in their efforts to extirpate idolatry.

Moreover, Guaman Poma did not reject Andean notions of spirituality. He dismissed the leaders of Taqui Onkoy as false shamans who had subverted traditional healing rituals, which he viewed as valid and beneficial. He recommended that dances customarily performed for the old gods be continued, but now in honor of "the true God and all that the holy Roman church demands." Indeed, he believed his people had been part of the Christian story of redemption all along. One of the three magi who visited the Christ child at Bethlehem, he claimed, was an Andean.

Nearly 1200 pages in length and featuring 398 pen-and-ink drawings, Guaman Poma's manuscript was lost for three centuries until scholars discovered it in the Royal Danish Library in Copenhagen. Historians and anthropologists have used his chronicle as a rich primary source about the indigenous people of sixteenth-century Peru.

Questions for Discussion

Felipe Guaman Poma de Ayala's book, including all 398 of his illustrations, can be viewed on the Internet, with commentary in English and in Spanish, at www.kb.dk/elib/mss/poma/. What do these images tell us about the times in which he lived?

CONCLUSION

Over the course of three centuries, indigenous peoples responded to their colonization by Spain and Portugal in ways that ranged from open defiance to self-serving accommodations detrimental to their long-range personal and collective interests. Whatever tactics they chose, they succeeded at least in capturing the attention of colonial authorities. The Spanish and Portuguese governments had to spend substantial revenues on subsidies for missionaries whose job it was to teach the natives to obey proper authorities, on courts to handle native complaints, and on military forces to repress overt challenges to colonial rule. Likewise, the Church expended time and money on periodic prosecutions of natives accused of idolatry. Nor could the owners of the mines, haciendas, plantations, and obrajes ignore nearby native peoples. Heavily dependent on Indian labor, owners of these enterprises spent considerable time and effort finding the right mix of compulsion and compensation that would turn reluctant natives into dependable workers.

Without question, natives of the Americas suffered mightily under Spanish and Portuguese colonial rule, but they also played a crucial role in shaping the history of Latin

America. Meanwhile, they borrowed selectively from the cultural baggage that the Iberians brought with them. Over the course of three centuries, they formed a new cultural synthesis, one that made sense of their changing world and that enabled them to survive and to preserve their families and their communities. For most Indians, life as colonial subjects was a complex mix of accommodation and resistance to European norms and institutions.

LEARNING MORE ABOUT LATIN AMERICANS

Ganson, Barbara. *The Guaraní Under Spanish Rule in the Río de la Plata* (Stanford, CA: Stanford University Press, 2003). An excellent history showing how the Guaraní adapted to life in the Jesuit missions of Paraguay, Argentina, and Brazil.

Knaut, Andrew. *The Pueblo Revolt of 1680: Conquest and Resistance in Seventeenth-Century New Mexico* (Norman, OK: University of Oklahoma Press, 1995). Examines the causes and consequences of the Pueblo rebellion.

Schroeder, Susan, ed. *Native Resistance and the Pax Colonial in New Spain* (Lincoln, NE: University of Nebraska Press, 1998). Six leading historians discuss resistance to colonial rule in Yucatán, Chiapas, Oaxaca, and northern Mexico.

Stern, Steve. *Peru's Indian Peoples and the Challenge of Spanish Conquest: Huamanga to 1640,* 2nd ed. (Madison, WI: University of Wisconsin Press, 1992). Describes the internal changes that occurred in indigenous society during the first century following the Spanish conquest.

Yannakakis, Yanna. *The Art of Being In-Between: Native Intermediaries, Indian Identity, and Local Rule in Colonial Oaxaca.* (Durham, NC: Duke University Press, 2008). An award-winning recent study of indigenous adaptation to colonialism in southern Mexico.

6

A NEW PEOPLE
AND THEIR WORLD

LATIN AMERICAN SOCIETY began with a handful of European sailors landing on the shores of tropical America from the Bahamas to Brazil. To them, the natives they encountered were simply *indios*. Within a short time—usually not much more than 9 months—the ethnic mix became more complicated as the first mestizos and mamelucos were born to native mothers and European fathers. Most early voyages also included a few African-born slaves, and colonists soon began importing large numbers of slaves to work their fields and perform household chores. New Christians (recent converts from Judaism) and a scattering of non-Iberian Europeans also made their way to the colonies despite official pronouncements excluding them. Along the west coasts of Mexico and South America, one could find Asians who had crossed the Pacific on the Manila galleons. Meanwhile, more and more people of mixed African, Indian, and European ancestry appeared. Many terms were coined to describe them. In Spanish America they were often simply called *pardos,* meaning dark-skinned people, or *castas,* or people of *color quebrado* ("broken color"). Other labels included *lobos* (literally, wolves) and *coyotes* in the Spanish colonies and *cabras* (goats) in Brazil.

Colonial Latin America was, then, a racially diverse society, but not everyone enjoyed equal access to power and privilege. Spanish and Portuguese immigrants and their American-born descendants claimed the premier positions for themselves and attempted to keep "inferior" people in their places. Ethnicity was not the only determinant of a person's standing in colonial society, however. Wealth was important too, and while the richest people were usually white, ambitious mestizos and mulattos could sometimes advance their positions if they were successful in mining or trade. Another criterion was honor, measured by the degree to which individuals conformed, or at least appeared to

155

conform, with written and unwritten standards governing personal behavior. These rules were highly gender specific and relegated women, regardless of their wealth or ethnicity, to subordinate positions in colonial society.

Colonial Latin Americans lived in a hierarchical society where they were expected to defer to their social betters, command respect from those who ranked beneath them, and above all to adhere to the norms of conduct appropriate to their class, gender, and ethnicity. Yet many people found ingenious ways to flout the rules or bend them to their own advantage. In the process, they created a vibrant and ever-changing society and culture.

THE MAKING OF MULTIETHNIC SOCIETIES

The first Europeans arrived in the Americas with a very clear sense of "us" and "them." They believed that the natives of this new world were so different from themselves that some of them doubted whether these strange people even had souls. From the very beginning, authorities of church and state began dictating how Europeans and "Indians" should relate to one another. Some of these rules were intended to protect the natives from exploitation, and others stipulated taxes and labor obligations that they owed to their new masters, but all of them upheld the sharp distinction between indigenous Americans and European newcomers. Law and custom also set African slaves apart from people who were free.

Officially, then, the Iberian colonies in the Western Hemisphere began with the assumption that there were three sharply distinguished categories of people: Europeans, Indians, and African slaves. Social reality was far more complex. European immigrants did not always identify with those who came from a different region of Spain or Portugal, and they usually viewed themselves as socially superior to people of European stock born in the Americas. Not everyone of African descent was a slave. The appearance of so many people of mixed ancestry further complicated the picture.

Spanish and Portuguese Immigrants

The influx of Spaniards and Portuguese continued throughout the colonial period and was especially strong whenever and wherever new mining bonanzas or other get-rich-quick opportunities appeared. These immigrants are often called *peninsulares* because they came from the Iberian Peninsula, but to their contemporaries they were *españoles europeos* (European Spaniards) or *españoles de los Reinos de Castilla* (Spaniards from the kingdom of Castile) in Spanish America, *europeus* (Europeans) or *reinóis* (from the kingdoms) in Brazil. A majority of these immigrants were male, especially during the early years. Between 1509 and 1519, only about 10 percent of the European immigrants to the Spanish colonies were female. By 1600, that proportion had grown to more than 30 percent, but in the eighteenth century, a time of heavy immigration, women constituted only about 15 percent of those arriving in the Spanish colonies.

The ratio of women to men among Portuguese immigrants to Brazil was always significantly lower—so low, in fact, that in 1549 a leading Jesuit even suggested that the numbers of white women in the colony could be increased if prostitutes were allowed to emigrate from Portugal. Not until the late seventeenth century did Portuguese authorities permit the founding of a convent in Brazil, preferring that white women choose marriage and procreation rather than a life of celibacy.

Many of the Spanish and Portuguese immigrants were young bachelors eager to make their fortunes in the Indies, while others were married men whose wives remained in Europe, at least until their husbands established themselves in their new homes. While immigrant men often had casual sex and longer-term relationships with Indian, African, and mixed-race women, when it came to marriage they usually preferred women of European descent, often the daughters or nieces of previous newcomers. Spanish and Portuguese immigrants formed tightly knit communities, often settling near relatives or people from their own hometowns.

Europeans never constituted more than a tiny minority in any given place—typically less than 2 percent of the population in major cities and even less in smaller towns and rural areas. Their economic, social, and political influence far outweighed their numbers, however. High-ranking positions in the church, the government, and the military typically belonged to peninsulares, and town councils were often top-heavy with Europeans. The most powerful merchant companies were headed by peninsulares, many of them New Christians in the sixteenth and seventeenth centuries. Europeans also figured heavily in the landowning class. More than 60 percent of Bahia's sugar planters in the period from 1680 to 1725 were either Portuguese immigrants or the sons of immigrants.

Those born in Spain and Portugal based their claims to power and prestige on their presumed purity of blood, which in the colonies meant European ancestry untainted by African or Indian mixture. European immigrants could be found in many social ranks, however. Many were master artisans, government clerks, and itinerant merchants, but some were vagabonds and criminals. Whatever their place in society, they often displayed arrogance toward those born in America. For their part, Americans of all racial groups mocked the immigrants for their speech and their unfamiliarity with the culture and terrain of the colonies. Mexicans called them *gachupines*, while Peruvians used the word *chapetones*.

Creoles

Far more numerous than the peninsular immigrants were those born in the colonies who claimed pure Spanish or Portuguese ancestry on both the paternal and maternal sides. Historians usually label these people "creoles," though in practice Spanish Americans usually just called themselves *españoles* (Spaniards). In Brazil, Americans of Portuguese descent were known as *americanos* or *brasileiros*. Some Americans of European stock became quite wealthy, as merchants and owners of mines, haciendas, and plantations. A select few attained high offices, serving as judges of the superior courts and occasionally even as viceroys. Other prominent creole families formed business partnerships or marriage alliances with high-ranking peninsular officials, even though both the Spanish and Portuguese crowns explicitly forbade such practices.

Large numbers of creoles occupied lower positions in the civil and ecclesiastical bureaucracies, while many others were artisans, petty merchants, and small landowners. Peninsular immigrants often scoffed at their pretensions to "pure" European descent. In fact, many people successfully hid their Indian and African ancestors and "passed" as whites. Those creoles who had little else going for them in the way of wealth or connections often proved the most touchy in defending their "whiteness," their sole claim to preferential status in society.

Mestizos and Mamelucos

The first Spanish American mestizos and Brazilian mamelucos were the offspring of European men and native women. Virtually all of them bore the stigma of illegitimacy, and colonial authorities viewed their growing numbers with alarm. Young males in particular were seen as troublemakers. As time passed, however, more and more mestizos and mamelucos were simply the children of racially mixed people. If their parents were married in the church, they could claim legitimacy, an important marker of social standing.

By the seventeenth and eighteenth centuries, large numbers of mestizos lived in the cities and towns of Spanish America, and even in many "Indian" villages. They worked at many different kinds of jobs. In cities, many were skilled craftsmen, even though artisan guilds often tried to exclude them. Urban mestizos also worked as domestic servants, shopkeepers, and street vendors, while in rural areas they were small farmers, overseers of haciendas and plantations, cowboys, muleteers, and itinerant peddlers (see Plate 11). Spanish law, with its neat division of colonial society into separate "republics" of Spaniards and Indians, had no official place for mestizos, so by default they became part of the Spanish community. As such they were considered *gente de razón,* or "people of reason," and they were exempt from tribute and other obligations required of Indians. Mestizo men of legitimate birth could become priests, especially if they were fluent in an indigenous language. Higher positions in the church were closed to them, however, and they were most often assigned to poor parishes in the most remote rural locations.

The situation of mamelucos in Brazil differed somewhat from that of their counterparts in Spanish America. Most of colonial Brazil's principal cities were located along the coast, where the drastic decline of the native population left comparatively few Indian women available to give birth to the first generation of mamelucos. In frontier areas farther inland, however, people of mixed European and indigenous ancestry were more numerous. They served as cultural intermediaries between the Portuguese and the natives.

African Slaves

Wherever sufficient numbers of dependable native workers could not be found, proprietors of plantations, mines, and haciendas relied on slave labor of Africans or of their American born, often racially mixed descendants. Slavery was especially common in

Brazil, the Caribbean, and the coastal areas of Central and South America. With the important exceptions of Cuba, Santo Domingo, Puerto Rico, and Venezuela, the importation of Africans into the Spanish colonies began to slow after 1650, as the developing British colonies in the Caribbean and eastern North America outbid Latin American buyers. In Mexico, the native population began to rebound ever so slightly after about 1650. They and the growing numbers of racially mixed people supplied more and more of the colony's labor needs, so that by the eighteenth century slavery had virtually disappeared in many parts of Mexico. In Brazil and Cuba, on the other hand, the importation of slaves and the institution of slavery remained viable until well into the nineteenth century (see Plate 10).

Slaves occupied key positions in the colonial economies. Recent arrivals from Africa performed heavy unskilled labor, while American-born slaves often acquired specialized skills. On plantations, slave men often held the coveted post of sugar master, entrusted with overseeing the entire process of sugar manufacture. Master artisans such as shoemakers, blacksmiths, and tailors acquired slaves and employed them in their own shops. In urban areas, masters often found it profitable to hire out skilled slaves and pocket their earnings. These slaves might enjoy considerable control over their own time and living conditions. One observer noted that slaves in Havana "go about as if they were free, working at whatever they choose, and at the end of the week or the month they give the masters the *jornal* [wages] ... some have houses in which they shelter and feed travelers, and have in those houses, slaves of their own."

Slaves in Brazil and Spanish America were usually baptized as Catholics, sometimes at their point of departure in Africa and sometimes on arrival in the colonies, but received very little formal religious instruction. In Brazil and other areas with high concentrations of slaves and a continued influx of new Africans, slaves managed to retain many elements of African culture, including religious practices and beliefs, diet, music, dance, and traditional medicine. African women played especially important roles in the transmission of their native culture to future generations of slaves and free blacks. Slaves could marry in the church, although Brazilian sugar planters often discouraged their slaves from receiving the sacrament of matrimony, especially if it involved a partner who belonged to another master. Marriage between slaves and free persons was also permitted, with children of these unions taking the status of their mother, slave or free. Family ties could be ruptured, of course, when slaves were sold.

As Catholics, slaves were subject to prosecution by the Inquisition, and inquisitors often looked askance on their continued practice of African folkways and their incomplete grasp of orthodox Catholic teachings. Because there was no Inquisition tribunal in Brazil, slaves were sometimes taken to Portugal for trial and punishment and then returned to the colony. Such was the fate of José, a mulatto slave who worked in a sugar mill in northeastern Brazil. In 1595, he was convicted of denouncing God and cursing the church when his master refused to give him enough to eat. His sentence included a public whipping in the streets of Lisbon. After he returned to Brazil, his blasphemous protests continued, so vehemently that local officials ordered him to serve 4 years on the king's galleys.

Slave Resistance

Slaves found various ways to resist or protest their condition. Many employed what scholars have called the "weapons of the weak," subtle acts of defiance that included feigning illness and sabotaging work routines. Slaves could appeal to government authorities if they were mistreated, and they might persuade a judge to order them sold to a more lenient master. In extreme cases, women resorted to abortion and infanticide to save their children from a life of slavery. Slaves also used African spiritual practices, actions the Europeans called "witchcraft," to assert some degree of power over their masters and other whites. Some Brazilian slaves became so well known for their powers of divination and casting spells that they were able to sell their services to other slaves and even to whites.

Collective slave rebellions also occurred from time to time. In the region around Córdoba in eastern Mexico, some 2000 slaves from several different sugar and tobacco plantations rose in revolt in 1735. They killed plantation overseers, destroyed crops, and carried off equipment used in processing sugar. Only after 5 months of fighting did militia units succeed in quelling the rebellion, but 6 years later another slave upheaval again brought the local economy to a standstill. Still other slaves found freedom through escape, often to frontier areas where they might easily gain paid employment with no questions asked. In some cases, especially during the early years of European colonization, runaways joined Indian communities and helped the natives resist conquest. As early as 1503, Governor Nicolás de Ovando reported that some of Hispaniola's slaves had escaped and were living with native rebels.

Maroon Communities

Sometimes runaways (known as *cimarrones* in Spanish, maroons in English) formed their own settlements in remote jungle or mountain locations. Known as *palenques* in Spanish America, runaway communities could be found in eastern and western Mexico, the Isthmus of Panamá, and especially in Venezuela, where the runaway population reportedly reached 20,000 in the early eighteenth century. The region around Cartagena in present-day Colombia was another favored location. In eastern Cuba, palenques proliferated in the mountain range known as the Sierra Maestra, where Fidel Castro's rebels would launch their resistance movement in the 1950s.

Maroon communities supported themselves through subsistence agriculture, by bartering their produce for other needed items at local markets, and by raiding nearby haciendas and towns. In coastal areas, they traded with pirates of many nationalities and sometimes joined them in sacking towns and plundering treasure ships. They augmented their population by inviting Indians and other marginalized people to join in their communities. In some parts of Mexico, male residents of palenques seized Indian women from neighboring villages.

Hundreds of runaway settlements known as *quilombos* formed in the vast interior of Brazil. The Dutch occupation of northeastern Brazil in the mid-seventeenth century prompted many masters to desert their plantations, creating especially favorable opportunities for slaves to flee the sugar zone. Perhaps the most famous of all Brazilian quilombos was Palmares, whose population may have numbered 30,000 or more at its height around 1670. Despite repeated attacks from both Dutch and Portuguese forces, Palmares endured for most of the seventeenth century until it was finally routed in 1694. Zumbi, one of its last leaders, is today honored as a hero by Afro-Brazilians, who observe the anniversary of his execution on November 20 as a National Day of Black Consciousness. Even though Palmares was destroyed, the remnants of numerous maroon communities survive to this day in many parts of Latin America. Brazil has as many as 1,000 former quilombos, whose residents have struggled in recent years to gain title to their lands. The town of Cuajiniquilapa in the Mexican state of Guerrero had its origin in a colonial palenque. Today, the descendants of the original settlers maintain a small museum dedicated to the town's history.

Free Blacks and Mulattos

Some slaves found their way to freedom through a legal process known as manumission. Owners might free an especially favored slave, perhaps a female domestic servant, in their wills. Slave children fathered by masters frequently won manumission as well, especially if their fathers lacked legitimate heirs. Some slaves were able to purchase their own freedom. In the mining regions of Brazil, slaves were often required to deliver a stipulated quantity of gold to their masters each day but could keep anything over and above that amount. Female slaves who worked as street vendors could also pocket a portion of their receipts, and free blacks might buy the liberty of their kin. In contrast to the southern United States in the nineteenth century, Latin American society assumed a relatively permissive attitude toward manumission.

Manumission, flight, and intermarriage between slaves and free persons all contributed to the growing numbers of free blacks. Many of these people were racially mixed, with Native American and/or white ancestry. They were usually called mulattos, though a host of other terms existed. Colonial authorities everywhere viewed mulattos as a socially disruptive group, even more so than mestizos. A governor in Minas Gerais summed up this attitude: "Mulattos being unstable and rebellious are pernicious in all Brazil; in Minas they are far worse because they are rich, and experience shows us that wealth in these people leads them to commit grave errors, chief among them being disobedience to the laws." Free blacks and mulattos experienced multiple forms of discrimination. Often, they were mistaken for slaves, and they had to go to great lengths to assert their status as free men and women. In the Spanish colonies, they were required to pay tribute, just as Indians were. Although artisan guilds tried to exclude them, free black craftsmen played prominent roles in the colonial economy, and some managed to accumulate considerable wealth (see Plate 9).

Free persons of African descent were vital to the defense of the Iberian colonies. Skilled black stonemasons helped construct the heavy fortifications that guarded

Blacks in Trujillo, on the northern coast of Peru, drawn in the 1780s by an unidentified Indian artist.

Cartagena, Havana, St. Augustine, and other ports. Some free blacks served in racially integrated militia units, but many more filled the ranks of black and mulatto militia companies. They fought alongside Spanish and Portuguese units in defending coastal regions against enemy attack and helped maintain order in major cities. In Mexico, black militia forces helped repel pirates from Veracruz in 1683. Military service gave free blacks important advantages, including pensions, certain legal rights, and exemption from tribute in Spanish America.

Free people of color built a sense of group solidarity in their militia companies and in the many religious brotherhoods they established in cities and towns throughout Brazil and Spanish America. The brotherhoods often included slaves as well as free blacks and mulattos. Salvador, Brazil, had six such organizations for blacks and five for mulattos at the beginning of the eighteenth century. Like the Indian *cofradías* of Spanish America, these groups sponsored religious celebrations and provided members with many social services, including funeral expenses, dowries for young women, and help in times of illness. In the Brazilian district of Minas Gerais, functions sponsored by these organizations provided the only opportunities for large numbers of blacks to assemble legally. Events sponsored by the brotherhoods often featured African rituals.

RACE AND CLASS IN COLONIAL LATIN AMERICA

Colonial Latin America was a racially stratified society, with what might seem to be a straightforward pecking order. Whites usually occupied the most prestigious ranks, followed in descending order by mestizos, free mulattos, Indians, and slaves. Social reality, however, was not that simple. Wealth, skills, and connections to powerful people could help an individual advance beyond the status held by others of his or her race. Some enterprising mestizos could and did enjoy a social standing superior to that of their creole neighbors, and in fact they often came to be regarded as white, even when their physical features suggested otherwise.

Still, society placed a high premium on whiteness, and people of mixed ancestry often took care to distance themselves as much as possible from their African and Indian origins. Consider, for example, Beatriz de Padilla, a woman accused of murdering her lover in Guadalajara, Mexico, in the mid-seventeenth century. She insisted that court records list her as a *morisca,* meaning that she was more white than black. Although her mother was a mulatta, Padilla proclaimed that her father belonged to one of the city's leading white families. In similar fashion, lighter-skinned mestizos began calling themselves *castizos,* supposedly indicating that they were three parts white and only one part Indian. A sure way to insult someone was to cast doubt on his or her pretensions to whiteness.

Social and Cultural Definitions of Race

Beatriz de Padilla's claim to be a morisca shows that some people created subcategories when defining their racial identity. By the mid-eighteenth century, artists were producing the so-called castas paintings, images that depicted a bewildering range of possibilities

A casta painting, *De Español y Mestisa, Castiza*, by Mexican artist Miguel Cabrera, 1763.

De Español y Mestisa. Castisa.

that could result when people of different categories produced offspring. In fact, very few of these fanciful terms were ever used in everyday conversation, and the paintings were curiosity pieces coveted by European art collectors rather than accurate representations of social reality in the colonies.

Few people could trace their lineage as precisely as the subjects in the castas paintings or even as well as Beatriz de Padilla. Members of the high elite proudly touted genealogies that spanned many generations and included conquistadors and peninsular grandees, but most people were lucky if they knew their family's history at all. Like most Indian commoners, many blacks, mulattos, and even mestizos lacked surnames. Migration, the death of parents, and the abandonment of children all worked to erase memories. Because there was no civil registry of births, people could "prove" their ancestry only by obtaining a copy of their baptismal record or producing witnesses who could attest to their parentage.

In any case, ethnic identities were fluid and highly subjective, depending on personal appearance, reputation, hearsay, occupation, and who was making the identification. If several different people were all asked to specify the race of an individual, they might all give different answers. Historians have discovered numerous cases in which the same individual might be listed as a mestizo in one document, an español in another, and a mulatto in yet another. Priests could be persuaded to go back and alter a baptismal record, and a person moving to a new place might be tempted to "whiten" his or her ancestry, especially in areas where there were few European immigrants who might contest their claims.

In fact, racial identity was often defined as much by behavior and culture as by biology. Someone called a mestizo might look very much like an Indian, but if he or she spoke Spanish and functioned as a member of the república de españoles, then he or she was not an Indian. "Indians" were people who lived in Indian communities, paid tribute, spoke indigenous languages, and dressed like Indians, regardless of their actual parentage. Mestizos residing in Indian villages sometimes found it advantageous to "pass" as Indians in order to gain access to community land or office. When factional disputes erupted within Indian communities, a sure way of discrediting an adversary was to accuse him or her of being a mestizo or a mulatto.

An example from the province of Latacunga in the Ecuadorian Andes shows how cultural artifacts served as markers of ethnic identity. Indians were supposed to belong under the ecclesiastical jurisdiction of the Franciscans, while secular clerics ministered to españoles, but church officials quarreled over where mestizos should worship. In 1632, the bishop ordered that all mestizos who wore Indian-style clothing to go to the Franciscan church. Even this seemingly simple solution did not settle the issue, however, for many Indian and mestiza women favored a skirt known as a *faldellín,* a style that combined native and European elements. An arbiter finally decided that all women who wore a *lliclla,* a shawl widely used by indias and mestizas alike, should belong to the Franciscan parish.

Ethnicity, therefore, was imprecise and subject to modification throughout a person's lifetime. How much or how little an individual cared about his or her ethnic classification varied as well. People with tenuous claims to whiteness were often especially sensitive to any aspersions cast on their ancestry. Race also mattered to someone like Beatriz de Padilla, perhaps because she could better defend herself against criminal charges if the court regarded her as almost white. Many others, however, realistically perceived that they had little likelihood of moving up the social ladder, and thus no reason to quibble about their racial identity.

Class and Ethnicity

Great wealth could buy many status symbols in colonial Latin America—a spacious townhouse, a rural estate, fine clothing, jewelry, an elegant coach, and slaves. Such luxuries went a long way toward convincing one's neighbors that anyone who could afford them

How Historians Understand   PARISH REGISTERS AND THE STUDY OF COLONIAL SOCIETY

Written sources available to historians are heavily weighted in favor of the literate, the wealthy, and the powerful. The Catholic Church's insistence that everyone be baptized, however, assured virtually every person at least a cameo appearance in the documentary record. Priests were required to keep careful records of all the baptisms, marriages, and funeral rites they performed, regardless of the social standing of the individuals involved. The Genealogical Society of Utah in Salt Lake City has microfilmed many of these parish registers, and copies are available to researchers worldwide.

Parish registers are extremely valuable for people wishing to trace their own family genealogy, but historians have learned a great deal about colonial Latin American society by using these materials. Baptismal records give the infant's parents' names and ethnicities and note whether or not their parents were married. Some children, however, were listed as *hijos de padres no conocidos* ("children of unknown parents") or *espósitos* ("abandoned"). Still other records give one parent's name while omitting the other. From these notations, historians have been able to gather information about fluctuations in the rates of illegitimacy and abandonment.

Baptismal registers also name the child's godparents, offering important clues to patron–client relationships and other social networks. Even the names chosen for newborns indicate important trends. Historians have traced the growing devotion to the Virgin of Guadalupe in Mexico by noting the increasing popularity of the name "Guadalupe" in eighteenth-century baptismal registers. Contrary to the popular belief that this cult arose first among Mexican Indians, the name was initially more popular with españoles.

Burial registers offer grim reminders of recurrent epidemics—page after page of hastily scribbled notations, with many of the deceased described as infants or small

deserved an elevated standing in the community. Money could also buy other less tangible but perhaps more important markers of social distinction. Men could purchase a seat on the town council or even the governorship of an entire province. Wealthy parents could provide their daughters with sizable dowries and increase their chances of marrying into a prominent family. Those with fortunes to spare could greatly enhance their prestige by becoming patrons of a convent or hospital. Even titles of nobility were for sale, although as we saw in the case of Antonio López de Quiroga in Chapter 4, not everyone who entered a bid actually got a title.

Further down the social ladder the benefits of financial success were more modest but still significant. The mulatto muleteer Miguel Hernández of Querétaro, Mexico, used his hard-won earnings to acquire rural property, a slave, and a membership in one of the city's most prestigious cofradías. Blacksmiths, tailors, jewelers, and other craftsmen who children. If time and energy permitted, priests might include the cause of death. Many women died in childbirth and were buried alongside their newborns. Priests in frontier areas might note that a person had been killed by hostile Indians. Often too, priests noted whether a person was buried with a simple ceremony or with more elaborate pomp—an indicator of wealth and social status.

Marriage documents have proven particularly useful to historians. When a couple presented themselves to a priest asking to be married, they had to show documents proving that they were not close blood relatives of one another or already married to others. If they were not natives of the place where they were marrying, they had to prove where they had previously resided, which has enabled historians to track migration patterns. The frequency of marriage across racial lines offers important clues to social mobility.

There are limits to what we can learn from these documents, however, especially about specific people of lower social standing. Indian commoners, slaves, and many racially mixed people either had very common surnames or none at all, thus making it difficult to trace an individual from one record to another. Many people of limited means also spared themselves the expense of a church wedding. Still, our knowledge of colonial Latin American society is immeasurably richer thanks to these sources.

Questions for Discussion

Consider again the case of Juan and María, the hypothetical Mexican couple we thought about in the "How Historians Understand" section of Chapter 4. Using the church records from their home parish along with the documents we found in that imaginary "trunk," how full a picture of their lives could we reconstruct?

accumulated enough funds to acquire their own shop advanced their standing in the community. A mestiza or a mulatta with a modest dowry might hope to marry a respectable artisan or shopkeeper. By the eighteenth century, class—a person's access to wealth—was becoming an increasingly important criterion of social status. Yet there were clear limits to the upward mobility of Indians, mestizos, blacks, and mulattos, and limits also to the downward mobility of people who could plausibly claim pure European ancestry. Lighter-skinned people had more chances to marry "up" and found it easier to get loans to finance a daughter's dowry or the purchase of a shop.

Wealth and ethnicity also played a role in patron–client relationships. A person's patron was someone of higher social standing who provided help of many kinds. A peninsular immigrant seeking a job in the colonial bureaucracy, a journeyman carpenter hoping to set up shop for himself, a free black seamstress or cook trying to round up enough money to buy a loved one's freedom—all of these people would look to someone a rung or two higher on the social ladder to assist them in achieving their goals. The higher up one stood to begin with, the more powerful patron he or she could summon and the more generous favors he or she could expect. Both class and ethnicity were crucial in setting the upper and lower boundaries of a person's social mobility.

HONOR, GENDER, AND PATRIARCHY

If class and ethnicity set the parameters of social mobility, a person's reputation could raise or lower his or her standing within those parameters. Reputation depended in large part on how much one adhered to a comprehensive code of honor that prescribed rules of proper behavior for males and females at all stages of their lives. The rules covered nearly every aspect of a person's life, from marriage and sexuality to honesty in business dealings. People had endless opportunities to become familiar with these rules: Priests expounded on them from the pulpit and in the privacy of the confessional, and civil officials echoed the same message as they carried out their duties.

For many people, a strict adherence to all of these norms was impractical given the circumstances of their lives. Others simply went their own way. Those who enjoyed relatively high social standing might try to conceal their transgressions, but men and women who had little to lose had less reason to cover them up. Still, people at even the humblest ranks of society often cared very much about their personal reputations. For many, it was the only way they could gain a measure of respect in the eyes of their neighbors and perhaps the support of a patron.

Honor and the Patriarchal Family

Central to the notion of honor was the principle of patriarchy, the idea that all authority is society rested in the hands of fathers or father-like figures. The patriarchal nuclear family, headed by a male with all women, children, and servants subject to his governance, was considered the building block and the prototype of a stable society. The king and his appointees were supposed to rule their jurisdictions in paternal fashion—firmly but benevolently. In theory, each male head of household acted as the king's deputy, charged with controlling the behavior of everyone under his roof. His prerogatives included administering corporal punishment, within certain limits, to errant family members and servants.

Priests and civil officials stressed how important it was that men monitor and discipline their wives, daughters, and female servants, paying special attention to their sexual behavior. As daughters of Eve, women were seen as morally inferior to men—dangerous temptresses who, if left unsupervised, could easily lead men to "the precipice of perdition," as one observer in eighteenth-century Mexico put it. Ideally, wives and unmarried daughters were expected to observe what Spanish Americans called *recogimiento*, or seclusion within the walls of their homes, leaving only to attend mass or family gatherings, and then only when chaperoned by a male guardian. Widows and women who never married were urged to join the household of some male relative— father, uncle, brother, even an adult son.

Unseemly conduct by a man's wife, daughters, servants, or other female relatives reflected negatively on his honor and therefore on his standing in the community. Spanish Americans used the phrase *hombre de bien*, literally, man of good, to describe the honorable head of household. Such a man was fair and honest in his business dealings, loyal to the king, and conscientious in fulfilling his civic obligations. He was also expected to support his family as best he could. Most of all, he effectively "governed" his household. The surest way to insult a man was to suggest that he was a cuckold, unable to control the sexual behavior of his own wife. A man who caught his wife in an adulterous affair could kill her or her lover with little fear of prosecution. In short, a man's honor depended on his family's conduct and reputation, while a woman's honor was contingent on her submission to her father or other adult male relative.

Marriage and the Family

Because the nuclear family was considered so important to the stability of society, both church and state paid careful attention to marriage. In theory, men and women were free to marry whomever they chose, but in practice, parents—especially those with great wealth and or even slight pretensions to elevated social status—often exerted powerful pressure on their children to make matches advantageous to the family's honor. In their efforts to ensure that their sons and daughters chose "proper" spouses, they often petitioned the church for exemptions to customary bans on marriages between first cousins or other relatives.

Families of means provided their daughters with a dowry in money or other property. This endowment might consist of a few animals, furniture, dishes, and other household items, but the wealthiest brides brought to their marriages huge fortunes, including haciendas or plantations, slaves, and abundant silverware and jewelry. The daughter of the Bolivian silver magnate Antonio López de Quiroga received a dowry valued at 100,000 pesos when she married in 1676. In general, the more lavish the dowry, the better the woman's chances of marrying someone of high social standing.

Almost without exception, once the marriage ceremony was performed, the union was for life. It was possible to secure an annulment if one could prove that the marriage had been invalid in the first place, in the case, for example, that one party proved physically incapable of performing the conjugal act or was found to have another spouse living somewhere else. A husband or wife could also secure an ecclesiastical divorce, which permitted one to live apart from an abusive spouse but did not include freedom to remarry as long as the spouse survived. Such concessions were quite rare, however. Priests and civil officials alike generally tried to keep couples together for what they saw as the greater good of society. Colonial archives are full of complaints of domestic violence, almost always from women, who sought recourse when their husbands exceeded what society considered appropriate levels of physical "correction." More often than not, authorities of both church and state summoned the husband and exhorted him to use more "gentle" means of persuasion in governing his household. They would then urge the wife to return home and take special care in performing her domestic and conjugal duties. The authorities reasoned that a woman allowed to live apart from her husband would have no means of support for herself and her children and would become a burden to the community.

Honor and Sexuality

The church forbade all sexual activity outside of marriage or not intended for procreation. Women were expected to be virgins at the time of marriage, although it was assumed that men would have had prior sexual experience. An honorable man was permitted, indeed expected, to break an engagement if he learned that his fiancée was not a virgin. In practice, however, many couples saw nothing wrong with having sex once they had become engaged.

When a pregnancy resulted before a marriage ceremony actually took place, what happened next depended a great deal on the relative social status of the man and the woman. If both parties held similar standing in the community and their families approved the match, the marriage proceeded as planned, with few consequences for anyone's reputation, and the child was considered legitimate. If the woman's parents considered her fiancé socially inferior, they faced a dilemma: Which would do greater damage to the family's honor—to have their daughter bear a child out of wedlock or to accept a man of questionable status as a son-in-law? When the man's social rank was notably higher than the woman's, his family might well pressure him into breaking the engagement and leaving her to fend for herself. She could, however, sue him for breach of contract, and force him to marry her or at least provide her with a dowry to enhance her chances of marrying someone else.

Women who bore children out of wedlock suffered great dishonor, and those with pretensions to some standing in the community often went to great lengths to conceal their pregnancies. Abortion and even infanticide were not unknown, but it is difficult to determine how frequently these practices were employed by desperate women—certainly often enough to prompt repeated comment from the clergy. Much more commonly, a woman who could manage to do so kept hidden from view throughout the pregnancy, and then either "adopted" the child as if it had been born to another woman, gave the baby to someone else to raise, or left it on the doorstep of a church or convent. Most major cities had foundling hospitals for abandoned infants. Mortality rates in these institutions often ranged as high as 90 percent.

Even the more fortunate of children born out of wedlock bore a social stigma. The priesthood and other prestigious careers were usually closed to men of illegitimate birth, while women might find fewer chances of marrying into an elite family. It was possible, however, for a person to gain legitimacy after the fact, if the biological parents subsequently married. Those who could afford the long paper trail involved could also obtain an official certification from the Spanish crown declaring them legitimate, regardless of the circumstances of their birth.

Men's sexual activities were far more difficult to monitor than women's, of course, and even men who openly acknowledged that they had fathered children out of wedlock suffered few consequences, as long as they provided for their offspring's care. In some cases, fathers took their illegitimate children into their own homes and never publicly revealed the identity of the mother. Respectable bachelors could preside over their own patriarchal households, exercising control over servants and others who lived under their roof. This double standard did not mean that men's sexual indiscretions went completely unpunished. Rape was prosecuted, but the rigor of the prosecution varied according to the social standing of the victim and her male relatives. The victim usually bore the burden of proof, and her past sexual history weighed heavily in determining the guilt or innocence of the accused. Authorities of church and state were especially concerned with the problem of bigamy, which most often involved married men who migrated across the ocean or to a new part of the Americas and took new wives, passing themselves off as widowers or bachelors.

Honor and Homosexuality

Homosexual behavior was punished in the civil and church courts, and punishment sometimes went as far as the execution of those found guilty. In 1658, authorities in Mexico City rounded up more than 120 men on charges of homosexuality, and 14 of these were executed. Men reputed to be homosexuals also became targets of gossip and ridicule. The social standing of the accused definitely played a role in determining his fate, however. Doctor Gaspar González was a priest in La Plata (today, the city of Sucre, Bolivia) prosecuted for sodomy in 1595 and again in 1608. The jobs he held during his long and distinguished ecclesiastical career included the conduct of a general *visita*, or inspection, of the entire diocese of La Plata. His open affair with a young man named Diego Mexía caused quite a scandal. They lived in the same house, shared sleeping quarters, and publicly displayed their affection. Mexía accompanied González on his inspection tour, and the priest later purchased him a seat on the city council of La Plata and many expensive gifts.

Had González been more discreet, his education and occupation might have spared him from the consequences of his actions. Indeed, some witnesses hesitated to reveal evidence against him because of his standing in the community. Ecclesiastical authorities normally preferred to handle such matters quietly in order to protect the church's reputation, but González's outright defiance of accepted standards left them little choice but to prosecute. When the church court in La Plata found him guilty of sodomy, González used his connections to appeal the sentence before a superior tribunal in Lima. That court ruled that there was insufficient evidence to convict him, but because he had scandalized the community, he should be banished from the diocese of La Plata. He did not, however, lose his claim to the privileges and benefits accorded to priests.

As for Diego Mexía, his lower social rank and prior legal troubles brought him stiffer penalties. He had been a prisoner in the Potosí jail before González befriended him and secured his release. As a layman, Mexía faced prosecution in the stricter civil courts rather than the ecclesiastical tribunals that handled González's case. During the course of the investigation, authorities tortured him, hoping to convince him to admit his transgressions. The procedure left him permanently disabled in both arms. Although he refused to confess, the court found him guilty and sentenced him to 6 years' unpaid service on the galleys. He also lost his city council position. The man with whom González had been involved at the time of his earlier trial, a 20-year-old apothecary's assistant, fared even less well. He was convicted and publicly executed.

The Limits of Patriarchy

However much the clergy, civil officials, and families might stress the importance of observing the norms of honor and patriarchy, many people found these rules impractical or irrelevant. Often, couples ignored the teachings of the church and never formally married, even though they lived together for many years and had several children. A church wedding cost money, including fees for the priest who performed the ceremony and the expense of getting certified copies of documents required to prove eligibility for the sacrament. In many communities, between one-fourth and one-half of all children baptized were listed as illegitimate. Ironically, it was only at the highest and lowest rungs of the social ladder where formal marriage was close to universal—among the elites and among Indians living in missions or villages under the strict control of the clergy.

The demands of daily life meant that most women simply could not remain secluded in their homes, even if they did live with a husband or other male relative. Women who lacked servants left the home several times a day just to perform their domestic chores. They walked to the market and hauled water from streams or from public fountains in larger cities. They gathered at the rivers to do their laundry as well. Those who lived in crowded urban tenements, where an entire family might share a single room, spent much of their time in the streets and plazas of their neighborhoods. Women in rural areas did most of their work outside as well.

Many women, wives as well as widows and single women, also had to go out and earn a living. Rural women took produce from their gardens and fields to markets in town. Women also operated businesses, such as bakeries, taverns, inns, and retail stores, while others worked as midwives and healers, seamstresses, and cooks. Elite families hired young mothers as wet nurses. Wives of shopkeepers and artisans worked alongside their husbands and often carried on the business themselves if their husbands died. A few women even became members of artisan guilds. In Lima, for example, the potters' guild counted 1 woman among its 14 members in 1596, and another woman was an active member of the hatters' guild. By the late colonial period, a few cities even had guilds comprised entirely of female artisans. In 1788, Mexico City's guild of women silk spinners included 23 masters, 200 journeymen, and 21 apprentices. The port of Cartagena, Colombia, had a guild of female brandy producers.

Working women could not easily conceal an out-of-wedlock pregnancy, and in general they had a harder time defending their honor and reputation than women who remained secluded. Even women who stayed home and supported themselves by taking in laundry or mending might be accused of having illicit relationships with their male clients. Some women did resort to prostitution, in brothels in the larger cities and on a more freelance basis elsewhere, perhaps because they could earn much more by selling sexual favors than they could in other occupations. Ana María Villaverde, for example, was a young widow who worked in Mexico City's tobacco factory in the late eighteenth century. When she was laid off from her job, she turned to prostitution, tripling her earnings. Despite the social stigma they suffered, prostitutes seldom ran the risk of prosecution by civil or church authorities.

If they survived the dangerous childbearing years, women usually outlived men, especially because wives were often much younger than their husbands. Iberian inheritance laws provided widows with half the property that the couple had accumulated during the marriage, with the other half divided equally among all children, sons and daughters alike. A woman also retained full rights to any goods she had brought to the marriage as a dowry. Wealthy widows lived comfortably and sometimes wielded enormous economic influence as owners of mines, haciendas, and plantations. If they cared to marry again, they usually did not lack for willing prospects.

For poor women, however, generous inheritance laws meant nothing, and their relatives were often unable to take them in. Unmarried women, including many single mothers and wives abandoned by their husbands, often lived on their own. By choice or necessity, large numbers of women lived in households headed by females, especially in urban areas where it was easier for women to find work. Often, two or more women might pool their meager resources to form a single household. Eighteenth-century censuses taken in the cities of Mexico show that women headed as many as one-third of the households. In the Brazilian town of Ouro Prêto, women were in charge of 45 percent of all households as of 1804, and 83 percent of these women had never been married.

LATIN AMERICAN LIVES

JUANA DE COBOS, BAKER IN CHIHUAHUA

ON THE EVENING of September 3, 1752, Mariana Muñoz de Olvera went for a walk through the streets of the Mexican mining town of Chihuahua. Passing by the home of a prosperous widow named Josefa García de Noriega, she caught the eye of Miguel Rico de Cuesta, a peninsular Spanish merchant and García de Noriega's fiancé. He called out to Mariana, taunting her with questions about how she could afford the new clothes she was wearing and insinuating that she had traded sexual favors for the money to buy them. She responded with a couple of choice insults. A few hours later her mother, Juana de Cobos, heard about the incident and confronted Josefa García de Noriega about her fiancé's rude remarks and questioned the widow's own sexual conduct.

The next morning, García de Noriega filed criminal charges against the "troublesome and scandalous" Cobos and her daughter. Thus began a legal battle that would last for several months and eventually result in their being ordered to move their home and business to the other side of town, where they would be less likely to have further altercations with Rico de Cuesta and García de Noriega. The local authorities were clearly biased against Juana de Cobos. Indeed, the official who first heard García de Noriega's complaint served as a witness when she and her fiancé married a few months later.

Juana de Cobos and Mariana Muñoz de Olvera were easy targets for scorn, for they lived outside the confines of patriarchal households. Though both were married, both lived apart from their husbands without official church permission. Juana, born in a farming community south of Chihuahua in 1706, had migrated to the town with her husband Juan Muñoz de Olvera during its silver boom of the late 1720s. Sometime thereafter, she and Juan separated, and for the remainder of her long life she supported herself, her children, and several grandchildren by operating a bakery. Like so many other women of her time, she never learned to read or write, but one of her adult sons took care of the necessary paperwork. Mariana married in 1746, when she was 21, but within a few years, she too left her husband and went to live with her mother with her two young children.

By refusing to live in patriarchal households, Cobos and Muñoz de Olvera forfeited a good measure of their claims to honor and respectability. Their frequent quarrels with other people in town did not help their reputations any, and Juana's rivals in the bread trade did not appreciate her periodic attempts to undercut prices set by the town's cabildo. She found it hard to compete with male bakers, many of whom were well-placed peninsular Spaniards who ran larger operations. Her competitors routinely asked her to contribute to activities of the town's loosely organized bakers' guild, but allowed her and other female bakers no say in the proceedings. Not surprisingly, Cobos often refused to help. In 1748, for example, she declined to help underwrite a comedy that the guild sponsored during festivities belatedly marking King Ferdinand VI's accession to the Spanish throne.

Despite her many difficulties, Juana de Cobos managed to win a certain standing in her community. Most people took her for an española, although a few documents refer to her as a mestiza, and Josefa García de Noriega called her a mulatta during their protracted feud. At least some of the time, people addressed her using the honorific title of "Doña." Perhaps the greatest measure of her social standing came when city officers decided that she was sufficiently respectable that they could use her bakery as a place where young women accused of sexual misconduct might be disciplined while learning a useful trade. When she died in 1797, at the age of 91, she was buried "de cruz alta" ("with a large cross"), an honor reserved for those able to afford a deluxe funeral.

Questions for Discussion

Did Juana de Cobos and Mariana Muñoz de Olvera violate all of the gender norms of their society, or only some of them? What mattered most in determining their social position in Chihuahua: class, ethnicity, or gender?

Women who headed their own households could still not escape the fact that they lived in a patriarchal society. While widows certainly enjoyed somewhat greater respectability than unmarried women, any woman not under some kind of male supervision had to overcome public suspicions that she lived dishonorably. Still, many women had no choice but to live with this stigma and concerned themselves more with the practical necessity of supporting themselves and their children than with what their gossipy neighbors had to say about them.

Convents: "Islands of Women"

Life in a convent provided some women with a respectable alternative to living in a male-dominated household. In fact, convents amounted to what one historian has called "islands of women," with populations as high as 1000 in some of the larger establishments in Mexico City and Lima. These women had little or no contact with men other than the priests who administered the sacraments or perhaps members of their immediate families. Nuns took perpetual vows of poverty, chastity, and obedience to their superiors. Cloistered nuns were supposed to spend their time almost exclusively in prayer and contemplation. Contact with outsiders occurred in the convent's *locutorio,* a meeting room where an iron grille separated the cloistered nun from visitors. The public might also attend mass at a convent chapel, but here too the nuns remained sequestered behind a grille.

Life in the convents, however, was not always as austere as these rules might suggest. Nuns' failure to observe proper decorum and their refusal to live in strict accord with their vows of poverty was a frequent subject of concern for church officials. Many nuns, especially those who came from wealthy families, eschewed communal dormitories and lived in comfortably furnished private rooms or even small apartments, some complete with private patios and gardens, within the convent. In her quarters, a nun could create what amounted to a matriarchal household that might include several servants or slaves, one or more orphan girls whom she personally raised, and perhaps a female relative or two.

The locutorios of major convents often witnessed lively social events featuring spirited conversation, music, and other entertainment. Visitors at these gatherings were treated to fine delicacies from the convents' kitchens. Popular legend maintains that the famous Mexican mole—a flavorful sauce combining American ingredients such as chiles, chocolate, and tomatoes with cloves, cinnamon, peppercorns, coriander, and other Old World spices—originated in one of Puebla's principal convents.

Not everyone who lived inside a convent was a nun. In addition to servants, slaves, and orphans, one could find young girls from respectable families who were there to learn reading, writing, arithmetic, needlework, and other basic skills in a society that offered few other formal educational opportunities for females. Victims of domestic violence, widows, and other women on their own might find temporary or permanent shelter within the convents' walls, sometimes of their own accord and sometimes "deposited" by their male relatives. Church authorities might also remand a woman to a convent as punishment for sexual improprieties or other wrongdoing.

Within the convents' walls nuns had certain opportunities not customarily available to them in the outside world. Convents as institutions typically controlled substantial wealth. As "brides of Christ," novices brought dowries when they entered religious life, and these became the property of the convent. Through bequests and other donations, nunneries acquired assets in the form of real estate, both rural and urban, and they figured among the most important sources of credit in the colonial economy, making loans to merchants and landowners and garnering an annual interest rate of 5 percent. Women who headed the convents exercised considerable leverage in managing these assets, along with power over the internal operation of the nunneries. These positions thus provided leadership opportunities available nowhere else to women in colonial society. Abbesses and other convent officers were chosen in periodic elections by the

Portrait of Sor Juana Inés de la Cruz, at work in her library.

highest-ranking nuns themselves, and elections were sometimes hotly contested. Powerful creole families took an active interest in convent elections because of the prestige and economic benefits that might accrue to them if a family member were elected abbess of a wealthy convent.

Convents also afforded a select few women a chance to pursue intellectual interests. The most famous colonial nun was Sor Juana Inés de la Cruz (1648–1695) of Mexico. Although universities and other institutions of higher learning were closed to women, she studied on her own. Her interests ranged from music, physics, and mathematics to theology and philosophy. She corresponded with leading intellectuals of her time and wrote poetry, drama, and essays, often with a decidedly feminist spin. One of her most widely quoted verses, for example, posed the question of the relative morality of prostitutes and their male clients. Who sins more, Sor Juana asked, she who sins for pay or he who pays for sin? Hundreds of other nuns also left numerous writings, including poetry, plays, histories of their convents, and lengthy spiritual autobiographies written at the suggestion of their confessors. Still others became expert musicians, singers, and composers.

Convents and Colonial Society

No matter how much economic power or intellectual distinction these favored nuns received, they could not escape the fact that they lived in both a patriarchal and hierarchical society. They always remained subordinate to male church authorities, from their personal confessors to the bishops of their dioceses. Toward the end of her life, Juana Inés de la Cruz renounced her intellectual pursuits, giving away her books and scientific instruments, in part because a bishop had warned her that these activities put her soul at risk. Cloistered nuns also had to rely on male majordomos, who were often close relatives of the abbesses, to take care of their business affairs.

Convents also reflected the class and ethnic divisions of society. Only women able to provide a dowry could become professed nuns. In addition, their families usually had to provide an annual stipend to cover their living expenses. Smaller towns, especially in frontier areas, usually lacked convents, thus restricting the options of many women. In Brazil, the religious life was out of reach for all but the most affluent women. Until 1677, when Salvador's first convent opened, wealthy families sent their daughters to convents in Portugal.

Inside the convents, there were numerous social distinctions. The most prestigious nuns were those who wore the black veil. They came from respectable and often wealthy families of Spanish or Portuguese descent. Only they were eligible to vote and hold office, and they were exempt from all menial work. Next came the sisters of the white veil. Their dowries were lower and their social backgrounds less distinguished than those of black-veiled nuns. To them fell many of the housekeeping duties inside the convent. The convents also housed many Indian, mestiza, and black women known as *donadas*. They took informal vows of chastity and performed the most onerous chores.

A few convents were specially created for Indians and mestizas, but these institutions did not escape the strictures of a racially stratified society either. As we saw in

Chapter 3, even though Cuzco's convent of Santa Clara had been founded originally for mestizas, within a few decades nuns of Spanish origins had captured control of the convent's leadership and relegated mestiza sisters to second-class status. Mexico City's convent of Corpus Christi, founded in 1724 for Indian women, was reserved for the legitimate daughters of caciques and other Indian nobles. It owned no property. The nuns survived exclusively on alms they gathered and were not permitted to have private quarters or servants.

Women unable to enter a convent but still wishing to pursue a religious life might find shelter in a *beatario,* an informal institution that resembled a nunnery but had no recognized standing in the church and none of the prestige associated with convents. The Catholic Church eventually conferred sainthood on two colonial *beatas,* Rosa of Lima and Mariana de Jesús of Quito. In general, however, church authorities distrusted these women for seeking spiritual enlightenment outside of official ecclesiastical channels. Many beatas found themselves accused of heresy and brought before the Inquisition.

CONFORMITY AND DEFIANCE IN COLONIAL SOCIETY

Colonial Latin Americans received constant reminders that they lived in a society that made fine distinctions of ethnicity, honor, class, and gender. Whenever they appeared in court, whether as defendant, plaintiff, or witness, a notary carefully noted their ethnicity, or at least what he perceived it to be. Church records also stipulated the race of persons baptized, married, or buried. Class differences were clearly visible. The wealthy paraded about in elegant coaches and dressed in fine clothing while the poor were lucky if they had a roof over their head. And while class and ethnic identification could sometimes change, gender distinctions were the most obvious and enduring. Outside of convents, women held no official positions in the church, nor were they eligible for public office or admission to higher education or the professions. Men and women alike were repeatedly exhorted by priests and civil officials to behave in ways appropriate to their gender.

For most people the routines of daily life entailed interaction with people who ranked above them or beneath them socially, and elaborate rules of etiquette supposedly governed these encounters. On special occasions, the pecking order of colonial society went on public display as high dignitaries of church and state marched in procession through city streets, followed by representatives of other groups, all lined up according to rank. Men, women, and children also regularly witnessed what happened to those judged to be social outcasts. Executions and whippings were carried out in public, as were the punishments of nonconformists condemned by the Inquisition, to provide object lessons for all. Despite all these rules and lessons, however, people found ways to defy the conventions of their society, sometimes in full view of their presumed social betters, more often in safer, more private settings.

The Social Etiquette of Everyday Life

The rules of etiquette began with the forms of address used in everyday conversation but also included grammar and general demeanor. "Remember to whom you are speaking" was a frequent admonition to people of lower social standing whenever they found themselves in contact with people who ranked above them. In Spanish America, men and women who possessed a certain measure of social standing presumed that the title "Don" or "Doña" would precede their names whenever anyone talked to or about them. Government officials expected to be addressed with even loftier terms, such as "Your Excellency" or "My Most Excellent Lord." Even in casual conversation, Spanish and Portuguese speakers were expected to use the appropriate version of the pronoun "you," as each language has two words for the term. One connotes respect, or at least social distance between the speaker and listener, and the other is used among equals or when the speaker considers himself or herself superior in rank to the listener. Men were also expected to doff their hats in the presence of their social betters.

As clear as these guidelines might seem, situations might arise, particularly in the world of petty commerce, where the rules were not at all straightforward. Peninsulares or creoles often owned tiny retail shops that sold a wide variety of merchandise to people of many different ethnic backgrounds. By virtue of their own rank in society, shopkeepers expected deferential behavior from Indians and mulattos, but their livelihoods depended on treating their customers with a certain amount of respect. The merchants' clientele often understood that spare cash in their pockets gave them the leverage necessary to defy customary social conventions.

One such encounter took place in the shop of the Spaniard Martín de Echaquibel in Chihuahua, Mexico, in 1753. A mulatto came into the store, asked to see some merchandise, and then turned to leave without buying anything. Insulted, Echaquibel exclaimed, "Look, dog, you are a mulatto and I am very much a Spaniard," using the familiar second-person pronoun. The customer could hardly dispute the difference in their racial identities but defiantly pointed out that he was not the shopkeeper's slave and that he would do as he pleased.

Other people were just as disrespectful as Echaquibel's customer, though less openly. In the privacy of their homes and in other protected spaces, they surely mocked the pretensions of those who claimed to be their social betters. They found safety in numbers, too. The lower classes in late colonial Buenos Aires, for example, often gathered to watch the creole militia drill, and laughed whenever these weekend warriors made a mistake. And, as we shall see, public celebrations offered ideal opportunities to mock any and all symbols of rank and authority in colonial society.

The Administration of Justice

Authorities of church and state found plenty of occasions to remind everyone who was in charge and how those in subordinate positions should behave. The administration of justice, vested in city councils, in local officials serving in rural districts, and in the

An eighteenth-century drawing of an open-air tavern or *pulquería* in Mexico City.

viceroys and high courts in major cities provided numerous such opportunities. In the sixteenth century, the central square of every newly founded Spanish American town had a *picota,* a stone or wooden pillar that symbolized the king's authority. Whenever local officials set out to arrest someone, they carried with them a special baton that signified their right to mete out justice.

Punishments for crime varied according to one's social standing. Whites were usually spared corporal punishment and ordered to pay a fine. Whippings and executions were usually carried out in the central plaza of town. Petty criminals such as thieves and those found guilty of assault might be given dozens or even hundreds of lashes. Convicted murderers were often executed, but only after they were paraded through the streets of town, accompanied by members of the clergy, representatives of the civil authorities, and a town crier who publicly announced their crimes. Their corpses were then left on display for the presumed edification of those who had not witnessed the actual execution.

Civil and church officials were certainly concerned with impressing people with the long arm of the law, but they also had to convince the public that they were wise and just rulers. For this reason they tempered the administration of justice with a fair amount of leniency and attention to prescribed procedures. Although there was no trial by jury, the accused were usually provided with a defender who summoned witnesses to testify on the defendant's behalf and argued in favor of leniency when guilt was not in doubt. Civil authorities and inquisitors resorted to the death penalty only occasionally. Serious crimes were often punished by banishment from the community or a term of forced labor in a textile factory, silver refinery, bakery, or sugar mill. Men might also be sent to serve in a remote military post for ten or more years.

The Inquisition and Deviant Behavior

In addition to the civil government, the Holy Office of the Inquisition played a role in enforcing many of society's rules. The formal establishment of tribunals in Lima and Mexico City came in the early 1570s, although monastic orders and bishops had previously conducted inquisitorial proceedings, particularly against Indian converts accused of backsliding into their old ways. After the 1570s, Indians were exempt from the Inquisition's jurisdiction, but the church found other ways to prosecute native "idolaters." Every other baptized Catholic, from the most prestigious ranks of the Spanish nobility to mestizos, slaves, and free people of color, was fair game for Inquisition scrutiny, however. Brazil never had a formal tribunal, but Inquisition authorities from Portugal paid occasional visits to the colony, and sometimes the accused were sent to Portugal for trial.

The Inquisition's official charge was to root out deviant beliefs and behavior, including heresy, blasphemy, bigamy, witchcraft, superstition, and the secret practice of Jewish rites. Powerful New Christian merchant families were rounded up in a series of trials held in Lima and Mexico City in the late sixteenth and early seventeenth centuries. Women, especially those who claimed to have special spiritual or magical powers, were often subject to prosecution. Scores of English pirates captured at Veracruz, Cartagena, and other ports were brought to trial as "Lutheran corsairs."

In fact, however, the Inquisition proved less oppressive in the colonies than in Spain and Portugal. Given the territorial expanse of Spanish America and Brazil, it could reach only a small number of people. The tribunals of Mexico City and Lima, as well as a third one set up at Cartagena in 1610, covered huge areas, with agents in principal cities who were supposed to report offenses to their superiors. The inquisitors followed regular procedures, carefully questioning witnesses, punishing those who falsely accused others, and dismissing many charges for want of sufficient evidence. Those found guilty faced penalties that ranged from wearing penitential garb in public for those who reconciled themselves to the faith to confiscation of their property and even execution for those who stubbornly refused to recant their errors. Executions were rare—about 50 were ordered by the Mexico City tribunal in the 250 years of its existence, another 30 in Lima, and probably not more than 100 in all of Spanish America. According to one estimate, not more than 1 percent of all persons prosecuted by the Inquisition received death sentences. Others, however, died in Inquisition jails while awaiting trial. Sentences were carried out in public ceremonies so that all could see the consequences of violating religious and behavioral norms.

Rituals of Rule

Public executions and whippings offered gruesome reminders of the power of the church and state, but other occasions provided more pleasing portrayals of the social and political order. On religious holidays the pecking order of society went on public view in the colorful processions that passed through the streets and plazas of all major towns. These occasions also provided good opportunities to portray the teachings of the church in brilliant visual fashion to the assembled crowds. Reenactments of the medieval battles between Christians and Muslims underscored the message that the church had triumphed over its enemies.

In many cities, the feast of Corpus Christi was the most spectacular of these religious holidays. Celebrated in late May or early June, this holy day honored the sacrament of the Eucharist. A solemn procession carried the consecrated host, displayed in a golden and bejeweled monstrance, through the streets and plazas, accompanied by representatives of many different segments of society. Participants included the viceroy in capital cities, the bishop and the rest of the secular clergy, the city council, members of male religious orders, Inquisitors, cofradías, trade guilds, Indians, blacks, and mulattos, all carefully arranged according to their rank in society, with places closest to the Eucharist considered the most prestigious. The Mexico City procession was often more than a mile long and even included students from the school of San Juan de Letrán. City governments went to great expense to mark the occasion. In 1621, for example, Mexico City spent 21 percent of its budget on the Corpus Christi celebration.

Other occasions provided opportunities to reinforce the allegiance of the people to their king. The death of a monarch and the coronation of his successor called for solemn funeral rites, followed by public demonstrations of loyalty to the new king. Lavish and costly spectacles marked the arrival of a new viceroy, or a marriage or birth in the royal family. Others heralded Spanish successes in warfare. In Mexico City, an annual observance was held on the anniversary of Cortés's victory at Tenochtitlan in 1521. All of these rituals were designed to teach the king's subjects that they lived in a great empire. To symbolize the benevolent, paternal generosity of their sovereign, those who marched in the processions often tossed coins or other trinkets to the crowds.

Scatological Songs and Dances of Defiance

Solemn processions were only part of the festivities that marked special religious and civic occasions. There was plenty of popular entertainment, including fireworks, theatrical pieces, cockfights, and bullfights. Many festivals gave people the opportunity to dance in the streets, drink heavily, and ridicule the powerful and pretentious. Their songs and dances often had explicit sexual content. In the streets of eighteenth-century Mexico, men and women favored a lascivious dance called the *chuchumbé,* performed while singing suggestive verses, such as this one: "A monk is standing on the corner, lifting his habit and showing the chuchumbé." Holidays also allowed people to don costumes and act out ritual inversions of the social order. Men dressed as women, and laymen disguised as members of the clergy pretended to bless the crowds. The pre-Lenten carnival season was especially noted for such excesses.

Authorities worried that these large gatherings might spill over into popular riot. In June of 1692, such fears materialized when an angry crowd stormed the viceroy's palace and set the building on fire during the Corpus Christi celebration in Mexico City. People were angry because food prices had skyrocketed and the viceroy had failed to provide the relief they expected. Their protests soon gave way to generalized looting. The authorities responded by rounding up alleged ringleaders and ordering several of them to be executed. They also attempted to ban the sale of the popular intoxicating beverage known as *pulque*.

Religious and civil festivals certainly brought large numbers of people together and allowed them a temporary escape from the drudgery of their daily routines, and a chance to play at turning the social order upside down, with plenty of all-around carousing. These "time out" settings may also have reinforced rather than destabilize existing social and political hierarchies. Those who witnessed lavishly staged processions may well have come away convinced that the existing order of things was inevitable, even if they entertained questions about its legitimacy. Then too, the opportunity to "let off steam" at festival time may have served as a useful safety valve in keeping the lower classes in their subordinate places. When the party was over, they went back to work and their accustomed outward show of deference to those who ranked above them.

Slice of Life   CORPUS CHRISTI IN CUZCO

THE FEAST of Corpus Christi was a celebration of Catholicism's victories over its enemies. Everywhere the processions included figures representing Muslims, Turks, and others vanquished by militant Christians. Cuzco, built literally on the foundations of the Inca capital, provided an ideal platform on which to stage this annual tribute to the faith triumphant. The immense fortunes generated by silver mining permitted local elites to put on a lavish show, and the willing participation of native Andeans seemed to signify that Spanish hegemony and the Catholic Church rested on firm foundations.

The bishop, city council, and other dignitaries who presided over the Corpus Christi rituals had definite ideas about which native people should play an active role in the solemn procession of the Eucharist. Like the representatives of Spanish society who took part, those chosen to march were all male. They were also presumed to be direct descendants of the pre-Hispanic Andean nobility. Conspicuously absent were those related to Incas who had resisted the imposition of Spanish rule and held out at Vilcabamba for more than 30 years after Pizarro's conquest (see Chapter 3).

Spanish authorities intended that the procession display the social, political, and religious order that had prevailed in Peru ever since the 1530s, but Cuzco's Andean leaders added their own messages to the script. Even though they usually wore

Spanish-style clothing, on festive occasions they put on costumes that invoked their glorious past. They dressed as specific rulers, such as the legendary first Inca Manco Capac and his descendant Huayna Capac, the last to occupy the throne at Cuzco before the Spaniards arrived in Peru. On their foreheads the marchers wore red-fringed headbands once reserved for the exclusive use of the Inca ruler himself, but in colonial times these headbands were the ultimate status symbol for native Andeans. Those who claimed the right to wear them carefully guarded their privilege. Each year they elected 24 men whose duties included making sure that no one "illegally" donned the fringe.

Corpus Christi and other public celebrations permitted native Andeans many other ways of publicly reenacting what they understood to be their history. Among Cuzco's native population were descendants of Cañaris from southern Ecuador who had been forcibly relocated to the Inca capital in the late fifteenth century. They had sided with the Spaniards during the conquest and from then on had cited that alliance in claiming special status in the new colonial order. Cañaris served as armed guards to Spanish authorities, and on Corpus Christi and other special days they marched in the processions as military companies, armed with arquebuses and pikes. Those who called themselves descendants of the Incas often disputed the Cañaris' exalted position in official ceremonies. Although the Corpus Christi procession was supposed to symbolize the unity of all Christians in submission to the body of Christ in the Eucharist, the feast also mirrored and perpetuated the many divisions in the social and political order.

Questions for Discussion

Suppose that Felipe Guaman Poma de Ayala (see Chapter 5) had witnessed one of the Corpus Christi celebrations in Cuzco. What would he have thought? Would he have approved of the role given to the descendants of the Incas? Why or why not?

CONCLUSION

Colonial Latin Americans lived in a hierarchical society that assigned privileges and obligations according to ethnicity, class, honor, and gender. Priests and officers of the law tried to get people to pay proper respect to authority, and they seemed constantly on the lookout for violations of the boundaries that separated one group from another. Some authorities even experimented with sumptuary laws that forbade Indians and blacks from wearing clothing supposedly reserved for Europeans and their American-born descendants, but people persisted in wearing whatever they could buy or otherwise acquire.

Other rules proved somewhat easier to enforce, but everywhere people of all social classes got away with far more than laws, sermons, court rulings, or Inquisition proceedings might imply. Racial labels were attached to people whenever they appeared in the official records of church or state, and whiteness counted for a lot, but in fact all ethnic identities were quite flexible, especially for those who were economically successful. Many slaves found ways to escape their bondage. Often out of practical necessity and sometimes out of personal choice, women disregarded the strict standards that theoretically placed them firmly under the thumbs of husbands and fathers. People of the lower classes found periodic release from their workaday routines and occasions when they could safely mock or even challenge those who claimed precedence over them. However rigid and specific the rules of social interaction might seem to have been, they were everywhere subject to constant renegotiation.

LEARNING MORE ABOUT LATIN AMERICANS

Bennett, Herman. *Africans in Colonial Mexico: Absolutism, Christianity, and Afro-Creole Consciousness, 1570–1640* (Bloomington, IN: Indiana University Press, 2003). Looks at free blacks and slaves and the ways their lives were affected by the government and the church.

Boyer, Richard. *The Lives of the Bigamists: Marriage, Family, and Community in Colonial Mexico*, abridged ed. (Albuquerque, NM: University of New Mexico Press, 2001). Examines the lives of people tried by the Inquisition for bigamy, giving details about family life, education, and migration.

Burns, Kathryn. *Colonial Habits: Convents and the Spiritual Economy of Cuzco, Peru* (Durham, NC: Duke University Press, 1999). An insightful case study of Cuzco's nunneries and their relationships with the larger society.

Curcio-Nagy, Linda A. *The Great Festivals of Colonial Mexico City: Performing Power and Identity* (Albuquerque, NM: University of New Mexico Press, 2004). A richly detailed history of the public civil and religious rituals in the capital of New Spain.

Few, Martha. *Women Who Live Evil Lives: Gender, Religion, and the Politics of Power in Colonial Guatemala* (Austin, TX: University of Texas Press, 2002). Shows how mestiza, black, Spanish, and indigenous women wielded power through witchcraft and healing.

Katzew, Ilona. *Casta Painting: Images of Race in Eighteenth-Century Mexico* (New Haven, CT: Yale University Press, 2004). Hundreds of color and black-and-white illustrations provide a fascinating visual tour of colonial Mexico.

Lavrin, Asunción. *Brides of Christ: Conventual Life in Colonial Mexico* (Stanford, CA: Stanford University Press, 2008). The most comprehensive and thoroughly researched study of life in colonial convents.

Myers, Kathleen, and Amanda Powell, eds. *A Wild Country Out in the Garden: The Spiritual Journals of a Colonial Mexican Nun* (Bloomington, IN: Indiana University Press, 1999). The writings of Madre María de San José, a nun who lived in Mexico from 1656 to 1719, edited and annotated by two well-known literary scholars.

Socolow, Susan Migden. *The Women of Colonial Latin America* (Cambridge, MA: Cambridge University Press, 2000). A comprehensive survey that draws on the best recent scholarship.

Sweet, James H. *Recreating Africa: Culture, Kinship, and Religion in the African-Portuguese World, 1441–1770* (Chapel Hill, NC: University of North Carolina Press, 2003). Shows how slaves in Brazil were able to maintain African religious beliefs and practices and use them to mitigate the suffering of slavery.

7

THE SHIFTING FORTUNES OF COLONIAL EMPIRES

IN 1700, THE CROWNED HEADS of Europe waited anxiously as King Charles II of Spain lay dying without a direct successor ready to assume his throne and his vast colonial possessions. The last of the Spanish Hapsburgs, Charles had ruled since 1665, but his reign bore little resemblance to the brilliant successes of his namesake who had presided over the realm in the time of the great conquests of Mexico and Peru. Spain's population was actually smaller than it had been a century before, the flow of American treasure to the royal coffers had fallen off precipitously, and Spanish merchants reaped diminishing profits in trade with the colonies. Spain's rivals, especially England and France, stood by eager to enrich themselves at its expense, and soon fell to fighting one another over who should inherit Charles's domains.

Thus began a long struggle between France and England, the superpowers of the eighteenth century, a conflict that ended only with the final defeat of the French general Napoleon Bonaparte in 1815. The wars of the eighteenth century and the resulting emergence of Great Britain as the premier economic, political, and military power in Europe and the world had profound consequences for Latin America. Spain often sided with France, even while trying to thwart French incursions in North America. The English therefore viewed the Spanish colonies as fair game for attack, while also coveting entrance into the huge markets of Spanish America. Portugal, on the other hand, maintained close economic and political ties with England, which made Brazil the occasional target of French assaults. Spain had always accused Portugal of encroaching on its territory in South America beyond the line of demarcation that the two nations had agreed upon in 1494, but clashes between them accelerated as they found themselves on opposite sides of the conflict between the superpowers of their time. The conflict between France and England also led indirectly to three great revolutions, the first in England's

North American colonies, the second in France, and the third in the French sugar colony of Saint-Domingue, today's Haiti. Each of these upheavals was so significant that historians often refer to this period as the "Age of Revolution."

Spain and Portugal had to overhaul their colonial empires to shore up their own competitive position in the high-stakes game of eighteenth-century world politics. New imperial policies coming out of Lisbon and Madrid reordered everything from taxes and trade to the position of the church, to the benefit of some and the detriment of many others. Representatives of many different social classes voiced their opposition to these changes in written petitions, town meetings, riots, and armed uprisings.

THE SPANISH AND PORTUGUESE EMPIRES IN EIGHTEENTH-CENTURY POLITICS

The opening round in the wars of the eighteenth century was the War of the Spanish Succession, which lasted for 13 years following the death of King Charles II in 1700. Charles had named Philip, a French duke and a member of the House of Bourbon, as his heir. Philip was a grandson of King Louis XIV of France, and other European powers feared that one day a single person might rule France and Spain and their huge colonial empires. England and Austria therefore went to war to prevent Philip from assuming the throne. For England, however, the War of the Spanish Succession was about much more than who would occupy the throne in Madrid. As King Louis XIV proclaimed in 1709, "The main object of the present war is the Indies trade and the wealth it produces." British access to the growing markets of Latin America was a major objective in this and all of the other conflicts of the eighteenth century.

Great Britain and Latin America

The eighteenth century witnessed the beginning of the Industrial Revolution in Great Britain. British makers of textiles, tools, and other manufactured goods eagerly sought new customers among the growing population of Latin America. Some of this trade operated legally through Spanish intermediaries, and England's colonies in North America and the Caribbean provided ideal bases for smuggling additional merchandise, but Great Britain also flexed its political and military muscle to gain greater direct access to these lucrative markets. In 1703, England and Portugal signed a treaty that guaranteed preferential treatment for British woolens in Portugal and Brazil. Although Portuguese winemakers received similar concessions in British markets, this arrangement crippled Portugal's already struggling textile industry, and Brazilian gold flowed northward, helping to underwrite Great Britain's continued economic growth. According to one estimate, fully 80 percent of the gold that circulated in Europe in the eighteenth century came originally from Brazil.

TIMELINE

1700
Death of King Charles II of Spain, accession of
Philip V and beginning of the Bourbon dynasty

1700–1713
War of the Spanish Succession

1703
Commercial treaty between England and
Portugal

1718
Founding of San Antonio, Texas

1739
Creation of viceroyalty of New Granada

1739–1748
War of Jenkins' Ear, War of the Austrian
Succession

1740
Spain begins abandonment of fleet system

1756–1763
Seven Years' War

1759
Expulsion of Jesuits from Brazil

1763
Treaty of Paris: France surrenders North
American possessions; Spain gets Louisiana;
England gets Florida

1767
Expulsion of the Jesuits from Spanish America

1776
Separate military command created for northern
frontier of New Spain; creation of viceroyalty of
Río de la Plata

1776–1783
American Revolution

1780–1781
Revolt of Tupac Amaru II; Comunero revolt in
New Granada

1788–1789
Conspiracy in Minas Gerais, Brazil

1789
Beginning of the French Revolution

1791
Haitian Revolution begins

1798
Conspiracy in Bahia (Salvador) in northeastern
Brazil

1803
United States acquires Louisiana

1815
Defeat of Napoleon

1819
Spain cedes Florida to the United States

    In 1713, the Treaty of Utrecht formally ended the War of the Spanish Succession. England and its allies agreed to accept Philip as King of Spain, but in many other ways England came out the victor. The Spanish and French Bourbons agreed that the two nations would never be united under a single monarch, and England gained other concessions crucial to its entry into Latin American markets. King Philip V granted British merchants permission to send one ship bearing African slaves and other cargo each year to the Spanish colonies, a concession that continued until 1748. The ship was authorized to call at the most important ports on the Caribbean and the Gulf of Mexico, including Cartagena, Portobelo, Veracruz, and Havana. Eager traders used this privilege as a cover to import a wide variety of merchandise to Latin America and to scout out additional prospects for contraband. Portugal got control of Colônia do Sacramento, a settlement in present-day Uruguay on the Río de la Plata estuary directly across from Buenos Aires. British merchants and Brazilian cattlemen used this port to smuggle goods into the

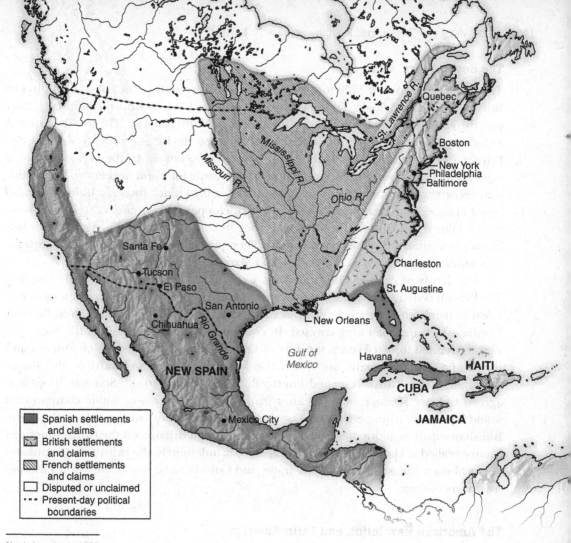

Legend:
- Spanish settlements and claims
- British settlements and claims
- French settlements and claims
- Disputed or unclaimed
- - - - Present-day political boundaries

North America in 1750

Spanish colonies in southern South America throughout the eighteenth century, even after Portugal ceded it back to Spain in 1777.

Continued contraband trade involving British and a growing number of Anglo-American merchants brought Britain and Spain to armed conflict in 1739 in the War of Jenkins' Ear, so named because Spanish authorities captured English sea captain and smuggler Robert Jenkins and cut off his ear. British naval forces held Portobelo for 2 months and nearly seized Cartagena, while North American vessels serving as privateers captured numerous Spanish ships at sea. The contest later merged into the larger conflict between England and France and their respective allies, which lasted until 1748. During the brief interval of peace that followed, the flow of British and North American merchandise into Spanish America continued unabated.

The Seven Years' War

The Seven Years' War of 1756 to 1763 brought a decisive shift in the colonial empires of Britain, France, and Spain. Fighting actually began in 1754, as British colonists clashed with the French and their Indian allies for control of North America. The war then spread to Europe, where the principal point of contention was the long-standing rivalry between Prussia and Austria, allies of Britain and France, respectively. In the end it became a significant turning point in the long Anglo-French battle for world hegemony. The British won decisively, capturing Quebec in 1759 and defeating French forces in India. They also seized France's Caribbean sugar colonies of Guadeloupe and Martinique. Spain's decision to join France had enormous consequences for its colonial empire. The British now had an excuse to attack key Spanish possessions. They quickly took Havana, linchpin of Spain's mercantile system, as well as Puerto Rico and Manila in the Philippines.

The Treaty of Paris of 1763 ended the war and redrew the map of North America. The French ceded Canada and their claims to everything east of the Mississippi River to Great Britain, but got their Caribbean islands back. The British also received Spanish Florida, which they had long coveted. In compensation, Spain was given the huge and vaguely defined former French territory of Louisiana, extending from New Orleans and the Gulf Coast to Canada and from the Mississippi River westward to the Rocky Mountains. The British returned Puerto Rico and Manila to the Spanish. They also agreed to leave Havana, but only after instituting important economic changes that would have far-reaching effects on Cuba's subsequent history. During 11 months of the British occupation, more than 700 merchant ships from Britain and the North American colonies called at Havana. Hoping to hold Havana indefinitely, the British also stimulated the local sugar industry and the slave trade, and Cuba became one of the world's leading producers of sugar.

The American Revolution and Latin America

Britain's stunning victories in the Seven Years' War were expensive, and as a result Parliament imposed new taxes on the colonies. Parliament also forbade Americans to settle west of the Appalachian Mountains and stationed British troops in Boston to subdue the city's unhappy residents. These measures and a growing sense of American nationalism drove the colonists to open revolt. Armed clashes began in Massachusetts in 1775, and representatives of the 13 colonies signed a formal declaration of independence in 1776.

The French saw an opportunity to avenge their losses in the Seven Years' War by allying with the 13 colonies in 1778, and a year later encouraged Spain to declare war on Britain. Although King Charles III of Spain could not openly support American independence for fear that his own colonial subjects might follow the example of their neighbors to the north, he welcomed the chance to regain some of the ground Spain had lost in 1763. Most U.S. history textbooks pay relatively little attention to the Spanish role in the American Revolution, but both Spain and France contributed to the colonists'

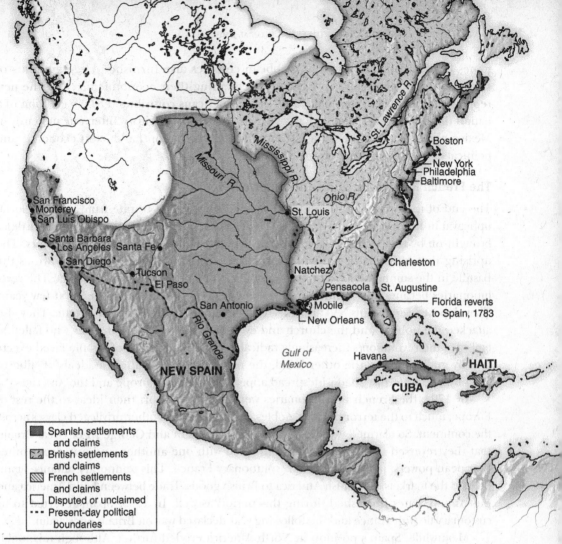

San Francisco
Monterey
San Luis Obispo

Santa Barbara
Los Angeles   Santa Fe
San Diego

Tucson
El Paso

San Antonio

Rio Grande

Missouri R.

Mississippi R.

Ohio R.

St. Louis

Natchez

Pensacola

Mobile
New Orleans

Gulf of
Mexico

NEW SPAIN

St. Lawrence R.

Boston
New York
Philadelphia
Baltimore

Charleston

St. Augustine

Florida reverts
to Spain, 1783

Havana

CUBA

HAITI

Spanish settlements
and claims

British settlements
and claims

French settlements
and claims

Disputed or unclaimed

Present-day political
boundaries

North America after 1763

victories on the battlefield. The Spanish smuggled guns, ammunition, and crucial information to the Anglo-American rebels and struck at strategic British positions in North America and the Caribbean. Led by Bernardo de Gálvez, the energetic young governor of Louisiana, Spanish troops dealt decisive blows to the British at Pensacola and Mobile and at Natchez on the Mississippi River. They also repelled an assault on Saint Louis and defended New Orleans against a possible attack.

In the Treaty of Paris of 1783, Great Britain formally recognized the independence of the United States and returned Florida to Spain. The success of the American Revolution certainly encouraged Latin Americans to think in terms of one day forming their own independent nations, but Spain's involvement in the struggle had other more immediate consequences as well. Spanish military operations were financed with steadily mounting taxes paid by colonial subjects from California to Buenos Aires and with silver from the mines of Mexico. The Spanish Caribbean colonies also furnished large amounts of supplies to the American cause, further cementing their economic ties with the new republic to the north. Ironically, then, Latin Americans contributed to the creation of a nation that would one day seize half of Mexico's national territory, intervene militarily in Mexico and several Caribbean and Central American nations, and exert economic and political dominance throughout the hemisphere.

The French Revolution and Latin America

The end of the American Revolution provided only a brief respite from war and social upheaval in Europe and the Americas. The French people faced mounting tax burdens, brought on by their monarchs' involvement in the wars of the eighteenth century. The uprising that officially began with the storming of the Parisian prison known as the Bastille in the summer of 1789 was much more than just a tax revolt, however. The revolutionaries became more and more extreme in their demands over the next few years. They deposed King Louis XVI and executed him and Queen Marie Antoinette. They also attacked the nobility and the church and even their old comrades in arms who failed to embrace the revolution's increasingly radical agenda. Thousands of people faced execution by guillotine. On the other hand, the revolution's appeal to the ideals of "liberty, equality, and fraternity" had widespread appeal throughout Europe and the Americas.

By 1793, the French revolutionaries were ready to export their ideas to the rest of Europe, much to the terror of kings, nobles, churchmen, and other privileged classes across the continent. So alarmed were Kings Charles IV of Spain and George III of Great Britain that they reversed their usual policy and sided with one another, and numerous other European powers, in a war against revolutionary France. This temporary alliance again opened the markets of Spanish America to British goods. Trade between Latin America and the United States flourished during this period as well. In 1795, Spain reverted to its customary tie with France and the following year declared war on Britain once again.

Meanwhile, Spain's position in North America eroded further. Although missionaries, soldiers, and settlers had recently occupied California as far north as San Francisco, they could not keep the British and North Americans away from the coast of what is now Oregon, Washington, and British Columbia. In 1789, a Spanish officer arrested the captain and crew of a British naval ship at a remote location on Vancouver Island and sent them to Mexico City for trial. Great Britain threatened war, knowing that internal turmoil in France would prevent Spain from turning to its traditional ally, and Spain agreed to share the region north of California with the British.

Trouble also loomed with the young and expansive United States. After 1783, Americans poured into the area between the Appalachian Mountains and the Mississippi River. Farmers in the Ohio River Valley needed an outlet to the Gulf of Mexico through Spanish New Orleans, and a disagreement over the northern boundary of the Florida territory created additional friction between the two countries. Here too, Spain adopted a policy of appeasement, just as it had done with the British in the Pacific Northwest, ceding the disputed part of Florida to the United States and granting Americans permission to use the port of New Orleans. As Anglo-Americans cast covetous eyes on Louisiana, Spain returned that territory to France, now headed by Napoleon Bonaparte, on the condition that it would never be given to a third party. Napoleon quickly went back on his word and sold the heartland of North America, from New Orleans north to Canada and west to the Rocky Mountains, to the United States in 1803. Spain yielded all of Florida to the United States in 1819. Its once proud empire was clearly in retreat.

Under Napoleon, French armies again took the offensive against the other nations of Europe. War continued with only brief interruptions until he was finally defeated in 1815, and England emerged as the world's undisputed power. Spain sided with France until 1808, when Napoleon invaded the Iberian Peninsula and imposed his brother Joseph Bonaparte as king of Spain, an event that led indirectly to the independence of Latin America. The Napoleonic Wars disrupted Spanish trade across the Atlantic, and Spain opened its colonies to ships coming from neutral powers. Traders from the United States eagerly took advantage of this opportunity to strengthen their position in Latin America.

The Haitian Revolution

The French Revolution's most profound repercussions in the Americas took place on Hispaniola. In 1697, Spain had ceded the western portion of the island to France, and the colony known as Saint-Domingue became one of the world's leading producers of sugar over the next several decades. Thousands of slaves were imported from Africa to work the plantations. By 1789, nearly 90 percent of the colony's 520,000 people were slaves, another 28,000 were free people of color, and about 40,000 were white. Events in France divided the colony's whites between those loyal to the king and those who sympathized with the revolutionaries, while free people of color seized on the more radical ideas of the French Revolution, the notions of liberty and equality, and demanded an end to various forms of discrimination.

In August of 1791, the slaves of Saint-Domingue took advantage of these splits within the upper and middle classes. They revolted, slaughtering their former masters and torching a thousand plantations. White reprisals were equally vicious. Great Britain and Spain sent forces to intervene, each hoping to seize control of the colony for itself. The revolutionary government of France declared the abolition of slavery in 1794 and rebuffed the British and Spanish attacks with the help of François Dominique Toussaint L'Ouverture, an ex-slave and a key leader of the rebellion. The rise of Napoleon Bonaparte inaugurated a shift in the mother country's racial policies, culminating in his public reinstatement of slavery in 1802. Meanwhile, Toussaint L'Ouverture declared independence from France, whereupon Napoleon dispatched a military expedition to crush his revolt. Although the French forces captured him, new black leaders emerged to fight in his place. They defeated Napoleon's troops and killed or expelled all remaining whites from the colony. On January 1, 1804, they proclaimed the independence of the new nation of Haiti—using the name the original Taino Indians had used for their land. The declaration voiced their determination "to enjoy the liberty consecrated by the blood of the people of this island" and to "forever renounce France, to die rather than to live under its domination."

How Historians Understand   LATIN AMERICA AND THE ATLANTIC WORLD

You are probably reading this book because you are enrolled in a course on "Latin American History." Historians have traditionally divided their work into a series of geographic "fields," such as U.S. History, European History, or Latin American History, and in their graduate studies and research, professors of history usually specialize in one or two of these sorts of fields. Dividing history in this way enables us to examine different parts of the world on their own terms and look for patterns that distinguish, for example, the lived experience of Latin Americans from those of Africans or Europeans or Asians.

Sometimes, however, these divisions interfere with our understanding of larger developments that cut across cultural or political lines. Take, for example, the history of the Caribbean islands. Various European powers, including Spain, France, Britain, and the Netherlands all developed Caribbean colonies, with economies based on sugar cultivation and African slave labor. Teachers of Latin American history often debate whether to include former English colonies like Jamaica or Barbados, or former French colonies like Saint-Domingue or Guadeloupe, in their discussions of plantation agriculture, slavery, or the political and social upheavals of the "Age of Revolution." Then there is the question of territories like Louisiana, first colonized by France but part of the Spanish empire from 1763 to 1803, and Florida, long a Spanish colony but a region that experienced significant change during England's 20-year hold on the colony.

Historians have come to grips with these dilemmas by thinking in terms of an "Atlantic World," a geographic space that embraces western Europe, the Americas, and western Africa. Beginning with the first Portuguese voyages to the African coast in the fifteenth century, these lands became increasingly tied together. In what historians have called the "triangular trade," ships carried tools, cloth, and weapons to

Events in Haiti terrified slaveowners and, indeed, all privileged classes throughout the Americas, while inspiring slaves and free people of color. As early as 1805, Afro-Brazilian soldiers were wearing medallions with images of Jean-Jacques Dessalines, one of the new republic's leaders. Afro-Cubans invoked the Haitian example in their own unsuccessful revolt less than a decade later.

THE BOURBON AND POMBALINE REFORMS

The dramatic shifts in world power politics during the eighteenth century moved the Bourbon kings in Spain and the Braganzas in Portugal to change the way they ruled at home and in their colonies. They adopted governing philosophies and practices from the absolutist Bourbons of France and attempted to bring the Catholic Church more

Africa, where they traded these goods for slaves, transported the slaves to markets in the Americas, and finally carried American products such as tobacco and sugar back to Europe. Ideas traveled these same routes, and as news of the American, French, and Haitian revolutions circulated rapidly through this Atlantic World, some people considered challenging the political and social status quo, while others recoiled in horror at the prospect of revolutionary upheavals.

The concept of an Atlantic World is useful for understanding the history of many people who traversed geopolitical boundaries many times during the course of their lives. Consider the case of Prince Whitten, born in West Africa in the mid-eighteenth century. As a young man he was enslaved and taken to South Carolina. Shortly after the American Revolution he and his family fled to Spanish Florida, where they obtained their freedom and converted to Catholicism. Prince joined the free black militia and fought against U.S. incursions into Florida, at one time serving under the command of Georges Biassou, a former leader of the Haitian Revolution who had sided with Spain and eventually sought refuge in Florida. After Spain ceded Florida to the United States, Prince evacuated to Cuba, where he spent the remainder of his life. Prince Whitten's story is part of African history, but it also belongs to United States and Latin American history as well. Only an Atlantic World perspective can do justice to the lived experience of Whitten and countless others like him.

Questions for Discussion
How does the history of Cuba fit into an "Atlantic World" perspective? What about the history of Brazil? Should courses on Latin America include such places as Saint-Domingue, Jamaica, Florida, Louisiana? Why or why not?

firmly under royal control. They tried to stimulate trade and economic development and imposed new taxes in an effort to generate more revenues to underwrite offensive and defensive military operations. Crown monopolies on such commodities as tobacco, gunpowder, and playing cards constituted another major source of revenue for the Bourbon kings of Spain. As the American, French, and Haitian revolutions unfolded, the Spanish and Portuguese governments attempted to suppress the spread of seditious ideas among their colonial subjects.

Above all, the monarchs of Spain and Portugal worked to tighten their hold on their overseas territories in the face of mounting foreign pressure to gain access to the thriving markets of Latin America. They reorganized colonial administration and sent growing numbers of peninsular bureaucrats to keep potential rebels in line. The Spanish kings revamped colonial defense policies, especially in areas vulnerable to British intrusions. They built stronger fortifications in ports such as Havana, San Juan, and Veracruz and promoted the settlement of California to ward off Russian fur traders moving southward from Alaska, as well as the British and the North Americans.

All of these changes, collectively known as the "Bourbon Reforms" in the Spanish empire and the "Pombaline Reforms" in Portugal and Brazil, carried huge consequences for Latin Americans. Although the first of these changes occurred during the reign of Philip V, the most sweeping innovations took place during the second half of the eighteenth century, as the conflict between Britain and France reached its climax and Spain's position in the Western Hemisphere became increasingly precarious. King Charles III, who assumed the Spanish throne in 1759 and reigned until 1788, spearheaded the reforms in his empire, with the energetic assistance of his minister of the Indies, José de Gálvez (see Plate 12). In Portugal and Brazil, Sebastião José de Carvalhoe Mello, better known as the Marquis of Pombal, served as chief minister during the reign of King José I (1750–1777) and masterminded the overhaul of the Portuguese colonial empire.

Vue de la Ville de Havanne en Amérique

The fortified port of Havana, captured by the British in 1762.

Defending the Spanish Empire

Prior to the eighteenth century, Spain maintained a rather minimal military presence in its American colonies. The Hapsburg kings were reluctant to spend much money on colonial defense, even as they squandered huge sums on their military exploits in Europe. In New Spain, as of 1700, fewer than 6000 poorly equipped regular army troops guarded the northern frontier and strategically located ports that had been traditional targets of foreign pirates. The crown preferred that career soldiers from Spain man these garrisons. By the late seventeenth century, however, not enough Spaniards were willing to serve overseas, so growing numbers of creoles, mestizos, and free blacks filled the ranks, often conscripted from among vagrants and criminals. Citizen militias, organized in cities and small towns throughout the empire, supplemented the regular army forces. Often, the militia members had to supply their own uniforms and weapons.

As imperial rivalries accelerated in the eighteenth century, the kings of Spain devoted more resources to the defense of their colonies. In the aftermath of the Seven Years' War, sturdier fortifications were built at San Juan, Cartagena, Havana, Veracruz, and other ports that had been such tempting targets for the British. In 1767, the king created a standing colonial army to augment the meager frontier garrisons and local militias. Sales taxes were increased from 2 to 6 percent to offset the cost. Young men of all social classes except Indians were liable for conscription. Throughout the empire, militia forces were also expanded, with regular army officers assigned to monitor these units. Ambitious creoles found new opportunities as officers in the regular army and the militia units. Growing numbers of career military officers were appointed to administrative positions.

The Bourbon monarchs also sponsored new settlements to bolster Spanish claims to frontier regions. Even though they often allied with France in the world conflicts of the time, they actively resisted French encroachments on their territory in North America. The presence of French missionaries and fur traders in the Mississippi Valley and the establishment of substantial French settlements at New Orleans and along the Gulf Coast prompted Spain to tighten its grip on Texas. King Philip V made the permanent occupation of Texas a top priority, fostering the establishment of missions, military garrisons, and civilian communities clustered around what is now the city of San Antonio, founded in 1718. Settlers were recruited from adjacent parts of northern New Spain and from as far away as the Canary Islands.

Although the French presence in North America was clearly a menace to Spain, it also served as a buffer against the even more troublesome British. After 1763, however, Spain found itself face-to-face with Great Britain along the Mississippi River. The situation called for a thorough revamping of defense policies all along the northern frontier. In 1776, King Charles III ordered the creation of a separate military command to oversee the security of the entire northern frontier of New Spain. Meanwhile, Franciscans were setting up a chain of missions up the coast of California from San Diego to San Francisco and military presidios and civilian settlements appeared at select locations, all in an effort to secure Spain's hold on the west coast of North America.

Administrative Restructuring and New Viceroyalties

Both the Spanish and the Portuguese governments also reorganized colonial administration. Beginning in 1764, Spain installed men known as intendants to represent the
crown's interests, supervise fiscal and military affairs, and implement the Bourbon
reforms at the local level. The intendants were like miniature viceroys operating out of
major provincial towns. Peru had 8. Subordinate to the intendants were *subdelegados*
(subdelegates) in charge of Indian villages. The intendants and subdelegados received
better salaries than the alcaldes mayores and corregidores they were supposed to replace,
so that they might be less tempted to corruption. In fact, they appear to have continued
the same old practices, and many of them were military officers and peninsulares who
alienated local creoles. They also proved to be more efficient tax collectors than their
predecessors, to the consternation of the taxpayers.

The Spanish government also created two new viceroyalties in South America. The
first, known as New Granada, was established at Bogotá in 1739 and had jurisdiction over
present-day Ecuador, Colombia, Panama, and much of Venezuela. In 1776, Buenos Aires
became the seat of the viceroyalty of La Plata, which included Upper Peru and the mines
of Potosí (present-day Bolivia) as well as Argentina, Uruguay, and Paraguay. The creation
of new high courts (*audiencias*) in cities such as Caracas and Buenos Aires also signified
the crown's desire to increase its presence in areas that were once considered peripheral
to the empire but were now of growing economic and strategic importance.

Meanwhile, comparable developments were occurring in Brazil. The discovery of
gold in Minas Gerais at the end of the seventeenth century shifted the colony's economic
axis southward, away from the sugar-growing region of Bahia. Accelerating conflict with
Spain heightened the strategic importance of the south as well. Although all of Brazil
remained under the jurisdiction of a single viceroy, in 1763, he moved his headquarters
from Salvador to Rio de Janeiro in the south. Salvador continued to be the seat of a high
court, but a second court was set up in the new capital. Like his counterparts in Spain,
Prime Minister Pombal also appointed peninsular military officers to many high-level
government posts in Brazil.

The Power of the Church

The absolutist kings of eighteenth-century Europe increasingly viewed the Catholic
Church as a rival power. Although the Pope had long ago conceded the Spanish and
Portuguese monarchs the right to name bishops and otherwise supervise church affairs
in their colonies, the wealth and political power of the church had grown steadily from its
humble missionary origins in the sixteenth century. From the perspective of Lisbon and
Madrid, the church enjoyed far too tight a hold on people's loyalties and its extensive
property might be better diverted to more utilitarian ends.

The Society of Jesus represented a particularly great threat to ministers of state like
the Marquis of Pombal and José de Gálvez. The Jesuits had accumulated enormous real
estate holdings and thousands of slaves. From Paraguay in South America to Sonora, Baja

California, and Arizona on the northern frontier of New Spain, Jesuit missions constituted veritable kingdoms outside the sphere of crown control, while Jesuit colleges
trained the sons of colonial elites throughout Spanish America and Brazil. Moreover,
along with the customary monastic commitments to poverty, chastity, and obedience to
superiors, they took a special vow of loyalty to the Pope. Ambitious monarchs throughout
Europe feared that the Jesuits might work in concert with the pope to subvert their own
power. Members of the order were accused of inciting popular riots in Madrid and plots
against the king in Lisbon.

Slice of Life   THE ROYAL TOBACCO FACTORY IN MEXICO CITY

THE CREATION OF A CROWN monopoly on tobacco in 1765 was a key component of the
Spanish Bourbon Reforms. Tobacco production was restricted to specified areas,
growers were required to sell their crops to agents of the monopoly, and royal factories were established to replace independent makers of cigars and cigarettes. The
monopoly's most obvious objective was to increase crown revenues, but it served
other purposes too. Reformers saw the cigarette factories as vehicles to control the
growing masses of poor people and to use their labor for the betterment of the
empire. As one monopoly official put it, "The man without an occupation is a dead
man for the State; those who work are like living plants which not only produce but
propagate . . . wherein lies the true increase of the population and prosperity of the
State." Although they couched their objectives in terms of men, in fact the Bourbons
hoped to tap women's productive potential as well. They believed that women's small
hands and manual dexterity ideally suited them to the task of rolling cigarettes, and
that women workers were more conscientious and less likely to get drunk or steal
from their employers than men. The reformers also hoped that factory jobs would
get women off the streets, away from prostitution and into useful activity.

The tobacco factory of Mexico City employed up to 9000 workers, many of them
women and children. Factory jobs were especially appealing to single women and
widows without other means of support. Most employees were either españoles or
mestizos, but some were Indians and mulattos. They worked Monday through
Saturday, with the exception of religious holidays, and they were paid on a piecework
basis. A workers' cofradía provided burial insurance and other benefits, and there
was even a kind of on-site day care for young children.

Factory work usually implies a fixed routine. Employees show up at a specific time
and work more or less nonstop for a stipulated number of hours. Administrators of
the tobacco factory aimed to impose this kind of discipline on the riffraff they
recruited from the streets of Mexico City. In theory, workers arrived on the job early
in the morning and stayed for a 12-hour shift, but in fact they often came and went
as they pleased. Many subcontracted their daily quotas to family members or dependents

and then went about other, more profitable activities. They also took some of their work home so they could attend to household responsibilities along with their paid employment.

Nor were tobacco workers always the obedient, docile labor force envisioned by Bourbon planners. They voiced their concerns in frequent petitions to monopoly administrators and occasionally took to the streets to get their grievances heard. Their most notable success came in 1794 in the so-called paper riot. The imported paper used for making cigarettes was becoming increasingly expensive as war in Europe disrupted shipments from Spain. In an attempt to prevent waste and theft of this precious commodity, factory managers forbade the workers' usual practice of taking paper home in the evening and preparing it for the next day's work. Outraged workers marched in protest to the viceroy's palace and got their customary rights restored. The Bourbons wanted to reorder colonial society to the benefit of the state, but they often had to make concessions to reality.

Questions for Discussion

The Bourbon Reforms have sometimes been portrayed as a second Spanish conquest of America. Would the people who worked in the Mexico City tobacco factory have agreed? Why or why not?

In 1759, the Marquis of Pombal ordered the society expelled from Portugal's overseas territories, and a similar decree went out to Spanish America in 1767. The Jesuits were given just a few days to gather up their personal belongings and embark for Europe, while crown officials seized the order's assets and began selling them off to the highest bidders, many of them drawn from local elites who had long coveted these choice properties. Jesuit missions were placed under the control of secular clergy or other religious orders. In northwestern New Spain, for example, Franciscan priests took over the missions of Sonora, Baja California, and present-day southern Arizona.

The eighteenth-century kings of Spain and Portugal also attempted to curb the wealth and power of other ecclesiastical institutions. The early evangelization of the native peoples of Latin America had been entrusted largely to the regular clergy—that is, the Franciscans, Dominicans, Augustinians, Jesuits, and other religious orders. Their control of these mission parishes was supposed to be temporary, with secular clergy expected to replace them within a decade or two of the initial conversion of a given area. The regulars would then move on to new mission fields on the frontiers of Spanish settlement. In practice, however, the regular clergy continued ministering to many centrally located Indian parishes well into the eighteenth century.

Because the secular clergy answered directly to their bishops, who were in effect royal appointees, the absolutist monarchs of the late colonial period renewed their efforts to secularize Indian parishes. High-handed Spanish bureaucrats forcibly ejected Franciscans, Augustinians, and Dominicans from their sixteenth-century monasteries, and the secular priests who succeeded them often rented out portions of the mission

San Xavier del Bac mission, Tucson, Arizona, built by Franciscans in 1776.

complexes to serve as stables and tenements. Pombal removed the regular clergy from their control over the assets of Indian villages (*aldeias*) in Brazil, although they were allowed to remain as pastors. The Spanish crown restricted the jurisdiction of church courts, forbade the establishment of new nunneries, and tried to convince nuns residing in existing convents to adhere more closely to their vows of poverty.

Economic Development

The Spanish and Portuguese monarchs of the eighteenth century also endeavored to stimulate economic development at home and in the colonies and generate a greater stream of revenue into the royal treasuries. To increase silver mining in Spanish America, the Bourbon kings offered tax incentives, reduced the price of mercury used in processing silver, and established a college for training mining engineers in Mexico City. These changes failed to bring any great bonanza in South America, but the output of Mexican silver mines in 1800 was eight times what it had been a century earlier, and Mexico was producing as much silver as the entire rest of the world. Other measures targeted those select places in the Spanish colonies where gold could be found. Miners in certain parts of present-day Colombia, for example, were permitted to import greater numbers of slaves to assist them in panning for gold.

In both Spanish America and Brazil, royally chartered companies were created to boost production of desired commodities and to lure Spanish, Portuguese, and colonial investors into new ventures. The Basque merchants of the Caracas Company, for example, received a monopoly on cacao exports from Venezuela, a trade that grew substantially as demand for chocolate spread in Europe during the eighteenth century. Pombal created the Companies of Pernambuco and Grão Pará e Maranhão to stimulate the northern regions of Brazil. The latter company received a 20-year monopoly on slave imports to the area.

The Bourbons also experimented with liberalizing trade within the Spanish empire. As we saw in Chapter 4, policies adopted in the sixteenth century had limited trade with the colonies to a single port in Spain, required ships to travel in convoy, and permitted them to call only at Havana, Cartagena, Portobelo, and Veracruz. First to be abandoned was the fleet system. The last convoy bound for Panamá sailed in 1740. A new era of *comercio libre*, or free trade, began after the Seven Years' War, and eventually merchant vessels were permitted to sail from anywhere in Spain to any port in the colonies. Meanwhile, as we have seen, foreign trade with the colonies also increased, sometimes legally permitted, sometimes not.

Pombal's economic policies aimed at reducing Portugal's dependence on Great Britain, but within the constraints posed by the strategic alliance of the two nations. He sent inspectors to Brazil's chief ports to impose quality control standards on exports of sugar and tobacco, thus hoping to guarantee a favorable world market share for these traditional products. In 1773, he ordered an end to discrimination against New Christians, whose capital and mercantile experience he hoped to enlist for his economic development schemes. He also imposed tighter controls aimed at forcing gold miners to pay their taxes.

The relaxation of trade restrictions within the Spanish empire and other policies of the home governments in Lisbon and Madrid brought spectacular growth to certain regions that had previously been considered marginal parts of the colonies. Buenos Aires, now capital of the viceroyalty of La Plata and the seat of a newly created high court, was especially favored in the new commercial order. The city became the principal outlet for silver from Upper Peru and hides and salted beef from the vast plains known as *pampas* in Argentina, Uruguay, and southern Brazil. The population of Buenos Aires soared from about 10,000 in 1750 to almost 40,000 by the beginning of the nineteenth century.

Havana, of course, had long been important as the hub of the Indies trade, but the rest of the island had remained an economic backwater. Once its deposits of placer gold were exhausted in the early sixteenth century, Cuba's exports had consisted principally of tobacco and hides. The shipbuilding industry was the only other major employer. The British occupation of 1762 inaugurated a new phase in Cuba's economic history. Hoping to hold the island indefinitely, the British fostered sugar production during their brief tenure, and Spain continued to encourage the industry after it regained control of Cuba. The destruction of plantations in Haiti after 1791 gave an additional stimulus to Cuban production. The island rapidly became one of the world's leading sources of sugar, a position it held during a good part of the century to come. With the expansion of the sugar industry came a huge influx of African slaves to Cuba—more than 300,000 between 1780 and 1820 and another 200,000 in the next 40 years. Cuba would remain a slave society for much of the nineteenth century.

Under the auspices of the Company of Grão Pará e Maranhão, the region near the mouth of the Amazon in northeastern Brazil also developed rapidly. Pombal sent his own brother to the area as governor, explicitly assigning him the task of building a plantation colony to replace old mission complexes. These efforts proved exceptionally successful in Maranhão, where cotton plantations developed rapidly, worked by a fresh supply of slaves imported from Africa. "White cotton turned Maranhão black," people said. Rio de Janeiro also flourished in its new status as capital of Brazil after 1763. Its population grew from just over 20,000 in 1775 to more than 100,000 by 1820. The city became Brazil's most important port, exporting gold, cotton, rice, coffee, and indigo while importing slaves and manufactured goods.

Other areas experienced marked downturns in the new economic order. Panama and Cartagena declined following the dismantling of the fleet system, and Cartagena's audiencia was abolished. Some colonial industries could no longer compete with the increased volume of imports that accompanied the relaxation of trade restrictions. The textile trade of Quito and the region known as the Bajío, northwest of Mexico City, were among the most severely affected as British and other foreign cloth flooded American markets in the age of free trade. Other manufacturers weathered the changes more successfully, as population growth generated new markets.

LATIN AMERICAN PEOPLES IN THE AGE OF REVOLUTION

The reorganization of colonial government, the promotion of economic development, new intellectual currents, and the shifting world politics of the "Age of Revolution" brought important changes to the people of Latin America. Economic growth and an influx of immigrants from Spain and Portugal added new dimensions to the region's already complex hierarchies of class and ethnicity. Intellectuals in the colonies eagerly read and discussed the works of Enlightenment philosophers despite the efforts of the Inquisition to thwart the circulation of these potentially subversive ideas. At the same time, the kings of Spain and Portugal actively promoted the Enlightenment's more pragmatic, strictly scientific side. They encouraged innovation in agriculture and industry and sponsored research expeditions to learn more about the flora, fauna, and physical environment of their colonies. They also undertook a systematic makeover of urban space in the Americas, in an effort to make Mexico City, Rio de Janeiro, and other cities look more like the sophisticated metropolises of Europe. Even if they had no access to the news coming out of Philadelphia or Paris, the people of Latin America could find plenty of other evidence that they were living in an Age of Revolution.

Social Change in the Late Colonial Period

One of the most visible social changes of the late colonial period was the marked influx of peninsulares. During the seventeenth and early eighteenth centuries, growing numbers of creoles had gained entry into the ranks of the bureaucracy in the Spanish colonies. Between 1700 and 1759, 108 of the 136 men appointed judges of the audiencias were American born. As part of their effort to bring the colonies under firmer control of the mother country, the Bourbons began to reverse that trend, especially during the reign of Charles III. Choice positions in the church also increasingly went to peninsulares. The growing volume of trade between Spain and the colonies attracted other Spaniards, many of them Basques, eager to make their fortunes as merchants. Ambitious creoles perceived a clear threat to their own chances for political and economic advancement, and the divisions between Spanish born and Americans deepened.

In Brazil, the numbers of Portuguese immigrants also increased in the late colonial period, especially in the rapidly developing frontier regions. The Marquis of Lavradio, a Portuguese nobleman who served as viceroy of Brazil during the Pombal regime, often accused Brazilians of being lazy and ill-suited to carrying out the crown's agenda. In general, however, tensions between foreigners and those born in America were not as marked in Brazil as in the Spanish colonies.

If the distinctions between creoles and peninsulares became sharper in many places, other social barriers were undermined by the economic and political changes of the times. The newly rich eagerly spent their fortunes on landed estates and other status symbols, including titles of nobility and certificates of legitimate birth issued by the crown. Even people of questionable social and ethnic backgrounds sported elegant clothing, built impressive townhouses for themselves, and aspired to marry into prestigious families. More Spanish Americans were using the titles "Don" and "Doña," an indicator of social prestige. Some of the older established elites felt threatened by these changes and attempted to protect their privileged status against these upstarts by exerting even greater control over the marriage choices of their children. The Spanish crown obliged them in 1776 by issuing a law requiring anyone under the age of 25 to have their parents' consent and permitting parents to disinherit any son or daughter who disregarded their wishes.

In many places—with the notable exception of Cuba and some parts of Brazil—the number of slaves declined in the late colonial period. Just about everywhere, the number of free blacks and mulattos grew. In the gold mining region of Antioquia in New Granada, for example, free blacks outnumbered slaves three to one according to a census compiled in the 1770s. In Venezuela and elsewhere, slave revolts and runaway communities became more numerous. A select few free blacks even obtained official government documents granting them the legal status of whites regardless of their color.

Military necessities of the Age of Revolution also chipped away at old social distinctions between blacks and whites. Blacks and mulattos who helped defend the Spanish empire won new privileges in colonial society. In Mexico, the people of the maroon community of Nuestra Señora de los Morenos de Amapa, most of whom were slaves who

LATIN AMERICAN LIVES

JOSÉ ANTONIO APONTE, SCULPTOR OF HAVANA

On March 19, 1812, local officials in Havana arrested José Antonio Aponte, a free black man in his early 50s, on charges of fomenting a series of slave uprisings that were sweeping across Cuba. Aponte was literate and a skilled carpenter and sculptor by trade. Like many other artisans of the Age of Revolution, Aponte had served in the free black militia, attaining the rank of captain before his retirement in 1800. A highlight of his military career was his participation in a campaign against the British in the Bahamas during the war for U.S. independence. Aponte was proud of his military service and kept copies of Spanish royal ordinances that conferred special privileges on veterans.

A key piece of evidence used in prosecuting Aponte was a scrapbook found in his home. Although the book has been lost, testimony taken at his trial revealed that it contained maps showing locations of military garrisons and sketches of depicting his military exploits, along with those of his father and grandfather. Another series of illustrations, hand-copied from printed engravings or cut from published books, included portraits of George Washington and various leaders of the Haitian Revolution. Perhaps even more disturbing to authorities were drawings that depicted black soldiers fighting whites and an image of the king of Spain informing two black soldiers that they need not remove their hats in his presence—an open challenge to militia regulations that required black members to show deference to white soldiers. Another illustration showed a crown and scepter overrun by vipers. The subversive content of his scrapbook was enough to convince the judges of that Aponte was indeed the ringleader of a plot to stage in Cuba a revolution comparable to the one that had swept Saint-Domingue. He was convicted and executed, along with several coconspirators, just 3 weeks after his arrest.

Cuba's slave-based plantation economy had grown substantially since the 1760s, while the position of free blacks like Aponte had deteriorated. While not all free blacks supported the abolition of slavery, and a few even owned slaves themselves, Cuban elites panicked at the suggestion that the two groups might collaborate in a revolutionary enterprise and an outspoken black man like José Antonio Aponte served as a convenient scapegoat. The so-called Aponte rebellion helped convince several generations of Cuban whites that they needed the continued presence of Spanish authorities to prevent the island from going the way of Haiti. While the rest of Spain's American colonies became independent by the 1820s, Cuba and Puerto Rico—another burgeoning slave society, retained their colonial status until 1898.

Questions for Discussion

Why would free people of color support a slave revolt? Why might they oppose such a revolt? How might Aponte have been affected if Cuba had experienced a revolution like the one in Haiti? Is the term "Age of Revolution" appropriate when referring to Afro-Cubans? Why or why not?

had run away from sugar plantations in the area around Veracruz, received their freedom after their men joined the forces defending the port city against a possible British attack in 1762. In other ways, however, the defense reforms of the late colonial period undermined the role of free blacks in the military. In Mexico, white regular army officers were put in charge of free colored militias, undermining the authority of black officers who had previously commanded these forces, and in the 1790s the black units were disbanded altogether.

The cultural differences between Indians and others continued to erode as well. Late colonial censuses show declining numbers of Indians as growing numbers of people "passed" into other ethnic categories and participated more fully in the market economy, while more non-Indians took up residence in Indian villages. These changes were welcomed and encouraged by the Spanish and Portuguese crowns. Hoping to increase the population of the sparsely settled frontier regions, Pombal promoted intermarriage between Indians and non-Indians. He also encouraged Indians in these areas to work for wages and to speak Portuguese. The secular clergy who replaced the religious orders in many Indian parishes were seldom proficient in indigenous languages, and many of them probably agreed with the newly appointed bishop of Oaxaca who in 1803 lamented the fact that the people of his diocese still spoke 18 different "rough, unknown tongues." Teaching Spanish and Portuguese therefore became a matter of practical necessity, and schoolmasters were appointed to Indian villages in central and southern New Spain for precisely that purpose. By the end of the eighteenth century, few Indian villages kept official records in indigenous languages.

In rapidly developing frontier regions, the distinction between "Indians" and non-Indians was even less pronounced than in Mexico or the Andes. By the beginning of the nineteenth century, Indians comprised only 13 percent of the population of central Venezuela, for example. Two-thirds of the people in Buenos Aires were classified as españoles, one-third as black or mulatto, and only about 1 percent as Indians.

The Changing Face of Colonial Cities

The economic changes of the late colonial period spurred a marked increase in the size of cities and towns all across Latin America. Mexico City, for example, had a population estimated at 137,000 in 1803, easily dwarfing such North American cities as Philadelphia, Boston, and New York. Urban growth presented city councils and imperial authorities with mounting challenges in the areas of food supply, public health, and safety. The Bourbon monarchs attempted to end what they considered the insalubrious practice of burying the dead in churches and promoted the use of new cemeteries located outside of town. After Edward Jenner developed the smallpox vaccine in Britain in the late 1790s, the practice quickly spread to Latin America.

Other measures addressed the problem of crime in the streets. Mexico City expanded the capacity of municipal jails and divided the city into 32 police districts, each with its own magistrate. The number of arrests increased from about 1000 per year in 1783 to 10 times that number a decade later. Bogotá established its first police force in the 1790s. Mexico City, Veracruz, and other cities also began lighting the streets at night and providing for more efficient garbage disposal. Many town councils enacted ordinances against vagrancy and begging in the streets and attempted to gather the destitute into orphanages, poorhouses, and other social welfare institutions. They also tried to control public drunkenness by imposing tighter controls on taverns.

The Bourbon kings of Spain were also concerned with the threat to public order posed by popular religious festivals, and their determination to lessen the influence of the church added further incentive to reduce the number and extravagance of these observances. Efforts to suppress pre-Lenten carnival festivities began in Mexico City early in the eighteenth century. Other campaigns followed, but with limited success, for the city's elite continued as before to use festivals as a chance to flaunt their wealth, the lower classes looked forward to a change in their daily routines, and people of all social classes viewed religious holidays as a central part of their spiritual lives.

Meanwhile, urban residents enjoyed more amenities. Streets and plazas at the center of many towns were now paved, and public fountains made water more easily available.

A 1763 drawing of Mexico City's central park, the Alameda.

Mexico City doubled the size of the Alameda, its public park, and inaugurated a new theater known as the Coliseum in the 1750s. Caracas even boasted a symphony orchestra. The naming of city streets and the numbering of buildings reflected the growing concern with imposing order on urban space.

The Enlightenment in Latin America

Cities and towns were also hubs of intellectual activity in the late colonial period. Educated elites avidly read and discussed the new ways of thinking coming out of Europe and North America. The U.S. Declaration of Independence, Tom Paine's pamphlet *Common Sense,* and the Federalist Papers circulated throughout Latin America, along with the British economist Adam Smith's highly influential *The Wealth of Nations,* a book that argued for free trade, and the French revolutionaries' Declaration of the Rights of Man and of the Citizen. Many others read Voltaire, Rousseau, Montesquieu, and other French Enlightenment philosophers, as well as Spanish writers who also disseminated the new ideas.

The kings of Spain and Portugal tried unsuccessfully to stop the spread of such potentially subversive ideas, especially after the French Revolution took its radical turn in the 1790s, but they enthusiastically embraced the Enlightenment's practical side and actively promoted scientific research. In 1737, Philip V sent a team of French scientists to Quito to measure degrees of latitude near the equator. Between 1799 and 1804, the German scientist Alexander von Humboldt traveled throughout Latin America. He explored Venezuela's Orinoco River and a good portion of the Amazon Basin, climbed Mount Chimborazo in Ecuador, and reported on mining and other industries in Mexico. The Marquis of Pombal dispatched investigators to learn about the flora and fauna of Brazil. The presence of so many scientists helped Latin American intellectuals stay abreast of the latest developments in Europe.

Educational institutions also began placing greater emphasis on science and reason in place of theology, especially after the ouster of the Jesuits. Many clergymen were in fact quite receptive to these new ideas and introduced them into the curricula of the schools they operated. The Bishop of Pernambuco, for example, set up a seminary with a program of study modeled after that of Portugal's University of Coimbra, which had become a center of the new learning under Pombal's influence. Schools operated by the Franciscans in Rio de Janeiro began offering courses in physics and natural history. New universities established at Caracas and Santiago, Chile, had medical schools.

By the late colonial period, newspapers disseminated scientific learning throughout Spanish America. The *Mercurio Peruano,* edited by the physician Hipólito Unanue, carried numerous articles on medicine, while José Antonio Alzate y Ramírez used the *Gaceta de México* to discuss ways of coping with widespread famine that resulted after a premature frost destroyed much of the maize crop in central Mexico in 1785. The papers

Alexander von Humboldt.

also included political news, including substantial coverage of the events of the American Revolution. European and North American newspapers brought by trading vessels kept Spanish Americans and Brazilians informed about current events.

Meanwhile, intellectuals in the Spanish colonies and in Brazil met in informal gatherings called *tertulias* to discuss the political and scientific ideas of the age. They also established more formal clubs to explore ways to stimulate local economic development. In Spanish America, these associations were usually called "Societies of Friends of the Country." The Havana society established Spanish America's first public library in 1793, and within a year it had 1500 circulating volumes. The group in Cartagena sought ways to promote the cultivation of cotton in the surrounding region.

RESISTANCE AND REBELLION IN THE LATE COLONIAL PERIOD

The enormous economic, political, and social changes of the late colonial period, the increased flow of information, and the critical spirit of the Age of Revolution prompted Latin Americans from a variety of social backgrounds to take a hard look at the situations in which they found themselves. Privileged classes objected to the high-handed tactics of colonial administrators, the preferential treatment given to peninsulares, and the taxes and other restrictions imposed on their economic activities. Creole intellectuals expressed a new pride in their homelands and looked for ways to promote true prosperity and progress at the local level. A select few suggested that their compatriots borrow a lesson or two from the North American and French revolutionaries.

People further down the social ladder had neither the education nor the leisure to ponder the works of French philosophers or the latest news from Philadelphia and Boston, but many of them were clearly aware that the changing times were making life more difficult. Taxes and military conscription hit them hard, while population increase strained land and water resources and depressed their real wages. They expressed their dissatisfaction in quite a few popular revolts in the late colonial period. For Latin Americans, the Age of Revolution was a time to evaluate their status as colonial subjects and to resist injustices both old and new.

Developing Creole Consciousness

As they became more familiar with the leading thinkers of the European Enlightenment, Latin Americans were appalled to learn that some of these supposedly great minds held the Western Hemisphere and its people in disdain. The French natural historian George-Louis Leclerc Buffon, for example, argued that the New World's climate and environment made people lazy and decrepit. For Buffon, the pre-Columbian inhabitants of the Americas were "stupid, ignorant, unacquainted with the arts and destitute of industry," and creoles were not much better. Another French writer, Guillaume-Thomas Raynal, questioned the accounts of early Spanish conquistadors who were dazzled by what they saw at Tenochtitlan and Cuzco. The Aztec capital, he wrote, was not a great city but "a little town, composed of a multitude of rustic huts," and its highly touted temples and palaces were crudely thrown together.

Creoles took these criticisms personally. They wrote lengthy treatises on the grandeur of ancient American civilizations in an effort to prove that the Western Hemisphere could nurture cultural achievements second to none. Homesick Jesuits exiled in Italy were among the leading proponents of these views. Francisco Javier Clavijero penned what he called "a history of Mexico written by a Mexican, expressly designed to answer the slanders" of writers like Buffon and Raynal. He drew on his fluency in Nahuatl to counter charges that indigenous languages lacked words to express abstract concepts and praised the intellectual abilities of Indian students he had taught at the Colegio de San Gregorio in Mexico City. His fellow Jesuit, the Ecuadorian Juan de Velasco, wrote a history of the kingdom of Quito that extolled pre-Hispanic society in the Andes. The Chilean Juan Ignacio Molina cited the fertile soil and benign climate of his homeland and pointed out that Araucanian poets rivaled those of the Celts in Europe.

Creole intellectuals also grappled with the question of why the Americas had seemingly been overlooked by the Twelve Apostles after Jesus had told them to go out and "preach to all nations." They revived the sixteenth-century notion that St. Thomas had in fact traveled to the New World, and that he was the person whom Mesoamericans called Quetzalcoatl. Others argued that the greatness of pre-Columbian Mexico owed nothing to any outside sources, not even an apostle.

Still another manifestation of growing creole self-awareness was the spread of the cult of Our Lady of Guadalupe in Mexico. Tradition claims that the Virgin Mary appeared to an Indian named Juan Diego on a hillside near Mexico City in 1531. Although historians have confirmed that some kind of shrine had been built on the site by the latter part of the sixteenth century, they have found no evidence that the Juan Diego story actually circulated in New Spain before 1648. Thereafter, however, devotion to the Virgin spread, not initially among Indians but rather among creoles who viewed the apparition as proof of divine favor for Mexico and its people. In 1754, Pope Benedict XIV proclaimed her as the patroness of all New Spain.

Resistance to the Bourbon Reforms

The new taxes and other administrative changes ordered by Charles III sparked protest and debate throughout Spanish America. In many towns and cities, leading male citizens convened to discuss issues of concern. One such gathering took place in the town of Concepción in Chile in 1794. Those present voiced their objection to new taxes proposed by the audiencia in Santiago. Concepción's town council had not been consulted, and they were protesting taxation without representation. Creole elites everywhere argued that as descendants of conquistadors and early settlers they should be appointed to government posts in place of upstarts just off the boat from Spain. Meanwhile, merchants' guilds in many towns called for an even greater liberalization of trade.

Other protests were more violent. Riots occurred in Quito in 1765, following the introduction of new taxes and other "reforms." In Mexico, popular uprisings followed the expulsion of the Jesuits in 1767. Spanish officials responded with exceptional force in the mining district of San Luis Potosí, ordering the execution of 85 people and the imprisonment of hundreds more. In 1781, the people of New Granada staged a somewhat more successful opposition to the Bourbon Reforms in the so-called Comunero Revolt. They attacked tax collectors and agents of royal monopolies on tobacco, cane alcohol, and playing cards, while also demanding the appointment of more creoles to government offices. Some 20,000 rebels threatened to march on Bogotá, which was poorly defended because most of the Spanish military forces had been sent to the coast to guard against British attacks. They won a reprieve from certain taxes, and a general amnesty for most participants in the rebellion, except for four alleged ringleaders who were executed.

Conspiracies in Brazil

Brazilians also registered their complaints in the volatile climate of the Age of Revolution. An attempt by zealous bureaucrats in Lisbon to collect overdue tax revenues in the mining district of Minas Gerais prompted a few dozen landowners, military officers, heavily indebted tax contractors, and intellectuals in the town of Ouro Preto to conspire to revolt in 1788 and 1789. Influenced by the example of the American Revolution, the rebels proposed to create an independent, democratic republic in Minas Gerais and to do away with colonial taxes and restrictions on diamond mining and manufacturing. They offered freedom to slaves who joined the plot and planned to defend their government with a citizen militia made up of blacks and mulattos. When colonial authorities got wind of the plot, they exiled five of the conspirators to the Portuguese African colony at Angola. The principal ringleader, a military officer named Joaquim José da Silva Xavier, alias Tiradentes ("tooth-puller"), was publicly executed in 1789.

Another abortive conspiracy occurred about 10 years later in northeastern Brazil, when handwritten proclamations of the "supreme tribunal of Bahian democracy" appeared on churches and other public buildings in Salvador. These rebels came from lower ranks of society than their counterparts in Minas Gerais. Echoing the rhetoric of the French Revolution, they promised freedom for slaves, abolition of monasteries, and equality of all people. They also proposed free trade and an end to the "detestable metropolitan yoke of Portugal." The leader of the group was João de Deus do Nascimento, a 27-year-old free mulatto tailor. Asked about his visions for the future, he proclaimed that with "everything being leveled in a popular revolution, all would be rich, released from the misery in which they were living, discrimination between white, black, and mulatto being abolished; because all occupations and jobs would be open and available without distinction to each and every one."

Local authorities moved quickly to thwart the conspiracy, arresting 49 alleged participants. Most of those apprehended were free mulattos in their 20s, many of them tailors or other artisans, although 11 were slaves, and 10 were white; 5 of those detained were women. The movement also included a number of enlisted military personnel and militia members. Many of the conspirators were able to read and write, in a city where 90 percent of the population was illiterate. In 1799, colonial authorities ordered the public execution of Nascimento and three other key participants, while others received public whippings and some were exiled to Africa.

The Great Rebellion in Peru

The most widespread and violent of the late colonial rebellions occurred in the Andes in the early 1780s. The uprising had multiple causes. Population growth over the past several decades had left many native communities without sufficient land. Many Indians also harbored long-standing resentments over their continuing obligation to provide labor at the silver mines of Potosí and over the *repartimiento de mercancías,* the system that allowed local officials to profit from the sale of merchandise to native communities. Specific policies recently introduced by the Bourbon monarchy fueled additional unrest among creoles and mestizos. Buenos Aires rather than Lima had become the principal outlet for the silver of Potosí in 1776, stifling economic activity along the traditional trade routes linking Upper Peru with the Pacific Coast. Greater efficiency of local administrators meant that it was harder for everyone to evade payment of taxes both old and new.

The trouble began at Tinta, just south of the old Inca capital of Cuzco, where rebels led by the mestizo kuraka José Gabriel Condorcanqui killed the corregidor Antonio de

Arriaga in November of 1780. For the next 6 months, they threatened much of highland Peru and nearly took Cuzco. The movement's leadership included many other mestizos and creoles, including many muleteers and Condorcanqui's mestiza wife, Manuela Bastidas, but Condorcanqui chose to tout his native Andean heritage. He changed his name to Tupac Amaru II, after his putative ancestor who had resisted Spanish domination and faced execution on orders of Viceroy Francisco de Toledo in 1572, and attracted thousands of Indians to his cause.

In May of 1781, Spanish authorities captured Tupac Amaru, along with several of his close associates, and sentenced him to death in the main plaza of Cuzco, precisely where his namesake had met a similar fate 200 years before. The death of Condorcanqui did not restore peace to the region, however. The rebellion continued for another 2 years in present-day Bolivia, where it became more radical, marked by repeated calls for the extermination of what Quechua speakers called *puka kunka,* or "red necks," their derogatory term for Spaniards. Sometimes they indiscriminately killed anyone caught wearing Spanish-style clothing. Order returned only in 1783, when forces loyal to the regime rounded up the movement's leaders and put them to death.

Not all native Andeans took part in the rebellion. Ethnic rivalries dating back hundreds of years left some groups reluctant to join a movement that championed the cause of the Incas. Many natives simply saw it to their advantage to support Spanish authority, or found that they could continue get their needs met through traditional, less radical means, such as legal petitions and face-to-face dealings with local authorities. Notable kurakas remained loyal to the crown and even helped defeat the rebellion.

The rebellion of Tupac Amaru and his successors terrified Spanish authorities. After 1783, they tried to suppress native historical memory that exalted the Incas. They banned the reading of the sixteenth-century mestizo historian Garcilaso de la Vega because his book idealized the old days and drew too critical a picture of the Spanish colonial system. When the new audiencia was established in Cuzco in 1788, local Andean nobles were invited to participate in the inauguration ceremonies, but only if they agreed to leave their traditional costumes at home and dress as Spaniards. From this point onward, racial tensions deepened in the Andes, with disastrous consequences for the formation of any kind of national unity after Peru and Bolivia became independent.

CONCLUSION

The changing political climate of the eighteenth century, especially in the period after 1763, drove the governments of Spain, Portugal, and Great Britain to reorganize their overseas empires, often to the consternation of their American subjects. In 1776, Anglo-Americans declared their independence, but their neighbors to the south responded much more cautiously to changes in colonial administration. Despite their numerous and highly vocal complaints and occasional recourse to violence, few Latin Americans supported a complete break with Spain or Portugal before 1800. A familiar refrain used by Spanish colonists was *"Viva el Rey y muera el mal gobierno"* ("Long live the king and death to bad government"), signifying their continued allegiance to the crown while protesting against specific abuses and particular officials. Even Tupac Amaru II invoked this rhetoric.

Various reasons have been cited to explain why Latin Americans were slower to assert their independence than Britain's North American subjects. Some have suggested that English colonists had more experience in self-government and were therefore less willing to accept new rules imposed by Parliament after 1763, but perhaps we should not carry this interpretation too far. After all, the Spanish and Portuguese colonial systems allowed considerable latitude for local officials, city councils, and ad hoc citizens' groups to protest, ignore, modify, or defy edicts sent from Madrid and Lisbon. In theory, any subject could address his or her grievances directly to the king, over the heads of colonial bureaucrats.

Other more compelling factors definitely favored the cautious stance of Latin Americans. Geography played an important role. The British settlements were clustered along the Atlantic seaboard, making it relatively easy for news to travel by ship from one town to another. Most major cities of Spanish America were located inland, separated by weeks or months of arduous overland travel. South Carolinians could coordinate plans with New Englanders far more readily than residents of Mexico City could share concerns with their counterparts in Lima or Bogotá. Even in Brazil, where many important settlements were located near the Atlantic coast, the vicissitudes of ocean currents prevented towns from communicating easily with one another. Residents of Pará and Maranhão could send messages more quickly to Portugal than to Bahia or Rio de Janeiro.

The self-perceived vulnerability of Latin American elites also made them hesitant to tamper with the status quo. Many of them lived surrounded by Indians, mestizos, mulattos, and other groups whom they despised and feared, and the gap between rich and poor tended to be much wider than in the British colonies. George Washington was a wealthy slaveholder, but his three-story residence at Mount Vernon in Virginia was quite modest in comparison with the splendid homes of the great landowners and silver miners of Mexico. The slightest suggestion that the dispossessed masses might be unleashed was enough to terrify anyone with anything to lose. The ferocity of Tupac Amaru II's rebellion triggered a conservative backlash in the Andes, and Toussaint L'Ouverture's uprising in Haiti alarmed slaveholders everywhere.

Moreover, many of Latin America's elites both old and new managed to prosper in the troubled times of the Age of Revolution. Brazil, for example, experienced an economic boom as competing sugar plantations in Haiti were destroyed and wartime conditions in Europe created a huge demand for all manner of tropical produce. As we shall see in Chapter 8, only when events in Europe appeared to provide them with few other options did Latin American elites turn to the formation of independent republics.

LEARNING MORE ABOUT LATIN AMERICANS

DuBois, Laurent. *Avengers of the New World: The Story of the Haitian Revolution* (Cambridge, MA: Harvard University Press, 2004). A detailed recreation of the day-to-day events in Haiti revolution in the context of the "Age of Revolution."

Stavig, Ward. *The World of Túpac Amaru: Conflict, Community and Identity in Colonial Peru* (Lincoln, NE: University of Nebraska Press, 1999). A close look at the lives of ordinary men and women in the region that spawned Tupac Amaru II's rebellion.

Vinson III, Ben. *Bearing Arms for His Majesty: The Free-Colored Militia in Colonial Mexico* (Stanford, CA: Stanford University Press, 2001). Traces the formation of Mexico's black and mulatto militias and explores the roles they played in the larger society.

Viqueira Albán, Juan Pedro. *Propriety and Permissiveness in Bourbon Mexico* (Wilmington, DE: Scholarly Resources, 1999). An examination of popular culture in eighteenth-century Mexico City, including bullfights, dancing, gambling, ball games, and popular religious devotions.

Weber, David J. *Bárbaros: Spaniards and Their Savages in the Age of Enlightenment* (New Haven, CT: Yale University Press, 2005). A leading scholar of the Spanish American frontier examines attitudes and policies toward unsubdued Indians in the eighteenth century.

8

THE NEW NATIONS OF LATIN AMERICA

FOR 300 YEARS, Spain and Portugal ruled their enormous American empires with few serious challenges from people living in the colonies. But within less than two decades between 1808 and 1824, Brazil and most of Spanish America won independence, leaving Spain with just two islands, Cuba and Puerto Rico, and Portugal with nothing. From Mexico to Argentina, the new nations of Spanish America emerged from drawn-out, hard-fought wars, costly both in terms of lives lost and damage to the economic infrastructure (roads, buildings, mines, and agricultural estates). Brazil's independence came somewhat less violently, in 1822, when a son of Portugal's king agreed to become emperor of the new nation, but there too the years since 1808 had witnessed considerable political turmoil.

The movements for independence in Latin America resulted from the convergence of two sets of factors, one international and the other internal to the individual colonies. Although the most important cause of the rebellions for independence was the demand from Latin Americans to obtain more control over their daily lives, as manifested in local governance and practice of traditions, the timing of the independence movements depended to a considerable extent on events that occurred in the metropolises and in the rest of Europe.

The specific character of the struggles for independence and the kinds of nations that emerged varied greatly across Latin America, reflecting the tremendous geographical and historical diversity of the region. The independence movements were bitterly divided along class and racial lines. Wealthy creoles (people who claimed European descent, though born in the Americas) needed tactical support from the lower classes to win the battles against Spain and Portugal and in the political struggles of nation building that ensued. But they despised the masses of poor Indians, blacks, and *castas*

TIMELINE

1788
Charles IV takes the throne of Spain

1789
French Revolution

1791
Haitian Revolution

1807–1808
Napoleon's armies invade Portugal and Spain

1810
Hidalgo begins Mexican War of Independence

1812
New Spanish Constitution

1814
Restoration of Spanish monarchy

1821
Mexican independence

1822
Brazilian independence

1824
Battle of Ayacucho ends wars of independence

(racially mixed people) that surrounded them. One of the principal reasons why the Spanish and Portuguese empires endured so long was that upper-class whites were terrified that any act of rebellion against the mother country might unleash popular unrest that could easily turn against them.

Creole fears were anything but groundless. The colonies were sharply split between the haves and the have-nots, and the gap had widened in many parts of Latin America during the last few decades of the eighteenth century. Popular discontent had mounted accordingly, usually meeting brutal repression by colonial governments and the creole upper class. When external events finally began unraveling the ties that bound the colonies to Spain and Portugal, lower classes joined the battles, but with their own agendas in mind. Their specific objectives varied from place to place, but included the abolition of slavery, an end to special taxes levied on Indians, and land reform.

The movements for Latin American independence divided on geographical lines as well. The racially and ethnically diverse people of the countryside thought mostly in terms of local autonomy at the village level and at least initially paid relatively little heed to the ideas of nationhood formulated by the creole upper classes in the larger cities and towns. The upper classes had their own local and regional loyalties as well. Peruvians and Venezuelans and Argentines all distrusted one another, and people who lived in towns across southern South America resented the domination of Buenos Aires. All of the divisions—racial, social, economic, and geographical—that became so evident during the wars for independence were to shape Latin American politics for much of the nineteenth century.

SPANISH AMERICA AND THE CRISIS OF 1808

During the last half of the eighteenth and beginning of the nineteenth centuries, upheavals in the Caribbean, Europe, and North America profoundly affected events in Latin America and contributed to the development and success of independence movements in the region. The French Revolution (1789) and subsequent conquest of Europe by the Emperor Napoleon, the slave rebellion in the French sugar colony Saint-Domingue (1791) that caused the birth of Haiti, and the uprising of British colonists in North America that created the United States deeply transformed how Latin Americans viewed contemporary society and the colonial governance of Spain and Portugal, causing them to question the underlying principles and structure of colonial rule that had lasted for 300 years. These revolutions disrupted the international balance of power and the uneasy equilibrium in domestic society. Most immediately, the Napoleonic invasion of Portugal and Spain in 1807 and 1808 provided the catalyst for the emergence of the Latin American independence.

Spain, the Napoleonic Invasion, and Representative Government, 1808–1814

From the 1788 death of energetic King Charles III, who had instituted widespread administrative changes in the empire, Spain experienced considerable political turmoil. No sooner had the dimwitted Charles IV ascended to the throne than revolutionaries overthrew the French monarchy, setting off a reign of terror, executing King Louis XVI, and going to war against the rest of Europe. From 1793 to 1795 Charles took up arms as an ally of traditional foe England in order to stem the French revolutionary tide. He quickly reverted to the old alliance with France once the revolutionary fervor there abated. The disruptions and war took a heavy toll on both Spain and its American colonies, for the burden of taxation was high and British naval blockades ruined commerce. The crisis came to a head in 1808, when faced with domestic opposition and an impending invasion by Napoleon, Charles IV abdicated. His son, Ferdinand VII, who had secretly plotted against his father, succeeded to the throne, only to have the French force him out to make way for Napoleon's brother Joseph Bonaparte to take over as king.

Spaniards resisted the imposition of a Frenchman as monarch, fighting a guerrilla war and claiming that sovereignty lay in the hands of the people. They experimented with various forms of representative government on both sides of the Atlantic. But with the defeat of Napoleon, the victorious European powers forcefully returned Ferdinand to the throne in 1814. Six years of self-rule, however, had convinced many Americans, particularly the creoles, that they were quite capable of governing themselves and that Spanish colonial rule was far too costly and the benefits too few.

At the same time that Spaniards rose to fight the invading French in 1808, municipalities throughout the country formed *juntas* to govern in place of the monarch. They also set up a central junta that claimed to represent the entire nation and its overseas territories. Spaniards soon called for the reestablishment of the Cortes, a parliamentary body that had existed during medieval times, but had not met in three centuries. Looking for support among Spanish subjects in the colonies, the organizers invited Americans to send representatives to the central junta and the Cortes. The Cortes first met in Cádiz in September 1810 and over the next few years enacted a series of sweeping political changes for both Spain and its American colonies. Most important was the writing of a constitution in 1812, which considerably limited the powers of any future restored monarchy. The absolute kingship was to be no longer.

Americans needed no prodding from Spain to take matters into their own hands in this time of political crisis. Juntas comprised mostly of creoles appeared in cities and towns throughout the empire as soon as news of Ferdinand's captivity reached them. All of these bodies proclaimed their loyalty to Ferdinand. Many, however, objected to any form of subservience to the ad hoc government in Spain, arguing that they were not colonies but separate kingdoms fully equal to Castile, León, Navarre, Catalonia, and the other peninsular territories that comprised the realm of the Spanish monarch. They were technically correct, for only in the time of Charles III had Spanish bureaucrats begun using the term "colonies" in reference to the overseas possessions.

This sentiment for self-rule gathered strength in early 1810, when Americans favoring local autonomy feared that the French armies might overwhelm all Spanish resistance and then Napoleon might impose his regime on the overseas kingdoms. In some places, politically active groups moved quickly to an outright break with Spain. Town councils in Venezuela, for example, convened a national congress that declared independence in July of 1811.

Other Americans preferred to cooperate with the ad hoc government in Spain and welcomed the opportunity to send spokesmen to the sessions of the central junta and the Cortes. Men in cities and towns all over Spanish America participated enthusiastically in elections. The Constitution of 1812 permitted the formation of elected municipal councils (cabildos) in all towns with 1000 or more residents. Hundreds of cities exercised that option. In Mexico, for example, only 20 communities had had cabildos prior to the enactment of the Constitution, while afterwards that number rose to nearly 900. Eighteen new cabildos were formed in Puerto Rico, and dozens more in the highlands of Ecuador. This process empowered men in Latin America as never before. Women, however, were excluded from participating in elections until well into the twentieth century.

The "American Question"

The disruptions to the rule of the monarchy between 1808 and 1814 provided the first practical demonstration of the principles of popular sovereignty and a taste of active political participation for the colonies. Autonomy without independence, however, proved impractical. Moreover, the inherent distrust that both creoles and Spaniards felt toward indigenous and casta peoples permeated the discussions.

The first objections to American autonomy arose in the heated debates over how many American delegates the Cortes would include. Authors of the Constitution of 1812 assumed they would allocate representation according to population. Americans easily outnumbered Spaniards, but they included large numbers of Indians and racially mixed people. Were all of these groups to be allowed to vote or even to be counted for purposes of representation? The Constitution of 1812 gave the franchise to Indian and mestizo men but not to castas, whom it defined as people with any trace of African ancestry (Latin Americans themselves used this term to describe many types of racially mixed people). It also excluded felons, debtors, and domestic servants—provisions that might eliminate many Indians and mestizos, and even some people of Spanish extraction, from the

How Historians Understand   WERE THE WARS OF INDEPENDENCE THE TURNING POINT?

Periodization—the dividing of history into segments and identifying crucial turning points—is a major device historians use to explain and simplify the past. Traditionally, historians have considered the Latin American wars of independence between 1808 and 1825 as the crucial watershed in the region's history, and many Latin American history courses are divided into terms focusing on the colonial and national periods. This interpretation inferred that Latin America abruptly ended its colonial era and entered into modern times with a sharp break from Spain and Portugal. We know, however, that while independence hastened many transformations already underway during the previous century, all vestiges of the colonial order did not disappear in the 1820s. Slavery and discrimination against indigenous peoples endured well past independence, and many laws and government procedures carried over from the colonial regimes to the new nation states. Puerto Rico and Cuba remained colonies of Spain until after 1898. The traditional

Bernardo O'Higgins, Chilean leader who symbolized the efforts of the colonial elite to maintain its power after Independence.

division of eras obscured critical continuities and made it difficult to assess the effects of change.

During the 1960s, an alternative approach arose, viewing the independence era as part of a broader period stretching from approximately 1720 or 1750 to 1850. This "Middle Period" incorporated the transition from traditional to modern society and from colonial to independent politics. The newly configured century allowed historians to trace the evolution of the trends and forces that caused the independence movements and to evaluate the impact of the end of colonial rule.

Investigating the half-centuries before and after independence has elucidated a number of new themes and hypotheses. First, traditional assumptions that the Spanish Empire was peaceful in the century before 1810 were incorrect. In the Mexican countryside, for example, there was constant unrest. Second, colonial rule was far from omnipotent. Historians had long ago documented corruption and inefficiency, but recent explorations have revealed the considerable extent of local autonomy. We have only scratched the surface of understanding to what degree the innovations introduced by the Spanish Bourbon kings and their counterparts in Portugal not only disrupted accommodations reached earlier but also began processes of change that independent governments built on after 1830. The Iberian monarchs of the eighteenth century, for example, took steps to reduce the power and political influence of the Catholic Church in Latin America. Many independent governments in the nineteenth and twentieth centuries continued to pursue this objective. Economic development, especially that of frontier regions, was a major concern of late colonial kings and independent governments alike.

While the inclusion of the wars of independence as part of a longer period and as part of longer historical processes has provided much new knowledge and many new insights, the more traditional periodization (adopted by the authors of this text) has considerable advantages. First, the break with Spain and Portugal had an enormous political impact. As we will see in Chapter 9, it set off decades of conflict over who was to rule and how. Independent governments tried for a century to establish their legitimacy and control. Moreover, there is little doubt that the wars of independence were economically cataclysmic. The damage to property and people over the course of nearly two decades of fighting was massive. It required nearly the entire century to recover to the level of production and prosperity in 1800. Independent Latin America had broken significantly from the past and begun a new era.

Questions for Discussion

What examples of significant historical turning points can you think of that have occurred during your own lifetime? What has changed? What continuities are there? Is periodization a useful tool for understanding history? Why or why not?

political process. Many American upper-class people feared the empowerment of castas and others they considered their social inferiors. Thus, the creoles were torn between their need to assure that their own concerns would receive ample hearing in the emerging political debate and their overwhelming fear of the lower classes. Full representation of all people regardless of ethnicity would have given the Western Hemisphere a three-to-two majority in the Cortes. Not surprisingly, Spaniards opposed this prospect.

The Spaniards prevailed on the question of representation, retaining control of the new parliament and using that advantage whenever their position differed from that of the Americans. One particularly divisive issue was the freedom to trade with all nations, a right that Spain's American colonies had never enjoyed. Spanish merchants preferred to maintain existing rules that allowed Americans to trade legally only with other Spanish subjects. Other American demands included the abolition of crown monopolies and, most crucially, equal access to jobs in the government, the military, and the church.

As they witnessed Spanish intransigence on issues such as representation and freedom of trade, even those Americans who initially favored some degree of cooperation with the new government moved toward a stance of greater self-determination for the overseas territories. Once they began to assert themselves politically, few Spanish Americans were willing to go back to old routines of subservience to the mother country. In the words of Simón Bolívar, a major leader of the independence movement in South America, by 1815 "the habit of obedience . . . [had] been severed."

SPANISH AMERICAN GRIEVANCES AND THE CRISIS OF 1808

The French invasion of Spain exacerbated decades of festering political and social tensions. Population growth, which had begun in the previous century, intensified during the 1700s, increasing the pressures on scarce land and water resources. There were an estimated 150 village riots in central Mexico from 1700 to 1820, as a result. In the early 1780s a dangerous rebellion, led by a man who claimed to be a descendant of the last Inca emperor, had shaken the viceroyalty of Peru.

The so-called Bourbon Reforms (named after the ruling dynasty of Spain installed after the Hapsburg line had expired in 1700) introduced by Kings Charles III and IV added to the undercurrents of dissatisfaction. The new monarchs sought to tighten Spain's control over its colonies to improve its defenses against threats from England and France, curb the influence and wealth of the Catholic Church, and increase the flow of revenues into the royal coffers. The reforms adversely affected Americans across all classes, with new taxes hitting everyone, conscription for the new standing armies striking fear into the vulnerable lower classes, and the arrival of swarms of Spanish bureaucrats thwarting the rising expectations of creoles. Riots protesting high prices erupted from Mexico to Ecuador. The Crown further agitated Americans by expelling the Jesuits, a powerful religious order, from the empire in 1767.

The disruption of Spanish sovereignty in 1808 brought all of these grievances to the forefront and sparked different kinds of revolts in the colonies. Three of the most important of these upheavals, each with its own special character but all with important implications for the future independence of Latin America, occurred in Mexico, Argentina, and Venezuela.

Mexico

The kinds of political, social, and economic changes that Latin Americans experienced at the beginning of the nineteenth century were especially apparent in the region of Mexico known as the Bajío, located between 100 and 200 miles northwest of Mexico City. As the colony's population grew in the late colonial period, wealthy individuals had invested in the commercial production of wheat, maize, and other crops, taking advantage of the area's rich soil and its proximity to the principal urban markets of New Spain. To expand their estates, these landowners forced many poor sharecroppers and other small farmers off the land.

At the same time, people who had worked in the region's many cloth factories and artisans who had made textiles in their own homes lost their livelihoods when the Spanish crown eased trade restrictions and opened the Mexican market to cheaper

An 1812 flyer recruiting Mexican women to join in the struggle for independence. The caption reads: "To war, American women, let's go with merciless swords to kill Callejas [a royalist commander] and to join up with Señor Morelos."

merchandise manufactured abroad. Production at the Bajío's silver mines also declined sharply as the new century began, leaving thousands of workers without jobs. Meanwhile, droughts and crop failures added to the misery. In the worst of these agricultural crises, from 1785 to 1786, almost 15 percent of the Bajío's population died of hunger. A new round of crop failures struck the region in 1809. The combined effects of economic change and natural disaster left thousands of people with little left to lose as the nineteenth century began.

Father Miguel Hidalgo y Costilla was a priest in the Bajío, in the town of Dolores, about 20 miles from the old silver mining town of Guanajuato. Born in 1753 to a middle-class creole family, Hidalgo had his own grudges against Spanish authority. He had received his early education at the hands of the Jesuits, and their expulsion from Mexico angered him and many others of his class. As an adult, he read the books of French Enlightenment thinkers who disputed the divine right of kings to exact unquestioning obedience from their subjects. His unorthodox ideas got him dismissed from his position as rector of a college in Valladolid (today, Morelia), one of the principal towns of the Bajío, and he narrowly escaped prosecution by the Inquisition. Policies of the Spanish king also hurt him in the pocketbook. He owned a small hacienda, but in 1804 royal officials seized his property when he could not pay special taxes levied to meet Spain's rising costs of defending itself against Napoleon. Meanwhile, Hidalgo took up his post as parish priest in Dolores. There he tried to promote new industries such as ceramics, tanning, and silk production to help his parishioners to weather the economic hard times they were facing. He also continued to meet with other intellectuals conversant with Enlightenment ideas and disgruntled with the Spanish monarchy.

Hidalgo's concerns and those of many other people in the surrounding region merged with the international crisis provoked by Napoleon's invasion of Spain. Since 1808, the government in Mexico City had been in the hands of conservative forces who favored maintaining ties with Spain at all costs. Father Hidalgo joined one of many conspiracies to overthrow them, and when authorities learned of his plans he decided to take the preemptive strike of declaring open revolt in his famous "Grito de Dolores" on September 16, 1810. Word of his rebellion quickly spread among the desperate and dispossessed classes in the Bajío. Within a few days, Hidalgo enlisted thousands of supporters who held a variety of grievances against the status quo. At its height, his army included 60,000 people, of whom about half were Indians and 20 percent were mestizos. In the words of historian Eric Van Young, many rural people joined Hidalgo's insurgency, and the many revolts that followed because they were "driven by hunger and unemployment, pulled into the maelstrom of violence by the prospect of daily wages in the rebel forces, the easy pickings of looting, or simply to escape from depressed conditions at home." The Indian rebels also wanted to retain control over their own communities, and for the most part, they did not stray far from their homes to fight. Their concern was less with independence from Spain than with local power and traditional values.

Hidalgo's forces sacked several towns and killed hundreds of Spanish men, women, and children who had taken refuge in the municipal grain warehouse in Guanajuato.

Creole elites, some of whom had once flirted with the cause of autonomy, recoiled in horror at the violent turn of events and joined forces with pro-Spanish authorities in Mexico City to crush the insurrection. Within a few months, they captured and executed Hidalgo, but another priest, José María Morelos, continued the fight, controlling virtually all of southern Mexico from 1811 until his defeat in 1815. Followers of Morelos, in particular the casta Vicente Guerrero, then continued guerrilla operations against Spanish authorities for several more years, but continued Spanish control seemed almost certain. It would take another round of events in Spain to propel Mexico toward the final step of independence.

Venezuela

The Bourbon Reforms included an emphasis on the economic development of formerly peripheral parts of the empire. Venezuela was one such region. Cacao production flourished as the popularity of chocolate grew in Europe during the eighteenth century. Its principal city, Caracas, became the seat of a new *audiencia,* or court of appeals, created in 1786.

Creole upper-class men in Caracas began efforts to create a self-governing junta in 1808 but succeeded only in the spring of 1810, when they overthrew the audiencia and the Spanish governor. A year later, they officially declared independence, created a three-man executive body, and drafted a constitution that excluded the lower classes from political participation. The new government lasted just a year. After a powerful earthquake hit Caracas in 1812, royalists regained control after convincing the popular classes that God was punishing Venezuela for its disregard for divinely constituted authority.

The young creole aristocrat Simón Bolívar took command of the forces favoring independence and began a campaign to retake Venezuela in the spring of 1813. Like so many others of his social standing, Bolívar detested the lower classes, and his enemies eagerly took advantage of this situation. In 1814, he suffered a humiliating defeat by royalist armies led by a black man José Tomás Boves and comprised largely of black and mulatto *llaneros* (plainsmen, cowboys by trade) angered at the harsh treatment they had received at the hands of those favoring an independent republic. Boves himself had suffered imprisonment by the insurgents in 1810. Now 4 years later, his "Legion of Hell" slaughtered wealthy creoles. Boves died on the battlefield, but his troops routed Bolívar and forced him into exile. In Venezuela as in Mexico, the outlook for independence looked grim as Ferdinand VII returned to power in Madrid in 1814.

Argentina

Like Venezuela, southern South America and the port town of Buenos Aires reaped significant benefits from the Bourbon kings' efforts to develop the empire's periphery. Formerly subject to the authority of the Spanish viceroy in Lima, Peru, in 1776, Buenos Aires became the seat of a newly created viceroyalty. The port now became the principal outlet through which silver from Bolivia and hides and tallow from the vast plains of Argentina and Uruguay reached markets abroad. The town's merchants also enjoyed abundant opportunities for contraband with British and Portuguese traders. The population of Buenos Aires quadrupled in the last half of the eighteenth century, reaching almost 40,000 by 1800.

Merchants and civic leaders took pride in the growing prosperity of their community. That sentiment deepened in 1806, when local citizens organized themselves and many of Buenos Aires's blacks and mulattos to drive out a British naval force that had taken control of the city. The following year, this combined militia thwarted yet another British invasion and forced the British to evacuate the city of Montevideo, across the Río de la Plata estuary from Buenos Aires, as well.

Creole militia officers thus positioned themselves to play key roles in the politics of Buenos Aires in the volatile years that followed the Napoleonic invasion of Spain. They figured prominently in a gathering of some 250 members of the town's upper class in May of 1810. That meeting produced a new governing junta that proclaimed nominal allegiance to Ferdinand VII, but in fact Spanish authority had ended in Buenos Aires, never to reappear. Those who dared to voice opposition to the patriot agenda were soon silenced.

SPANISH AMERICAN INDEPENDENCE

Buenos Aires was the exception, however. Only there, at the southernmost extreme of the empire, did prospects for the political independence of Spanish America seem good when Ferdinand resumed the throne. Everywhere else, the cause of independence appeared doomed. Hidalgo and Morelos were dead in Mexico, and within a few years thousands of those who had fought beneath their banners accepted amnesty from the crown. Bolívar had fled to Jamaica and King Ferdinand sent new armies to crush the Venezuelan rebellion once and for all. Once again, however, the determination of Latin Americans to assert control over their own affairs combined with events in Europe to bring about independence.

The Final Campaigns

When Ferdinand returned to power, he dissolved the Cortes and rejected the Constitution of 1812. These actions reinforced the determination of those Americans who had decided to break with the mother country and disillusioned those who had hoped he would be a just and fair monarch attentive to the concerns of all his subjects. Despite the many setbacks they had experienced, Americans persisted in their efforts to wear down the strength and morale of Spanish military forces.

By 1820, liberal politicians and army officers, fed up with Ferdinand's absolutist policies and the unpopular war in America forced the king to accept the 1812 Constitution and reconvene the Cortes. This led to the formation of provincial governments and elections to the Cortes in areas loyal to Spain. But the metropolis's new leaders proved unwilling to grant the overseas kingdoms an equal voice in government or the liberalization of trade.

The way now lay open for the Americas to break with Spain. In Mexico, the flurry of political activity among the lower classes, once again enfranchised by the resumption of constitutional government, alarmed Mexican conservatives who remembered the excesses of Hidalgo's forces in Guanajuato and elsewhere. Nonetheless the upper classes needed the support of the lower classes to obtain independence. In February 1821, the royalist general Agustín de Iturbide switched sides, forming an alliance with the rebel leader Vicente Guerrero, who had carried on guerrilla operations against royalist forces following the death of Morelos. Iturbide's proclamation of independence, known as the Plan de Iguala, was designed to calm conservatives. He proposed independence for Mexico and the creation of a constitutional monarchy. He also promised protection to the Catholic Church and to all Europeans in Mexico who agreed to support him. Over the next several months, Spanish authority simply collapsed in New Spain. In September of 1821, exactly 300 years after the Spanish conquest of Mexico, Iturbide entered Mexico City in triumph.

In South America, Simón Bolívar returned to Venezuela in 1816 and scored major victories against the Spanish, in part because he incorporated black troops, a tactical reversal of his prior refusal to allow them a role in the struggle for independence. Thousands of llaneros also joined with Bolívar at this critical juncture. By 1822, he had assured the independence of the Republic of Gran Colombia, consisting of present-day Colombia as well as Venezuela and Ecuador.

Meanwhile, the cause of independence won new victories in southern South America, led by José de San Martín, an Argentine-born officer in the Spanish army who

Independence or Death, the Shout of Ipiranga on September 7, 1822.

LATIN AMERICAN LIVES

MANUELA SÁENZ, 1797–1856, LIBERATOR OF SOUTH AMERICA

The life of Manuela Sáenz demonstrates how South Americans, and women in particular, experienced the transition from colony to independence. Manuela was born in Quito, the illegitimate daughter of a Spaniard who served on the city council and a woman from a prominent creole family. Her father provided for her upbringing in the largest and most affluent of Quito's convents, where she learned to read and write. In 1817, her father arranged for her to marry one of his business associates, the wealthy British merchant James Thorne, some 20 years her senior.

Manuela relocated to Lima with her husband and over the next few years helped manage his business affairs. Meanwhile, she became involved in Lima's political intrigues. She joined other women who supported Peruvian patriots' efforts to overthrow Spanish rule and actively helped recruit men to serve in José de San Martín's armies, even though both her husband and her father supported the royalist cause. In 1822, she paid a visit to her native Quito, in part because she wished to claim a portion of her mother's estate. She observed Simón Bolívar's triumphant arrival in the city on June 16, 1822, and shortly thereafter met him in person. The two soon began an intimate relationship that would last the remaining 8 years of Bolívar's life. She left Quito for Lima and from there accompanied Bolívar on his final campaigns against royalist forces in the Andes, serving as his personal archivist. After independence, she continued to support Bolívar against the many enemies who opposed his dominance of the newly emerging nations of northern South America. In 1828, when they were both living in Bogotá, she foiled an assassination attempt against her lover, winning for herself the title of the "Libertadora del Liberatador."

Bolívar resigned the presidency of Gran Colombia in 1830 and died of tuberculosis later that same year. Manuela's subsequent years were difficult. Bolívar's political adversaries in Ecuador refused to let her return to Quito, citing her unbridled ambition, outspoken nature, and past sexual improprieties. In 1835, she settled in Paita, a small port on the northern coast of Peru, not far from the Ecuadorian border. There she lived in poverty for the remainder of her life, depending on proceeds from the sale of handicrafts, occasional remittances from property in Ecuador, and the generosity of friends. A debilitating hip injury eventually confined her to a wheel chair. Her involvement in politics continued, however. She connived with other exiles and provided intelligence to her long-time friend, Ecuadorian President Juan José Flores, alerting him to Peruvian plots afoot to seize Ecuadorian territory and topple him from power. Even after Flores left office in 1845 she continued to maintain ties with other prominent conservative politicians in Quito. Gabriel García Moreno, a future president of Ecuador, was a frequent guest at her home during his period of political exile in Peru.

While in Paita Manuela began corresponding with her estranged husband, whom she had not seen since her departure for Quito in 1822. Thorne was murdered in 1847 at his hacienda in Chancay province, some 500 miles to the south of Paita.

Manuela was devastated when she heard the news, dressing in black and demanding that authorities identify and punish the perpetrators of the crime. She corresponded with her attorney in Lima, hoping to claim the dowry she had brought to their marriage and a share of Thorne's assets. Her husband's executor dismissed her pretensions, citing her notorious affair with Simón Bolívar. She died in 1856, as a diphtheria epidemic swept through northern Peru.

Sáenz has long been a controversial figure in Latin American history, denounced in her own time and subsequently for transgressing societal norms of proper feminine conduct. She smoked cigars, rode horseback, sometimes wore men's military uniforms, and was exceptionally outspoken, but many other literate and well-connected women, less flamboyant in their personal style than Manuela, participated in Latin American political life in the turbulent years surrounding national independence. Although Manuela and other women of her generation could neither vote nor hold office, their social networks proved vital for the emergence of new political ideas. They hosted political gatherings, and in the words of historian Sarah Chambers, "were active in social spaces between the public and private spheres, where philosophies were discussed, plots hatched, and alliances formed."

In recent years a novel by Colombian Nobel laureate Gabriel García Márquez, a film by Venezuelan director Diego Rísquez, and a carefully detailed biography by historian Pamela Murray have portrayed Manuela Sáenz as a strong, intelligent woman who made important contributions to the independence of Latin America. Feminists in her native Ecuador and elsewhere in Spanish America have seen her as a role model and a precursor of women's emancipation. She has also become a symbol of Ecuadorian patriotism. In 2007, she was posthumously promoted to the rank of general in the national army.

Questions for Discussion

Why do you think Manuela Sáenz is considered a national hero in Ecuador? Does her life story suggest that the independence era was a time of significant change for women? Why or why not? If Sáenz were alive today, how would her status as the mistress of a prominent male politician affect her involvement in political life?

had fought against Napoleon in Spain but returned home to join the independence struggle in 1812. After years of careful preparations, in January of 1817, San Martín led 5500 troops through treacherous mountain passes, some at altitudes approaching 15,000 feet above sea level, to Chile. Decisive victories over Spanish forces then paved the way for Chile's final independence in 1818.

San Martín's plan to liberate Peru stalled, because of distrust between the Peruvians and the invaders from Argentina and Chile. Although, Peruvian creoles declared independence and accepted San Martín as their military and civil ruler in 1821, royalist forces remained firmly in control of much of Peru. The following year San Martín and Bolívar met in Guayaquil, Ecuador, to determine how to complete the Peruvian campaign and realign the continent. As a consequence, San Martín withdrew and retired, leaving

A monument at the waterfront in Guayaquil, Ecuador, commemorating the meeting of South American independence leaders Simón Bolívar and José de San Martín there in 1822.

Bolívar to occupy Lima in 1823 and Bolívar's lieutenant Antonio José de Sucre to the secure victory at the Battle of Ayacucho in 1824.

Regional Conflicts in the Spanish American Struggle for Independence

The surrender of the royalist armies in Upper Peru in 1825 ended Spanish sovereignty in all of the Americas except for Cuba and Puerto Rico. The new republics that replaced the Spanish empire were taking shape, although their final boundaries underwent numerous alterations throughout the nineteenth century and beyond. The nation-states that emerged were the products of age-old local rivalries that drove Spanish Americans apart even as they fought for the common cause of independence. The movement for independence remained rooted in the desire of people from many different social classes to remain in control of their own communities.

Throughout the struggle for independence, the ad hoc governments created in major cities claimed to speak for entire provinces, but smaller towns resisted their domination. Declarations of "independence" proliferated, but the authors of these manifestos often meant independence from Lima or Buenos Aires or Mexico City, and not necessarily from Spain. Under royalist control in 1810, Quito formed a superior

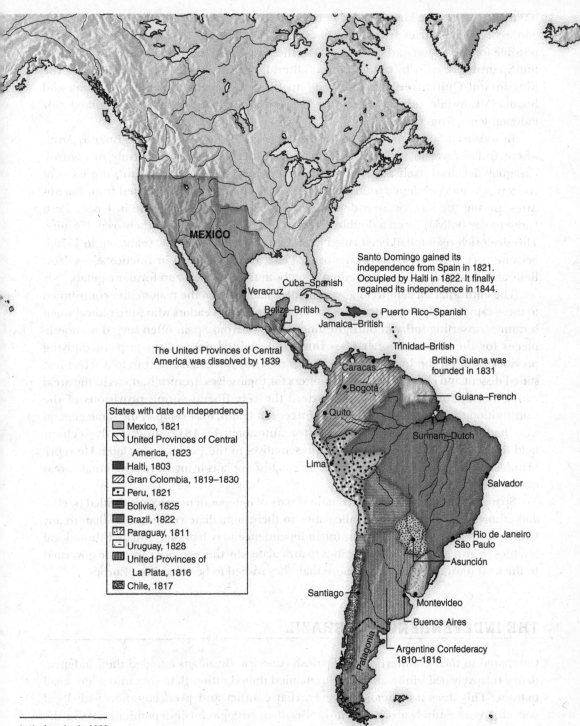

MEXICO

Cuba–Spanish

Veracruz

Belize–British

Jamaica–British

Puerto Rico–Spanish

Santo Domingo gained its
independence from Spain in 1821.
Occupied by Haiti in 1822. It finally
regained its independence in 1844.

The United Provinces of Central
America was dissolved by 1839

Trinidad–British

British Guiana was
founded in 1831

Caracas

Bogotá

Quito

Guiana–French

Surinam–Dutch

Lima

Salvador

Rio de Janeiro

São Paulo

Asunción

Santiago

Montevideo

Buenos Aires

Argentine Confederacy
1810–1816

Palagonia

States with date of independence

- Mexico, 1821
- United Provinces of Central
  America, 1823
- Haiti, 1803
- Gran Colombia, 1819–1830
- Peru, 1821
- Bolivia, 1825
- Brazil, 1822
- Paraguay, 1811
- Uruguay, 1828
- United Provinces of
  La Plata, 1816
- Chile, 1817

Latin America in 1830

junta to preserve the kingdom for Ferdinand VII to defend the Catholic faith against godless revolutionaries from France, and, as they put it, "to seek all the well-being possible for the nation and the *patria*." For them the word "nation" meant all subjects of the Spanish crown, while the "patria," literally translated as "fatherland," was the Kingdom of Quito, free and independent from the viceregal capitals of Lima and Bogotá. Meanwhile, other towns in the Ecuadorian highlands in turn proclaimed *their* independence from Quito.

In southern South America, many places resisted the hegemony of Buenos Aires, where forces favoring autonomy from the mother country were firmly in control. Paraguay declared itself an "independent republic" in 1813, but again, the issue of concern was independence from Buenos Aires. Montevideo also separated from Buenos Aires, paving the way for an independent nation of Uruguay. People in Upper Peru (present-day Bolivia) faced a double threat to their ability to control their own destinies. This silver-rich region had been ruled from Lima for more than 200 years, but in 1776 it became part of the new viceroyalty of La Plata, headquartered in Buenos Aires. Now Bolivians took up arms to win freedom from both their present and former capitals.

The authoritarian actions of governments established in the major cities contributed to these rapidly multiplying struggles for local autonomy. Leaders who were radical when it came to asserting full and outright independence from Spain often served as mouthpieces for the colonial upper class intent on maintaining a firm grip on outlying provinces and on the Indian and casta masses. They restricted the vote to a select few, stifled dissent and claimed dictatorial powers for themselves. Ironically, it was in the areas controlled by forces loyal to Spain where the very liberal voting provisions of the Constitution of 1812 were most often enforced. In Quito, for example, the same general who had crushed a local movement for autonomy in 1812 supervised elections held throughout Ecuador to choose representatives to the Cortes a year later. He reprimanded a local official who tried to disenfranchise Indians living in remote jungle areas east of the Andes.

Spanish Americans emerged from their wars of independence sharply divided by class and ethnicity and with far more allegiance to their immediate communities than to any larger entity. If anything, the fight for independence may have accentuated those local loyalties by giving people opportunities to articulate why they did not care to be governed by the next town or province any more than they wished to be ruled from Europe.

THE INDEPENDENCE OF BRAZIL

Compared to their counterparts in Spanish America, Brazilians attained their independence relatively peacefully, and Brazil remained united rather than split into many small nations. This does not mean, however, that conflict and preoccupation with local concerns were entirely absent from the Brazilian struggle for independence. As in the case of Spanish America, Brazilian independence was triggered by events in Europe.

The Portuguese Monarchy in Brazil

Napoleon's invasion of the Iberian Peninsula was meant to sever Portugal's long-standing alliance with Great Britain. For decades, policymakers in Lisbon had toyed with the idea of removing themselves from the vicissitudes of European power politics by making Brazil, rather than Portugal, the center of the empire. The rapid approach of French troops in November of 1807 persuaded the government to consider this radical proposal as a temporary expedient in the face of a national emergency. The Crown decided to move the court and its entourage, numbering perhaps 10,000 people, sailing with a British naval escort. Queen Maria and her son, the de facto ruler Prince João, arrived in Rio de Janeiro in 1808. King João VI continued to reside in Brazil after his mother's death in 1816.

The presence of the royal court brought dramatic changes to Portuguese America. Intellectual activity flourished with the long-overdue introduction of printing presses at Rio de Janeiro and Salvador, the expansion of education at the primary level, and the establishment of two medical schools and a military academy to train officers for Brazil's new army. Rio de Janeiro thrived as never before, as local merchants found a market providing the court with its many needs. Most important, Brazilians took pride in their homeland, touting its greatness in new periodicals that circulated in major cities. As one young man from Bahia put it, "Brazil, proud now that it contains within it the Immortal Prince, . . . is no longer to be a maritime Colony . . . but rather a powerful Empire, which will come to be the Moderator of Europe, the arbiter of Asia, and the dominator of Africa." In 1815, Portuguese America was proclaimed the Kingdom of Brazil, fully equal with the mother country.

Other changes proved less welcome, however. Brazilians had to shoulder new tax burdens to pay for the expanded bureaucracy and the costs of waging war against the French in Portugal. Willingly at first but with increasing reluctance as time passed, prominent citizens of Rio de Janeiro vacated their homes to accommodate the courtiers and bureaucrats who accompanied the king to Brazil. People in Bahia in the northeastern part of the country chafed under Rio de Janeiro's growing dominance. Although the government in exile officially encouraged trade with all nations, it also bound Brazil more closely than ever before to an economic dependence on Great Britain that stifled the growth of local manufacturing.

Popular Unrest in Brazil

Some Brazilians dared to express their opposition to the adverse effects of the Portuguese occupation, and King João was no more sympathetic to their concerns than King Ferdinand was to the grievances of his American subjects. In March of 1817, a revolt began in Pernambuco in the northeast after royal authorities arrested a number of army officers and others suspected of harboring treasonous sentiments. The rebels destroyed images of the king and his coat of arms, proclaimed a republic, and trumpeted ideals voiced by their contemporaries in Spanish America, among them personal liberty, equality before the law, support for the Catholic religion, and devotion to their homeland, or patria. They also expressed their hatred toward the many Portuguese-born Europeans who had settled in Brazil in the years since 1808, but vigorously denied rumors that they advocated an immediate end to African slavery, a mainstay of the Brazilian economy. The revolt spread throughout the northeastern part of Brazil, the area that most resented the heavy hand of the royal government based in Rio de Janeiro.

King João was aghast at what he called "a horrible attempt upon My Royal Sovereignty and Supreme Authority." His forces suppressed the rebellion within just 2 months and about 20 of its leaders were executed, but the king could no longer take his Brazilian subjects for granted. He brought new armies over from Portugal and stationed them in Rio de Janeiro, Salvador, and Recife.

The Culmination of Brazilian Independence

Indeed, King João had cause for concern that the people of Portugal might attempt to throw off his authority. Discontent within the military sparked a revolt in August 1820 that strongly resembled the Spanish coup of that same year. The participants called for the convoking of a Cortes and the writing of a constitution modeled after the Spanish document of 1812. They also demanded that King João return to Lisbon, and he prudently acquiesced. Before embarking from Rio de Janeiro in April of 1821, he placed his 22-year-old son, Pedro, in charge as prince regent of the Kingdom of Brazil.

This was a period of important political change in Brazil. With the blessing of the Portuguese Cortes, many towns and cities formed juntas, asserting their local autonomy rather than accepting the continued domination of the government in Rio de Janeiro, much as Spanish Americans of their time tried to free themselves from the control of

Coronation of Emperor Pedro I, Rio de Janeiro, 1822.

capital cities. The Cortes also ordered the dismantling of superior tribunals created during King João's residency, and the local governing juntas refused to send tax revenues to Rio de Janeiro. The cumulative effect of these changes was to reduce Prince Pedro's authority, so that, in effect, he functioned as little more than the governor of the capital city and its immediate surrounding area. Affluent residents of Rio missed the good times their city had enjoyed between 1808 and 1821, and those imbued with a sense of Brazilian national pride fretted over the splintering of the great Kingdom of Brazil into a series of petty autonomous provinces, each under the jurisdiction of a separate local junta.

Meanwhile, delegates in the Cortes worried with considerable justification that those opposed to these constitutional changes might rally around Prince Pedro. The Cortes therefore commanded the prince regent to return to Portugal, as his father had done several months previously. In January of 1822, Pedro announced his decision to stay in Brazil,

Brazil States and Their Capitals

The final break came on September 7, 1822. Pedro I became the "constitutional emperor and perpetual defender" of Brazil, a position he held until 1831, when he abdicated in favor of his son, Pedro II, who in turn ruled until Brazil became a republic in 1889.

THE MEANING OF INDEPENDENCE

As they went about setting up governments, leaders of the new nations of Latin America borrowed very selectively from the egalitarian rhetoric of the North American and French Revolutions. They eagerly invoked ideas of representation and freedom of expression when it came to claiming a voice for themselves in governing their homelands. Taking their cues from France and the United States, Latin America's leaders forged a new concept of citizenship, calling on all who lived within their borders to place loyalty to the nation above any ties to their church, family, or local community.

Slice of Life   THE 16TH OF SEPTEMBER:
INDEPENDENCE DAY IN MEXICO

THE LEADERS OF LATIN America's new nations not only had to set up governments and rebuild economies disrupted by the independence wars; they also had to convince their people to pay allegiance to the nation. Historians sometimes speak of nation-states as "imagined communities" in which people who do not have face-to-face contact with one another and who may not have much in common all see themselves as citizens of the nation. In practical terms, forging these new communities in Latin America meant getting people as diverse as, for example, pampered creole aristocrats in Mexico City, Zapotec-speaking Indians in Oaxaca far to the south, and farmers who eked out a living on the far northern frontier of New Mexico, to set aside their racial, economic, linguistic, and cultural differences and swear loyalty to the new republic of Mexico.

Most Latin Americans of the early nineteenth century, whatever their backgrounds, did in fact see themselves as part of a universal community, that of the Catholic Church. Those who took command of the new national governments strove to persuade their citizens to transfer their loyalties from the church to the nation, and they borrowed some of the tools the church had used for centuries to instill a sense of community among the faithful. National holidays now competed with religious ones, and the heroes of the independence wars were invoked as examples of patriotism, much as saints had served as examples of Christian piety.

Leaders of Mexico lost little time in setting up a new ritual calendar intended to enkindle a sense of nationalism from Oaxaca to New Mexico. Foremost among the days they chose to commemorate was September 16, the anniversary of Father Hidalgo's "Grito de Dolores" of 1810, the proclamation that had ignited the first phase of Mexico's wars for independence. The initial celebration of September 16

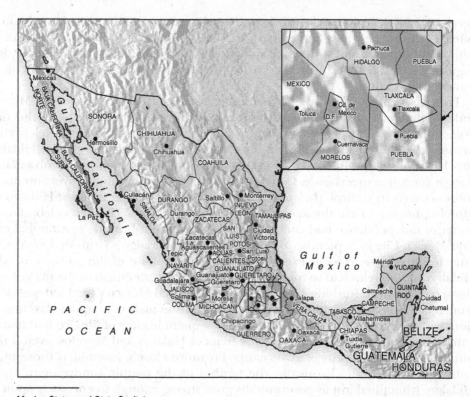

Mexico States and State Capitals

took place in Mexico City in 1823. The festivities included the ringing of church bells, a splendid parade with music supplied by a military band, and speeches extolling the virtues of the new nation. The remains of national hero José María Morelos were brought to Mexico City for burial. Just as saints' days had offered a variety of secular entertainments in addition to the religious observances, the independence celebrations of September 1823 featured music and theatrical presentations in the Alameda, the city's centrally located park. Fireworks shows at the *zócalo,* the main plaza facing the cathedral, lasted far into the night.

From 1825, a private, voluntary organization supervised the celebration in Mexico City. For 30 years, with only one exception, when U.S. troops occupied the city in 1847, the *Junta Patriótica* (patriotic committee) oversaw the events. Beginning on the night of September 15 and continuing throughout the next day, there were patriotic speeches, artillery salutes, music, theater, and fireworks. The junta, the president of the republic, and other dignitaries marched through the city's streets on the morning of the 16th. Schoolchildren sang patriotic hymns specially commissioned for the occasion. The people of Mexico City turned out in droves dressed in their best. The junta also marked the day with charitable works such as cash payments to disabled or impoverished veterans and to widows and orphans of rebels who died in the wars. In the 1820s, poor children received new clothes. Every prisoner in the Mexico City jails received a good meal, a packet of cigarettes, a bar of soap, and one *real* (a coin, worth one-eighth of a peso) on September 16. In the provinces, the holiday was marked with equal fervor, if not with equal splendor. In San Luis Potosí, for example, local dignitaries marched and tossed coins to the assembled crowds, who also enjoyed music and fireworks.

From the 1820s to the present, the timing, scale, and specific content of Mexico's independence festivities varied according to the political climate of the time. Sometimes, members of the nineteenth-century upper class muted the celebrations because they feared a rekindling of the same kind of popular unrest that Hidalgo's proclamation had unleashed. On some occasions, they suspended all observances except for a few speeches in Congress. In times when national governments felt more securely in control, they praised the revolutionary aspirations of Hidalgo and Morelos, hoping to win the allegiance of the lower classes. The first celebrations of Mexican independence had commemorated Agustín de Iturbide's triumphal entry into Mexico City in September of 1821 along with Hidalgo's Grito de Dolores, but later leaders chose to focus exclusively on the first phase of the movement, when Hidalgo and Morelos had so forcefully articulated the grievances of the masses, even though it had been Iturbide's actions that had secured Mexico's final independence from Spain. Iturbide's victory represented the consummation of upper-class negotiations with insurgents—a backroom deal. Subsequent leaders of Mexico had more to gain politically if they claimed to be the heirs of Hidalgo and Morelos, even if their outlook and their means of governance far more closely resembled those of the conservative Iturbide. Ironically, the symbol of the people's movement, Father Hidalgo, triumphed just as governments grew strong enough to encroach upon the very local autonomy for which the people had fought.

Questions for Discussion

Are patriotic holidays effective in promoting a sense of national loyalty? Why or why not? What are some other means that governments use to win people's allegiance? Are there means that are available to governments today that were not available to the leaders of the new Latin American governments in the early nineteenth century?

The kind of equality proclaimed by the more radical factions of the French Revolution, and the specter of the bloody slave revolt that had brought independence to the former French colony of Haiti, terrified Latin American political elites. At the same time, fighters both for and against independence sought to enlist the lower classes on their side. Various insurgent leaders in Spanish America promised to abolish the tribute, a special tax on Indians and blacks levied by on the colonial state. In Peru, the insurgents also ordered an end to the mita, a highly oppressive system of forced labor that had sent thousands of Indians to work in silver mines and other enterprises. The tribute and the mita both symbolized the power of the colonial state that the insurgents were anxious to destroy. Indians often had few reasons to trust privileged creole patriots and sided with the Spanish. In Peru and Bolivia, for example, Indians comprised the bulk of the royalist armies. After independence, many leaders declared that the people formerly known as "Indians" were now citizens of the new national states. In practice, however, many forms of discrimination lingered long beyond the end of colonial rule.

Royalist commanders throughout the hemisphere promised freedom to slaves who helped them fight the rebel forces. Similar offers went out from insurgent camps as well, but sometimes blacks were advised that they would have to wait patiently for these promises to be fulfilled. In 1812, for example, the revolutionary junta at Buenos Aires told the city's slaves, "Your longed-for liberty cannot be decreed right away, as humanity and reason would wish, because unfortunately it stands in opposition to the sacred right of individual liberty." By "individual liberty," the Argentine patriots meant the property rights of slaveowners. Even when the offers of freedom were genuine, creole leaders of the independence movement often showed extreme prejudice toward blacks even as they tried to recruit them, and many people of color cast their lot with the royalists. After independence, victorious creoles devised means to deny blacks access to the political process in their new nations. Only in places where slavery was no longer economically viable did they carry through with their wartime promises to abolish slavery.

Both sides in the independence struggle also sought the support of women. Women often accompanied soldiers into battle, preparing meals, nursing the wounded, and sometimes taking up arms themselves. In South America, Bolívar's companion Manuela Sáenz played a prominent role in the final battles for independence. Throughout the Americas, women served as spies for royalist and patriot armies alike. María Josefa Ortiz de Domínguez, wife of a royal official in the Bajío and nicknamed "La Corregidora," alerted Father Hidalgo and his coconspirators that the authorities had learned of their plot. Women smuggled weapons, and—in one instance in Mexico—a printing press, to insurgents and persuaded soldiers in the royalist armies to desert. In Mexico City, however, a women's organization called the *Patriotas Marianas* drummed up support for the royalist cause. Despite the active involvement of many women in the independence movement, the new leaders of Latin America, like those who commanded the United States and all the nation-states of nineteenth-century Europe, included only males in their definition of who was entitled to play an active role in civic affairs.

CONCLUSION

In most of Latin America, the wars of independence were long-drawn-out, brutal contests. The Spaniards had defeated the insurgencies in the first phase by 1815. Popular and creole movements (in New Spain and northern South America, respectively) failed because of the deep-seated mutual distrust between the upper classes on one hand and Indians and castas on the other. Upper-class fear of the indigenous and mixed population cut short Hidalgo's campaign, and the unwillingness of creoles to make concessions to the lower classes in New Granada ensured Bolívar's initial defeats. Undercurrents of class and race war added a vicious, murderous aspect to the fighting.

Beginning about 1817, the tide turned in favor of independence, in part because the creoles learned from past mistakes and reached temporary arrangements with the lower classes, such as the llaneros of Venezuela and Vicente Guerrero's guerrilla forces of southern Mexico. Politics in Europe also played a role in pushing the colonies toward the final break with the mother countries. Following his restoration to the Spanish throne, King Ferdinand VII had paid little attention to colonial concerns, and the representative assemblies that reemerged in Spain and Portugal in 1820 proved intransigent on issues of vital concern to Latin Americans. Colonial upper classes finally felt confident they could declare independence and contain popular discontent without help from overseas. From 1817 to 1824, Spanish and Portuguese authority yielded to independent governments from Mexico to southern South America.

Soon after taking power, leaders of the new Latin American governments began declaring national holidays that honored the heroes of independence and their victories on the battlefield, but more than a decade of war left most Latin Americans with little to celebrate. Parts of the region were in ruins, and hundreds of thousands had died. Many survivors, armed and mobile, had nothing to which they could return. Facing an uncertain future, those who did have resources hesitated to invest in new enterprises. It would take much of Latin America a century to recover economically from the wars of independence. Poverty in turn undermined the political stability of the new republics.

And while it was easy enough to create new symbols of nationhood such as flags, monuments, and coinage, much more difficult was the task of forging new national identities, "imagined communities" in which racially and culturally disunited peoples who thought mostly in terms of their own towns and villages could live together and come to see themselves as Mexicans or Peruvians or Brazilians. The resulting tensions would undermine the stability of Latin American politics for a half century.

LEARNING MORE ABOUT LATIN AMERICANS

Bethel, Leslie, ed. *The Independence of Latin America* (New York: Cambridge University Press, 1987).

Chambers, Sarah C. *From Subjects to Citizens: Honor, Gender and Politics in Arequipa, Peru, 1780–1854* (University Park, PA: Pennsylvania State University Press, 1999). A look at how ordinary people in one Peruvian community experienced the transition from colonialism to independence.

Graham, Richard. *Independence in Spanish America: A Comparative Approach*, 2nd ed. (New York: McGraw-Hill, 1994). Comprehensive coverage of the wars for independence.

Henderson, Timothy J. *The Mexican Wars for Independence* (New York: Hill and Wang, 2009). Succinct survey.

Kinsbruner, Jay. *Independence in Spanish America: Civil Wars, Revolutions, and Underdevelopment* (Albuquerque, NM: University of New Mexico Press, 2000). Good overview of the process of independence.

Kraay, Hendrik. *Race, State, and Armed Forces in Independence-Era Brazil: Bahia, 1790s–1840s* (Stanford, CA: Stanford University Press, 2001). An examination of independence and early state-building in one of Brazil's historic sugar-producing regions.

Méndez, Cecilia. *The Plebeian Republic: The Huanta Rebellion and the Making of the Peruvian State, 1820–1850* (Durham, NC: Duke University Press, 2005). This study of a rebellion by peasants, muleteers, landowners, and military officers shows the kinds of challenges facing the new governments of Latin America in the era of Independence.

Murray, Pamela. *For Glory and Bolívar: The Remarkable Life of Manuela Sáenz* (Austin, TX: University of Texas Press, 2008). A definitive biography of Manuela Sáenz that dispels the many myths surrounding Simón Bolívar's mistress.

Rodriíguez, O., Jaime E. *The Independence of Spanish America* (New York: Cambridge University Press, 1998).

Schultz, Kirsten. *Tropical Versailles: Empire, Monarchy, and the Portuguese Royal Court in Rio de Janeiro, 1808–1821* (New York: Routledge, 2001). How the temporary presence of the Portuguese monarchy transformed life in the capital of Brazil.

Van Young, Eric. *The Other Rebellion: Popular Violence, Ideology, and the Mexican Struggle for Independence, 1810–1821* (Stanford, CA: Stanford University Press, 2001). A learned exploration of the reasons why Mexicans rebelled against Spanish authority.

Walker, Charles F. *Smoldering Ashes: Cuzco and the Creation of Republican Peru, 1780–1840* (Durham, NC: Duke University Press, 1999). Gives key insights into the roles played by the indigenous people of Cuzco in forging independence and a new national state.

9

REGIONALISM, WAR, AND RECONSTRUCTION:
POLITICS AND ECONOMICS, 1821–1880

THE NEWLY INDEPENDENT COUNTRIES of Latin America confronted two enormous challenges. The first was the need to persuade people who lived within their boundaries to render allegiance to the nation-state. Second, they had to rebuild their economies following the widespread destruction of the prolonged wars of independence. But before they could undertake these efforts, they had to resolve endless, seemingly intractable, disputes over who was to rule and what type of government was most appropriate. Most important, the new nations had to overcome the fact that the majority of people thought about politics in terms of their village, town, or province. Their concerns centered on how best to earn their livelihoods and maintain their local traditions, and for centuries, they had stubbornly resisted outsiders' attempts to meddle in their affairs. As we saw in Chapter 8, this regionalism shaped the independence struggle in many parts of Latin America, and it would continue to frustrate the efforts of nineteenth-century politicians bent on forging national communities.

Class and ethnic divisions further stymied nation-building, as people of different social classes fought for control of the new national governments. Underlying all politics was the deep fear the white upper classes had for the lower classes—comprised of African Latin Americans, native peoples, and mixed bloods—in part the result of a series of Indian and slave rebellions during the half century before the end of colonial rule.

Nor was there any kind of consensus about the form that governments should take. Some called for monarchy as the only way to guarantee stability, while others favored representative government. Among the advocates of democracy, some wanted a broad franchise, while others preferred to limit political participation to a select few. Often, charismatic strongmen, called *caudillos,* who were able to impose order by either mediating or coercing the various competing groups, took the reins for long periods. Finally, for many Latin Americans the struggle for independence was just the beginning of a cycle of intermittent and devastating warfare that would last for much of the nineteenth century. Civil conflicts, wars with neighboring Latin American nations, and invasions launched by nations outside the region all took an enormous toll in human lives, wreaked economic havoc, and undermined all efforts at achieving some kind of national political cohesion.

Building strong economies proved equally daunting. The damage caused by the wars of independence was extensive. The lack of continuity caused by changes in the form of government and turnover in personnel made economic development difficult.

DILEMMAS OF NATIONHOOD

The new leaders of Latin America embarked upon nationhood with many ideas about political life, but no clear blueprint of the forms their national governments should take. They all had recent experience with kings, much of it unfavorable. The principal model of self-government at the national level was that of the young United States, but some political leaders found it unsuitable for Latin America. Like their neighbors to the north, the larger nations grappled with the question of whether to create a strong central government or to leave substantial power in the hands of state, provincial, or local governments. Given the profound attachment that many Latin Americans had to their own regions and towns, this dilemma of centralism versus a loose confederation proved especially vexing. Then, too, Latin Americans disagreed about how much change their societies needed. What institutions and practices left over from the colonial period should they retain, and what colonial legacies should they discard? In particular, they quarreled over the proper role of the Catholic Church in their societies and how best to make their economies more productive. But before they could address any of these questions, they had to settle the argument over who was to control the new national governments.

Who Governs and What Form of Government?

From Independence through the 1870s, four broad groups vied in the political arena. At the top were wealthy, influential whites, such as prosperous merchants, large landowners, mine owners, and church officials, who expected to rule their nations for their own benefit. Military, comprised of national armies, provincial militias, and locally based private forces, formed the second contender. Mostly, the latter allied with the interests of the upper class, but on occasion had their own goals. The nineteenth century's many wars reinforced the role of the military. A small middle sector made up of professional bureaucrats, who allied with the upper classes and ran the everyday operations of government, lower-level clergy, and merchants, also competed. Lastly, the lower classes, which included sharecroppers, tenant farmers, small-scale merchants,

1814–1840
Dr. Francia rules Paraguay

1822–1831
Pedro I rules in Brazil

1829
Gran Colombia breaks up

1828–1852
Juan Manuel de Rosas dominates the Río de la Plata

1836–1838
Peru–Bolivia Confederation

1846–1848
Mexican War with the United States

1857–1860
War of the Reform in Mexico

1862
Argentine unification
French Intervention in Mexico

1865–1870
Paraguayan War or War of the Triple Alliance

1879–1883
War of the Pacific (Chile vs. Peru and Bolivia)

unskilled and skilled workers, artisans, street venders, and domestics, demanded a say in the political debates. Although the upper class dominated politics and commanded most of the economic resources, the lower class wielded some influence at the local level. The upper class feared the lower classes but also needed their support, especially in times of internal conflicts or external war. The lower classes could negotiate, trading their assistance in return for local autonomy or other concessions.

The type of government was also under discussion. Mexico and Brazil first adopted monarchies. In Mexico, Emperor Agustín I (Iturbide) lasted little more than a year (1821–1822). The Brazilian monarchy, however, endured for 67 years (1822–1889) and two emperors, Pedro I (1821–1829) and Pedro II (1839–1889). For the most part, Latin Americans chose the republican model of government with three branches, the executive, the legislature, and the judiciary, with political participation limited to literate male property owners. For much of the nineteenth century, dictators who did the bidding of the upper classes ruled.

Federalism/Centralism and Liberalism/Conservatism

Regionalism was at the core of the political discourse with the political ideologies of the times focused on the roles of government at the various levels. On one side were the federalists who advocated weak national governments and strong provincial (state) governments. On the other were the centralists who favored strong national governments and weak provincial governments. Each counted landowners among their ranks, but the centralists also included urban merchants, top-echelon government bureaucrats, military officers, and high clergy. Neither factions trusted the lower classes, but nonetheless relied on their support, particularly at the local level.

During the middle decades of the nineteenth century, the political discourse expanded to include the role of the Roman Catholic Church in the economy and politics, the place of collective landholdings as practiced by Indian and mestizo villages, and the relative merits of free trade and protectionism. Federalism became subsumed in Liberalism (except in the Río de la Plata) and centralism in Conservatism. Each of these new factions for the most part incorporated the followers of their predecessors. The Liberals vehemently opposed the position of the Church as a large landowner, insisted on individual rather than collective property holding, and advocated free trade. They sought to create a nation of small farmers, practitioners of capitalism, who would form the backbone of the republic. Regional elites tended toward Liberalism, because it would maintain their traditional autonomy. Large-scale merchants were Liberals because they favored deregulation of commerce. Ironically, the Liberals discovered by century's end that their goals for economic development were incompatible with federalism, so they became centralists. They found too that free trade did not further modern industrial development. Conservatives fought most fiercely for the rights and privileges of the Church, which they believed served as the protector of social stability.

Whether Liberal or Conservatives, privileged groups distrusted, even despised, the lower classes, while at the same time they eagerly solicited their support. For most people in the countryside the struggles of everyday life remained paramount; access to good land and avoidance of oppressive taxation were at the center of their agenda. Keeping local community and religious traditions free of outside interference were also of utmost importance. Most country people had joined independence movements in order to reassert the local autonomy lost to the administrative reforms of the late colonial era. To them ideology meant far less than did control over local affairs. They often changed their allegiances, establishing links to whatever regional and national forces that seemed least likely to intrude on local prerogatives.

THE CHALLENGE OF REGIONALISM

The histories of almost every nation in Latin America recount decades of struggle to forge regions into larger entities and build national identities. The centuries-old desire for local autonomy on the part of many lower-class people lay at the heart of Latin American regionalism, but many other factors also worked against any quick achievement of national unity. Geography played a decisive role. Mountains, deserts, and jungles often impeded easy overland transportation and communication and made it difficult to determine clear national and provincial boundaries. In Mexico, the lack of navigable rivers further hindered contact among people across its vast territory that extended from present-day California to Central America. Linguistic differences and racial antagonisms divided many countries as well. Although a small group of upper-class whites in each country by the 1810s had imagined nationhood, the vast majority of the people owed loyalty to their home villages or cities. Mexico, Central America, northern South America, and Argentina all required a series of civil wars to create nations from regional conglomerations. Bolivia, Paraguay, and Uruguay owed their status as separate nations to their efforts to escape from the control of Argentina. Brazil avoided the ravages of civil war but still experienced serious conflicts among its many regions. Only Chile did not struggle to unify. It maintained orderly politics for 60 years, and Chilean presidents succeeded one another at 10-year (two 5-year terms) intervals until 1890.

Argentina, Mexico, Colombia, and Central America

Four areas, Argentina, Mexico, Colombia, and Central America, required a series of civil wars to amalgamate nations from their disparate regions. The rivalries between federalists and centralists and Liberals and Conservatives were often bitter and brutal. Independent Argentina (originally the Viceroyalty of Río de la Plata) consisted of four regions: the city and environs of Buenos Aires, the area along the coast north of Buenos Aires, the territory across the river (present-day Uruguay), and the interior (west of Buenos Aires to the Andes mountains). From the outset of independence, the people of the Río de la Plata struggled among themselves based on regional loyalties. Centralists, primarily export-oriented landowners and merchants in Buenos Aires, favored a unified, secular nation with an economy based on free trade. They earned their fortunes by exporting animal products, such as salted meat, to Europe. They also sought to limit the influence of the church and advocated religious freedom. Against them stood the regional bosses, usually landowners with armed cowboy (*gaucho*) followers, who objected to a strong central government and supported the church and fiercely fought to maintain their provincial autonomy.

The old Viceroyalty of Río de la Plata disintegrated as a political entity immediately after independence. It would take more than four decades to unite what is today Argentina. The northeast (Corrientes, Entre Ríos, and Santa Fe provinces) sought to throw off the domination of Buenos Aires as early as 1810. Upper Peru (now Bolivia) broke away in 1810, followed by Paraguay in 1811. Montevideo (across the river in present-day Uruguay) simultaneously rejected the rule of Buenos Aires. In 1819, several coastal and interior provinces declared themselves independent republics, each ruled by a local warlord.

The city of Buenos Aires, which was the strongest political and military entity in the Río de la Plata, led the struggle for centralization. Bernardino Rivadavia (1821–1827) and Juan Manuel de Rosas (1829–1852) established Buenos Aires's dominance until the provinces reasserted their autonomy, overthrowing Rosas in 1852. After nearly a decade of warfare, Buenos Aires finally defeated provincial forces in 1861 and imposed unification. Delegates from the provinces elected Bartolomé Mitre (1862–1868), the victorious general, Argentina's first president in 1862. He then used war with Paraguay (1865–1870) to further strengthen the power of the national government at the expense of provincial autonomy. By the mid-1870s, the government had eliminated the last of the regional bosses. The achievement of a centralized nation-state had been costly, however, requiring two civil wars and an external war.

Regionalism was also at the core of nineteenth-century Mexican politics. In Mexico, centralists and federalists alternated in power through the 1850s. The experiment with monarchy immediately after independence was short lived. Emperor Agustín I, who as Agustín de Iturbide had forged the negotiations between the upper classes and rebel guerrilla leaders that obtained independence from Spain in 1821, failed to unite the country and fell to a federalist insurgency. Mexico's first elected president, Guadalupe

Victoria (1824–1829), a hero of the guerrilla wars of independence, managed to balance the two factions. From 1829 until 1855, as the battle between federalism and centralism teetered back and forth, Antonio López de Santa Anna dominated the political landscape. Santa Anna began as a federalist, but quickly changed views when confronted with the fragmentation of his country. The centralists ruled for a decade from 1836 to 1846, lost out to the federalists from 1846 to 1853, and reasserted themselves in 1853. The loss of Texas in 1836 and defeat in the war with the United States (1846–1848) badly discredited the centralists led by Santa Anna. The federalist–centralist struggle was then subsumed in the new conflict between Liberals (who were federalists) and Conservatives (who were centralists). A terrible civil war erupted, which ended only in 1867 with the defeat of the centralists-Conservatives. Mexico began to come together under the presidency of Benito Juárez (1858–1872), a Liberal, who unified the nation through his heroic struggle against the French Intervention from 1862 to 1867. The Conservatives allied with the French and, as a result, suffered devastating defeat. Like Argentina, the emergence of Mexican nationhood had required a series of brutal civil wars and an external war in which there were hundreds of thousands of casualties.

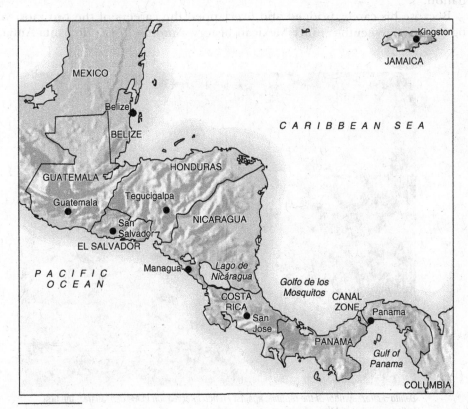

Central America

How Historians Understand   BENITO JUÁREZ: THE MAKING OF A MYTH

Benito Juárez was president of Mexico from 1858 to 1872. Mexico's first Indian head of state led the nation through its bloodiest civil war, the War of the Reform (1858–1860), and its longest foreign war, the French Intervention (1861–1867). During his distinguished career, Juárez served at every level of government in both elected offices and the courts: from city councilor, to state legislator, national congressman, state governor, cabinet minister, and president, and from district judge to chief justice of the Supreme Court of the nation. Almost single-handedly, by force of his own determination, Juárez assured the triumph of Liberalism as the dominant political ideology and began the process of creating Mexico as a nation from the conglomeration of regions that had emerged from independence. Despite his obvious importance in nineteenth-century Mexican history, the myth of Benito Juárez has changed over time to reflect its creators' needs at the time. In the words of historian Charles Weeks: "…what Mexicans say about Juárez represents what they want to believe about themselves, as individuals and as a nation."

Because his career bridged and overlapped the careers of the two most vilified figures of nineteenth-century Mexican history, Antonio López de Santa Anna, who

Benito Juárez, symbol of the republic against French intervention in Mexico. Juárez, the first Indian president of Mexico, was a controversial figure.

dominated politics from 1828 to 1855, and Porfirio Díaz, the dictator from 1876 to 1911, Juárez should have attained the status of the nation's greatest hero. But mythical status came hard. In the fragmented politics of the era, his leadership was never uncontested. Two rivals vied for the presidency against him in 1861. He faced opposition to his continuation as president, during a time when the nation was at war, after his term ended in 1865. Two opponents confronted him in the elections of 1868 and 1872. (In the latter year he died shortly after his reelection.) Despite having defeated the French and their figurehead, the emperor Maximilian, Juárez found himself demonized by his enemies as a dictator.

For the first 15 years after his death, Juárez was almost forgotten. His successor, Porfirio Díaz, had tried twice to overthrow him by force, and the two men had ended as enemies. Díaz initially sought to get out from under Juárez's shadow. A radical change in attitude toward Juárez took place in 1887, when Díaz sought reelection for the first time. Díaz had served as president from 1877–1880, sat out for a term, and had run for election again in 1884 and also in 1888. Díaz needed to place himself as the heir to Juárez of the mantle of Liberal leadership, and it legitimized him for Juárez also to have run for reelection in a time of national crisis. The opposition to Porfirio Díaz supported the myth of Juárez, as well. They saw him as the champion of anticlericalism (anti–Roman Catholic Church), a strong legislative branch of government, and individualism. The celebration of Juárez the hero peaked in 1906 with the centennial of his birth.

Juárez then became a symbol of the radical opponents of Díaz, who sought to revive his program—democracy, and anticlericalism—that Díaz had betrayed. The major opposition to Díaz, which arose in 1910 led by Francisco I. Madero, named its political clubs after Juárez. Ironically, they called themselves anti-reelectionists. Madero deeply admired Benito Juárez as the epitome of legality. Madero's followers called him the modern-day Juárez. During the Revolution (1910–1920), Juárez emerged in yet another reincarnation as the model of a strong president. Amid the chaos and episodic tyranny of civil strife, Juárez stood for strength and law. The revolutionary leaders eventually constructed a centralized state led by a president with vast powers. They raised Juárez to hero status in order to legitimize strong presidential rule.

Questions for Discussion

Was Juárez a popular figure among common folk or just an icon created by the ruling class to suit its own purposes at various times? In the contest for control over their everyday lives, where did Juárez and his politics fit in? How do you think it is possible for historians to separate themselves from their times and to evaluate historical figures evenhandedly?

Regionalism destroyed independence hero Simón Bolívar's grand dream of a unified northern South America. From 1821 to 1830, Bolívar, as president, built Gran Colombia out of Ecuador, New Granada (present-day Colombia), and Venezuela. But by 1830, despite his enormous efforts, the three nations had separated and were individually beset by centrifugal forces. In Ecuador, the height of its regional divisions occurred in 1859, when no fewer than four governments with capitals in four different cities claimed to rule. Colombia was more divided than Ecuador. There were six major regions, five with an important city at its center: Cauca (Popayán), Antioqueña (Medellín), the coast (Cartagena), the Central Highlands (Bogotá), the northeast (Vélez), and the llanos (coastal plains). Francisco de Paula Santander, one of Bolívar's important lieutenants who was president from 1832 to 1837, maintained an unsteady peace. But after he left office, federalists and centralists fought a series of bitter civil wars from 1839 until 1885. Venezuela, through the skills of José Antonio Páez, another important lieutenant of Bolívar, resisted regional fragmentation into the 1850s. However, the nation erupted into the so-called Federal Wars from 1859 to 1863, which resulted in a federalist victory. The triumph was short lived, however, because in 1870 Antonio Guzmán Blanco (1870–1877, 1879–1884, and 1886–1888) reestablished centralized rule. In neither Colombia nor Venezuela did civil wars settle the conflicts between federalism and centralism.

Central Americans struggled against each other for much of the nineteenth century. In 1821, they put their fates in the hands of Mexico, joining the newly independent empire of Agustín de Iturbide. With the fall of Iturbide, a Central American congress met to declare the independence of the United Provinces of Central America in 1823, but the government of the United Provinces never gained control as the region plunged into civil war. Although the central government continued, the individual states increasingly expanded their influence. By 1865, Guatemala, under the rule of José Rafael Carrera (1844–1848, 1851–1865), defeated unification once and for all. In Central America, as in Argentina and Mexico, it took civil war to establish nation-states. Nothing, however, could unite the region.

Brazil and Chile

Although Brazil experienced no widespread civil wars, it, too, suffered deep regional divisions. Regional leaders never ceased their opposition to the nation's first ruler, Pedro I, and finally forced him to abdicate in 1831. Regional rebellions erupted during the 1830s, when a regent ruled during the minority of the heir to the throne. (Pedro I abdicated when his son was only 4 years old.) With Brazil seemingly on the verge of dissolution in 1840, Pedro II became emperor at age 14. War with Paraguay (1864–1870) to some extent served to push some Brazilians to think in national terms. Pedro II kept Brazil together until he abdicated, when regional tensions again overwhelmed the monarchy in 1889. Thus, to a large extent, regionalism determined Brazil's political fate, though the nation did not have to pay as great a price in bloodshed as had Mexico and Colombia.

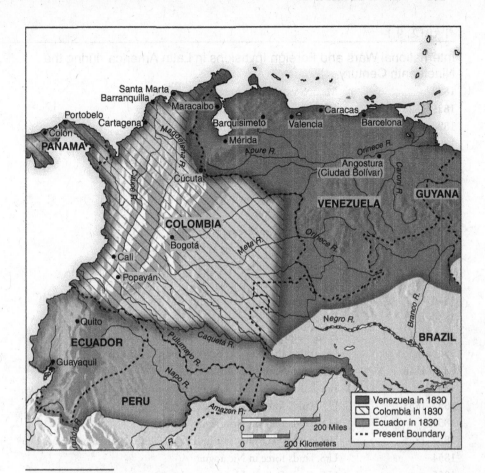

Gran Colombia: The failed experiment

A CENTURY OF WAR

War was the second major factor in the political instability in Latin America, as well as the primary reason for the lack of economic development. Hardly a year went by when there was not a war or some kind of military action somewhere in Latin America (see Table 9.1). Warfare inflicted enormous physical and economic damage; disrupted commerce, communications, and transportation; and drained governments of scarce financial resources. Political scientist Brian Loveman has identified four categories of wars in Latin America: transnational wars of political consolidation; international wars between Latin American nations; wars against foreign military intervention; and civil wars.

Wars of Political Consolidation

The best examples of wars of political consolidation were actually unsuccessful in unifying the contesting countries, leading instead to the dissolution of large confederations.

TABLE 9.1

International Wars and Foreign Invasions in Latin America during the Nineteenth Century

1823	Mexico vs. Central America
1825–1828	Cisplatine War: Brazil vs. Buenos Aires
1828–1830	Gran Colombia vs. Peru
1829	Spain vs. Mexico
1833	Great Britain takes Falkland Islands
1833	U.S. force in Buenos Aires
1836–1839	Chile vs. Peru–Bolivia Confederation
1836	Mexico vs. Texas
1838	Pastry War: Mexico vs. France
1838–1840	France blockades Río de la Plata
1838–1851	La Guerra Grande: United Provinces vs. Uruguay
1838–1865	Central American Wars
1840	Peru vs. Bolivia
1840–1841	Panama vs. New Granada
1840–1845	France and Great Britain blockade Río de la Plata
1843–1850	Great Britain occupies parts of Central America
1846–1848	Mexico vs. United States
1851	Brazil, Río de la Plata, and Uruguay vs. Buenos Aires
1852–1853	U.S. lands force in Argentina
1853	U.S. lands force in Nicaragua
1853–1854	William Walker filibuster in Baja, California, and Sonora, Mexico
1854	U.S. lands force in Nicaragua
1855	U.S. lands force in Uruguay
1855–1856	William Walker conquers Nicaragua
1856	U.S. lands force in Panama
1857	U.S. lands force in Nicaragua
1858	U.S. lands force in Uruguay
1859	U.S. displays force in Paraguay
1859	U.S. force in Panama
1860	William Walker filibuster in Honduras
1861	Tripartite (Great Britain, France, Spain) intervention in Mexico
1861–1865	Reoccupation of Santo Domingo by Spain
1862	Great Britain in Central America
1862–1867	French intervention in Mexico
1863	Guatemala vs. El Salvador
1864–1866	Peru, Chile, Bolivia, and Ecuador vs. Spain
1864–1870	War of the Triple Alliance: Paraguayan War

(Continued)

TABLE 9.1 (*Continued*)

International Wars and Foreign Invasions in Latin America during the Nineteenth Century

1864–1871	Guatemala and Honduras vs. El Salvador
1865	U.S. force in Panama
1868	U.S. lands force in Uruguay
1868	U.S. lands force in Colombia
1876–1885	Central America
1879–84	War of the Pacific: Chile vs. Peru and Bolivia
1885	U.S. force in Panama
1888	U.S. force in Haiti
1890	U.S. force lands in Argentina
1891	U.S. force in Haiti
1891	U.S. force in Chile
1894	U.S. force in Brazil
1895	U.S. force in Colombia
1896	U.S. force lands in Nicaragua
1898	U.S. force in Nicaragua
1894–1895	Great Britain in Central America
1898–1899	United States vs. Spain (Cuba)

Sources: C. Neale Ronning, ed. *Intervention in Latin America* (New York: Knopf, 1970); David Bushnell and Neill Macaulay, *Latin America in the Nineteenth Century*, 2nd ed. (New York: Oxford, 1994), pp. 305–309; and Brian Loveman, *For La Patria: Politics and the Armed Forces in Latin America* (Newark, NJ: SR Books, 1999), pp. 45–47.

Uruguay emerged as a separate nation as a result of the war between the Argentine Confederation and Brazil from 1825 to 1828. One of the longer wars of political consolidation took place in Central America, where the struggle for unification dragged on from 1824 to 1838, ending in failure. Peru and Bolivia, once together as part of the Viceroyalty of Peru, also failed to unify, engaging in a fruitless war from 1836 to 1841.

Intra-Regional Wars

The most important wars between Latin American nations were the War of the Triple Alliance (1864–1870) and the War of the Pacific (1879–1883). The War of the Triple Alliance, or Paraguayan War, in which Paraguay fought against the alliance of Argentina, Brazil, and Uruguay, was the most prolonged and destructive. The war began when Brazil invaded Uruguay (which Brazil claimed was part of its territory) and Paraguay responded by crossing a sliver of Argentine territory to attack the Brazilian province of Rio Grande do Sul. Argentina, Brazil, and Uruguay (with a government that was a puppet of Brazil) then allied and turned on Paraguay in May 1865. The war devastated Paraguay. It lost between 8 and 18 percent of its population and over one-third its territory. After the peace, alliance troops occupied parts of Paraguay for 8 years. All of the progress of the previous half-century toward a self-sufficient, relatively economically egalitarian society ended. Political instability followed for the next six decades.

Another extremely destructive conflict between Latin American nations was the War of the Pacific. Chile fought Peru and Bolivia over access to nitrate fields. Chile and Bolivia had a long-standing disagreement over the territory—located in a disputed area in northern Chile, southern Peru, and western Bolivia—while Peru and Chile disputed control over the taxes on nitrate deposits. Chile won a drawn-out struggle and occupied Peru from 1881 to 1883. Peace brought a substantial victory for Chile, for it acquired the nitrate fields and thus a monopoly on the world's supply of this fertilizer. Bolivia lost its access to the Pacific Ocean, which was a serious detriment to its future economic development.

Foreign Wars

The most devastating war with a nation outside the region was the Mexican War with the United States (1846–1848). Mexico had lost its northern province of Texas in 1836 to

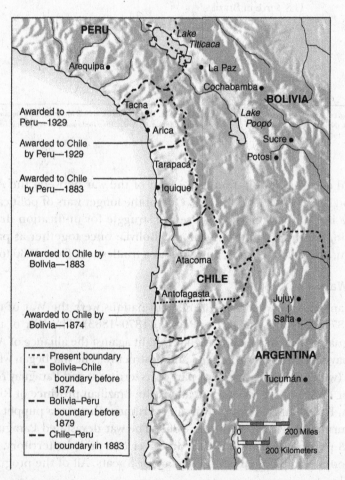

The War of the Pacific, 1879–1883

North American settlers, who had revolted against Santa Anna's imposition of centralist rule. Mexico never recognized the independence of the Republic of Texas and warned the United States that any attempt to annex Texas would be considered an act of war. In late 1845, the United States, ignoring Mexico's protests, annexed Texas. A few months later, a clash between Mexican and U.S. forces in south Texas led to war. In a relatively short but costly conflict, the United States eventually captured the major cities of Monterrey, Veracruz, and ultimately Mexico City. Mexico lost half its national territory, including present-day Texas, Arizona, New Mexico, and California.

In addition to the actual wars themselves, the potential for war with neighbors over boundaries and other issues was continuously present. Argentina and Chile disputed each other's rights to Tierra del Fuego. Peru and Ecuador were at odds over their Amazonian territories. The threat of foreign intervention was constant. For a decade after independence, Mexico feared Spain would attempt to reconquer it. It also anticipated invasion by the United States for almost a century after the two ended their war in 1848. Central America and the Caribbean lived in the shadow of U.S. intervention from the 1850s.

Civil Wars

The small civil wars that plagued Latin America in the nineteenth century were innumerable. There were 11 "national level rebellions" in nineteenth-century Colombia alone. From 1831 to 1837, Brazil endured continuous rebellions in Maranhão, Bahia,

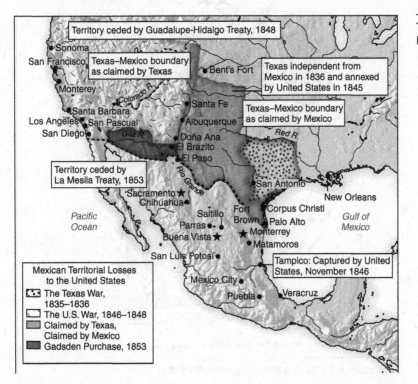

The Wars for Northern Mexico, 1836–1853

Territory ceded by Guadalupe-Hidalgo Treaty, 1848

Texas–Mexico boundary as claimed by Texas

Texas independent from Mexico in 1836 and annexed by United States in 1845

Texas–Mexico boundary as claimed by Mexico

Territory ceded by La Mesila Treaty, 1853

Tampico: Captured by United States, November 1846

Mexican Territorial Losses to the United States
The Texas War, 1835–1836
The U.S. War, 1846–1848
Claimed by Texas, Claimed by Mexico
Gadsden Purchase, 1853

Minas Gerais, Mato Grosso, and Río Grande do Sul. Thirteen military uprisings occurred in Peru in the months between June and October 1840. From 1852 to 1862, there were 117 uprisings of one type or another in the Río de la Plata.

The struggles between Liberals and Conservatives in some countries, Mexico and Colombia for instance, erupted in brutal warfare during the middle decades of the century, as the conflicts over the place of the church in society, politics, the economy and over collective landholding intensified. These were emotional issues, for at stake were the very essence of day-to-day life—control over one's religion and livelihood. In Mexico, neither Liberals nor Conservatives were willing to compromise. From 1854 to 1867, they fought a series of vicious civil wars, including the Plan of Ayutla Revolt (1854–1855), which ousted Santa Anna for the last time, the War of the Reform (1858–1860), and the French Intervention (1862–1867). The Liberals ultimately won the struggle because they won over the people of the countryside. Communal villages sided with the Liberals despite the fact the Liberals advocated destruction of communal landholding because the Liberals, as federalists, also advocated local autonomy in governance. Villagers calculated that it did not matter what laws the Liberals enacted nationally, as long as the villagers controlled their own local governments, they could evade them. The crucial factor was local autonomy.

Soldado de línea con su dotación de campaña y combate

A soldier in the Río de la Plata in the nineteenth century.

The Impact of War

The effects of warfare were profound both politically and economically. Wars militarized society, gave political prominence to military leaders, and undermined democracy; widened ethnic divisions; diminished daily life; killed tens of thousands of people; destroyed property, transportation, and communications; and squandered scarce resources. They made economic development nearly impossible and thus prevented any substantial improvement in living conditions for most Latin Americans (see Chapter 10).

Constant warfare militarized society as formal national and informal regional armed forces proliferated. The regular army functioned at the national level to defend the nation against external threats, but often its units attempted and succeeded in over-throwing the national government. In addition, there were local militias that formed the power bases of regional bosses who challenged national unity and authority. It seemed at times that everyone was armed.

Warfare spawned countless military leaders who dominated high government office in many countries. Six civilians and 16 generals served as president of Mexico between 1821 and 1851. Three of the civilian presidents lasted just a few days. Two generals, Antonio López de Santa Anna and Anastasio Bustamante (1830–1832, 1837–1841), dominated Mexican politics for the first half of the nineteenth century. The men who overshadowed all others in the politics of the Río de la Plata were in the military. Juan Manuel de Rosas was a noted military commander. Bartolomé Mitre (1862–1868) won fame for winning the decisive battle for Argentine unification in 1861. Despite its reputation as perhaps the most stable of the continent's republics, Chile was ruled by military officers through its initial three decades.

The presence of so many military figures gave politics an authoritarian air. Moreover, in times of war, governments often suspended civil liberties, such as freedom of the press and freedom of speech. National legislatures, when confronted with war emergencies, regularly chose to temporarily suspend the rule of law in order to bestow extraordinary powers on the president.

In addition, wars rubbed raw old ethnic and class divisions. The civil wars at mid-century in Mexico exacerbated local rivalries in the countryside to the extent that vengeance became an integral part of everyday life in the villages. There had been too many atrocities to be forgotten. In Mexico in the 1840s, the Caste War of Yucatán nearly resulted in the overthrow of white rule on that peninsula. In Peru, the War of the Pacific ripped open ethnic scars as Chinese coolies and rural blacks in the south sought vengeance for mistreatment. These conflicts only accentuated the fears of the upper classes.

Economically, wars were devastating. Lack of reliable sources makes it impossible to accurately assess the damage wreaked by a century of wars, but there is sufficient anecdotal evidence to suggest that in some areas it was debilitating. The mining sector was initially hardest hit. It took decades for production in the mines of Bolivia, Peru, and Mexico to regain their colonial levels. The destruction of mine shafts by flooding, scavenging of equipment, and deteriorating roads impeded redevelopment. No better example exists than Bolivia. It emerged from the wars of independence with its mining industry in ruins. The human cost of war in terms of casualties was sometimes catastrophic, as in the case of Paraguay in the War of the Triple Alliance. In Yucatán, in Mexico's southeast, more than 100,000 people lost their lives in the vicious rebellion during the late 1840s. Perhaps 300,000 people lost their lives in Mexico's War of the Reform a decade later. The tremendous losses among young males profoundly altered family structures and gender relations (see Chapter 10).

Wars and military preparedness bankrupted national governments. Armies drained scarce, precious financial resources that would have been better spent on roads and schools. The cost of the military was nowhere more evident than in Mexico. In 1836, the Mexican military expended 600,000 pesos a month, while government revenues totaled only 430,000 pesos. These figures did not include the cost of the Texas War (1836), which added another 200,000 pesos a month! Needless to say, this left no money for other functions of government. Dictator Rosas of Buenos Aires maintained a standing army of 20,000 and a militia of 15,000, the cost of which accounted for one-half to three-quarters of his annual budgets. In both these examples, the threat of foreign invasion was constant. Mexico feared Spain and the United States, while Buenos Aires worried about the Brazilians, the British, and the French.

Because armies regularly expanded and shrank in size, there were always a substantial number of out-of-work soldiers who were unwilling to return to their former homes to toil as tenants or peons on a hacienda or the communal holdings of their villages. Many became bandits, and lawlessness followed. From the 1820s to the 1860s, it was virtually impossible to travel between Veracruz, Mexico's major port, located on the Gulf of Mexico, and Mexico City without being held up. Some stagecoaches were robbed several times over the course of a single trip. It was not uncommon for passengers to arrive at their destination wrapped in newspapers, having been relieved of all their worldly possessions en route. This disorder greatly discouraged commerce and thus impeded economic development.

Not all of the effects of war were adverse, however. The military provided unparalleled upward social mobility. Indians, mulattos, and mestizos obtained unprecedented opportunities for economic and social advancement through war. Many of the national leaders who emerged from the wars of independence and subsequent conflicts had lower-class origins. Notable among them was Porfirio Díaz, who was dictator of Mexico in the last quarter of the century. Mobilization in Brazil during the Paraguayan War had conscripted mostly black and mulatto troops. The war probably assured the end of slavery as an institution, for slaves earned their freedom through military service. Returning soldiers were not the docile workforce they had been when they went to war. Some veterans received money bonuses and land grants. Others who had received nothing for their service refused to return to the status quo before the war.

Constant warfare undoubtedly eroded the fabric of everyday life and politics. Ironically, however, a few international wars may have actually contributed to the creation of nationalist sentiment and helped forge a sense of nationhood. Its two wars against Peru and Bolivia unquestionably helped consolidate sparsely populated Chile. These clear victories boosted popular association with the nation. The War of the Triple Alliance, which came only 3 years after unification, promoted a sense of Argentine national identity. The valiant fight of Benito Juárez against the French Intervention in Mexico also produced the first extensive sense of nation and Mexicanness.

POPULAR PARTICIPATION

Regional fragmentation, divisions among the upper classes, and war provided unusual opportunities for lower-class participation in political affairs during the first five decades after independence. Although Latin American civil conflicts rarely involved more than a few thousand troops, local and regional bosses required regular retainers recruited from their areas. Workforce requirements necessitated concessions and inducements. While personal loyalties were sometimes sufficient to secure followers, lower-class supporters demanded not only personal gain, such as wages, war booty, and promotions, but more importantly, maintenance of local autonomy for villages and protection from laws against collective landownership and taxes.

Popular participation in the politics of nation building resulted from the need of the lower classes at the very least to exert some influence over their everyday lives. As we have discussed, the policies of neither upper-class factions were acceptable. Country people increasingly opposed both Liberal and Conservative policies to develop the economy. The struggle to maintain control over their daily existence in the countryside manifested itself in the vast conflict over local autonomy, which translated into the national conflict between federalism and centralism. This in turn led the lower classes into broader political participation. In search of supporters, national leaders courted the concerns of everyday people, who comprised the armies of various competing factions.

In the cities, local issues revolved around food prices and employment. Riots were important expressions of political involvement in urban settings. Protests erupted in Latin American cities as a result of the high cost of corn and beans. For example, in 1831, the populace of Recife, Brazil, attacked Portuguese merchants believed to have been price gouging.

There were also a number of instances where the urban lower classes played crucial roles in national politics. Mexico City's lower classes formed the backbone of Iturbide's support during his last days. However, he was unwilling to use their support to maintain power, so strong was his sense of solidarity with the upper class and his fear of the lower classes. Mexico City dwellers erupted again in 1828 in the Parián Riot (see Slice of Life: The Parián Riot) in support of Vicente Guerrero, the hero of the war of independence, in his campaign for president. Mobs in the streets of Rio de Janeiro helped to force Pedro I to abdicate in 1831.

Slice of Life   THE PARIÁN RIOT: MEXICO CITY, 1828

IN NINETEENTH-CENTURY Latin America, common folk struggled constantly both to sustain themselves—furnishing sufficient food, adequate shelter, and safety for their families—and to maintain some measure of control over their everyday lives. During the first five or six decades after independence, the lower classes exercised a degree of political influence because the upper classes were divided, and in some places, periodically at war among themselves. Urban and rural working-class folk participated in the politics of the time in several ways: as voters in local elections, soldiers in civil wars and revolts, allies of upper-class factions, and perpetrators of specific, directed incidents of urban violence. Upper-class Latin Americans needed the lower classes to fight their battles and as allies. Nonetheless, the wealthy and powerful were wary, often fearful, of the lower classes, knowing fully well that to arm the masses risked unleashing the dangerous forces of centuries of pent-up resentment. The Parián Riot, which occurred in Mexico City in 1828, was an instance in which the lower classes took part in political events, leading to a tumultuous episode that shook the Mexican upper classes to their very core.

As in most history, the upper classes wrote the narrative of the riot, and, consequently, the actual events of the day were slanted in a way unfavorable to the masses. On the early afternoon of Thursday, December 4, 1828, simultaneous to and probably in association with a popular revolt that broke out against President Guadalupe Victoria (1824–1829), a crowd of 5000 assaulted and looted the luxurious shops located in the Parián Building in Mexico City's Zócalo. It ended sometime the same evening. Upper-class chroniclers of the era depicted the riot in graphic terms, such as a "savage invasion," "murders in cold blood," and a "stain on the pages of our history." We know that the rioters were people of the lower classes and some soldiers, probably part of the troop sent to bring the tumult under control.

There were two murders, neither committed by the lower classes (but by the upper class), and there was considerable damage to stores and houses around the Zócalo. Most of the heavy destruction actually resulted from 3 days of street fighting that preceded the riot. Considerable disorder followed, with the wealthy of the city notably absent from the streets.

The revolt against President Victoria began on November 30. The lower classes rushed to support the upheaval led by Vicente Guerrero, a hero of the long guerrilla war that had led to independence. One observer estimated that 30,000 to 40,000 people, 20 to 25 percent of the population of the capital, fought on the side of the rebels. Most soldiers abandoned the government and joined the rebellion.

Upper-class Mexicans disdained Guerrero, an uneducated, dark-skinned casta. Guerrero advocated two policies that were especially popular among the capital's poor. He propounded protective tariffs for the native textile industry, where many lower-class and artisan city dwellers earned their living. He also proposed to expel the remaining Spaniards, many of whom were quite wealthy and, given the dire straits of the Mexican economy, were bitterly resented. It may have been that some rioters shouted "Death to the Spaniards" as they stormed into the Parián. Many of the merchants in the building were Spaniards.

The Parián riot was indicative of the politics of lower-class mobilization in the first decades after independence. Mexican upper classes both in the cities and in the countryside needed popular support. But this came at a price—sometimes mobilization got out of control. In the countryside lower classes demanded local autonomy for their villages and delay in the implementation of many of the modernizing policies so dear to upper-class hearts. By mid-century it was clear to the Mexican upper class that the price of lower-class cooperation was too high. The Parián riot remained an indelible memory for Mexico's rich and powerful. Their fear of the masses, to their mind, was justified.

Questions for Discussion

Both during the colonial and early independence eras, Mexico had a long history of urban riots as a means for the common people to express their dissatisfaction with their governments. What were the alternative strategies for the lower classes in negotiating with the upper classes?

The lower classes also influenced national politics in some instances when they were willing to fight foreign invaders long after the upper classes, who, while looking after their own self-interests, surrendered to or collaborated with the enemy. After the United States army had defeated Santa Anna's army in a series of battles on the outskirts of Mexico City in 1847, the general withdrew from the capital. The population of the city continued to fight, however, sniping and throwing debris from the rooftops at the North American troops. During the War of the Pacific (1879–1883), after the total defeat of the Peruvian army, the civilian country people of the central sierras and the south of Peru continued to fight under the leadership of General Andrés Cáceres against the invading Chileans. Upper-class Peruvians collaborated with the invaders. In both Mexico and Peru, the upper classes signed disadvantageous peace treaties at least in part because they feared the expansion of popular upheavals.

Throughout the nineteenth century, the upper classes faced a decided dilemma. They needed support from the lower classes, but they were not always pleased with their allies, for the masses were not easy to control once an uprising began. They lost control of the 1831 revolt in Recife, Brazil, when slaves joined in hoping to obtain their freedom. In 1835, outraged blacks and Indians in Belém, Brazil, joined and then overwhelmed an upper-class–led revolt seeking independence for their province, engaging in widespread destruction of property and attacking wealthy whites. It took the government 5 years to finally quash the rebels. The death toll for this bloody uprising reached 30,000, approximately one-fifth of the provincial population.

The new rulers of Latin America were more successful at reimposing traditional gender roles in politics. Females were crucial participants in the wars of independence on both sides. This, of course, upset long-held views that women's place was in the home in the private sphere. The male casualties endured during the decades of war in some areas, however, created demographic imbalances that threatened male domination (see Chapter 10). In Argentina, females were in the majority until mid-century. The upper classes realized full well that in times of war and disruption, families rather than governments would hold society together. They therefore insisted on the model of a male-dominated family. In order to maintain stability, the upper classes sought to maintain long-established gender roles.

CAUDILLOS

Strong leaders, known as caudillos, often emerged to bridge the gap between the upper and lower classes and temporarily bring order to disrupted politics. The term *caudillo* refers to a leader whose notoriety and authority arose from the local level, where he had attained a reputation for bravery. The caudillos of the nineteenth century, who first emerged from the wars of independence, often obtained their economic and popular bases from landowning. A caudillo's army comprised the workers on his hacienda, and a web of patron–client relations (informal and personal exchanges of resources between parties of unequal status) served as the base of his support. Typically, a landlord expected labor, deference, loyalty, and obedience, while the employee, in turn, received a basic level of protection and subsistence. Many caudillos solicited support among the lower classes and consequently earned their fierce loyalty.

Juan Manuel de Rosas, who dominated Buenos Aires and allied provinces from 1829 to 1852, embodied the qualities of the nineteenth-century Latin American leader. He was rough, brave, ruthless, tyrannical, and a sharp political strategist. Rosas was a military leader with a common touch. Growing up on a large cattle estate (*estancia*) he shared the austere life and learned the ways and language of the people who inhabited the vast plains of the Pampas. Although he became a large landowner, Rosas presented himself as one of the people. He adhered to their "code" of honesty and discipline. It is said that he once ordered his servant to give him 20 lashes for being a bad gaucho, and when, unsurprisingly, the servant balked, Rosas threatened him with 500 lashes if he did not comply with the order. Virtually unchallenged through the 1840s, Rosas succumbed to his provincial opponents in 1852.

Like many other caudillos, Juan Manuel de Rosas had a crucial base of support among Indians and blacks. He organized a personal retinue from the poor of Buenos Aires and had a wide following among the gauchos of the Pampas. The lower classes regarded Rosas as the protector of their way of life. Rosas negotiated fairly with the Indians of the plains, thereby gaining their respect.

Rosas turned Afro-Argentines into a pillar of his regime, relying on them for his war machine. Through his wife, Encarnación, he worked with African mutual aid societies. Rosas lifted the previous bans on African street dances that reached the pinnacle of their popularity during his rule. His daughter Manuela attended dances and danced with black men. Once when the provincial government was strapped for money, 42 black nations (mutual societies) made special contributions to it. Rosas named his urban home after the black saint Benito de Palermo. His propaganda was written in African Argentine dialects. By 1836, Buenos Aires ended the forced draft for freed slaves and in 1839 ended the slave trade. Rosas promoted blacks to high military rank and took others as personal retainers. His large military force provided jobs for the chronically underemployed lower classes. He distributed land to the poor who were willing to live on the frontier and rewarded loyal soldiers with land.

LATIN AMERICAN LIVES

FRANCISCO SOLANO LÓPEZ

Some historians of Latin America have labeled the nineteenth century the "Age of Caudillos," when these often charismatic leaders imposed order through either negotiations or violence. The most notable examples, such as Antonio López de Santa Anna in Mexico and Juan Manuel de Rosas in the Río de la Plata (Argentina), dominated the histories of their nations, especially during the first decades after independence. In every instance the caudillos were controversial. This was particularly true in the case of Paraguay, whose three successive leaders—Dr. José Gaspar Rodríguez de Francia (1811–1840), Carlos Antonio López (1844–1862), and Francisco Solano López (1862–1870)—determined their nation's fate for 60 years. Historians have gone so far as to call two of them, Dr. Francia and Francisco Solano López, madmen. But to others both were national heroes.

At independence, Paraguay had carved itself out of the Spanish Viceroyalty of Río de la Plata (which also included current day Argentina and Uruguay). Its first caudillo Dr. Francia isolated the nation. The scrupulously honest dictator established a highly efficient government and a relatively egalitarian society, carefully curtailing the wealthy landowning class. He operated unusually successful educational programs and profitable state enterprises. He also created a strong military, ever in fear of larger neighbors Argentina and Brazil. His successor Carlos Antonio López for the most part continued his policies. López, in addition, broadened the rights of the nation's indigenous people, the Guaraní, expanded export agriculture, and developed independent military industry. His son Francisco Solano López took over after Carlos Antonio's death in 1862.

Francisco Solano López (1826–1870) was the material from which writers make great novels. Brought up as the privileged eldest son of a powerful dictator, to whom no one ever said no, the young López was a brigadier general at 18 and his father's chief advisor while barely in his twenties. Carlos Antonio sent him to Europe to be his chief procurement agent in 1853 and 1854. The experience yielded a close-up view of balance of power diplomacy and an Irish mistress, Elisa Alicia Lynch, who eventually bore him five sons. Many observers thought the beautiful Lynch the dark power behind the dictator; she was well hated by the local elite. López's mercurial temperament added to the drama.

Shortly into his 10-year term as president, López became enmeshed in the complicated politics of civil wars in both Argentina and Uruguay. As a result, Paraguay

Francisco Solano López.

entered into a 5-year long, catastrophic war against the Triple Alliance of Argentina, Brazil, and Uruguay. Uruguay was the 1828 creation of diplomatic compromise between Argentina and Brazil, both of which claimed its territory. At stake was access to the Río de la Plata-Parana-Paraguay river system. After more than a quarter century during which each nation turned inward, civil wars in Argentina that eventually resulted in its unification under the leadership of Buenos Aires, and in Uruguay restarted the rivalry between Argentina and Brazil over influence in the region. López became quite concerned that one or the other of his larger neighbors would upset the balance of power in the Rio de la Plata, endangering Paraguay. He attacked Brazil in late 1864 to prevent it from interfering in Uruguayan politics. In April 1865, he invaded an Argentine province, setting off war with the second neighbor. Although they had overwhelming advantages in population and resources, neither Argentina nor Brazil succeeded in taking advantage. López held them off until he died in battle in 1870.

Although often vilified by the victors and proclaimed a national hero by Paraguayans, recent scholarship has discussed more judiciously López's strengths and weaknesses, concluding that his motives for war were not unsound—he should have indeed feared his neighbors; he clearly commanded the loyalty of his people, who stayed with him to near extinction; he could have ended the war in 1866, but refused because the terms of the peace included his resignation; and as the war continued and his desperation intensified, he resorted to ever more brutal methods to maintain discipline.

The end result for Paraguay was, however, indisputably a catastrophe from which the nation never recovered. Although recent demographic studies have debated how many Paraguayans died in the tragic war, there is ample evidence that perhaps half the total population was lost and a much higher percentage of the male population. The nation also ceded tens of thousands of miles of territory to Argentina and Brazil. Brazilian troops occupied the country until 1878. Perhaps the most prosperous, stable, and egalitarian nation on the continent in 1865, Paraguay never came back from the debacle. Whether a madman or sound strategist, Francisco Solano López had led his homeland to ruin.

Questions for Discussion

How does the War of the Triple Alliance compare with other major wars in Latin America during the nineteenth century, such as the War of the Pacific or the Mexican war with the United States? Given the case of Francisco Solano López, do you think that colorful personalities were the dominant factor in nineteenth-century Latin American history?

Heroism and charisma were no guarantees for a long or successful political career. Several of the foremost figures of the wars of independence suffered tragic fates. Bernardo O'Higgins won independence for Chile, but as ruler, he lasted only until 1822. Antonio José de Sucre, one of Bolívar's best generals, was the first president of Bolivia (1825–1828), but he failed in his efforts to end the oppression of the Indian population.

THE CHALLENGE OF ECONOMIC RECOVERY

Regionalism and war adversely affected Latin American economic development. Regionalism created an uncertain political environment, which frightened investors, while war unproductively consumed vast human, material, and financial resources.

In Mexico and Bolivia, the loss of territory deprived the nation of valuable resources. During the years from 1810 to 1870, Latin American economies, with a few exceptions, stagnated due to the inability or unwillingness of the upper classes to establish governments that could create stable environments for commerce and industry. Institutional obstacles left from the colonial period, the widespread damages and disruptions caused by the wars of independence and subsequent upheavals, and the lack of capital further stifled economic growth. After 1850, the situation slowly began to change, as booming markets for Latin American agricultural staples and minerals, along with European capital investment in mining and transportation, brought renewed economic growth. From 1850 until World War I (1914), most nations in the region attached their economic fortunes to the burgeoning export markets in Western Europe and the United States. Still, economic development of Latin America faced substantial obstacles.

Obstacles to Development

In many regions, geography was a major obstacle to development. Most of Latin America lacked inexpensive transportation and easy communications. The lack of transportation greatly limited the establishment of national and regional markets. The cost of moving products to market was prohibitive. The Spanish colonial government had never invested much in roads, and the wars of independence left existing roads in disrepair. With the exception of the Río de la Plata, few major waterways ran through population centers. Coastal trade was not important in the nineteenth century.

Laws, attitudes, and institutions inherited from the colonial period further hindered growth after independence. These included local and regional autonomy; overregulation and underenforcement of rules; indifference to long-term planning and preference for short-term benefits; concentration on the export of precious minerals; state monopolies of commodities such as liquor and tobacco; strict limitations on international trade (including with neighboring nations); widespread corruption; a tradition of smuggling; and failure to invest in roads and ports. Three-hundred-year-old colonial habits and tendencies were not easy to break.

There were considerable institutional constraints to economic enterprise. Laws were often arbitrary and capricious, changing from regime to regime, and easily subverted through corruption. Laws often differed from region to region within the same nation. Each region also imposed its own taxes. Perhaps most important was the lack of modern systems of banking. The lack of credit handicapped both industry and agriculture. The shortage of capital prevented the repair and maintenance of mines and haciendas. The church, which had acted as a major source of credit during the colonial era, lost its primary base of income when the new governments abolished the tithe (an annual tax of 10 percent on all income collected by the colonial government from individuals for the church). The church's funds were still considerable, but they were tied up in land and virtually unredeemable loans to landowners. Europeans, with the exception of a few brief (mad) years in the 1820s, were unable or unwilling to invest in Latin America. Governments also experienced chronic revenue shortages because the newly independent states did away with many royal taxes and, because of their incompetence, were unable to collect those taxes that remained. The flight of Spaniards with their capital in the aftermath of the independence wars drained Latin America of crucial investment funds.

The new nations sought to make up for the lack of capital during the 1820s by borrowing funds abroad in the form of government loans. Several of the founders, like Bolívar, obtained loans from British investors, which they used to buy arms. From 1822 to 1825, seven Latin American nations (Brazil, Buenos Aires, Central America, Chile, Colombia, Mexico, and Peru) contracted for more than 20 million (British) pounds debt. Not surprisingly, economic difficulties prevented repayment. All the Latin American nations except Brazil remained in default of these debts for a quarter century. This foreclosed the possibility of attracting external capital to the region. After 1850, Europeans were attracted once again with the upturn of Latin American agricultural and mineral exports.

Export Economies

Although the general trend for the region as a whole was bleak for much of the first half of the nineteenth century, as continuous war and periodic political disruptions impeded economic growth, several nations prospered because of increasing demand for agricultural commodities. Buenos Aires became one of the remarkable economic success stories of nineteenth-century Latin America. Even when fighting raged, its foreign trade expanded. Markets for hides and cattle by-products flourished. A new industry arose to process hides and salt meat. The Río de la Plata provided the slaves of Brazil and the working class of Europe with their food. Entrepreneurial landowners began to raise sheep to provide cheap wool for the carpet factories of New England and Great Britain. Buenos Aires evolved into a complex of stockyards, slaughterhouses, and warehouses. The vast plains around Buenos Aires, the Pampas, became an enormous, efficient producer of agricultural products. In a more modest example, Venezuela experienced a coffee boom that brought two decades of prosperity from the 1830s through the 1840s.

After mid-century, European markets expanded rapidly. The increasing affluence of a growing population in Europe, a crucial aspect of which was the transfer of people from agriculture to industry, created a demand for Latin American products. Because most European nations were self-sufficient in basic agricultural staples, at first demand centered on luxury and semi-luxury commodities such as sugar, tobacco, cacao, coffee, and (later) bananas. Salted and dried beef also became a preferred part of the European diet. As industrialization in Europe accelerated, so too did the demand for raw materials. Cotton production grew rapidly during this period to meet the demand for inexpensive clothing. As the population continued to grow in Europe, there was less land available for raising livestock, and Europeans looked abroad for their tallow, hides, and meat. As Europe required more and more efficient agricultural production, the demand for fertilizers rose. Latin America had the natural resources to fill these demands.

The Haitian revolution of 1791, which destroyed the island of Hispaniola as the major sugar-producing region, sharply altered the trends of sugar production. Cuba and Brazil were the main beneficiaries. Brazil, which once had been the world's largest producer of sugar but whose ability to compete on the world market had atrophied by the end of the colonial era, was presented with new potential markets. Production doubled in the 1820s and nearly doubled again the following decade. Perhaps the most spectacular case of the rise and fall of an export economy occurred in Peru. The demand for fertilizers in Europe created an enormous demand for the natural fertilizer guano (bird excrement) found on Peru's offshore islands. Beginning in 1841, shipments of guano for export rose sharply. The Peruvian government used the prospects of future revenues from guano to compile an enormous debt. It also used guano funds to build the country's major railroad lines. By the early 1880s, however, guano deposits were nearly exhausted, and nitrate came on to the market as an alternative fertilizer. Consequently, the guano boom ended. Peru was left with huge debt to foreign companies and no possibility of repaying it because the revenues from guano had ceased.

A pattern of boom and bust cycles emerged. Latin America's national economies reacted to market forces using their competitive advantages in the production of agricultural and mineral commodities. Before 1850, when the market demanded

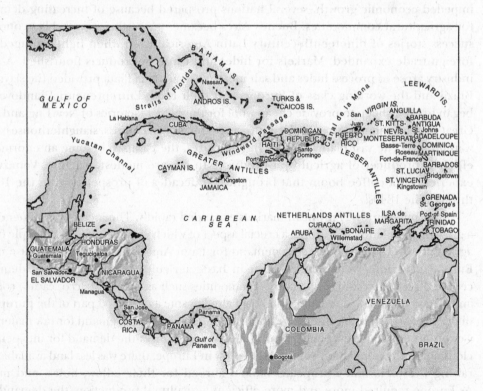

The Caribbean

mostly agricultural products, domestic entrepreneurs responded. Later in the century, however, when the demand was for minerals, foreign investors played an ever-increasing role. Latin American nations became increasingly dependent on foreign capital and vulnerable to fluctuations in world markets as the nineteenth century closed. Economic recovery from a century of war and political upheaval rested on an extremely precarious base.

CONCLUSION

The nineteenth century was a difficult time for governments and ordinary people in Latin America, but some progress occurred nonetheless. Once established, nations displayed remarkable continuity and cohesion in the face of strong regional forces. Despite the high turnover among high officeholders and the occurrence of civil wars, there were elements of stability in Latin American politics. Not infrequently, one or two figures dominated for a decade or more, though not continuously occupying the presidency. For example, Mexico had 49 national administrations between 1824 and 1857, and only one president, Guadalupe Victoria (1824–1829) finished his term. However, five chief executives held office on three or more separate occasions. Two, Anastasio Bustamante and Antonio López de Santa Anna, headed the nation for approximately half this period.

The high turnover was deceptive elsewhere as well. Though at times upheavals beset its politics, four men dominated Venezuela, José Antonio Páez (1831–1835, 1839–1843, 1861–1863), the Monagas brothers (José Tadeo and José Gregorio, 1847–1858), and José Guzmán Blanco (1870–1877, 1879–1884, 1886–1888). Pedro I (1822–1831) and Pedro II (1831–1889) ruled Brazil for more than six decades. Chilean presidents followed successively by election from 1831 to 1891. Rosas ruled the Río de la Plata from 1829 to 1852. Argentina's presidents followed one another by election from 1862 to 1930. Three dictators ruled Paraguay from 1815 to 1870.

Peru was perhaps the worst case of unstable politics. From its independence in 1821 to 1845, there were 24 major regime changes and more than 30 presidents. Strongman Agustín Gamarra (president 1829–1833 and 1839–1841) established some measure of order, interrupted only by Bolivian caudillo Andrés Santa Cruz's attempt to conquer Peru and establish the Peru–Bolivia Confederation from 1836 to 1838. During the early 1840s, Peru came apart. Finally, General Ramón Castilla reestablished order from 1845 to 1862 (as president 1845–1851 and 1855–1862), despite fighting a vicious civil war in 1854 and 1855.

Stability was more evident at the regional and local levels of politics. In Mexico, state (regional) politics were mostly in the hands of locally prominent merchant and landowning families who ruled for generations through control of municipalities and courts. In the Río de la Plata, provincial leaders like Estanislao López in Santa Fe ruled for decades. In Brazil, local bosses, known as colonels, and their families ran roughshod for generations.

Moreover, this era was in some ways the most democratic era in Latin America until nations introduced unlimited universal suffrage and mass voting after World War II. The lower classes not only participated in government, particularly on the local level but also took part indirectly in national politics and helped shape the political debates. It was also the period of the most extensive economic equity in Latin American history. In some areas, large landholdings suffered from disruptions and uncertainties. War and the expansion of the armed forces provided opportunities for upward mobility for the lower classes, including people of color.

Postindependence Latin America, as we will see in the succeeding chapter, was by no means the Garden of Eden, but common people had control over their everyday lives, a role in national politics, and often a chance to get ahead. The next 50 years were not to be as kind.

LEARNING MORE ABOUT LATIN AMERICANS

Barman, Roderick J. *Citizen Emperor: Pedro II and the Making of Brazil, 1825–91* (Stanford, CA: Stanford University Press, 1999). This is the best biography of the man who had the longest rule in Latin American history.

Fowler, Will. *Santa Anna of Mexico* (Lincoln, NE: University of Nebraska Press, 2007). Presents a balanced view of the most vilified Mexican ruler of the nineteenth century.

Graham, Richard. *Patronage and Politics in Nineteenth-Century Brazil* (Stanford, CA: Stanford University Press, 1990). Graham delves into the intricacies of politics in Brazil.

Guardino, Peter. *The Time of Liberty: Popular Political Culture in Oaxaca, 1750–1850* (Durham, NC: Duke University Press, 2005). A very good rendition of popular participation in Mexico.

Halperin-Donghi, Tulio. *The Aftermath of Revolution in Latin America.* Trans. Josephine de Bunsen (New York: Harper Torchbooks, 1973). Halperin has written a brilliant exposition of the impact of the wars of independence.

Jacobsen, Nils. *Mirages of Transition: The Peruvian Altiplano, 1780–1930* (Berkeley, CA: University of California Press, 1993). Traces change in the Peruvian altiplano.

Mallon, Florencia E. *Peasant and Nation: The Making of Postcolonial Mexico and Peru* (Berkeley, CA: University of California Press, 1995). Studies the ins and outs of rural local politics in communities in Mexico in Peru.

Thurner, Mark. *From Two Republics to One Divided: Contradictions of Post-Colonial Nationmaking in Andean Peru* (Durham, NC: Duke University Press, 1997). A study of the relationship between country people and the state in the early postindependence era.

10

EVERYDAY LIFE IN AN UNCERTAIN AGE, 1821–1880

IN LATIN AMERICA during the 60 years after independence, the uncertain political environment and frequent warfare adversely affected the material well-being of a large number of people of all social classes. The absence of consistent rules and regulations, the widespread lawlessness, and the loss of life and physical damage to property resulting from armed conflict often made day-to-day living quite difficult. It also substantially transformed important aspects of society, most importantly gender relations. Much changed profoundly over the course of the nineteenth century, but as much—good and bad—stayed the same. Despite these ofttimes troubled conditions, ordinary folk continued to earn their living and conduct their private lives much like their ancestors had for decades, even centuries. Ordinary people and to some extent their wealthier neighbors, particularly in the countryside, resisted the transformations sought by centralizers and modernizers.

The vast majority of Latin Americans during the nineteenth century lived in rural areas either as residents of large estates or villages with collective or small individual landholdings. Only a minority of country dwellers owned their own lands, though many were tenants or sharecroppers. In Brazil, most people in the countryside were slaves, forcibly brought in large numbers from Africa until 1850, when the trade in slaves from Africa ended as the result of enormous pressure put on the Brazilian government by Great Britain. A significant minority of Latin Americans lived in large cities, such as Mexico City, Buenos Aires, Lima, Rio de Janeiro, and São Paulo. Wherever they resided, most common folk lived in poverty, often barely surviving. Work was never easy, whether one was employed on a large estate, on one's own plot of land, in the mines, or as a domestic in a wealthier family's home in the city. Latin Americans toiled long and hard for their sustenance. However difficult their labor, they took pride in their jobs and did them well (no matter how much their bosses may have complained about them). Latin Americans, no matter how poor they were, mostly enjoyed their lives. There were *fiestas* (festivals) and other entertainments, the comfort of one's family, and the pageantry and solace of the Catholic Church.

The contrasts between rich and poor were enormous. Wealthy landowners often lived in palatial splendor in the cities, while only blocks away workers struggled in filth and squalor. Moreover, the well-to-do often had little sympathy for those less fortunate than they.

Let's turn, now, to the lives and work of Latin Americans, rich and poor.

THE PEOPLE

Who were the people who populated the newly independent nations? Latin America emerged from the colonial era with an ethnically diverse population, which had, during the eighteenth century, recovered from the horrific losses suffered in the sixteenth century, when the number of people had fallen by as much as 90 percent, mostly as a result of epidemic diseases brought by the Europeans. The vast majority of Latin Americans were Indians, Africans, or castas. Typical of Mexico at the turn of the nineteenth century, the population of the state of Puebla was 75 percent Indian, 10 percent white, and 15 percent castas. Less than one-third of Brazil's population was white, the rest black or mulatto. More than 30 percent were slaves. In the early 1820s, out of a total of 1.5 million Peruvians the white population counted only about 150,000. Mestizos numbered between 290,000 and 333,000. The African slave population was an estimated 50,000. The remaining million people were Indians. Approximately 65 percent of the people of Central America were Indian, 31 percent ladino (mestizo and mulatto), and 4 percent white.

The disruptions that followed independence slowed demographic growth (see Table 10.1), and, as a consequence, the region's economies stagnated. Mexico's population grew only at an average annual rate of 1 percent. Its population increased from 6 million in 1820 to 7.6 million inhabitants in 1850. Brazil's population rose from between 4 and 5 million inhabitants at independence (1822) to 7.5 million by the early 1850s. Unlike the other new nations, Argentina experienced rapid population growth, as its half-million people in the 1820s increased to 1.8 million by 1869. Latin America experienced growth after 1850, as Mexico's population rose to 15 million and Brazil's to 22 million by 1910.

In contrast, during the first half of the nineteenth century the population of the United States rose from less than that of Mexico in 1800—just over 5 million—to 92 million in 1910. The United Kingdom grew from 11 million to 45 million during the same period. These differences in population growth accounted for a large portion of comparable difference in economic progress between Latin America and these industrial leaders. While Latin America failed to grow economically, the United States and the

TABLE 10.1

The Population of Latin America in the Nineteenth Century

Nation	1820	1850	1880
Argentina	500,000+	1,800,000 (1869)	
Bolivia		1,378,896 (1846)	
Brazil	4–5,000,000	7,500,000	
Chile	1,000,000 (1835)		2,100,000 (1875)
Colombia			
Ecuador	496,846 (1825)		1,271,761 (1889)
Mexico	6,000,000	7,600,000	
Paraguay			
Peru	2,488,000	2,001,203	2,651,840
Uruguay			
Venezuela	760,000	1,660,000 (1860)	2,080,000
Costa Rica	63,000	101,000	137,000 (1870)
El Salvador	248,000	366,000	493,000 (1870)
Guatemala	595,000	847,000	1,080,000 (1870)
Honduras	135,000	203,000	265,000 (1870)
Nicaragua	186,000	274,000	337,000 (1870)

United Kingdom's economies expanded exponentially. Latin America has never been able to make up for these 50 or so years of economic and demographic stagnation.

The colonial heritage of large, dominant cities continued in postindependence Latin America. Mexico City's population fluctuated between 150,000 and 200,000. Rio de Janeiro experienced growth from 100,000 inhabitants in the 1820s to 275,000 in the 1850s. Buenos Aires blossomed from 50,000 inhabitants in 1810 to 189,000 by 1869. As we will see later in this chapter, the expansion of the cities outpaced governments' ability to provide a healthy and prosperous environment for their residents.

THE LARGE ESTATES: HACIENDAS, ESTANCIAS, PLANTATIONS, AND FAZENDAS

Most Latin Americans earned their living on the land, planting, maintaining, and harvesting crops and tending to the livestock of their wealthier neighbors. Other Latin Americans toiled on lands owned either collectively by the residents of their home villages or individually by themselves and their families. Some worked as both employees and owners. Whichever the circumstances, the land represented more than just a living: Farming or ranching was a way of life. As we will see, life in the countryside in the nineteenth century was difficult. Sometimes, as in the case of slaves, conditions were oppressive and cruel. But even those worst off, including slaves, made lives for themselves often with humor, love, and grace.

A large number of Latin Americans resided on large estates (known as *haciendas, estancias,* or *fazendas* in Mexico, Argentina, and Brazil, respectively), where they worked for the landowner or leased land as tenants or sharecroppers. In rural areas, the owners of these large properties (known as *hacendados, estancieros,* and *fazendeiros*) controlled much of the land. Conditions on these large estates varied widely according to era, region, property size, and crops under cultivation.

At the top of hacienda society in Mexico was the owner, the hacendado, and his family. Beneath him were the supervisors and administrators, headed by the chief administrator or *mayordomo.* Usually males headed haciendas, but occasionally a widow operated a large property. Mayordomos in the Río de la Plata managed the larger estancias, directing employees, keeping records, and communicating with the owner about all estate-related matters. The mayordomo controlled his workers through subordinate foremen (*capataces*). On smaller ranches the foreman took the role of the mayordomo. The living conditions of the capataces were hardly better than those of the workers. The mayordomo, however, was well paid.

Work Life

Estate employees worked long, hard hours. On the Mexican haciendas, there were two types of employees: permanent and temporary laborers. Permanent labor included resident peons (unskilled laborers), tenants, and sharecroppers. A hacienda's temporary labor came from neighboring villages, whose residents supplemented their incomes from communally held land or family plots by working seasonally at planting and harvest. Commonly, the hacienda's sharecroppers and tenants earned extra money by working for their landlord.

While some hacendados farmed their own land with their own employees, the most common arrangement was for owners to combine farming their lands with sharecropper- or tenant-cultivated lands. Tenants paid their rent to the hacendado in the form of cash or a portion of the harvest. Though most tenants leased small plots, there were a few who leased entire haciendas. Sharecroppers paid the landowners with a preset part of the harvest, usually 50 percent. A possibly typical such arrangement in the central region of Mexico included resident peons earning wages and rations of corn to feed their families and receiving the use of small plots of land for cultivation. Tenants received a hut, firewood, seeds, and some pasturage, along with their plots, in return for half their crop. Occasionally, tenants worked for the hacendado and earned additional cash. For peons, the crucial part of the arrangement was the corn ration. Custom obligated hacendados in some areas to provide peons with the ration, regardless of the market price of corn. Because corn comprised 75 percent of a peon family's diet, this arrangement ensured the peon's most important staple, even in periods of drought and crop failure, and partially insulated him and his family from the effects of inflation, which resulted from shortages of staples arising from crop failures. Tenants and sharecroppers had no such security, so their well-being depended on the vagaries of the weather. A good-size plot with oxen and plenty of rain might turn a profit, but there were no guarantees. We know little about the situations of such day laborers other than that agricultural wages varied according to the available supply of labor.

Conditions on the haciendas varied according to region, depending on the availability of labor. A relatively dense population, concentrated in mestizo or Indian villages, as in central Mexico, meant a large pool of potential workers and, therefore, low wages and less-favorable terms for tenants and sharecroppers. Labor shortages, as in the far north and the far south, produced one of two outcomes: heavy competition for workers, which raised wages and added benefits, such as advances on wages; or intensified coercion to retain employees.

Debt peonage was the most notorious aspect of hacienda labor relations. In this system, peons went into debt to the hacienda in order to pay church taxes and fees; expenses for rites of passage such as marriage, baptism, and burial; or for ordinary purchases at the hacienda store. Peons then were obligated to work until they repaid the debt—but, of course, they often could not repay it. In some regions, multiple generations were tied to the hacienda, because children were expected to repay their parents' debts. Debt peonage in a few areas was nearly indistinguishable from slavery. On one of the great estates of northern Mexico, the owner dispatched armed retainers to hunt peons who tried to escape their obligations. Some historians have observed, however, that debt was not always to the disadvantage of the debtor, for in some areas debt served as a kind of cash advance or bonus, attracting peons to work on a particular hacienda. In these instances, it was understood by both debtor and creditor that the debt was not to be repaid. Debt, in these situations, became a device to attract and keep workers.

The Hacienda del Maguey, a grain and livestock estate in central Mexico, provides us with an example of relatively benign living and working conditions. The normal workday on this hacienda lasted from 6 A.M. to 6 P.M. There were breaks for breakfast and a traditional midday dinner followed by a resting period, or *siesta*, which lasted for 2 to 3 hours. The complete workday was 8 to 9 hours long, which, compared to the contemporary industrial workforce in the United States and Western Europe, was not arduous. The workload was heaviest at planting, weeding, and harvest times.

Peons on the Hacienda del Maguey, according to the calculations of historian Harry Cross, were relatively well treated. The average peon laboring in the fields probably needed 2150 calories a day. His family, two adults and two children, required 9000 calories. The ration of corn provided by his employer contained 75 percent of this caloric need. The rest of the diet consisted of *frijoles* (beans), chile peppers, lard, salt, and meat. The peon added to these staples wheat flour, rice, and sugar, which he bought at the hacienda store. (Usually, there were no other stores in the area. Sometimes employers allowed employees to purchase goods only at the hacienda stores.) The typical family also gathered herbs, spices, and cacti from the countryside at no cost. Alcoholic beverages, particularly *pulque*— the fermented juice of the maguey plant—were consumed in large quantities, providing vitamins. The combination of beans and corn produced most of the diet's protein.

LATIN AMERICAN LIVES

THE GAUCHO

THE HISTORY OF the *gauchos* (cowboys) of the Argentine plains, known as the Pampas, reflects the evolution of the region's politics and economy in the postindependence era. Gauchos were the symbol of regionalism, fierce local independence, the crucial role of the lower classes in politics, and the importance of the export economy. Originally a product of the vast growth of wild herds of horses and cattle on the Pampas during colonial times, gauchos were skilled horsemen who roamed far and wide, taking the livestock that they needed to survive. Viceroy Arredondo, in 1790, considered them "vagabonds" who "live by stealing cattle from the estancias and selling the hides . . . to the shopkeepers . . . ." Like other members of Latin America's working classes, cowboys in the Río de la Plata and Venezuela were important participants in the wars of independence and the uncertain politics and warfare of the early nineteenth century. During the wars, gauchos were among the rebels' best troops. After the wars, they comprised the local private armies of the numerous regional chiefs who ruled in the Río de la Plata. As the Argentine economy grew by exporting hides, tallow, and dried salted beef, gauchos worked on the expanding estancias. During the first half of the nineteenth century their services were in such demand, both as soldiers and as ranch hands, that they escaped worker discipline.

To many upper-class Argentines, however, the mixed-blood gauchos were a symbol of backwardness. Domingo F. Sarmiento, in his famous polemic (*Life in the Argentine Republic in the Days of the Tyrants*) against Juan Manuel de Rosas, the notorious gaucho leader who ruled Buenos Aires from 1829 to 1852, defined the gauchos as representatives of "barbarism." He saw them as impediments to Argentine development.

Dressed in little more other than a poncho, mounted on horseback, armed with rope and knife, the gaucho was a formidable sight. He subsisted on meat, a bit of tobacco, and strong yerba mate (a strong, tea-like beverage) and lived in simple huts roofed with straw and possessing neither doors nor windows: "The walls were sticks driven vertically into the ground, and the chinks were filled with clay . . . ." Furniture in a gaucho's hut consisted of perhaps "a barrel for carrying water, a horn out of which to drink it, a wooden spit for the roast, and a pot in which to heat the water for mate." There were no chairs or tables or beds, and cutlery consisted of only a knife, for gauchos ate only meat. To cook and keep warm, gauchos burned dung, bones, and fat. Their clothing, shelter, and food made the gaucho no different from other Latin Americans who struggled to make their living in the nineteenth century.

Compared to most Latin American workers, however, gauchos retained a relatively high degree of freedom, because Argentina's growing economy increased demand for their services. For example, gauchos attained the right to enjoy leisure time on the numerous fiesta days. Often, cowboys worked for a few months, asked for their pay, and moved on. Offering them higher wages only delayed the inevitable. There was always another job somewhere for a gaucho to fill.

Time was against the gauchos, and their glory days did not last long. The export economy demanded their subordination, and the undisciplined gauchos, who were enthusiastic brawlers, and loved to sing, gamble, and drink, were not acceptable employees in the modern economy. In addition, modern technology, in the form of barbed wire, and a glut of immigrant agricultural labor in Buenos Aires province also worked to end their independence. The history of the Argentine gaucho parallels that of many other lower-class Latin Americans, who defended their local prerogatives, customs, and traditions in an ever more difficult struggle against government centralization and economic modernization.

Questions for Discussion

How did the life of an Argentine gaucho compare with that of a Mexican worker on a hacienda? Why were gauchos able to exert their independence and, thus, control over their daily lives so successfully during the first half of the nineteenth century?

Gauchos comprised the lower-class political support for local bosses of nineteenth-century Argentina.

But not all haciendas treated their peons so well. A passerby noted the conditions for resident peons on the Sánchez Navarro estate in northern Mexico in 1846: "The poor peon lives in a miserable mud hovel or reed hut (sometimes built of cornstalks, thatched with grass). He is allowed a peck of corn a week for his subsistence, and a small monthly pay for his clothes . . . ." Peons generally earned 2 or 3 pesos a month and 1 or 2 pecks (a peck equals a quarter bushel or 8 quarts) of corn a week. The Sánchez Navarro family paid their highly valued shepherds and cowboys (*vaqueros*) a bit more, 5 pesos a month and 2 pecks of corn a week salary, but these modest wages hardly covered an average family's necessities.

The Hacienda de Bocas, located 35 miles north of San Luis Potosí, also in central Mexico, for which we have extensive records for the 1850s, illuminates another example of hacienda life. Bocas had between 350 and 400 permanent workers. The better-off minority of these had free title to land they used for a house, corral, and farming. The best-treated permanent workers also received a corn ration. A resident earned 6 pesos a month, slightly less than $1.50 a week, with a corn ration of 15 liters a week. Because this was not enough to feed his family—1 liter a day per adult was necessary for sustenance— he purchased another 7 or 8 liters a week, on account, for 0.125 pesos each, leaving him with roughly 50 centavos a week to cover all the family's other expenses. The worker received a plot of 3000 square meters for which he paid no rent. He bought seed for planting from the hacienda. Other purchases during the year included food, sandals (*huaraches*), leather pants, and a burial. His expenditures totaled just over 72 pesos for the year, approximately the same amount as his annual salary. The circumstances for temporary workers on the Hacienda de Bocas were not quite as favorable as those for permanent workers. Despite earning 10 pesos a month (if they labored 30 days), versus permanent workers' 6 pesos, temporary employees were not guaranteed subsistence rations. Regardless of employee status, however, few of the 794 tenants and 200 sharecroppers at Bocas in 1852 made ends meet without supplementing their incomes with temporary work for the hacienda.

Work was equally hard in the Río de la Plata, where most of the employees on the estancias were wage labor called in for cattle branding and horse breaking. There were a few permanent workers who tended cattle or sheep and rode the perimeter looking for strays. Each of these workers maintained a hut and a corral in his area. Routine work consisted of tending to the herds and rounding them up every morning. Shepherds' chores were to wash and shear, brand, and slaughter, as well as to tend the herd. Cowboys earned wages, while shepherds shared in the profits. Some owners gave their shepherds one-third to one-half the increase in their flocks per year. Other sheepherders earned up to one-half of the sale of wool, grease, and sheepskins. Cowhands, in addition to their flat wage, received rations of salt, tobacco, *yerba mate* (a very strong tea-like beverage), and beef, and perhaps a small garden plot.

The estancias employed Europeans, mixed bloods, and both free and enslaved blacks. Part-time workers came from the interior of Argentina and Paraguay. Native-born mestizos and mulattos, migrants from the interior, tended cattle, while immigrants raised sheep, farmed, and traded. Labor for the cattle roundup and sheep shearing came from nearby rural communities. When labor was scarce, temporary workers earned more. Estancieros had to pay high wages to skilled workers, such as sheep shearers, who could demand as much as 40 to 50 pesos a day plus food. A native-born laborer, with his own string of horses, could hire himself out at 20 to 25 pesos a day in cattle-branding season. Some estancieros offered advances and credit at the ranch store to attract laborers. These workers, however, were often paid irregularly or in scrip to be used at assigned stores. Agricultural wages remained relatively high until the late 1880s, when immigration and improved stock-raising methods ended the labor shortage.

Domestic Life

The differences between the affluent and the poor were particularly evident in the conduct of their everyday lives. Daily routines for upper-class women and men focused on work and meals. Wealthy women on the hacienda began their day around nine and spent much of the morning doing needlework together in the drawing room in what was called "virtuous silence." After the midday meal, each female family member carried out chores before retiring for a nap (siesta). During the mid-afternoon, the women gathered again to continue their needlework. Males and females joined at eight in the evening to say prayers and eat the evening meal. Afterward, the women put in another hour of needlework, while one of the men read aloud to the family.

Women administered the domestic sphere and may have acted as heads of family when their husbands were away. Girls stayed at home while boys went to school. Young women learned needlework and enough reading skills to enable them to read the Bible and carry out religious observances. A curious relationship existed between wealthy families and their household servants, who simultaneously were part of and separate from the family. A hacienda's rich and poor children grew up together, even shared confidences, but real friendship was never possible, because the social barriers between classes were too great.

Slice of Life   URBAN SLAVES

MANY SLAVES WORKED in the plantation fields, but a few toiled in their master's home, and others had skilled occupations processing sugar and coffee. A surprising number of slaves worked in the cities, primarily as domestic servants, but also as artisans and in other jobs.

Slaves comprised 11 percent of the Brazilian industrial workforce in 1872. Approximately 13,000 slaves worked in textile factories. Slaves also made up 15 percent of construction workers, and slave women represented 8 percent of all seamstresses. Many of these slaves lived in the cities, numbering some 118,000 in total, or roughly 15 percent of the population.

Urban slaves usually found themselves in one of three working situations (or some combination thereof): the traditional relationship with a master; a largely traditional relationship with a master but which included being rented out to a third party; or self-employment (the latter arranged housing for themselves). Self-employed slaves generated considerable income and were a lucrative enterprise for their masters. Such slaves worked as bakers, barbers, carpenters, masons, porters, and prostitutes. It is likely that slaves in the cities had more control over their everyday lives than their counterparts on the plantations. Nonetheless, urban slaves were no less subject to abuse or the other hazards of survival. Thomas Ewbank, a traveler from the United States, observed at mid-century: "Slaves are the beasts of draught as well as of burden. The loads they drag . . . are enough to kill both mules and horses."

In Rio de Janeiro, the constant demand for domestic servants arose from the need for services later supplied by urban utilities and public works. As late as 1860, homes in the city had neither piped water nor a sewerage system. Residents also had no refrigeration, and perishable food could not be stored, because it spoiled easily in the tropical climate. Servants carried water, shopped, and did laundry. Most indoor chores were centered around the kitchen, where slaves were skilled cooks. Other household slaves saw to the considerable volume of cleaning required in the dusty, dirty city in houses chockful of furniture and other objects. Still other servants emptied chamber pots and wet-nursed babies. Trusted servants were so valued by wealthy families that parents sometimes passed such workers down to their children to ensure that the younger generation had a reliable staff when it established households of its own.

While a significant minority of slaves worked independently in the cities or held relatively privileged positions in their owners' households, they, nonetheless, remained in bondage. Their master still controlled their fate.

Questions for Discussion

How did the lives of urban slaves compare with those on the plantations? How and to what extent were slaves able to shape their own living and working conditions (and thus exert some control over their daily lives)?

Plantations and Slavery

Brazilian slaves lived perhaps the hardest lives of all the Latin American poor. About two-thirds of Brazilian slaves worked in agriculture. And of these, the largest group, one-third, worked on coffee plantations in the environs of Rio de Janeiro or São Paulo. Others toiled on sugar plantations in the northeast. On plantations, particularly in the south, masters practiced swift, brutal discipline. They regarded slaves as "by nature the enemy of all regular work." Planters lived in constant fear that their slaves would rebel.

At the beginning of the nineteenth century, Brazil had 1 million slaves and during the next 50 years imported another million. Perhaps surprisingly, slaves' life expectancy was not much different from that of the rest of the population: 23 to 27 years. The crucial difference, however, was the odds of a child born into slavery surviving infancy. One-third of all male slave babies died before the age of 1, and a little less than one-half died before the age of 5. If a male slave reached the age of 1, he was likely to live until he was 33.5. If the slave child survived until age 5, then he could expect to live more than 43 years. Twenty-seven percent of female slave children died before reaching the age of 1, and 43 percent died before age 5. If the female lasted until age 1, she could expect to live until 25.5, and if she endured to age 5, she would likely reach 39 years.

Slaves born in Africa had difficulty in adapting to the new climatic and biological environments of Brazil, and, as a result, their mortality rate was high. In the northeast, the climate was very humid and hot, but sudden drops in temperature were common.

Many Africans, unaccustomed to such swings in temperature, suffered chills, which, in turn, often resulted in pulmonary illness. Diseases such as tuberculosis, scurvy, malaria, dysentery, and typhus were endemic. Slaves lived in unhygienic conditions and medical care was crude or unavailable. The number of slave deaths in Brazil always exceeded that of births, and only the continual importation of newly enslaved people from Africa permitted the slave population to increase.

The flow of slaves to Brazil ended in 1850, a decision made as a result of pressure from the British. This brought about a massive transfer of slaves from the cities and towns to the countryside and from regions where markets for export crops were in decline to those areas where exports flourished. Regardless of a slave's age, the dynamics underlying every slave's relationship with his or her fazendeiro were coercion and violence. Owners required slaves to be loyal, obedient, and humble. In return, slaves might expect to be made part of the patron's family, with all the accompanying benefits and protections: Slaves who attained "family" status could become skilled artisans and attain positions as overseers.

Most slaves worked in the fields in regimented gangs closely supervised by overseers. Corporal punishment—being whipped or placed in stocks, for example—was common. The workday lasted 16 to 17 hours. Overnight work was rare, except when sugar had to be milled and coffee dried. Surprisingly, slaves did get breaks during the day. And while everyday work was always hard, it may have been truly unbearable only for short periods during harvest.

Many slaves had occupations other than being field hands. Men were given the skilled positions repairing equipment, constructing buildings, and sewing clothing. Planters even rented the services of slave artisans to other landowners. As a result, fewer male slaves and more women planted, weeded, and harvested. Slaves were also domestic servants. Slaves who worked in the masters' houses or as artisans experienced better living conditions than those in the fields.

In the nineteenth century most slaves worked in the São Paulo coffee region. The typical plantation had 70 to 100 slaves, though the largest coffee fazendas contained as many as 400. The average adult slave took care of well over 3000 coffee trees and produced approximately 1000 kilograms of coffee.

Slaves' daily routine began before dawn with breakfast, which consisted of coffee, molasses, and boiled corn. They then said prayers and divided into work teams, which were led by supervisors who were themselves slaves. At 10 A.M., slaves ate a meal of corn porridge, black beans, and pieces of lard covered with a thick layer of manioc flour. Sometimes they also ate highly seasoned sweet potatoes, cabbage, or turnips. At 1 P.M., there was another break for coffee and a corn muffin. Dinner was eaten at 4 P.M. Work then went on, often until well after dark, as late as 10 or 11 P.M. Finally, before retiring, slaves received a ration of corn, a piece of dried meat, and some manioc meal.

Slaves usually lived in a single unpleasant building. Some were given the use of a plot of land to raise coffee or vegetables and were even allowed to sell these crops and keep the proceeds. Coffee planters did not give slaves Sundays off because they feared that

How Historians Understand   THE CONSTRUCTION OF RACISM

The upper classes' fear of the lower classes that so impeded political developments in Latin America during the nineteenth century was founded in racism. Africans and Indians were people of color and, as such, were widely disdained, if not hated, by the white descendents of European colonials. Nineteenth-century historians, many of whom were prominent intellectuals and politicians, were the generators and pillars of this racism.

By mid-century, pervasive racism had overwhelmed Argentina. In their desire to modernize, Argentines firmly believed that European immigration was the only "civilizing" influence on their nation. Juan Alberdi, one of Argentina's leading intellectuals and author of the Constitution of 1853, disdained nonwhites, writing that to populate the Pampas with Chinese, Asian Indians, and Africans was "to brutalize" the region's culture. Domingo Sarmiento, another notable Argentine intellectual and later president of the nation from 1868 to 1874, also advocated the benefits of European immigration, because he believed that Africans and people of mixed blood were inferior. These men and others thought that Argentina in the 1850s was a mestizo country and that it would not progress unless it was Europeanized. Part of the consequent "whitening" campaign was having Argentine historians and government bureaucrats make Afro-Argentines disappear from the country's history and be excluded from its census. Similarly, Chileans saw to it that Africans disappeared from their history. They, too, firmly believed that development would come only with the Europeanization of local culture.

In Peru, intellectuals retained their hostility to Afro-Peruvians long after that country's abolition of slavery in 1861; one even insisted that "the Negro [is] a robber from the moment he is born . . . ." Another thinker decried that "in South America, civilization depends on the . . . triumph of the white man over the mulatto, the Negro, and the Indian."

The failure of Latin American governments to abolish African slavery at independence was not only an indication of the powerful political influence of planters, but also of the underlying fear and contempt the white upper classes felt for Africans.

Abolition of Slavery

Country	Year	Country	Year
Argentina	1861	El Salvador	1825
Bolivia	1831	Honduras	1825
Brazil	1888	Mexico	1829
Chile	1823	Nicaragua	1825
Colombia	1850	Paraguay	1870
Costa Rica	1825	Peru	1854
Cuba	1886	Uruguay	1846
Ecuador	1852	Venezuela	1854

Free and enslaved Africans were not the only victims of racism. In Argentina, Mexico, and Chile, governments conducted campaigns of extermination against nomadic indigenous peoples, who white officials believed also stood in the way of progress. Indians were perceived as barbarians and obstacles to the betterment of society by Latin Americans of European descent. These indigenous peoples fought back fiercely. In the north of Mexico, for example, the Apaches, Yaquis, Comanches, Mayos, and Tarahumara resisted incursions until the end of the century. In Yucatán the Maya Indians came close to eliminating whites from their peninsula in a bloody rebellion that began in 1847. (Historians did not confirm stories of this resistance until the late twentieth century, however.) Mexican historians of the era, such as Lucas Alamán and Carlos María Bustamante, had a predictably low regard for the nation's Indian peoples, even though by virtue of Mexico's first Constitution (1824) all Mexicans were equal before the law. Alamán once said that "it would be dangerous to enable the Indians to read the papers."

How could these historians legitimate such inaccurate and destructive beliefs? Historians, like everyone, are products of their times: Nineteenth-century historians such as Alamán, mostly from upper-class origins, shared the same prejudices and fears of the others of their status.

Questions for Discussion

Why do you think that historians in nineteenth-century Latin America, like Domingo Sarmiento and Lucas Alamán, were so biased against people of color? Why do you agree or disagree with the assertion that race underlay all of the region's politics during the century after independence?

Mistreating of a slave in Brazil in 1839.

religious or social gatherings of the entire slave population would lead to trouble. Instead, to prevent the possibility of any kind of unified revolt, rotating groups of slaves were given different afternoons off during the week.

Within the larger plantations, African slaves established their own communities, resembling small villages. There they established families and forged a new culture adapting African ways with those of the Americas. Almost all native-born slaves married. And though they were not usually married by the church, the fazendas commonly recognized the marriages. Maintaining a family was difficult, however, for there was always the possibility that one or more family members would be sold, thus permanently separating the family. And the reality of high mortality rates among slaves was a perpetual threat to family stability. On the plantations, enslaved women were subordinate in marriage to their husbands (like their free counterparts). As with every aspect of slaves' existence, their family and social lives were both separate from and intimately attached to the world of their masters.

Like marriage and family, religion played an important part in plantation slave communities. Slaves practiced godparenthood (*compadrazgo*), in which close friends of the parents of a child became godparents, which meant that they were obligated to care for the child if its parents died. Slaves also synthesized their African religions with Catholicism, producing a folk Catholicism and religious cults, such as *candomblé, voudoun,* and *santería.* In these hybrid spiritual practices, African deities often took on the guise of Catholic saints.

Ultimately, however, slaves confronted and resisted their conditions: They refused to surrender either their cultural heritage or their dignity. Slaves resisted passively, by slowing the work pace, working shoddily, or refusing to do work that did not fit their described assignment (i.e., work that was not in their "job descriptions"). Cooks would not do housework, for example. Occasionally, slaves struck back violently at their masters. More commonly, slaves tried to gain their freedom by running away. Those who fled sometimes found haven in isolated communities, known as *quilombos.* Whatever the approach—harsh or paternalistic—taken by the planters, few were entirely successful in controlling their slaves.

VILLAGES AND SMALL HOLDERS

The majority of the rural population in Mexico and Peru consisted of Indians, who continued to live in relatively autonomous villages, as they had during colonial times. The small, individual plot of land used for family subsistence farming was the basis of rural life. Villages had simultaneously symbiotic and conflicting relationships with haciendas: Villagers relied on the estates for work to supplement earnings garnered from farming their own lands. Haciendas, in turn, depended on village residents for temporary labor and tenants. Nonetheless, haciendas and pueblos frequently clashed over land and water rights. The relationship was, perhaps, most equal in the years from

1821 to the mid-1880s, a period when war and uncertain political conditions badly weakened the haciendas economically. Villages traded their political support for increased local autonomy and protection of their lands.

It is important not to idealize rural life, particularly in the villages. In Mexico, the *pueblos* (villages) had their own forms of social stratification, with local bosses (*caciques*), municipal officeholders, and lay leaders of religious organizations comprising the upper level. Small traders, muleteers, and some of the larger tenants (in terms of the amount of land they rented) at times entered the top group. At the bottom were poorer residents who worked permanently or temporarily as hacienda peons and tenants.

Generally, village leadership came from elder males, who nominated people for local offices, made decisions in times of crisis, and oversaw all dealings by local officeholders with the wider society. Elders attained their elevated status through hard work on the community's behalf or, perhaps, through economic achievement. As the century wore on, the ability of the elders to act justly and to reach community consensus lessened, as state and national governments intruded on their autonomy.

Politically, residents of all villages concerned themselves primarily with protecting their individual and collective landholdings, minimizing taxes (both of which required local autonomy), as well as maintaining the right to govern their everyday affairs without interference from state or national governments. Taxes oppressed country people, and throughout the nineteenth century taxes were a never-ending source of friction between pueblo residents and the various levels of government. Country people also bitterly opposed coerced military service. It was not uncommon for the armies of various factions to raid villages in order to drag off their young men, the loss of whom badly disrupted the local economy and society.

A considerable measure of competition, petty bickering, and serious disputes often existed among villagers. In many places, such as Oaxaca in southeastern Mexico, intervillage conflict was endemic, as rival pueblos fought perpetually over land and water.

For most rural dwellers in Mexico and elsewhere, life revolved around their land and their families. Country people lived in two worlds: the first was the traditional subsistence economy, which retained ancient practices, and the second was the modern money and wage economy, the incursion of which country people carefully limited. Indian people, such as the Maya of the Yucatán peninsula of Mexico, fiercely resisted the discipline and values of the plantation and the industrial workplace. North American John Lloyd Stephens, who traveled extensively in the peninsula in the 1840s, reported that "The Indians worked as if they had a lifetime for the job." Working slowly, though, was only one strategy for resisting the demands of overbearing employers. Unlike Brazil's slaves, however, passive resistance was not the only tactic available to rural folk: Attempts to alter existing custom or wages were met by strikes or mass migrations.

In many parts of rural Latin America, the family was an economic unit, both on small plots and on the large estates. Families worked together in the fields, especially during planting and harvest. The men worked their 8- to 9-hour days at the hacienda or, perhaps, even longer on their own land or in helping neighbors at planting and harvest times.

Families' small fields were watered only by erratic rainfall. If the rains did not come, crops failed, and people either starved or went deeper into debt to the hacendados in order to purchase their food. Often, the plots were cultivated by the slash-and-burn method, whereby a field was cleared of forest or scrub, the debris burned to create ash fertilizer, and the land tilled with a wooden digging stick. Crops quickly exhausted such lands' nutrients after only 2 or 3 years, whereupon the farmer abandoned it. Usually, it took 7 years for the land to restore itself for cultivation.

In Argentina, small, family landowners comprised the most common productive unit on the vast plains of the Río de la Plata. Most farmers lived in comparative modesty on land they worked with family members and a few hired hands. In one sector of Buenos Aires province, almost 70 percent of the landholdings were smaller than 5000 hectares in 1890. The typical rural residential unit was a farm or small ranch with six to eight persons: a man, his wife, their children, a peon, an orphan, and perhaps a slave or *liberto* (a slave born after 1813 who was to remain a slave until age 21). In the Brazilian northeast, small farmers eked out a living raising the region's staple crop, cassava. To plant cassava, farmers cleared the land with an iron axe and set fire to the brush, then the farmers' slaves used hoes to heap the earth into small mounds. These prevented the cassava roots from becoming waterlogged and rotting during the winter rainy season. Two or three pieces of stalk cut from growing plants went into each little mound. Corn or beans were planted in the rows between the mounds. In about 2 weeks, the cuttings took root and poked through the soil. For several months, slaves guarded the crops from weeds and other natural enemies, such as ants, caterpillars, and live-stock. After 9 to 18 months, the central stalks sprouted small branches. Below ground, each plant put down five to ten bulbous roots, which the farmer harvested.

The slaves then prepared the cassava for processing into coarse flour (*farinha*). Most important was to eliminate poisonous prussic acid from the roots, which involved scraping, washing, grating, pressing, sifting, and toasting. Workers first scraped the roots with blunt knives and washed them. Then they grated or shredded the roots with a grating wheel. The pulp fell through the wheel and dried overnight to remove the prussic acid. The fine white sediment that collected at the bottom of the trough, when dried, washed, and sifted, became tapioca. The grated pulp of the cassava root was sifted into a coarse grain with the texture of moist sand. Slaves placed the sifted cassava on a large griddle made of glazed clay or copper and then lightly toasted it over an open hearth, stirring often to prevent burning. Toasting made it taste better and removed the last of the prussic acid. Cassava was a crop that could be planted or harvested at any time. Harvesting, moreover, could be delayed for a year before the roots would spoil.

Regardless of where they lived, nonslave women's workdays and responsibilities went far beyond those of men. Women rose well before dawn to prepare the family's food. The backbreaking work of making tortillas took hours, and because men had to take both breakfast and lunch with them to the fields, women had to prepare enough food for both meals early in the day. Women drew the water, gathered wood for the fire, cared for the children, prepared three meals for their households, did the wash, spun thread and wove cloth, and made clothing. They also made pottery and then hauled it to the Sunday market. When men were hired on to a hacienda, it was common for the women in their families to function either as field hands or as domestics in the hacienda house—work for which they received no pay. All was not drudgery, however: The weekly market day provided a welcome respite from the dull daily routine, giving the women vendors the opportunity to meet, gossip, and laugh with friends. Despite the enormous amount of work done by pueblo women, employment opportunities for women in rural areas were very limited. Consequently, a large number of young women migrated to the cities, where, for the most part, they entered domestic service.

Religion

Religion occupied a central place in rural Latin American life, and permeated popular culture. The influence of Catholicism was everywhere. Almost every small town had at least one chapel, and many had several churches. Perhaps the most important religious institutions in the countryside were the *cofradías,* the village organizations that maintained the church and funded religious celebrations. Much of a village's social life revolved around these celebrations and rites of passage. Priests often lived only in the larger villages or towns, and so traveled periodically through the villages in their districts to perform masses (Catholic religious services) and sacraments (baptism, marriage, and burial). Though clergy were among the most important figures in Latin American society, most country people rarely encountered a priest. As a result, the folk Catholicism practiced in the countryside retained many indigenous customs from pre-Christian times. The characteristics of Christian saints were often indistinguishable from those of gods worshipped by pre-Columbian peoples. Religion was a daily presence in the lives of all villages, rich and poor. The literate wealthy, for example, read primarily devotional literature, and their houses were decorated with religious artwork. The huts of poor families were blessed by corner altar bearing candles, flowers, and the likenesses of saints.

URBAN LIFE AND SOCIETAL TRANSFORMATION

During the nineteenth century, most of Latin America may have been rural, but Latin American cities rivaled any in the world in size. These cosmopolitan centers were at once splendiferous and horrifying. Often situated in physically beautiful settings with impressive colonial architecture, they also were unsanitary and dangerous, filled to overflowing with poverty-stricken people. The cities were crucibles of change, for it was in the urban areas that modernization most directly confronted tradition—especially in the realm of gender roles and relations. It was in the cities that the transformation of the role of women was most dramatic.

The Cities

Mexico City was the largest city in the Western Hemisphere and the fifth largest city in the Western world during the early nineteenth century: Its population was 168,846 by 1811. Half its population was of Spanish descent, with the rest comprised of Indians, mixed bloods, and African Mexicans. During the next three decades, through the 1850s, the city's population fluctuated between 160,000 and 205,000 because of periodic epidemics, and migration from the countryside, rather than natural increase, accounted for the net population growth. At the beginning of the nineteenth century, Rio de Janeiro had between 50,000 and 60,000 residents. But its population rose to 423,000 in 1890. The city's residents included immigrants from Portugal, Spain, and Italy, free blacks and mulattos, and white Brazilians from the hinterlands. Buenos Aires was the fastest-growing large city in Latin America during the second half of the century, becoming the largest city in the region by 1890. By 1914, in all the Americas, only New York exceeded it in number of inhabitants. Half of Buenos Aires' population was foreign-born.

As mentioned previously, the physical spaces of the cities were impressive, but their beautiful buildings and picturesque settings hid the dismaying conditions of most of their inhabitants. Mexico City was laid out in a grid with an enormous central plaza, the Zócalo. The great cathedral stood at the north end, with the palace of government on the east, and the offices of the municipality on the south. Five causeways furnished access to the city over the lake beds that surrounded it. A legacy from Aztec times, the city was divided into distinct sections, known as barrios. The outer margins of the city were left to

View of Mexico City from northwest, taken from the terrace of the Mining School, ca. 1870.

the poor, while the affluent lived in the central area. Rio de Janeiro was located in a setting of overwhelming physical beauty but was just as shabby and disease ridden as Mexico City. With narrow, stinking streets and crowded tenements, it was jam-packed with poor people. In contrast, Buenos Aires at mid-century was little more than a large village, possessing none of Rio de Janeiro's topographical beauty or Mexico City's impressive architecture. One Scottish traveler remarked that there was a "filthy, dilapidated look" to the houses. Pastureland, adorned with grazing livestock, lay 20 blocks from the central plaza.

All these cities were unsanitary and unhealthy. The Spaniards had built Mexico City on the ruins of the great Aztec capital Tenochtitlan and surrounding dry lake beds. During rainy season, these beds flooded, frequently transforming the outlying districts into lakes, dumping mud, garbage, and human feces into the houses, and leaving the central plaza knee-deep in stagnant water. Buenos Aires also had poor drainage, making even paved streets difficult to pass when rains were heavy. Much of Rio de Janeiro was built on filled-in swampland, so its inhabitants suffered similar problems.

Mexico City never had enough water for any purpose or sufficient waste disposal (nor does it today). Walking its thoroughfares was dangerous to one's health. The air smelled horribly from the sewage and piles of garbage. The city dumped trash into Lake Texcoco, which, unfortunately, was one of the primary sources of municipal drinking water. These unsanitary conditions had an enormous cost. Diseases such as smallpox, scarlet fever, measles, typhoid, and cholera were endemic. In 1840, smallpox killed more than 2000 children, while cholera killed almost 6000 in 1833 and 9000 in 1850. Cholera killed 15,000 in Buenos Aires in 1870. These diseases and others, such as diarrhea and dysentery, were closely associated with the wretched living conditions. Rio de Janeiro also was chronically short of water. In the 1860s, the city built a new system of reservoirs to hold water from mountain streams. This did not solve the problem, however.

Governments, whose minimal resources were used up to finance their armies, were simply unable to provide the public works necessary to make the cities healthy and safe.

Life in the cities in early nineteenth-century Latin America differed in many respects from that in the countryside, but many of the societal dynamics were much the same in urban settings as in rural ones. The social structure was just as rigidly stratified in the cities as in the country, the work was equally hard and as badly paid, and the gap between rich and poor was comparably wide. And, the vast migration of the populace from the countryside to the city made these conditions worse, especially during the last half of the century, when the migration intensified. But this migration also made possible the transformation of certain aspects of Latin American society, particularly that of women's roles.

Society in Mexico City was divided into very small upper and middle classes separated by vast differences in wealth and status from the majority of people, who were tremendously poor. The upper classes were comprised of high civil government and ecclesiastical officials, merchants, and wealthy mine owners and landowners. The next layer of the strata, upper middle class, was inhabited by professionals, such as doctors, lawyers, prosperous merchants, civil servants, industrialists, and other business people.

This group was closely associated in circumstance and outlook with the uppermost class. The "true" middle sectors consisted of small shopkeepers, tradesmen, artisans, and the better-off skilled workers. At the bottom lived 80 percent of the city's population: the unskilled workers, peddlers, artisans of low-prestige trades, and others who lived at the margins of society, such as prostitutes and beggars (*léperos*). These urban dwellers tried desperately to live on wages barely sufficient for subsistence. There was never enough steady employment; only 30 percent of those employed had full-time jobs. Only 1.4 percent of city residents owned property.

A large number of tiny businesses supplied consumer goods; many of these merchants conducted their commerce on dirty blankets in the filthy main market. The most common occupations, much like on the haciendas and in the pueblos, were domestic service, manual labor, and artisanship. Shoemakers, carpenters, and tailors were the most common types of skilled workers, while bricklayers, domestics, and street peddlers made up the majority of unskilled laborers. The average daily salary was .5 to 1.0 peso per day for skilled workers and .25 to .50 for unskilled, while the minimum cost of subsistence was .75 to 1.0 peso per day. (Until late in the century, the peso was equal in value to the U.S. dollar.) The region's stagnant economy and a labor surplus ensured that wages did not rise much, if at all, through the 1830s.

Transformations

The nineteenth-century migration from rural to urban life transformed the situation of women. These brave, determined women, many of whom were single and aged 15 to 29, left their rural birthplaces in search of a better life. They often came to urban areas without a father or a husband and suddenly found themselves having to lead self-reliant lives of unprecedented, even undreamed of, independence. Now, they had to function in public spaces (such as factories and markets), make their own living, and even act as head of their own household.

Women made up between 57 and 59 percent of the inhabitants of Mexico City and the majority of the migrants from the countryside throughout the first half of the nineteenth century. As with the men, almost all were castas or Indians who came from the densely populated regions around the capital.

Work

A quarter of all women in Mexico City worked, accounting for one-third of the total work force in the capital. More than a third of casta women and almost half of Indian women worked. Sixty percent of women worked as domestic servants; 20 percent sold food from their homes, on the street, or in the markets. Other occupations ran the gamut from midwife to peddler to waitress. Women fared no better than men regarding the conditions and remuneration of employment. Work was hard to come by and wages were paltry. Even those who found employment were underemployed. Worse still, women were limited to the worst-paying occupations. The jobs most easily obtained, in domestic service, were regarded as humiliating. Some servants were well treated, but all owed their employers "submission, obedience, and respect." They were on call 24 hours a day and were often paid no more than their room and board. Because there were so many young women available for domestic service, the labor market precluded any improvement in these conditions. Factories paid no better. And, although work there was considered more honorable than domestic service, conditions in the textile and tobacco industries, large employers of women, deteriorated considerably over the course of the 1820s and 1830s. Women were not allowed into the clergy, the military, or government bureaucracy—which were, of course, the main paths to upward mobility in Mexico.

In Rio de Janeiro in 1870, 63 percent of free women and 88 percent of slave women were gainfully employed. Only a very few, however, were professionals, working as midwives, nuns, teachers, or artisans. Women were prohibited from holding jobs in the government bureaucracy and in law and medicine. Women found work in commerce only as street vendors or market sellers because employers preferred to hire men as clerks and cashiers. More often women found jobs in the textile and shoe industries. By far and away the most common occupation for women in Rio de Janeiro was, as in Mexico City, domestic service. More than 60 percent of free working women and almost 90 percent of urban slave women were servants.

Marriage and Children

As previously noted, urban women often were separated from their families and became necessarily independent, though desperately poor. Not surprisingly, then, many women did not conform to the traditions of their male-dominated society. In Mexico City, slightly less than half were married. Eighty percent of females married at some point, either in formal or informal unions, but most spent only a small portion of their lives married. If they migrated from the countryside, they delayed marrying. Because of the higher mortality rate among men, it was likely that they would be widowed. One-third of adult women were single or widowed at the time of the censuses (1811 and 1848). Seventy percent of married women between 45 and 54 had outlived their husbands. Rich or poor, women spent much of their lives on their own.

An average woman in the Mexican capital bore five children. With infant mortality (death before age 3) estimated at 27 percent, it was likely that she would outlive at least one of them. Although two-thirds of adult women bore children, less than half of these women had children at home.

For much of their lives, therefore, a substantial proportion of Mexico City's women headed their own households as widows. Widowhood afforded wealthy women a degree of independence. This, of course, should not be exaggerated, for in many wealthy families, an adult son or son-in-law controlled the finances and negotiated with the outside world for the woman. Half of white women headed their own households in 1811, while only a third of casta or Indian women did so. Wealthy widows benefited from inheritance laws, which forced the division of an estate among spouse and children. The wife would always have at least some control over the estate. Because affluent males commonly married late, the number of offspring was often limited, thus keeping the widow's share of the estate larger. These kinds of calculations, of course, were of no consequence to the poor. Poor women barely subsisted. They had few alternatives other than to turn to men for support. Even then survival was uncertain. Children were such women's only old-age insurance; it was hoped that children would care for and support their parents in their old age.

Marriage and motherhood did not end a woman's work outside the home. Poor women worked out of necessity, because families could not subsist on men's incomes without the addition of women's earnings. So, poor women, married or not, worked. Marriage may, however, have changed a woman's occupation. Domestic service, for instance, was not possible for a married woman because it required that she live apart from her husband, in the residence of her employer. Self-employment, on the other hand, allowed women to care for their children while generating income. They could prepare food for sale, sew, operate small retail establishments, or peddle various wares. The result was that women dominated the markets.

Marriage, an entirely patriarchal institution, was an unequal relationship for women. A wife was expected to submit to her husband and to "obey him in everything reasonable." Domestic violence was common. Sexuality was another arena defined by double standards: It was perfectly acceptable for men to engage in extramarital relations, but totally unacceptable for women to do so.

FOOD, CLOTHING, SHELTER, AND ENTERTAINMENT

For most Latin Americans the fabric of everyday life—the food they ate, the housing that sheltered them, and the clothes that covered them—remained much the same throughout the tumultuous decades of the nineteenth century. Nowhere were disparities between social classes as clear as in these three basic aspects of daily existence.

Food

The staples of the Brazilian diet were black beans, dried meat, and manioc flour, occasionally augmented by game, fruit, molasses, and fish. The average Mexican's diet consisted of maize, beans, squash, and *chiles,* with small amounts of eggs, pork, meat, and cheese, with the corn tortilla as an essential staple. Women shucked corn and soaked the kernels in water with small bits of limestone, which loosened the sheath of the corn, imbued it with calcium, and increased its amino acid content. The latter created proteins from the mix of corn and beans, crucial in a diet that lacked meat. Next, the women beat the corn in the grinding bowl for hours. Finally, small pieces of the resulting dough were worked between the hands—tossed, patted, and flattened—until they were no thicker than a knife blade, after which they were thrown on a steaming-hot griddle (*comal*). The combination of maize tortillas and beans (tucked inside the folded tortilla) was not only delicious, but also provided almost all of the eater's required daily protein. (The more prosperous could afford to obtain more of their protein from meat, mostly pork.) Squash, which is 90 percent water, supplied badly needed liquid in an arid land and filler (fiber) to make meals more satisfying. Chiles were added to the beans as the source of crucial vitamins A, B, and C. The capsaicins in chiles, the chemical elements that make chiles "hot," killed bacteria that caused intestinal disorders. Water or pulque was drunk with the meal, and lump sugar provided a sweet. The urban poor took few meals at home for there was no place in their crowded rooms for cooking appliances. Instead, they purchased inexpensive food from vendors and ate it on the street.

The diet of the middle class, while also modest, was more varied and nutritious. In a respectable house in Rio de Janeiro, residents woke to a cup of strong coffee. Later in the morning they ate bread and fruit. The afternoon meal consisted of hot soup, then a main course of fish, black beans sprinkled with manioc flour, rice, and perhaps vegetables and, on occasion, well-cooked meat or stewed or roasted chicken. Two favorite dishes that took hours of preparation were *feijoada*, which required black beans to be soaked overnight and cooked for a long time with fatty pork, and cod (*bacala*), which was soaked for 20 hours and then baked. Desserts were sweets, such as fruit glazed with a paste made from guavas and sugar, or candy made from egg yolks, egg whites, and sugar, and was accompanied by highly sweetened strong coffee.

In Mexico City, breakfast started with a hot drink—chocolate for the adults or corn gruel (*atole*) for the children—and then toast, biscuits, or pastries with coffee and milk. At 11 A.M., chocolate or atole was drunk again, but this time flavored with anisette. The large meal, served in mid-afternoon, consisted of bread, soup, a roast, eggs in chile, vegetables, and beans flavored with pickled onion, cheese, and sauce. Dessert was honey with grated orange on a toasted tortilla. A light dinner in the evening consisted of a spicy sauce (*mole*), stewed meat, and a lettuce salad. A small staff served the meals.

For wealthy Mexicans, food was plentiful, varied, and rich, and meals were leisurely. At 8 A.M., the well-to-do partook of a small cup of chocolate with sweets. Two hours later, they ate a hearty breakfast of roasted or stewed meat, eggs, and beans (boiled soft and then fried with fat and onions). Dinner was served at 3 P.M. It began with a cup of clear broth, which was followed by highly seasoned rice or some other starch; a meat course consisting of beef, mutton, pork, fowl, or sausages; various vegetables and fruits; and dessert. After such repast a siesta was in order. At 6 P.M., families enjoyed a warm drink of chocolate during the cooler months or a cold, sweet beverage in summer. Cigars and conversation or a walk followed. Wealthy families ate "light" supper at 10 P.M. consisting of roasted meat, salad, beans, and sweets. Domestics served all meals on elegant china and silverware with tablecloths and napkins.

Clothing

Differences in dress between the affluent and poor were as striking as the differences in their diets. Rich urban women conformed to the latest fashions from France, often adding traditional Spanish garb, such as the *mantilla* (a shawl, usually made of lace, worn over the head). European diplomat Brantz Mayer described one woman in church in

Mexico in the 1840s: "She wore a purple velvet robe embroidered with white silk, white satin shoes, and silk stockings; a mantilla of the richest white blond lace fell over her head and shoulders, and her ears, neck, and fingers were blazing with diamonds." The dandies who frequented the fashionable spots in Mexico City might wear a "French cutaway suit, American patent leather shoes and an English stovepipe hat." The more sedate wore broadcloth suits and silk hats.

Few Mexicans, of course, could afford rich silk and woolen apparel. Travel writer Frederick Ober described mestizo dress in the early 1880s: "In the warmer regions he wears (on Sundays) a carefully plaited white shirt, wide trousers of white or colored drilling, fastened round the hips by a gay girdle, brown leather gaiters, and broad felt hat, with silver cord or fur band about it." Ranchers wore "open trousers of leather ornamented with silver, with white drawers showing through, a colored silk handkerchief about the neck, and a *serape*—the blanket shawl with a slit in the centre . . . ." The women "seldom wear stockings, though . . . feet are often encased in satin slippers; they have loose, embroidered chemises, a woolen or calico skirt, while the *rebozo*—a narrow but long shawl—is drawn over the head, and covers the otherwise exposed arms and breast."

Poor Mexicans dressed in simple, practical clothes. They went barefoot or wore sandals (*huaraches*) made simply from rawhide or plaited fibers. Despite the laws that demanded they wear pants and hats in public, Indian men usually wore only a breechcloth. Other rural Mexicans wore cotton shirts without collars and buttons and pants with long legs that covered their feet. Belts were strips of rawhide or cloth. The serape, a brightly covered woolen blanket, was an all-purpose garment that protected its wearer from the elements. The one common luxury among poor men was a straw hat. Rural women's apparel was no fancier than that of men. Indian women often wore only a few yards of cloth wrapped around their bodies. Rebozos were used similarly to serapes, protecting women from the elements and providing modesty. When folded the right way, the rebozo also was used to carry small children. Other women wore a scarf bound at the hips with a girdle that extended to the feet, accompanied by a broad mantle that covered the upper part of the body. This wool garment had with openings at the head and arms and was often ornamented with colorful embroidery. Wealthier Indian women wore a white petticoat with embroidery and ribbons. Some girls wore simple white cotton dresses with the head, neck, shoulders, and legs below the knees left bare. Women also wore heavy earrings and necklaces of cut glass. Their feet bore the same sandals worn by men or nothing. For the most part, women went without head coverings. Both men and women often carried rosary beads.

Shelter

As in the case of diet and clothing, housing, too, sharply differentiated the classes. The wealthy lived in opulence. In larger cities, houses of the affluent often had two stories. The ground floor in these buildings was for shops or other businesses, while the second floor was the family home. The house of Vicente Riva Palacio, well-known soldier-statesman, had 50 rooms. One entered through an impressive stairway leading to the living quarters.

The stairs and the floors of the corridors were made of the finest Italian marble. Tropical plants decorated the halls, and an aviary was filled with singing birds. Of the numerous rooms, there were three parlors, a grand salon, and two smaller salons. There was also an impressive private chapel adorned with luxurious drapes and beautiful religious ornaments. Mirrors and massive sideboards took up the walls of the dining room, measuring 100 by 50 feet. On these shelves were thousands of pieces of china, crystal, and silver. The brass bedsteads in each of 30 bedrooms bore an elegant bedspread of velvet, silk, lace, and crochet; hand-stitched linens; and canopies. The large living room, whose ceilings were 30 feet high, contained furniture decorated with gold trim, fabulous mirrors and chandeliers, and rich carpets. The family had its own 200-seat theater. Maintaining this remarkable establishment required 35 servants.

Guillermo Prieto, a noted social critic, described the typical middle-class home in Mexico City, which was considerably more modest:

A steep stairway led to a corridor paved with red varnished millstones. (The middle class usually lived on the second floor . . . because of the flooding that periodically afflicted the city, and the servants occupied rooms on the first floor.) The corridor was embellished with cages filled with stuffed birds, squirrels, wind chimes, and earthen crocks packed with stored foods and vegetables. Landscapes . . . adorned the walls. Comfortable chairs and couches . . . furnished the principal chamber. . . . In the bedroom were a large bed of fine wood, easy chairs, and wardrobes. The small children of the family slept in the halls. Those of a small family slept with their parents in curtained compartments of the main bedroom. The dining room contained a washstand holding towels, soap, straw, and a scouring stone for scrubbing. Colored vegetables, pots and pans, and jars lined the kitchen walls . . . with strips of garlic and pepper for a festive air.

In contrast to the domestic comfort enjoyed by the urban well-to-do, housing for farmers in the countryside was little more than a hut. Because wood for construction or fuel was prohibitively expensive in these deforested or arid areas, neither lumber nor bricks were practical building materials. (Wood was too costly to use in ovens to bake bricks.) Consequently, in temperate climates, country people constructed their huts with adobe made from sun-baked straw and mud blocks. In the highlands, where wood was more plentiful and affordable, houses consisted of brick (or stones plastered with mud rather than mortar) walls and a flat roof of beams laid close together and covered with finely washed, carefully stamped clay. In the tropics, farmers built their huts with saplings and leaves held together with mud. Occupants drove hewn logs into the ground to support the beams and roof and used bamboo sticks for the walls. The normal hut measured 20 by 15 feet and contained one room with no windows and a floor of packed earth mixed with ashes. Doorways (without doors) provided ventilation and light. Roofs were commonly made either with thatch or by laying rows of poles across the tops of walls that were covered with 1 or 2 feet of dirt and a layer of pine boards. Where it was colder, roofs were covered with shingles. Native vegetation, such as palm leaves or straw, served as roofing material in the tropics.

The kitchen area, where a fire burned continuously, was outside or in a separate, smaller building. The metate for tortillas was beside the fire. Huts had no furniture. Mats known as *petates* served as sleeping pallets. Better-off rural dwellers might have a bed consisting of four mounds of clay crossed with rough boards. No one could afford bedding or mattresses. Men and women slept in their clothes, wrapped in serapes and rebozos in cold weather. Because most people owned only the clothes they wore, there was no need for chests or closets. Pottery and baskets stored food and whatever other possessions the family owned. The only decoration in the hut was a picture of the Virgin of Guadalupe or a saint. Most regions were warm enough that homes did not require heating—and even if heat was needed, no one could afford it. The more prosperous rancheros lived in slightly less simple abodes. They might have a few pieces of furniture, such as a bench, a table (perhaps with low stools for seating), and board beds with mats and skins for pillows.

Poor people in Mexico City lived in rooms rented in crowded tenements (*vecindades*). Because the city endured periodic flooding, ground-floor rooms were continually damp. Badly ventilated, filthy, and crowded, the vecindades were breeding grounds for disease. Apartments lacked cooking facilities, which meant most of the poor took all their meals from street vendors. Not everyone was fortunate to have a roof over his or her head. Joel Poinsett, the United States Minister in 1824, estimated that 20,000 people slept on the streets. In Buenos Aires, most of the poor lived in small, ugly houses on the outskirts of the city. About a quarter of the residents in 1887 lived in tenements (*conventillos*), where they and their many children inhabited tiny rooms piled high with garbage and filth. In Rio de Janeiro, many of the new immigrants and internal migrants lived in crowded slums known as *corticos*. As in Mexico City the fashionable suburbs sprang up on the periphery, while the core of the city became the ever more crowded home of the poor.

Entertainment

Statistics and anecdotal evidence depict everyday life in nineteenth-century Latin America as being unpleasant or even miserable (if one were poor or a slave), but people found ways to enjoy themselves. The church, family, drinking, and gambling provided the most common entertainment for people of all classes. Solemn church masses were great spectacles, offering the best entertainment of the time, a theater of rites and rituals, resplendent priests, and majestic music. While no parish in the capital or anywhere else duplicated the magnificence of the great cathedral in Mexico City, many churches elsewhere stirred and inspired the people. Even in a modest village chapel, a visiting clergyman might put on a good show despite the lack of an opulent setting.

Religious fiestas took up a large number of days; in Aguascalientes, Mexico, for example, in the 1860s, there were 40 per year. These occasions provided both solemn consideration and joyous fun. Cities, towns, and villages prepared carefully for these celebrations by repairing and cleaning the streets, so that the processions that marked the special days were fit for the event. The Palm Sunday march represented Jesus' entrance into Jerusalem. On Good Friday, the crucifixion procession took place. Repentant sinners paraded through the roads half-naked and wearing crowns of thorns.

Mexico City celebrated Corpus Christi in unusual splendor. The archbishop conducted mass in the great cathedral in the Zócalo after which he led a grand parade from the church through adjacent streets, walking under a canopy of white linen, decorated with a red border. Everyone who was anyone—presidents, generals, cabinet ministers—appeared in full regalia. The procession was a time to show off. The wealthy displayed their fine clothes, perhaps imported from Paris. The surrounding homes were decked out with carpets, flowers, flags, and streamers. And a vast crowd of costumed people of different races and colors watched as the spectacle passed before them.

One of the most important holidays in Mexico was the Day of the Dead, celebrated in late October and early November. The celebrants burned massive numbers of candles and consumed large quantities of food. Poor Indians expended years of earnings in remembrance of departed loved ones. The night of the last day of October, families decorated their homes with flowers and candles and set out a colorful mat on which they lay a feast to lure the dead children back. The next day, the family repeated the ritual, adding dishes too hot for children, such as turkey mole and tamales. On this day, liquor also was offered. The Day of the Dead celebrations indicated that Mexicans knew death well and did not fear it.

Drinking was an important aspect of religious celebrations and, perhaps, for many, a crucial method of alleviating the pain of daily life. Alcoholism became a serious problem among the poor, however, as the alienation of urban life and industrialized working conditions became widespread at century's end. Pulque was the alcoholic beverage of choice. The *maguey* (agave) cactus has leaves of up to 10 feet in length, 1 foot wide, and 8 inches thick. After some years, it sends a giant flower stalk 20 to 30 feet high, on which grow greenish yellow flowers. The plant dies after it blooms. Just before it is about to emit its stalk, the Indians cut into the plant to extract the central portion of the stem. The incision leaves only the thick outside rind, forming a natural basin 2 feet deep and a foot and a half in diameter. The sap that would feed the stem, called *aguamiel* (honey water), oozes into the core and is extracted. A small amount is taken to ferment for 10 to 15 days. This becomes the *madre pulque,* which acts as a leaven inducing fermentation in the aguamiel. Within 24 hours it is pulque. As one draws off the pulque, one adds aguamiel to the mix. A good maguey yields 8 to 16 liters of aguamiel a day for as long as 3 months. Although the pulque has a lumpy consistency, tastes something like stale buttermilk, and smells like rotted meat, it is quite nutritious, and many believe it helps digestion.

Another popular diversion was gambling, which many observers of the time believed was a Mexican obsession. Cockfighting was a passionate outlet for gamblers and necessitated considerable preparations. Handlers bred and selected the cocks (roosters) carefully, fed them strictly, and trained them assiduously. The event required an arena 6 feet in diameter fenced in by 3-foot boards with benches around it. From the gallery, spectators urged on and bet on their favorites. The spectacle of the birds was bloody and brutal. The brave cocks exhausted themselves, but would not quit until one of the two contestants lay dead. Money then changed hands.

Of the different types of entertainment available in Mexico during this period, bull-fighting was the most famous. Thousands frequented the Sunday afternoon spectacles in Mexico City. Although it was a sport shared by all classes, one's status was made clear by virtue of seating. The wealthy sat in the shade, while the masses suffered the searing sun. The spectacle proceeded in traditional stages: The bull entered to have *picadors* and *matadors* goad and tease him with lances and red cloaks. These men had to be agile to avoid death on the animal's horns. Then, amid trumpet sounds, the bull's tormentors stuck small lances into his neck. The bull, snorting, thundering to no avail, attacked anyone and anything. Finally, the chief matador emerged, accompanied again by trumpets, to do battle armed with his red cloak and long blade. After some flourishing, the matador plunged his weapon between the bull's shoulder blades and into its heart, putting the animal out of its misery.

CONCLUSION

Life in Latin America during the first seven decades of the nineteenth century was enormously difficult for all but the wealthiest classes. The huge majority of Latin Americans struggled in poverty. Most people resided and worked in the countryside, either on large estates, in communal villages, or on small farms. A small percentage found employment in mining camps. As the century progressed, growing numbers of the populace migrated to the great cities in hopes of creating a better future for themselves. Inept and corrupt governments, war and banditry, and stagnant economies tormented nearly everyone, most profoundly, of course, the poor.

In the face of such dauntingly difficult lives, Latin Americans sought to preserve their customs and traditions. The best means at their disposal was to defend local governance. As we learned in Chapter 9, political and economic instability ironically allowed the lower classes to maintain their autonomy, at least in the countryside, for several decades after independence. Political centralization and economic development during the latter half of the century, however, undermined local prerogatives and eroded the practices of everyday life that had been sustained for centuries. New forms of work emerged, and modernization made life worse, rather than better, for most of the population.

LEARNING MORE ABOUT LATIN AMERICANS

Arrom, Silvia. *The Women of Mexico City* (Stanford, CA: Stanford University Press, 1985). Pathbreaking study of the changes in the conditions for women during the nineteenth century.
Barickman, B. J. *A Bahian Counterpoint: Sugar, Tobacco, Cassava, and Slavery in the Recôncavo, 1780–1860* (Stanford, CA: Stanford University Press, 1998). Explores economics and society in the Brazilian northeast.

Beezley, William H. *Judas at the Jockey Club and Other Episodes of Porfirian Mexico* (Lincoln, NE: University of Nebraska Press, 1987). Explores popular culture at the end of the century.

Burns, E. Bradford. *The Poverty of Progress: Latin America in the Nineteenth Century* (Berkeley, CA: University of California Press, 1980). Classic argument against the European notion of progress.

Calderón de la Barca, Frances. *Life in Mexico* (Berkeley, CA: University of California Press, 1982). Sometimes biting observations by foreign diplomat's wife.

Fowler-Salamini, Heather, and Mary Kay Vaughn, eds. *Women of the Mexican Countryside, 1850–1990* (Tucson, AZ: University of Arizona Press, 1994). Essays on the social history of women in everyday life.

Francois, Marie Eileen. *A Culture of Everyday Credit: Housekeeping, Pawnbroking, and Governance in Mexico City, 1750–1920* (Lincoln, NE: University of Nebraska Press, 2006). Details the struggles of everyday people.

Graham, Sandra Lauderdale. *Caetana Says No: Women's Stories from a Brazilian Slave Society* (New York: Cambridge University Press, 2002). The lives of a woman slave owner and a woman slave.

Graham, Sandra Lauderdale. *House and Street: The Domestic World of Servants and Masters in Nineteenth-Century Rio de Janeiro* (Austin, TX: University of Texas Press, 1992). A study of lower-class women who worked as domestics.

Johns, Michael. *The City of Mexico in the Age of Diaz* (Austin, TX: University of Texas Press, 1997). Mexico City, warts and all.

Mattoso, Katia M. de Queirós. *To Be a Slave in Brazil, 1550–1888* (New Brunswick, NJ: Rutgers University Press, 1986). The most thorough analysis of what it was like to be a slave in Brazil.

Stein, Stanley J. *Vassouras: A Brazilian Coffee County, 1850–1900* (Princeton, NJ: Princeton University Press, 1985). Classic study of a coffee plantation.

Wasserman, Mark. *Everyday Life and Politics in Nineteenth Century Mexico: Men, Women, and War* (Albuquerque, NM: University of New Mexico Press, 2000). A lively rendition of what life was like in nineteenth-century Mexico.

11

ECONOMIC MODERNIZATION, SOCIETY, AND POLITICS, 1880–1920

THE PERIOD FROM 1880 to 1920 was a time of momentous changes in the world economy. Railroads, steamships, telegraphs, and telephones made it possible for people, goods, ideas, and money to move rapidly across oceans and international boundaries. In Western Europe and the United States, most people now lived in cities and earned their livelihoods in industry rather than agriculture. The population of these areas grew in both numbers and affluence, creating demand for a wide range of agricultural products, such as beef and grains for consumption and cotton and wool for wear. New industries required minerals, such as copper for electric wire, and other commodities, such as petroleum for internal combustion engines. Large corporations emerged to provide the capital, technology, and administrative know-how in a global process of economic modernization.

These transformations had especially profound economic, political, and social consequences in Latin America. Beginning in the 1870s and continuing to the 1920s, Latin America experienced an extraordinary export boom. The construction of thousands of miles of railroads and the refurbishment of seaports eased the flow of products from Latin American mines and fields to waiting North Atlantic markets. Europe and the United States not only provided expanding markets but also new technologies and capital to facilitate the extraction of agricultural and mineral resources. Economic growth brought a measure of prosperity, but it was unequally distributed. Workers in the region's mines and nascent industries experienced harsh working conditions and often received scant compensation for their contributions to the growing economies. Poor farmers, usually indigenous peoples who still held their land communally, often lost their holdings to large estates that sought to increase their acreage in order to produce more agricultural commodities for export. Aided and abetted by national governments, who looked unfavorably on collective landholding as an impediment to progress, land expropriations created a large class of landless rural people, whose customs and mores had for centuries revolved around collective and individual landownership. Meanwhile, as the region became more closely tied to the world economy, it became exceptionally vulnerable to fluctuations in overseas markets. The resulting boom and bust cycles wreaked havoc in many countries. Major depressions in the world economy in the 1890s and again in 1907 sparked political conflict in various Latin American countries.

Export-led modernization brought enormous political and social changes to Latin America. Emerging from the violent decades that followed independence, many nations experienced long periods of political stability, dominated by land-based upper classes ruling through rigged elections or dictatorships. This political stability was vital to the modernization process, but economic development generated forces that disrupted the status quo. The export boom created two new, crucial social classes—an urban middle class and an urban industrial working class—whose demands for equality and equity eventually brought an end to the rule of the large landowners. The export economy expanded the size and role of governments, which needed a growing number of white-collar workers who obtained middle-class status. These workers formed one component of the new middle class. Economic opportunities in boom times created an entrepreneurial group of small-scale businesspeople, who also joined the ranks of the middle class. This middle sector commonly formed the foundation of rising political parties.

Meanwhile, railroads, mining, food processing, and other new industries stimulated by the export economy required growing numbers of workers. In some countries, massive immigration—made possible by rapid development of railroads and steamship lines—helped fill the demand. The new export economies needed large numbers of unskilled workers, but the new technology also required many workers with specialized skills. Workers of all ranks, but particularly those who were highly skilled, organized labor unions and joined political parties in search of improved living and employment conditions.

Workers' grievances joined with those of dispossessed farmers to form an increasingly volatile political climate. The crisis, known in some countries as the "Social Question," intensified after 1900. Those who ruled struggled to maintain their position. Some upper classes grudgingly made concessions to the middle and lower classes, while others stubbornly refused. During the first two decades of the twentieth century, many cities and mining regions witnessed violent protests against upper-class oppression, but only in Mexico did these protests lead to revolution. Almost everywhere, however, the rule of large landowners drew to a close.

Export-led development brought with it not only profound economic and political dislocations, but wrenching social changes as well. The old ruling classes faced the

TIMELINE

1876
Porfirio Díaz takes power in Mexico

1888
Abolition of slavery in Brazil

1889
Empire overthrown by military in Brazil

1891
Chilean civil war ousts President José Manuel Balmaceda; parliamentary rule begins

1910
Mexican Revolution begins

1912
Sáenz Peña Law in Argentina extends male suffrage

1912
Foreign investment in Latin America reaches US$8.5 billion

1916
Election of Hipólito Yrigoyen as president of Argentina

1917
Mexican Constitution

1919
Semana Trágica in Buenos Aires

erosion of the patriarchal norms that underlay their positions of power. The urbanization, industrialization, and migration that accompanied export-led development undermined traditional gender roles and family structures that cast fathers and husbands as the heads of families and men as the sole actors in the political sphere. Women's positions in the family, the workplace, and the public arena changed. Feminism rose to demand that women be recognized as important contributors to the construction of modern nations. Women sought equality under the law, both inside and outside the family. Not only was the public rule of the upper classes under attack, but the private basis of their position as well.

Economic change notwithstanding, the core of the political struggle remained control over everyday life. Urbanization and industrialization merely shifted the locations, altered some of the methods employed, and broadened some of the goals. In the countryside, struggle continued much the same as it had before against the intrusions of central authority. To country people, modernization and centralization meant a widespread assault against their culture and traditions.

ECONOMIC MODERNIZATION

After nearly a half-century of stagnation with interludes of export boom, much of Latin America entered into a period of economic growth from the 1880s through World War I, resulting from the influx of new technologies and capital, mostly from abroad, and the advent of domestic peace. Massive new railroad networks were both the products of modernization and the engines of further economic development. They also facilitated national consolidation in ways unimaginable before 1880.

Exports

The development of export agriculture and industry was at the core of the economic, social, and political transformations of the era. The export boom displayed several notable characteristics. First, most nations concentrated on one or two export commodities. Second, the booms were not sustainable, for the most part, for more than a decade or two at a time. International markets for primary products were cyclical, and busts inevitably followed booms. Third, the question of who actually benefited from the expansion of exports is subject to unending debate. Finally, linkages between the export economy and domestic sectors of the Latin American economies were not consistent. As a result, the growth of exports did not necessarily stimulate overall economic development.

The industrialized nations of the North Atlantic (Great Britain, France, Germany, and the United States) greatly increased their population and general prosperity after 1850. Annual income per capita doubled. The market demand for agricultural staples, such as grain, meat, and wool, exceeded locally available supplies, while increased affluence stimulated demand for more "exotic" products, such as coffee, cacao, sugar, and bananas. Simultaneously, technological advancements in agriculture and industry created additional demands for primary materials. New farming techniques required fertilizers, for example. Intensifying industrialization created a need for mineral ores such as lead, silver, gold, tin, zinc, and copper. The invention and widespread use of the internal combustion engine expanded demand for petroleum. Technological improvements in metallurgy and mining made it possible to extract minerals from previously unusable sources and cut down on the bulk and cost of ore shipments. New railroads and communications and the introduction of steamships facilitated the transportation of raw materials. The new ships reduced the Buenos Aires to Europe route to weeks. Refrigerated shipping made it possible to send even fresh meat and other delicate commodities across the ocean.

Latin American nations possessed the natural resources to help satisfy the North Atlantic market for food and minerals. The industrialized nations supplied capital, technological expertise, and administrative organization to extract and transport these commodities. A vast inflow of foreign investment stimulated the expansion of exports. By 1912, foreign investment in Latin America reached $8.5 billion, of which railroads accounted for $2.9 billion. The largest other sectors of investment were in government obligations (bonds), mining, and public utilities.

Great Britain accounted for the largest share of foreign investment in Latin America, nearly $5 billion. Between 1900 and 1914, the British doubled their holdings in the region. The British were a notable presence in Chilean nitrate mining and Mexican petroleum. U.S. capital was second in importance to the British and concentrated in Mexican railroads and mining, Cuban sugar production, and Central American plantations and railways. Between 1900 and 1914, U.S. investment in Latin America quintupled. Mexico received the most capital, more than $1 billion. U.S. investors mostly sought export industries. Before 1914, the third largest source of foreign investment was Germany. Germans invested heavily in Argentina, Brazil, and Mexico (more than $100 million in each). World War I, however, broke most of Latin America's commercial and financial ties with Germany.

Growing demand in the North Atlantic economies, transportation improvements, and massive foreign investment all combined to increase Latin American exports enormously. Some of this growth began as early as the mid-nineteenth century, but the pace accelerated greatly after 1880. Between 1853 and 1873, Argentine exports grew sevenfold. By 1893, they had doubled again. Brazilian coffee exports more than doubled in the years between 1844 and 1874 and quadrupled between 1874 and 1905. Colombian, Costa Rican, and Venezuelan coffee exports also increased spectacularly. Total Mexican exports rose nearly 700 percent from 1878 to 1911. Bolivian tin exports jumped by 1200 percent from 1897 to 1913.

The burgeoning export economy had important positive effects. In 1916, Argentina's per capita national wealth stood at approximately 10 percent less than that of the United States, but 62 percent higher than that of France. By 1914, Argentina's per capita income exceeded that of Spain, Italy, Switzerland, and Sweden and compared with that of Germany, Belgium, and the Netherlands.

The Downside of Export-Led Modernization

Despite overall growth, export-led modernization proved a mixed blessing for Latin Americans. The rise in per capita income was statistically impressive, but the numbers masked the fact that this wealth was not equitably distributed. Wealthy landowners became fabulously rich, while the situation of the rest of the population remained the same or deteriorated.

Moreover, few Latin American nations were able to sustain steady high growth. Only Argentina and Chile expanded their exports at a rate averaging more than 4 percent from 1850 to 1914. Argentina averaged more than 6 percent, a truly impressive accomplishment. The other nations had spurts of growth followed by long periods of stagnation. By World War I, however, exports seemed to reach a ceiling, because either the products of these nations dominated the world market to such an extent that little room for growth remained or severe competition had arisen and market share inevitably fell.

Latin America's vulnerability to world market fluctuations was exacerbated by the fact that most nations continued to rely on a limited number of export commodities. To be sure, in the first decade of the twentieth century, there were a number of efforts to diversify from the model of one or two raw material exports, but concentration of exports persisted. In five Latin American nations (Bolivia, Chile, Cuba, El Salvador, and Guatemala) in 1913, one commodity comprised more than 70 percent of exports. In five more nations (Brazil, Ecuador, Haiti, Nicaragua, and Panama), one product accounted for more than 60 percent of exports. And in three others (Costa Rica, Honduras, and Venezuela), one commodity accounted for more than 50 percent. The most diversified export nations were Argentina, Colombia, and Peru. Argentina was the most successful at diversification, exporting grains (wheat, linseed, rye, barley, and maize) and livestock (chilled and frozen beef, lamb, wool, and hides).

Most Latin American export economies became dependent on a handful of consuming nations and therefore found themselves vulnerable to economic fluctuations in those countries. Four markets, the United States, Great Britain, Germany, and France, together accounted for 90 percent of the exports in 10 countries and more than 70 percent in 18. Only Argentina avoided this heavy dependence on the four markets.

The foundation of Latin American trade was the shipment of primary commodities in return for manufactured goods. Historians have long debated the equity of this system. Some have maintained the terms of trade were unfair because manufactured goods constantly rose in price while commodity prices declined. This is difficult to determine conclusively, however, because the statistics for trade and prices are not very reliable and those that are available do not show firm trends. The advantage, however, was not always with the industrialized nations.

The impact of export-oriented development strategies is also heatedly argued among historians and economists. Advocates claim that these strategies stimulated the other sectors of the economy, particularly industrialization. Some export commodities require processing, such as butchering and chilling meat, tanning hides, and milling flour. Sugar production, as we have seen, is as much an industrial as an agricultural enterprise. Exports drove the construction of railroads and other transportation. At the same time, however, export commodities often drained the nation of resources, leaving little or nothing for other economic activities. In nations where capital was chronically scarce, precious few resources trickled from the export machine. Some export economies, notably petroleum drilling, operated in enclaves without enhancing the overall economy.

The rapid rise of the various export economies of the region did not necessarily lead to development of the nonexport economy. Industrialization, the usual measure of economic modernization, did not automatically derive from increased primary exports. In general, the nations with the most varied export product base were the most likely to develop. Those economies that relied on one product were the least likely to develop.

Finally, export booms inevitably ended. Agricultural commodities wore out the soil, causing production gradually to decline. This was particularly the case for coffee in Central America, Venezuela, and Haiti around 1900. Bananas were vulnerable to disease and natural disasters. More important, world market demand was fickle. For example, demand for Brazilian rubber skyrocketed at the turn of the century, creating fabulous fortunes, only to fall precipitously when competitors from Southeast Asia flooded the market and, later, chemists invented a substitute.

Railroads

Railroads were, perhaps, the greatest technological agents of change during the nineteenth century, and as such they provide a good illustration of the benefits and drawbacks of modernization. They were the "backbone" of the export economy, bringing unparalleled prosperity to some regions and unmitigated misery elsewhere. The expansion of the railways was spectacular (see Table 11.1). The railroad system of Argentina increased from 1600 miles in 1880 to 21,200 miles in 1914. Mexico had less than 400 miles of railroads in 1880, but by 1910 it had constructed nearly 15,000 miles of track.

Railroads provided inexpensive transportation for agricultural commodities, minerals, and people. The rail networks opened up new lands for cultivation. In Argentina, they made it possible to cultivate grains on the rich soil of the Pampas and to push livestock raising farther and farther south into the semiarid region of Patagonia. Brazilian planters spread coffee cultivation to the vast interior of São Paulo. Railroad transportation facilitated the recovery of the Mexican mining industry.

The new transportation systems brought together nations torn by regionalism. They enabled governments to exert their authority in previously autonomous areas. What once were months-long journeys for armies now took only days, and former day trips now took only hours. Railroads enabled people to travel farther and at less cost than ever before.

TABLE 11.1

Railways in Latin America, 1880–1920 (Number of Miles)

	1880	1900	1920
Argentina	1,600	10,400	21,200
Brazil	2,100	9,500	17,700
Chile	700	8,300	13,000
Peru	1,100	2,700	5,100
Latin America	7,200	34,500	62,900

Source: Copyright © 2000 Frederick Stirton Weaver. Reprinted by permission of Westview Press, a member of the Perseus Books Group.

Walking to the mines of northern Mexico from the center of the nation was an impossible dream, but the railroad carried passengers to potentially better lives for minimal expenditure. It also created truly national markets for the first time.

Despite the obvious benefits they generated, railroads also were a symbol of unwanted modernization, one that people frequently resisted. In Mexico during the last quarter of the nineteenth century, there was violence in almost every region where tracks were laid for the first time. It was not unusual for people anywhere in Latin America to throw rocks at the train cars as they passed, so hated were the engines of progress. The railroads disrupted old patterns of landholding. Their presence raised the value of land. In areas where indigenous people owned lands collectively and individually and grew subsistence staple crops, government officials and large landowners forced them off their properties. The greedy landowners then converted production to commercial crops, which they sent to urban and international markets by means of the railroads. This process created a large, landless class of poor rural people, and thus a pool of inexpensive labor, and cut the total production of staple crops, which in turn caused the prices of basic foodstuffs to rise. The subsequent inflation undermined the living standards of both the middle and working classes.

MODERNIZATION AND SOCIAL CHANGE

The economic and technological transformations described in the preceding section triggered great changes in Latin American society. First, improved diets and medical care, coupled in many countries with a steady stream of immigrants, brought a substantial increase in population, most particularly in urban areas. Second, new social classes arose, complicating the social hierarchy and political agendas for the region. Third, discontent mounted in the countryside. Finally, people were on the move—from rural areas to cities and mining camps, from overseas to Latin America, from one country to another. All these changes had a profound impact on the daily lives of men, women, and children throughout Latin America.

Population Increase

As we saw in Chapter 9, the decades following national independence were pervaded by warfare throughout Latin America. These conflicts cost many lives, and the population growth that many areas had experienced in the late colonial period came to a halt. By the 1880s, however, the populations of Latin American nations began to grow once more. The population of Argentina doubled between 1895 and 1914, from 3.9 to 7.8 million. Brazil's population went from 10.1 million in 1872 to 30.6 million in 1920. Cities exploded. The population of Buenos Aires went from 178,000 in 1869 to nearly 1.6 million in 1914. Other than Hamburg, Germany, it was the fastest-growing city in the Western world. Lima, which because of the War of the Pacific and subsequent civil wars, did not begin to grow until the 1890s, jumped from 104,000 in 1891 to 224,000 in 1920. Guayaquil, Ecuador, grew from 12,000 to 90,000 between 1870 and 1920.

New Classes, New Voices

The increase in population and the development of industry created both a bigger, more complex middle sector and an industrial working class, while at the same time providing opportunities for women. Each of these groups would in turn seek to add their voices the political discourse begun in the decades after independence.

There had been from colonial times a *gente decente* (decent folk) that comprised light-skinned people who did not work with their hands. In great part their status depended on their race. Few Indians, blacks, or mulattos found acceptance into the middle class (although there were, of course, exceptions). The new middle class that arose from the export boom and industrialization was quite varied. In Buenos Aires, the mostly immigrant middle class operated small businesses, such as bakeries, breweries, print shops, and retail shops. The number of small-scale manufacturers doubled from 1853 to 1914. These remained vulnerable to the fluctuations in economic conditions. The depression of 1907, for example, devastated small-scale entrepreneurs in northern Mexico, erasing a decade of gains. Oftentimes the middle class depended on the goodwill and good fortune of their bosses, not necessarily their own merits. Proprietors of small businesses rarely had any other assets other than their own skills. In the cities few middle-class people owned property.

White-collar employees occupied the most complicated and difficult position among the middle classes. Not always earning income sufficient for full-fledged middle-class status, they, nonetheless, sought respectability. They lived precariously on the edge of ruin, fearing above all the prospect of falling back into poverty. In Lima in 1908, the census revealed that half the 6600 white-collar employees were white, 25 percent were mestizo, and 15 percent Asian. Only 1 percent of white-collar employees in Lima were women. According to D. S. Parker, they were "marginal figures at best. With no family connections, they were only capable of moving into the lowest rung of the commercial ladder. Poorly paid for long hours, ruthlessly exploited, and lacking any job security, their highest realistic expectation was to receive a steady pay check and to wear a clean shirt."

The rapidly emerging industrial working class was also quite diverse. In mining, its members ranged from unskilled peons, who carried 200-pound sacks of ore up rickety ladders from deep tunnels to the surface, to experts in explosives. On the railroads, common pick-and-shovel men toiled with locomotive engineers. In meat packing there were unskilled meat carriers and skilled butchers. Although in Argentina meat-packing plants were large enterprises, thousands of small workshops manufactured an enormous variety of products. European immigrants comprised from one-half to two-thirds of the workers. The number of workers in Lima, Peru, rose from 9500 in 1876 to more than 44,000 in 1920, and in Callao, Lima's port, their number doubled between 1908 and 1920. Women and children comprised one-fifth of the working class employed.

Expanding literacy rates among the middle classes and some sectors of the working classes gave these groups greater access to information about national affairs and emboldened them to demand a voice in political debates. In Brazil, to cite one example, only 19.1 percent of all Brazilian men and 10.4 percent of all women were literate in 1890. By 1920, literacy had improved to 28.9 percent for men and 19.9 percent for women. Literacy was much higher in the cities. By 1920, 65.8 percent of the men and 54.5 percent of the women in São Paulo and Rio de Janeiro had learned how to read and write.

The emergence of these new middle-class and working-class groups added new voices to the political debates in Latin America by the early twentieth century. A growing number of these voices were female. Although women comprised a tiny percentage of white-collar employees, they entered the urban workforce and gained access to at least a rudimentary education in unprecedented numbers. As factory workers, operators of small businesses, and heads of households, they acted independently of traditional family ties and increasingly sought equal treatment in both private and public spheres. Feminists among them asserted their equality with men, while insisting on their differences as well. They used the regard society had for them as females to establish their role in the public sphere and their position as working women to campaign for societal reforms. Feminism called for a redefinition of the traditional notions of the home as women's space and the street as forbidden. At stake were the long-held values of honor and the double standard. They challenged the basic structure of the family, seeking to end the legal subordination of women and the illegality of divorce. Ultimately, women sought to obtain suffrage. Initially, however, they focused on securing equality under the law and better health care for women and children. Their active voices changed the nature of political discourse in the modernizing nations of Latin America.

Rural Discontent

Although the emergence of middle and industrial working classes had limited impact in rural areas, other disruptive trends affected people living in the countryside. Generally, conditions for rural working people deteriorated. In central Mexico, for example, wages had stagnated while purchasing power declined. In Mexico, land expropriations by politicians and large landowners left many rural dwellers landless, who toiled either for

---

Slice of Life   A CHILEAN MINING CAMP

LIFE IN THE MINING camps of Brazil, Chile, Mexico, and Peru was difficult, dangerous, and expensive. Spanish and Portuguese colonial enterprises had little success in attracting voluntary labor to the camps without substantial monetary inducements or coercion. The indigenous peoples steered clear of the mines as much as possible. The advent of a freer labor market and the introduction of modern technology during the nineteenth century did not improve the living and working conditions. As one observer noted, "Labor in the copper mines of the nineteenth century was harshly disciplined, intense, and brutal."

Chilean copper mines were small and totally lacking in modern technology. Mine owners had no capital, suffered poor transportation, and lacked a dependable labor supply: Who would want to work in a copper camp? The mines were usually isolated, accessible to the outside world only by several days of hard travel through rugged terrain. Most were located in the mountains, which were buffeted by inhospitable weather.

The miners were treated abominably. The physical labor was arduous and included working with heavy hammers and chisels and carrying 200-pound sacks of ore up rickety ladders. Charles Darwin observed that the miners were "truly beasts of burden." Miners had little time for meals, working from dawn until dusk. Adding

Mining camp. The work was backbreaking and dangerous.

insult to injury, armed guards patrolled the camps, and if miners were caught stealing ore, they were subject to corporal punishment.

Conditions changed somewhat during and after World War I, when copper prices rose because of increased demand. After the war, large international corporations invested in the copper industry. They brought in new technology, such as the widespread use of dynamite. The big companies paid relatively high wages and provided better living conditions than the small Chilean operations. This was not saying much, however.

Better wages were offset by the skyrocketing cost of living in the camps. And slightly improved working conditions did not change the fact that life in the mines was unendurable: The mine tunnels were hell-like, either unbearably hot from the venting of underground gases or cold and wet. Copper dust swirled in the air, making it nearly impossible to breathe and causing rampant respiratory disease. Miners were often injured or killed by cave-ins, falls, asphyxiation, and dynamite explosions. Housing for single workers was makeshift; in the smaller camps, it usually consisted only of tents. Often, 20 men were packed into one room. Families fared no better, residing without ventilation, electricity, or light in hovels made of wood and aluminum boards. There was no heat, and the cold was unbearable. Two families often shared two-room, dirt-floored apartments in the barracks.

The mines recruited workers from the southern agricultural regions, especially the Central Valley, where the concentration of landholding pushed landless people to seek work in the mines and cities. *Enganchadores* (less-than-honest recruiters) haunted the bars and plazas, buying drinks for hungry, desperate men, getting them drunk, and convincing them to sign work contracts. The following morning, these men woke up, hung over, only to find themselves on a train bound for the north, often having been advanced money from the enganchadores that had to be worked off. Because the mining companies needed workers who were at full strength to do the arduous work, they often rejected men supplied by these recruiters.

Agricultural labor went back and forth between the farming regions and the northern mines, and levels of turnover in the labor force were high. Many rural workers spent a year in the mines to earn the relatively high wages and then returned home to pay their debts or settle on a plot of land. Others migrated to the mines during the agricultural off-season to accumulate enough money to buy their own land. Still others worked just long enough to amass some cash and then left without notice. The companies did not always pay departing workers what they were owed. In 1917, El Teniente employees averaged only 18 to 20 days' work. The high job turnover had numerous causes, including the harsh working conditions; exhaustion, injury, and illness; and racial discrimination, especially from foreign supervisors employed by the large companies.

Women moved in and out of the camps, working as domestic servants, preparing and selling food and alcohol, and working as prostitutes. Women came to the camps mostly independent of men, looking to earn and save money, perhaps to start again elsewhere. They ran their own households, raised children, and struggled mightily to make ends meet. Formal marriage was infrequent, because life at the mines was too transient.

Both men and women resisted the efforts of large foreign companies to institute labor discipline. Mobility and independence were highly valued by the workers and widely opposed by the companies. It took decades to instill the industrial work ethic into rural workers.

Workers and bosses frequently clashed over control of aspects of everyday life. This struggle was a microcosm of the relationship between the upper classes and lower classes throughout Latin America during the nineteenth century.

Questions for Discussion

Compare the lives of Chilean miners to those of Argentine gauchos. What were the social and economic processes that gradually limited their independence? How did the miners assert their control over their own lives?

small remuneration on the great estates or abandoned their villages to labor in the mines and cities or across the U.S. border. The ownership of land was concentrated among the upper classes. At the same time, in some areas, such as northern Mexico and the Argentine Pampas, the number of owners of small farms increased. In the Mexican north, small holders were a vocal and prosperous group that deeply resented unfairly high taxes and government centralization.

In Argentina, rural conditions for farm tenants, gauchos, shepherds, and seasonal laborers varied. Landowners no longer recognized any traditional, patriarchal obligations to look after the welfare of their employees, in return for which they had received both labor and loyalty. As in Mexico, there was a sector of small farmers, mostly tenants, who increased their numbers and prospered. By the 1910s, however, many tenants, chronically in debt to suppliers, lived in desperate conditions.

In both rural Argentina and Mexico, the onslaught of centralization grew more intrusive, because landowners and governments sought not only to extend their control to local governance but also to modernize owner–labor relations. This meant that the ruling classes attempted to transform age-old customs and traditions that lay at the core of rural society. Regional autonomy remained strong in Argentina, but rural society changed to suit the needs of the estancieros. In Mexico, however, where the traditional village structure remained strong despite unending assaults by the national government, rural protests led to revolution in 1910.

Mass Movements of People

Latin American leaders, even before independence, had dreamed of populating their vast nations with immigrants from Europe as part of their effort to modernize their economies. For the upper class and intellectuals, disdainful of their indigenous and mestizo brethren, an influx of Europeans was the way to "get rid of the primitive element of our popular masses." Domingo Sarmiento, the liberal ideologue who was president of Argentina (1868–1874), claimed that only mass immigration could "drown in waves of industry the Creole rabble, inept, uncivil, and coarse that stops our attempt to civilize the

TABLE 11.2

Destination of European Emigrants to Latin America, c. 1820–1932

Country	Number of Immigrants
Argentina	6,501,000
Brazil	4,361,000
Cuba	1,394,000
Uruguay	713,000
Mexico	270,000
Chile	90,000
Venezuela	70,000
Peru	30,000
Paraguay	21,000

Source: Copyright © 1998, The Regents of the University of California.

nation." Despite the fervent wishes of upper classes almost everywhere, few Latin American countries attracted many immigrants. Five nations, Argentina, Brazil, Uruguay, Cuba, and Mexico, drew the preponderance of the new arrivals.

From 1860 to 1920, 45 million people left Europe to go to the Western Hemisphere (see Table 11.2). Massive immigration occurred in Argentina, Brazil, and Cuba. From 1904 to 1914, on average, 100,000 immigrants a year found their way from Italy and Spain to Argentina. Much of the new middle and working classes derived from the immigrant and migrant population. The export economies demanded labor and, consequently, Peruvian cotton and sugar industries brought in Chinese coolies, the construction of the Panama Canal drew British West Indians, and the Dominican Republic exploited Haitian workers for plantations. By the beginning of the twentieth century, then, an increasingly diverse population demanded a say in the affairs of Latin American nations.

POLITICS IN THE AGE OF MODERNIZATION

The spectacular growth in Latin America's national economies in the late nineteenth and early twentieth centuries was accompanied by an equally impressive degree of political stability that stood in marked contrast to the recurring political upheavals that had occurred during the first few decades after independence. Political stability fostered economic growth by guaranteeing a safe climate for domestic and foreign investment. Economic growth, in turn, gave the ruling classes the tools they needed to maintain order—professionalized and better-equipped armies to repress dissidents and sometimes act as arbiters of political disputes, railroads to carry troops quickly to the scene of any potential disorder, and jobs to keep the middle classes happy. The philosophy of positivism was the ideological underpinning of the ruling classes during this era.

Developed by Frenchman Auguste Comte (1798–1857) and infused with social Darwinism by Herbert Spencer (1820–1902), positivism emphasized reason, science, order, and progress, which fit nicely into the efforts of the Latin American upper classes to modernize their nations.

The political stability of the age of modernization assumed a variety of forms. In Argentina and Brazil, ranchers and planters played a dominant role in national politics. Chile demonstrated a fair degree of democracy, while in Peru an "Aristocratic Republic" held sway. The long dictatorships of Porfirio Díaz (1876–1911) in Mexico and Antonio Guzmán Blanco (1870–1888) in Venezuela brought a measure of peace and prosperity at least for those who enjoyed the favor of the regime in power.

The rise of the new middle and urban working classes and the widespread encroachments on traditional rural politics and society undermined this stability. In 1910, Mexico burst into revolution that tore it apart for nearly a decade. In other countries, political parties representing the new classes and labor unions formed to contest upper-class rule. By the first decade of the twentieth century, the challenges to the ruling classes were profound.

A Modernized Military

Latin American military establishments reflected the transformations of the times. In Argentina, Brazil, Chile, and Peru, upper classes sought to modernize and professionalize the armed services. Latin American governments imported European consultants to update and professionalize their militaries. These foreign missions inculcated a sense of separateness, nationalism, and impatience, which reconstructed the military in a way that ultimately made it the major threat to democracy in the region. The military was a crucial ally of the upper classes, for the two groups envisioned similar futures of order and economic development. As the social pressures from below increased, self-proclaimed professional, apolitical, incorruptible military officers came to despise civilian politicians. Concurrently, middle-class people entered the armed services as a route toward upward mobility. As a result, Latin American militaries were integral participants to the struggles over the "Social Question."

The revamped militaries recreated their officer corps through education at special military academies and a career system based on merit. The new career routes were meant to keep the young officers away from politics. Technology changed the military, as it did society as a whole. Railroads, cannons, rifles, machine guns, and telegraphs altered warfare. Ironically, professionalization took place when the region was at peace. After the War of the Pacific, there were no more external wars until the Chaco War between Paraguay and Bolivia in the 1930s. Nonetheless, militaries expanded their role in society and politics.

Isolated and confident (though untested in most cases), Latin American militaries set themselves up as arbitrators of their nations and saw themselves as saviors of their fatherlands. One Argentine army officer wrote in 1911: "The army is the nation. It is the external armor that guarantees the cohesive operation of its parts and preserves it from shocks and falls." No constitutional guarantees, moreover, could dissuade the military from its duty to ensure that governments responded to the needs of the nation. But the military was far from unified. As in the upper classes, there were divisions between those who those who wanted to crush all dissidents and those who were willing to compromise with the new urban classes. In Chapter 12, we will see how these disagreements evolved as the militaries asserted more power and influence.

The Rule of the Ranchers and Planters: Argentina and Brazil

A pattern emerged across Latin America in which export-dominated economies experienced successive booms and busts, with the downturns leading to political unrest and sometimes rebellion. This pattern was evident in Argentina and Brazil during the depression of the 1890s, though none of the resulting rebellions overthrew the existing order. The large landowners of Buenos Aires and the Pampas and the coffee planters of Brazil who dominated politics in their respective nations from the mid-nineteenth century until the 1920s were willing to concede very little, if anything, to the new groups. In Argentina, the large landowners accommodated only the middle classes, while harshly repressing the urban working class. The Brazilian upper class stubbornly refused any compromise. Eventually, it would split over tactics toward the new classes.

General Julio A. Roca dominated Argentine politics at the end of the century, first through puppets from 1892 to 1898 and then as president from 1898 to 1904, using a combination of patronage and force. He advocated economic growth financed through foreign investment in the export sector. Eventually his support base among landowners split into two factions, one that supported him and his hard line toward the lower classes and the other that sought progressive reform. Fortunately for the upper classes, the new classes also divided. The middle class took refuge in the Radical Party (Unión Cívica Radical), while the working class divided its allegiance among various leftist parties centered in Buenos Aires.

The Radical Party challenged the rule of the landowners, staging two revolts during the 1890s. In response the upper classes consented to expand voting rights to all males through the Sáenz Peña Law of 1912. The Radicals changed their violent tactics and triumphed in the presidential election of 1916 with Hipólito Yrigoyen (1916–1922, 1928–1930).

The Buenos Aires working class divided into anarchists and socialists. The anarchists sought to obtain better conditions for workers by means of the general strike. In 1910, a government crackdown against threatened demonstrations at the nation's centennial broke the movement. Argentine socialists were moderates, who supported democracy and sought primarily to raise living standards by raising wages and lowering prices. They also advocated women's suffrage. Neither anarchists nor socialists made more than a passing mark on Argentine electoral politics. Nonetheless, they frightened enough of those in power into making some concessions to the lower classes.

Yrigoyen proved a masterful politician, building a formidable political machine founded on patronage. However, the Radicals, never in control of both houses of Congress, were neither able nor inclined to implement extensive reforms. Yrigoyen confronted his greatest crisis in 1919, when strikes in Buenos Aires led to widespread violence. The Radicals sided with the upper classes and crushed the unions in what became known as the Tragic Week (*Semana Trágica*). This instance of the middle class siding with the upper class in confrontation with workers set the pattern for the next century of politics in Latin America.

In Brazil, the emergent classes were weaker and the upper classes stronger than in Argentina. Regionalism remained a major force, with state governments more influential than the national government. In the 1880s, Brazil experienced two enormous political and economic shocks. First, the monarchy proclaimed the abolition of slavery on May 13, 1888. Then, on November 15, 1889, the army overthrew the Empire, thus beginning the First Republic (1889–1930). Thereafter, a fragile alliance of state upper classes ruled Brazil until this arrangement broke down in 1930 at the outset of the Great Depression.

At first, the military ruled. The Republic's first two presidents were military officers. Eventually, large landowners took the reins of power, sharing control with state-level alliances of local political bosses, known as colonels, who presided over the rural hinterlands through a strict system of patron–client relations. The colonels' clients obligated themselves to vote as ordered in return for patronage and protection.

An alliance of São Paulo coffee planters and Minas Gerais cattle barons controlled the national government. By agreement, the major states, Minas Gerais and São Paulo, alternated their representatives in the presidency. (This agreement was the so-called *café com leite* alliance.) Of 11 presidents during the First Republic, 6 came from São Paulo and 3 from Minas Gerais. A third state, Rio Grande do Sul, muscled its way into the mix after the turn of the century. Brazilian states exercised control over their own finances and militaries. The State of São Paulo had a well-equipped state militia with as many as 14,000 men. State governments could even contract foreign loans. The coffee planters openly used government for their own economic gain, relying on the national and state governments to buy their surplus crops. Brazil's slower industrialization delayed the development of pressure from below for a decade or two after other Latin American nations confronted the social question.

Democracy in Chile

Chile's landed upper class ruled until 1920. But it, too, was vulnerable to the downturns of the export economy. As in Argentina and Brazil, the depression of the 1890s brought unrest. President José Manuel Balmaceda (1886–1891) encountered unparalleled rancor because to many Chileans he symbolized the corrupt, coercive system so long in power. Balmaceda's opposition, which sought to hold free elections and modify the balance of power, stalemated Congress in 1890, virtually paralyzing the national government. When the president closed Congress (which was legal), it established a rival government, and its forces defeated Balmaceda in an 8-month-long civil war.

During Chile's so-called Parliamentary Republic from 1891 to 1920, Chilean politics reached an impasse. The government's inability to meet the demands of the emerging classes led to recurring crises during the 1920s. The working class increased in numbers as people moved into the mines and cities from the countryside. Inevitably, they sought ways to protest their brutal labor and living conditions through unions. In the 1890s, there were riots in the nitrate fields, where conditions were unimaginable. Conflict worsened in the first decades of the new century. Disturbances in Santiago in 1905 cost the lives of 60 people. There were economic depressions in 1907–1908 and after World War I. The worsening economic crisis led to terrible strikes in 1919; one in Santiago involved 50,000 workers. Arturo Alessandri emerged in 1920, promising to accommodate the demands of the new classes, and won election to the presidency. The upper class continued to be unwilling to compromise, creating a political stalemate. Reformist military officers, impatient for change, overthrew Alessandri in 1924. Only then was the impasse broken, but only temporarily.

The Aristocratic Republic: Peru

Thirty or 40 families, consisting of large landowners and businesspeople tied closely to the export sector, dominated Peruvian politics at the turn of the century. These upper-class families often were more familiar with Paris than with the Peruvian countryside. Racist, as well, they viewed Indians and castas as barbarians. Nonetheless, from the mid-1890s until 1919, Peru experienced an era of relative peace and stability, known as the "Aristocratic Republic." Like everywhere else, however, the inevitable downturns eventually brought discontent and unrest.

The War of the Pacific (1879–1883) left the nation's economy and politics in ruins. Exports fell sharply. Andrés Avelino Cáceres, a hero of the War of the Pacific, brought some order to Peruvian politics and government finances from 1885 to 1895, first as president and then through puppet rulers. His successor Nicolás de Piérola (1879–1881, 1895–1899) presided over a considerable measure of development, by expanding exports of agricultural commodities and minerals. However, increased agricultural exports caused landowners to expand their territory at the expense of individual and communal landholdings, which created widespread unrest.

During World War I, Peru experienced rebellions in the countryside, uprisings of Chinese immigrant laborers, and protests by university students. Social unrest exploded in 1919 with huge strikes in Lima and Callao. The presidential election in 1919 returned to power former president Augusto B. Leguía (1908–1912, 1919–1930), who ruled for the next 11 years. His solution to the nation's economic problems was an extensive program of public works construction that was devised to provide employment.

Dictatorship: Mexico

In Mexico, dictator General Porfirio Díaz ruled for 35 years (1876–1911), in conjunction with the landed upper class, the military, and a cadre of professional bureaucrats. Building his regime on a shrewd combination of consensus and coercion, Díaz wove an intricate web of alliances among once fragmented regional upper classes. He bound them together using the revenues generated by his export-based economic strategy. Don Porfirio, as he was called, was a masterful politician who was simultaneously admired and

LATIN AMERICAN LIVES

EVARISTO MADERO (1829–1911), PATRIARCH OF THE NORTH

In 1910 a 37-year-old rancher and industrialist from the northern state of Coahuila, Mexico, Francisco I. Madero, led a political movement against the long-term regime of Porfirio Díaz, setting off what was to become the Mexican Revolution. Defying enormous odds, he overthrew the dictator and became president. Not 2 years after his victory, he fell to assassins' bullets. The martyred Madero achieved perhaps the highest rank in the pantheon of Mexico's heroes.

Sometimes forgotten is the fact that Francisco I. Madero was the scion of one of the richest families in Mexico. The Madero, based in Parras, Coahuila, and Monterrey, Nuevo León, were at the fulcrum of the crucial network of northern entrepreneurs who were crucial to the Mexican economy from the mid-nineteenth century through the Porfiriato, Revolution, and postrevolution. Evaristo Madero, its patriarch, built a great empire through shrewd entrepreneurship and familial and political connections. In 1910, the *El Paso Morning Times* referred to him as a "Mexican Croesus." He had a personal fortune estimated at US$20,000,000. The Madero were important cattle raisers, cotton growers, and guayule producers in the Laguna region of Coahuila, and were involved with many industrial and banking concerns, among which was the largest Mexican-owned mineral smelting operation in the nation. Family members reportedly owned 7 million acres of land, with holdings in Chihuahua, Coahuila, Durango, San Luis Potosí, and Zacatecas.

Despite their vast economic resources, the Madero's influence in politics was limited by the patriarch's difficult relations with dictator Díaz and his representative in northeastern Mexico, General Bernardo Reyes. The family's ambiguous relations with Díaz at times thwarted its economic interests. Subsequently, family members stood at the forefront of local and statewide opposition to the national regime during the 1890s and the first decade of the twentieth century. Eventually, this led to Francisco I. Madero's seemingly quixotic campaign for the presidency in 1910.

The patriarch of the family, Evaristo, was born in the late 1820s. He began his career as a freighter along the recently drawn border between Mexico and the United States in the years after the war between the two nations. At first he operated mule and wagon trains in Coahuila, soon moving on to trading contraband silver bullion, wool, and hides across the border in return for dry goods and manufactures. Evaristo Madero earned a fortune in border trade, in particular generating enormous profits from Confederate cotton during the U.S. Civil War in the1860s, when the Union Navy blockaded southern ports, leaving only outlets through Mexico to export to markets in Europe. In his illicit trade, Madero benefited from the protection of Santiago Vidaurri, then the political boss of Nuevo León and Coahuila. Evaristo used the income from his mercantile business to buy land and expand into industry and banking. His first investments were a huge ranch in Coahuila that included an old winery, then a number of flour mills, and a textile mill. From the late 1860s to the 1880s he bought large haciendas in the Laguna region.

The Madero relied heavily on their family connections. Evaristo Madero had 18 children, and between them his children, grandchildren, and great grandchildren numbered 124. Many married into prominent families. His first marriage in 1847 brought him his brother-in-law and long-term business partner Antonio V. Hernández. Also important were his son Francisco's marriage to Mercedes González Treviño, a member of a family of important landowners and politicians in Nuevo León, and his daughters' marriages to Lorenzo González Treviño, Melchor Villarreal, and Viviano Villarreal. He also had marriage ties to prominent Monterrey families such as Zambrano and Sada Muguerza. With nine sons and numerous sons-in-law, he had a substantial pool of managers to succeed him.

Evaristo was governor of Coahuila from 1880 to 1884, when Porfirio Díaz, whose rebellion in 1876 he had opposed, allied with rivals to force him out. The Madero family retained local influence in Parras and continued to compete in state politics but was unable to reestablish itself at the top. Despite maintaining cordial relations with the científico faction within the national regime, the Madero found themselves badly disadvantaged by a series of decisions made by the old dictator during the first decade of the twentieth century. This quite likely led to considerable disgruntlement among family members toward Díaz and may very well have led to Evaristo's grandson's revolution. Evaristo died in 1911 before Francisco I. became president.

Questions for Discussion

Do you think that there was a link between the Madero family's exclusion from political power in Coahuila by Díaz and Francisco I. Madero's opposition to the regime? What is more important in causing revolutions, the desire for political access or for economic gain?

feared. He was a war hero, recognized as one of the commanders at Puebla, where Mexican troops won a great military victory against French invaders on May 5, 1862. (The *Cinco de Mayo,* or Fifth of May, is a national holiday in Mexico.) Díaz was often magnanimous in victory, when it was to his political advantage. He could be equally ruthless, however. When, early in his regime, a subordinate asked him what to do with captured rebels, Díaz told him to "kill them in cold blood." His rural police, the *Rurales,* kept order in the countryside. (One practice was to shoot prisoners, even those guilty of minor offenses, while allegedly trying to escape.)

During Díaz's rule, Mexico's economy grew spectacularly. Domestic peace and the end of foreign invasions combined with burgeoning markets for Mexican agricultural commodities and minerals and the inflow of international capital to cause unprecedented economic expansion. The Díaz government oversaw the investment of $1 billion in U.S. capital and a ninefold increase in trade from 1877 to 1911 and sponsored the construction of more than 10,000 miles of railroad.

Despite peace and prosperity, however, Mexico's economy and politics had a dark underside. As did other export economies, Mexico endured periodic booms and busts. There were downturns during the mid-1880s, the early 1890s, and from 1907 to 1909.

"The Liberal Party under the regime of Porfirio Diaz" (1910).

The booms brought prosperity, but the busts caused widespread suffering among the urban and rural working class. Economic depressions caused political disruptions by undermining the conditions of the emerging working and middle classes and by unbalancing the delicate system of political arrangements between Díaz and regional upper classes. Díaz's web of political alliances depended on his ability to reward cooperation with jobs, tax exemptions, subsidies for businesses, and other benefits. The economic downturn in 1907 allowed him insufficient resources to pay for cooperation. Ungrateful upper-class allies looked for opportunities to free themselves from the dictator.

While the economic crisis undermined his support among the upper classes, the countryside had reached the point of rebellion. Improved transportation and widened markets for agricultural commodities both in Mexico and abroad had sharply increased land values. Political officials and large landowners, particularly in the mid-1880s and in the decade after 1900, undertook to expropriate the lands of small owners and the communally held lands of Indian villages in order to expand both their landholdings and the pool of cheap, landless labor. As a result, there was an undercurrent of agrarian discontent throughout the dictatorship. This discontent evolved into crisis in 1907, when the economic downturn and the upper classes' land grabbing limited the alternative employment possibilities of landless people in rural areas. Previously, they had found jobs in the mines, the cities, and the United States, but the depression deprived them of these employment opportunities. The Díaz dictatorship also had eliminated elections to local offices by creating a system of appointed district leaders (*jefes políticos*). Some of these district bosses proved extraordinarily intrusive, meddling even in private matters. Not surprisingly, country people protested this loss of local autonomy.

Coinciding crises helped bring down the dictatorship after 1900. The most immediate was the furor over Díaz's succession. Díaz was 74 when he was reelected as president in 1904. His vice president, Ramón Corral, was given the post because he was one of the most unpopular officials in Mexico and was, therefore, no threat to Díaz. None of the obvious successors dared to show ambition, despite the fact that if Díaz was reelected again in 1910 at 80, few expected he would live out his term. The second crisis was the depression of 1907, which erased many of the gains of Díaz's economic miracle and ruined the businesses of the emerging middle class. The middle class had suffered discrimination in taxation, the courts, and the banking system under Díaz's regime, and this rampant unfairness was laid bare by the economic downturn. The last crisis was the squabbling among and eventual division of the upper classes. Enemies of the dictator, who had bided their time and been content to be bought off, saw an opportunity to even old scores. These combined crises left the urban and rural working classes with little to lose, the embryonic middle class falling back toward poverty, and the upper classes uninterested in supporting the dictator, at best, or quietly working against him, at worst. The oil that greased the wheels of the dictator's political arrangements evaporated. It was time to fight, and Díaz was ousted, as we shall see later.

MODERNIZATION AND RESISTANCE

The situations described above specifically caused the disintegration of the Mexican dictatorship, but similar conditions existed generally throughout Latin America during the early part of the twentieth century. The export boom presided over by the upper classes disguised inherently unfair societies everywhere, because the prosperity accrued to only a small minority. The new middle classes were extremely vulnerable to economic downturns and saw their modest gains erode during the depression following the turn of the century and the inflation of World War I. The mines and new factories paid pitiful wages and offered miserable working conditions for new migrants from the countryside and immigrants from abroad. Workers agitated not only for better compensation and working conditions but also against the regimentation that domestic and foreign employers tried to impose upon their daily lives. Meanwhile, rural people lost their lands and livelihoods to the forces of the export economy. Some migrated in search of better opportunities elsewhere, but others stayed where they were and revolted in an attempt to regain or retain their landholdings and their control over their daily lives. National leaders in a number of countries grappled with the question of how best to draw indigenous peoples into the new capitalist nation-state. Resistance then was inevitable in the face of the intrusion of the world market and national authorities.

Indigenous Peoples

Many Latin Americans of the upper class and urbanized middle classes regarded the indigenous population as a serious impediment to national progress. Positivists in Mexico shared this view, and the Díaz regime alternated between ignoring and trying to exterminate indigenous peoples. Apaches in the north of Mexico were at times subject to bounties on their scalps. Conversely, some of the victorious factions in the revolution that overthrew Díaz adopted a conscious policy of glorifying the nation's indigenous heritage. Archaeologists and historians rediscovered the great cultures that had existed in Latin America before the arrival of the Europeans, while the brilliant muralists of the 1920s and 1930s illuminated the Indian past.

The place of indigenous peoples also provoked much discussion in Peru, where the humiliating defeat in the War of the Pacific caused a reevaluation of the nation's priorities and policies. Peruvian intellectuals concluded that Indians required "reform." Fired by the 1889 novel *Aves sin nido* by Clorinda Matto de Turner, which exposed the harsh exploitation endured by Indians in a small Andean town, a new movement, *indigenismo,* resolved to rediscover Indian Peru. U.S. archaeologists rediscovered Machu Picchu, the long-lost Incan city, further fueling interest in pre-European Peru. After World War I, the indigenismo movement shifted from willingness to study Indians to a more revolutionary stance. A few envisioned a new nationalism that glorified the Indian past. A second strain of indigenismo arose from José Carlos Mariátegui, the noted Marxist intellectual, who tied indigenismo to socialism. He advocated radical land reform to end the centuries-old oppression of Indians by the hacienda system.

Resistance in the Countryside

Not everyone accepted the notion that modernization and economic development were good, as is illustrated by the Latin Americans who threw stones at passing railroad cars. The first, and perhaps most crucial, source of opposition to modernization arose in the countryside. During the first half of the nineteenth century, political disruptions and inadequate transportation kept land values down. As we observed in Chapter 9, after mid-century, Liberals, following the models of England and the United States, attempted to create a class of small farmers that they believed would form the basis for both capitalism and democracy. Their efforts to break up the landholdings of the Catholic Church and communal indigenous villages backfired, however, because politicians and large landowners inevitably ended up with much of this property. A number of nations, notably Argentina and Mexico, gave away vast tracts of public lands to the politically well connected, which concentrated landholding even further.

Unlike the peaceful, political attempt to create social equity described above, country people sometimes violently resisted modernization. Two such movements erupted in Brazil. The first occurred in Canudos, an estate in the northern part of the state of Bahia, where Antônio Conselheiro and his followers set up a community in 1893. Located deep in the backlands, it grew into a considerable city of 20,000 to 30,000 people. The local upper class—and eventually the national government—viewed Canudos as a threat. Several military expeditions were sent to Canudos in an effort to oust the residents and break up the community, but the residents defeated the soldiers. Finally, in October of 1897, the federal army destroyed the city and slaughtered its last 5000 residents. The events were made famous by the book *Rebellion in the Backlands* by Euclídes da Cunha. Another movement, the *Contesdado*, took place in the border area between the states of Paraná and Santa Catarina in southern Brazil. The rebellion began in 1911, led by José María, who his followers regarded as a saint. The processes of modernization in rural and urban areas had alienated many of the people who joined the movement, including small farmers who had been thrown off their lands as railroads spread across the country and railroad workers who were abandoned to unemployment when their contracts expired. Despite the deaths of their leaders, including José María, rebels continued to fight until late 1915. Meanwhile, widespread banditry swept Brazil during the period of the Canudos and Contesdado rebellions. Many of the poor dark-skinned people who made up the majority of the rural population had lost their lands or ended up on the wrong side of local political disputes, and they filled the bandits' ranks, having few other options.

The Mexican Revolution

Nowhere was the impact of the rapidly developing export economy dominated by foreign investors clearer than in Mexico, where a diverse coalition of profoundly discontented people waged a revolution of unprecedented duration and cost. In 1910, a multiclass alliance of dissidents from the upper class, middle-class people who had suffered financial ruin in the depression of 1907, country people whose lands the upper class had expropriated, and unemployed workers rallied around Francisco I. Madero, a disaffected, wealthy landowner, who toppled Porfirio Díaz from power. As we have learned, the depression of 1907, the uncertainty of succession, and the deteriorating state of the army and police had badly weakened the Díaz regime. In the spring of 1911, the coalition ousted Díaz, who prudently embarked on a comfortable retirement in Paris, never to return to Mexico. But the consensus among Madero's followers soon crumbled as landowners and landless country people clashed over land reform and the middle and lower classes disagreed over the importance of property rights. Dormant regionalism, suppressed temporarily by Díaz, reawakened as well.

In 1913, supporters of Díaz took advantage of the disintegration of the revolutionary coalition and the resurgence of regionalism to briefly reestablish the old regime without Díaz. General Victoriano Huerta, Madero's most important military commander, took over the reins of the counterrevolutionary movement, betraying Madero and ordering his execution. Others then formed a loose partnership of revolutionary movements to defeat Huerta in 1914. Their leaders included Venustiano Carranza, another alienated northern landowner; Pancho Villa, a bandit-businessman from Chihuahua (also in the north); and Emiliano Zapata, a village leader from the state of Morelos (just south of Mexico City). This alliance did not last even as long as Madero's. Carranza, representing the dissident landowners, clashed with the *Zapatistas* (followers of Zapata) who advocated wide-ranging land reform. Villa and Carranza disliked each other intensely. Villa and Zapata allied since they both stood for the lower classes. The three factions set upon each other in a brutal civil war that lasted until 1917. In those 3 years, there was virtually no functioning government in Mexico.

By 1917, however, Carranza emerged triumphant with the brilliant assistance of his best general, Álvaro Obregón, another northerner. Carranza owed much of his victory to his ability to win over the working class and some rural people with promises (later unfulfilled) of reforms. Carranza also appealed to members of the middle class because he defended private property rights and offered political patronage. The revolutionaries promulgated the Constitution of 1917, which provided for extensive land reform, workers' rights, and other wide-reaching reforms. Carranza then split with Obregón over the extent to which the government would implement the provisions of the constitution. Obregón, who favored reforms, overthrew Carranza in 1920 and made himself president. Meanwhile, Zapata and Villa continued guerrilla warfare until 1919 and 1920, respectively. Mexico's bloody struggle had lasted a decade and cost the lives of between 1 and 2 million people. The revolution also devastated the nation's economy. It would be well into the 1930s before most economic indicators recovered to 1910 levels.

CONCLUSION

In 1920, middle-aged and elderly Latin Americans could look back on the enormous changes that had occurred in their lifetimes. Those who lived in the cities saw signs of "progress" all around them—streetcars, automobiles, modern office buildings, banks, and factories. In the more fashionable parts of towns, they could marvel at the lavish homes and other symbols of the upper classes' conspicuous consumption. More people could read and write than ever before. Outside the cities, railroads crisscrossed the countryside, although they were concentrated along routes that served the new export economies. Large estates and modern farm machinery produced crops for sale in nearby cities and overseas markets (while small farmers, however, found it increasingly hard to produce the subsistence crops they needed to support themselves and their families).

With the notable exception of Mexicans, this generation of Latin Americans had seen fewer wars than their parents or grandparents, but only the most naïve among them would have predicted that this peace would last indefinitely. Some of them had witnessed massive strikes by urban workers in the turbulent aftermath of World War I.

How Historians Understand   WHY DO PEOPLE REBEL?

The era from 1880 to 1920 was a tumultuous one for Latin America. Emergent working and middle classes jostled for a place in politics, economy, and society. Upper classes struggled to maintain their positions. Country people sought a return of the protection they had enjoyed under the Catholic monarchs of the Iberian empires. Technological innovations disrupted society at all levels. The international movement of ideas, people, and money reinvented the ways that men and women worked, lived, and interacted. Yet, despite all these upheavals and rapid changes, only in one country, Mexico, did the people rise up in revolution. It is an enduring and important question in Latin American history as to why only the Mexican the lower and middle classes allied to destroy the old regime.

Most people in Latin America had lived with a (sometimes considerable) degree of day-to-day oppression. The daily struggle to subsist consumed their days; they had little time or energy to plan, let alone carry out, a rebellion. At some points in history, however, individuals have ignored survival in order to rise up against their oppressors (though such occurrences are rare). Historians have almost universally failed to discern what causes such rebels to risk everything.

In the case of the Mexican Revolution, as in any social revolt, historians and sociologists have numerous questions: Why did some groups or individuals rebel and

Ordinary people from central and southern Mexico rose up against Porfirio Díaz in 1910.

others did not? Why did some country people, such as permanent residents on the haciendas, remain uninvolved, while northern small landowners led the overthrow of Porfirio Díaz? Why did some large land-owning families join the revolution, while others fought it to the death?

Most difficult to answer, perhaps, is the question of why individuals participated in uprisings, because very few sources exist to give scholars insight into individuals' motivations. Historians researching the Mexican Revolution have compiled many oral interviews and discovered criminal court records, both of which reveal personal stories. But these sources are not available for all regions or eras.

Of all the groups that rose in rebellion against Díaz in 1910, the most elusive have been country people. Everyone concedes that rural people were central to the Mexican Revolution, but there is disagreement as to why exactly they revolted. Did country people fight to restore their lost lands? Did they resist the encroachments of centralized government on their local prerogatives? Do people risk their lives for land or religion or local autonomy? It is extremely difficult for twenty-first–century historians to penetrate the worldview of late nineteenth-century rural dwellers.

Historians and social scientists have formulated various theories, based on such factors as rising expectations, class conflict, moral economy, and mob behavior, to try to understand why people rebel. The paucity of evidence, however, has made it impossible for scholars to validate or confirm any of these theories of motivation. Analysts have tried to circumvent the lack of direct evidence (also called *primary sources*, such as accounts of participants' actual words) by examining the possible grievances, the economic circumstances, and the political crises that might have alchemized discontent into revolution. Thus, historians build circumstantial cases without proof of causality.

Perhaps the most convincing and plausible attempts to understand the mental and emotional states of various revolutionaries have appeared in the works of fiction written during and after the Mexican Revolution. The works of such authors as Mariano Azuela (*The Underdogs*), Martín Luis Guzmán (*The Eagle and the Serpent*), and Carlos Fuentes (*The Death of Artemio Cruz*) give insights into the rebels' reality through the imagined conversations and thoughts of their characters. The novelists often portray the revolutionaries as petty, greedy, and murderous, with few heroes among them. (For instance, Azuela's Demetrio Macías was less than admirable.)

How, then, do historians obtain an accurate picture of the revolutionaries and their motivations? It is unlikely that we ever can: Pieces of the puzzle will always be missing.

Questions for Discussion

Without benefit of an extensive written record to which to refer, how do you think historians can understand the thinking of working-class and country people? How can the twenty-first–century historian "get into the heads" of people who lived decades, even centuries, in the past?

Rural discontent was in evidence everywhere as well. Intellectuals and some political figures began to carve out a more active role for indigenous peoples, and women began to demand changes in the home, the legal system, and society as a whole. In Chapter 12, we shall see how Latin Americans met these and other serious challenges in the coming decades.

LEARNING MORE ABOUT LATIN AMERICANS

Azuela, Mariano. *The Underdogs*. Trans. Frederick H. Fornoff (Prospect Herights, IL: Waveland Press, 2002).

Dore, Elizabeth, and Maxine Molyneux, eds. *Hidden Histories of Gender and the State in Latin America* (Durham, NC: Duke University Press, 2000). Essays on women, the state, and society.

Gwynne, Robert N., and Cristobal Kay, eds. *Latin America Transformed: Globalization and Modernity*, 2nd ed. (New York: Arnold, 2004). The impact of vast change in the twentieth century.

Haber, Stephen, ed. *How Latin America Fell Behind: Essays on the Economic Histories of Brazil and Mexico, 1800–1914* (Stanford, CA: Stanford University Press, 1997). Essays that attempt to account for the lack of Latin American economic development.

Hart, John Mason. *Revolutionary Mexico: The Coming and Process of the Mexican Revolution* (Berkeley, CA: University of California Press, 1987).

Knight, Alan. *The Mexican Revolution*. 2 vols. (Durham, NC: Duke University Press, 1994). The best history of the Revolution in English.

Lavrín, Asunción. *Women, Feminism, and Social Change: Argentina, Chile, and Uruguay, 1890–1940* (Lincoln, NE: University of Nebraska Press, 1995). Traces the feminist movement in the Southern Cone.

Poniatowska, Elena. *Las Soldaderas: Women of the Mexican Revolution* (El Paso, TX: Cinco Punto Press, 2006).

Wasserman, Mark. *Everyday Life and Politics in Nineteenth Century Mexico: Men, Women, and War* (Albuquerque, NM: University of New Mexico Press, 2000).

Weaver, Frederick Stirton. *Latin America in the World Economy* (Boulder, CO: Westview Press, 2000). An overview of the role of external economic factors in Latin American economic development.

12

BETWEEN REVOLUTIONS:
THE NEW POLITICS OF CLASS AND THE ECONOMIES OF IMPORT SUBSTITUTION INDUSTRIALIZATION, 1920–1959

THE ERA FRAMED by the end of the Mexican Revolution (1910–1920) and the beginning of the Cuban Revolution (1959) continued, augmented, and refocused the conflicts and dilemmas of Latin America's politics and economy, which emerged from the transformations experienced in the preceding four decades. Battered by recurring crises—two world wars and a debilitating depression—and the exigencies of the superpower confrontation we know as the Cold War, Latin America struggled to answer the questions raised at independence and discussed in Chapter 9: Who was to govern (and for whom) and how were they to govern? Latin American upper classes fiercely resisted the strident demands of the middle and urban working classes, whose rise we studied in Chapter 11. Refurbished and reformed militaries established themselves as crucial participants in politics, mostly as conservatives, but on occasion as moderate and even radical advocates of social justice. For the most part, however, the upper classes allied with the military against labor organizations and popularly based political parties, the primary advocates of the lower classes. Armed forces anointed themselves as the ultimate arbiters of civil society, intervening periodically when differing versions of democracy faltered.

The profound changes brought about by urbanization and incipient industrialization altered relationships not only between classes but also between men and women. Women entered the public political and economic arenas, forcing readjustments to traditional patriarchy. Old notions of women's role, sexuality, and honor underwent important transformations. During this period, women fought for and eventually won suffrage.

Constant battles between moderates and hard-liners in the upper classes and militaries were reflected in the rise and fall of democracy and dictatorship. Many members of the upper classes and allied military officers realized the necessity of altering the economic and political systems, at least so as to minimally satisfy the demands of the lower and middle classes for better living and working conditions and for electoral and economic fairness. Compromise was difficult because the ruling classes of most nations were no longer homogeneous, making consensus virtually unattainable, and intransigent elements of the upper class—military alliance were unwilling to make concessions. The most notable divisions arose because export economies had created a brash new class of industrialists and entrepreneurs whose interests were not always in harmony with the landowning class. The militaries were divided as well, usually between old-line upper-class senior officers and up-and-coming middle-class junior officers.

The lower classes strove for their voice in politics and the economy by joining labor unions, though these mostly served skilled workers. With expanded male suffrage, workers were valuable allies for rival middle- and upper-class political parties. Left political groups, such as the Socialists and Communists, experienced only modest success. With the exception of the brief Socialist Republic proclaimed in Chile in 1932 and Chile's and Cuba's popular front (alliances of Left and center political parties) governments of the late 1930s and early 1940s, none of the leftist parties ever shared national power. The working class more commonly attached itself to a rising political leader, such as Colonel Juan Perón (1946–1955, 1974–1976) in Argentina, who traded concessions, such as wage increases, for support. A number of other democratic leaders and dictators also relied on the support of the middle and lower classes. Thus, populism, comprised of cross-class alliances brought together by a charismatic leader advocating social reform, dominated the politics of the era.

The struggle for control over their everyday lives continued to be at the center of lower-class demands. Although the increasing migration of people to the cities muted somewhat the demands for local autonomy in the countryside, they remained at the core of Mexican politics into the 1940s (and perhaps longer). The strength of regionalism forced even dictators like Juan Perón in Argentina and Getúlio Vargas in Brazil to ally with provincial and state political bosses, who obtained the support of the people of the countryside by defending local customs and traditions.

At the same time, important sectors of the national ruling classes came to realize that they could not obtain their goals of modernization without national governments becoming more active in the economy. The prolonged economic crisis of the 1930s strengthened and expanded governments' role. Concerned with the industrial base of national security, the new industrialists and organized labor joined elements of the military to institute extensive tariff protection for domestic manufacturing. The resulting resurgent drive for modernization became known as import substitution industrialization.

Nonetheless, exports fueled the economies of Latin American nations throughout all the crises. The plight of the region depended on the booms and busts of the international markets for agricultural commodities and minerals. Political instability or stability and the choice between dictatorship and democracy often (though not always) derived from the status of the economies of the individual nations.

THREE CRISES AND THE BEGINNINGS OF INTENSIFIED GOVERNMENT INVOLVEMENT IN THE ECONOMY, 1920–1945

As we observed in Chapter 11, the export boom from the 1870s to the 1910s stimulated industrialization, mainly in the form of processing agricultural commodities. The boom ended after 1920, however, when three great crises—the two world wars and the Great Depression—disrupted international trade and capital markets for prolonged periods (1914–1919, 1929–1941, and 1939–1945). Latin American upper classes reassessed their nations' reliance on exporting commodities and importing consumer goods.

The Aftermath of World War I

World War I revealed the extreme uncertainties and costs of the booms and busts associated with economic reliance on exports. The war should have stimulated exports and benefited the region, as European countries placed their economies on a wartime footing. Instead, the war exposed Latin America's vulnerability to temporary stoppages in the flow of goods and capital back and forth across the Atlantic Ocean. During the early part of the war, the demand for Latin American commodities plummeted. Government revenues dropped sharply, which led to government deficits. When the demand for strategic materials finally rose, other factors, such as the rising cost of imports, mitigated the benefits. Latin American exports earned high prices, but only for a short period.

This brief boom proved detrimental to Latin American agriculture in the long term, because many farmers tried to respond to the temporary increase in demand by borrowing money to increase the amount of land under cultivation. When Europe recovered its agricultural capacity and the rest of the world regained access to European markets, these farmers faced ruin. The most startling case of this agricultural boom and bust was the Cuban "Dance of the Millions." In 2 years, sugar prices soared from 4 cents to more than 20 cents a pound, only to plunge to prices even lower than where they had begun. In anticipation of booming demand and prices, Cuban sugar growers greatly expanded landholdings and production, only to confront disaster when prices dropped.

With competition from abroad cut off by the war, domestic manufacturing seemingly had unprecedented opportunities. Unfortunately, machinery and capital

TIMELINE

1914–1918
World War I

1919–1930
Augusto B. Leguía, dictator of Peru

1924
Young military officers overthrow President Arturo Alessandri in Chile

1929–1941
Great Depression

1933
Cuban Revolution ousts dictator Gerardo Machado

1937
Getúlio Vargas overturns his own government and establishes the Estado Novo

1938
Lázaro Cárdenas expropriates foreign oil companies in Mexico

1939–1945
World War II

1946
Juan Perón elected president of Argentina

1952
Fulgencio Batista returns to Cuba as dictator

were not available. The United States furnished an alternative market, but during the war it could not supply Latin America with all the needed industrial equipment, materials, and capital.

Despite the lessons of the world war and the nasty, though brief, depression in 1920 and 1921, Latin American economies remained export oriented throughout the decade. Unfortunately, overall international trade grew far more slowly than it had in the previous decades. From 1913 to 1929, the volume of trade rose an average of only 1 percent per year. To make matters worse, Latin American nations confronted harsh postwar competition for this stagnant global market. It was nearly impossible to increase market shares of primary commodities because there were other, often cheaper, producers elsewhere. Latin American nations were already operating at high efficiency, so they could not significantly decrease costs.

Circumstances were right for the development of modern manufacturing. Urbanization had brought together a relatively more affluent population that demanded consumer goods. The expanding middle and laboring classes furnished a growing market. Improved transportation and communications expanded the market to the countryside. Domestic manufacturing, however, could not compete successfully against its external rivals unless protected by government. Internal markets were simply too small to obtain economies of scale.

The Great Depression

As the 1930s began, Latin American economies remained highly concentrated on a few export commodities sent to a handful of markets. For 10 countries (Bolivia, Brazil, Colombia, Cuba, the Dominican Republic, El Salvador, Honduras, Guatemala, Nicaragua, and Venezuela), one product in each accounted for at least 50 percent of the exports. Four nations, the United States, Great Britain, Germany, and France, provided 70 percent of the trade. This concentration put the region in serious jeopardy when the century's worst economic crisis hit.

The worldwide Great Depression wrecked havoc with Latin American economies. Between 1928 and 1932, export prices tumbled by more than half in 10 countries. Mineral producers in Bolivia, Chile, and Mexico were hit the worst, as both unit volume and prices declined. Argentina's exports fell from about $1.5 billion in 1929 to $561 million in 1932. The Cuban sugar industry was all but ruined.

Recovery from the depression began between 1931 and 1932. The fastest recoveries, where the gross domestic product (GDP) rose 50 percent or more from 1931 to 1939, took place in Brazil, Mexico, Chile, Cuba, Peru, Venezuela, Costa Rica, and Guatemala. Argentina, Colombia, and El Salvador came back more slowly, with their GDPs increasing 20 percent in these years. The countries worst off were Honduras, Nicaragua, Uruguay, Paraguay, and Panama. Real GDP in Colombia exceeded its predepression level in 1932. The same was true for Brazil in 1933, Mexico in 1934, and Argentina, El Salvador, and Guatemala in 1935, while Chile and Cuba, where the depression was most severe, recovered later in the decade. Honduras, solely dependent on bananas, did not regain its

Slice of Life   COLOMBIAN COFFEE FARM IN 1925

COFFEE IS PRODUCED in two distinct ways: on plantations (fazenda in Brazil, *finca* or hacienda elsewhere) and on small, family-operated farms. Two nations, Costa Rica and Colombia, are particularly known for the latter. Between 1920 and 1950, small producers came to dominate Colombian coffee production. Small holdings required, as one historian observed, a "lifetime struggle in which ingenuity, hard work, and a good measure of luck . . ." were crucial elements.

The small operators did not always own their own property. On the huge plantations in the older coffee regions, permanent workers (*arrendatarios*) obtained the right to farm a small parcel on which they grew corn, yucca, plantains, and sugarcane and raised fowl or livestock. In return for the use of the land, the worker undertook an obligation to labor ranging from a few days to nearly a whole month on the plantation, depending on the size and quality of his plot. The coffee estates also employed temporary workers, small farmers from other areas, contracted for harvest and paid according to the amount of coffee beans they picked. Temporary labor weeded the groves as well. A third type of worker, the *colono*, contracted to open up new lands for coffee production, clearing the land, planting new trees, and caring for them for 4 years. The colono then sold the trees to the plantation owner and renounced all rights to the land. The colono also cultivated food crops between the trees for family subsistence.

In the newer coffee regions, small- and medium-sized family farms predominated, the latter operated by sharecroppers or renters. The sharecroppers received half the harvest in return for caring for the trees and processing the beans. They received only one-third, however, if they did not dry and depulp the beans. Although some medium-sized farms were worked with the help of sharecroppers, these operations mostly relied on family labor.

Small farmers had to adapt to the environment and the family's limited resources. The topography of Costa Rica and Colombia made it impossible to use mechanized machinery, so farmers used axes and fire to clear the land and hoes to weed it. Colombian farmers planted their crops in vertical rows on the severely steep slopes so they could weed standing upright. (Weeding bent over is excruciating work.) The farmers planted using a *barretón,* a heavy wedge-shaped implement with an iron tip and a long, straight wood handle that the farmer poked into the soil. The farmer then placed corn or a coffee seedling into the resulting hole in the ground. Clearing was done with a *peinilla* or *machete*. They planted food crops between the rows of coffee trees not only to provide sustenance for themselves but also to help prevent erosion. Shade trees, such as plantain, also were planted to inhibit erosion and provide leaves that were used as fertilizer for the coffee trees. Shade also slowed the growth and ripening of the coffee beans, so that they matured at the proper pace. Pigs and fowl wandered in the fields, eliminating insects and supplying fertilizer. Family farms grew many crops, but the smallest farms concentrated on subsistence staples such as plantains, bananas, manioc, corn, and beans. Corn was grown on the least fertile land.

The work of growing coffee was hard and long. Men usually did the heavy work of clearing, planting, and weeding. Women and children helped with the harvest, including depulping, washing, fermenting, drying, and selecting. Once this process was complete, women and children were responsible for putting the coffee beans into burlap sacks and transporting the sacks by mule or horse, on difficult trails, to coffee towns, where the coffee was sold to merchants and traders.

Farm families lived simply. Corn, eaten in soups and bread, was the staple of their diet. It also was fed to the fowl and pigs, which, in turn, were eaten by the family on special occasions. The usual meal was soup and then some kind of starch with small bits of salted beef or pork purchased in town. The farmers also bought most of their vegetables. Many farmers grew citrus and mango trees and, in the warmer zones, sugarcane. From this sugarcane, they produced brown sugar cakes called *panelas* and the molasses that was later fermented and distilled to yield *aguardienté* or rum. These provided sweets and alcoholic beverages.

To survive, the families had to be frugal and self-sufficient. They usually produced most of what they needed, except for some of the men's clothing (pants, shoes, and boots). Poor children wore little or no clothing. The women made baskets, mattresses, and candles.

Small-farm coffee growers lived in houses consisting of bamboo walls, thatch roofs, and dirt floors. Washing was done in local rivers and streams. Human waste was dropped in the fields; this unsanitary practice fouled water supplies and resulted in the transmission of intestinal diseases, including intestinal parasites, which were common.

In Colombia, small producers engaged in constant, often violent, competition with their neighbors. The prevalent *clientelist* politics, in which country people owed allegiance to local political bosses, usually powerful landowners, forced them to participate in partisan wars, such as *La Violencia*. It had been the hope of Latin American liberal politicians during the nineteenth and twentieth centuries that small farmers would form the bedrock of a democratic society, as they had in some parts of Europe and the United States. In Colombia, however, they were at the heart of conflict.

Questions for Discussion

Compare the lives of Colombian coffee farmers with other small farmers, such as cassava growers in Brazil. Why was violence so integral a part of conditions in the countryside? Was violence a result of the local loss of autonomy?

precrisis GDP until 1945. The recovery of external trade in the 1930s was at least partly the result of a shift away from markets in Great Britain and the United States to those in Germany, Italy, and Japan.

The depression acted much like World War I in that it impeded the flow of imports to Latin America. But again, manufacturing did not necessarily flourish. Low productivity, the result of shortages of cheap power, the lack of skilled labor, the lack of credit, obsolete machinery, and overprotection (tariffs that were too high), hindered industrial development. The depression also shut off the flow of capital into the region from Europe and the United States. The only way for Latin American countries to modernize, therefore, was through some form of government intervention. National governments established agencies such as CORFO (Chilean National Development Corporation) in Chile to foster industrialization that the private sector was unable or unwilling to undertake.

World War II

World War II hit Latin America harder than the depression and previous world war. The British market shrunk when it went on war footing, and the British blockade of Europe cut off recently expanding continental European markets. U.S. programs such as Lend-Lease and the Export-Import Bank never replaced the shortfall in either finance or commerce. Some of the lost market was made up with inter–Latin American trade.

The drop in U.S. and European imports after 1939 should have provided impetus for further Latin American industrialization, but wartime inflation eroded real wages and purchasing power. Nonetheless, industrialization expanded in several nations. The United States fostered industry by supplying technical assistance. Governments established nonconsumer industries, such as the Volta Redonda steel works in Brazil. Latin American nations accumulated tremendous reserves from the sale of exports during the war, which led to inflation. Very few workers' wages and middle-class salaries could maintain their real earnings in the face of rising prices. Those who had assets, on the other hand, saw them appreciate. This increase in the cost of living had created social unrest by the end of the war.

PEACETIME ECONOMIES

Peacetime solved few of the region's problems. First, as in the aftermath of the World War I, Latin America suffered from the decline of U.S. purchases of primary products and the elimination of the cooperative mechanisms for funneling technical assistance and capital into Latin America. Second, to make matters worse, the inter–Latin American markets gained during the war were lost as cheaper European and U.S. products flooded Latin America. Latin American nations were further disadvantaged because their governments did not devalue their currencies, making their exports more expensive abroad. Third, the United States, confronted by the threat of Soviet communism, turned its attention to rebuilding Europe, so U.S. government resources were no longer available, and Latin America had to rely on insufficient private sector capital investment. Fourth, slow European recovery (until the advent of the Marshall Plan for European recovery in 1948) limited potential markets. (The outbreak of the Korean War (1950–1954) sent prices up again, but only briefly.) Fifth, Latin American nations faced a dilemma as to how to spend the large foreign exchange reserves they had built up during the war before those reserves were eroded by inflation. Some, like Argentina, repaid external debt. Argentina also purchased its foreign-owned railroads. Mostly, however, Latin American governments spent the reserves, setting off a wave of inflation.

Facing dismal market opportunities and with only limited resources available from abroad, Latin America turned inward in the late 1940s. Most governments instituted tight restrictions on imports, both to end the spending spree and to protect domestic manufacturing. Postwar depression in Europe erased traditional markets with no prospects for quick recovery. Latin America shared only minimally in the vast postwar expansion of international trade. The growing consensus among government officials and intellectuals was that Latin America could no longer rely on the export model. Some nations sought to diversify their exports, others adopted the policies of import substitution industrialization (ISI), and another, smaller, group attempted both. These goals proved illusive. In the most advanced countries (Argentina, Brazil, Chile, Colombia, Mexico, and Uruguay), the easiest steps toward industrialization were already taken. The next stage was to be far more demanding in terms of capital and technology. Domestic enterprise was unable or unwilling to risk capital. This left the field open to either multinational corporations (which were eager to enter protected markets) or state-owned companies.

Unfortunately, the ISI strategy for development was critically flawed. Domestic manufacturers were hard pressed to compete with multinational companies, because the former were so highly protected by tariffs that they were extremely inefficient. To make matters worse, the small size of domestic markets meant there were no economies of scale. Often, domestic manufacturers operated at less-than-full capacity. They could not compete outside their home countries. Moreover, industrialization was itself import intensive; it needed capital goods available only from abroad. Foreign exchange paid for technology, royalties, licenses, and profits, creating a further drain of scarce capital. With the exceptions of Brazil and Mexico, the 1950s were a time of economic stagnation in the region. Meanwhile, the developed nations were on the path to unprecedented prosperity, leaving Latin America behind.

DICTATORS AND POPULISTS

The Social Question remained preeminent in Latin American politics throughout the years of world wars and economic crises. The constant conflict and negotiation among the upper, middle, and lower classes (at least the organized elements) and between genders defined political parameters. The region's nations alternated between limited democracy and dictatorship, for the most part, but not always, in correlation with the booms and busts of the world market. Good times allowed democracy to function; bad times increased conflict between classes and led to the imposition of coercive governments by the upper class allied with the military.

During the 1920s a wave of popularly elected leaders prepared to make concessions to the new aspiring classes and the changing circumstances of women. Unfortunately, both Hipólito Yrigoyen, the head of the Radical Party in Argentina, and Arturo Alessandri in Chile eventually fell victim to military coups. Augusto B. Leguía in Peru and Gerardo Machado in Cuba turned from populism to dictatorship when economic depression eroded their support.

The 1920s and 1930s were troubling times for the traditional social order. The upper and, to some extent, the middle classes feared their societies were coming apart as challenges by the lower classes increased. Perhaps the greatest uncertainties evolved from the transformation of women's roles. Women worked in visible urban settings in factories and offices. They organized and staged strikes. The new "free" woman— sexually active, cigarette smoking—was not the reassuringly pliant, passive mother of old. As in the case of those who were agitating for the improvement of working- and middle-class conditions, however, feminists found it difficult to obtain their goals in the face of resistance from the male hierarchies that composed the government and religious and financial establishments. Feminists' major objective, to obtain equality in law, was not achieved until the 1930s, and suffrage (the right to vote) took even longer.

E' coisa certa e patente
Que toda "élite,, elegante
Adopta unanimamente
O "Guaraná Espumante,,;

E não contente com isso,
A gente chic se mata
Para gosar o feitiço
Dos finos bonbons do "Lacta,,.

Modern women in Brazil.

Women's organizations received assistance from liberal and populist political parties. A handful of liberals viewed changing laws to reflect women's new roles to be part of the modernization process crucial to societal development. Women were active participants in the multifaceted campaigns for social reform all over the region. They sought not only the right to vote but also better working, sanitary, and health conditions for everyone. As Latin American governments haltingly involved themselves in public welfare, women made these activities their own as social workers and teachers.

In both Argentina and Peru, the upper classes, through populist leaders Yrigoyen and Leguía, shared power with the middle class. As long as the export economy stayed strong and the national government did not attempt far-reaching reforms, this tension-filled alliance held. The Great Depression of the 1930s, however, put the upper and middle classes into competition for rapidly shrinking resources. Ultimately, the upper classes used coercion (by the police, thugs, or the military) to maintain their status. In Chile, politicians could not reach consensus about the Social Question. As a result, the younger elements of the military twice intervened to force reforms that would improve conditions for the middle and lower classes.

The 1920s

In Argentina, the Radical Party alliance between the middle class and elements of the landowning upper class dominated the country's politics during the 1920s. A major accomplishment was the 1926 enactment of the law of women's civil rights, which provided that women had all the rights of men, thereby removing gender limits to the exercise of all civil functions (but, crucially, not the vote). Heavily reliant on government patronage to bolster their support, the Radicals required prosperity to generate the revenues to pay for their strategy. The economic downturn that began in 1928, however, sharply curtailed the ability of the Radicals to provide patronage employment for their followers. In September 1930, the military, overthrew Yrigoyen, who had won a second term in 1928.

Yrigoyen's case clearly illustrates that populist politics succeeded only when government revenues were sufficient to fund patronage and that the precarious alliance between the upper and middle classes disintegrated rapidly when the two groups had to compete for scarce resources or when their interests clashed. Their ties, forged from their mutual fear of the lower classes, proved unstable. When there was conflict, the side with the strongest links to the armed services, most often the upper classes, won out.

Peruvian politicians, like Argentina's Radicals, sought to find answers to the Social Question by appealing to the middle class and by adopting a vast program of patronage. Former president Augusto B. Leguía (1908–1912, 1919–1930) returned from exile in 1919 to topple the "Aristocratic Republic." With strong backing from middle- and lower-class voters, he proclaimed *La Patria Nueva* (the new fatherland). He proposed a stronger interventionist state, which would modernize and grow the economy, financed by foreign investment and increased exports. The center of his administration was a massive program of public works. He rebuilt Lima into a beautiful modern city and constructed nearly 10,000 miles of roads. Leguía's plan was successful until 1930, when the depression sharply limited the funds available.

Leguía focused on the middle class and country people as his bases of support. To appeal to the former, he vastly expanded the government bureaucracy and the educational system, quadrupling the number of public employees and doubling the number of students. Leguía took advantage of growing unrest in the Indian countryside, where indigenous peoples and landlords were at bitter odds, to undermine landlords whom the president regarded as impediments to his drive to centralize power. The end of Leguía's efforts to forge an alliance with country people came when the army and local authorities killed 2000 small farmers and landless residents during two uprisings in 1923. Like Yrigoyen and so many after him, Leguía learned that populism was only as successful as its economic program. Leguía could not survive the crisis of the depression. He was ousted in August 1930.

The Chilean upper classes, unlike some of their counterparts in Argentina and Peru, steadfastly refused concessions to the middle and lower classes. As a result, Chile's Parliamentary Republic (1891–1920) simply did not work. Social unrest escalated as the government was unable to ameliorate the economic crisis and hardship brought on by the World War I. Strikes tore apart the northern nitrate region. Out of the turmoil of the late 1910s rose veteran politician Arturo Alessandri Palma. Drawing support from the working class, promising sweeping reforms, and professing an interest in women's issues, Alessandri won the presidential election of 1920. For 4 years, however, he was unable to overcome congressional opposition to his program. Impatient junior officers, led by Major Carlos Ibáñez del Campo and Major Marmaduke Grove Vallejo, seized the government in 1924. In 1925, their administration decreed a law that extended the property rights of married women; they also penned a new constitution that restored strong presidential rule (lost in the 1890 civil war). Ibáñez took office as president in 1927, and his foreign loan–financed spending spree brought a measure of prosperity. The impact of the Great Depression, however, was especially harsh in Chile, which was heavily dependent on mining exports. Massive street demonstrations forced Ibáñez to resign in mid-1931.

In Cuba, populism also evolved into dictatorship in response to the depression. The 1920s were plagued by the terrible collapse of sugar prices in 1920, and a two-decade-old tradition of ineffective, corrupt government, exacerbated by the Platt Amendment to the Cuban Constitution of 1902, which had installed the United States as the island's protector. Gerardo Machado became president in 1925. Like other populists he initiated a massive foreign loan–financed public works program. But in 1929, sugar and tobacco prices crashed, and the ensuing crisis wore away Machado's popularity. His regime thereafter was increasingly brutal. He lasted until August 1933, when a coalition of students and military officers forced him out of office.

In Argentina, Peru, Chile, and Cuba, leaders with reform programs had emerged, supported by the urban middle and working classes. Yrigoyen, Leguía, Ibáñez, and Machado encountered difficulties when economic depression limited their ability to provide employment in government and build public works projects. All turned to

How Historians Understand

RECONSTRUCTING THE *SEMANA TRÁGICA* (TRAGIC WEEK) IN ARGENTINE HISTORY

Class conflict, as we have seen in Chapters 11 and 12, was always just beneath the surface in Latin America. And as we will see in Chapter 14, the political outcomes of these confrontations depended to a considerable extent on the middle class. When the demands of the lower classes threatened the middle class (which they nearly always did), its members sided with the upper class–military alliance against workers and country people.

One of the first instances of this was *Semana Trágica,* which occurred during the "red scares" (Communist scares) after World War I. The middle class panicked, believing the government had lost control over the lower classes. But class conflict was not the only factor in the horror, it also focused on the festering prejudices Argentines felt toward the vast wave of new European immigrants that had poured into their country over the preceding half century. In particular, it exposed Argentine anti-Semitism, for much of the violence Argentines committed was against the Jewish community.

The events began in December 1918 with a strike in a metallurgical factory in Buenos Aires. As the month wore on, the single factory strike spread throughout the city. It continued into January of 1919. Fueling the tension, rumors flew about plots

Jewish synagogue in Buenos Aires in the early twentieth century.

BUENOS AIRES.   Iglesia Judaica.

from abroad, and the badly frightened urban middle and upper classes believed the government had "lost control" of the situation and allowed a communist conspiracy to run amok. This led to violent reprisals from the upper classes, carried out by vigilantes who formed militias to protect their neighborhoods from the workers. President Hipolito Yrigoyen sent police and the army to subdue the strikers.

The situation culminated horribly in the Semana Trágica, which lasted from January 10 through 14. Many upper-class Argentines blamed Jews for the troubles. The upper classes identified Jews with the Left, because most Jewish immigrants in Buenos Aires had come from Russia, where a Communist revolution had recently (1917) taken place. Acting on their fears, groups of vigilantes took to the streets. Allied with the police, they attacked Jewish neighborhoods, arresting people and destroying property. The Argentine Navy played a crucial role in encouraging, arming, and leading these middle- and upper-class vigilante groups.

In mid-January, the government finally brokered an agreement that ended the strike and the conflict. In light of the universality of the anti-Left riots of the post–World War I era (the Palmer Raids in the United States, for example), historians paid little attention to the anti-Semitic aspect of the event. Later, Argentina, like most of the world, closed its doors to Jews fleeing Nazi Germany during the 1930s. Again, because the situation was commonplace, historians found this unremarkable. Many did comment, however, on the military rightist regime's affinity for Germany during World War II; Argentina had steadfastly refused to declare war against the Axis powers until the last day of the conflict.

Anti-Semitism reappeared publicly during the dire crisis of the 1960s and 1970s. The military governments (1966–1973 and 1976–1983) fired Jews from positions of prominence. In the early 1970s, rightist paramilitary groups killed Jews suspected of Left sympathies. When the army instigated the "Dirty War," Jews bore the brunt of the violence disproportionately. The harrowing story of newspaper publisher Jacobo Timerman's imprisonment and torture was, perhaps, the least daunting, for many Jewish young people filled the rolls of "the disappeared ones."

Looking back through the context of Argentina's growing anti-Semitism over the course of the twentieth century, historians are reevaluating the initial assessment of Semana Trágica, which too easily dismissed the tragedy.

Questions for Discussion

Given the propensity of Argentines, particularly of the Right, for anti-Semitism in times of domestic strife, should historians look for patterns within that society? Are the Argentine Right's acts, some decades apart, indicative of wider aspects of the country's history that historians should explore? Why did the Argentine middle class turn on the lower classes in the period after World War I? Why do people in crisis look for scapegoats? Why were Jews convenient scapegoats in 1919 Argentina?

coercion. Each of these leaders lost the confidence of the middle and working classes and was toppled by the military.

Mexico's situation differed from these other cases because its middle class, allied with workers and country people, had won the revolution and controlled the national government. The new ruling group, comprised of middle-class northerners (from the state of Sonora in particular), did not share power with the upper classes because it was ruined by the civil war. The main problems facing the revolutionary regime were rebuilding the economy, satisfying the demands of the victorious revolutionaries, and unifying an army fragmented by regional and personal loyalties.

From 1920 until the mid-1930s, Mexicans struggled to balance reconstructing their nation's economy after a decade of destructive civil war against satisfying the various revolutionary factions. Middle-class demands for equal and fair access to education, employment, and economic opportunities were, perhaps, the easiest to meet. The middle class sought, in particular, the expansion of government to provide them with jobs.

The needs of country people and urban workers, however, encountered more government resistance because they threatened private property rights, of which their middle-class allies were the firmest advocates. Landless villagers had fought in the revolution to regain the lands stolen from them and their ancestors by hacendados. The Constitution of 1917 guaranteed the return of these lands. Nonetheless, the revolutionary government redistributed land only when politically necessary, because government leaders feared that land reform might undermine private property rights and decrease agricultural production and thereby impede economic recovery. Moreover, during the 1920s a new landowning class, many of them ex-revolutionary military officers, emerged

LATIN AMERICAN LIVES

ELVIA AND FELIPE CARRILLO PUERTO

ELVIA CARRILLO PUERTO (1876–1967) and her brother Felipe Carrillo Puerto (1874–1924) were, respectively, among the foremost feminist and radical leaders of the postrevolutionary era in Mexico. Elvia once said that "I want ... women to enjoy the same liberties as men ... to detach themselves from all the material, sensual, and animal, to lift up their spirituality and thinking to the ideal ... to have a more dignified and happier life in an environment of sexual liberty and fraternity." As the radical governor of the state of Yucatán (1922–1923), Felipe carried out the most extensive redistribution of land outside of Morelos. In their brief time in power, the siblings created the most progressive state government in postrevolutionary Mexico in terms of women's rights.

Elvia and Felipe Carrillo Puerto were 2 of 14 children born in the heart of the *henequen* region. (Henequen was used to make twine.) Their father was a small merchant. Both lived and worked during their formative years among the poor Maya of the region, learning their language, customs, and traditions.

Elvia Carrillo Puerto was a feminist, an activist, a politician, an administrator, and a teacher for the first two-thirds of the twentieth century. She was a controversial figure in Yucatán as the governor's sister, and her activities defined Yucatán feminism during the 1920s. Married at 13 and widowed at 21, she scandalized Yucatán's traditional society by living with men to whom she was not married, as well as marrying three times. When her brother was killed during a rebellion in 1924, she had to flee the state and returned only once during the next 40 years.

Elvia worked as a rural schoolteacher to support herself and her son after her first husband died. She saw firsthand the horrors of poverty and malnutrition in the countryside. She was well read (Marx, Lenin, and others), especially for a woman of her status and time. She joined the movement against the dictator Porfirio Díaz in 1909 and continued her work as a teacher and organizer through 1915. In 1912, she organized the state's first feminist league. In the late 1910s, she moved to Mexico City, for a short time sharing a house (1921–1922) with her brother, who was then a deputy in the federal congress. She married again, divorcing in the early 1920s and remarrying in 1923. In 1921, Elvia was the first woman elected to a seat in the state congress of Yucatán. After her exile from Yucatán, Elvia held a series of administrative posts in the capital. She continued to organize feminists, founding a succession of important feminist groups.

Felipe, as the governor of Yucatán, led one of the failed "Laboratories of the Revolution" during the 1920s, only to be killed in a brief rebellion that failed nationally but succeeded in Yucatán. As a youth, Felipe was a small landholder, mule driver, trader, and railroad conductor. During the 1910s, he spent time with Emiliano Zapata's agrarian movement in Morelos before attaching himself to General Salvador Alvarado, the socialist governor of Yucatán. Felipe took over the Socialist Party of the Southwest, the governing political party of Yucatán, when Alvarado left the state in 1918. Felipe encouraged the people to become involved in politics, and he advocated Mayan culture and history. Felipe, however, was too radical for the so-called Sonoran Dynasty made up of presidents Álvaro Obregón and Plutarco Elías Calles. They readily abandoned him during the revolt by army officers, led by Adolfo de la Huerta, in 1923.

The Carrillo Puerto siblings symbolized the unfulfilled promise of the Mexican Revolution at its turning point during the 1920s. A series of local and state radical initiatives all fell victim to the harsh practicalities of rebuilding a war-ravaged nation and the hard-eyed greed of the victorious generals. Elvia, however, who lived into the late 1960s, never gave up her dreams of women's equality.

Questions for Discussion

In some ways, the careers of the Carrillo Puertos were microcosms of the failures of both the Mexican Revolution and Mexican feminism. Why did both movements fail? Or, do you think that one or the other did not fail? Do you think that the Carrillo Puertos had the same goals as their constituents in the latter's battle for control over their everyday lives?

to oppose the implementation of land reforms. The revolutionary regime was willing to allow industrial labor to organize as long as the unions affiliated with the Regional Confederation of Mexican Workers (CROM). Presidents Álvaro Obregón (1920–1924) and Plutarco Elías Calles (1924–1928) balanced reconstruction and reform and survived a series of major rebellions. Obregón won reelection in 1928, but an assassin's bullet killed him before he took office. Calles ruled from behind the scenes, as three puppet presidents filled out the 6-year term until 1934. He solved the problem of the fragmented army by founding (1929) and building a new political party, the National Party of the Revolution (PNR), which brought together the disparate factions and wayward generals.

Brazil's middle and lower classes were the politically weakest in Latin America in 1920. Nonetheless, the old order fell apart when it experienced the depression. The power-sharing arrangement among the upper classes of the largest states gradually broke down during the course of the succeeding decade. When the upper classes of São Paulo (the other participants were the states of Rio de Janeiro and Minas Gerais) refused to alternate out of the presidency in 1930, their action set off a rebellion. Plummeting coffee prices added to the crisis. A coalition of dissident regional upper class, disgruntled mid-rank army officers, and disparate members of the urban middle class revolted to overthrow the old republic. Out of the uprising, Getúlio Vargas, governor of Rio Grande do Sul and the defeated presidential candidate of 1930, emerged to rule Brazil for the next 15 years.

Depression and War

To meet the crisis of the Great Depression of the 1930s, most of Latin America turned from democracy to military dictatorship or to civilian dictatorship with strong military support. The major exception was Mexico, which, instead, constructed a one-party regime. A number of important experiments took place during this period, such as the *Concordancia* in Argentina, the Socialist Republic in Chile, the *Estado Novo* in Brazil, and the revolutionary administration of Lázaro Cárdenas in Mexico. Almost all were short lived, and although each aimed to end conflict between classes, only Cárdenas's reforms succeeded.

Leftist ideologies, such as socialism and communism, often flourished as intellectual exercises, particularly among university students, but they were no match for upper-class and military opposition. More eclectic, and at times relatively radical, leftist political parties, such as the American Popular Revolutionary Alliance (APRA) in Peru and the National Revolutionary Movement (MNR) in Bolivia, proved more enduring and influential. In the short term, local variations of rightist ideologies, most importantly corporatism and fascism, had greater impact, but quickly receded.

By 1932, the moderate military, led by General Agustin Justo (1932–1938), formed an alliance (known as the Concordancia) comprised of old-line conservatives, independent Socialists (primarily from Buenos Aires), and, most importantly, anti-Yrigoyen Radicals. The new conservative alliance confronted the depression by balancing the budget, paying the foreign debt, encouraging exports, and discouraging imports. The Justo administration introduced Argentina's first income tax, which substantially cut the government's reliance on trade taxes for revenues, and established a central bank, which gave the government unprecedented influence on the management of the economy. The depression did not hit Argentina as hard as it did other Latin American nations, and, as a result, the upper-class regime was relatively benign. The moderate Concordancia continued to govern when Roberto M. Ortiz took over as president in 1938.

In Chile during the 1930s, the upper classes made concessions to urban workers and women but were unwilling to accommodate demands for land reform in the countryside. For a year and a half after the fall of Carlos Ibáñez, Chileans stumbled from one government to another. One of these was the Socialist Republic, led by Marmaduke Grove, which lasted for 100 days in 1932. Former president Arturo Alessandri won a new term in 1932. By 1935, Chile had recovered from the economic crisis, which allowed Alessandri to make overtures to the lower classes. He permitted extensive labor union organization and instituted a very effective process of mediating employer–employee disputes. A law in 1934 expanded women's freedoms and property rights, though men still maintained legal authority in the family. Alessandri cracked down hard in the countryside. Pedro Aguirre Cerda, the candidate of a coalition of center and Left parties known as the Popular Front, captured the presidency in 1938. His administration established the National Development Corporation (CORFO).

Brazil's social ferment and economic crisis led it to dictatorship. Like the postrevolution Mexican government during the same period, Brazilian dictator Getúlio Vargas (1930–1945) obtained the support of white-collar and industrial workers. He was unable to create a wide political consensus, however, instead ruling by decree. Vargas's appeal to the masses was more show than substance. Three years after winning election as president by vote of a constituent assembly (1934), Vargas engineered a coup against his own government to prevent new elections and established the *Estado Novo* (New State) in 1937. At this point, he no longer made even a pretense of having popular support.

In Peru, various forms of populism failed because the military remained steadfastly opposed. Sánchez Cerro represented the same middle class that had formed the core of Leguía's following. His "Conservative Populism" promised to restore the old social and economic structure, but at the same time offered the lower classes land reform, social security, and equal rights for Indians. After a bitter election campaign in 1931 against APRA's Víctor Raúl Haya de la Torre, Sánchez Cerro survived 16 terrible months of civil war and economic crisis until he was assassinated. General Oscar Benavides (1933–1939), a former provisional president (1914–1915), took over. Despite issuing a general amnesty, he engaged in a continuing struggle with Haya's followers in APRA. Peru recovered more quickly than other nations in the region from the depression, as exports surged beginning in 1933. Benavides cancelled the 1936 elections when it became apparent he was losing and ruled as dictator for the next 3 years. Modest conservatives inclined toward slightly expanding the role of government served as presidents from 1939 to 1948. Like Brazil, Peru experienced short periods of stability, but the Social Question remained unanswered.

Mexico experienced the most far-reaching reforms and consequently the longest era without upheaval. By 1934, the Mexican Revolution (set forth in detail in the Constitution of 1917) had seemingly reneged on its promises. Seventeen years after revolutionary victory, however, the country's new president, Lázaro Cárdenas, finally implemented long-awaited reforms. His major accomplishment was to redistribute 49 million acres of land to 15 million Mexicans, one-third of the population. As we discussed in Chapter 11, rural Mexicans had fought the revolution for land, and Cárdenas fulfilled Emiliano Zapata's promises to return these lands to the lower classes. As a result, the president bestowed an aura of legitimacy on the postrevolution regime that lasted for half a century. The Cárdenas administration more than doubled the average wage of urban workers. In 1938, Cárdenas expropriated the foreign-owned petroleum companies operating in the country when they refused to obey a Supreme Court order to increase the wages of their employees. In addition, the president undertook major efforts in public health and education. He also reorganized the official party in 1938, transforming it from a loose alliance among revolutionary generals, regional bosses, and labor leaders into an organization responsive to four major sectors: labor unions, rural organizations, the military, and government bureaucrats (middle class). Cárdenas did not, however, fulfill his promise to amend the Constitution to ensure equal rights for women.

Reform reached its acme in 1937. Land redistribution had disrupted food production, worsening conditions for the lower classes. Cárdenas had gone as far as he could, for there was enormous opposition among the postrevolution upper class to any further radical policies, and the nation did not have sufficient resources to carry out further reform.

During the 1950s, the Revolution moved to the center and shifted to policies for economic growth and produced the second great Mexican economic miracle (the first occurred under Porfirio Díaz). Mexico flourished as the official party consolidated its support among the middle class by providing large numbers of jobs in the government bureaucracy and government-operated businesses and free education at the fast-expanding National University (UNAM).

In all of Latin America, only in Mexico was the ruling group substantively responsive to the demands of the middle and working classes. Country people and the urban middle class obtained the land and opportunities for which they had fought so long and hard. As a result, Mexico prospered until the 1960s and maintained unparalleled political stability.

Cubans rose up in popular rebellion against Gerardo Machado in 1933. The victorious revolutionaries, comprised of a coalition of university students, noncommissioned military officers (sergeants, corporals), and political opponents of Machado, encountered strong disapproval from the U.S. government. Sergeant-stenographer Fulgencio Batista emerged from the plotting and violence as the power behind the scenes. Batista used methods similar to those of other populist leaders of the era, appealing to the working class from which he had come. He won election as president in 1940 and led the island through World War II. He retired peacefully and moved to Florida in 1944. Cuba, like Mexico, had achieved a measure of stability through concessions by a government run by the middle class (with a few leaders from the lower classes as well) to the needs of the middle and working classes.

Argentina became the setting for the most notorious populist regime in the Americas during the twentieth century, when the charismatic Juan Domingo Perón and his wife Evita Duarte de Perón emerged from a series of wartime political crises. The two towered over postwar Argentine politics. Perón, though the military ousted him in 1955, was a major influence until his death in 1974. *Peronism* was the most important example in Latin America of an alliance between a dictator and the lower classes. Perón built a base of support among organized labor, known as the shirtless ones (*descamisados*), in 1943 and 1944. Military hard-liners pushed him out of the government in 1945, but a massive demonstration by workers in October of 1945 rescued him, and he won the presidential election in 1946. Unlike Yrigoyen and Leguía, both of whom drew support from the middle sectors, Perón's politics was based on the urban working class with strategic allies among conservative bosses in the provinces. Perón repaid the working class for its support, greatly improving working conditions and benefits. The president opened the way for massive government involvement in business enterprise with the establishment of one state agency for marketing all of the nation's agricultural exports and of another that administered industries confiscated from German citizens during the war. His government also operated shipbuilding and steel firms. He nationalized the railroads and telephone service. After 1950, however, postwar prosperity ended as stagnation and inflation tormented the economy. Like the other populists, Perón found that he was unable to pay for his programs in times of downturn and lost support. In response, he shifted his strategy from popular appeal to repression, generating bitter opposition from the middle and upper classes. Nonetheless, he maintained his hold on the masses, overwhelmingly winning reelection in 1951. The economy stagnated, inflation rose, and his regime grew increasingly harsh, leading to a military coup in 1955.

A unique aspect of Perón's rule was the crucial role played by his wife Eva Duarte de Perón, a former actor. Evita, as she was known, exerted enormous influence through her Eva Perón Foundation, which funded medical services and provided food and clothes for the needy. She had come from the lower classes, and she became Perón's connection to them. Unfortunately for Perón, Evita died in 1952.

Peacetime Politics

The first major revolutionary movements to arise from the ashes of World War II took place in Guatemala in 1945, when a group of young, reformist military officers overthrew the long-running dictatorship of Jorge Ubico (1930–1945), and in 1951 in Bolivia, when a coalition of country people, miners, and the middle class, under the banner of the National Revolutionary Movement (MNR), toppled the conservative government backed by landowners, industrialists, and the military. The Bolivian Revolution implemented widespread land reform, destroying the traditional landowning class; nationalized the tin mines, the producers of the nation's major export; enfranchised all males and females; and virtually eliminated the military.

More common was a profound shift to the Right, as the upper class–military alliance, in the midst of the international Cold War between the communist Soviet Union and the capitalist United States, struck hard against the threat of communism in Latin America. Anti-Left dictators arose in Chile, Colombia, Cuba, and Venezuela in the early 1950s.

After a number of years under the rule of Left and Left-center coalitions, in 1948 Chile turned to former dictator Carlos Ibáñez, who took advantage of widespread discontent to bring together an odd coalition of Socialists, feminists, the middle class, and deserters from various parties to win the election of 1952. Unable to build consensus, he repeated his earlier policies of repression. His major innovation was to vastly intensify and broaden government involvement in the economy, establishing a central bank and also state enterprises in major industries such as sugar, steel, and petroleum. Colombians looked to Conservative General Gustavo Rojas Pinilla, as dictator of Colombia, who tried to bring peace to a nation wracked by civil war, but he could not survive through an economic downturn. Fulgencio Batista returned to rule Cuba in 1952, overthrowing a corrupt, democratically elected regime, and presided over a measure of prosperity on the island until the late 1950s. Batista, like Ibáñez and Rojas Pinilla, used harsh repression to govern instead of his earlier appeal to the masses. A young lawyer, Fidel Castro, led a rebel band in the mountains of southeastern Cuba, which gradually attracted support and allies among the middle class and workers in the cities to defeat Batista's army in late 1958. Reformers alternated with dictators in Venezuela. A group of officers, calling themselves the Patriotic Military Union, overthrew the president of Venezuela in 1945, but the Democratic Action Party (AD), led by Rómulo Betancourt, outmaneuvered the officers and installed a civilian government. Three years later, Marcos Pérez Jiménez took the reins as dictator until 1958, when the military overthrew him and returned Venezuela to democracy. In Brazil, GetúlioVargas joined Batista and Ibáñez as former presidents, once discredited, who returned to power. He won election as president in 1950 mainly because of the support given him by the working class of the big cities. Economic stagnation and inflation, however, badly eroded real wages and drastically undermined his base among workers. Amid a scandal over his role in the attempted assassination of a political rival, Vargas killed himself on August 23, 1954. Ironically, his death at his own hands prevented a military coup and paved the way for the continuation of civilian rule under Juscelino Kubitschek (1955–1960).

In each of these cases, neither populism nor coercion succeeded in establishing social peace. Reform was possible only in times of economic boom. Populism disintegrated during economic downturns. Efforts to win the support of the middle and lower classes through public patronage and concessions to labor unions required booming economies to pay for them. Coercion was unsustainable without some concessions to the middle and lower classes. The upper classes and military were willing to make only superficial accommodations. The basic unfairness and unjustness of Latin American society remained.

FAILURE OF THE LEFT AND RIGHT

The major populist experiments all failed in the long term. Their success, as we have seen in the cases of Yrigoyen's Radical Party and Perón's movement (known as *peronismo* or *justicialismo*), were tied closely to the fortunes of their nations' export economies and the unbending opposition of the hard-line elements of the military and upper classes.

Perhaps the most auspicious failure of populism in Latin America was that of the American Popular Revolutionary Alliance (APRA) in Peru. Victor Raúl Haya de la Torre founded APRA in 1924. He gained support among labor unions and the middle class. APRA's program consisted of opposition to U.S. imperialism, unification of Latin America, internationalization of the Panama Canal, nationalization of land and industry, and solidarity for oppressed peoples. Although its leadership was middle class, the party extolled the Indian past and sought to adapt the majority of Peruvians, who were Indians, into modern life. Haya believed that socialism was not possible in Peru, with its tiny industrial working class. He envisioned, instead, the middle class leading a cross-class alliance.

With the upper classes and military adamantly opposed to Haya, he was never to gain the presidency, though APRA was often an influential force in Peruvian politics. After losing in the election in 1931, Haya led an unsuccessful revolt, which led to the party being outlawed. Haya moved APRA to the center during the 1940s, ending its plotting and eliminating its anti-imperialist rhetoric to the point of exhibiting a favorable attitude toward the United States. During much of the 1940s and 1950s the government banned APRA.

The most successful and extensive social reforms in Latin America took place in Bolivia. Bolivia's National Revolutionary Movement (MNR) sought to create a strong centralized state with middle-class leadership of a cross-class alliance. In 1943, the MNR helped Major Gualberto Villaroel overthrow a conservative military government. Villarroel, in turn, fell in 1946 without accomplishing much reform. Conservative governments followed until 1951, when the MNR, which adopted a much more radical program, won the presidential election with its candidate Victor Paz Estenssoro. After the military intervened to prevent Paz's victory, the MNR rose in rebellion in 1952 allied with organized labor. The MNR carried out extensive land reform; nationalized the tin mines, which produced the nation's most important export; and enacted universal suffrage without literacy requirements. For the first time in centuries, the Indian population had access to land and politics. After these initial radical transformations, the MNR balanced the rival interests of small landowners, who had become conservative when they received land, and tin miners, who sought more radical changes. The MNR maintained its power until it was overthrown by the military in 1964.

The APRA failed in Peru and the MNR succeeded in Bolivia because the APRA alienated the military, which remained unalterably opposed to it, while the MNR initially defeated the Bolivian military. Just as importantly, the MNR, unlike the APRA, enjoyed a cross-class alliance between the middle and urban and rural lower classes.

Women's Suffrage

Industrialization and urbanization transformed the place of women in society. As we have seen, women always worked, whether inside or outside the home, and were often single heads of households in the nineteenth century. At times, women were crucial participants in politics, as in the military aspect of the Mexican Revolution from 1910 to 1920. The white upper-class men who controlled governments had to find satisfactory ways to recognize the realities of these transformations. This required a reassessment of such concepts as public and private space, honor, and gender (see Chapter 13).

Latin American feminists of the early to mid-century (the first wave of Latin American feminism) were comfortable with defining themselves as mothers and wives, emphasizing their childbearing and nurturing capacities. They did not seek to gain equality with men but rather to eliminate laws and conditions that impeded their traditional roles. They also used their status as mothers and teachers to further their argument for their participation in the public sphere. Feminists' early successes included revising civil codes to eliminate the legal inequality of married women and raising

Acción Femenina in 1922.

TABLE 12.1

Women's Enfranchisement

Nation	Year	Nation	Year
Ecuador	1929	Argentina	1947
Brazil	1932	Chile	1949
Uruguay	1932	Bolivia	1952
Cuba	1934	Mexico	1952
El Salvador	1939	Honduras	1955
Dominican Republic	1942	Nicaragua	1955
Panama	1945	Peru	1955
Guatemala	1945	Colombia	1957
Costa Rica	1945	Paraguay	1961
Venezuela	1947		

important social welfare issues. Because elections were meaningless in many Latin American nations, suffrage was not an important issue to feminists until the 1920s. Furthermore, not all feminists agreed on the value of women participating in the corrupt male world of politics. In fact, some doubters believed that the female vote would be overwhelmingly conservative and thus impede their progress. Thus, prior to World War II women obtained suffrage in only four Latin American nations (see Table 12.1).

CONCLUSION

Import substitution economics and populist politics dominated the era from 1920 to 1959. Latin American ruling classes sought to industrialize and modernize their nations, while maintaining the political status quo. The urban middle and working classes simultaneously looked to better their living and working conditions and to have a meaningful say in government. In the countryside, small property owners and landless workers wanted either to maintain what they had or to acquire lands previously stolen from their ancestors by the greedy upper class and to defend their control over their local traditions and values.

Import substitution, which protected Latin American manufacturing from foreign competition, did not succeed in stabilizing economic conditions, despite the opportunities for improvement afforded by two world wars and the depression. Most Latin American countries were too poor to constitute markets extensive enough to enable domestic industries to achieve economies of scale. The capital required for industrialization was available from only three sources: domestic private credit, domestic public funds, or foreign investment. Given the high risk involved with such enterprises, domestic private capital was unwilling to invest. Although Latin American banking had emerged by 1900, it had only a scattered impact on import substitution industrialization (ISI).

Foreign investment was unavailable through much of the period because of the world wars and economic crises. As a consequence, Latin American upper classes had to turn to domestic public funds, expanding the role of government in economic enterprise. Both public and private capital, however, relied almost entirely on the export sector to generate revenues for investment. And as we have seen, the export sectors were subject to booms and busts and therefore unreliable.

As for the Social Question during this era, the answer seemed at times to be populism, with its cross-class alliances. Charismatic leaders such as Yrigoyen and Perón, who were willing to distribute patronage and other economic benefits to their loyal followers, enabled years of social peace. The price was high: sham elections and loss of institutional independence for popular organizations. More importantly, populism, like ISI economic policies, was built on sand. It relied on booming exports to pay for the public works, expanded bureaucracy, and higher wages and benefits. When export booms ended, populism often deteriorated into oppressive dictatorship.

The struggles of ordinary Latin Americans remained much the same as they had since independence. The upper classes, as always, sought to maintain their wealth and power and were reluctant to share either. Those at the bottom of the economic scale fought to preserve their control over their everyday lives: to feed, clothe, and shelter their families and to maintain their local values and traditions.

The inability of Latin American economic policies and politics to lead to development and to answer the Social Question intensified societal tensions. When combined with the threatening specter of the Cold War struggle between communism and capitalism, these tensions would produce the conditions that in turn created two decades of tyranny and civil wars.

LEARNING MORE ABOUT LATIN AMERICANS

Bergquist, Charles. *Labor in Latin American History: Comparative Essays on Chile, Argentina, Venezuela, and Colombia* (Stanford, CA: Stanford University Press, 1986). Places workers at the center of Latin American politics.

Besse, Susan K. *Restructuring Patriarchy: The Modernization of Gender Inequality in Brazil, 1914–1940* (Chapel Hill, NC: University of North Carolina Press, 1996). Traces the changes in gender relations in the first half of the twentieth century.

Caulfield, Sueann. *In Defense of Honor: Sexual Morality, Modernity, and Nation in Early Twentieth Century Brazil* (Durham, NC: Duke University Press, 2000). Explores the role of public honor in gender relations.

Chant, Silvia, with Nikki Craske. *Gender in Latin America* (New Brunswick, NJ: Rutgers University Press, 2003). Excellent overview.

Craske, Nikki. *Women and Politics in Latin America* (New Brunswick, NJ: Rutgers University Press, 1999). Another insightful overview.

Dore, Elizabeth, ed. *Gender and Politics in Latin America: Debates in Theory and Practice* (New York: Monthly Review Press, 1997). Provocative essays.

Dore, Elizabeth, and Maxine Molyneux, eds. *Hidden Histories of Gender and the State in Latin America* (Durham, NC: Duke University Press, 2000). A collection of essays on the nineteenth and twentieth centuries.

Fraser, Nicholas, and Marysa Navarro. *Evita: The Real Life of Eva Perón* (New York: W.W. Norton & Company, 1996).

Gwynne, Robert N., and Cristobal Kay, eds. *Latin America Transformed: Globalization and Modernity*, 2nd ed. (New York: Arnold, 2003). Examines changes from all angles.

Krauze, Enrique. *Mexico: Biography of Power* (New York: Harper Collins, 1997).

Levine, Robert M. *Father of the Poor: Vargas and His Era* (New York: Cambridge University Press, 1998). A short, comprehensive biography.

13

PEOPLE AND PROGRESS,
1910–1959

IN THE ERA FROM the 1910 to 1960, Latin America underwent a vast transition from rural, agriculturally based traditions to urban middle- and working-class "modern" life. This transformation manifested not only in the politics of popular organizations and upheavals but also in all aspects of everyday life, such as employment, housing, food, popular entertainment, and art. The prolonged processes of altering gender roles, begun in the nineteenth century, continued. The struggle by common people for control over their everyday lives, particularly in the countryside, became as much cultural as political, though no less intense as a result.

Change, as always, was contested. In the countryside, especially, people resisted transformations of their long-held values and practices. Interestingly, not only rural dwellers, who would seem to most benefit from change, struggled against modernity, but also many members of the upper classes, the nominal promoters of change. The latter looked on mass popular culture as vulgar—the products of the slums—and regarded with suspicion the repercussions of migrations and industrialization. The wealthy and powerful were torn between their goals to transform their nations and the lower classes and their worries about whether they could control these changes.

The transition from countryside to city and from rural agricultural to urban industrial worker or middle class did not transform the attitude of the upper classes toward the lower, whom the rich and powerful continued to fear. The wealthy, as we have seen in previous chapters, grappled with the Social Question in politics and economics and allied with the armed services and the middle class to control the masses. This seeming contradiction was reflected in a Brazilian saying: "The social question is a question for the police." It was not enough, however, for the upper classes merely to maintain their control over the lower classes through government coercion. The wealthy tried mightily to force all aspects of social life and culture to conform to their need to rein in the urban lower classes. They sought to transform immigrants and migrants into a quiescent proletariat loyal to the nation (sometimes known as the *patria,* or fatherland). Moreover, they attempted to exert similar influence over the transformation of gender roles, particularly the place of women, in the rapidly changing urban society. Through the state, Latin American upper classes sought to shape the families, relationships, homes, leisure time, and tastes of workers to maintain their (male) hegemony (patriarchy). This meant potentially massive intrusions into local and personal prerogatives.

The movement of people from the countryside to the cities was and continues to be the most crucial process in Latin America. In 1950, 61 percent of the population was still rural. But from 1950 to 1960 alone, nearly 25 percent of rural Argentines abandoned the countryside for the cities; 29 percent of Chilean country people and 19 percent of Brazilian rural folk did the same. They left their homes because neither land nor jobs were available to them. Increasing concentration of land ownership severely limited their opportunities to obtain their own plots. "Land reform" projects distributed only marginally productive properties and did so without the opportunity to obtain credit to purchase equipment and make improvements. Burgeoning populations added to the pressures on the accessible land. Making matters worse, large landowners required fewer year-round laborers because of technological innovations and changes in crops. Many export commodities needed only seasonal workers, at planting and harvest. In contrast to the deterioration of conditions in rural areas, cities offered more employment, better opportunities for education—and therefore upward mobility—and improved health care. However miserable the living conditions in the slums of the cities, they were infinitely better than in the countryside, and however limited the possibilities in the metropolises, they were shining rays of hope compared to the darkness obscuring economic opportunities for the poor on large estates and in villages.

Even in the cities, of course, everyday life remained a constant struggle, as it had in the nineteenth century. Most Latin Americans continued to be poor and uneducated. Literacy rate for those older than 15 years of age was 50 percent. Only 7 percent of the people possessed a secondary education. As for work, if anything, it became harder. Large companies rather than small, family-operated workshops now employed most industrial workers. Impersonal bureaucracies replaced personal relations. City streets, noisy and smelly, polluted and unsanitary in the previous century, deteriorated further. The vast influx of people from the countryside and from abroad increased the pressures on existing facilities and public works beyond the breaking point. Like the Europeans and North Americans before them, Latin Americans who advocated modernization cared little that their relentless drive for economic development decimated their forests and pastures and polluted their water and air.

The contrasts between rich and poor, and the ironies they generated, were striking. Latin American upper classes during the first half of the twentieth century rebuilt the cores of the largest cities to emulate London or Paris. Governments built the Teatro Nacional (now the Palacio Nacional de Bellas Artes) in Mexico City and the Teatro Colón in Buenos Aires and constructed the elegant avenues of Rio de Janeiro and the Avenida de Mayo in Buenos Aires. While resplendent buildings and gleaming boulevards appeared in the cities' centers, however, more and more people crammed into the decaying tenements in the vast tracts of the city untouched by renovations.

SOCIALIZATION IN THE FACTORY AND THE MINE: PROLETARIANIZATION AND PATRIARCHY

Conditions in rural areas had deteriorated steadily for the lower classes since independence, and life for farm tenants and other workers was as precarious as in the preceding century. Work on the farms and ranches, if available at all, remained as hard and as badly paid as ever. Employment was erratic or seasonal. It was impossible to do more than scratch out the barest living. Most rural workers faced lifelong indebtedness to their bosses or landlords. At a ranch in the northwestern part of the state of São Paulo, in Brazil, in 1929, for example, 50 laborers rose at 4 A.M. to eat a breakfast of bread and coffee, after which they cleared fields to plant pasture for cattle. The men ate lunch at 8 A.M. and consumed their third meal consisting of beans, rice, and pasta at 2 P.M. Their toils did not end until dusk. Although the food was plentiful, no more was provided after the early dinner. Famished at the end of their long day, workers purchased additional food—perhaps cheese and bread or candy—from the ranch store, buying it on credit to be charged to their salaries. On Chilean estates, tenants were provided with a house and a small parcel of land in return for their labor. But the landlord could change the arrangements at a moment's notice and evict or move the tenants. Protest was futile, for the police and military were at the service of the landowner. In short, conditions for rural workers had not changed at all since the nineteenth century.

Living in any one of thousands of small villages in Peru or Mexico was little better. The villages were often isolated, reachable only over muddy or dusty potholed roads hours from any city. There was no electricity. Many of the inhabitants of the Indian and mestizo villages, especially women, spoke only their Indian language, such as Quechua and Aymara in the Andean nations or Nahuatl in Mexico.

It was nearly impossible to feed a family on the produce of small, individually owned plots, despite the families' modest meals—Andeans, for example, ate simple stews of potatoes, other vegetables, and, in good times, shreds of chicken, beef, or pork, accompanied by wheat or barley bread. As a result, country people sought work on neighboring estates and farms, in mines, and in cities. The movement of people from place to place was continual from the mid-nineteenth century on. Country people in Chile, for instance, often left their farms for short periods to work in the mines, drawn by high wages and the possibility of saving enough to buy their own land. After a few months, when the farmer-miner had accumulated enough money, he returned to his own parcel of land or to the estate where his family members were tenants. Manuel Abaitúa Acevedo, who first traveled to Chile's El Teniente copper mine in 1924 from his home in an agricultural town, was typical of the early migrants, who traveled back and forth between farm and mine. Initially, Abaitúa Acevedo worked 9 months in the mine before going home. The next year, he mined for 4 months, and in the following 2 years, 1 month each. In 1928, he worked in the mine for 5 months. His dream, of course, like that of others in his situation, was to someday save enough money to buy his own land.

Rural working conditions improved somewhat early in the twentieth century, in large part due to the arrival of two machines that had significant impact on country life. First, in Mexico, the *molino de nixtamal,* which ground soaked maize kernels into damp flour to make tortilla dough, revolutionized the everyday lives of women, allowing them to escape the centuries-long practice of grinding corn by hand, which required hours and hours of work. Second, the sewing machine, many of which operated through foot power rather than electricity, facilitated home piecework production, thus permitting women to work and tend to their families, and forming the basis of the cottage clothing industry. Sewing machines also eased the transition from wholly traditional to more western-style, modern clothing. (Access to electricity and the radio would have enormous effect on rural life, as well, but they were not universally accessible until the 1950s. Only 40 percent of the residents of Huaylas, a village in Peru, for example, had electricity in 1963.)

Despite these improvements, however, rural life in the first half of the twentieth century was so difficult that vast numbers of country dwellers left their homes and migrated to the mines and cities in hopes of finding better work. These women and men bravely left their villages and estates in order to improve their situation by entering the unfamiliar culture of mining camps and urban landscapes and acquiring new skills. When necessary—and it often seems to have been—they moved from job to job.

The history of María Elisa Alvarez, a Medellín textile worker, illustrates this situation. Alvarez arrived in Medellín, Colombia, at age 16 after toiling on a coffee plantation for 5 years. She had also sold cured tobacco, sweets, and produce on the streets of her hometown. In the city, Alvarez worked in domestic service for a year and then went to the textile mills. She worked there for a few months and then labored at a small dyeing shop and a local hospital. Having learned enough as a nurse's assistant to care for a patient, she gained employment caring for the invalid son of a wealthy family. After quitting because the son was unpleasant, she obtained employment in the factory she had worked in years before and then found a position in another mill, where she stayed until retirement.

Migrants from the countryside, such as Alvarez, arrived in the cities or mining camps only to face a long process of socialization and accommodation. The very sights, sounds, and smells were different, and as if this weren't disorienting enough, the newly migrated workers became immersed in struggles over their customs, traditions, and demeanor with their employers.

The conflicts between laborer and company are evident in the histories of two important industries, textile manufacturing in Medellín, Colombia, and copper mining in Chile. In both cases, companies required a reliable body of workers, but this proved difficult. Medellín textile workers were known for being uncooperative and mobile.

Slice of Life   VILLAGE LIFE IN PERU

HISTORIAN FLORENCIA MALLON conducted extensive research in the villages of the neighboring Yanamarca and Mantaro Valleys, in the central highlands of Peru, that illuminates the lives of rural people. The land is fertile and well watered by the Yanamarca and Mantaro rivers. The area lies on the major transportation routes to both important mining regions and the tropics, which meant that the mines furnished a market for the area's livestock and produce.

At the beginning of the twentieth century, the region was predominated by small- to medium-size farms, the proprietors of which enlisted the help of family labor to grow alfalfa, wheat, and vegetables. In the higher altitudes around the valley, people raised livestock and grew potatoes and quinoa. The holdings were much larger in this area. They drew labor from local villages.

Some proprietors owned plots in three zones: the humid lowlands located in the center of the valley, the valley slopes, and the flat lands on the other side of the mountains. This practice, of course, replicated the ancient Incas' approach to farming and commerce. To illustrate how the country people diversified, Mallon tells us the story of Jacoba Arias, an Indian who spoke only Quechua, from Acolla in the Yanamarca Valley. She owned 14 hectares (2.47 acres = 1 hectare) divided into small parcels scattered in different growing regions. She had 40 sheep, three teams of oxen, six bulls, and one cow. These animals provided the family with milk, cheese, meat, and lard, as well as wool for Arias's family's clothes. She also owned three mules, which allowed her to engage in small-scale commerce.

Farming the valley's slopes was no easy task. The environment often changed radically even within a single plot, resulting in variations in soil and climate. Farmers had to intimately understand their land and to meticulously adapt their methods and crops to it, according to the soil composition, the temperature, and the amount of sunlight and rain. Families also adjusted to the needs of the farm and the capabilities of their members. Young children and the elderly tended the livestock because these duties required less arduous work. No time was wasted. The shepherds, for instance, spun wool thread while they watched the flock.

Family farmers diversified their economic activities to make ends meet. Agricultural work was seasonal. Everyone participated in planting and harvest. Spinning thread, weaving, and household chores were major year-round tasks. Some men, usually those who were young and single, worked in the mines or as muleteers, transporting goods, during the off-season. Others made handicrafts, such as shawls, hats, ponchos, blankets, or woodcarvings. In good years, there was an agricultural surplus that could be used for purchasing extras, perhaps coca and alcohol. In bad years, the family was required to sell handicrafts or even some livestock.

Agriculture was a risky enterprise under the best of circumstances. An early frost, hail, or too little or too much rain could bring disaster. Because family size was not planned, inheritance eventually divided up the land into such small plots that no single family could subsist on them. Some families augmented their property's produce by working the farms of other owners in return for splitting the harvest between them. Some families tended other livestock owners' animals in return for half the newborn sheep or cattle. Another arrangement included cooperation between a farming household and a livestock-raising household: The latter's sheep fertilized the fields of the former, and the two families tended to and shared the crops.

Godparenthood enhanced cooperation among local families. On the occasions of a baby's first haircut, baptism, marriage, and roofing of a new house, children obtained six godparents, who, tied with the bonds of affection and respect, looked out for them in difficult times. Usually, one of the families was better off, but the arrangement worked to the benefit of both families because the wealthier had access to labor (and perhaps political support), while the less affluent could expect assistance in case of poor harvests or conflicts.

Governance in each village in the region consisted of two or more administrative units with their own officials. These entities oversaw community projects such as cleaning the irrigation ditches or planting community fields. There were also *cofradías,* religious lay brotherhoods, that sponsored the local saint's celebrations. Each of these organizations had a mayordomo to administer the celebration. He had to pay for the expenses not covered by the income from cofradía lands. The people of the community came together in these shared tasks. There was, of course, always conflict, ranging from petty arguments to more serious disputes over landownership.

Questions for Discussion

Compare village life in Peru with that of village life in Mexico. Why do you think the upper classes so mistrusted villagers even though the former need the latter's support in the politics of the nineteenth and twentieth centuries? Which of the villages in Peru and Mexico were more successful in retaining their autonomy over time?

At the El Teniente mine in 1922, an exasperated foreman fired close to 100 employees for "disobedience, laziness, fighting, insolence . . . leaving the job, carelessness, sleeping on the job, gambling, thieving, and incompetence." Companies sought to transform rambunctious and itinerant country bumpkins into passive, stable, productive workers. Workers resisted mightily. With the new century came critical changes in labor relations and market conditions, technology, and gender relations. In response to these changes, large companies attempted to control workers' lives to an extraordinary extent.

First, labor strikes during the mid-1930s in Medellín led company owners to formulate new strategies to instill stronger discipline into their unruly workers. Second, firms had grown larger and more bureaucratic, so owner families no longer supervised their operations from the factory floor, which, in turn, meant that they no longer fostered personal relations with their employees. Third, large looms capable of weaving much more cloth at one time began to be commonly used in textile mills. These new machines increased productivity, but—together with the industry's attempt to keep women "in their places"—caused a drastic shift in the gender makeup of the workforce. Bosses believed the looms were best operated by men, which resulted in a large number of women employees being fired. Medellín's textile and clothing factories, like most in Latin America, had heavily employed women through the 1930s, but by the end of the 1950s men far outnumbered women textile workers.

These transformations left employers struggling to reacquire control over the workplace during the 1940s by devising a new, two-pronged strategy: on one hand, providing desirable benefits for their employees, and on the other hand, seeking to influence all aspects of their employees' lives.

The first part of this strategy included improving working conditions and keeping salaries relatively high. The corporations that owned the mills and mines hoped that good pay would ensure a steady supply of able laborers, but it soon became clear that high pay would not persuade workers to abandon their freedom of movement or reform their behavior. Repressive tactics also were tried, but they proved to be equally ineffective at creating a body of compliant, respectable workers.

This led industries to the second part of the strategy: to influence every aspect of their employees' lives. Thus, corporations adopted paternalistic (fatherly) practices, making workers' lives more comfortable—and the job more attractive—by providing bonuses for attendance, establishing social and cultural organizations, setting up schools, and offering inducements to form traditional nuclear families.

As a result, Colombia's mill workers were paid well and were provided with such amenities as cafeterias that served subsidized meals and were surrounded by landscaped patios. The companies subsidized housing and grocery stores and paid for medical care, chapels, and schools. Similarly, in Chile, the foreign-owned mining companies sought to ensure a stable, resident, skilled labor force by offering workers schooling, movies, libraries, organized sports, and clubs—the last of which were to substitute for labor unions—in hopes of simultaneously attracting and altering them.

The Chilean state became involved in the socialization of workers during the 1930s in order to incorporate the middle and lower classes into the new conception of the nation. The government sought to build a citizenry of disciplined and responsible people. This, of course, coincided exactly with the goals of the foreign copper companies. Thus, both the government and the corporations were vested in successfully implementing new responsibilities for the lower classes, who were to be "disciplined, educated, and responsible [in order to] fulfill the demands of citizenship for the national community." Workers, nonetheless, wanted to rule their own lives. Miners resented attempts to control them by both the companies and the unions, and they continued to get drunk, play cards, and fornicate.

The efforts made by the Chilean government and mining companies, as well as by the Colombian textile industry, to reform workers quickly became the aggressive reassertion of traditional, patriarchal definitions of gender roles.

With the encouragement of the Chilean state, the mining companies, for instance, created a masculinized culture of work. The difficulty and danger of the labor was to be overcome by the sense of dignity. Pride was to overwhelm the dehumanization that accompanied modern mining.

Masculinizing work was one-half of the process; the other half was reemphasizing women's traditional roles. Latin American culture at the time—like most cultures— viewed female workers as a threat to the "proper" relationship between men and women, because when women earned wages, they redefined narrow definitions of gender. Further, owners believed that patriarchal and paternalistic authority could not be maintained in the factory if it no longer functioned in the family setting—that is, if employment in mills or mines provided women with the means to be independent of the authority of fathers, husbands, brothers, and sons.

Crucial to patriarchal beliefs and authority is the notion of female "virtue," specifically virginity. If women worked only when they were (theoretically) virgins—and the comforting assumption was that all unmarried women were—the factory maintained its patriarchal standing as "father" figure. So, mills and mines stopped hiring married women and single mothers. This way, women were allowed to work only while awaiting marriage, rather than working as independent females who would provide for themselves and potentially remain unincorporated into the family system.

Thus, in the midst of modernization, women's status in the mines and mills was altered to conform to centuries-old beliefs, but practicalities stood in their way. Women in the mining camps played a large part in helping the camps function. Women worked as domestics, as petty traders, and in the bars and brothels (which they sometimes owned) that sprouted like mushrooms around every camp. Like the men, many of these women hoped to save some money and move on. They usually came to the camps alone and often entered into sexual and domestic arrangements with men.

The foreign companies that owned the mines believed that this transient and unruly population of women, especially prostitutes, in the camps added to the instability and lack of discipline among the miners by adding to and exacerbating the problems caused by rampant alcohol use and gambling. Thus, the companies sought to regulate the sex lives of the workers and the women in the camps. The mine managers even went so far as forcing men and women found alone together either to marry or to leave their jobs. During the 1930s, some companies offered a monthly bonus and an extra allowance to workers who had families and were willing to formalize their relationships. This induced many couples to enter into civil unions and legitimize their children.

In addition, the companies sought to "civilize" the women in the camps, as they did the men. Company-sponsored programs, for instance, taught housekeeping skills to wives. Especially important in these lessons were the pointers in managing money and making ends meet, because the companies feared that poverty would tear apart the nuclear families they were trying so hard to create. As for single women who became pregnant or had abortions, the companies' solution was simple—the women were fired.

All of these policies, programs, and attempts to reinforce traditional gender roles succeeded in creating a stable mining workforce during the 1930s and 1940s. They could not, however, eliminate the difficult working conditions in the mines. And, what neither the companies nor the state anticipated was that their efforts to masculinize the work culture would generate not only an increased sense of pride on the part of male workers, but an equal increase in their disdain for authority.

Therefore, the miners never became entirely passive. Union activity continued, as did women's economic activities. Women sold food and beverages from their homes, took in laundry, and brought in boarders. Some even operated as female bootleggers (smugglers of illegal alcohol). Worst of all, some married women managed to obtain a degree of economic independence through their involvement in the informal market sector.

The ways in which the companies' tactics failed is well illustrated by the story below.

Ana (Nena) Palacios de Montoya worked as a domestic in Medellín when she met Jairo, who would become her husband. He was a driver for the local textile factory and used his contacts to obtain a position for her in the factory. Palacios de Montoya loved working in the mill. With funds cobbled together from yearly bonuses, mill loans, and the help of friends, she and her husband bought land and built a house. She gradually built her dream home, adding to the original structure as the family saved enough money for more construction. Amazingly, she managed to marry and have a child without being discovered and fired from her job. The bosses obtained two good workers, and their employees earned a good life—but, precisely contrary to the companies' efforts, Nena and Jairo clearly maintained their independence.

A Miner's Day at El Teniente

Work at the copper mines paid better than any other occupation in Chile. By the mid-1940s, miners earned 50 percent higher wages than from any other employment. Despite this, mines frequently experienced labor shortages until the relative stabilization of the workforce during the 1930s. When demand for labor grew, the companies dispatched unethical recruiters (*enganchadores*) to the rural areas. These recruiters got farmers drunk and told them about all the money to be made in the mines. When the desperate, drunken men "agreed" to become miners, the enganchadores had them sign contracts (which they could not read) and then loaded them onto a train headed to the mines. The farmers woke up, hung over, only to find themselves at a mine miles away from their villages, contractually bound to their new employers, and in debt to the recruiters, who often advanced them funds on their wages—which, of course, had to be repaid by working in the mines. If the farmers protested or tried to leave, the threat of police intervention persuaded them to cooperate. Despite these recruiting practices, turnover was a continual problem.

Regardless of how they had arrived at a mine, however, most miners' lives were similar to the description of the daily work at El Teniente, described below.

At four or five o'clock in the morning, a Chilean copper miner would rise and have breakfast at a cantina or the house of a family. By six, he was on his way to the train, completely enclosed and dark, that would take him up to the mine. When he arrived, the miner reported to the foreign supervisor, who recorded his time of entry. A giant elevator then transported the miner and some 600 of his fellow workers to the different levels of the mine, where they joined their teams, which consisted of 15 people, and began work in the tunnels.

The lead miners entered the designated tunnel first, laying pipes and tubes that brought in compressed air and water for the drills. As the miners drilled, the machines sprayed water on the work site to prevent dust from filling the cavern. (Despite this precaution, the tunnels were perpetually filled with so much dust that the miners could see only 5 or 6 feet ahead.) Dynamite was inserted into the drilled holes—a delicate, highly skilled process—and the walls were blown up, creating access to the veins of ore. Other team members then lay rails in the tunnels for cars that hauled in timbers to support the shaft's walls and ceiling, and then hauled out the ore. Once a vein was accessed, miners began the grueling work of chopping the ore out of the rock walls. The ore was loaded into the railcars, which were pushed to and emptied into chutes that carried it to the concentrating plants.

Mining was brutal work in terrible conditions. Foremen, under relentless pressure from the companies to increase productivity, pushed the workers hard. Miners learned these varied skills—all of which were dangerous and required enormous strength—on the job. When they exhibited proficiency, they moved on to better positions, though some refused to take the most dangerous assignments. A few became foremen. Work in the concentrating mills also required a great deal of skill and was even more dangerous than work in the tunnels, because the refining process released toxic fumes. There was never sufficient protective equipment, so the miners who labored in the plants inevitably acquired silicosis, a respiratory disease. Concentrating plant workers were lucky to survive a dozen years.

Living conditions in the El Teniente mining camp were generally abhorrent. Lodgings for families had no electricity, light, or ventilation. ". . . [T]he barracks for single workers [were] so awful as to be irrational." Miners with their families lived in two-room apartments in barracks buildings. Often, two families shared one apartment. A member of a family consisting of nine children and parents wrote: " . . . [W]e women had the bedroom because there were six girls and three boys, so in the big bedroom there were only women, in the other were my father with the boys, and in the other the kitchen." The company did not allow electric heaters or irons, so families used small wood- and kerosene-burning stoves, but both were expensive. There were common taps for water and toilets.

The worst disadvantage of living in the camps, perhaps, was the extraordinarily high cost of living, which badly eroded the real value of the nation's highest wages. Food was especially expensive, which meant that workers' and their families' nutrition suffered. Monopoly prices were at the heart of the problem. Miners often resisted the difficult conditions. New miners often skipped work after a few days to recover from their aches and pains. Ultimately, because miners were in perpetually short supply, they had the advantage of being able to find another job if the work environment was unacceptable.

URBANIZATION AND SOCIAL CHANGE

The transformations sweeping through Latin American society during the first half of the twentieth century were nowhere more apparent than in the growing cities of Latin America. They were particularly evident in the conditions of the middle class and attitudes toward women.

The Cities

Latin American cities were overcrowded, unsanitary, overrun by epidemic diseases, and teeming with uneducated migrants from the countryside and abroad. At the beginning of the century, the upper classes in Rio de Janeiro, Buenos Aires, and other cities determined to dramatically alter their metropolises' physical and social space while simultaneously inculcating moral values in the masses. Urban redevelopment, electrified public transportation, and massive population growth transformed the cities economically, spatially, and culturally.

The divide between the wealthy and the lower classes widened and grew more obvious. Rio de Janeiro, for example, was really two cities, whose population was half Afro-Brazilian and where immigrants flooded in by the thousands: the poor, on whom the authorities cast suspicious eyes, and "decent" upper- and middle-class folk, who made up less than 20 percent of the population. The upper classes imposed their will on the lower classes through cleaning up downtown spaces by instituting new health and housing codes, regulating recreation, and strictly enforcing laws against public nuisances such as prostitution.

Massive urban renewal took place in Rio de Janeiro from 1902 to 1910. Working-class neighborhoods were cleared and their inhabitants moved to the city's outskirts. As migrants continued to flow into the city, urban services remained woefully inadequate. Terrible epidemics tormented the city. By 1920, the downtown streets were ravaged by disease and littered with abandoned girls, beggars, and prostitutes.

The most startling example of superurbanization during this era may be Mexico City. Country people have thronged into the city in increasing numbers from 1940 to the present. Much of the nation's new industry was established in Mexico City—one-fourth of the country's factories were located there by 1970. Thus, between 1940 and 1970, millions of people left the countryside to seek their fortunes in the metropolis, increasing the capital's population from 1.5 million to 8.5 million. The number of automobiles jamming city streets also grew exponentially during that time, choking the city with carbon monoxide fumes. The government erected architectural splendors such as the National Autonomous University and the Museum of Anthropology. Skyscrapers sprouted in the core of the city and along the beautiful, tree-lined, statue-ornamented Paseo de la Reforma, while migrants overflowed burgeoning barrios, such as Netzahualcóyotl.

Generally, life was better in the city than in rural areas and offered more opportunity to improve one's conditions. In 1960, *capitalino* (resident of Mexico City) family income was 185 percent more than a rural family's income.

Life on the Edge: The Middle Class

The middle class expanded because government bureaucracies grew larger, the presence of foreign businesses multiplied opportunities trickled down in growing economies, and education became available to more than just the wealthy. What mattered to the members of the middle class, as it had to the gente decente in the nineteenth century, was maintaining their respectability and their distance from the lower classes. Because their economic situation was chronically precarious, middle-class people—who were only marginally more financially well off than the working class—concerned themselves primarily with keeping up the appearance of their status (see Table 13.1).

White-collar workers lived perpetually on the edge; their paychecks barely covered basic living expenses (see Table 13.1). Pawnshops were the only source of ready credit. White-collar workers found it nearly impossible to buy a home. It was difficult to save money, whether to build a down payment or create a financial cushion in case of emergency, and there were no banks to keep savings, even if they had existed, or to provide mortgages.

Their health was barely better than the working class. Lima's white-collar workers were less likely than poorer Peruvians to die of epidemic diseases such as typhoid, cholera, bubonic plague, or yellow fever, but they did succumb to tuberculosis. This disease accounted for one-third of all white-collar mortality in Lima and resulted from working in badly ventilated spaces or residing in damp, overcrowded apartments. It is likely that they were malnourished as well.

Despite these obstacles to financial security, white-collar workers tried to emulate the rich and were mostly concerned with appearance. Middle-class women followed European fashions, while men who worked in commerce in Lima during the 1920s

TABLE 13.1

A Typical Middle-Class Budget in Mid-Twentieth-Century Peruvian Soles

	Soles
Rent	100
Food	240
Soap, toothpaste	20
Transportation	36
Water, electricity, garbage	14
One servant	50
Kerosene	12
Movies, once a week	20
School fees for oldest child	80
Total	572 on income of 600 (a meager sum at the time)

Source: Ya! No. 16 (July, 1949), pp. 18–19, cited in D. S. Parker, *The Idea of the Middle Class: White Collar Workers and Peruvian Society, 1900–1950* (University Park, PA: Penn State University Press, 1998), p. 212.

How Historians Understand   THE VOICE OF THE LOWER CLASSES

The most difficult task historians confront is the construction of the past of the rural and urban lower classes. Mostly illiterate, they did not often record their own histories. The upper classes, whose fear of the masses we have discussed extensively in these pages, were in charge of governments, universities, and media and excluded the stories of those who were not of their own status in national histories. The less well-born, among them the poor, country people, urban workers, and nonelite women, appeared in official history books only as no-account, lazy subjects of justifiable oppression, exotic objects of sympathy, criminals, or irrational protestors. As in the cases of the well-known Mexican historian Lucas Alamán and the liberal historians of nineteenth-century Argentina and Chile, upper-class fear and disdain of the lower classes was clearly evident.

Foreign visitors, the most famous of whom was Fanny Calderón de la Barca, the wife of the Minister of Spain to Mexico, who recorded her observations of nineteenth-century Mexico, were perhaps the best sources for glimpses into the lives of everyday people. They tended, however, to see Latin Americans through the narrow focus of wealthy, white Europeans or North Americans, with their racism and condescension undisguised. Their best-selling books provided pictures of half-naked gauchos and tropical villagers, noble at their best, savage at their worst.

Pressured by the events of periodic, violent upheavals during revolutions in Mexico (1910), Bolivia (1952), Cuba (1959), and Nicaragua (1979) and the challenges of Marxism, populism, and feminism, twentieth-century historians of Latin America

Women workers on strike in Mexico in the 1920s.

delved into the histories of lower-class people. The first efforts used traditional methods, exploring national institutions, such as labor unions, which had records to consult.

Traditional sources seemed to provide neither description nor insight. Newspapers of the day, unless in opposition to the government—and these were rare—hardly paid attention to the poor. Few treated the lower classes with any degree of fairness. Strikes, for example, were seen as the result of the manipulations of outside agitators. Not many reporters explored the lives of the people driven to these radical actions.

In the 1960s, dismayed by the massacre of 300 civilian protestors in Mexico City by government secret police forces, and in the 1970s, horrified by the emergence of vicious, repressive military regimes in Argentina, Chile, and Brazil, historians pushed harder to write the stories of everyday people. Local records provided the sources for this history.

The best sources for the history of common people lie in judicial, police, notary, and municipal archives, located in villages, towns, and cities. In addition, most recently, historians have discovered illuminating materials in the records of large companies. There are also some records from modern large estates. Foreign mining companies in Brazil and Chile, in particular, have proven rich depositories. Most of the archives contain "official" documents, of course, which reflect views of events that are hardly impartial.

Historians, despite the difficult conditions in local archives, such as poor lighting and ventilation, the threat of dangerous parasites from dust, and uncooperative bureaucrats, have discovered invaluable materials. Judicial archives, for example, contain the records of suits concerning marriage, criminal trials, tax protests, litigation between heirs, and land disputes. Notarial records reveal family economic holdings, wills, business transactions, and contracts. Police documents tell us what crimes were committed and by whom. Municipal records detail taxes, rules, and regulations, the activities and tactics of local officials, and the reactions of the citizenry to official actions.

Although police and court records are not always representative samples of the general population, by using them historians can uncover the extent of such activities as drunkenness, wife beating, prostitution, and banditry. They can also estimate the extent of government interference in everyday life in its efforts to discipline the lower classes.

The picture produced by these records is, of course, never complete, but they have created history where none had existed previously.

Questions for Discussion

Why do you think that historians in recent decades have focused on the lower classes? Why do you think that historians ignored the masses for so long?

joined shooting clubs or played billiards or wore English cashmere. Because living spaces were so small and unpleasant, many people frequented cafés and streets. Walking the streets of Lima was a way to show off their respectability—of seeing and being seen. Crucial to the middle-class psyche was the notion that they were demonstrably different from the working class. Thus, middle-class workers were willing to commute for hours so they could reside in respectable areas of the city. The middle class sought forms of entertainment beyond films, radio, and sports—all favored by the working classes—and began to travel.

Women made up only 1 percent of the white-collar workforce in 1908 in Peru and did not enter this sector in numbers until the 1910s, when they began to fill positions in post offices, telegraph offices, and telephone companies. In the 1920s, they moved into retail, then banking, insurance, and commerce. Five percent of all working women were white collar by 1931. The typical images of white-collar workers, however, remained those of a young bachelor or of a family man whose wife did not work. Respectability demanded wives stay at home, even if the result of living on one salary meant that the family lived more modestly than it otherwise might have. Despite this tacit cultural injunction, however, it is probable that married middle-class women worked outside the home.

In Peru and elsewhere in Latin America, the number of white-collar workers expanded from 1930 to 1950 as businesses grew larger and more complex and public bureaucracies swelled. As in Chile's mines, traditional paternalism gave way to hierarchies and impersonal relations. As mentioned previously, many more women entered the white-collar ranks during this period, although usually at the lowest-paid levels. After the 1930s in Lima, mestizos comprised the largest number of white collars. And white-collar workers' children eventually gained access to university educations.

La Chica Moderna

Urbanization and industrial work, with its accompanying financial freedom, instilled a new attitude in women, many of whom became what the era called "the modern woman." (They were known in Mexico and elsewhere as *las chicas modernas,* or modern girls.) Although at the beginning of the twentieth century women office and factory workers—that is, women holding nontraditional jobs—were only a small minority of the female workforce, they caused much public discussion. At that time, most working women still toiled as domestics, as they had in the previous century. The 1920s, however, brought with them the notorious flapper—self-confident women who were racy, flirtatious, and assertive. This unprecedented image of the independent, sensuous female shook male culture, because female "virtue" was the very center of patriarchy—and such virtue certainly did not include self-reliance, self-determination, or a sense of self-worth that was inherent rather than bestowed by a father or husband. In Latin America, as elsewhere in the Western world at that time, modernity indicated economic progress and healthy, rational sexual and family relations when applied to men, but it meant a dissolute lifestyle and loose morals when applied to women.

In Brazil, as in other Latin American countries, the upper classes, government officials, and conservative Catholics worried about the low rate of marriage among the poor, the high rate of infant mortality, and the increasing numbers of women and children in the industrial workforce.

The irony, of course, was that middle-class women in Brazil (and other nations) were entering the white-collar workforce because it had become harder and harder for families to make ends meet on one salary. Thus, given this reality and despite governmental policies designed to keep women in their place, more and more middle-class women took advantage of educational opportunities and went into the professions. By the 1920s, women's employment did not elicit the disapproval among the middle class that it had in the past.

Women's fashions of the 1920s disconcerted the upper-class males who dominated Brazil (and probably disconcerted a significant percentage of middle- and working-class males and some females). Compared to the clothing of the previous century and the turn of the century, during the early part of the decade, women wore lighter, shorter, and more comfortable dresses. Later in the decade, hems came up all the way to the knee and were worn with silk stockings and high heels. Less-cumbersome bras and panties replaced corsets. Short haircuts and the use of makeup were the style. Bare arms and legs were exposed on the beach. Women were revealing themselves physically as never before.

Fashion wasn't the only aspect of women's lives that was changing drastically. Women now smoked cigarettes in public. Films and magazines celebrated a glamorous, decadent life and encouraged women to aspire to it. Dances and music became scandalous: The tango, foxtrot, Charleston, and shimmy were all the rage.

To upper-class males, women's virtue was under attack, and the Brazilian state, like the Chilean state, sought to defend patriarchy from these challenges. The regime of Getúlio Vargas (1930–1945) adopted policies that were intended to adjust the traditional role of women to meet the new economic and cultural conditions of the twentieth century while maintaining the patriarchal structure of society. Its targets, of course, were women and the poor, the groups believed to pose the greatest threat to upper-class men's—and thus the state's—status. The goal was to strengthen traditional marriage. Women were, after all, crucial to society not only because they reproduced but also because they educated their children. Therefore, it was necessary to "re-educate" women and reemphasize traditional values, so that women would inculcate their offspring with the "proper" values and attitudes. To accomplish this, the government adopted protective legislation limiting women's access to the workplace. It was hoped that this would, in turn, limit women's ability to support themselves, thus essentially forcing them to find husbands simply to survive. The government also instituted social service agencies to monitor the urban poor. In addition to these governmental policies, industrialists even set up model villages to control the domestic lives of their workers.

The Brazilian ruling class and government were, however, willing to make minimal concessions to women. Early in the century, Brazilian legislation altered the wife's status to "companion, partner, and assistant in familial responsibilities." (Nonetheless, this legislation firmly maintained the husband as head of household, and women still did not have the power to control their own property.) In 1940, the government's penal code eliminated the distinctions between male and female adultery. There was also an attempt to end the legal tolerance of crimes of passion. (Law permitted a husband to kill his wife, if he caught her in adultery.) Thus, women, like the middle class, had struggled enormously to better their conditions, and succeeded somewhat, but their situation remained precarious. As the middle class had not achieved equal status with the wealthy and powerful, neither had women obtained legal, economic, or cultural equality with men.

POPULAR AND HIGH CULTURE

The vast movement of people from the countryside to the cities and from the rest of the world to Latin America during the first half of the twentieth century deeply affected the region's popular culture (folk songs, dance, and crafts) and its so-called high culture (orchestral music, theatrical dance, painting, sculpture, literature, etc.). Improved communications and transportation not only brought more people together domestically but facilitated travel among countries and, thus, the introduction of foreign influences. The arts were closely tied to the constructions of national identities, and Latin Americans struggled to find their way in the space between their own artistic traditions and those of Europe and North America, which were much admired by upper classes. The changes wrought by industrialization, migration, and urbanization on Latin American dance, music, and painting, in particular, are discussed below.

The tango, which was born in the slums of Buenos Aires, Argentina, during the late nineteenth century, was a fitting symbol for the profound transitions mentioned above. Before World War I, the tango was performed primarily in the outskirts of Buenos Aires, where rural tradition was still stronger than in the heart of the city. It was connected with rural music and songs that protested the miserable conditions in the teeming tenements and the industrialization of urban work. Rural people, newly transplanted, despised city ways as exemplified by the *cajetilla,* or dandy.

The tango melded various aspects of Argentine society, combining the music of the rural milonga, the Spanish *contradanza,* and influences of African Buenos Aires. Its very form was a protest against conventional mores: Danced by couples whose bodies were closely entwined, the tango was modern, urban, and explicitly sensual, eschewing more innocent traditional (folk) dances performed in groups. Radio and film made the tango part of popular culture, and the upper and middle classes, who disdained the dance for the first several decades of its life as being symbolic of the poor, later embraced it as a symbol of Argentina.

The Brazilian samba, too, was an object of upper-class scorn during the nineteenth century. In fact, the Brazilian government outlawed it for a time. Nonetheless, the samba became the symbol of Brazil's mixed heritage of African and European culture. Arising from the poor Afro-Brazilian neighborhoods of Rio, during the 1920s samba clubs took over Carnival (the festival before Lent). The clubs' leaders were able to shed the bad reputations of their predecessor organizations and convince parents in the poor neighborhoods to allow their daughters to participate. Thus, not only did samba—the dance of the poorest Brazilians—become the symbol of the nation, but it also illustrated how women, who were now active and public participants in Carnival, were no longer restricted to private spaces.

In painting and literature, the conflicts inherent in the processes of urbanization, modernization, and finding national identities emerged at the turn of the twentieth century in movements such as *modernismo* and *indigenismo* (nativism). Nicaraguan poet Rubén Darío founded modernismo, a literary movement that sought to express the Latin American experience. The visual arts followed, also seeking a uniquely Latin American presentation of the region's culture. Latin American artists, most of whom trained in Europe, set aside the perspective of the continent and began to look at their homeland up close. Mexican artist Saturnino Herrán (1887–1918), for example, depicted Indians and mestizos living and working in their local environs in such paintings as *El Trabajo* (*Work*) (1908) and *La Ofrenda* (*The Offering*) (1913). Herrán, who never studied in Europe, was one of the first twentieth-century Mexican artists to look to the country's pre-Columbian past for subject matter. Similarly, Ecuadorian painter Camilo Egas (1899–1962) depicted the life of Indians over the centuries since the conquest in huge horizontal panels, such as the *Fiesta Indígena* (*Indian Festival*) (1922).

At the heart of the Mexican search for national identity and art's place within it was Geraldo Murillo, widely known as Dr. Atl (1875–1964). He was a crucial link among European movements (such as impressionism), Mexican popular culture, the famous Mexican muralists, and the revolutionary government. Dr. Atl was an important sponsor of the muralist movement in the 1920s, and he brought *arte popular* into the forefront in 1921 when he organized an exhibition of popular art and wrote its accompanying text, *Las artes populares en Mexico*. A talented painter in his own right, Dr. Atl's works, such as *El Volcán Paricutín en erupción* (1943), for instance, showed his eclectic approach to art. Uruguayan Pedro Figari (1861–1938), son of an Italian immigrant, depicted life on the vast plains of the Pampas, as well as creole and black dance. He, like Herrán and Egas, painted the lower classes in the countryside, as one critic observed, "never before represented with such boldness and candor. . . ."

Perhaps the most well-known and the most important artistic movement that grappled with the intertwined dilemmas of modernization and national identity—most crucially the place of indigenous peoples within the revolution—were the Mexican muralists. The most famous of these were Diego Rivera (1887–1957), David Alfaro Siqueiros (1896–1974), and José Clemente Orozco (1883–1949), but the group also included Alva de la Canal, Charlot, Fernando Leal, Xavier Guerrero, Roberto Montenegro, and Dr. Atl. According to one art historian, Jacqueline Barnitz, "The artists faced two major challenges: that of introducing a new public monumental art requiring special technical skills, and that of creating an effective visual language for propaganda purposes." José Vasconcelos, the minister of education during the administration of

José Clemente Orozco's *La Clase Obrera* (*The Working Class*).

President Álvaro Obregón (1920–1924), set out quite pointedly to incorporate and indoctrinate the masses through public art. Vasconcelos sought to educate the mostly illiterate Mexican population about their country's culture and identity—in short, to make them Mexicans.

Siqueiros's manifesto of 1923 set out the muralists' goals: "the creators of beauty . . ." must ensure that "their work presents a clear aspect of ideological propaganda." The muralists introduced workers and country people into their art on a grand scale and rewrote Mexican history in their enormous paintings on walls. The stairwell murals in the National Palace in the Zócalo (central plaza) of Mexico City depict Mexico's history from the conquest through the Cárdenas (1934–1940) era. Art, to the muralists, was inherently political. In a nation in flux during the 1920s, art seemed a way to help construct a sense of nationhood in a country blown apart during the previous decade's revolution.

During the 1930s, artists' concern for the lower classes intensified. In Mexico and Peru, indigenismo art took center stage as these nations struggled, as they had for centuries, over the place of the Indian population in their societies. The Mexican muralists were the primary purveyors of the new indigenous image, which romanticized pre-Columbian

The Exploiters by Diego Rivera.

LATIN AMERICAN LIVES

FRIDA KAHLO

FRIDA KAHLO (1907–1954) was a tortured artist famous for her striking self-portraits and her stormy marriage to muralist Diego Rivera. Long after her death at 47, she became celebrated for her incorporation of distinctively female concerns, such as reproduction, children, and family, into her paintings. Critics consider her avowedly feminist in her treatment of her own body. She, like Elvia Carrillo Puerto (see Chapter 12), was a prominent example of Mexico's "new" woman who defied convention. Kahlo has reached cult status among feminists for her merging of personal emotions and politics.

Her life was determined by four factors: a terrible automobile accident that left her with a fractured spine and pelvis and constant pain throughout most of her life, her tumultuous marriage to Rivera, her inability to bear children, and her prodigious talent (though unrecognized, for the most part, while she was alive).

When she was 15, a bus she was riding collided with a trolley. The crash inflicted terrible injuries, which resulted in 35 hospitalizations and operations. The remainder of her life was spent in constant physical torment. Kahlo and Rivera married in 1929. They divorced in 1939 and remarried in 1940. They were international stars, consorting with world-famous artists and leftist politicians and thinkers. Rivera's notorious philandering marred their dreamlike lives, though Frida, herself, had affairs as well.

Personally and professionally, Kahlo was in the forefront of the movement to incorporate popular culture into art. She was flamboyant in her dress, wearing the traditional garb of the women of Tehuantepec, the isthmus in southern Mexico, and styling her hair in indigenous coiffures with bows, combs, and flowers. She bedecked herself in jewelry. She was an avid collector of popular, folk, and pre-Columbian art. Her artistic work was rooted in pre-Columbian and colonial sources. Some commentators regard her as the Mexican artist who best combined popular art with the "modernist avant-garde." The merger of her concerns as a woman and her feeling for country people manifest themselves in her painting *My Nurse* (1937), in which she suckles on the breasts of a dark-skinned Indian woman.

In her most famous paintings, we can observe her obsessions with her pain, her love, and her barrenness. In her work *Raices* (*Roots*, 1943), she portrays herself with vines growing out of her chest as she lies in barren land. Despite her inability to bear children, she insists on herself as part of and a contributor to the "natural environment." In *El abrazo de amor del universo, la tierra* [Mexico], *Diego, yo y el señor Xolotl* (*The Love Embrace of the Universe, the Earth [Mexico], Diego, Me and Señor Xolotl*) (1949), she holds a baby with Diego's face in her arms, combining both her obsession with motherhood and her love of her husband. *Las Dos Fridas* (*The Two Fridas*, 1939; see Plate 17) resulted from her divorce from Rivera. The two women depict her traditional and urbane sides, only the former loved by Diego.

In the male-dominated art world, Frida Kahlo was unappreciated until the 1980s, when her striking depictions of motherhood and her body fit into the new feminist art history. Some historians, however, have criticized the treatment of her as a victim, obsessed with her physical and emotional pain. Overlooked, they maintain, is "her active role in the formulation of the language of art, which questioned neo-colonial values." Interpreted as "'the other,' the feminine and the unconscious," she is marginalized in a similar way in which Latin America finds itself made exotic. Kahlo, however, does not interpret Mexican women (or herself) as victims, but rather as "an assertive presence with the power of life and death."

Questions for Discussion

Discuss how you think that art reflects its time. Why is art such an effective instrument of social protest?

civilizations and denigrated Spanish colonial culture. Indigenismo, both in art and literature and as a political problem, was a complex phenomenon. On one hand, intellectuals sought to extol the great heritages of the Indian civilizations. On the other hand, modernizing upper classes saw the Indians as backward rustics. At best, the more thoughtful members of the upper class sought to place the Indians in industrializing society. Pride in the accomplishments of native peoples dovetailed nicely with intensifying nationalism, which was a crucial aspect of populism, the political answer to the Social Question during the 1930s and 1940s. Nonetheless, to the upper and middle classes, modern Indians were impediments to progress.

Brazil had to confront its national and cultural identity not only in terms of Indians, but of African peoples, as well. Traveling the path of the Mexican muralists, Tarsila do Amaral (1886–1973) returned from her European training in the early 1920s to paint the everyday existence of poor Brazilians, who comprised the nation's largest population. Another Brazilian painter, Candido Portinari (1903–1962), according to Barnitz, also depicted the "poor and the dispossessed, haggard and weak, with the staring eyes and distended stomachs of the malnourished."

During the 1920s, with a movement centered in São Paulo, modernist Brazilian artists ended the nation's denial of its past and set about incorporating it into a national culture. They rejected regionalism and sought to make Brazil Brazilian. Novelist Mario de Andrade became a leader of the search for what constituted "Brazilianness."

Similarly, sociologist Gilberto Freyre sought Brazilianness in the country's various traditions and regions. Brazil could be whole, he argued, only by allowing regional differences to flourish within the nation. Both men rejected foreign models, none of which had stood up to Brazilian requirements.

CONCLUSION

At the core of Latin American struggles during the first half of the twentieth century were economic and physical survival. Most people were poor and struggling day by day to survive. Although great gains were made in education and health care—more people were literate and they lived longer—Latin Americans' standards of living lagged far behind those of people living in Western Europe and the United States.

Latin Americans also grappled with the widespread effects of industrialization and urbanization. Everyday people, particularly in the countryside, fought to retain their cherished traditions and control over their daily lives. The onslaught of the factories, railroads, highways, telephone, radio, electricity, and centralized government, however, was too strong. Nonetheless, the urban and rural working classes and small landowners were remarkably independent and resilient. They selectively adopted new ways and adapted to new conditions. Their resistance to the dictates of the upper classes and military, however, caused the latter to seek drastic solutions to the decades-old Social Question. Two decades of violence and trauma ensued.

LEARNING MORE ABOUT LATIN AMERICANS

Baily, Samuel L., and Franco Ramella, eds. *One Family, Two Worlds: An Italian Family's Correspondence across the Atlantic, 1901–1922* (New Brunswick, NJ: Rutgers University Press, 1988). The story of Italian immigrants in Buenos Aires.

Barnitz, Jacqueline. *Twentieth-Century Art of Latin America* (Austin, TX: University of Texas Press, 2001). An interpretive history of the region's brilliant art.

De Jesus, Carolina Maria. *I'm Going to Have a Little House: The Second Diary of Carolina, Maria de Jesus*. Trans. Melvin Arrington, Jr., and Robert M. Levine (Lincoln, NE: University of Nebraska Press, 1997). The sad story of a favela dweller.

De Jesus, Carolina Maria. *The Unedited Diaries of Carolina Maria de Jesus*. Ed. Robert M. Levine and Jose Carlos Sebe Bom Meihy. Trans. Nancy P. S. Naro and Cristina Mehrtens (New Brunswick, NJ: Rutgers University Press, 1999). The story of a favela dweller.

Farnsworth-Alvear, Ann. *Dulcinea in the Factory: Myths, Morals, Men, and Women in Colombia's Industrial Experiment, 1905–1960* (Durham, NC: Duke University Press, 2000). Women factory workers.

Fowler-Salamini, Heather, and Mary Kay Vaughn, eds. *Women of the Mexican Countryside, 1850–1990* (Tucson, AZ: University of Arizona Press, 1994).

French, John D., and Daniel James, eds. *The Gendered Worlds of Latin American Women Workers* (Durham, NC: Duke University Press, 1997). Essays on working-class women.

Herrera, Hayden. *Frida: A Biography of Frida Kahlo* (New York: Perennial, 1984).

James, Daniel. *Doña María's Story* (Durham, NC: Duke University Press, 2000). A woman in the meatpacking plants of Argentina.

Klubock, Thomas. *Contested Communities: Class, Gender, and Politics in Chile's El Teniente Copper Mine, 1904–1951* (Durham, NC: Duke University Press, 1998). Life in the mining camps.

Moya, José C. *Cousins and Strangers: Spanish Immigrants in Buenos Aires, 1850–1930* (Berkeley, CA: University of California Press, 1998). Traces the immigrant experience from Europe to Buenos Aires.

Parker, D. S. *The Idea of the Middle Class: White Collar Workers and Peruvian Society, 1900–1950* (University Park, PA: Penn State University Press, 1998). A rare view into middle-class work and society.

Parodi, Jorge. *To Be a Worker in Peru: Identity and Politics*. Trans. James Alstrum and Catherine Conaghan (Chapel Hill, NC: University of North Carolina Press, 2000). The hard life of the Peruvian working class.

14

REVOLUTION, REACTION, DEMOCRACY, AND THE NEW GLOBAL ECONOMY:
1959 TO THE PRESENT

THE POSTWAR WORLD'S promise of equitable politics and societies and prosperous economies went unfulfilled in Latin America. The region's leaders still grappled with the Social Question, seeking to satisfy the demands of the expanding middle and urban industrial working classes. In the early 1950s, as we saw in Chapter 12, Latin Americans turned to old dictators, such as Carlos Ibáñez in Chile and Getúlio Vargas in Brazil, or looked to new strongmen, as in Colombia and Venezuela. There seemed to be no answers, only failed formulas, tired politicians, and angry, impatient military officers. The major innovation of the era was the vast expansion of the electorate. Women at last won full suffrage, although the vote by no means ensured them an equal voice in political affairs. Governments eliminated literacy qualifications for political participation. The Cold War rivalry between communists in the Soviet Union and China on one side and capitalists in the United States and Western Europe on the other provided international context for the internal struggles.

The victory of the 26th of July Movement in Cuba in 1959 and the subsequent adoption of communism by the Revolution struck fear into the upper class–military alliance in Latin America. During the next 20 years, the Latin American Left surged and experienced an unprecedented degree of success. Chileans elected Socialist Dr. Salvador Allende (1970–1973) as president, and the *Sandinista* Revolution in Nicaragua (1979–1990) held power for a full decade. Major leftist insurgencies took place in Colombia, El Salvador, Guatemala, and Peru. Salvadoran and Peruvian rebels came within a hairbreadth of winning their wars. But at the same time, politics polarized into brutal violence. Leftist guerrillas staged robberies and kidnappings, attacked police, and bombed buildings, and, in response, Latin American militaries embarked on a vicious reign of terror from the mid-1960s through the mid-1980s. Neither Left nor Right governments delivered sustained economic growth or social peace. Militaries ruled the major nations of the region through the 1970s and 1980s, seeking, at least in the beginning, to formulate new societies without popular organizations and political parties.

Eventually, if reluctantly, the armed forces, at times humiliated by defeat or scandal, withdrew from direct control over governments in the 1980s, pushed out to a large extent by the citizens of the nations they ruled. Democracy returned to every country in the region (except Cuba) by the 1990s. As the new century began and the new democracies struggled with widespread poverty and severely inequitable income distribution, a number of Latin American nations elected left-of-center leaders in a phenomenon known as the "Pink Tide." ("Pink" indicated that the leaders were not so far left as to be communist.)

At the outset of the post-1959 era, Latin American regimes continued to adhere to the import substitution industrialization (ISI) model of economic development. As we saw in Chapter 12, as the Right triumphed, it had presided over increasing government involvement in the economy. By the 1980s, however, ISI had failed resoundingly. Starting with Chile's military rule after 1973, Latin America gradually embraced free market economics. With the fall of communism in the Soviet Union and Eastern Europe in the late 1980s, there was no longer a Left alternative to capitalism. By the 1990s, it was clear that both the most extreme Left and Right regimes had ended in unmitigated disaster for most middle- and lower-class Latin Americans. The new left-of-center governments in several nations, such as Argentina, Brazil, Chile, and Peru, continued neoliberal economic policies, but modified their application by paying more attention to issues of social welfare. New programs have achieved some success in alleviating the worst poverty.

THE REVOLUTIONS: CUBA, NICARAGUA, EL SALVADOR, GUATEMALA, PERU, AND COLOMBIA

The Cuban Revolution shattered the fragile political equilibrium of the late 1950s in Latin America. The victory of Fidel Castro and his 26th of July Movement in Cuba introduced a whole new set of factors into Latin American domestic political equations. The "fall" of Cuba to communism mobilized the United States to intense involvement in the region. Fidel Castro's call for revolution throughout Latin America intensified the fears of the upper class–military alliance. Revolutionary insurgencies rose all over the region in the 1960s and 1970s, some obviously inspired by Cuba and others the result of entirely domestic factors. Often encouraged by the United States, Latin American militaries increased their political and economic activity in response.

Cuba

Cuba seemed an unlikely location for communist revolution in the late 1950s. After all, it was only 90 miles from the United States, filled with U.S. investment and tourists, dependent on the United States as a market for its sugar, and ruled by the Caribbean's strongest dictator, Fulgencio Batista. It also boasted one of the wealthiest, healthiest, and best-educated populations in Latin America. Nonetheless, on January 1, 1959, the revolutionary 26th of July Movement, led by Fidel Castro and other opposition groups, overthrew Batista (1940–1944, 1952–1959).

Batista had dominated the island's politics since 1934. He spent 7 years of comfortable, voluntary exile in Florida after the completion of his first term as president in 1944, and then returned as dictator in 1952. He and his followers hoped to regenerate Cuba, but, as his fellow former strongmen Ibáñez and Vargas discovered, ruling was harder the second time around, even if one was now a dictator. Fidel Castro was one of Batista's early opponents. Castro had grown up in the rough-and-tumble of Cuban student politics during the late 1940s and early 1950s, an era of blatant corruption, open violence, and deep disillusionment. On July 26, 1953, Castro led a small band in a disastrous attack on the army barracks at Moncada on the southern part of the island, barely escaping with his life. He was captured a few days later, however, and avoided execution only by luck. Amnestied after 2 years in prison in 1955, he left for Mexico, where he plotted and raised money to mount a new invasion of Cuba. He returned in late 1956, making his way with a small group of rebels to the mountains in the southeastern part of the island. There he established a small guerrilla movement, supported by local rural people. During the next 2 years, Batista's regime crumbled as the 26th of July movement and others, mostly urban rebels, grew stronger.

On the day the rebel army rolled into Havana, Castro declared that "This time the Revolution will truly come to power. It will not be . . . [as in the past] . . . when the masses were exuberant in the belief that they had at last come to power but thieves came to power instead. No thieves, no traitors, no interventionists! This time the revolution is for real."

Glorious victory soon gave way to grim reality, and Castro faced a number of daunting obstacles. First, the relatively small 26th of July Movement had to consolidate its power, because the group had never numbered more than a few hundred. Other rebel groups looked to share the victory. Second, at 32, Castro was the oldest of the revolutionaries. The revolutionaries' relative youth, which had stood them well during the rigors of guerrilla warfare, was a glaring disadvantage when the rebels became rulers: Neither Castro nor his followers had administrative experience, nor did they have a plan for governing. Castro thus needed reliable allies with expertise in governance. Third, Castro had to neutralize the United States, which had cut short Cuba's previous revolutions in 1898 and 1933.

Castro resolved these problems in the early 1960s by proclaiming his revolution socialist, breaking relations with the United States, allying with the Soviet Union, and taking on the Cuban communist party as a partner in governance.

His actions led to two confrontations with the United States that ultimately solidified his regime. In April 1961, his army defeated an informal force of U.S.-trained and U.S.-supported Cuban exiles who invaded the island at the Bay of Pigs, making him an even greater hero than previously. Then, in October 1962, the United States and the Soviet Union nearly went to war over the installation in Cuba of Soviet offensive intercontinental ballistic missiles. The U.S. Navy blockaded the island to prevent the arrival of additional weaponry. After a tense 13 days, the superpowers reached agreement: The United States promised not to invade Cuba if the Soviets removed the missiles from the island. The United States, however, has maintained an embargo on trade with Cuba from that time to the present day.

The Cuban Revolution has met with mixed success. Its economic program during its first two decades was marked by a series of unsuccessful attempts at diversification from its dependence on sugar exports and quixotic efforts to create a "New Socialist" Cuban who would work for the general good rather than individual gain. Castro then created a Soviet-style inflexible bureaucracy, the failures of which led him to occasional experiments with free markets and private enterprise. Cuba relied heavily on billions of dollars provided by the Soviet Union and the Communist bloc in Eastern Europe, which purchased most of the island's sugar. The collapse of the Soviet Union and its satellites in 1989 and the subsequent loss of their financial support caused an enormous crisis from which the nation recovered only slowly. There have been periodic shortages of staples and rationing. Nickel exports and tourism (mostly Europeans) have augmented the economy since 2000. Sugar has been in decline, with the 2009 harvest the smallest in a century. Despite the ups and downs of the economy, Cubans have been the best-educated and healthiest Latin Americans. The distribution of wealth is the most equitable in the region.

Politically, Fidel Castro, ailing at age 82, resigned as president of the Council of State in 2008, stepping aside for his younger brother (by 5 years) Raul. Fidel remains the First Secretary of the Communist Party.

Nicaragua

Central America suffered major upheavals after World War II, when long-term dictators, pressured by U.S. diplomacy, retired or were overthrown by more progressive forces.

The prolonged guerrilla wars and counterinsurgency in the region began in the aftermath of the Cuban insurrection and resulted in the deaths of hundreds of thousands of people and the displacement of millions more during the 1970s, 1980s, and early 1990s. By 2000, the nations of the region, their civil wars fought to stalemates, were at peace, and democracies governed all.

The road to this eventual outcome was long and agonizing, however. In 1979, the Sandinista National Liberation Front (FSLN) in Nicaragua overthrew Anastasio Somoza Debayle, making Nicaragua's leftist revolution the only one other than Cuba's to win power through force of arms. Later, however, it became the only leftist revolution in Latin America to lose control of the government through fair elections. The Somoza family, Anastasio Somoza García (1935–1956) and his sons Luis Somoza Debayle (1956–1967) and Anastasio Somoza Debayle (1967–1979), ruled Nicaragua for 46 years through control of the National Guard, which devolved into a lucrative criminal enterprise. Like many other Latin American insurgencies, the Sandinista National Liberation Front began in the early 1960s. It took its name from Augusto Sandino, who had led guerrillas against the U.S. occupation of Nicaragua during the late 1920s and whom Somoza's henchmen had assassinated in 1934. It attracted rural people, students, and the disillusioned children of upper- and middle-class families, perhaps numbering only about 3000 in 1978.

The Somoza regime began to disintegrate when it misappropriated relief funds after a catastrophic earthquake in 1972. Anastasio Somoza Debayle lost the support of the upper classes 6 years later when he ordered the assassination of longtime rival Pedro Joaquín Chamorro. The FSLN then took control of the National Palace in a daring raid, an action that clearly indicated the regime had lost its iron grip. Somoza fled on July 19, 1979. An estimated 50,000 Nicaraguans died in the brief but bloody civil war.

The Sandinistas ruled for the next decade. They governed without national elections until 1984, when FSLN leader Daniel Ortega won the presidency. Unfortunately for the Sandinistas, they encountered implacable opposition to their regime from the United States during Ronald Reagan's administration, which clandestinely and illegally backed the rival *Contras,* a conservative coalition, in a vicious civil war from 1981 to 1989 that cost another 40,000 Nicaraguans their lives. With the help of the other Central American presidents, the FSLN and the Contras finally reached a peace agreement in 1989.

The Sandinistas, again, like the 26th of July group, committed serious economic and administrative blunders mostly due to their inexperience. The civil war took an enormous toll not only in lives but also in billions of dollars in damages. The military draft, instituted to supply soldiers to combat the Contras, was very unpopular. But the single most important mistake of the Sandinista leadership was its failure to fully incorporate women. Much of the Sandinista guerrilla leadership was female, and many women heroes were wounded, raped, and tortured during the war for control of the country. The FSLN could not have won without the efforts of its women leaders and soldiers, but many of the movement's women felt dismissed and disdained after 1979, when the work of battle shifted to the work of governing. The Sandinistas also angered women in traditional roles, who did not want their children drafted into the army. This massive loss of women's support during the 1980s played a large part in the Sandinistas loss of the 1990 election.

Almost everyone in Nicaragua and abroad was surprised when Violeta Barrios de Chamorro, the widow of the martyred Pedro Joaquín Chamorro, won election as president that year. Nicaraguans were exhausted from years of civil war and sought an alternative to the ineffective Sandinistas. The FSLN remained a powerful influence in the National Assembly, where it was the largest single party, and in the army. Nonetheless, Nicaraguans were so disillusioned with the Sandinistas that they elected two more Conservative presidents to succeed Chamorro in 1996 and 2002, the first instances in Nicaraguan history when one democratically elected president succeeded another. However, in 2006, amidst the regionwide Pink Tide, Daniel Ortega staged a stunning political comeback, when he won election as president.

El Salvador

In El Salvador, a leftist insurgency nearly won control of the country in the 1980s. The nation's troubles dated back to the early 1930s, when the brutal dictatorship of General Maximiliano Hernández Martínez ordered the slaughter of 30,000 rural Salvadorans. The upper classes, fearing another uprising, backed Hernández Martínez (1930–1944) until his overthrow in 1944. Thereafter, an alliance between wealthy coffee planters and the military governed through electoral fraud and violent repression. El Salvador held its first open election in 1972, but the government nullified the results when it became clear that José Napoleón Duarte, the opposition candidate, had received the most votes. Twelve years passed before the next legitimate election, and this time Duarte (1984–1989) won (again) and took office in 1984.

Despite the democratic outcome of the election, a vicious civil war tore the country apart for the next 5 years. Guerrilla groups appeared in El Salvador in the late 1960s, drawing their support from El Salvador's vast, exploited, migratory rural working class. Between 1979 and 1989 the Augustín Farabundo Martí Front for National Liberation (FMLN) mounted a strong challenge to the military–upper class alliance, nearly winning the civil war, but for the massive assistance to the Salvadoran army provided by the United States. At their peak, the FMLN had an estimated 8000 combatants.

Exhausted by years of civil war, Salvadorans went to the polls in 1989 and elected Alfredo Cristiani, the candidate of the National Republican Alliance (ARENA), a coalition of right-wing groups. Much as in Nicaragua, people turned to the Right to bring peace. Cristiani reached agreement with the guerrillas in 1991, and three ARENA presidents succeeded each other in 1994, 1999, and 2004. In 2009 Salvadorans elected Maurisio Funas, a member of the FMLN, as president. As in Nicaragua, the guerrillas of the 1980s had in the new millennium taken power.

Guatemala

In 1944, Guatemala's longtime dictator, Jorge Ubico (1930–1944), was overthrown by a reformist group, led by young military officers, that redistributed land and fostered labor. This process ended in 1954, however, when the U.S. Central Intelligence Agency sponsored a successful revolt by Colonel Carlos Castillo Armas, who brutally overturned a decade's worth of improvements in the lives of the working classes. His successor, Miguel Ydígoras Fuentes (1958–1963), likewise served the interests of the upper classes, but without the repression practiced by Castillo.

In 1960, a guerrilla movement calling itself the Rebel Armed Forces, heartened by the Cuban example, took up arms. The military, in an effort to combat the guerrillas, ousted Ydígoras in 1963 and then ruled behind the scenes for the next decade, waging a campaign of terror and murder. Two successive generals ruled for the next 8 years. They intensified repression and presided over a measure of economic gains and an orgy of corruption. Death squads, determined to crush the rural insurgency, stalked the countryside, killing Indians, who supposedly supported the guerrillas. The scale of murder reached genocidal proportions. The war continued through coups and a string of presidents until 1996, when the government reached an accord with the rebels, ending nearly four decades of warfare that had caused 200,000 deaths. A semblance of democracy followed with democratically elected presidents in 2000, 2004, and 2008. As in the cases of Nicaragua and El Salvador, Guatemala lies in ruins, only slowly recovering from decades of violence and destruction.

Peru

From the late 1960s through the 1990s, Peru experienced three distinct revolutionary movements. The first in 1968 consisted of reformist military officers who implemented far-reaching reforms. During the 1980s and 1990s, a violent guerrilla organization terrorized the country and nearly toppled the government. Lastly, a third upheaval occurred when the president who had defeated the guerrillas ruled as an elected dictator in order to rebuild the economy.

Each of the revolutions resulted from the long-term, frustrating impasse in Peruvian politics that pitted the military–upper-class alliance against APRA (see Chapter 12) and its leader Victor Raúl Haya de la Torre. The precipitating event for this series of upheavals was the election of 1962, which first resulted in a military coup to prevent Haya from becoming president. Fernando Belaunde Terry (1963–1968) won the new election, but governed ineffectively, paving the way for another coup, led by General Juan Velasco Alvarado, who set out to establish a "third way," neither communism nor capitalism. Velasco redistributed more land from 1968 to 1975 than either the Mexican or Bolivian revolutions, giving over half the nation's land to 375,000 families, one quarter of all rural dwellers. He also vastly expanded the government's role in the economy, financing his program through massive borrowing abroad. But Velasco became ill in 1975 and stepped down. His successor Francisco Morales Bermúdez rolled back some of the reforms and adopted austerity policies to repay the debt. New elections took place in 1980 with

Belaunde winning the presidency, again with little to show for his term (1980–1985). These years, however, marked the emergence of the Sendero Luminoso (Shining Path), in the Andes mountains.

Abimael Guzmán, the self-proclaimed "Fourth Sword of Marxism" (Marx, Lenin, and Mao were the first three), was the mastermind of the movement, which began in 1970 as a splinter of the fragmented Peruvian Communist Party. The name derived from a quote from José Carlos Mariátegui, Peru's leading communist thinker, which proclaimed that "Marxism-Leninism will open a shining path to revolution." Guzmán dismissed other leftists in Latin America as traitors. He called the Cuban Revolution, for example, "a petty bourgeois militaristic deviation." He also believed in violence. The Sendero brutally murdered thousands of political officials, especially small landowners and those regarded as do-gooders. The awful violence not only intimidated many Peruvians but also earned the group many enemies.

The Sendero organization was extremely disciplined and cohesive, in part because it offered its members opportunities they did not have otherwise. Sendero drew its strength from young people with poverty-stricken backgrounds in the countryside and the shantytowns of Lima. Many of these youths had achieved a university education only to find that neither government nor the private sector could provide them with satisfactory employment. This made the Sendero, which paid its soldiers well by Peruvian standards (by using large amounts of money from taxes on narcotics traffickers), extremely appealing. In addition, the Sendero was fairly egalitarian in terms of gender: Half of its leadership was female. At its height, the Sendero had perhaps 10,000 guerrillas under arms and as many as 100,000 sympathizers.

By 1992, Sendero Luminoso had brought Peru to the verge of demoralization and collapse, and the war had cost 30,000 lives. Guerrilla victory appeared inevitable as the military seemed to fall apart and panic gripped the nation. Then on September 12, 1992, the tide turned, when the army unexpectedly captured Abimael Guzmán and much of the Sendero leadership. Without its highest echelons, the movement disintegrated. The Shining Path had brought Peru to its knees. Like the FMLN in El Salvador, the guerrillas came very close to victory, and the war cost the country dearly in terms of human life and economic destruction.

The third Peruvian "revolution" occurred in 1990, when Peruvians, desperate for a savior as Sendero violence devastated the country, elected little-known Alberto Fujimori president (1990–2000). Having used the military and rural community organizations to defeat the Sendero, Fujimori won reelection in 1995. Fujimori governed autocratically, but with the nation finally at peace, the Peruvian economy grew rapidly. This third "revolution" ended when Fujimori had to flee the country in 2000 in order to avoid arrest amid major scandals. In 2001, Alejandro Toledo became the first Indian to be elected president. In 2006 Peruvians elected Alan García to be president once again.

Colombia

In Colombia during the middle of the twentieth century, as in Peru, dysfunctional politics led to prolonged guerrilla warfare, which, predictably, exacted a heavy toll on its people and economy. Colombian history had long been marred by bloody civil wars between its two major political parties, the Liberals and Conservatives. Following the overthrow of the dictator Gustavo Rojas Pinilla (1953–1957) in 1957, the two political parties formed the National Front. They agreed to alternate the presidency every 4 years and to distribute elected and appointed political offices equally. This arrangement endured for 16 years, finally ending the long-running violence between the two parties.

But Colombia was hardly democratic during these years, given that the National Front permitted little dissent. Lacking outlets for peaceful protest, some citizens banded together into a number of guerrilla groups sprung up during the early 1960s. By the 1980s, the M-19 (founded in 1972) and the Revolutionary Armed Forces of Colombia (FARC) had become the largest and most effective of these groups. The guerrillas often controlled various regions of the country, but they were fragmented and unwilling to unite to obtain victory. In the mid-1980s, there was a brief peace, but from 1986 to 2001, an estimated 300,000 Colombians perished in the violence and an additional 2 million were displaced. By the end of the century, the FARC, its army numbering 15,000, controlled nearly half the country. The Colombian government often seemed on the brink of collapse. The election and reelection of Alvaro Uribe as president in 2002 and 2006 reinvigorated the government's struggle against the rebels, but the FARC remained the largest Marxist insurgency in the world.

THE TYRANNIES: BRAZIL, ARGENTINA, AND CHILE

Beginning in the mid-1960s and lasting through the late 1980s, several Latin American nations endured prolonged rule by rightist, military governments that seized power illegally and maintained control by using terror. Unlike past military regimes, these governments determined to remain indefinitely and to remake their societies, seeking to return to traditional patriarchal values with women subordinate to men and dedicated exclusively to caring for the home and their children. The military regimes sought and achieved the elimination of leftist organizations, including political parties, labor unions, and university students and faculty. Tens of thousands of people perished in the onslaught, many of them tortured. They spared no one, as rich, poor, men, women, children, bureaucrats, priests, and nuns were victims. Most citizens of these countries looked the other way in the face of the horror, fearing leftist takeovers more than their loss of freedoms.

The support for the rightist governments came from the armed forces, which despite their internal divisions united in common fear of the Left, the middle classes, whose members were terrified by the threatened disorder brought on by protesters, and the U.S. government, which regarded the Latin American military as the last bastion against communism in the resurgent Cold War against the Soviet Union. The military relied on well-educated technocrats to operate the government bureaucracy and state-owned enterprises, creating a political structure that became known as "bureaucratic authoritarianism."

The military regimes also looked to further economic development through a strategy that included attracting foreign investment by keeping wages low and enabling the accumulation of vast wealth by the domestic upper classes. State-run businesses proved enormously inefficient and corrupt. Moreover, their economic policies were often detrimental to their core constituencies, the middle classes.

Brazil

The Brazilian military took over in 1964 after a tumultuous 3 years during which President Janio Quadros (1961), an eccentric independent with no political party backing, abruptly resigned after only months in office and was succeeded by João Goulart, the vice president, a former close ally of Getulio Vargas, whom the military despised. Goulart lasted less than 3 years.

The first military governments were led by General Humberto de Alancar Castello Branco (1964–1967) and General Artur de Costa e Silva (1967–1969), who severely limited civil rights and established the wage suppression–foreign investment economic development policy. The war on the Left intensified under Emílio Garrastazú Médici (1969–1974), who also presided over the so-called Brazilian "economic miracle." By the late 1970s, however, the military had proven as inept and corrupt as its civilian predecessors, and it began a slow transition to democratic government. The first elected president in two decades, Tancredo Neves (1985), died after 2 weeks in office, but his successor José Sarney (1985–1990) managed his way through difficult economic times. Since 1985 Brazil has maintained its democracy.

Argentina

After the coup that overthrew Juan Perón in1955, Argentina experienced a decade of alternating military and civilian governments with neither the armed forces nor the various factions of the Radical Party able to find a way to accommodate the Peronists.

In 1966, General Juan Carlos Onganía overthrew Arturo Illia (1963–1966) and set about to renovate society. He outlawed political parties and expelled leftist students and faculty from the universities. These actions resulted in widespread protests, led by automobile workers and students in the interior city of Córdoba in May 1969. Within a year, these protests were followed by series of spectacular kidnappings by guerrillas known as the *Montoneros*. Although it proved ineffective, the group provoked an unprecedented, vicious response from rightwing military and upper-class-sponsored gangs. Argentina descended into murder and chaos. With the nation disintegrating, it turned once again to Juan Perón, then long exiled in Spain. Even though in failing health, 78-year-old Perón won election as president in 1974. He died in July after only a few futile months in office. His third wife María Estela Martínez de Perón ("Isabelita") succeeded him with no better results until she was overthrown in early 1976.

From 1976 to 1983 was the darkest chapter in Argentine history. Under the brutal rule of General Jorge Videla (1976–1981) due process of law vanished and was replaced by torture and murder. By 1978 the military had eradicated the guerrillas and killed most labor union leaders, even shop stewards. The cost was dear, for the armed forces, police, and right wing gangs killed an estimated 30,000 people. Known as the "disappeared" ones (*desaparecidos*), they were executed without trials or public records.

As in Brazil, however, the military's popularity waned over time as they proved inept economic managers. In a desperate measure to regain support, the regime went to war against Great Britain in April 1982. Argentine forces occupied the Malvinas in the South Pacific, a territory that the British had seized 150 years earlier and which had remained in dispute ever since. President Leopoldo Galtieri (1981–1982) badly miscalculated both the British response and the reaction of the United States, expecting the former not to fight for the islands and the latter to back Argentina. The war was disastrous, resulting in 2000 casualties and $2 billion in expenditures. The humiliating defeat discredited the Argentine armed services and forced them to relinquish power.

Raúl Alfonsín (1983–1989), who had long opposed the military dictatorship, won election as president in 1983. His term was difficult, because the Peronists were uncooperative and the armed forces staged a number of rebellions. He had begun the healing, however, and paved the way for the peaceful succession of Peronist Carlos Menem (1989–1999) in 1989. It was the first time since 1928 that one elected Argentine president followed another. Menem served two terms. Four presidents fulfilled the next term, as an economic downturn buffeted the nation. Left-leaning populist Néstor Kirchner (2003–2007) and his wife Cristina Fernández de Kirchner (2007–2011) were Argentine versions of the "Pink Tide" that swept South America after the turn of the millennium.

Slice of Life   ON THE STREETS OF NUEVO LAREDO

MORE THAN ONE-FOURTH of all working Latin Americans are employed in the informal sector of the economy, which includes petty entrepreneurs selling a broad range of items and providing services, as well as small-time criminals, prostitutes, and street children. In Peru, more than half of the working people toil in the informal sector. High unemployment rates, especially among unskilled, inadequately educated people, many of whom are recent migrants from the countryside, have left millions of Latin Americans on the economic margins, struggling daily to make a living.

Perhaps the most well-known of these petty business people are the street vendors seen almost everywhere in the large cities, where they fill the public spaces outside of the underground (subway) and bus stations and the sidewalks of busy neighborhoods. But there are several hundred thousand more who scratch out their subsistence as trash pickers, known as *pepenadores* in Mexico, *cartoneros* in Argentina, *catadores* in Brazil, and *moscas* in Peru. They constitute an extensive recycling enterprise throughout the region, scavenging bottles, cans, and cardboard. One study in 2002 estimated that 150,000 Brazilians earned their living collecting aluminum cans, some 9 billion of them a year. In some cases, trash picking has moved beyond the informal economy. In Mexico City, the pickers have their own union which controls the municipal dumps.

The cardboard pickers, known as *cartoneros,* of Nuevo Laredo, Mexico, while not entirely typical of the informal economy, nonetheless, provide us with a graphic insight into its operations. Nuevo Laredo is a city of 400,000, in the State of Tamaulipas, in northeastern Mexico directly across the Rio Grande River from its twin city Laredo, Texas. For a century and a half Mexicans have recovered wastes from both cities. According to Martín Medina, who has meticulously studied the cartoneros in Nuevo Laredo, Mexican scavengers have collected cardboard in Laredo since before World War II. Medina's informants describe a large number of cartoneros collecting in Laredo and bringing the cardboard across the border during the 1940s. Because U.S. sanitary regulations did not permit them to bring their horses into the United States, the collectors had to use pushcarts. They use horse carts in Nuevo Laredo to the present day.

As a result of the considerable expansion of Laredo as a retail center and the establishment of border manufacturing plants, known as *maquiladoras,* in northern Mexico, the amount of cardboard boxes has grown enormously over the past few decades. During the 1950s, a Catholic priest in Laredo helped found a cartonero cooperative, the Sociedad Cooperativa de Recuperadores de Materiales de Nuevo Laredo, and to negotiate a legal working arrangement with local government in Laredo. The scavengers suffered a setback in the 1960s, when the Mexican government outlawed importation of waste cardboard. The cartoneros innovatively smuggled the material by throwing the cardboard into the river and having accomplices pull it out on the other side. During the 1980s, the Mexican government instituted a quota system, requiring an expensive permit to transport cardboard within Mexico. The cartoneros, however, circumvented and outlasted all these impediments.

Recycling of paper products in Mexico has become an important business. The paper industry has been chronically short of raw materials, as the consequence of the high cost of logging in Mexico (paper is made from wood). By the 1990s, only a quarter of the fiber used in Mexican paper came from wood pulp. The rest was from recycling. Therefore, what began as an illustrative case of the informal economy has become attached (and vital) to the formal economy, the paper industry. Middlemen connect the two sectors, with the cartoneros selling to the middlemen and the middlemen selling to the industry.

Medina cites a survey conducted in 1994, which presents a picture of the average cartonero: He is a 40-year-old married male and is literate in Spanish, despite having had only 4 years of education. Most cartoneros are male, because the usual method of transporting the cardboard is a three-wheeled cart, known as a *tricicleta,* which requires strength enough to move more than 800 pounds of cardboard at a time. The cartoneros work 8 or 9 hours a day, 6 days a week. Many augment their income by collecting aluminum cans and other salvageable materials, and occasionally helping smugglers move their goods, mostly electronics, across the border. According to the 1994 survey, three-quarters of the cartoneros owned homes and had a higher median income than the average resident of Nuevo Laredo.

Although some observers sometimes dismiss the informal economy as having marginal economic value, it is clear, at least in the instance of the cartoneros of the

Another occupation in the internal economy is begging. In the words of one mother: "Shame is for those who steal, not for those who beg for their children."

two Laredos that the operators of the informal economy not only perform a valuable economic function but also allow a better-than-average standard of living for themselves and their families.

Questions for Discussion

What are the obstacles to entering the informal economy? What are the obstacles to making a decent living? Do you think that the cartoneros are part and parcel of an inherently corrupt political and economic system?

Chile

The tyranny that emerged in Chile during the 1970s was as shocking as that in Argentina and lasted a decade longer. Chile's long-held reputation for democratic, nonviolent politics was forever shattered.

In the 1950s, Chileans had turned to familiar names for their leaders, Carlos Ibáñez (1952–1958), a former president, and Jorge Alessandri (1958–1964), a son of a former president, with little results. Fearing that Socialist Salvador Allende, who had narrowly lost the 1958 election, would win in 1964, the moderate and conservative parties coalesced to support Christian Democrat Eduardo Frei (1964–1970). Despite considerable assistance from the U.S. Alliance for Progress, he could not sustain economic development, paving the way for Allende's election in 1970.

The first elected socialist head of state in the Americas, Allende, had a promising start, but his regime ended in tragedy. He ultimately failed, because he was unable to rein in the most radical factions of his coalition; he lost the support of the middle classes, which were wary of his radical program; and, lastly, the military abandoned its commitment to civilian constitutional rule. High prices for copper, Chile's leading export, boosted the economy during his first year, but the fierce opposition of the upper classes, the opposition of the U.S. government and foreign corporations, the loss of middle-class backing, and deteriorating economic conditions led to a military rebellion on September 11, 1973. Allende died in the fighting.

The commander of the army, General Augusto Pinochet, led the coup. He set out to not only depose the socialist president but, like the Argentine military, also to renovate Chilean society by eliminating the Left. The armed forces and their right-wing allies imprisoned, tortured, and murdered thousands. Pinochet closed congress and outlawed political parties and labor unions. He also privatized government-run enterprises and deregulated the economy. During his 16 years of dictatorship, however, Pinochet never suppressed Chileans' democratic tradition. A national plebiscite in 1988 ended military rule. Moderate Christian Democrats succeeded each other in the 1990s, accompanied by a measure of economic prosperity.

THE EXCEPTION: MEXICO

Only in Mexico, among the largest nations of Latin America, did the military play a subordinate role, though it too experienced a hidden "dirty" war against the Left during the 1970s and 1980s. As we learned in Chapter 11, after the revolutionary decade 1910 to 1920, a single-party political system evolved that began relatively responsive to the middle and lower classes, but which over time cared less and less about its constituents and became more and more corrupt. The regime used selective violence and patronage to maintain its power. From the 1940s through the 1960s, Mexico underwent a prolonged era of economic growth that redistributed wealth downward from the upper-income strata and upward from the lowest strata. The middle classes and skilled working class enjoyed a measure of prosperity. The Institutionalized Revolutionary Party (PRI) ruled unchallenged.

By the 1960s, however, the PRI had lost touch with the common folk. Growing protests from students and workers in 1968 caused PRI leaders to panic, leading to the slaughter of an estimated 500 people in the Plaza of the Three Cultures in Mexico City on October 2. Mexico was to host the Summer Olympic games, and the government feared embarrassment. The massacre at Tlateloco, as it became known, discredited the regime at home and abroad.

The discovery of vast oil reserves in the 1970s seemed at first as the way to continue economic growth and maintain the PRI in power. But mismanagement and corruption squandered the oil revenues. In order to continue the orgy of spending and theft the government borrowed heavily abroad, which left the nation with a mountain of debt, which, when oil prices fell from the boom time heights, was beyond Mexico's ability to repay.

The PRI continued to elect presidents through 2000, when the conservative *Partido de Acción Nacional* ended 70 years of one-party rule with Vicente Fox (2000–2006), a former executive with Coca Cola, winning the presidency. He was succeeded by another Panista Felipe de Jesús Calderón Hinojosa (2006–2012). Faced with a national legislature split between the PRI, PAN, and PRD (Party of the Democratic Revolution), neither Fox nor Calderón have accomplished very much reform. Calderón also confronted the drastic economic downturn in the United States, Mexico's largest trading partner, and the debacle of the war on drugs. The latter led to a widespread outbreak of violence, especially along the northern border.

LATIN AMERICAN LIVES

AN ARGENTINE MILITARY OFFICER

THE YEARS FROM 1976 to 1983 were Argentina's nightmare. The military, police, and vigilantes kidnapped, tortured, and killed thousands of its citizens. Military officers threw naked, drugged civilians from airplanes over the South Atlantic Ocean. Squads of white Ford Falcons arrived at homes in the middle of the night and took away their occupants, whom no one ever saw again. Soldiers raped female prisoners. Terrorist gangs kidnapped pregnant women, taking the babies and killing the mothers. Even today, few military officers are repentant for the deeds of this era. Who were the soldiers who could have committed such acts? What was it about the institution of the military that led it to turn viciously on its own people?

In 1995, retired Naval Captain Adolfo Scilingo and a half dozen other ex-officers publicly confessed to murder. While stationed at the Navy Mechanics School as a junior officer in 1977, Scilingo had flown on two flights during which he personally threw more than 30 living people into the ocean. He reported that his superiors had told him that these were extraordinary times requiring unusual actions.

The Argentine military was at almost every point before 1976 divided into two main groups: those who would maintain the constitutional order, even if they opposed the policies of the civilian government, and those who would overthrow any civilian government. There were also splits between the generals and the lesser-ranking officers. They argued over personalities and management styles. Finally, there were disagreements between the Army, Navy, and Air Force. The military previously had taken over the government in 1930, 1943, 1955, 1962, and 1966. Although their divisions never entirely disappeared, the armed forces unified from 1976 to 1983 in what they believed was a holy mission to save their fatherland. This time they vowed to remain in control.

Prior to 1976, Latin American officers trained at their individual nation's military academy. They chose their branch (cavalry, infantry, or artillery) during the first year of their 4-year course. Supply officers attended the academies, but they did not develop the same bonds as the line officers. The rigorous training emphasized character and tradition. The academies turned out men who had "a very subjective and very romantic . . ." worldview.

New officers experienced rigid discipline. They fell under the complete authority of their commanding officer, who often took an interest in the junior officer's social life and whose approval was necessary to marry. They earned promotions periodically: sub-lieutenant to lieutenant in 4 years, to captain in 8. Officers attended new schools at regular intervals. Selection to the status of general staff officers through examinations assured higher ranks. Those who reached the rank of colonel after about 20 years had received a year of higher military studies, which educated them in important national concerns. They also traveled abroad, often to the United States. The Argentine military was heavily influenced by German practices prior to World War II and by U.S. doctrine thereafter.

An officer's experience throughout the twentieth century would also include eroding salaries, outmoded equipment, and an intensifying sense of loyalty to the military. The officer corps believed itself above civilian petty politics in the abstract, but was mired in them in reality. Officers saw their duty was to defend their nation, but they disdained the civilians they swore to protect.

The generation of officers that came of age during the 1970s was either from small towns in the interior or sons or grandsons of immigrants. The previous cohort of officers had included many second-generation Argentines (half of the generals in 1950). As ethnic Argentines, they were often superpatriotic. Many sons of officers followed their fathers into the military. They lived to great extent in an insular world with military friends and family, which created a mentality of the military against the world. These officers did not trust civilians. The burst of leftist terrorism in the 1970s struck hard at their psyches, traditions, and beliefs. They saw themselves under siege by international communism.

By 1976, the Argentine military was desperate. It had intervened repeatedly in politics since 1930 to no effect. The nation seemed to regard the military with respect. Peronism was a sore that would not heal, but after his death in 1974, bringing back the dictator clearly was not an option. The international situation frightened the military, for insurgencies were everywhere: Vietnam, Africa, and other parts of Latin America. Fidel Castro had sponsored guerrillas (unsuccessfully) in neighboring Bolivia. Reflective of their middle-class backgrounds and decades of indoctrination, the office corps struck hard against its real and imagined enemies. The results scarred Argentina forever.

Captain Adolfo Scilingo, one of the Argentine military officers who admitted murdering civilians during the "Dirty War" (1976–1983).

Questions for Discussion
How did the Argentine military become so integral to the years of terror during the 1970s and 1980s? What factors caused the struggle between Left and Right to degenerate into brutality? How would you compare the years of the terror with some of the internecine strife during the nineteenth century, such as the civil wars between Liberals and Conservatives?

RESURGENT DEMOCRACY AND THE "PINK TIDE"

Latin Americans freed themselves from right-wing tyrannies beginning with the fall of the Argentine military in the wake of the humiliation of the Malvinas War in 1983, the Brazilian *Abertura* (democratic opening) during the mid-1980s, and the Chilean plebiscite (1988) and end to Pinochet's dictatorship in 1990. With the exception of Colombia, the terrible civil wars and insurgencies that had raged in the region ended by the mid-1990s. The new democracies that replaced the dictatorships, however, confronted overwhelming problems, such as the increased number of poor and the extreme maldistribution of wealth, which were the results of the inability of Latin American economies and societies to create sufficient employment or to provide crucial elements of social welfare, including basic education and health care. The exuberant return to free elections, unfortunately, did not bring about immediate amelioration of the harsh conditions many Latin Americans endured. Consequently, in some nations, though notably not Colombia, Mexico, or those in Central America, by the turn of the twenty-first century voters turned leftward for solutions.

The first of the new, elected leftist leaders was Venezuela's Hugo Chávez, a former military officer who had attempted to forcefully overthrow the government in 1992. He took office in 1999. Over the course of the next 7 years, left-of-center Ricardo Lagos and Michelle Bachelet in Chile, Luiz Inácio "Lula" da Silva in Brazil, Néstor Kirchner in Argentina, Alejandro Toledo in Peru, Evo Morales in Bolivia, and Tabares Vázquez in Uruguay ascended to the presidencies of their countries, comprising what became known as the "Pink Tide." Daniel Ortega's election in Nicaragua in 2006 and the FMLN's Mauricio Funes winning the presidency in 2009 continued the leftward trend.

Hugo Chávez quickly became notorious for his bellicose oratory, loudly berating both his domestic enemies—all political parties—and the United States, and for his friendship with Fidel Castro. The rapid increase in world oil prices after the terrorist attack on New York City in September 2001 heralded a bonanza for Venezuela, which had the largest petroleum reserves in the world outside of Saudi Arabia, providing Chávez with billions to implement his programs. Despite a slow start, his regime lowered the poverty rate to 39 percent from 50 percent, and the rate of extreme poverty by half. Inequality also fell substantially. There was a one-third decline in infant mortality and a doubling of the number of students in higher education. Inflation, however, remained a critical problem, remaining at over 30 percent. The country continued to be at the mercy of erratic oil prices. Chávez pushed through a number of political reforms that concentrated power in his hands and limited the rights of his opposition.

Latin American political leaders who came from the socialist and communist Left were somewhat more successful in alleviating the extreme inequities in income and the widespread poverty that plagued the continent. They were also less likely to challenge the neoliberal economic programs of their predecessors. In Chile, a left-of-center coalition of Christian Democrats and Socialists governed after the end of the Pinochet regime in 1989. Ricardo Lagos (2001–2006) and Michelle Bachelet (2006–2011) came from the old Socialist Party of Allende. The Left alliance brought a considerable measure of prosperity to Chile, reducing poverty, growing the economy, and investing in human capital (education, for example). Christian Democrats and Socialists alike continued the neoliberal policies of their predecessor Pinochet. Chile, however, suffered a major setback in 2010 when an enormous earthquake struck in the vicinity of the port city of Valparaíso. In Uruguay, Tabares Vázquez (2005–2010) won the presidency with the support of the old Left, including many former guerillas, but nonetheless did not tamper with the neoliberal economic program that had resulted in his nation having the lowest rate of poverty in the region. Uruguayans elected a former Tupamarú guerrilla José Mujica as president in 2010. Alejandro Toledo (2001–2006) in Peru, another socialist, restored stability to the nation's ruined politics in the aftermath of Fujimori's resignation in 2000. But he, too, did not alter the neoliberal economic policies of his predecessor. Peruvians then rejected further movement leftward by electing Alan García, the former president who had allowed the Shining Path insurgency to expand, as president in 2006. Both Uruguay and Peru experienced steady economic growth from 2003 through 2008.

"Lula" da Silva (2003–2011) in Brazil, perhaps, more than any other Latin American leader, epitomized the new wave of Left politics. He had founded the Brazilian Workers' Party in 1980 at the height of the military dictatorship. But he, too, did not adopt a radical program as president. His economic record has been cautious. Lula chose to continue the policies of his predecessor Fernando Henrique Cardoso (1995–2003), emphasizing fiscal conservatism and maintaining low inflation. The centerpiece of his social program was the Bolsa Família, which involves direct payments to poor families in return for their sending their children to school and taking advantage of preventive medicine programs. There has been as a result a halving of the number of Brazilians living in extreme poverty. Nonetheless, income distribution remains the most unequal in Latin America with the top 10 percent controlling 50.6 percent of the wealth and the bottom 10 percent 0.8 percent. In the new millennium, Brazil has emerged as one of the most important economic powers in the world, particularly as a leader in the production of food.

The most obvious old-line populist to emerge in the Pink Tide was Néstor Kirchner (2003–2007), a Perónist like Saul Menem, in Argentina. Kirchner rescued his nation from the depths of economic crisis and employed many of the familiar redistributive policies that made Perón popular among the working class. This resulted in a considerable reduction in the rate of poverty and extreme poverty and an improvement in the unequal distribution of wealth, though Argentina remains one of the most inequitable societies in the region. His wife Cristina Fernández de Kirchner, a prominent politician in her own right, succeeded him as president in 2007.

Perhaps the most radical of the emerging left leaders was Evo Morales (2006–2014) in Bolivia, the first elected indigenous president. Morales, contradicting a generation of political economic policies in the region, nationalized Bolivian natural gas resources in his first months in office. He also severed Bolivia's long-standing relationships with the International Monetary Fund and the World Bank. Taking over the revenues from hydrocarbon production provided the government with windfall revenues to finance its programs. Bolivia remains the poorest country in South America.

Democratization has proven inefficient in Latin America (as it has everywhere else), with presidents often at odds with their legislative bodies. In Venezuela, impatience with indecisive and often corrupt politics resulted in a popular president enhancing executive powers. A tendency toward authoritarian politics has also marked Nestor Kirchner's career. But for the most part, the Left has maintained a strong commitment to democracy.

The Left has not surged to power everywhere in Latin America, however. In Colombia, dissatisfaction with the displacements of decades of guerilla warfare led voters to elect conservative hard-liner Álvaro Uribe (2002–2010) as president twice. In Central America, the people of El Salvador, Guatemala, and Nicaragua elected conservatives as presidents for a decade after their prolonged civil wars. Mexico turned to the rightist Partido de Acción Nacional (PAN) and Vicente Fox, rather than to the Left to break the hold of the long rule of the PRI, and then elected another PAN president, Felipe Calderón, in 2006 (by a razor-thin margin in a bitterly disputed vote).

THE STRUGGLE FOR CONTROL OF EVERYDAY LIFE

Have Latin Americans given up the struggle to control their everyday lives? For two decades, terror overwhelmed this struggle, and currently, globalization threatens to eliminate differences between nations and peoples. Nonetheless, many Latin Americans retain their sense of locality, and they certainly continue to seek control of their lives. Local loyalties may have helped to save the nation-state from disintegration. The strong sense of local governance and tradition in the Peruvian highlands, for example, was the bulwark of opposition to the Shining Path guerrillas during the 1990s. The Shining Path thoroughly alienated much of the countryside by killing village leaders and priests and by brutally intruding on local prerogatives. The local organizations brought together to protect villages against the guerrillas were crucial participants in the eventual defeat of the insurgency. In Mexico, the deterioration of the official revolutionary political party (PRI), which led to its loss of power in 2000, was caused in large part by its unresponsiveness to local needs and sensibilities. Power had grown overcentralized in a nation where local traditions were so strong. The victorious opposition party, the National Action Party (PAN), was to considerable extent a product of Mexico's peripheral states, particularly in the north.

Unquestionably, contemporary factors have altered this unending struggle for control of everyday life. It was transformed by the vast migration from the countryside to the cities (see Chapters 13 and 15), which shattered the old ways. The migration resulted in far more people residing in urban slums, barrios, or squatter settlements than in villages. Thus, village life and identity were no longer the basis for people's politics, and the struggle for local (village) autonomy became largely irrelevant for urban dwellers. Instead, people formed neighborhood organizations to obtain services, such as water, electricity, schools, and roads. Also, new arrivals in the cities found it difficult to maintain the traditions of their country homes in the face of mass media that perpetually touted the benefits of a consumer culture.

In the workplace, the new migrants discovered that most workers had to negotiate their own way; only the fortunate might join a labor union. Those who were self-employed, as street vendors, for example, faced similar conditions, though a very few joined associations that represented them.

For those who remained in the countryside, much of the isolation that once defined rural life disappeared. Few could earn a living solely in agriculture, and, as a result, even those who stayed in the villages often had to supplement their income by working elsewhere. Mexicans regularly crossed the border to the United States to work on farms during planting and harvest seasons and then returned home. Rural dwellers' lives were also made difficult by bureaucratic-authoritarian and dictatorial regimes that determinedly undermined local prerogatives the 1970s and 1980s, perceiving local political efforts as impediments to the government's mission. The end of tyranny and the resurgence of democracy, however, have given new life to local autonomy.

INDIGENOUS POLITICAL MOVEMENTS

One of the most extraordinary developments arising from the democratization of Latin America since 1990 was the emergence of indigenous political movements. They have taken up the struggle to enhance local autonomy and to preserve their traditions. Indigenous peoples comprise approximately 11 percent of Latin America's population or 60 million. They are the majority in Bolivia and Guatemala and significant minorities in Belize, Ecuador, Honduras, Mexico, and Peru. Most live in rural communities, barely subsisting by farming their own plots and augmenting their incomes by working elsewhere or by crafts production.

Some historians have surmised that the movements originated with the guerrilla insurgencies of the 1960s and 1970s. Dormant during the years of the terror, they reorganized in thae space afforded them by more open democratic governments. By the 1990s the organizations had adopted up-to-date strategies that included sustained protests and use of mass media. The most famous of the efforts took place in Mexico in 1994, when the Zapatista Army of National Liberation (EZLN) rebelled in Chiapas, a state in southern Mexico, ostensibly against the implementation of the North American Free Trade agreement. Indigenous protests pushed out governments in Ecuador in 1997, 2001, and 2005 and in Bolivia in 2003 and 2005.

A striking aspect of the new movements was their creating new political parties that won considerable success in Colombia, Ecuador, and Bolivia. Peasant and indigenous groups (most notably coca growers) became part of the Movement to Socialism (MAS) that won the presidency in Bolivia in 2005; Evo Morales became the first indigenous elected leader of a South American nation in 2006.

In some ways the indigenous movements are a throwback to the struggles of the nineteenth and early twentieth century, when country people fought to retain their control over their everyday lives. The issues remain much the same: local control, national government interference, taxes, and land alienations. It was no accident that the EZLN took the name of Zapatistas.

THE NEW GLOBAL ECONOMY

As the new millennium began, democratic elections and relatively smooth transitions of power prevailed throughout Latin America. But these new regimes still faced the daunting economic challenges and mounting social tensions that had proven the downfall of the military dictatorships that preceded them. During the half century after World War II, the countries of the region pursued three general strategies to achieve economic development. The first was to promote and diversify exports, either by finding new primary products (oranges in Brazil or petroleum in Mexico, for example) or by using the advantage of inexpensive labor costs to manufacture goods for European or the U.S. markets. The second was import substitution industrialization. There were two versions of ISI: one set forth by democratic governments and the other by military dictatorships. Both export enhancement and ISI required extensive government involvement, costly importation of capital goods, heavy foreign borrowing, and massive foreign investment. Widespread poverty sharply limited domestic markets, placing a brake on economic development based on ISI. The third strategy, neoliberalism, adopted after policymakers declared ISI a failure, threw open Latin American markets, and removed governments from direct participation in the economy.

Despite so-called economic miracles in Mexico from the 1950s through 1970, in Brazil during the late 1960s and early 1970s, and in Chile during the 1990s, major problems hampered sustained economic growth in Latin America in the post-1959 era. The region experienced increasingly volatile cycles of booms and busts because all of the strategies for development depended on external markets, capital, and technology. Periodic downturns cost many people their jobs. Prolonged periods of steep inflation eroded the standard of living of the working and middle classes. Staggering foreign debt

How Historians Understand   THEORIES OF ECONOMIC DEVELOPMENT AND HISTORY

Since World War II, successive theories of economic development not only have greatly influenced the policies of Latin American governments, the behavior of businesspeople, and the plight of hundreds of millions of people but also the interpretation of historical events and trends.

During the nineteenth century, ideas advocating free trade and comparative advantage dominated. Accordingly, Latin American nations were to produce agricultural and mineral commodities for export and open their markets for imports of manufactured goods. The Great Depression of the 1930s challenged these perspectives. Economists no longer universally believed that the export of primary products was sustainable as a means to develop. In the late 1940s, the United Nations Economic Commission for Latin America (UNECLA or CEPAL), led by Raúl Prebisch, an Argentine, put forward the center-periphery paradigm, also known as structuralism. This view dominated Latin American economic thinking through the 1970s. It argued export economies tended in the long run to suffer from a decline in the terms of trade. In other words, the prices received for primary goods decreased because the demand for primary products would not rise as fast as income, while at the same time the prices of industrial products rose over time. The only way structuralists believed that Latin

Women sorting coffee beans on a fazenda in Brazil. Coffee was Brazil's leading export for more than a century.

America could develop was to substitute domestic for imported manufactures. This encouraged import substitution industrialization (see Chapters 12 and 14) as the development policy widely adopted in Latin America after World War II.

By the 1960s, however, ISI had clearly failed. Dependency analysis arose to explain Latin America's lack of development. There were two schools of *dependencia*—the neo-Marxist and the reformist. Dependency advocates believed that peripheral (underdeveloped) countries, like those in Latin America, and center nations (the United States, Western Europe, and more recently Japan) were involved in an unequal exchange that would always exploit the former and benefit the latter. Consequently, the only way to change the system was to either overthrow it, which the Marxist school advocated, or reform it. The most important translation of dependency into policy resulted in further government involvement in the economies of Latin American nations to mitigate the influence of the developed center. Ironically, in order to finance their economic interventions, governments borrowed huge sums from the industrialized nations.

In opposition to the dependency school, the diffusionist model maintained that technology, capital, trade, political institutions, and culture spread out from the advanced nations to the backward countries. Within the underdeveloped nations, there also were dual societies in which a more advanced urban sector and a backward rural sector coexisted. The diffusionists maintained that ideas and capital spread from urban to rural. Accordingly, they believed that policy should be directed so that the more advanced nations cooperate with the middle classes in less advanced nations to modernize the latter. Contrary to the diffusionists, the *dependentistas* believed that the diffusion of ideas and capital made the less developed nations dependent on the giving country and therefore widened the gaps between developed and less developed nations. This situation was duplicated in the dual domestic society.

Because no Left regime (with the exception of Cuba) endured for more than a decade in Latin America after 1945, due to the opposition of upper class–military alliances throughout the region, the intervention of the United States, and communist regimes everywhere falling into economic crises by the 1980s, Latin Americans became disillusioned with governments' strong involvement in the economy. Pressured heavily by the United States and international lending agencies such as the International Monetary Fund and the World Bank, Latin American policy makers turned to the century-old liberal paradigm, now known as neoliberalism. The idea that market forces will eventually bring equity dominated once again.

How did these differing views affect historians? These theories overwhelmingly emphasized outside factors as causes of Latin American underdevelopment. This tended to lessen the importance of domestic circumstances. In a sense, these theories removed culpability from the upper class–military alliance, from individual leaders, political parties, traditions, and culture. They reduced the lower classes to

(*continued on next page*)

THEORIES OF ECONOMIC DEVELOPMENT AND HISTORY (*continued from previous page*)

meaningless nonparticipants. The emphasis on international factors tended to push aside the consideration of the regional and local, which had predominated in Latin America since pre-Columbian times, leaving out the most meaningful aspects of culture and society, and overemphasizing economics. Finally, dependency, especially, did not incorporate change over time, perhaps the most crucial aspect of an historian's purview.

In recent times, historians have reduced their concerns with economics and turned to the occurrences of everyday life and culture. This has placed the lower classes in a more central place in their studies. There has been a shift from international to local and from great forces to people.

Questions for Discussion
Why have the various models of economic development failed in Latin America? How has the struggle for control over daily life fit into the various models of development?

interest payments absorbed the preponderance of government revenues, leaving little or nothing for social welfare. The already sharp inequalities in the distribution of wealth and income widened, as the rich grew ever richer and the poor even poorer. Corruption ran rampant.

The world petroleum crises of the 1970s constituted a twofold curse for Latin America. Not only did the rise in oil prices cause general inflation and economic downturn, but it also exacerbated the debt crisis in many countries. The members of the Organization of Petroleum Exporting Countries (OPEC) earned enormous sums from the increases in oil revenues, which they deposited in Western financial institutions. The banks faced the dilemma of where to invest this money. Latin American nations (mostly Argentina, Brazil, Mexico, and Venezuela) required vast funds to develop. Latin American nations were able to pay the interest on the debt as long as their economies grew. Badly damaged by the second oil crisis, however, Latin American countries could not pay by the early 1980s. Mexico nearly defaulted in August of 1982. Rescheduling the debt and a short-lived upturn avoided the collapse of the international banking system, but the enormous burden for Latin America was not lessened in the long term. From 1978 to 2000, Argentina increased its foreign debt tenfold. Brazil quadrupled it. Mexico increased it by 500 percent. Argentina, Brazil, and Mexico in 2000 owed more than a half billion dollars abroad.

There are some indications the new millennium has brought some interesting changes. First, the vast movement of peoples, particularly to the United States, has had some surprising consequences. Funds sent by Latin American workers to their families back home, known as remittances, have had an enormous economic impact. In Mexico, remittances (*migradollars*) constitute the third-largest source of income after oil exports and tourism. In a number of the poorest Latin American nations, remittances account for more than 10 percent of the Gross Domestic Product. Until the economic crisis that began in 2008, remittances had grown at a rate of 15 percent per year for a decade, reaching an estimated $70 billion, 80 percent of which came from the United States. These funds have mitigated the harsh conditions in much of the region, lessening the precariousness of survival in many instances. It is not clear to what extent the remittances have alleviated poverty, however.

Second, there are several examples of nations that have diversified sufficiently to no longer suffer as badly from the swings of the world economy. Brazil with its array of agricultural commodity exports would be a prime case. Third, Brazil among others has also succeeded in diversifying its export customer base. As of 2010, China was its leading trade partner. Lastly, with Brazil again the major case, Latin America has begun to expand its domestic markets, lessening its dependence on markets abroad.

CONCLUSION

Momentous changes marked the half century after the Cuban Revolution in Latin America. Guerrilla wars and military reigns of terror caused the deaths of countless thousands and dislocated hundreds of thousands more. At times, it seemed as if the region had descended into madness. An era of democracy followed those dark days. The end of insurgencies in Guatemala and Peru in the 1990s left only one major rebellion—that in Colombia.

Though democracy rules almost every nation of Latin America, there are threatening clouds overhead. Who can guess what will happen when Fidel Castro finally passes from the stage in Cuba? Mexico at times seems near to descending into chaos as a result of the economic crisis in the United States from 2008 to 2010 and the U.S.-sponsored war on drugs. In 2010, violence on the northern border had reached epic proportions. Colombia with its still-strong insurgencies remains precarious. The Pink Tide's social programs offer at least the threat of inflation. Latin America continues to be deeply in debt. Most important, however, is the problem of how Latin America can assure the continuation of democracy when, as we will see in Chapter 15, poverty and misery pervade the region.

LEARNING MORE ABOUT LATIN AMERICANS

Diamond, Larry, Plattner, Marc F., and Abente Brun, Diego, eds. *Latin America's Struggle for Democracy* (Baltimore, MD: The Johns Hopkins University Press, 2008). Reasoned analysis of the Pink Tide.

Domínguez, Jorge I., and Shifter, Michael, eds. *Constructing Democratic Governance in Latin America* (Baltimore, MD: The Johns Hopkins University Press, 2008). An analysis of the recent wave of democracy in the region.

Gwynne, Robert N., and Cristobal Kay, eds. *Latin America Transformed: Globalization and Modernity*, 2nd ed. (New York: Arnold, 2004). Filled with statistical data and interesting analyses.

Masterson, Daniel. *Militarism and Politics in Latin America: Peru from Sánchez Cerro to Sendero Luminoso* (New York: Greenwood, 1991). Clarifies the role of the military in Peru.

Menchú, Rigoberta. *I, Rigoberta Menchú: An Indian Woman in Guatemala*. Trans. Ann Wright (New York: Verso, 1984). Heart-breaking story of rural women in Guatemala in the midst of civil war.

Miller, Francesca. *Latin American Women and Social Justice* (Hanover, NH: University Press of New England, 1991). Relates the participation of women in organized social movements.

Pérez-Stable, Marifeli. *The Cuban Revolution: Origins, Course, and Legacy*, 2nd ed. (New York: Oxford University Press, 2003). Fair-minded assessment of the revolution.

Smith, Lois, and Alfred Padula. *Sex and Revolution: Women in Socialist Cuba* (New York: Oxford University Press, 1996). Explores the disappointing treatment of women in Cuba.

Stern, Steve, ed. *Shining and Other Paths: War and Society in Peru, 1980–1995* (Durham, NC: Duke University Press, 1998). Essays on the Sendero Luminoso and its relations with people in the countryside.

15

EVERYDAY LIFE:
1959 TO THE PRESENT

THE UNPRECEDENTED REIGN of terror perpetrated by rightist military dictatorships in Argentina, Brazil, Chile, and Uruguay, and the vicious civil wars between rightist militaries and rightist and leftist guerrillas in Central America, Colombia, and Peru, described in Chapter 14, created an era of deep political tensions and economic hardships across Latin America. Not only were hundreds of thousands of people killed, wounded, and displaced, but nearly everyone else suffered uncertainty. Latin Americans risked imprisonment, torture, or death for speaking their minds in public. In countries such as Argentina and Guatemala, few people were not related to or familiar with someone who had been "disappeared": taken away in the middle of the night, never to be seen again, or killed by leftist guerrillas or rightist death squads. To make matters worse, military regimes often installed nonpolitical technocrats as the managers of their governments. Because neither the military nor the technocrats saw themselves as accountable to voters, they disregarded the potential repercussions their new economic programs might have on the middle and lower classes. They instituted policies that dismembered direct government involvement in business enterprises and opened national borders to free trade and foreign investment. As a result, many Latin Americans suffered extensive job losses and a large-scale erosion of their standard of living.

The end of the terror and the ensuing democratization of the region over the course of the 1980 and 1990s did not immediately improve economic conditions. Almost every nation in the region experienced periods of sustained economic growth, which after the new millennium lessened the dire inequalities between the wealthiest and the rest of the population and decreased the numbers of desperately poor. The Pink Tide governments that won elections after 1998 adopted a number of programs aimed at alleviating the worst poverty. In Venezuela, Chávez used the increased revenues derived from the government takeover of the national oil company in 2003 to lower the poverty rate from 54 to 26 percent of the population. Extreme poverty fell by 72 percent to under 10 percent. Inequality lessened as well. However, with the exception of Venezuela and Bolivia, the new left governments were extremely cautious financially, maintaining surpluses, which limited to a considerable extent their ability to alleviate the plight of the poor. Nonetheless, they benefitted almost uniformly from the boom in export commodities after 2003 that raised their revenues. Thus, from 2003 to 2008 Latin America enjoyed a period of economic growth and low inflation. Despite the significant improvement in the lives of Latin Americans, in 2008, 33 percent of the region's population or 180 million people lived in poverty and 12.9 percent or 71 million lived in extreme poverty.

In the new millennium, globalization transformed not only the economies but also the material culture and communications of Latin America. The impact of U.S. consumerism and popular culture, carried by the mass media all over the region, was widespread. (Even in the most remote villages, for instance, one could find Coca-Cola.) Indigenous Latin Americans, much like their ancestors in the sixteenth century, had to choose which aspects of their tradition and which aspects of the modern culture generated, in part, by globalization they would use to construct new and unique cultures. In art, as well as in politics and everyday life, Latin Americans sought to make sense of their shifting reality. When brutal regimes suppressed their creativity, artists found new means of expression, while at the same time melding their views and techniques with those from abroad to construct distinctly Latin American art.

The last quarter of the twentieth and first decade of the twenty-first century brought on extraordinary challenges for the people of Latin America. Their efforts to pull themselves upward economically produced unanticipated adverse consequences for the environment. And natural disasters, such as hurricanes, floods, and earthquakes added to their struggles.

THE REIGN OF TERROR

Dictatorships and guerrilla insurgencies tormented Latin America from the mid-1960s through the mid- or late 1980s. Citizens in all of the nations discussed in Chapter 14 lived in fear of the police, military, guerrillas, and informal paramilitary death squads. The human and physical damage that resulted from this long era of terror was breathtaking. There were tens of thousands of casualties. Hundreds of thousands of people were dislocated from their homes. If this were not enough, civil and human rights were nonexistent. Regimes, such as in Chile, ruled under a state of siege, eliminating due process of law.

The human toll exacted during this period surpassed that of the incessant conflicts of the nineteenth century. Between 1975 and 1995, 33,000 Colombians were casualties of the civil war. In 1997 alone, 200,000 people had to abandon their homes because of intensified fighting. El Salvador suffered 70,000 civilian deaths in its terrible civil war during the 1980s. The guerrilla war and counterinsurgency in Guatemala destroyed

LATIN AMERICAN LIVES

WOMEN REBELS

IN THE CUBAN REVOLUTION and subsequent movements, women have mobilized in response to widespread political oppression. They have led the resistance to dictatorships in Argentina, Brazil, and Chile. They have joined the revolutionary organizations in Guatemala, El Salvador, and Nicaragua. In Bolivia, Mexico, and Peru, women have actively participated in rural and urban protest movements. They have fought time and again to protect themselves and their families from economic crises and political mistreatment and to end long-standing gender-based oppression.

Two of these women, Vilma Espín and Doris María Tijerino, are examples of the endurance, sacrifice, and extraordinary courage and leadership women have provided to the movements for social justice.

Vilma Espín Guillois (1930–2007) was a chemical engineer with degrees from the University of Oriente (in Cuba) and the Massachusetts Institute of Technology, whose father was a high-ranking executive in the Bacardi Rum Company. In 1955, she joined the 26th of July Movement in Cuba, led by Fidel Castro. As a student, she had participated in protests against Batista, written and distributed antigovernment pamphlets, and joined the National Revolutionary movement. She was in Mexico briefly when Castro was in exile there, and when the 26th of July struggled in the Sierra Madre Mountains during 1956 and 1957, she was a member of its national directorate, along with two other women, Haydée Santamaría and Celia Sánchez (later Fidel Castro's longtime companion). Working in the cities, she went underground, narrowly escaping arrest in May 1957. Espín coordinated the group's work in Oriente province and then took over much of the overall leadership in the province when police killed Frank País, her boss. Espín was one of the leaders of a national strike in April 1958, which failed. She married Fidel Castro's brother Raúl, one of the rebel commanders, after the triumph of the revolution in 1959 (the couple reportedly separated in the 1980s). In 1960, she became director of the Federation of Cuban Women (FMC), a post she held through the 1990s. The FMC eventually included 3 million women, 80 percent of the women in Cuba. She also served as a member of the Central Committee, the Council of State, and the Politburo, the highest leadership group of the Communist Party. Espín was outspoken against the sexual double standard and other gender inequities that were still prevalent in Cuban society. She was one of only a small number of women to hold the top leadership posts in the government and Communist Party, which is clear indication of the mixed success achieved by the Cuban Revolution in granting equal rights to women.

Doris María Tijerino Haslam (b. 1943) was one the earliest Sandinistas. Her father worked as an engineer for the Nicaraguan National Guard, which was notorious for its corruption and oppressive tactics. A veteran of the guerrilla insurgency from the late 1960s, Tijerino was arrested, jailed, and tortured in 1969 by the Somoza regime. She was imprisoned until 1974, when the infamous Sandinista raid on a high-society Christmas party obtained the release of political prisoners. The government captured her again in 1978. Another daring raid, which took over the National Palace, secured her release. Tijerino received the rank of full commander in the Sandinista army, the only woman to do so. She paid a terrible personal price for her achievements, however—the Somoza government murdered two of her husbands. In postrevolutionary Nicaragua, she headed the National Women's Association, was head of the national police, and was a member of the national legislature. She kept her seat as a Senator even after the Sandinista defeat in 1989. Tijerino, like Espín, suffered from discrimination by the very revolutionary government she helped place in power and then helped lead, because its men would not allow women to attain the highest ranks within the government, despite their obvious ability to lead and the wrenching sacrifices they had made.

Questions for Discussion

Given the traditional role of women in Latin America, why do you think women were such important contributors to the revolutions in Cuba and Nicaragua from the 1950s through the 1990s?

440 hamlets. Hundreds of thousands fled into exile in Mexico and the United States. Forty thousand died in the civil war in Nicaragua during the 1980s. Between 1980 and 1995 in Peru, the Shining Path guerrilla movement and the government counterinsurgency led to the deaths of more than 20,000 people and produced perhaps 200,000 internal refugees.

The economic cost of all this destruction was staggering. The Shining Path, for example, caused an estimated $15 billion in damages. The real income of Peruvians dropped by one-third just in the period from 1990 to 1992: One million people lost their jobs in Lima alone. In the late 1990s, because of the long civil war, three-quarters of the people of Guatemala lived in poverty, more than one-half of these in extreme poverty.

THE QUALITY OF LIFE

The terror visited upon Latin America by the right-wing regimes and leftist insurgencies brought unspeakable misery to the region. Latin Americans, after two decades of economic growth and equalization of income after World War II, plunged once again into overwhelming poverty. Latin America and the Caribbean suffer the most unequal distribution of income in the world.

The deterioration of Latin Americans' well-being was all the more tragic in light of the fact that after World War II several decades of relative growth and prosperity had offered hope to millions by reducing poverty in terms of percentage of the population and redistributing wealth to the middle and lower classes. From 1950 to 1980, per capita income rose by an average of 3 percent a year. This pushed down the percentage of the population living in poverty from an estimated 65 percent in 1950 to 25 percent in 1980.

Between 1970 and 1982, the share of the income of the wealthiest 20 percent fell, and the share of the poorest rose 10 percent.

By 1980, however, after a decade of dictatorships, sustained growth ended and during the next 10 to 15 years the widespread adoption of free market, neoliberal strategies badly exacerbated conditions. From 1982 to 1993, the number of people living in poverty in Latin America increased from 78 million to 150 million. Relatively speaking, the wealthiest nations in the region, Argentina, Uruguay, and Venezuela, experienced the sharpest increase in poverty. Economic stagnation or decline, rampant unemployment, widespread underemployment, and inflation characterized the years of the terror and incipient democracy. During the 1980s, the per capita gross domestic product fell more than 20 percent in Argentina, Bolivia, Nicaragua, Peru, and Venezuela. The only countries that did not suffer net decline in gross national income from 1980 to 1992 were Chile, Colombia, and Uruguay. In Latin America, 1990 per capita income was 15 percent below the 1980 level. As a result, the number of poor rose to 210 million by the mid-1990s. There was a clear correlation between the establishment of right-wing regimes or the presence of a prolonged insurgency and the impoverishment of the population. The percentage of people below the poverty line in Chile, for example, went from 17 in 1970, the first year of the government of Salvador Allende, to 45 in 1985 after a dozen years of Agustin Pinochet's dictatorship. Thirty years of war in Guatemala immersed 60 percent of the total population of 10 million in poverty.

The onset of democratization has improved the lot of the poor. Current poverty and indigence rates are far below those of 1990, the approximate date by which the terror had ended. Peru's rate of poverty went from 48 to 36 percent since 2006. In Uruguay, under Pink Tide president Tabare Vázquez (2005–2010), the unemployment rate fell to 6.4 percent, the lowest ever recorded.

What Does It Mean to Be Poor?

The poor in Latin America are overwhelmingly rural, female, and Indian or black and most likely live in Brazil, Mexico, or Peru. Poverty levels in the countryside are twice those in the cities. Women are more likely to be poor than men. The percentage of the indigenous population living in poverty in Bolivia in 2002 was 72, in, Mexico 90, and Peru 65 (see Table 15.1).

Malnourishment, disease, and high infant mortality are an inescapable fact of life for the poor. In 1980, more than 50 million people in the region had a daily calorie intake below the standards set by the World Health Organization (WHO). Twenty million of those were seriously malnourished. In Mexico, the diets of an incredible 52 percent of the population did not meet WHO standards. Urbanization and globalization increased malnourishment. In 1960, for example, Mexicans mostly ate tortillas, beans, bread, and small quantities of vegetables, eggs, and meat. Two decades later, poor city dwellers consumed more processed food (such as white bread) and soda. Consumption of milk in Mexico declined about 10 percent during the 1980s, while consumption of beans dropped even more. Mexicans ate only minimal amounts of eggs, fruits, and vegetables, and 60 percent

TABLE 15.1

Latin Americans Living in Poverty and Extreme Poverty, 1980–2002

Country	Percentage of Population in Poverty			Percentage of Population in Extreme Poverty		
	1980	2002	2006	1980	2002	2006/7
Argentina	10.5	45.4 (Urban)	–	2.8	20.9	–
Bolivia	–	62.4	–	–	37.1	31.2
Brazil	45.3	37.5	33.3	22.6	13.2	8.5
Chile	45.1	18.8	13.7	17.4	4.7	–
Colombia	42.3	51.1	19.2	17.4	24.6	–
Costa Rica	23.6	20.3	–	6.9	8.2	5.3
Ecuador	–	–	43.0	–	–	16.0
El Salvador	–	48.9	–	–	22.1	–
Guatemala	71.1	60.2	54.8	39.6	30.9	–
Honduras	–	77.3	71.5	–	54.4	45.6
Mexico	42.5	39.4	31.7	15.4	12.6	8.7
Nicaragua	–	69.4	–	–	42.4	–
Panamá	41.0	–	29.9	19.7	–	12.0
Paraguay	–	61.0	–	–	33.2	31.6
Peru	34.0	54.8	44.5	17.4	24.4	–
República Dominicana	–	44.9	–	–	20.3	–
Uruguay	14.6	–	–	4.0	–	–
Venezuela	25.0	48.6	30.2	8.6	22.2	8.5
Latin America	40.5	44.4	–	18.6	19.4	–

Source: Economic Commission for Latin America and the Caribbean (ECLAC), Statistical Yearbook for Latin America and the Caribbean, 2004 (LC/G.2264-P/B), Santiago 2005, figure 50.0, pp. 118–119. United Nations Publications, Sales Nº E/S.05.II.G.1.

ate no meat at all, leaving them easy prey for dysentery, malnutrition, and anemia. Their diets were marked by consumption of less protein and more sugar. The complex combination of corn (tortillas), beans, and chili (hot sauce), which had provided their sustenance since the beginning of civilization, gradually gave way to widely advertised Pan Bimbo (the equivalent of Wonder Bread) and Coca-Cola. Maternal malnutrition has been the primary cause of high child mortality rates, which in 1996 stood at 102 per 1000 births in Bolivia. In Nicaragua, the infant mortality rate in the 1990s was a stunning 138 per 1000 births among the poorest sector of the population. Ironically, at the same time, overall life expectancy improved: It was 47 years in 1950 and 68 in 1990.

To be poor not only means that you would not have enough to eat and that your children would likely die before they were a year old but that you would have limited or no access to health care, sanitation, and housing. Routine health services are not available to one out of three Latin Americans. An estimated 1.5 million people under the age of 65 die each year from causes that are avoidable. Unfortunately, neoliberal policies have cut expenditures for health care, and, as a result, the incidence of diseases associated with poverty, such as dengue, cholera, hepatitis, typhoid, and tuberculosis, has risen. Access to safe drinking water and adequate sanitation is badly limited, leading to the proliferation of disease. Less than 2 percent of Latin American sewage is treated, resulting in the proliferation of typhoid and cholera. The lack of health and sanitation facilities in indigenous communities allows outbreaks of influenza, measles, dengue, and respiratory infections to quickly become epidemics. Between 20 and 30 percent of all Latin American children grow up in overcrowded lodgings (three or more in a bedroom). In Brazil, perhaps 200,000 children live on the streets.

The biggest hope for Latin Americans to struggle out of poverty is education, but it is seemingly unattainable beyond the first few grades. While overall educational enrollment expanded from the 1960s through the 1970s and the percentage of children ages 6 to 11 in school reached 71 in 1970 and 82 in 1980, the percentage of children ages 12 to 17 in school only went from 15 to 24. Today in Guatemala, a poor child will complete on average just 1 year of schooling. In Bolivia, only one-third of those who enter primary school finish. Even in Chile, a poor child will complete only 6 years of school. The situation worsened with the neoliberal reduction in government expenditures as Latin American per capita public expenditures on education fell 12.5 percent during the hard times of the 1980s. Latin Americans are imprisoned in their poverty.

Some observers saw the rapid population growth after World War II as a major cause of the increase in poverty. During the post–World War II boom, reproductive rates rose so that by 1960 the region's population was increasing at the rate of over 3 percent per year, more than doubling between 1950 and 1980. It became clear, however, that Latin American economies could neither sustain sufficient economic growth to provide employment for the increased number of workers nor could governments provide services, such as health care, housing, and education, for them. Consequently, Latin American governments have implemented policies to lower the birth rate, expecting that this would alleviate poverty. Since 1980, in fact, the population growth rate in the region has declined as a result of the expanded use of contraception. The Mexican government program to encourage the use of contraceptives resulted in more than a twofold increase in their use from 1976 to 1995 (30.2 percent in 1976 to 66.5 percent in 1995). However, the poorest Latin Americans have resisted contraception use and maintained high levels of fertility. Geographer Sylvia Chant provides the example of Melia, a 27-year-old woman who lived in a one-room hut in a barrio in Puerto Vallarta, Mexico, with her husband, a construction worker, and six children ranging from ages 3 to 9 years. Melia is a devout Catholic who had not used nor planned to use contraception, calling her offspring "gifts from god."

Although the sharp increase in population contributed to unemployment and poverty, no other phenomenon of the post-1959 era has damaged the status and well-being of the lower and middle classes more than inflation. Inflation reached staggering rates during the 1970s and 1980s (see Table 15.2). Bolivia's consumer price index, for example, rose an average of 610 percent between 1980 and 1985, with the largest

TABLE 15.2

Inflation (Average Annual Rate)

	1970–80	1980–85	1985	1992	1995	2000	2003
Argentina	118.5	322.6	672.2	17.6	1.6	−0.7	13.4
Bolivia	18.8	610.9	11,749.2	10.5	12.6	3.8	3.3
Brazil	34.2	135.1	301.8	1,149.1	22.0	5.5	14.7
Chile	130.2	21.3	30.7	12.7	8.2	4.7	14.7
Colombia		22.3	24.1	25.1	19.5	8.8	7.1
Mexico	16.5	60.7	57.8	11.9	52.1	8.9	4.5
Peru	30.3	102.1	163.4	56.7	10.2	4.0	2.3
Latin America				414.4	25.8	8.7	

Source: ECLA, *Statistical Yearbook for Latin America and the Caribbean,* 1990, pp. 98–99; ECLA, *Statistical Yearbook for Latin America and the Caribbean, 2000,* p. 751, and *2005,* p. 136.

increase in 1985 at over 11,000 percent. Brazil's inflation topped 1500 percent in 1989, Nicaragua's 9700 percent in 1988, and Peru's 3398 percent in 1989. Only Colombia, Guatemala, Honduras, Panama, and Paraguay escaped inflation rates of more than 30 percent per year during this era. Inflation badly eroded real wages. No one could live without difficulty during these periods of hyperinflation. Fortunately, in the first decade of the new century the Pink Tide governments have, for the most part, reined in inflation with only Venezuela's rate above 10 percent in 2010.

It is perhaps not surprising that in an environment where the currency might decline 2 percent in value each day, conditions created desperation. Thus, to be poor also meant that one lives amid crime, which has risen sharply, further exacerbating the decline in the quality of everyday life. Crime in Mexico City, for example, rose by 40 percent from 1963 to 1980, by more than 40 percent more in the 1980s, and by more than 40 percent again in the first half of the 1990s. Many other cities in Mexico, such as Guadalajara and Tijuana, also suffered from surging lawlessness. Conditions deteriorated to the extent that police subjected passengers to weapons searches before the passengers were allowed to board first-class buses traveling between Mexican cities.

Latin Americans have proven extraordinarily resourceful in adapting to these difficult conditions. They have survived economically in great part because they have constructed an informal economy and because they have left their homelands to go elsewhere, sometimes to the cities, but often to other countries, in search of security and economic opportunities.

Informal Economy

The informal economy, which includes activities that take place outside of regulation and law, consists of small-scale, low-technology, family-run farms, mines, artisan shops, services, and vendors, nearly all of which are run by Indians, blacks, mulattos, and mestizos.

Neoliberal policies resulted in a substantial increase in the informal sector because 81 percent of the new employment they generated was in the informal or small enterprise sector. From 1980 to 1992, in Latin America as a whole, employment in small enterprises increased from 15 to 22 percent of the workforce. The informal sector's share of employment went from 19 to 27 percent. With domestic service (6.4 percent), these two accounted for over half the workforce. At the same time, employment in large- or medium-size businesses fell from 44 to 31 percent and public employment from 15.7 to 13.6 percent. La Paz, Bolivia, where the number of vendors in the markets jumped from 15,000 in 1967 to nearly double that number in 1992, provides a good example of the consequences of neoliberalism for the informal sector. The informal sector continued to grow through the era of democratization In Bolivia, Colombia, Ecuador, Paraguay, and Peru it accounted for more than 40 percent of the Gross Domestic Product. In Paraguay it amounted to nearly 70 percent.

The streets of Latin America's cities are filled with individual petty entrepreneurs, who will sell items ranging from gum and candy bars to hot food to appliances. These small businesses are usually the product of a continuum, in which migrants move to the cities, take jobs—if they can find them—as domestics and menial laborers, and then, when they are more established, begin their own enterprises, using the skills learned from parents and other family. They rely first on the unpaid labor of nuclear family, but also extended kinship networks. When necessary, they obtain additional labor from workers seasonally unemployed by the export sector, and illiterate, unskilled residents of urban slums. Some proprietors of informal-sector businesses manage to rise above the poverty level. Many others are not so fortunate, however, because the informal economy also includes street children, small-time criminals, and prostitutes.

The informal economy not only provides a living for increasing numbers of Latin Americans but also supplies the daily needs of much of the population. In the bustling central market of Cuzco, Peru, for example, vendors sell anything a consumer might want, such as watches, hats, medicinal herbs, clothes, and endless quantities of food, some prepared and hot. In Lima, the informal sector built most of the public markets and delivers 95 percent of Lima's public transportation. In Bolivia, half the economically active population works in small businesses. In Latin American cities, vendors set up shop anywhere that space is available. The sound of bargaining is relentless, as the market women and their customers dicker back and forth over prices. The noisy market, teeming with people and overflowing with smells of food, is still the very lifeblood of the city.

Women play exceptionally important roles in the informal economy. They dominate the markets today, much as they have since before the Europeans arrived in the sixteenth century. In Cuzco, women run the stalls, caring for children, gossiping, and helping their neighbors at the same time. Often, the women begin work as domestic servants, then move on to itinerant peddling, and lastly to the market. Necessary skills, including relentless haggling with customers to get the best prices for their merchandise, are passed on from mother to daughter or aunt to niece. Work in the market provides

MEDICAMENTOS
SUEROS
VACUNAS
ANTIBIOTICOS
ALIMENTOS
GRANILLO
SEMA
SALVADILLO

Women vendors in market.

women with income, flexibility to care for children, and autonomy from men. Some women work only part-time in the market so that they can hold additional jobs. Some vendors journey in from the countryside periodically to sell agricultural products, while others invest in a license for a permanent stall.

Life is by no means easy for market women, though. Most of them are single mothers or widows. Competition with other sellers is relentless. They must be shrewd in their dealings with local authorities. They depend heavily on family members to help them. They must be willing to work long hours. The pressure on them is enormous. As one market woman put it: "From the time I wake up until I go to bed, it's the preoccupation a mother has to feed her children, to find food for her children, whether we sell or not, because if we don't sell, there's no food to eat."

A few examples illustrate the complex adaptations required by men and women who earn their livelihoods in the informal economy. Doña Avenina Copana de Garnica is an artisan in La Paz, Bolivia. Born in the city, she nonetheless speaks Aymara, an indigenous language, as well as Spanish. She and her husband and their six children live in small, rented quarters above their small workshop in an artisan district of the city. The upstairs has one bedroom with bunk beds. They sleep and work there. The shop has a small stove for soldering and shares space with a cooking area demarcated by a piece of cloth.

The Garnica family uses metal, cardboard, and cloth to make numerous items used in rituals and celebrations, including masks, noisemakers, whips, and costumes for miniature figures. Avelina's parents live across the street, and the whole family works in the business. They learned their trades from relatives. Avelina comes from a family of costume makers. She embroiders the costumes for the miniatures. She also cuts and pastes the decorations for the costumes. Her husband, a tinsmith, apprenticed with her aunt and makes objects out of sheet metal. The family employs seasonal workers. Avelina keeps the books and supervises the workers, often making 40-minute bus rides to their homes. The Garnicas actively promote their products through sponsorship of local fiestas, selling to tourist stores in the city, and even traveling to Peru to expand their market further.

Slice of Life   The Barrio/Favela

THE VAST INCREASE in the population of Latin America's great cities is the most important development in the region since the 1940s. As we saw in Chapters 13 and 14, the enormous influx of migrants created gigantic, unmanageable urban areas, and shantytowns now dominate these megacities. Known as barrios in Mexico, barriadas in Peru, and favelas (also *mucambos*) in Brazil, they incorporate hundreds of thousands, sometimes millions, of poor people, most of whom have fled desperate conditions in the countryside. These huge, filthy shantytowns are noisy monuments to the resourcefulness and resilience of impoverished human beings who, seemingly against all odds, survive, and occasionally prosper, with dignity and humor. It is one of the mysteries of twentieth-century history that they have not erupted into bitterness, resentment, and widespread violence.

The shantytowns appeared in empty spaces owned by absentee landlords or by the local governments, arising overnight as people heard by word of mouth of any empty space and assembled to occupy it. After moving in from other parts of the city or from the countryside, residents constructed their abodes with materials salvaged from others' trash, such as scrap wood, corrugated metal, cement blocks, and, sometimes, cardboard and cloth. Unrecognized by city authorities, the settlements initially had no water, electrical, or sewage services, nor did they have schools or medical clinics. If lucky, inhabitants would line up for hours to fill cans and bottles with water from a public spigot or a visiting water truck. Inhabitants obtained electricity by stealing it—and paid exorbitant prices.

As cities expanded, the shantytowns always stayed on the outskirts, often on the steep sides of hills or in low regions susceptible to flooding. No one wanted these lands, for they were scarcely habitable. In some areas, shantytown residents organized and won self-government as municipalities. One such case is Netzahualcóyotl, now a city in its own right in the state of Mexico with 1.2 million residents, which began as a squatter settlement on the dried-out bed of Lake Texcoco, where strong winds swirl volcanic soil about and flooding is chronic. The government sold the land during the 1920s to developers whose project never materialized. Later, real estate promoters illegally sold 160,000 plots of land to low-income people. Ciudad Netzahualcóyotl incorporated 40 irregular settlements northeast of Mexico City in 1964. In the 1970s, still without services, residents protested by withholding mortgage payments. Eventually, the government furnished the services and granted legal titles to the residents. Similarly, in many other cities, squatters banded together to organize protests to acquire their properties legally and to obtain services. The fight was often hard, because governments and landlords frequently used violence against the protestors.

In Rio de Janeiro, the seemingly chaotic nature of the settlements hides innovation and resourcefulness. Dwellers employ clever techniques to maximize the use of difficult space. They build their homes literally brick by brick as they accumulate enough money to acquire more building materials and add to their structures, making them more permanent. The favelas are not obsolete, retrograde remnants of rural culture. Rather, they were and are places of transition and persistence.

The shantytowns in many ways are twenty-first-century urban versions of rural villages. Just as country folk fought to maintain their local autonomy and traditions in the nineteenth and much of the twentieth centuries, the residents of shantytowns have struggled to assert their control over everyday lives.

Questions for Discussion

How do the circumstances of twentieth- and twenty-first-century struggles for control over everyday life in urban shantytowns differ from those of villages in the countryside in the nineteenth and early twentieth centuries? How are they similar?

Like Avelina Copana de Garnicas, Sofía Velázquez grew up in La Paz, Bolivia, and earns her livelihood in the city's informal economy. She began her working life helping her mother sell candles in the markets and then sold vegetables in the market on days when there was no school. Later, she sold eggs, beer, onions, mutton, and pork. Separated from her husband, she earned enough to send her one daughter, Rocío, a teenager in the early 1990s, to private school. She continues to buy and sell pork, but she and her daughter now supplement their income by working as food vendors: Rocío cooks and Sofía sells the food in front of their home. Sofía also plays an active role in community affairs. She heads the organization that controls the local market, a position that carries with it the considerable expense of sponsoring local fiestas.

Narcotics

The most notorious aspect of the informal economy is the production and commerce in illegal drugs, primarily cocaine, marijuana, and methamphetamines. At various times over the past three decades, the United States has pushed for campaigns against the production and distribution of drugs in Bolivia, Peru, Colombia, and Mexico. The so-called "War against Drugs" has not appreciably diminished consumption. There have been, however, important ramifications to these efforts. By one estimate, illegal drugs just in Mexico generate $17 to $38 billion a year. The war has had mixed success. In Peru, cocaine production fell by 70 percent from 1995 to 2001, but experts attribute this drop to low prices for coca (the plant from which cocaine derives), and so when prices rose in 2002 acreage in production increased.

One of the unanticipated consequences of the antidrug campaign, U.S. antidrug intervention in Latin America has been an adverse impact on the environment. For example, erradication programs in Colombia have led to the clearing of over 1.75 million acres of Amazon rainforest. Aerial eradication efforts are responsible for the destruction of legal subsistence crops, and the pesticide glyphosate is suspected of causing a variety of health problems in Colombian children, including diarrhea, hair loss, and skin rashes.

The antidrug campaigns have affected primarily Bolivia, Peru, Colombia, and Mexico. But the most notable impact has been in Mexico, where in 2007 the newly elected president Felipe Calderón started a major campaign against the criminal cartels, called the Mérida Initiative, that caused an unprecedented outbreak of violence and by 2010 the deaths of 23,000 people, more than 7000 in 2009 alone. At one point Calderón sent an occupying army of 6500 to the state of Michoacán. By 2010 there were 45,000 Mexican troops involved in the national campaign. The militarization of the conflict resulted in widespread human rights abuses.

There has been a considerable economic and political cost, as well. Tourism, Mexico's third-largest enterprise (oil and remittances rank first and second, respectively), worth about $11 billion annually, has declined since 2007 because of the violence. The vast sums of money involved have led to widespread corruption at all levels of the police, military, and civilian government, which has eroded the respect for both the government and the law.

The Great Migrations

Since the 1960s, vast numbers of Latin Americans have left their homes to find security and work in other countries. This movement of people has to some extent alleviated the pressures on governments to provide employment for their citizens. It also has been an enormous source of funds for Latin American economies. Since 1960, more than 10 million people have immigrated from Latin America to the United States. Most came from Mexico, but hundreds of thousands arrived from the Dominican Republic, El Salvador, Cuba, Colombia, Guatemala, and Honduras. Cubans fled the communist regime. The Central Americans and Colombians sought to escape the region's civil wars.

The economic impact of this migration of people has been enormous, because the new immigrants have remitted billions of dollars to their home countries. In 2008, Latin Americans sent a total of $70 billion to the region, funds that benefited every country. Mexicans sent back more than $25 billion, and even Uruguayans remitted $116 million. The flow was set back somewhat by the worldwide economic downturn in 2009, which cut remittances. In some years, in countries such as the Dominican Republic, these remittances have kept the economy afloat during tough times.

A short summary of migration in Central America illustrates the importance of these movements of people. Before the 1960s, Central Americans moved within the region to find work. More than 350,000 Salvadorans, for example, made homes and found work in neighboring Honduras until the mid-1960s, when the Honduran authorities deported them. Guatemalan Mayan Indians crossed back and forth over the Mexican border for centuries to labor in the plantations in Chiapas. The civil wars of the 1980s, however, changed these patterns of migration, when endemic violence pushed hundreds of thousands to the United States and other nations.

One of the recent developments is the movement of people from Latin America to the nations of southern Europe (Spain, Portugal, and Italy) and the United Kingdom. A million people from Latin America and the Caribbean resided in Spain, for example, in 2010.

The impact of both the vast movement of people and the transfer of large sums of money from immigrants to their former homelands are much discussed. There is, for example, concern about the loss of workers in the prime of their lives economically, particularly the highly educated. In villages in Mexico it is not uncommon for the entire population of working age men and women to migrate at least for part of the year, leaving only the very old and very young. Remittances are a major source of income for many low-income families; in some places, as much as 40 percent of the households draw a substantial portion of their support from them. But the impact of the remittances is not certain. Beyond alleviating the worst conditions by allowing for the purchase of staples, there are few linkages that might lead to development.

THE CITIES

The massive movement of people to the cities that began in the nineteenth century has continued unabated. From 1950 to 1980, 27 million Latin Americans, almost all of them poor, left the countryside for the cities. The percentage of people living in urban areas rose from 40.9 percent to 63.3 percent. In the last third of the twentieth century, the people of Latin America moved to the cities in overwhelming numbers. By 1995, the proportion of urban dwellers reached 78 percent of Latin Americans. (In the United States, they comprise 76.2 percent.) Many Latin American nations' populations are predominantly urban: Argentina's is 87.5 percent urban, Brazil 78.7 percent, Chile 85.9 percent, Uruguay 90.3 percent, and Venezuela 92.9 percent. Furthermore, the population is concentrated in a very few enormous cities. Forty percent of Chileans live in Santiago. São Paulo and Mexico City each may have as many as 20 million inhabitants. With Buenos Aires and Rio de Janeiro, these cities make up four of the ten largest cities in the world.

The statistics for Mexico City are staggering. It is spread over 950 square miles, three times the size of New York City. Mexico City contains 25 percent of Mexico's population, 42 percent of all jobs, 53 percent of all wages and salaries, 38 percent of the value of all industrial plants, 49 percent of sales of durable goods, and 55 percent of all expenditures in social welfare. Its inhabitants consume 40 percent of all food production, buy 90 percent of all electrical appliances, use 66 percent of country's energy and telephones, and purchase 58 percent of the automobiles.

The great cities are virtually unmanageable. Less than half of Brazilian urban residents have garbage collection with almost all these waste materials dumped into streams or open spaces. The only factor that mitigates this enormous environmental problem is that poor people generate less waste than more affluent people. Many lack sanitation facilities. As of 1990, only 16 percent of the households of São Paulo were connected to municipal sewage treatment plants. Consequently, human wastes contaminate the water. In Brazil, it is estimated that 70 percent of all hospitalizations are the consequence of diseases that result from the lack of sanitation. Twenty-seven percent of Latin America's urban residents—80 million people—breathe air that does not meet World Health Organization guidelines. The only factor that keeps the cities from being overwhelmed by toxic emissions from automobiles is that Latin America has relatively few autos compared to the United States.

To Be Poor in the Cities

Latin American cities are really two cities—one for the rich and the other for the poor. Lima, for example, has a modern downtown with paved streets dotted with skyscrapers. Surrounding the center are millions of people living in *barriadas,* or squatter settlements. Many of the *barriadas,* also known as *barrios* or *colonias* elsewhere in Spanish America or as *favelas* in Brazil, were rural into the 1940s and even the 1950s. Gradually, as the city grew outward and as people searched for less expensive living quarters, farmland disappeared. The residents of these settlements have migrated from the Andean highlands. Dirt roads lead through the houses built from scrap lumber, woven mats, and other materials. The stink from open sewers is noticeable. The bustle is everywhere and noise abounds. The marketplaces are busy.

Beneath the apparent squalor, the odors, and the hustle are real communities. And it is here that the twenty-first century's version of the struggle for control over everyday life occurs. In Lima's barriadas and other squatter settlements throughout Latin America, people assist each other in much the same ways as they had when planting and harvesting on collectively operated farms in the highlands. Networks of relatives and friends from their home villages make life more bearable. When Jorge and Celsa settled in Lima's Chalaca barriada, for example, Jorge's sister and brother helped them build a house on the same plot where the sister and her husband lived. An aunt also provided support. Later, Celsa's sister, her husband, and four small children moved in.

Most barriada families started with next to nothing and have painstakingly built their homes. The typical house at first had one story and was built with reed matting or wooden boards. Later, residents reconstructed with wood or perhaps brick and cement. In the city of Callao, the port for Lima, dwellers salvaged bricks and wood from the buildings destroyed by an earthquake in 1967. There were a variety of furnishings depending on the economic status of the inhabitants. Barriada dwellers cooked over small fires or kerosene stoves. Only a few dwellings had electricity, initially pirated from main lines. Because there was no refrigeration, residents bought their food at the market every day, buying only what they needed. People shared space with goats, sheep,

How Historians Understand   FROM THE COUNTRYSIDE TO THE CITY

The vast movement of people from rural areas to the cities that has taken place since the 1940s in Latin America has left historians with many questions: Who were/are the migrants? From where did/do they come? Why did/do they leave the countryside? Three types of analysis have arisen to explain the phenomenon: The first interprets migration as a "rational" act by people seeking to better their economic situations; the second sees wider forces resulting primarily from capitalist market forces at work; and the third incorporates both individual motivations and structural causes. Generally, the latter, more eclectic approach has won the day. We realize now, thanks to a long series of case studies, that although the search for economic betterment is crucial to any decision to migrate, much more enters into it.

Migrants are difficult to characterize. At first glance, it appears that young, single males are the likeliest to move from rural villages. Some early observers concluded that these men migrated because they had fewer attachments and the best chance for employment. But, in fact, women have comprised the majority of migrants, especially in Mexico, Peru, Honduras, and Costa Rica. In general, however, there seems to be no pattern according to marital status or age. We cannot with certainty even maintain that the very poorest migrated. Some investigators believe that migration is selective and that only the "more dynamic members of the rural population" migrate to the cities. Nonetheless, women were less educated, were more discriminated against, and had fewer possibilities for employment, but were the majority of migrants.

There is considerable disagreement, too, over from where migrants originated. Some investigators have found that migrants overwhelmingly came directly to the cities from rural areas. Others claim a pattern of movement from village to a small town, such as a provincial capital, and then to the larger cities. Proponents of the first theory thought that migrants were totally unprepared for city life. Proponents of the second theory offer the opposite view, maintaining that the migrants were "preurbanized." Small cities, however, were not the same as large cities. Thus, while migration may be a step-by-step process, and this is debatable, acculturation was not so easy in any case. What seems the most likely conclusion is that migrants came from villages, small towns, small cities, and larger cities, depending on their particular circumstances. Geography and time period affected their plight and resulted in different migrants moving through different patterns.

Leaving one's home, abandoning what one knows for the unknown, was/is an act of enormous courage. But what were the reasons behind it? Were people "pushed" out of

and pigs and raised guinea pigs (a traditional South American delicacy) and rabbits in their kitchens.

The homes were functional with few possessions. A typical home might have a table and utensils hung from the walls. Sleeping areas had cots or beds with straw mattresses. Clothes were hung from poles or lines strung overhead. There were boxes or trunks for

Shantytown where newly arrived migrants make their homes.

their rural homes by shrinking access to and deteriorating quality of land? Or did they leave because of the unavailability of employment due to the adoption of large-scale agriculture and widespread use of technology? The first investigators thought the relentless poverty of the countryside provided the impetus for migration. Later studies, however, found that the process was not so simple. There were both "push" and "pull" aspects to migrants' decision making. One observer called what was involved no less than a "substitute for social revolution."

One survey found that the migrants themselves, when surveyed, mentioned economic concerns as a motivation factor less than half the time. Migration had more to do with family (to join a spouse, to find a partner, to escape civil war) or health. The same study was unable to get migrants to "describe the decision with any precision."

It seems there was/is no one reason why a person or family moves from the countryside to the cities: There is no typology for migrants. Nor was/is there a specific route of migration; it was too personal a process. The migrants themselves do not experience or depict their lives as linear. As historians, nor should we.

Questions for Discussion

If you lived in a rural area in Latin America, what would motivate you to migrate to the cities or immigrate to another country? Would you have the courage to leave your home?

storage. Larger animals, such as goats, sheep, and pigs, were kept in the courtyard and ate scraps. Nothing was thrown away, for everything had its uses. Nothing was fancy anywhere.

Little by little, these settlements and similar settlements throughout Latin America acquired community governance and services. Residents built cement basins with a number of spigots and a drain area at strategic points. There people waited in long lines in early morning and in the evening to draw water. Women washed laundry and bathed their children during less busy times.

An Urban Migrant's Story

The story of Percy Hinojosa (related by Jorge Parodi) of Lima, Peru, is typical of the hundreds of thousands of Latin Americans who left their rural homes and moved to the cities in search of better lives. Percy, like many others in Peru and elsewhere, left his village at 15 because the countryside offered nothing but endless poverty. Like most migrants who arrived in Lima from the countryside, he came with at best an elementary school education. In order to find work, it was important to have relatives or friends already in the city who could provide the migrant with contacts to obtain employment in factories, but Percy did not have any personal contacts. He toiled for 12 years in various jobs until he got a steady position in a factory. He began as a domestic servant and went to school at night. He then embarked on an odyssey very typical of migrants:

> I worked at Coca-Cola, at Cuadernos Atlas, and in the Italian bakery. Later on, I would work at Pepsi-Cola, in small shops, in furniture factories, and carpentry shops. I would work two months and a half or three and I'd be laid off. I think the companies didn't want you to have a steady job at that time.

Percy did everything from counting bottles to packing notebooks and sanding furniture. He earned enough to get by, though no more. In search of higher-paying, more secure employment, he entered the construction trade, but this meant enduring long periods without work. He then acquired a position as an apprentice auto mechanic. He had to quit that job, however, when he became too vocal about getting a raise. Percy returned to the countryside for a year. By the time he left for Lima again, jobs were even harder to come by. Eventually, he used a contact from his earlier employment as a domestic to obtain a factory job. Like so many Latin Americans, Percy did whatever was necessary.

THE ENVIRONMENT

The push for economic development in Latin America, as elsewhere, has come at a high cost to the environment. Air and water pollution, the deterioration of agricultural lands through overuse or misuse, and the destruction of tropical rainforest areas are among Latin America's chief environmental disasters. These conditions have exacerbated the health problems, especially among the poor that we discussed earlier.

Mexico City is one of the most disheartening examples of environmental degradation over the past half century. The air is dangerous to breathe and the smog is so thick that residents rarely see the beautiful mountains that surround the city. Three million cars clog the thoroughfares of Mexico City, often bringing traffic to a standstill—residents sometimes refer to their freeways as the "largest parking lot in the world." Motor vehicles are the primary contributors to air pollution, emitting enormous quantities of sulfur dioxide and other contaminants into the air every day. The government has tried to clean up the air by prohibiting cars from being driven into the city 1 day a week and by ordering emission tests and the use of cleaner fuels. These measures have helped a bit, but not enough. Motor vehicles, however, are only part of the problem. Erosion; exposed trash and feces; untreated water seeping into the subsoil; and emissions from electric plants, refineries, petrochemical plants, incinerators, and internal combustion engines spew tons of contaminants into the air each day.

Safe drinking water is hard to find. The sewage system filters only 70 percent of the city's water. Thirty percent of municipal solid waste is not collected, and people dump it into the streets, rivers, lakes, and open fields. Lake Guadalupe, the closest lake to the Federal District, is essentially a huge septic tank: Its 30 million cubic meters of residual waters are polluted with unspeakable wastes. Consequently, agricultural products produced in the region of the lake are dangerous because they are infested with harmful microorganisms from the lake water used to irrigate crops.

Outside the cities, conditions are no better. Tropical rainforests in Latin America are being depleted at an annual rate estimated between 113,000 and 205,000 square kilometers per year. This results mostly from the conversion of rainforests to open land suitable for agriculture, especially in the Amazon region of Brazil, as waves of immigrants have flowed into the area during the last third of the twentieth century. The population of the Amazon went from 3.6 million in 1970 to 7.6 million in 1980 and 18 million in 2000. The number of agricultural properties increased by 90 percent, and the number of cattle herds doubled. From 1973 to the mid-1980s, farmer colonists in the western Amazon region razed 60,000 square kilometers. Fewer than half of these settlers stayed more than a year. The cutting of wood for use in homes and industry has contributed considerably to the destruction of the rainforests. Oil wastes have devastated the tropical rainforests of Ecuador. Black slime formed in pools and slush filled with toxic wastes contaminated the countryside. Seventeen million barrels of oil spills ruined the rivers. The soil is so contaminated in some areas that it is crusty when poked with a stick.

Natural Disasters

From 1970 to 2000 there were, by one estimate by the Inter-American Development Bank, 972 natural disasters (hurricanes, floods, earthquakes, volcanic eruptions) in Latin America that caused 226,000 fatalities (an average of 32.4 disasters and 7,500 deaths per year), costing about $29 billion in direct damages and $21 billion in indirect damages. Just in the 1990s alone, these events made 2.5 million people homeless. The two most well-known disasters are the earthquake that struck Mexico City in 1985, which killed 10,000 people and damaged or destroyed thousands of buildings ($6 billion in damages), leaving countless people without shelter, and the 2010 earthquake in Haiti which caused the deaths of 200,000 people, erasing the entire infrastructure of Port-au-Prince. However, there have been other devastating tragedies, such as an earthquake in Peru in 1970 that killed 66,000, a 1976 earthquake in Guatemala with 23,000 dead, and floods/mud slides in

Venezuela that caused 30,000 deaths. There were also recurring events, such as the prolonged drought in Northeast Brazil (10 years of drought between 1970 and 1993) and *El Niño* on the Pacific Coast in Ecuador and Peru. El Niño is the variation in climate caused by change in the surface temperature of ocean water. The phenomenon occurs every 5 to 7 years and lasts several months to 2 years, causing droughts and/or flooding. The two climatic catastrophes have cost enormous sums in damages and lost production. In this suffering Latin America appears to follow a growing worldwide trend. In the same time period, the number of major natural disasters has risen by 300 percent globally.

THE GLOBALIZATION OF CULTURE

During the second half of the twentieth century, globalization shaped the lives of people in Latin America and everywhere else. Borders between rural and urban, local and national, and national and international culture have broken down. Massive migration from the countryside to the cities and across international boundaries has been one factor in this profound change. The advent of modern mass communications, especially television, has perhaps played an even more decisive role, touching the lives even of people who never ventured very far from their homes. Meanwhile, newspapers, comic books, magazines, popular theater, radio, movies, and television deeply influenced what were formerly entirely locally focused societies. The Internet has immeasurably widened the horizons of those fortunate enough to have the resources to use it. No culture exists in isolation anymore.

Brazil provides an excellent example of how mass media had transformed culture since the 1960s. Magazine circulation increased from 104 million to 500 million between 1960 and 1985. Between 1967 and 1980, the number of record players grew by more than 800 percent. The number of commercial records went from 25 million to 66 million just during the 1970s. The expansion of television was spectacular: In 1965, there were 2.2 million televisions in Brazil, but that number rose to 4.2 million in 1970 and to 16 million by the 1980s, when 73 percent of Brazilians had TV sets. By 1996, Brazil had become the seventh-largest advertising market in the world, with advertising expenditures at $10 billion, more than half of which was accounted for by television. The Brazilian television industry illustrates well how Latin Americans have used the mass media not only to increase their own cultural output but also to spread their culture across the world. From 1972 to 1983, the percentage of foreign programming decreased from 60 to 30 percent. Brazil exports its truly amazing soap operas all over the world (especially to Mexico and Portugal).

Without question, the globalization of popular culture brought a steady influx of movies, music, fast food, and fashions from the United States and Western Europe to Latin America. McDonald's golden arches are a familiar icon throughout the region, and Walmart operates 600 retail stores in Mexico, some under its own name and some under their original names, which were retained after Walmart acquired them. The mass media have heightened demand for consumer goods in the countryside, sometimes with negative consequences for the quality of life. According to the cultural commentator Néstor García Canclini, "The penetration of consumer goods into rural areas frequently generates a crisis. New needs for industrial goods are created, forcing the rural household to rationalize production and work harder, longer hours, thus making it difficult for the peasant family to continue participating in [traditional] magico-religious practices."

Latin Americans have found myriad and creative ways to blend old and new. On Sunday afternoon in the Praça de Se in São Paulo, Brazil, one can observe *capoeira* (a form of martial art used as self-defense, formerly practiced by slaves, now a dance), electric guitars playing rock music, and poetic duels by *cantadores*. In Peru during the 1980s, chicha music (*chicha* refers to an Andean maize beer often linked with traditional rituals) enjoyed widespread popularity. A combination of elements from Andean and tropical cultures, the music illustrated the mass immigration from the countryside into the cities. Although the mixture of electric guitars with tropical and Andean rhythms appears at first instance a degradation of tradition, it may in fact be a way of preserving the memory of the past within a practical acceptance of current reality. In Latin American homes, technology and tradition exist side by side. Television sets often rest on tables that stand right next to altars bearing religious images. In Brazilian favelas, residents paint their rooms pink to remind them of their rural homes.

Latin American popular culture has found worldwide markets and enthusiasts. Growing numbers of Latinos in the United States can watch soap operas on television, attend concerts of popular Latin American musicians, and celebrate traditional holidays. In June 2004, there were reenactments of *Inti Raymi,* the ancient Inca summer solstice festival, in cities as far away as Chicago, Seattle, New York, Brussels, Barcelona, and Budapest. The indigenous people of Otavalo in northern Ecuador have long been known as savvy marketers who sell their fine textiles to tourists visiting their picturesque community. Now a wide selection of their products is available on the Internet. Sometimes popular culture has changed its form to suit foreign tastes, while retaining cultural meaning at home. Andean music has shown a noticeable Western influence as it has become familiar to audiences around the world. In Peru and Bolivia, however, music has kept its place at the center of the annual cycle of ritual.

Transitions to the new hybrid folk art are ambiguous at times. In the late 1960s, the artisans of Ocumicho, Michoacán, in Mexico began to create ceramics depicting devil figures associated with elements of the modern world previously unknown in the village, such as police, motorbikes, and airplanes. Some observers have suggested that the devils provide a way of controlling the destructive effects of modernization, by placing them within a traditional repertory of symbols. Carlos Monsiváis, the Mexican essayist, reports an interesting twist on the intrusion of modernity into rural society that occurred when the Mexican government introduced video cameras to municipal meetings in the state of Hidalgo. The Otomí Indians, who comprised most of the population of the municipality, showed more enthusiasm about watching the videotapes of the meetings than attending gatherings in person.

International market forces and national political considerations have, without doubt, altered many local traditions. Mexican governments have encouraged handicraft production so as to provide sustenance for rural people and to thus keep them from migrating to the cities. Cultural commentator Néstor García Canclini maintains, for example, that the urban and tourist consumption of handicrafts "causes them to be increasingly decontextualized and resignified on their journey to the museum and the boutique. . . . Their uses on the land, in the household and in rituals are replaced by exclusively aesthetic appreciation," which in turn affects how they are made and the form they take.

Art

Latin American artists have continued to develop their innovative style and techniques in the age of globalization. The stark political art of the 1930s and 1940s gave way temporarily to geometric and abstract art by the 1950s, but neither proved satisfactory to artists concerned with contemporary conditions. In Mexico, there was a reaction against the muralists, led by José Luis Cuevas, who believed the world more complicated than that depicted by Rivera and Siqueiros. Instead of depicting a world of simple contrasts between heroes and villains, these artists portrayed humans as victims of greater forces. Perhaps the most famous artist to emerge from this era was Colombian Fernando Botero, who also dropped socialist realism. Like Cuevas, Botero was more comfortable using European painters' techniques, but he added exaggeration and parody to his portrayal of characteristic types in Colombian politics and society.

By the 1960s, Latin American artists again embraced social protest, but this new protest was more diversely applied than that of the earlier generation's socialist realists. According to art historian Jacqueline Barnitz, however, some artists working under the brutal regimes of the 1970s through the 1980s employed a "strategy of self-censorship" in which "they invented new symbols or invested previously used ones with new meaning." For example, Brazilian Antonio Henrique Amaral painted bananas in the 1970s as a parody of Brazil as a banana republic, a tinhorn dictatorship that deferred to the United States. Other artists challenged not the political state but the commercialization of art and official art institutions. This conceptual art, comprised of various media ranging from prints to performance, provided the means for ideological expression without actually confronting the terrifying regimes in power. Some artists, nevertheless, paid a high price for even veiled protests. After the Chilean coup in 1973, Guillermo Nuñez was arrested, imprisoned, tortured, let go, and then watched closely. After being jailed and tortured a second time 2 years later, he was forcibly exiled.

Latin American artists in the late twentieth century struggled and succeeded brilliantly in forging their own art out of the different strains of influence from their homelands and abroad. They fought to make sense out of a world of bitter poverty and profound disappointment. They explored their past and future with the same persistence, courage, and humor displayed by their ancestors for the preceding 600 years.

CONCLUSION

As they entered the new millennium, Latin Americans lived in a world very different from what their ancestors had known when they embarked on their journeys as independent nations nearly two centuries before. As we saw in Chapter 9, nineteenth-century governments struggled mightily to persuade their people to think of themselves as citizens of a nation rather than residents of a particular village, town, or region. Those who governed in Latin America after 1880 had a much easier time in getting people to see themselves as part of a national community. The coming of railroads, telegraphs, and telephones consolidated national territories as never before. Public education systems and mandatory military service provided ideal vehicles to inculcate patriotic values to students and raw recruits. Modernizing governments saw local governance and culture as impediments to their mission and took decisive steps to undermine both.

The development of modern mass communications in the twentieth century created national popular cultures as more and more people followed the same soap operas, read the same comic books, watched the same movies, and enjoyed the same music. Televised spectator sports also encouraged people to think of themselves as Peruvians or Mexicans or Costa Ricans as they cheered their national teams in international soccer competitions. Winning the World Cup in soccer has probably done as much as any government program to make Brazilians proud to be Brazilians and Argentines proud to be Argentines. In the age of globalization, even a nation's citizens who worked and lived abroad could partake of national patriotic observances and reaffirm their loyalties to their home countries. Each year on the night of September 15, for example, the medium of satellite TV permits Mexican citizens living in the United States to watch their president stand on the balcony of the National Palace in Mexico City and reenact Father Miguel Hidalgo's famous "Grito de Dolores," the spark that ignited the country's struggle for independence nearly 200 years ago. The Internet and cheap long-distance telephone service enable people living abroad to keep in touch with friends, family, and local happenings back home.

Meanwhile, globalization has also generated forces that weaken national loyalties. Traditional ways of life distinctive to a particular country are rapidly giving way to international consumer culture. At the same time, strong local and regional loyalties persist alongside wider national and international allegiances. In recent years, the end of tyrannies and the comeback of democracy have allowed more local autonomy. The rise of Mexico's most active opposition party, the Partido Acción Nacional, and its ultimate success in capturing the presidency in 2000 began in part as a resurgence of regional identity, particularly in the north. Ethnic and linguistic minorities continue to reassert their languages and traditions against homogenized national and international cultures.

Whether they work for multinational corporations or continue to work in the countryside, whether they never venture much beyond the localities where their ancestors have lived for centuries or travel great distances in search of work, education, or entertainment, whether or not they have access to the Internet, and regardless of their income levels, Latin Americans of the twenty-first century still see the struggle to retain control over their daily lives as their paramount objective, and one that is perhaps as unattainable today as it has ever been in their history. For a large majority of people in the region, poverty and its related ills—malnutrition, substandard housing, and disease—seriously interfere with that quest. Even those who live comfortably for the moment can remember all-too-recent times of political uncertainty, galloping inflation, and war and terror—and they fear a return to those conditions. The natural environment that nurtured the first civilizations in the Americas and provided a host of commodities used and valued all over the world faces the dire consequences of modernization. But ever since their first ancestors migrated across the Bering Strait thousands of years ago, Latin Americans have shown great ingenuity in meeting their needs for survival and for cultural autonomy. Their energy and cultural creativity will serve them well in the years to come.

LEARNING MORE ABOUT LATIN AMERICANS

Pacini Hernández, Deborah, Fernández L'Hoeste, Hector, and Zolov, Eric, eds. *Rockin' Las Américas* (Pittsburgh, PA: University of Pittsburgh Press, 2004).

Scheper-Hughes, Nancy. *Death without Weeping: The Violence of Everyday Life in Brazil* (Berkeley, CA: University of California Press, 1992). The author presents a gut-wrenching picture of favela life.

Tardanico, Richard, and Rafael Menjívar Larín, eds. *Global Restructuring, Employment, and Inequality in Urban Latin America* (Miami, FL: North-South Center Press at the University of Miami, 1997). The editors include all the dismaying statistics about the present state of Latin Americans.

Timerman, Jacobo. *Prisoner without a Name, Cell without a Number* (Madison, WI: University of Wisconsin Press, 2002). Argentine Jew who was jailed during the Dirty War tells his terrifying tale.

Ulloa Bornemann, Alberto. *Surviving Mexico's Dirty War: A Political Prisoner's Memoir.* Ed. and trans. Arthur Schmidt and Arora Camacho de Schmidt (Philadelphia, PA: Temple University Press, 2007).

Winn, Peter. *Weavers of the Revolution: The Yarur Workers and Chile's Road to Socialism* (New York: Oxford University Press, 1986). Winn gets inside the minds of workers to an unprecedented extent.

GLOSSARY

Aguardiente (ah-gwar-dee-EN-tay)   Sugar cane alcoholic beverage.

Alcaldes mayores (ahl-KAHL-days mah-YOR-ays)   In Spanish America, local officials who represented the authority of the king and exercised administrative and judicial functions; similar to corregidores.

Aldeias (ahl-DAY-ahs)   In Brazil, villages of mission Indians.

Arrendatarios (ah-rehn-dah-TAH-ree-ohs)   Permanent workers on Colombian coffee farms.

Atole (ah-TOH-lay)   Corn gruel eaten for breakfast in Mexico.

Audiencias (ow-dee-EHN-see-ahs)   In Spanish America, a court of appeal located in a major city.

Ayllu (ai-YOO)   The basic unit of indigenous society in Peru, a group of people who claimed descent from a single ancestor, worked lands in common, and venerated their own special deities.

Bandeirantes (bahn-day-RAHN-chees)   In Brazil, especially in the region around São Paulo, people who explored the back country and rounded up Indians to be sold as slaves.

Barretón (bah-ray-TOHN)   A heavy wedge with an iron tip and long, straight wood handle used to poke soil in order to insert seed.

Cabildo (kah-BEEL-doh)   A town council in Spanish America.

Cacique (kah-SEE-kay)   Originally, a traditional chief in Caribbean societies; later an indigenous local ruler in Spanish America; this term was also used to describe local political bosses in the nineteenth century, after Latin American independence.

Calaveras (kah-lah-VAY-rahs)   Skeletal figures used in celebration of the Days of the Dead in Mexico.

Candomblé (kahn-dohm-BLAY)   Afro-Brazilian religion.

Cantadores (kahn-tah-DOR-ays)   Singers.

Capataz (kah-pah-TAHS)   Foreman on a cattle ranch.

Capitalino (kah-pee-tah-LEE-noh)   Resident of Mexico City.

Capoeira (kai-poh-EH-rah)   Formerly a slave dance, evolved as form of self-defense in Brazil.

Castas (KAHS-tahs)   In Spanish America, people of mixed race; often specifically referring to people with some evidence of African ancestry.

Caudillo (kow-DEE-yoh)   Strong leader with a local political base.

Centralist   Favors strong national government.

Chica moderna (CHEE-kah mo-DEHR-nah)   Modern woman.

Chicha (CHEE-chah)   In South America, a fermented beverage made from maize.

Chicha (CHEE-chah)   Maize beer drunk in the Andean region.

Cofradía (koh-frah-DEE-ah)   In Spanish America, an organization of lay people devoted to a particular saint or religious observance; members maintained village churches and sponsored festivals.

Colono (coh-LOH-noh)   Temporary worker on a Colombian coffee farm; medium-scale Cuban sugar planter.

Compadrazgo (kohm-pah-DRAHS-goh)   Godparent relations; an individual who agrees to look after the child of another.

Concordancia (kohn-kor-DAHN-see-ah)   Argentine political coalition of the 1930s with Conservatives, Radicals, and Independent Socialists.

Conservative   Favors strong central government and the Roman Catholic Church.

Conventillos (kohn-vehn-TEE-yohs)   Buenos Aires tenements.

Corregidores (koh-ray-hee-DOR-ays)   In Spanish America, local officials who represented the authority of the king and exercised administrative and judicial functions; similar to alcaldes mayores.

Corticos (kor-TEE-kohs)   Crowded slums in Rio de Janeiro.

Creoles   People who claimed to be descended only from Europeans, but born in the Americas.

Debt peonage   Debt incurred by rural laborers on large estates in order to pay for baptisms, weddings, funerals, and to purchase supplies that debtor cannot repay.

Descamisados (des-kah-mee-SAH-dohs)   Shirtless ones; working class supporters of Juan Perón in Argentina.

Donatário (doh-nah-TAH-ree-oh)   In Brazil, the head of a proprietary colony.

Encomendero (ehn-koh-mehn-DAY-roh)   In Spanish America, an individual who received an encomienda.

Encomienda (ehn-koh-mee-EHN-dah)   In Spanish America, the right granted to an individual to demand tribute and/or labor from the Indians of a specific place; in theory, an encomienda also included the obligation to protect the assigned Indians from abuse and provide for their instruction in the Catholic faith.

Enganchadores (ehn-gahn-chah-DOR-ays)   Dishonest labor recruiters.

Engenho (ehn-ZHEN-yeu)   In Brazil, a sugar mill.

Español (ehs-pahn-YOHL)   A person claiming Spanish lineage, whether born in Spain or the Americas.

Estado Novo (eh-shta-doo-noh-voo)   Dictatorship of Getúlio Vargas in Brazil (1937–1945).

Estancia (eh-STAHN-see-ah)   Large estate in Argentina and Uruguay that generally raises livestock.

Estanciero (eh-stahn-see-EH-roh)   Large landowner in Argentina and Uruguay; owner of an estancia.

Farinha (fah-REEN-yah)   Coarse flour made from cassava.

Fazenda (fah-ZEHN-dah)   Large estate in Brazil.

Fazendeiro (fah-zehn-DAY-roh)   Large landowner in Brazil; owner of a fazenda.

Federalist   Favors weak national government with political power vested in states or provinces.

Finca (FEEN-kah)   Colombian coffee farm.

Frijoles (free-HOH-lays)   Beans, a staple of Mexican diet; usually combined with corn tortillas.

Gaucho (GOW-choh)   Argentine cowboy known for fierce independence.

Gobernador (goh-behr-nah-DOR)   In Spanish America, the governor of a province or the ruler of an Indian village.

Guano (goo-AH-noh)   Bird excrement used for fertilizer, collected from islands off Peru.

Hacendado (ah-sen-DAH-doh)   Large landowner in Spanish America.

Hacienda (ah-see-EHN-dah)   Any kind of large agricultural property in Spanish America.

Hectare   2.47 acres.

Hombres de bien (OHM-brays day bee-EHN)   In colonial Spanish America, men who had honorable reputations in their communities; in the nineteenth century, decent people; professionals of some means who often managed government in nineteenth century Mexico.

Huaraches (wah-RAH-chays)   Sandals.

Indigenismo (een-dee-hehn-EES-moh)   Admiration for the advanced culture of pre-1500 societies in Latin America; efforts to bring native peoples into the modern economy.

Indios ladinos (EEN-dee-ohs lah-DEE-nohs)   In Spanish America, Indians who could speak Spanish and were acculturated into Spanish ways.

Jefes políticos (heh-fays poh-LEE-tee-kohs)   District political bosses under Porfirio Díaz in Mexico.

Kuraka (koo-RAH-kah)   A traditional chief in Peru and other Andean countries both before and after the Spanish conquest.

Lavradores de cana (lah-vrah-DOR-ehs zhee KAH-nah)   In Brazil, small farmers who produced sugarcane.

Léperos (LEH-peh-rohs)   Beggars of Mexico City.

Ley fuga (Lay FOO-gah)   Shot while trying to escape; ruse used by Rurales.

Liberal   Favors weak central government, opposes the Roman Catholic Church, and encourages individualism rather than collective landownership.

Liberto (lee-BEHR-toh)   Slave born in Brazil after 1813 who was to remain a slave until age 21.

Mameluca (mah-may-LOO-kah)   In Brazil, a female of mixed European and Native American descent.

Mameluco (mah-may-LOO-koh)   In Brazil, a male of mixed European and Native American descent.

Manumission   The process whereby slaves could legally obtain their freedom.

Matador (mah-tah-DOR)   Bullfighter.

Mayordomo (mai-yor-DOH-moh)   Manager of an estancia or hacienda.

Mestiza (mehs-TEE-sah)   In Spanish America, a female of mixed European and Native American descent.

Mestizo (mehs-TEE-soh)   In Spanish America, a male of mixed European and Native American descent.

Mita (MEE-tah)   A forced draft of Indian labor in Peru, both before and after the Spanish conquest.

Metate (may-TAH-tay)   Grinding stone for corn used in making tortillas.

Mitayo (mee-TAI-yoh)   A worker drafted through the mita.

Molino de nixtamal (moh-LEE-noh day neex-tah-MAHL)   Corn-grinding machine.

Mulatta   A female of mixed African and European and/or Native American descent.

Mulatto   A male of mixed African and European and/or Native American descent.

Nahuatl (nah-WAHT-ul)   Language spoken by the Aztecs and other pre-Hispanic peoples of Central Mexico; still spoken today.

New Christians   Converts from Judaism to Catholicism and their descendants.

Obraje (oh-BRAH-hay)   Textile factory in Spanish America.

Panela (pah-NEH-lah)   Brown sugar cakes.

Patron–client relations   Unequal relationship between upper-class individual and lower-class individual (hacendado and peon, for example) in which the former obtains protection and patronage in return for loyalty.

Peinilla (pay-NEE-yah)   Machete.

Peninsulares (pay-neen-soo-LAH-rays)   Natives of Spain or Portugal.

Petate (pay-TAH-tay)   Sleeping pallet.

Presidio (pray-SEE-dee-oh)   In Spanish America, a military fort.

Pulque (POOL-kay)   In Mexico, a fermented beverage made from the agave cactus.

Pulque (POOL-kay)   In Mexico, a fermented beverage made from the agave cactus.

Quechua (KAY-chwah)   Language spoken by the Incas and other pre-Hispanic peoples of Peru, Bolivia, and Ecuador; still spoken today.

Quilombos (kee-LOHM-bohs)   Communities of runaway slaves in the interior of Brazil.

Rebozo (ray-BOH-soh)   Narrow, long shawl for women.

Regular clergy   Priests who belonged to a religious order such as the Franciscans, the Dominicans, or the Jesuits; they followed the rules established by the founder of their order.

Relação (ray-lah-SOW)   In Brazil, the highest court in the land.

Repartimiento (ray-pahr-tee-mee-EHN-toh)   In Spanish America, a forced labor draft.

Reparto de mercancías (ray-PAHR-toh day mehr-kahn-SEE-ahs)   In Spanish America, a practice whereby local officials engaged Indians in trade, often forcibly.

República de españoles (ray-POO-blee-kah day ehs-pahn-YOHL-ays)   In Spanish America, the Spanish community, supposedly separate from the Indian community.

República de indios (ray-POO-blee-kah day EEN-dee-ohs)   In Spanish America, the Indian community, supposedly separate from the Spanish community.

Rurales (roo-RAH-lays)   Rural police during era of Porfirio Díaz in Mexico.

Santería (sahn-tay-REE-ah)   Afro-Caribbean religion.

Secular clergy   Priests who did not belong to religious orders; they were directly under the supervision of their bishop.

Siesta (see-EHS-tah)   Nap after the midday meal.

Senhor de engenho (sayn-YOR zhee ehn-ZHEN-yeu)   In Brazil, the owner of a sugar mill.

Tithe   Contribution to the church of 10 percent of one's income.

Traza (TRAH-sah)   In Spanish America, the central portion of a city, reserved in theory for residents of Spanish descent.

Vaqueros (vah-KAY-rohs)   Cowboys in Mexico.

Vecindades (vay-seen-DAH-days)   Mexico City tenements.

Viceroy   Chief government official in the colonies; the personal representative of the king of Spain or Portugal.

Voudoun (VOO-doon)   Afro-Caribbean or Afro-Brazilian religion.

Yerba mate (YER-bah MAH-tay)   Strong tea in Paraguay and Argentina.

CREDITS

Front Matter
Opener Stamps: Fotolia, LLC and Flavia Morlachetti/Fotolia, LLC '
p. xxxii: Cheryl Martin
p. xxxii: James Wasserman Photography

Chapter 1
p. 6: Linda Schele/Mesoamerican Studies
p. 16: ©(Bettmann)/CORBIS All Rights Reserved
p. 17: Linda Schele/Mesoamercian Studies
p. 29: SGM/Stock Connection
p. 22: Imagebroker/Alamy

Chapter 2
p. 38: Oxford University Bodleian Library
p. 43: © (Werner Forman)/CORBIS All Rights Reserved
p. 45: Guaman Poma/Det Kongelige Bibliotek
p. 48: © (Hulton Archive)/CORBIS All Rights Reserved
p. 49: Picture Desk, Inc./Kobal Collection

Chapter 3
p. 70: © CORBIS All Rights Reserved
p. 72: William L. Clements Library/William Clements Library, University of Michigan
p. 78: © (Stapleton Collection)/CORBIS All Rights Reserved
p. 79: Courtesy of The Bancroft Library. University of California, Berkeley
p. 85: Tony Morrison/South American Pictures

Chapter 4
p. 102: Courtesy of the Library of Congress
p. 104: The Granger Collection, New York
p. 112: Special Collections/University of Texas at El Paso Library
p. 118: Courtesy of the Library of Congress
p. 123: © (G.E. Kidder Smith)/CORBIS All Rights Reserved

Chapter 5
p. 138: Det Kongelige Bibliotek.
p. 139: CORBIS All Rights Reserved
p. 140: McAfee Collection/UCLA Library
p. 142: Courtesy of the John Carter Brown Library at Brown University
p. 145: © (George H.H. Huey)/CORBIS All Rights Reserved

Chapter 6
p. 162: Virginia Foundation for the Humanities.
p. 164: Museo De America

p. 176: Courtesy of the Library of Congress
p. 180: The Hispanic Society of America

Chapter 7
p. 201: Cheryl Martin
p. 207: The Hispanic Society of America
p. 209: © (Bettmann)/CORBIS All Rights Reserved

Chapter 8
p. 220: CORBIS All Rights Reserved
p. 223: Stanford University Press
p. 227: The Bridgeman Art Library International
p. 230: © (Pablo Corral)/CORBIS All Rights Reserved
p. 234: Houghton Library/Harvard University, Houghton Library

Chapter 9
p. 248: The Bridgeman Art Library International
p. 256: Public Domain
p. 264: The Granger Collection, New York

Chapter 10
p. 277: Edward E. Ayer Collection/The Newberry Library
p. 283: Art Resource, New York
p. 288: Art Resource, New York

Chapter 11
p. 309: Donald c. Trupen/Center for Southwest Research
p. 319: Art Resource, New York
p. 324: © (Bettmann)/CORBIS All Rights Reserved

Chapter 12
p. 335: Courtesy of Susan Besse and the Author
p. 338: Edward Victor
p. 348: Biblioteca Nacional de Chile

Chapter 13
p. 364: © (Bill Gentile)/CORBIS All Rights Reserved
p. 370: Schalkwijk/ Art Resource, New York
p. 371: Art Resource, New York

Chapter 14
p. 387: © (Barry Lewis)/CORBIS All Rights Reserved/In Pictures
p. 390: © (Reuters)/CORBIS All Rights Reserved
p. 396: © (Johann Morit Rugendas)/CORBIS All Rights Reserved

Chapter 15
p. 410: © (Nik Wheeler)/CORBIS All Rights Reserved
p. 417: © (Paul Almasy)/CORBIS All Rights Reserved

COLOR PLATES (Front of book)

Plate 1: The Bridgeman Art Library International
Plate 2: Ira Black/National Geographic Image Collection
Plate 3: © (Danny Lehman)/CORBIS All Rights Reserved
Plate 4: © (Charles and Josette)/CORBIS All Rights Reserved
Plate 5: Cheryl Martin
Plate 6: © (Dave G. Houser)/CORBIS All Rights Reserved
Plate 7: Jason P. Howe/South American Pictures
Plate 8: Benson Latin American Collection/University of Texas at Austin.
Plate 9: Museo De America
Plate 10: Picture Desk, Inc./Kobal Collection
Plate 11: Elizabeth Waldo-Dentzel Collection
Plate 12: Derechos reservados (c) Museo Nacional Del Prado–Madrid
Plate 13: New York Historical Society/The Bridgeman Art Library International
Plate 14: Index/The Bridgeman Art Library International
Plate 15: The Bridgeman Art Library International
Plate 16: Erich Lessing/Art Resource, New York
Plate 17: Schalkwijk/Art Resource, New York
Plate 18: Time/Life Pictures/Getty Images/Time Life Pictures
Plate 19: Schalkwijk/Art Resource, New York
Plate 20: The University of New Mexico Press
Plate 21: © (Howard Davies)/CORBIS All Rights Reserved
Plate 22: © (Susan Gonzalas)/CORBIS All Rights Reserved
Plate 23: Art Resource, New York

INDEX

Note: The letters 'b' and 't' following the locators refers to boxes and tables cited in the text.